FOCUS ON THE FAMILY®

P9-EDD-194

COMPLETE GUIDE TO

Caring for Aging Loved Ones

THE OFFICIAL BOOK OF THE FOCUS ON THE FAMILY PHYSICIANS RESOURCE COUNCIL™

Foreword by Walter L. Larimore, M.D.

GENERAL EDITORS:
Henry Holstege, Ph.D.
Robert Riekse, Ph.D.

Tyndale House Publishers, Inc.
CAROL STREAM, ILLINOIS

Visit Tyndale online at www.tyndale.com.

Complete Guide to Caring for Aging Loved Ones

Edited by Linda Piepenbrink

Designed by Zandrah Maguigad

Library of Congress Cataloging-in-Publication Data

Focus on the family complete guide to caring for aging loved ones / endorsed by the Focus on the Family Physicians Resource Council.
    p. cm.
Includes bibliographical references and index.
    ISBN 0-8423-3588-9 (hc : alk. paper)
    ISBN 1-4143-0160-X (sc)
    1. Aged—Home care—United States.   2. Caregivers—United States.   3. Caring—Religious aspects—Christianity.
I. Title: Complete guide to caring for aging loved ones.   II. Focus on the Family Physicians Resource Council.
    HV1461 .F63 2002
649.8—dc21   2002000558

Printed in the United States of America

17   16   15   14   13
8   7   6   5   4   3

Table of Contents

Foreword

Why should you purchase, much less invest the time in reading, this complete guide? And why do I so exuberantly recommend it? After all, the shelves of the average bookstore have many other resources claiming to be complete. And some of them may be less expensive. So why should you choose *this* one?

The answer is simple. This volume deals with the aspects of successful aging from the viewpoint of the whole person—physical, mental, emotional, relational, and spiritual. If this guide did not address the spiritual aspect, it would be incomplete.

At the end of the twentieth century, doctors began to formally study the effects of religion and spirituality on successful health and aging. Now, after the publication of more than 1,200 medical studies on the subject, it is generally recognized that religious beliefs and practices are associated with a wide variety of healthy outcomes.

Many researchers have found that religious activity—particularly when it occurs in the setting of a caring community (e.g., involvement in worship services)—is associated not only with a longer life span but also with significant increases in overall quality of life. More importantly, for those wrestling with disease, studies have associated religious involvement with a greater ability to adapt to a medical condition, as well as with increased ability to care for those with disease. Religious involvement is, in general, linked with greater well-being and life satisfaction, greater purpose and meaning in life, greater hope and optimism, and less anxiety and depression. In fact, if religious activity were a medicine, it would be malpractice not to prescribe it for patients! Any health book purporting to be complete yet ignoring religion or spirituality is not only incomplete but also potentially misleading.

In addition, such "incomplete" books often overlook the role of religious organizations in providing support for the aging in communities and hospitals. Simply put, religious communities enjoy the active participation of society's most valuable resource—caring people. By supporting older adults and their caregivers, religious denominations, spiritually minded nonprofit organizations, ecumenical groups, and churches may reduce both the length and frequency of hospital and nursing-home admissions.

Nevertheless, any discussion of incorporating spirituality into medical care risks confusion and counterfeit, as the terms *faith, spirituality, religiosity,* and *religion* are defined in various ways by various people. As a Christian, I define spirituality as a personal, Christ-centered relationship with God, not bound by race, ethnicity, economics, or class, that promotes the wellness of self and others. The results are love, joy, peace, patience, kindness, goodness, faithfulness, gentleness, and self-control.

Having this type of relationship with God can produce significant physical, mental, emotional, and relational health benefits, especially in regard to coping with the difficult life circumstances that accompany aging. In one's private life, such a relationship may reduce the feeling of losing control and the helplessness that accompany chronic illness or disease. Private spiritual activities like prayer can reduce the sense of isolation that sometimes comes with age-related disease. Practicing one's faith in the public sphere, through such activities as participation in worship services, praying with others, social gatherings, and pastoral visits, also can improve health and increase the odds of successful aging.

This book focuses, however, not just on the spiritual aspects of aging. Successful aging includes the maintenance, as far as possible, of physical, emotional, mental, relational, and spiritual function, along with continued active engagement in social and productive activities. This book incorporates the critical "how-tos" of successful aging into its precepts and recommendations.

This indispensable guide will enlighten, equip, encourage, and enable you to care for those you love. Unlike most resources on the topic, this one recognizes that the aging process is extremely complex and consists of interdependent biological, psychological, emotional, mental, relational, social, and spiritual processes. Also, as any good guide should do, it directs you to resources for deeper study in any particular area that you might need.

Finally, this guide is sensitive to the wide range of Christian attitudes, beliefs, and practices. It wisely counsels that spiritual support and interventions should be offered only with sensitivity and with your loved one's permission—in ways that honor, cherish, and respect him or her. Any intervention utilizing Christ-centered spirituality for successful aging should be both biblically based and patient-centered. Wise caregivers must ethically and legally honor their loved one's wishes, follow their loved one's lead, and see to their loved one's needs.

My parents and my in-laws are now entering the stage of life in which my wife and I will be given the magnificent opportunity to return to them a small portion of the decades of care that they have given to us, our siblings, and our children. This wonderful resource will help to guide us down that uncertain and unpredictable path. I am thankful to have it available.

Walter L. Larimore, M.D.
COLORADO SPRINGS, COLORADO

Acknowledgments

Focus on the Family began the task three years ago of producing a book that would serve as an important resource to help current and future caregivers make wise decisions concerning their elders. An enormous group of skilled professionals dedicated countless hours and considerable expertise to bring *The Complete Guide to Caring for Aging Loved Ones* to its final form. Their work was a sacrificial act of love, and we are deeply indebted to everyone who contributed. It would be impossible to list every person or group who touched this project in some important way, but the following individuals deserve special recognition. Thank you all.

PROJECT EDITOR
Linda Piepenbrink

GENERAL EDITORS
Henry Holstege, Ph.D., and Robert Riekse, Ph.D.

FOCUS ON THE FAMILY BRAND MANAGER
Jane Terry

FOCUS ON THE FAMILY PROJECT MANAGER
Jim Mhoon

TYNDALE MANAGING EDITORS
Dan Elliott and Janis Long Harris

FOCUS ON THE FAMILY MANAGING EDITOR
Larry Weeden

PUBLISHER
Doug Knox

MEDICAL CONSULTANTS

Bradley G. Beck, M.D., Emergency Medicine/Preventive Medicine—Colorado Springs, Colorado
Margaret Cottle, M.D., Palliative Care—Vancouver, British Columbia
Robin Cottle, M.D., Ophthalmology—Vancouver, British Columbia
Douglas O. W. Eaton, M.D., Internal Medicine—Athens, Alabama
W. David Hager, M.D., Obstetrics/Gynecology—Lexington, Kentucky
Gaylen M. Kelton, M.D., Family Medicine—Indianapolis, Indiana
Walter Larimore, M.D., Family Medicine, Sports Medicine—Colorado Springs, Colorado
John P. Livoni, M.D., Radiology—Sacramento, California
Paul Meier, M.D., Psychiatry—Richardson, Texas
Mary Ann Nelson, M.D., Family Medicine—Cedar Rapids, Iowa

Special thanks to Dr. Margaret Cottle for her time and dedication to making this book the best it can be.

WRITERS

Marlee Alex, Ramona Cass, Rebecca Grosenbach, Linda Piepenbrink, Frank York
David P. Davis, M.S., Medical Research Writer
Carrie Gordon Earll, Writer/Bioethicist

REVIEWERS

Larry Burkett, Karin Stock Buursma, Joel Clousing, Ken Frenke, Scott Houser,
Lisa A. Jackson, Sharon Fish Mooney, Shana Murph, Eloise Schwarz, Jean Stephens

LEGAL CONSULTANTS

John C. Voorn, J. Thomas Witek

EDITORIAL SUPPORT

Anisa Baker, Tyndale Administrative Manager
Bonnie Franklin, Focus on the Family Copy Editor
Wendy Weaver Taylor, Tyndale Copy Editor
Sara Rogers, Focus on the Family Proofreader

BOOK DESIGN

Zandrah Maguigad

Introduction

Dear Reader,

Welcome to one of the fastest growing family categories in America—Caregivers for Elderly Relatives. As the U.S. Bureau of the Census has pointed out, never before in the history of America have we had so many middle-aged and young-old people (ages 65 to 74) caring for aging parents, and never before have we had so many older people. As people enter their oldest-old years, they are more likely to need help with the normal activities of daily living, such as dressing and bathing.

A *Newsweek* poll in a special edition (Fall/Winter 2001) revealed that persons aged 45 to 65 generally worry more about caring for aging parents and relatives than they do about the death of parents, the death of friends, losing their home or independence, separation from children, or marriage breakup. Only the death of a spouse created more worry than caregiving responsibilities did.

Of the 24 million family caregivers who utilized the Family and Medical Leave Act between 1999 and 2000, more took leave to care for elderly relatives than to care for ill children, to deal with birthing complications, or to care for ill spouses, according to the U.S. Department of Labor.

Who Cares for Our Elderly?
As medical research and technology continue to move ahead, we can expect to see more people living to the oldest-old ages (85 and older), but many will be living with chronic illnesses and physical and mental impairments. Caring for these people will become increasingly demanding. Who takes care of our elders? Contrary to some accounts in the newspapers about "granny dumping" in nursing homes, most of the long-term-care assistance for older people in America—whether by precedent, cultural orientation, or public policies—comes from family

members. Families provide 80 to 90 percent of all personal care and help with household tasks, transportation, and shopping for dependent older persons, according to the U.S. Census Bureau. Of these family caregivers, about 75 percent are women, including wives, daughters, and daughters-in-law. The rapid increase in the need for older-adult care in families has come at a time when vast numbers of women have entered or returned to the paid-labor force, adding more responsibilities to their traditional family roles.

A recent review of family caregiving by the National Alliance of Caregiving found that:

- More than 22.4 million households provide physical and emotional assistance to friends and relatives age 50 and older. This is nearly one in four households in America, a threefold increase from a decade ago.
- Up to 50 percent of the oldest-old (85 and older) need assistance with activities of daily living.
- For the first time in history, the average American has more living parents than he has children.
- Caregivers spend an average of 17.9 hours per week providing care for an aging loved one.

Effects of Caregiving

There are many consequences that family members, especially women, face as a result of long-term, in-home caregiving for elderly relatives. Some, according to data, are positive, but others are negative. Researchers have pointed out that family caregiving can provide personal satisfaction and can result in feelings of self-worth and usefulness. Most women feel caring for elderly parents is their duty. They do it out of devotion and love, but they often feel conflicting emotions such as frustration or guilt. All of these emotions get mixed together for family caregivers. "Guilt is such a primary emotion among caregivers," says Lynn Osterkamp, founder and editor of the *Parent Care* newsletter at the University of Kansas Gerontology Center. "Most people, no matter how much they do, never feel it is enough." Psychologist Marilyn Bonjean says, "And there is not one caregiver who doesn't feel it. . . .

Our emotions are not rational on this issue. It is human to resent parents for getting older and frail."

Elaine Brody, a leading researcher and author on caregiving, cites the following negative results of caregiving: depression, frustration, guilt, sleeplessness, demoralization, feelings of helplessness, irritability, lowered morale, and emotional exhaustion.

Caregiver Burnout

One of the reasons some disabled older persons are eventually placed in nursing homes is the wearing down of their caregivers. It is not difficult to understand why these family caregivers burn out in their caregiving roles. Women, for example, find it difficult to juggle a number of roles—wife, mother, daughter, caregiver, and worker. Unfortunately, many find that trying to carry out all these roles at the same time leads to stress and physical exhaustion. Too many sacrifice their own leisure interests and social lives along with time spent with their immediate families. Many end up neglecting their own health, which results in an inability to continue as caregivers.

Despite the sometimes dire consequences of caregiving, studies have clearly indicated that families do not flinch from providing care for dependent family members. Most families accept chronic conditions and physical impairments as a normal part of life and make adjustments accordingly.

Caregiving: Economic Issues

For many workers, caregiving for elderly relatives is a major threat to paid jobs outside the home. Numerous studies have documented the number and percentage of caregiving women who have rearranged or reduced their hours of work, or quit (or considered quitting) their jobs to care for elderly relatives. Employers, as well as employees, bear a large financial burden for personal caregiving. Lost productivity and the use of supervisors' time dealing with caregiving employees cost U.S. employers up to $29 billion a year. It is the purpose of this book to systematically lay out strategies, plans of action, and specific resources to turn to in order to assist family caregivers as much as possible. Pertinent to all this is understanding your own resources and your own limitations. It is a natural tendency for proud Americans to say, "We can take care of ourselves" or "We can take care of our loved ones by ourselves." This is fine as far as it is reasonable for each person. But this book is written from a Christian perspective, and part of being a Christian involves living in community, which means sharing one another's burdens. And we have already seen that there can be plenty of burdens in caregiving.

Caring for elderly relatives is very different from raising children. In child rearing the goal is to develop sound independence, which, with God's grace, leads to maturity. In elder care the pattern is reversed. Elders usually go from independence to greater and greater dependence on you and, ultimately, to physical death. Caregiving generally gets tougher the longer it continues.

Sources to Help: Spiritual Resources

How can we cope with elder care? The answer is clear. We need to turn to the supports that are available to us. First, spiritual supports, such as prayer, faith, and sharing burdens, can undergird our efforts. This book is written from a Judeo-Christian perspective with the understanding that its spiritual principles can benefit anyone. We hope that one of the outcomes of this book will be much more involvement by faith communities in supporting family caregivers through specialized ministries, support groups, specific services to elderly persons, and a better understanding of the aging process and its implications for the spiritual needs of the elderly and their family caregivers.

Sources to Help: Community/Program Resources

Second, we urge family caregivers to become aware of and use caregiver support services found in community-based resources provided by local, state, and national programs. One of the big challenges with these services is that they are not well-known and therefore not used by enough caregivers. Some of these programs are privately supported while others are government-funded. In the latter case, ultimately all are supported on a bipartisan basis in order to address some of the major issues facing older Americans and their family caregivers.

For example, the cost-of-living adjustment (COLA) for social-security benefits was added in the Nixon administration in 1972. This has been vital to the economic survival of millions of retirees. Many of the governmental community-support programs derive from the various titles of the Older Americans Act. This legislation has been reauthorized many times with strong bipartisan support. Its most recent version includes a new title, Title III E, which provides a range of family-caregiver support programs, which are so important to family caregivers. To obtain up-to-date information on these programs as well as others, you can contact an agency in your region called the Area Agency on Aging, which is listed in phone books across America.

In dealing with the necessity to take time off from work to care for an elder, the Family and Medical Leave Act of 1993, which we referred to earlier and which was signed in the Clinton administration, has been of enormous help to millions of family caregivers (over 24 million between 1999 and 2000).

An illustration of a private initiative to provide caregivers with information on available services in their localities is a Web site established in 2001 by the National Council on the Aging (NCA) and America Online. This program, called "BenefitsCheck*Up*," is a free public service that can help older persons and their family caregivers identify what services they qualify for in their region of the nation and how to obtain them. Over 5 million older Americans miss out on programs that can help with health care, transportation, income support, meals, and other important services. BenefitsCheck*Up* can be accessed at the Web address: http://www.benefitscheckup.org.

Sources to Help: Realizing Limits

Third, in spite of personal resolve, spiritual guidance and support, and community-based programs, it is important for family caregivers to know when they have reached the limits of their caregiving abilities. They should not sacrifice their own families or their own health to all-consuming caregiving. This is what long-term-care facilities and support programs—assisted-living arrangements, nursing homes, or home-delivered services—are for.

It is not uncommon to progress along the continuum of caregiving until you reach the stage where you can no longer cope due to an elder's multiple and/or progressively serious health conditions. This book deals with this problem and the guilt you may feel. You have done your best (most go beyond doing their best and experience personal burnout); you have been faithful to your biblically mandated calling as a caring child; you have identified and, as best you could, utilized community-based programs to help your aging loved one and to support you in your caregiving role. Now may be the time, as you continue to place your burdens in God's hands, to seek additional support, perhaps by placing your elder in a long-term-care facility. There are many ways to continue to be a caregiver after such a placement. With the practical and spiritual help of a book such as this, you will not only survive family caregiving, but you will also grow through it and help others to survive and grow as well.

We pray that God's peace, love, and grace will guide you in your caregiving journey, and we hope that you will utilize the spiritual and the community-based resources mentioned throughout this book.

Henry Holstege, Ph.D.
GERONTOLOGY PROFESSOR, CALVIN COLLEGE

Robert J. Riekse, Ed.D.
DIRECTOR, CALVIN COLLEGE—GRAND RAPIDS COMMUNITY COLLEGE
CONSORTIUM ON AGING

GENERAL EDITORS

CHAPTER I

And let us not grow weary while doing good, for in due season we

shall reap if we do not lose heart. Therefore, as we have opportunity,

let us do good to all, especially to those who are of the household of faith.

GALATIANS 6:9-10 NKJV

Facing a New Role
Becoming Your Loved One's Caregiver

DURING a career change, Karen moved in with her parents as a single adult. She planned to stay six months but never moved out. Instead, she eventually purchased the house and became her parents' primary caregiver as their health began to fail. "For the first 15 years I was footloose and fancy free, but as time went on, I had to learn to be a lot less selfish," says Karen, now 63. "It was quite a shift because they had always taken care of my needs and I'd been so involved outside of the home—at work and at church—but now it was my turn to care."

Her new role as caregiver developed gradually—from helping her arthritic mother climb the five steps to get to the bathroom and preparing meals for her parents to eat while she was at work to driving her blind father to organ concerts and cleaning up after her mother when she was incontinent.

Karen's help wasn't always immediately appreciated. When she brought home a commode to put on the first floor, her mother got angry. "She didn't want a 'potty chair' where others could see it, so she made me put it in the basement," says Karen, who respectfully complied. A couple weeks later, Karen gently raised the issue again. This time her mother agreed to put it next to her bed. "As a caregiver," says

Karen, "I learned not to impose or go any faster than what my parents were willing to accept, but I didn't ignore things either."

After working all day, Karen had to consciously slow her pace to half speed or less in order to avoid getting impatient with her parents or frustrating them. "If I talked too fast or moved too fast or expected decisions too fast, they would get upset. It could be a simple question, such as, 'Do you want coffee, tea, or milk for dinner?' Mentally they were okay, but it just took longer for them to decide."

Despite the challenges, Karen was devoted to caring for her aging parents. "My attitude is summed up in a motto I clipped out of a magazine years ago: 'The elderly need so little, but they need that little so much.'"

Is your mother, father, spouse, grandparent, aunt, uncle, or friend growing frail, becoming forgetful, or otherwise feeling the effects of aging? Have you taken on major responsibilities for an older loved one? Or do you fear that you may have to at some unexpected moment in the not-too-distant future? Do you feel perplexed or overwhelmed by decisions you must make, by information you do not have, or by feelings you do not understand? Do you wonder how God, faith, or the Christian community can be integrated into the life of your aging loved ones as they journey through their final years, or into your own life as you travel along this unknown path with them? If you answered yes to any of these questions, this book should assist you. It was designed to take a Christian approach in mapping and traversing the unfamiliar, complex, and sometimes overwhelming territory of caregiving for elderly loved ones.

CHANGING ROLES & RESPONSIBILITIES

Most people begin to experience the consequences of aging gradually. Since you are aging too, you may observe yourself having certain difficulties even as you attempt to help a loved one who may be further along in years. For example, you may need bifocals, just as your elderly loved one may need cataract surgery. We are all on the same journey toward our final destination. We just have different roles at different times. If your loved one is ahead of you in years or is growing frail more quickly, one of your roles for a while will be that of a caregiver.

Your loved one's difficulties may have increased slowly, making you a caregiver by degrees. Perhaps you first started driving Mom to her home after dinner at your place; then you had to write down important events on a calendar for her; now she needs daily visits so you can be sure she has taken her heart pills. As people live longer, many develop chronic ailments that require more hands-on assistance over a longer period of time. You may have become a caregiver precipitously, after your husband's stroke. Elders often take an abrupt downturn in health after an illness or accident that requires medical intervention and hospitalization.

Either way, you are finding that you must become a caregiver. The role means far more than caring about others or feeling concerned for their welfare. Most likely, you have always felt appreciative of and devoted to your parents, grandparents, aunts, uncles, spouse, or older friends. But now they need more than your time and tender feelings. They need help with concrete tasks—paying bills, grocery shopping, deciding when it is time to see a medical specialist, or even changing soiled bed linen at 3 A.M. You may need to arrange for professional services and transport your loved one to appointments and social activities. As your elder's health deteriorates, you might be called upon to supervise financial affairs and medical treatments while working with professionals such as physicians, attorneys, CPAs, and insurance agents. When you assume such tasks and accept major responsibilities for the well-being of elderly adults, you become a caregiver.

CAREGIVER PROFILES

The Spouse

When spouses are present as elderly people fall ill, they almost invariably become the principal caregivers. Elderly spouses are often enormously loyal to each other. But this arrangement can be tenuous. If you are a caregiving spouse—unless you happen to be a young one—you probably feel the effects of your own aging. What if you are asked to help your wife learn to walk again after her stroke, but you do not feel all that steady on your own feet? One devoted husband needed to help his wife to the bathroom several times during the night, even though he needed to take pills for his own difficulty sleeping at night. If you are such a caregiver, you might think privately, *We could both use help. But since I haven't had a heart attack in 10 years, nobody seems to notice my needs.*

The Female Relative

When elderly people become ill but do not have a spouse, most often the primary caregiver will be a female relative—usually a daughter or daughter-in-law. Female caregivers usually fill many additional roles in relationships, family, and career.

The largest group of caregivers is made up of employed women in their forties and fifties. But you may well be younger or older, married or single, not employed outside the home or working part-time. In any case, you have many demands competing for your time. You may have delayed your own professional aspirations until your children were grown. Perhaps now was the time you had hoped to go back to school or to devote time and attention to your career. You did not expect to become a new kind of caregiver, at least not so soon. Your employer might offer time off for maternity leave or crises with child care, but not for elder care.

The largest group of caregivers is made up of employed women in their forties and fifties.

Many times, a spouse can be a ready source of emotional support. You have someone to talk to about your parent-care problems; you have another adult in the house who can listen, understand, share decision making, and help out in many other ways. Still, caregiving responsibilities can become a source of conflict even in the best marriages. On the other hand, if you are a single caregiver, you may feel alone and isolated in your role.

Sooner or later most caregivers feel hemmed in by responsibilities on every side. Do you find yourself exhausted trying to balance the needs of your children with those of an elderly family member? If so, you are probably part of what experts call the Sandwich Generation, a term coined to describe caregivers who are assisting relatives on both ends—aging loved ones and their own children. Between 20 and 40 percent of caregivers are sandwiched between the caregiving needs of children at home and those of parents or older family members.[1] If you are a grandparent providing assistance to parents, children, and grandchildren, you are part of the Club Sandwich Generation, a term that refers to the numerous layers of responsibility many grandparents assume in today's complex and multigenerational culture.[2]

Wife, mother, grandmother, homemaker, volunteer, church worker, paid employee at a "real job." You may occupy all of these roles—or more—at the same time. You may fix meals; clean house; wash clothes; provide discipline and structure for youngsters; encourage and support your husband; arrange lessons and extracurricular activities; offer moral support and spiritual training; make peace out of conflict; put out "emotional brushfires"; and transport the young, the old, and yourself seemingly everywhere for everything.

The weight of the load may well be negatively affecting your marriage, your personal health, your career, and your emotional equilibrium. The risk of chronic fatigue, depression, and demoralization is high. Some caregivers decide to quit their jobs or eliminate certain responsibilities in order to restore balance to life. Still, most caregivers try not to complain under such circumstances.

The Sandwich Generation describes caregivers who are assisting aging loved ones and their own children.

The Male Caregiver

One single dad, raising two children and caring for an elderly mother, was ruthlessly honest about his experience. "We talk about the Sandwich Generation," he said. "But do you know what's in the middle of that sandwich? I'll tell you: chopped meat!"[3] If you are a male caregiver, like that single dad, you face your own unique challenges. You are in the minority; only about one in five caregivers is male. Perhaps this is be-

---

MINUTE MEN

My father's health declined so gradually that my wife and I were able to adjust to the changes. But just a few days before he died, I was surprised by a case of role reversal. It was a brisk autumn day and I encouraged Dad to take a walk outside with me—a wheelchair walk, actually. He loved scenic walks and agreed, but he was frail and easily chilled, so it required a great deal of bundling up to get him ready to go out. As the amount of time spent getting him ready, 45 minutes, exceeded the time we were able to walk in the cold, about five minutes, it reminded me of when I was a kid and the time my parents spent lovingly getting me bundled up to go outside. Five minutes later, I was often back inside again. Of course, I cherish that autumn stroll with my dad. I'm glad we took the time to do it, because now it's a precious family memory.

Timothy S.

cause women, when available, often automatically assume helping tasks. In general, society presumes caregiving is "women's work"; employers may frown on or penalize you for engaging in caregiving at the expense of your job performance.

Men may prefer tasks that reflect their traditional roles; for example, money management, home repairs, and making major decisions. But just like elderly husbands who are devoted to their aging spouses, sons love their parents and feel a strong sense of responsibility for them. When duty calls, many sons accept responsibility for direct, hands-on care for elderly parents.

What You May Be Feeling

Whether male or female, if you are like most caregivers, you did not plan for your new role. You might accept it with grace, but also with considerable fear and trembling. You probably do not feel prepared to address the myriad issues ahead. You want the best for your aging loved ones, but you recognize your lack of knowledge. You are not sure which symptoms are considered normal aging and which ones mean your elder should see a physician.

Nearly 7 million Americans travel at least one hour or more to provide assistance to older relatives.

You may wonder where you will get the time, strength, and energy to care for your elderly loved one in addition to your job and other roles. You might feel that your own mental and physical health are as much at risk as that of your elder. The more vulnerable your elder becomes, the more vulnerable you feel. In fact, many caregivers do encounter physical illness, psychological stress, spiritual discouragement, or all three.

If your aging loved one has not saved enough of his own money to support himself financially, you may fear that he will become dependent upon you and your resources. This could threaten your family's lifestyle. Your personal dreams may be delayed while medical costs for your aging loved one eat away at your savings—and your peace of mind.

You might feel frustrated, angry, or even resentful. There could be new restrictions on your personal freedom and new demands competing with your personal goals. Tensions may mount, not only within your immediate family, but also between you and your siblings. You may debate or quarrel with them about decisions concerning your elder's health care, living situation, or possessions. If you are a long-distance caregiver, you might feel guilty, anxious, or out of touch as you try to manage the care of your loved one with miles in between. In fact, nearly 7 million Americans travel at least one hour or more to provide assistance to older relatives.[4] This common situation has its own set of fears and challenges, yet with the proper help and resources, long-distance caregiving can be done successfully (see "Honoring a Loved One from Afar" on pages 33-38).

Perhaps becoming a caregiver has coincided with your own retirement. Just when you expected to be free of work obligations, instead of enjoying grandchildren, traveling, and hobbies, you are again facing more work, this time the mundane, practical tasks of caregiving. Or perhaps you are still in the midst of your working years and your children have only recently become independent. You have been looking

FACTS ABOUT CAREGIVERS

- Transportation, grocery shopping, and household chores are the most common tasks caregivers perform.
- Thirty-seven percent of caregivers help with medications, pills, or injections.
- Half of all caregivers help with at least one activity of daily living, such as bathing, dressing, or getting in and out of chairs.
- About half of all caregivers report they have less time for other family members, vacations, hobbies, or other activities.
- More than one in five caregivers take care of someone with Alzheimer's disease, dementia, or forgetfulness.
- Forty-one percent of caregivers are caring for children under the age of 18 at the same time they are caring for an elderly person.
- When asked what kinds of help, information, or support they could use most, 38 percent said they did not know.
- Only 7 percent of caregivers have participated in a support group.
- A majority of caregivers use positive words (e.g., *rewarding, happy*) to describe the caregiving experience.

National Alliance for Caregiving and the American Association of Retired Persons,
"Family Caregiving in the U.S.: Findings from a National Survey," March 1997.

forward to having time for other things: a delayed vacation, catching up on time with your spouse, reromancing your marriage, starting your own business, catching up on your sleep, or just having time to sit in a chair and do nothing for once in your life.

Experts say it is normal to experience anger at yourself, at your loved one, even at God. But in some communities and in some churches, such feelings are difficult to address and may be shunned. So in addition to your anger and resentment, you might also feel guilty just for having these feelings.

Caring for an elderly loved one is often the emotional opposite of raising children. You celebrated the passing of exciting milestones as you raised your children. But the significant milestones of an elder can be grim, leading to the inevitability of death. Simple tasks, like helping your loved one eat or washing her face, are constant reminders of decline, fraught with corresponding emotional overtones of grief and loss. You may feel deep pain and sadness about the way life is going.

At times, you may feel abandoned by family, friends, or community because they do not do enough to help. Or you may feel betrayed by the medical establishment when it fails to provide the assistance you expect from it. The culture, the community, and the church are often silent

SENIOR STATISTICS

The "baby boom" generation born following World War II is beginning to grow old while medical technology is moving forward at lightning speed. Since 1900 the number of Americans sixty-five and over has grown from 3 million to 34 million and is expected to double by 2030, one year after the last of the baby boomers reach the age of sixty-five.[1] Perceptions of aging are beginning to change; many Americans now think old age begins at age 70 or older. The U.S. Bureau of the Census generally divides seniors into three age levels:

1. The "young-old" are 65 to 74 years old.
   - By 2010 the baby boomers will become the "grandparent boom"—or, assuming that women continue to outlive men, 2010 will bring the "grandma boom."
   - By 2025, seniors will outnumber teenagers by more than 2 to 1.

2. The "aged" are 75 to 84 years old.
    *   Between 2010 and 2030, baby boomers will move from the first category—young-old—to the second category—the aged.
    *   Racial and ethnic diversity will expand. The African-American elderly population is expected to quadruple by 2050. The population of aging Latinos will increase eleven times, becoming 15 percent of the U.S. elderly.
    *   The percentage of the aged in nursing homes declined from 6 percent in 1985 to 5 percent in 1997, which may reflect a decline in disability rates and an increase in the availability of home health services over this period.[2]

3. The "oldest-old" are 85 years and older.
    *   Seventy percent of the oldest-old are females.[3] (Men tend to experience diseases that are fatal, whereas women are more likely to suffer diseases that lead to chronic, disabling conditions.)
    *   Disability increases substantially with age, with 18.1 percent reporting problems with two or more activities of daily living (ADLs), such as bathing or dressing.[4] Nevertheless, the percentage of the oldest-old in nursing homes declined from 22 percent in 1985 to 19 percent in 1997.[5]
    *   They are less likely to be married and more than twice as likely as the young to live in poverty. In 1990 four out of five were widowed. Of widowed men, 12.6 percent lived in poverty, compared to 24.1 percent of widowed women.
    *   They have less formal education than younger groups of elderly and the rest of the population. Research shows that with education come better health, higher incomes, and more self-sufficiency.
    *   They are projected to continue to make up the fastest-growing sector of the older population.

[1]The U.S. Administration on Aging, "AoA Announces New Elder Care Trends"; <www.demko.com/m000207.htm#one>. [2]Population Reference Bureau, *Older Women: Living Longer, Living Alone;* <www.ameristat.org> (click on "Older Population"). [3]U.S. Census Bureau, as reported by the Federal Interagency Forum on Aging-Related Statistics, *Older Americans 2000: Key Indicators of Well-Being* (2000). [4]Administration on Aging, *Number and Percent of Persons Reporting Problems with Two or More Activities of Daily Living (ADLs), by Age, Race, Gender, Poverty, Living Arrangements, Region, and Area of Residence. 1994–1995.* Based on the 1994–1995 National Health Interview Survey on Disability (Phase I), National Center for Health Statistics, Centers for Disease Control, U.S. Department of Health and Human Services. [5]Population Reference Bureau, *Older Women: Living Longer, Living Alone.*

about the difficult realities and challenges caregivers face. You may feel invalidated and ignored when social institutions take your efforts for granted or fail to articulate and meet your needs for assistance. Our social institutions affirm young parents and give solace to the bereaved after the death of a loved one. Caregivers often feel left out and left over. You might feel simply left alone—with too much responsibility, too little help, and not enough empathy.

In the midst of all these feelings, being a caregiver may, at times, bring out the worst in you. Very likely it will also bring out the best in you. In spite of overwhelming feelings of bewilderment, conflict, exhaustion, and even anger and resentment, you are likely to have some positive experiences: the sharing of burdens, growth in relationships, spiritual breakthroughs, forgiveness and reconciliation, feelings of satisfaction, and even a sense of joy and fulfillment because of the needed service you are providing.

Elderly people do much better under the care of family members, people who know their history and personality.

For your loved one, your presence will bring comfort and coherence to otherwise fragmented circumstances. Elderly people do much better under the care of family members, people who know their history and personality. They appreciate being cared for by someone they trust to treat them as real people, not just as an "old man" or an "old lady." They deserve and need to be included in discussions and decisions regarding their care. As their advocate, it is important for you to know their wishes. As you accept the burdens and challenges of being a caregiver, you will probably experience some strong negative emotions, and you will make mistakes and fall short of your own ideals. But as you become a caregiver—as you offer your labor, love, and prayer—remember this: For your elderly loved ones, your very presence is a model of commitment and compassion.

YOUR NEEDS AS A CAREGIVER

This book was designed to focus on your needs as a caregiver. Much of it explores various aspects of aging in order to give you the information you may need to fulfill your role as a caregiver. You will need a number of things: lots of information; ways to access appropriate support services; new skills; considerable help, encouragement, and inspiration; and—not to be forgotten—significant attention to your own self-care.

LIFELINES FOR CAREGIVING

When it comes to caregiving, you do not need to do it alone. Because of the needs of the aging population, a growing number of services and devices are available to help you, ranging from transportation services and adult day care to wheelchairs and home modifications. Yet one of the most frequent reasons caregivers give for not using a service is that they were not aware of it. Some caregivers report that they or their aging loved ones were "too proud" to use a service, such as adult day care (although some were confused about what adult day care is). Fewer people cite cost as a barrier to obtaining needed services.[1]

When you seek out caregiving options for your elder, community services (especially those coordinated through your elder's local Area Agency on Aging), help from family, or a support group for yourself, it is not a sign of defeat or weakness. You will need a break from caregiving from time to time. High on your list of resources should be services for respite care that will provide opportunities for relief from the day in, day out responsibility (see chapter 9: Finding Health, Medical, and Social Services).

You will also benefit from the practical guidance of other caregivers, whether they are friends from church or the members of a caregiver support group on the Internet. When a caregiver named George was trying to decide how best to care for his grandma, who could no longer live on her own due to Alzheimer's disease, he called his pastor for advice. Although his pastor had never been through the rigors of caring for an aging loved one, his father had. So George called his pastor's father. He ended up calling the man on a regular basis for advice and emotional support.

"You can read the printed word, look at research on the Internet, and learn about dementia or other diseases, activities that are all well and good for the purpose of educating you, but the best help often comes from someone who has walked a mile in your moccasins," says George. "Somebody who's been through it can tell you, 'Here's what I did right, and here are some mistakes I made.' They can speak from the heart."

On the bad days, look forward; give your complaints to God with an attitude of resting in His perfect will. Remember that God placed you in your particular family and is aware of your needs. He is "a very present help in trouble" (Psalm 46:1 NASB). You might feel that somehow you have to have all the answers, but you do not. Caring for elderly adults comes with some uncertainties and surprises. Accept your human frailty and ask God to provide the strength for each day.

[1] National Alliance for Caregiving and the American Association of Retired Persons, *Family Caregiving in the U.S.: Findings from a National Survey* (June 1997).

To understand your role and responsibilities in a Christian context, you need information from Scripture and firsthand application from other believers. You could probably use answers to questions like these: What biblical principles relate to caregiving and aging? How are we to apply these principles to the caregiving situation? (See chapter 2: Honoring Your Aging Loved Ones.) Christians believe in the sanctity of human life, yet today's world of high technology can extend not only life but suffering. How are we to apply the principle of sanctity of life to specific end-of-life treatment decisions? (See chapter 18: End-of-Life Issues.)

Biblical principles provide an essential foundation for caregiving, but you will need far more information, much of it quite technical in nature. This information will come from several fields, including medicine, nursing, insurance, finance, law, and ethics.

You do not need to go to medical school, but it would be beneficial to you to learn some basic facts and nursing skills.

Your situation is unique and depends on many factors about you and your elder, including your personalities, health, living situations, resources, and relationship. Your tasks may include familiar activities like meal preparation, housecleaning, and laundry—tasks for which you will not need much new information. But caregivers often need to make decisions or perform duties for which they do not feel prepared; they need specific and detailed information.

For example, your elder may need help arranging medical and professional services or transportation to appointments and social activities. Unless you have time to be a private chauffeur, you will want information about social-service agencies and services in your area. As your elder's health deteriorates, you may be called upon to supervise financial affairs, understand and organize insurance coverage, and make medical-treatment decisions. You may need to understand a variety of financial and legal matters, and you will want to know what resources are available. (See chapter 10: Financial Care, and chapter 11: Legal Care and Estate Planning.) You may need to work with and understand the functions of a variety of professionals, including physicians, physician's assistants, neurologists, registered nurses, nurse practitioners, gerontologists, neuropsychologists, social workers, attorneys, ombudsmen, and care managers. (See chapter 9: Finding Health, Medical, and Social Services.)

Now or later, your aging loved one could need assistance with eating, bathing, dressing, and toileting. You may need to help your elder get in or out of bed, get around the home, or take medications. If your loved one has Parkinson's disease, Alzheimer's disease, depression, diabetes, or some other specific illness, you will need to learn about that illness. You will need to understand its symptoms, your elder's daily needs, how to decide when your elder needs to see a physician, and how to help manage medications. You do not need to go to medical school, but it would be beneficial to you to learn some basic facts and nursing skills. (See chapters 5 and 6: Physical Changes in Aging—Parts 1 and 2.)

Equally important are the tasks of encouraging spiritual growth, emotional health, physical exercise, and good nutrition. But what food, spiritual sustenance, emotional stimulation, and physical activities would be most appropriate for your loved one? You may want information and guidelines for age-related care in each of these areas. (Read chapter 12: Church, Religious Activity, and Spiritual Life; chapter 8: Emotional Changes in Aging; and chapters 5 and 6: Physical Changes in Aging—Parts 1 and 2.)

Christians are not meant to carry their burdens alone. As a caregiver, you will need not only professional help and social services from the community; you will also need support, encouragement, and inspiration from your church or religious community. Some churches have explored specific ways to help caregivers; others might be open to pro-

CREATIVE RESPITE

Although I didn't want to, I planned to turn down a much-needed vacation because I couldn't take time away from my parents. And they were opposed to having any strangers taking care of them in their house. I'd mentioned the trip in passing to my brother and sister-in-law but didn't want to impose. Shortly after that, we were out for dinner and my sister-in-law, Sarah, said, "We've been talking, and we think we have a win-win situation." Sarah offered to take a leave of absence from her job in order to work on her master's thesis and assume the caregiving responsibilities while I was gone. I was so grateful! So Sarah moved into my bedroom temporarily, and I was able to take a memorable trip to England. *Janice F.*

viding more assistance if they knew how. Your role may include asking for help that is already available, learning how to receive it graciously, or suggesting ways the church can be more helpful or available.

Caregiving is, no doubt, only one of your many roles. The more the demands mount, the more exhausted you might feel—emotionally, physically, and spiritually. Other members of your family may be quite supportive; nevertheless, you may feel the strain of all your responsibilities and even come to resent some of the lifestyle restrictions imposed by your aging loved one's situation. Children, if present, may contribute both needed help and extra stress. If you and your family share a household with an aging loved one, the opportunities for interpersonal conflict increase for each family member. Your mental health may suffer.

As you tend to everyone else's needs, you may wonder what will become of your own needs. You may begin to feel restless, frustrated, depressed, overworked, unappreciated, physically exhausted, emotionally drained, and spiritually depleted. Even if many things hinge on you, you must consider your own needs at least as equal to the needs of the others you care for. Yet self-care is often a problem for Christians. We learn the importance of being a servant, like Jesus. We forget that our body is God's temple and that good stewardship includes taking care of it. If you are to survive and thrive as a caregiver, you will need to include yourself in your care and attention.

To survive and thrive as a caregiver, you will need to include yourself in your care and attention.

YOUR IMPORTANT ROLE

To be a caregiver is to manage a huge, complex process. It is time consuming and probably seems overwhelming. But with the help available today, you will grow with the responsibilities. As you become accustomed to making telephone calls to agencies and organizations, you will learn how to make telephone time most effective. As you seek advice from experts, you will learn how to ask for it so that you get exactly what you need. As you begin the hands-on care of your loved one, you will likely establish a closer bond than ever before that will be self-motivating and mutually rewarding.

The caregiving process will be different for every family because there is no single timetable for human aging.

The caregiving process will be different for every family, because there is no single timetable for human aging. Even as all of this begins to happen, your support may not be welcomed at first. Hang in there, and pray for harmony. You are much needed as your loved one begins to wrestle with the changes going on in body, mind, and spirit. When caregiving is difficult, keep in mind that it is hard for the one who is aging, too. It is important to be gracious.

No matter what your role is, caregiving involves lots of talking through issues and problems with your elder and other family members. Your role as a good listener is important. Equally important are the tasks of facilitating spiritual and mental stimulation, physical exercise, entertainment, and other forms of self-care for your aging loved one. When you engage your loved one in prayer or simple reminiscing, you help increase the contentment factor in his life, and that affects your elder's overall health in a positive way.

The journey through your loved one's final years can successfully be navigated. You will encounter challenges and difficulties along the way, but with the right information, resources, help, support, and especially the grace and wisdom of God, your experience as a caregiver can be rewarding and fulfilling.

When you engage your loved one in prayer or simple reminiscing, you help increase the contentment factor in his life.

———cvɔ———

"For I know the plans I have for you," declares the Lord, "plans to prosper you and not to harm you, plans to give you hope and a future." JEREMIAH 29:11 NIV

CHAPTER 2

If anyone does not provide for his relatives, and especially
for his immediate family, he has denied the faith
and is worse than an unbeliever. 1 TIMOTHY 5:8 NIV

Honoring Your Aging Loved Ones
Biblical Basics

As Mary's parents grew older and needed help with cooking and other activities of daily living, she did her best to honor them. "Honoring my mother was hard because she tended to become feisty and argumentative as time went on," says Mary. She wondered if her mom's incipient dementia had anything to do with it. "Sometimes Mom would apologize to me, but then she'd be right back to arguing and complaining about everything. That was hard on me, but it really pained my father."

To keep her cool, Mary prayed a lot, coordinated her visits so that she wasn't under heavy time constraints, and dropped nearly all outside commitments that required preparation work. She stopped teaching Sunday school, for example, but continued to lead the singing for a Bible class. When her employer planned to transfer her to another city, she started looking for another job that would keep her near her parents. This happened several times, but each time she found a better job than the last. "As a caregiver, you really do have to make a commitment to go as far as needed, and God will honor that," she says.

Honoring her father was easier because of his quiet, uncomplaining spirit. But after her mother died, Mary began to see how much he demanded of her. "That may have contributed to why my mom was crabby so often!" she says. Mary had to do a lot of "fetch and carry"—

fetching things and bringing them to him because of his arthritis and poor vision. "But I had eyes and legs and the chance to help my dad, so I didn't mind doing it."

Caring for your aging loved one often involves some sacrifice. It means taking care of another person's needs and not necessarily seeing an end in sight or being rewarded for your efforts. It may mean carving extra time from your own limited personal time to provide needed care. Over the long haul, you might feel the stress and strain of dealing with your elder's problems. With all the challenges involved in caregiving, what motivates a caregiver to keep on caring? What will keep you from complaining when weary? What will help you to persevere? Love goes a long way toward energizing and motivating you to care for your elders, but the key word is honor. In fact, honor is genuine love in action. It proves the sincerity of our love. When you seek to honor your parents or other elders, God is honored. And caregiving becomes a more gratifying experience.

DEFINING HONOR

When God gave the Ten Commandments to His people in the wilderness, He included this among them: "Honor your father and your mother, that your days may be long upon the land which the Lord your God is giving you" (Exodus 20:12 NKJV).

Honor implies choosing to give great respect and care to our elders—not grudgingly, but from a principle of love for them and their concerns. Service that is done willingly, with gentle words and a pleasing countenance, is a great relief and comfort to an elder who feels miserable. True honor is placing the highest value on our loved ones regardless of whether or not they deserve it. Once we have decided to honor them, affection for them often follows.

Other verses also support the commandment to honor our elders, including Mark 7:9-13 and Ephesians 6:1-3. The biblical mandate is clear: Our aging loved ones are not to be ignored or neglected. In fact, Jesus affirms the responsibility of children to honor their parents by not denying service or relief to them (Matthew 15:3-9). Instead, we ought to give them a special place in our hearts and lives, treating them with love, gratefulness, and higher-than-ordinary deference. When we honor our fathers and mothers, it glorifies our heavenly Father. It also comes with a promise attached.

The apostle Paul restates the fifth commandment (found in Deuteronomy 5:16) in his letter to the Ephesians: "Children, obey your parents in the Lord, for this is right. 'Honor your father and mother'—which is the first commandment with a promise—'that it may go well with you and that you may enjoy long life on the earth'" (Ephesians 6:1-3 NIV).

Why would God attach such a promise to this particular command-

BECAUSE I LOVE YOU

When Americans take care of their own, 77.6 percent acknowledge "a great deal" of satisfaction; only 17.1 percent claim "some" satisfaction, according to one survey. Those who claim "little or no" satisfaction numbered less than 4 percent. A majority of caregivers in another national survey used a positive word, such as *rewarding*, to describe their feelings about caregiving responsibilities.[1]

When asked why they take care of elderly loved ones, their number one reason was "because I love him/her" (26.2 percent). In this and all of the following replies, the concept of honor is part of the equation:

- "It's my family obligation" (20.8 percent).
- "That's what friends are for" (12.2 percent).
- "No one else will or can" (9.9 percent).
- "He's my husband/she's my wife" (8.8 percent).
- "I enjoy it" (8 percent).
- "It's my nature" (4.6 percent).
- "Religious beliefs" (1.8 percent).[2]

This all may seem stunning when you consider that caregivers are primarily middle-aged women and likely to be mothers—coping with competing financial and emotional demands of their own. Yet, loving and honoring our elders *is* worth the effort.

[1]*Family Caregiving in the U.S.: Findings from a National Survey.*   [2]F. G. Caro and S. A. Bass, *Patterns of Productive Activity among Older Americans* (Boston: Gerontology Institute, University of Massachusetts at Boston, 1993).

ment? While long life is often a blessing of God to a godly person, we also can understand the word *long* in its archaic meaning as "suitable" or "fitting."[1] In this sense, honor implies that we live *suitably* on this earth, so that we may *fit* God's plan. Honor is part of the Master Designer's plan for how families are to live.

The Lord, who "sets the lonely in families" (Psalm 68:6 NIV), chose this intimate community of family as the mode to pass on godly love, nurture, and a sense of belonging. While no parents are perfect, parenting is the chief responsibility God ordained to carry on the work of the world. It is through mothers and fathers that we receive the opportunity to breathe, work, and love on this earth. Surely, these originators of our lives—our parents—are due our highest loyalty. And extended family, whether they be aunts, uncles, grandparents, or godparents, are due our esteem as well.

The key issue, then, is knowing *how* to fulfill the biblical mandate to honor elderly loved ones. God's Word does not deal with nursing homes, pensions, or Medicare. There is no commandment that says you must take aging parents into your home or cancel your vacation plans to pay for their prescriptions. And what if your elder is not cooperative or grateful for your help?

The *act* of honoring means to live up to the terms of a commitment to love our elders. Knowing how to honor comes first from making a

SOAKING UP STORIES

As a little girl, when I first visited my grandma in the nursing home I was terrified. It smelled funny and people were yelling. I thought, *I don't want to be around these people.* But they were not there by choice, just like my grandma. I realized many of the elderly in the home were sharp as a tack mentally but not strong enough physically to do things for themselves. They had built a life, done things on their own, been responsible—then become like children, and it was devastating for them. They just wanted to be treated as if they were normal. They didn't want to be gawked at. They just wanted to be accepted for who they were. Toward the end of the four years my grandma was in the home, I learned to love talking to those old people and soaking up their stories. Young people miss out because there isn't an emphasis on respecting the elderly like there used to be.

Emily G.

commitment to God. You show honor by choosing to be present with your elder, emotionally if not physically, and treating her with tenderness and goodwill.

Finding ways to honor will grow out of your relationship with your aging loved one and from the way she perceives your love and respect. Ways to honor will emerge from the legacy you share as a family. You will discover what honor means in a practical sense as you progress in your journey as a caregiver. For some, it might mean sharing your home and offering financial support. For many others, it will mean seeking support services, filling out endless health/insurance forms, arranging for or providing transportation, arranging and talking with medical personnel, and all sorts of other support services. For most, it can mean sharing family contacts, assisting with religious supports, and having devotions with frail loved ones. Compassion is called for. Ask yourself, *What is the best way I can care for my elderly loved one?*

Honor implies choosing to give great respect and care to our elders—not grudgingly, but from a principle of love.

RESPECTING LOSSES

In order to practice honor, it helps to remember that our elderly loved ones have traveled a long pathway. As we age, we too will face a variety of obstacles. A representative of a company that designs products from an older person's perspective wanted to make a point with administrators at a California hospital.[2] He passed out dark glasses, earplugs, nose clips, and rubber gloves; then he directed the audience to don the accessories. Next he asked the administrators to sort out a confusing array of variously colored tiny pills.

One participant said afterward, "Suddenly our world didn't look the same." She noted that the colors were dim and dull, shapes and sizes were indistinct, sounds were muffled, and breathing was a chore.

Indignities like this are common by the time you reach old age. Physical disabilities often result in a diminishing return of life's simple pleasures and the letting go of one privilege after another associated with independence and autonomy. As life changes and losses accumulate, the personal identity of an elderly person also undergoes change. Imagine some of the important losses your aging loved one might endure:

- Cherished, active roles such as mother or father, youth sponsor or scout leader, provider, household manager, mentor, and friend
- Career or job that provided opportunities for interaction with other people, stimulating interests, a sense of belonging, making a difference
- Perceived usefulness, dependability, self-esteem
- Being needed—or being enjoyed by the people they love, one of the worst of the losses. Some older people lose even their memories of being needed, enjoyed, and embraced by family and friends.
- Siblings and lifelong friends, their deaths or relocation occurring at a time when friendships are more important than ever to help your aging loved one cope with all the changes
- A spouse; this loss is perhaps the most stressful of losses and is associated with losing the role of husband or wife, confidant, and lover.
- Home, sometimes a hometown or community; some elderly must move out of state.

SOCIAL LOSSES

I'm still healthy, but my husband isn't. We've lost a lot of our social life. Other couples our age are still able to do things that we no longer can. This is the stage in life when you still want to take a walk together—and he can't walk very well. So that eliminates a lot of things. We did go to the arboretum, but we drove through it. We have Bible studies with other couples, but it would be nice to be able to take a fun trip somewhere. One church has a PrimeTimers group and they're planning a trip to a Chicago museum that features old-time radios. But when you can't walk or keep up, it's hard to participate. I guess I could go by myself. I probably need to do that occasionally, but sometimes I have feelings of guilt for going. My husband will say, "Go, do what you want." But that doesn't always work out. He isn't driving anymore, either, which is hard on him. We drove to Florida twice, and I did all the driving. I'm not sure I want to do that anymore.

I cope by going back to the thought that the Lord is there. God is in charge. He knows what's happening to me. There must be some purpose in all this, and He won't let us down. *Phyllis H.*

- Children; they grow up and have their own families, get involved in their own communities and careers.
- Independence, a driver's license, and the ability to get around without assistance

When life is being turned upside down, there is a great deal of human passion and pathos involved. A person who has felt deeply about people, made achievements in a career, and spent energy to grow and learn will not have an easy time giving in to the limitations of old age. Each loss—a friendship, the right to drive, hobbies, and routine tasks—is a wound. In this context, personalities may appear to change. Frustration is evident. A person might act tough outwardly because he is hurting inside. A once-easygoing person may become cranky. A vigorous, independent person may respond to losses by resorting to self-pity. Complaining is common. And, as in any grieving process, one of the early stages of dealing with loss is anger, manifested in many different ways. To "go down fighting" is a natural instinct for many aging people.

Empathizing with the losses that come with age can help you to express honor, patience, and love for your elderly loved ones. Consider that the honor they used to receive through their reputation in social circles, church, and career might not be possible now. The respect they commanded as leaders in the workplace or as maintainers of their homes must come from other sources in old age, such as your thoughtful actions and affirming words.

As their own sense of value and usefulness deteriorates, it is more necessary than ever to reaffirm that your loved ones are, as always, worthy and full of dignity. Include other family members, relatives, and friends in their lives as often as possible. By modeling love and respect for your elders, your children and others will see that being loving and kind to older people is the right thing to do. Besides, we will be there soon enough ourselves!

As their own sense of value and usefulness deteriorates, reaffirm that your loved ones are, as always, worthy and full of dignity.

STEPS TO HONOR

According to researchers, most older people measure their personal worth by gauging how well they meet three goals: 1) dependability, 2) ability to maintain close family ties, and 3) self-sufficiency.[3] The key to honoring aging loved ones is to understand how to encourage them in these three areas. Most elderly people do not want to reach out for help, rely on government assistance, or have hired help in their homes. They want to do things independently, proving themselves dependable and responsible. Take time to show that you value the spirit and character of your aging loved ones even when getting outside help is necessary.

When one man's 89-year-old mother-in-law was caring for her ailing 99-year-old husband, she stated flatly, "I don't want Meals On Wheels; it's part of government welfare." The son-in-law explained that Meals On Wheels is not welfare but is a service to help people remain independent. He suggested that having balanced, nutritious meals delivered to the door was one important way she might care for her husband and herself. Thanks to that explanation, she consented. The more ways that older people feel they can be counted on to take care of themselves, help their loved ones, and stay connected to family, the more likely they are to remain optimistic. Consider the following eight ideas for honoring your loved ones:

Give your elders the opportunity to share their faith with children and grandchildren, telling the stories of hope that have sustained them.

Recognize their skills and successes. Honoring your aging loved ones entails recognizing them not only for who they are but for past achievements, abilities, and talents. Compliment your elderly loved ones for their accomplishments raising a family, contributing to the community and church, and being good citizens (e.g., participating in a war effort, exercising the right to vote, helping the underprivileged). Compliment them for knowing what is important in the context of personal morality, faith, and relationships. Watch for opportunities to recognize the significant part they are playing in your life.

Reminisce with them. Ask your older loved ones to review the successes and precious memories of their lives—the events that are most meaningful. Aging Christians love to recount how God has provided for and guided them through ups and downs, blessings and trials. Give your elders the opportunity to share their faith with children and grandchildren, telling the stories of hope that have sustained them. People with a Christian worldview can look back at failure, loss, and tribulation with a sense of divine meaning. Reviewing life in light of God's grace and unmerited favor is an exercise toward maintaining a healthy view of oneself.

Record your elders' stories on audiocassette or videotape. Capture their history, as well as their interactions with children and grandchildren, in photo albums or beautiful memory gift books. At family reunions, birthdays, and anniversaries, ask each guest to say something memorable about an elder or to retell a story that has been passed down. Include memories from your elders' spiritual heritage, such as how they became Christians or some ways in which their own parents served the Lord. These stories can become part of your family legacy to pass down to younger generations.

Reinvent memories. Send notes on special days that are meaningful to your aging loved ones, such as the anniversary of D day or VJ day, the day your elder became a Christian, or the birthday of a deceased sibling. Celebrate everything possible! Affirmations of life and love remind elderly people that they are appreciated. Create your own "Super Grandparent Day" or "Best Senior on the Block Award." Jot down positive things you remember about growing up. Then cut them into small scraps of paper, roll them into scrolls, and put them in a jar for your elders to read now and then.

ON THE ALERT

I tried to honor my parents by not taking over jobs they could do between the two of them. When my father was too blind to do the bookkeeping and keep track of investments, I encouraged my mother to do it. I reminded her that she had taught fifth-grade math and had the skills to do it. It took some time, but Mom came up with a system that worked. It helped keep her mental acuity sharp and it was one less thing I had to do. Later, Dad had a mild stroke that impaired his speech, but he worked hard to improve it. That's when I realized I could help speed his recovery by taking time to engage in his beloved crossword puzzles with him. He'd given them up because he could no longer see the words, but when I read the questions and gave the clues, he was eager to come up with the answers.

Karen A.

Remember friends and help your elders make new ones. Elderly people benefit from spending time with old companions as well as making new friends. Having a close friend in old age is sometimes more important than having a large family network. Friendships help people survive losses and move on. They also help people process loss, depression, and feelings of worthlessness. Arrange for your loved one to have access

---

CHOOSING TO CARE

I chose to purchase my mother's home and become her caregiver so that she could continue to live as independently as possible—not because I felt obligated as a single daughter but because I valued her and wanted to honor her.

I also wanted to get to know her. As a child, I felt I didn't like my mother much. She had a keen sense of humor, but she also was remote, inwardly angry, and seemed to be suppressing something. Well, I got to know her like nobody else. It started gradually. She began telling me delightful stories from her childhood. She had had a little red wagon just like I had when I was a little girl. She told the story of sitting on her mother's lap on the porch at night with her mother's apron tucked around her for warmth. Then she began telling some sad stories about her alcoholic father and other sorrows. She would say, "I don't know why I'm telling you this." Bit by bit Mom came to trust me. She told me some of the dreams she'd had at night, too, and I figured out what she'd been suppressing all these years. She asked me, "Do you think my dad abused me?" I said, "Yes, I do." She put her head down and just cried. I had never seen her cry, and she was 90 years old.

I felt so privileged to be there to walk through the pain with her. I feel pain is our greatest teacher. What we choose to do with our pain is one of the biggest choices we make in life. The resurrection can't come to us unless we deal with the cross first.

You know what? My mother became a really free person. She processed her life and found deep meaning in it. She stopped putting herself down and came to know and accept herself. She let go of some hurts in the family and accepted her children for who they were. At one point she watched a video that encouraged family members to be tender and hug each other. Mom, who never showed affection, took it to heart. She came to the breakfast table one morning with her cane, put her slender, bony arm around me, and said, "I love you." That was a precious moment among many in the nearly 12 years I cared for Mom, and I wouldn't trade it for anything. *Elsie N.*

to friends by phone, e-mail, or regular mail. You may need to provide transportation for friends to visit, if that will keep them close.

Renew their energy with regular exercise. Swimming, walking, or other light exercise improves circulation and keeps the **endorphins**—those "feel-good hormones"—coursing through the blood system. If possible, join your aging loved one regularly for a walk outside or down the hall, in an exercise facility, or in a shopping mall; you will both benefit. Some communities and congregate-living facilities have warm-water pools that are ideal for arthritis sufferers.

Report opportunities for senior volunteering in the community. Tell your aging loved ones about programs in which senior citizens may get involved. They are listed in local newspapers and magazines. Also, the federally funded Senior Companion Program works with nonprofit agencies to enable older adults with limited incomes to serve other seniors who are chronically impaired or frail.[4] For a few hours on weekdays, "senior companions" lend a listening ear and a helping hand (e.g., assisting with meals and personal care). In return, these volunteers receive a stipend, transportation assistance, lunch, and accident insurance. For volunteer opportunities, check with your city's Department on Aging, your local senior center, or your local Area Agency on Aging.

Remind them of latent talents. Encourage your loved ones to get back to painting, baking, writing, acting, or some other hobby or pastime, if possible. What about "scrapbooking," participating in a Senior Olympic event, becoming a foster grandparent, or taking part in a short-term missions project? Many aging people are becoming interested in computers, and classes abound for them to learn brand-new skills. Probe the interests of your elders until you see their eyes light up—then find a way for them to get involved.

Capture your elder's history, as well as her interactions with children and grand-children, in photo albums or beautiful memory gift books.

As Things Change, Revere Neutral Ground

Some adult children experience tension in their relationship with aging parents or other elders because of differences in opinion over music, entertainment, money, religious beliefs, even the roles of men and women in church and society. Don't allow differences to lead to unnecessary conflict and resentment. Listen respectfully to your elder and consider her words. On your own, examine God's Word regarding the topic or principle of discussion, and determine for yourself what is right. You might discover something you did not know before! Even when you agree to disagree with your elder, let no unwholesome word come out of your mouth. Only say what will edify your loved one (Ephesians 4:29).

You might also disagree over your elder's preferences for living arrangements, medical care, wills, eating habits, or other issues. Honor means trying to find neutral ground and then revering it. Respect your loved one's opinions and listen well, even as you talk about exploring some new services, options, alternatives, or other ways of maintaining independence. Give him credit for applying the wisdom he gained during his years of raising a family. For example, your dad may have saved most of the money he earned in a simple savings account. If he disputes your decisions about alternative ways to invest money, don't insist he understand completely. Your goal should be to preserve his dignity.

Preserving Your Elder's Dignity

Honoring the elderly is about maintaining their sense of personhood. Practical ways to preserve an elder's dignity include: making appropriate, clean clothes available at all times (such as after a spill at mealtime); keeping extra personal-hygiene supplies in stock (in case things like combs and toothbrushes get lost); providing a clock and a calendar (with large numbers for a visually-impaired elder) to help her keep oriented; and being sure glasses, medications, and telephones are within reach. Add a personal touch by giving your loved one the satis-

LOSING GRANDPA

My grandpa was a huge man, a really muscular coal miner, about six foot three. He used to pick me up and throw me in the air. I have watched him shrink, get thin, and lose his height and strength. He loses his glasses and forgets to take his medication. It just makes you realize how important your loved ones are to you. Your commitment to Christ has got to be there because loved ones can be gone in an instant.

Emily G.

faction of looking right and feeling comfortable with herself. A shampoo, a fragrant bath, a foot massage, and a manicure are classic ways to refresh and unwind. These should be routine, occurring on a consistent basis, but keep in mind that aging people may forget to ask or not want to trouble you. If modesty is an issue, find a nurse or someone else to help your elder with personal care, such as bathing and dressing. A few simple extras—fresh flowers on the dining-room table, soft lotions in the bathroom, patience, and a gentle touch—can make the difference between obligatory caregiving and the act of honoring. You will enjoy the responsibilities more, too, if color, fragrance, and a smile are a regular part of the day.

Allow your elder to do as much as possible for herself, even when you could do it more quickly or easily.

Preserving dignity also involves supporting your elder's sense of independence. It means not imposing decisions on your elder just because it might make things easier or more convenient for you. It means never assuming or acting as if an elder who is slow or hard-of-hearing is unable to understand what is going on around her. Do not shame your elder. Allow her to do as much as possible for herself in the area of personal hygiene, even when you could do it more quickly or easily.

Changing Roles

With increasing age or infirmity, your elder will begin to rely on you and your personal resources in many practical and emotional ways. It may seem as if you are reversing roles as you become a "parent" to your loved one. If you are caring for an aging mother or father, this can be

ALLEVIATING FEAR

I admire my mother's spunk at age 86. But the summer I went to England for my daughter's wedding—the longest I'd been away from Mom—she was on the phone saying, "I can't live by myself anymore. I don't know what I'm going to do."

When we got back, my husband and I decided that if Mom really meant that, I would spend three nights a week at her house making sure her needs were met. When I explained the plan, she said, "Well, I don't think that's necessary." Once she felt secure that I would really be there for her, she kind of backed off of being scared about being alone.

Lucy

distressing because role reversal is never clear-cut or complete. Adult children may remain in many ways dependent on their parents. But the truth is, we are interdependent; we need each other. There are riches to be mined and insight to be gained in the changing relationship between adult children and their parents or other aging loved ones.

In spite of your efforts to assist your aging loved one in living with some measure of independence, the time may come when you need to assume a more active decision-making role. This is the ultimate role reversal. It might feel threatening and unnatural. You may face a series of small endings. If you are now guiding the parents who guided you, how do you honor them in this?

It takes time to adjust the way you think and feel as your elder's caregiver. A transition may take place—that period when the old ways of relating to your loved one fade and a kind of emptiness takes their place. Be patient with yourself, especially when you must make difficult caregiving decisions, such as leaving the workforce to care for a parent who needs more assistance. Your attitude and spiritual values will affect your ability to cope with unplanned hardships. Are you trusting the Lord—whose mercies are new every morning—to refill your inner resources and to handle things you cannot control? Wait for the new way of relating to your aging loved one to become clear.

The relationship between adult women and their own mothers, for example, may be one of the most complex and emotionally charged of all family relationships. Mothers tend to have high expectations of their daughters—even more so when the mother is elderly and needs help. Yet there is no dress rehearsal to get comfortable with the change in

FREE AT LAST!

Mom was verbally and physically abusive to me while I was growing up. I resolved those issues years ago. But they do crop up occasionally, especially when I'm stressed out from family, work, and the two-hour drive to see her. Some time ago, I asked her forgiveness for all those years I treated her mean for mistreating me. It was so freeing for me! She never said, "Would you forgive me, too?" But I don't think she was capable of doing that. Mom has early stage Alzheimer's disease. Besides, I'm fairly convinced she, too, was abused—by her father—but has buried it. *Jane H.*

roles between an aging parent and an adult child. When an aging loved one can no longer handle ordinary skills necessary for living alone, it can be a scary time for everyone concerned. For the elderly person, the issue may be loss of control, which can produce stress, anger, and fear. For you, the issue may be fear that your elder is no longer safe on her own and frustration when she does not accept your recommendations. If this is the case, give her time and affirmation, and pray for God's protection.

Give your aging loved one as much freedom as possible under the circumstances. Guard against using a condescending tone when speaking with your elder. If your elder is still maintaining a home, simple offers to mow the lawn or clean the kitchen might sound like threats to a person who is struggling with the inability to do such tasks. One way around this dilemma is to hire outside help so your elder is not dependent on *you*. If your loved one balks at the expense, you and your siblings might privately subsidize the fee. There are many community-based agencies that can provide assistance and ease your burden at reasonable costs. Call the local Area Agency on Aging for information and referrals. (Also, see chapter 9: Finding Health, Medical, and Social Services.)

The relationship between adult women and their own mothers may be one of the most complex and emotionally charged of all family relationships.

Sometimes Honor Comes Hard

You did not choose your parents or other family members, of course. No one grows up with a perfect mother and father. No one is married to a perfect spouse. Perhaps your loved one has not lived up to the ideal. Some parents, guardians, and spouses simply are not supportive, responsible, mature, or good at providing. They might be irresponsible, mean-spirited, neglectful, or abusive. In those cases, love is hard to muster. But since honor is a gift we give to our elders, it is not really contingent on their actions or our emotions. (For more information, see "Dealing with Family Conflict" on pages 56-57 and "The Impact of Family Secrets" on page 48.)

Caring for the One Who Hurt You

Many individuals have been impacted by dysfunction and a disregard for the Word of God in their family of origin. You may feel disapointed or even bitter. Remnants of pain from childhood may still affect you. You may look back, even at the recent past, and remember only abuse and neglect from the people you are now supposed to honor. This is a tough assignment. Nevertheless, each life is precious and unrepeatable, even the life of someone who has sinned grievously against another person. God created each individual with certain gifts and abilities, even though these gifts may be left unopened and unused.

Only God can fully know the circumstances that molded a person's character. You cannot realign those events or alter another person's life choices. But you can refuse to give their problems power over you. You can set out to find the remnants of good in your parents or family, no matter how meager or unrefined. And you can choose to honor, to live in God's light and the illumination of your own conscience, and to respond with a Christlike attitude. When Jesus washed His disciples' feet, He demonstrated love and honor by being willing to stoop to the lowliest act of kindness for the good of undeserving people (John 13:5, 14, 34).

Being Realistic

When people have hurt you, it is difficult to give them the type of constant loving care they may need. Yet too often we have an unrealistic concept of caregiving. Honoring your parents does not mean bowing to every demand or neglecting the needs of your spouse or children in order

HONORING A DISTANT DAD

My father divorced my mom and disappeared from our lives when I was a child. Because he isn't a Christian, I guess I expect him to act like a sinner. So I don't hold a big grudge against him for not being Super Dad or even a visiting single dad. In spite of what happened, I try to find ways to honor him in his latter years. It's important for him, and it's a mandate from Scripture for me. My dad was really moved by a tribute I wrote and gave to him before his last surgery. It read, "I know your life hasn't gone the way you would choose if you could choose all over again. I know you did your best. I've got some great memories." I also try to verbalize things that honor him. I hope it will at least let him know he's not going to pass away with an angry son.

John T.

to be with them every moment. It does not mean tackling every caregiving task by yourself. Nor does it mean you must always agree with your elderly loved ones, become the doting daughter or son you never were, or make up for your own mistakes or disrespect of earlier years.

Honor does mean you do what you can to live at peace with your elders and other family members, even if you do not have a great affinity for each other. Regardless of your unique family circumstances, honor will come easier if you "get rid of all bitterness, rage and anger, brawling and slander, along with every form of malice. Be kind and compassionate to one another, forgiving each other, just as in Christ God forgave you" (Ephesians 4:31-32 NIV). When you seek to honor, God will show you the way to do it.

Attempt to make wise choices that will keep your own conscience clear. A woman named Margaret, whose mother died 16 years ago, is still comforted by the caregiving decisions she made. "When I read Bible verses about honoring my parents, I don't have to cringe," she says. "I did the things I needed to do. I realized that it isn't over when your parent dies. You always carry with you that relationship." This does not mean there is always a right or wrong decision, but it is important to step back and think about how you might feel years from now. (For more information on family dynamics, see chapter 3: Your Circle of Support.)

HONORING A LOVED ONE FROM AFAR

American families have always thought that taking care of their own was important. But in our mobile society, family members are more spread out geographically than ever before. It is not uncommon for aging loved ones to live one or more time zones away. In fact, there are an estimated 7 million long-distance caregivers in the United States, according to the nonprofit Family Caregiver Alliance. Caregiving becomes more of a challenge when miles separate you and your aging loved one.

Gather Information

Long-distance caregiving usually begins with a phone call from a neighbor or friend who has noticed a change in your aging loved one's behavior or is calling to report a crisis. Resist the urge to jump on a plane immediately to check on your aging loved one; instead, first gather as much information as possible from your elder's neighbors, relatives, friends, and doctor. Ask what kind of help your parent or loved one might need. Let the key people in your elder's life know how they can get in touch with you, and consider inviting them to call you collect in an emergency.

If a trip is warranted, try to arrange it so that you and your elder can meet with his doctor and other professionals who can advise you both about what to do next. This establishes a relationship with your elder's

SHOW AGING LOVED ONES YOU CARE

Try a few of these ideas for honoring your elders:

- Play the Question Game. Your loved one probably has a lifetime of stories you have never heard. Treat yourself and let him do the talking. Ask questions such as, "Who was your first best friend?" "What were you really good at in school?" "What is the scariest thing that ever happened to you?"
- Make the phone friendly. The right phone makes a great gift. Shopping suggestions: Look for jumbo buttons and easy-to-read numbers that do not wear off, cordless models, speed dials. Consider getting yourself a toll-free number so your aging loved one can call you without cost or hassle.
- Call your elder. Say, "I love you." Tell her, "I need your help," then ask her opinion about something, or ask, "Do you remember when . . . ?" Don't forget to add, "You're a great mom," or "You've always been a great uncle."
- Knock down walls. If your relationship with your aging loved one is not perfect, you are hardly alone. Difficult memories or painful emotions that have persisted through the years are hard to just forget about and put aside. Be honest. Sort out what you are angry about with a counselor or trusted friend. Face your own fears. Be willing to forgive and/or confess sins. Pray for wisdom and talk to your elder, beginning with "I love you."
- Laugh together. Laughter is like jogging for the spirit. Drag out the baby pictures, look for cartoons and jokes, watch a silly movie together.

Adapted by permission of Thomas Nelson Publishers from the book entitled 52 Ways to Show Aging Parents You Care, *copyright date 1992, by Tracy Green and Todd Temple.*

health-care team and shows that you care. Be specific with your questions, since time is at a premium. The doctor's office staff may be able to help you with some requests, such as test results and dates of upcoming treatments. Make an effort to meet personally with your elder's friends and neighbors, too, and exchange contact information.

Consider your elder's feelings before taking any major steps; most older people fear losing their autonomy or becoming a burden to family members or friends. And making a move can be traumatic for an elderly person. Try to weigh your elder's wishes to live independently against the potential risks of doing so. In cases where dementia is a factor, you may not be able to convince your elder you have her best interests in mind, but do your best to keep her feeling secure.

Keep in Touch

Honoring your aging loved one from a distance requires keen management and ongoing supervision. Here are some more tips that may make long-distance caregiving less complicated:

- Use your telephone to locate resources for seniors in your elder's community. Contact the local senior center or an outreach worker who will make a home visit and connect your elder to local services. Check with your elder's Area Agency on Aging (AAA) for references. Also, for future reference, compile a list of the names and telephone numbers of key people and places in your aging loved one's life: doctors, pastors, the pharmacy, neighbors, and close relatives, for example.

- Ask your elder to follow up on specific calls you have made. Legally, you will need to get your elder's permission before discussing his health with his physician. This also honors him and gives him a sense of control. If you ask for permission and are told no, find out why. Explain that because of your concern and the distance between you, you would like to talk to his physician. If your elder still says no, the doctor will not be able to share specifics about your elder, but you still can give information to the doctor. For example, if the building manager has called you three times to say your elder almost burned down

EIGHT PRACTICAL WAYS THEY HONOR AGING LOVED ONES

1. My mother visited my grandmother several times a week to give her a manicure, even though Grandmother didn't always know who she was. —*Lottie H.*

2. For Nana's 90th birthday I gathered stationery, cards, stickers, and postcards. Then I bought a big basket, painted it white, and trimmed it with small artificial roses. I filled it with 90 love notes written on the stationery and cards, all collected from friends and relatives. Nana was overwhelmed with surprise! She read them after the party at the retirement home and continued to read them over and over. —*Tami G.*

3. It's important to me that my mom knows she's still my mother even though as she gets old, she's becoming like a child. I still show respect for her ideas, her biblical knowledge, and her relationship with the Lord that is as strong as ever. I call and ask her, "What does the Bible say about this? What do you think God wants me to do?" Most of the time, Mom can still pull out the answers. —*Sharon T.*

4. My dad always told us that when you know someone is dying, be sure to tell him everything you want him to know. My sisters and I decided to make Dad an album. We each wrote him a letter, went through pictures, and made up a page for the album. It was one of the things he treasured most during his last few months. —*Joan W.*

5. Because so much of our lives revolved around our children's friends, we would always invite them to my mother's birthday parties. You can count on teenagers to make a big deal! Though Mother liked things quiet, she would get to where she would laugh out loud. One birthday we took her miniature golfing. We let her choose the holes she wanted to play. A couple of the big guys carried her over the obstacles. —*Sally B.*

6. When Nana "forgot" the good times and seemed to focus on life's difficulties, I created an ABC album to remind her of the beautiful person she is and all the wonderful things she has done over the years. It was an *A* to *Z* book of adjectives describing her, one alphabet letter per page, with a thought regarding that particular word. For example, *G* stood for *generous*. I found a picture of her holding some cash and included stickers of things I was able to do with the money she gave me (car, college, travel). I wrote a letter as an introduction to the album, took her out for a nice dinner, and presented the album to her. She laughed, cried, and enjoyed every minute of it. For a short time she sounded like the Nana I knew, and she continued to read the album constantly. —*Lottie H.*

7. We were always a family that played games. When we played with my mother, we would play teams. I insisted one of the kids be on the team with Mom. Mother's mind was still sharp. But instead of playing Jeopardy or Trivial Pursuit with the quickest answer winning, we'd give time for Mother to think, allowing time for each team to answer. —*Sally B.*

8. It was embarrassing for me to take my German grandmother to the store because of the strange things she would say. She would stop and talk to everybody she saw. Then I decided it was a good idea to change my perspective and just kind of go along and have fun with her. I listened to her banter on about how "they don't give you no good carrots anymore," and I started seeing the humor in it and not worrying about myself. That's one way I honored who she was. —*Elise C.*

the building, this is information the doctor ought to know about!

• Find a support person in your elder's community who can be trusted to monitor her condition, progress, and well-being. This may require making a trip to where your elder lives so you can talk to neighbors or interview candidates in person. Or you may pay for this help by hiring a case manager or a licensed social worker to locate and oversee appropriate services (contact the Eldercare Locator for information on referrals—see appendix). If your aging loved one has some cognitive or physical impairment but does not have a live-in caregiver, her neighbors and close friends might be willing to take turns discreetly checking in on her once a day.

• Keep a calendar to note your elder's doctor appointments and social activities. This will help you stay involved in his life.

• Get together with your elder as often as is feasible for you. Make regular telephone calls and listen closely to show your interest. Send letters, photos, audio- and videotapes, and little gifts to help your elder feel loved. E-mail is a supplemental way to stay in contact, but it is too impersonal to be your main mode of communication. Elderly people much prefer seeing their loved ones or hearing their voices.

• Consider having all bills sent directly to your own address so that your elder does not have to worry about them. Ask for permission first.

- Use catalogs to buy clothes and other necessities for your aging loved one. If your elder has the same catalogs, you can shop together by phone.

IT IS NEVER TOO LATE TO LEARN TO HONOR

No one wants to grow old. Few welcome it, but nearly all accept it. Caring for aging loved ones is all about *honor* in this process: Honor for God and His plan for humankind—human life, work, repopulation, aging, and passing on to eternal life. It is about honoring the people who brought you into the world, cared for you (in whatever degree), and watched you grow, leave the nest, and achieve. Caring includes honoring yourself—including body, soul, and spirit.

Honor is a gift you can give that will bring security, joy, and a sense of completion to your loved one's final years.

The first thing to do as you begin this journey is to pray for guidance and strength. Meet God each morning in His Word and in prayer, requesting the power of the Holy Sprit for the day. Picture yourself putting on the "full armor of God" (described in Ephesians 6:10-18) as you start the day: "Stand firm then, with the belt of truth buckled around your waist, with the breastplate of righteousness in place, and with your feet fitted with the readiness that comes from the gospel of peace. In addition to all this, take up the shield of faith, with which you can extinguish all the flaming arrows of the evil one. Take the helmet of salvation and the sword of the Spirit, which is the word of God" (NIV).

Most important, pray. Ask God for anything in line with the Holy Spirit's wishes. Ephesians 6:18 reminds us to be alert in prayer with all kinds of prayers and requests for Christians everywhere. Each night, commit yourself and your aging loved ones into God's protective hands. Exercise your faith by asking your heavenly Father to provide what you need when you need it: the money for a doctor's bill or the ability to be kind and gentle on a very bad day. Talk to a counselor, pastor, or friend when you feel drained or weak. Schedule a few hours or days of respite care when you need it. (If you do not have anyone else to look after your loved one temporarily, contact your local Area Agency on Aging, hospital, nursing home, or church for referrals.) No matter what, be faithful in the spiritual disciplines; they are a crucial part of honoring the people who need you.

"Middle-aged people need the elderly, although they may not know it or even believe it," says one 78-year-old woman. "To grow older themselves, younger people need the lessons that can be learned only from caring for their parents."

It is never too late, or too soon, to love and honor your elders. As you seek to honor them, your love for them will grow and your relationship with them will be enhanced. It will improve communication while creating an emotional environment for mutual trust. Honor is a gift you can give that will bring security, joy, and a sense of completion to your loved one's final years.

———— ✺ ————

Listen to your father, who gave you life, and do not despise your mother when she is old. PROVERBS 23:22 NIV

CHAPTER 3

Do not merely look out for your own personal interests,

but also for the interests of others.

PHILIPPIANS 2:4 NASB

Your Circle of Support
Family Dynamics in Caregiving

WHEN Christy's mother had a stroke, she and her siblings had a terrible time deciding what to do about their mom's house. They held on to it for about a year hoping she'd be able to go back, but finally realized that that wasn't going to happen. When they put it up for sale, Christy's sister cleared out some of their mom's things, saying she would put them in storage and sell them later at a garage sale. But when Christy visited her sister one day, she saw those same things incorporated into her sister's house. "If someone had asked me earlier how I would react, I wouldn't have imagined being angry—but I was," says Christy. "I could hardly talk to my sister."

While she was talking about it to her husband, he looked around at their nicely furnished house and asked, "If you had those things, what would you do with them?"

"I don't know," Christy said with a sigh. "Maybe I'm overreacting."

With that thought, she realized she was letting her emotions interfere with her relationship and needed to let go of the matter.

———— ✑ ————

A health crisis in the life of your aging loved one is a stressor that can put the whole family on alert. Your relationships with other family members can be severely strained as emotions run high and fears or resentments build. But ideally, a crisis that is properly handled will draw your family closer together to support your ailing elder.

This is not an easy task. There will be decisions to make and duties to divide. You may need to referee disagreements and identify unfair workloads. Outside expertise or counseling may be needed if discussions are too volatile or the issues regarding your elder are particularly complex. But the more prepared you are to handle a crisis when it occurs, the more successful you will be in resolving it.

FAMILY CAREGIVING

As the aging population grows, the ranks of family caregivers are swelling. One out of four U.S. households cares for a sick or disabled loved one who is age 50 or older.[1] Although there is usually one primary caregiver, the context of family—siblings, spouses, children, and extended relatives—provides a built-in network of partners for caregiving. This family network can offer emotional support and a kind of backup system, as well as the security of knowing that if something should happen to you, your aging loved one will not be left alone. Sharing a strong sense of family is a powerful motivator to share the caregiving responsibilities for elderly loved ones.

On the other hand, the stability of the family as a whole is affected by changes or disturbances among its members. In times of crisis, you need all the support you can get. But where do you find support when your aging loved one is incapacitated and your own siblings or immediate family members are in the vortex of the tempest with you? The time-consuming tasks, tough decisions, and caregiving arrangements for which typical caregivers are responsible can strain and drain the most loving of families, both emotionally and financially. Feelings of guilt, frustration, and resentment are common when the demands of caregiving are prolonged and family members disagree about caregiving decisions.

Those caring for someone with dementia are more likely than other caregivers to have less time for other family members or leisure activities.[2] In many situations, it seems one person does all the work and may feel tired, stressed, put-upon, and unappreciated (despite the fact that she is more than willing to care for her aging loved one). The other family members who are not serving as primary caregiver may feel left out, ignored, and guilty for not doing more. Some extended members prefer to stay out of the picture entirely, except to hear how their elder is doing. This can cause problems both with the family members and the elder and among the family members themselves.

Caregivers who are single or without siblings encounter less family interference, but they tend to feel overburdened and intensely lonely in the caregiving role. Caregiving daughters and sons who have no children of their own are sometimes plagued by uncertainty: *When I'm old, who will take care of me?*

To protect yourself and your loved ones, it may be helpful to expand your circle of support to include friends, neighbors, clergy, volunteers, and other professionals. You should not feel guilty because you cannot do everything. Be willing to delegate tasks and to turn to community programs and professional resources for help. Have discussions with your family and other supporters at the start of any acute situation in order to establish roles and responsibilities. Fostering good communication and solidarity will help keep finger-pointing to a minimum when it comes time to make life-changing decisions for your loved one.

Have discussions with your family at the start of any acute situation in order to establish roles and responsibilities.

The Role of the Spouse

If you have a supportive spouse, you have someone who will listen and sympathize with your elder-care problems—a gift in itself—even if he or she does not share in the hands-on care. Having a spouse also provides you with someone who can share in the decision making. However, spouses of caregivers may tire of the lifestyle restrictions—disruptions to vacation and travel plans, constraints on the family budget, increased household chores, and less time spent with each other and the children.

When Christine's aging mother lived with her family, it began to impact Christine's marriage. It helped build strength to depend on one another. "Sometimes my husband would say, 'Go to bed. I'll take care of your mom,'" Christine recalls. However, caregiving had a negative effect on intimacy. "My husband put up with my absence a lot when

Mom was in and out of the hospital, because we weren't really connected a lot physically," says Christine. "But you have to work with each other and support one another. This is part of life."

Children Will Reduce—or Add—Stress

Children in caregiving households are often silent witnesses to changing family dynamics. As children get older, they often become part of a caregiving backup system, both emotionally and practically. They can sense the importance of sacrifices made to care for grandparents or older relatives. They frequently are able to develop a special relationship with the older person, even if the aging adult has some form of brain deterioration. One family's teenage son voluntarily came home from high school each day to have lunch with his grandma, who was becoming forgetful. He enjoyed joking with her and was glad he could keep an eye on her in the kitchen.

As children get older, they often become part of a caregiving backup system, both emotionally and practically.

When children and adults share a household with an aging loved one, the potential for love increases with each additional family member. However, so does the possibility of interpersonal conflict. Children's social lives might be disrupted and their personal freedom restricted. They might feel uncomfortable bringing friends home. Parents find themselves mediating conflicts between the children and their aging loved one, especially when the elder's health is critical. Caregivers who are pulled in both directions—by the demands of their elder and their children—often feel restless, isolated, and depressed. As a caregiver, your desire to meet everyone's needs and set a good example of elder care for your children can contribute to the pressure you feel.

Whose Needs Come First?

Many caregivers ask this question. The answer: At times it will be the needs of an aging loved one who is coping with a health concern. At other times, the emotional state of a teenager will come into focus. A spouse's needs may go underground for a period of time, only to resurface later on. Perhaps the quality of your family as a whole will take first priority. But *your* needs also matter. If you neglect your personal health, your ability to care for your aging loved ones will suffer too. Take catnaps when possible and get regular periods of respite (short-term relief from constant caregiving) to help revive you for the task at hand. (For referrals for respite care, contact your local Area Agency on Aging, a nursing home, hospital, or church. Also, see chapter 4: Caring for Yourself.)

FAMILY FRICTION

In the course of caregiving, disagreements and differences sometimes arise between siblings and spouses as well as between parents and children. The illness of an aging loved one tends to bring unresolved issues to the surface. Siblings might not volunteer to help because they do not want to infringe on the primary caregiver's role or be told what to do. Family members might quarrel over a parent's finances or question a decision about an elder's medical treatment. Secondary or long-distance caregivers sometimes feel mixed emotions—guilt over their minimal involvement and relief that someone else is doing the bulk of the work, yet resentment toward the primary caregiver for his major role or decisions he has made.

There are no perfect people or perfect families. Each family has its own legacy and personality. Your unique family dynamics and history

SIBLING RIVALRY

When my mother was sick with a terminal illness last Thanksgiving, my sister was bound and determined to get her into a nursing home—against my wishes. (She's the oldest and always wants what's convenient for her.) My mother wanted to have hospice care at home in her apartment. Instead, she died after just six days in the nursing home.

My mom owned a lot of jewelry, so after the funeral I suggested we put her jewelry on a table so that my sister, my brother Bobby, and I could pick some. My sister responded, "Oh, Bobby doesn't deserve anything." Shortly after that, my sister emptied my mother's apartment and took all her jewelry and some other valuables for herself. That's when I realized she didn't think *I* deserved any of my mother's things either. Later she had the nerve to ask me about some watercolor paintings my mother had given me six months before she died. She apparently wanted those, too! We used to try and get along, but I'm done trying. I know that's not a very Christian attitude, but it's the way I feel right now.

Mary L.

add to the complexity of your responsibilities as a caregiver. Just as a family's strengths may rise to the occasion in a crisis, old conflicts and weaknesses also may surface. Knowing how to handle family conflicts and flare-ups before they explode will help you keep the peace.

Tensions

When unresolved tension exists between parents and children or siblings, time itself does not heal old wounds. In fact, the pressure of making caregiving decisions may bring out the worst in family members. Old feelings of envy, rivalry, or anger can be stirred up in a caregiving crisis, even when the family is scattered geographically. It is not unusual for an adult child to compete for a parent's affection or praise, trying to prove himself the favorite. His overly protective or doting behavior can cause the other siblings to feel cynical or left out. Friction might also result when a favored child is left to provide primary care for the parent, appointed by brothers and sisters in a kind of unofficial vote. The overburdened caregiver may feel suffocated, may take on a martyr complex, or may manifest smoldering resentment.

One woman who lives near her mother was glad to take on the role of primary caregiver, but she has grown frustrated by the lack of support from her siblings. "If I don't do it or at least direct it, it doesn't get done," she complains. "No one picks up the slack, and this is where the resentment comes in."

Sometimes a family member brings a personal agenda that may or may not be in the best interest of a frail or incapacitated elder. The person may have a hard time listening to the perspective of other family members.

Even family members who normally get along can clash over differing opinions or in response to stress. One sibling may be in denial, for example, about a mother's growing dementia and may resist taking steps to ensure her safety. Another might fantasize about rescuing an aging loved one and reversing the situation: *I can find a more hopeful diagnosis, a better doctor, a better-equipped hospital. When I move my parent in with me, everything will be just fine.* Yet another may chide the other family caregivers or the hospital, clinic, or nursing-home staff: "If only someone had been more alert, this wouldn't have happened. If only the nurse had given Dad more attention or noticed the symptoms, everything would have been fine."

Negligence can happen, but usually the problem is simply declining health and mortality at work. At some point, the family will be forced to acknowledge the truth about their aging loved one's condition. It might not be possible to pinpoint and untangle issues of denial, fantasy, or blame. But it is possible to stop blaming yourself or others when things go wrong and instead aim for deeper understanding and acceptance. When caring for elderly loved ones, it will be necessary for the family to communicate on more than a superficial level. If family members can jointly discuss the facts, concerns, and caregiving options regarding their elder, they can begin the process of cooperating as a team. (For tips about productive conversations, see "Communication in the Family Context" on pages 51-55.)

PLAYING FAVORITES

I am the firstborn daughter in my family. My sister came along 17 months later, then almost 11 years after that, my brother, Steve, was born. We started hearing our parents say they wished they had just one child, a boy. They raised my brother differently. Steve was more spoiled, more protected, and seemed to get into a lot of trouble in his younger years. Now single again, he lives with Mother, who lives next door to me. His two children come and stay every other weekend there.

My children and I hear a lot of comparison and favoritism from Mom for Steve's children. I talk to my kids a lot about how Grandma deserves the respect and love that you should give any aging person, especially a grandparent—even when she compares them to Steve's kids. I try to stress how fortunate we are to have Grandma right next door. I tell them over and over that she loves them, although she might not always treat them that way.

Steve helps Mom financially when he can and does household chores. But the errands, taking her to the hospital, and all the other things that go with caregiving are left up to me. Mom doesn't expect Steve to help. Since I'm the oldest and a nurse, I guess that's kind of natural. I left home at 16, when Steve was only 5 years old, so he and I never developed a close relationship. I try not to confront him now or ask that he do anything. Mom would be angry at me if I did. *Gayle T.*

The Impact of Family Secrets

Family caregiving is sometimes negatively impacted by the presence of family secrets—those sad or bad things no one wants to remember, much less talk about. These may include physical, verbal, or sexual abuse, addictions of many kinds, neglect or abandonment, mental illness, marital unfaithfulness, controlling behaviors, or personality quirks like a quick temper, excessive worry, or odd behaviors. Where any of these have occurred, perpetrated by one or more parents, the parent is almost always in a state of denial. The adult child may often experience underground rage. This is true even when family members are openly affectionate, attend church together, and talk often.

Karen, for example, grew up as an only child with an overly controlling mother. The situation was painful. When her mother had a stroke, Karen agonized over the decision to invite her to live in their home, even though Karen's family had plenty of room and time enough to care for her. Karen felt her blood pressure rise just thinking about her mother trying to tell her how to run her life. She dreaded hearing belittling remarks. As unresolved and long-buried anger rose to the surface, Karen feared it would affect both her marriage and her career as a teacher. She did not want to talk about it, however, and had trouble even admitting to herself that she was angry. Eventually, Karen decided to face the facts and confront them with a third party, learning practical ways to preserve her sense of self, even with her mother in her home.

Stop blaming yourself or others when things go wrong and instead aim for deeper understanding and acceptance.

Family secrets like Karen's are formidable barriers to communication and the caregiving relationship. Wounds that are hidden tend to fester and persist. Wounds exposed to the light heal faster and cleaner. The quality of caregiving will be adversely affected where family secrets are not allowed fresh air. A sibling may rationalize bad decisions based on the way he was mistreated as a child. Also, family secrets unconsciously but consistently affect the caregiver's attitude. Your relationship with your elderly loved one cannot be what it should be in the final years if dark secrets lie below the surface. When you recognize the disastrous effect that keeping secrets may have, you will be motivated to begin to process your past.

Telling the Truth in Love

Think about the family issues that you and your siblings or parents avoid talking about. When you begin to challenge your pain by admitting to others it is there, the pain will lose its power. But whom should you tell? First, talk to the Lord about it. Ask God to help you see the situation objectively rather than through the clouded eyes of your hurt. Test your motives. Examine your heart. If your elder hurt you in the past, do you desire restoration—or revenge? Remember, vengeance is God's domain, not yours. Above all, pray for truth and a spirit of compassion to prevail, as well as an end to any fear and bitterness. "Love suffers long and is kind; love . . . does not rejoice in iniquity, but rejoices in the truth" (1 Corinthians 13:4, 6 NKJV).

Next, consider the Bible's instructions about discipline and restoration. "If someone is caught in a sin, you who are spiritual should restore him gently. But watch yourself, or you also may be tempted. Carry each other's burdens, and in this way you will fulfill the law of Christ" (Galatians 6:1-2 NIV). A spirit of humility and gentleness is crucial when confronting another about sin.

Also, think about Matthew 18:15-17 (NIV): "If your brother sins against you, go and show him his fault, just between the two of you. If he listens to you, you have won your brother over. But if he will not listen, take one or two others along, so that 'every matter may be established by the testimony of two or three witnesses.' If he refuses to listen to them, tell it to the church; and if he refuses to listen even to the church, treat him as you would a pagan or a tax collector."

If you choose to speak to your loved one about the past, approach the subject with care and maturity, not impulsively. Briefly state your feelings about treatment from your childhood or adulthood. In this process, it will be important to name the hurt, which requires great courage. Even if you find the courage to do so, the person you tell might react with denial or anger if emotions, stuffed down for years, are touched like an open nerve. Openness may lead to more conflict, at least in the short term.

Be aware that some people might send mixed messages about family secrets, further bury their resentments, or deny the past. They may refuse to admit that a wound or secret exists. Do you force things? Do

Your relationship with your elderly loved one cannot be what it should be in the final years if dark secrets lie below the surface.

you let them go? If you are the one who wants to clear the air and defuse secrets of their power, it can be frustrating to meet a brick wall of silence from your family members. Try to empathize with them. Perhaps the timing is not right. One day, the topic may just open up and the tension will be released. Be patient with yourself, your siblings, and your elderly loved ones as you pray about it. "Above all, keep fervent in your love for one another, because love covers a multitude of sins" (1 Peter 4:8 NASB).

Even if you choose not to talk about family secrets with your elder or family members, you can and should talk to God about them. You also can journal about your situation and talk to a professional. For serious offenses, such as childhood sexual abuse, a neutral mediator (perhaps a counseling pastor or therapist) is crucial. A seasoned professional—one who shares your faith in Christ and will remind you of truth—can help you sort through your experience, set realistic goals, and even moderate the meeting with your elder. (For referrals to Christian counselors, contact Focus on the Family or the American Association of Christian Counselors [see appendix].)

Offering Forgiveness

To find true healing, it will be necessary to work toward forgiving your elder's past offenses. This does not come from forgetting what happened or from minimizing sin and its consequences but from remembering it, then learning from the pain. Indeed, the truth about the sin needs to be faced before you will know what needs forgiving.

Forgiveness is not something you can just produce; it is the work of God. It is best demonstrated by Jesus, who was pierced, crushed, wounded, rejected, and abandoned, yet He asked his Father to forgive those who hurt Him! The Son of God took the blows meant for sinners so that "everyone who believes in him receives forgiveness of sins through his name" (Acts 10:43 NIV).

Ask God to teach you how to forgive with the compassion of Christ. While forgiveness does not deny the truth, it does mean you surrender your right to retaliate or hold a grudge. When you forgive someone who has hurt you, you set yourself free from the bitterness and bondage of an unforgiving heart. Even if you do not feel forgiving, eventually your feelings will catch up with your words; don't let your actions be dictated by your feelings. Forgiveness can be a time-consuming spiritual process. Lean on God, "who has reconciled us to Himself through Jesus Christ, and has given us the ministry of reconciliation" (2 Corinthians 5:18 NKJV). He is looking for a willing heart and is merciful to those with a broken spirit.

Your forgiveness toward someone who has hurt you does its miraculous work every time you behave in a kind way toward that person. Loving action communicates the reality of love even when feelings of love are absent. You release the guilty party, just as you are set free in God's forgiveness for your own mistakes. Building trust takes time; sometimes it takes many years. Whether you need to forgive a sibling, an extended family member, or your aging loved one, let God's grace shine. His grace (unmerited, undeserved favor) transcends time, which is one reason why it is so amazing.

When you forgive someone who has hurt you, you set yourself free from the bitterness and bondage of an unforgiving heart.

COMMUNICATION IN THE FAMILY CONTEXT

No matter how you and your siblings or other family members get along, strive for honest, ongoing communication. If you want high-quality care for your parents or other elderly loved ones, it is crucial to get the cooperation and support of family members. This will call for joint meetings, followed by frequent one-on-one conversations. Work with these guidelines:

Plan a family meeting. Use that occasion to evaluate your elder's situation and air any concerns. You may want to consult community professionals first. Include your elder in the meeting, and if siblings live far apart, consider investing in speakerphones and three-way calling so you can all get the chance to talk. Prepare a brief agenda and don't expect to resolve every problem or disagreement the first time you get together. Trying to tackle too many items at once will cause unnecessary fatigue and irritation. (See "Practical Helps to Cooperation" on pages 53-55 for an effective meeting agenda.)

Invite a third party. At times the situation calls for loving confrontation. This should take place in a safe forum, preferably in the presence of a third party who has no investment in the outcome. A pastor may be willing to sit in quietly as a witness or be a moderator to guide the discussion and negotiations. Such a third party can reinforce honesty and dignity, as well as serve to inhibit any relapse into old familiar patterns of family dysfunction. Remind each other that you are together to discuss what is best for your aging loved one, not to argue with each other.

Seek solutions. As you begin, you may want to verbalize that feelings of vulnerability or fear are normal with change. Throughout the dialogue, make a sincere attempt to move toward a workable arrangement for each family member. Allow each sibling to express any frustrations or grievances as long as they relate to the reason for the meeting—to discuss your elder's care.

Show respect. Emphasize the importance of respecting each other's opinions. An embracing context means no one is put down for having a different opinion than anyone else. If a sibling is vocal about wanting Mom to receive medical treatment in the hospital rather than hospice care at home, it is important to talk through the issues, including your mother's wishes. If a family member is domineering or pushy, there may be deeper issues behind what the person is expressing. Is fear, exhaustion, or an old resentment at work? Try to see things through the

---

HOW'S MOM? HOW ARE YOU?

When I retired from my job and moved into my mother's house, I didn't expect my caring for her to last nearly 12 years. That was one of the tensions of it—the longevity of caregiving. I felt privileged to be there with Mom, but as her needs increased, I often felt at the point of emotional overload. My siblings, who lived nearby, would come over and say, "How's Mom?" I got so sick of answering that question. Sometimes I felt too tired to go to church because I wasn't ready to deal with the people. I was asked thousands of times about my mom but I could count on one hand the number of times someone asked how I felt. I felt so selfish for feeling that way, and even now I feel guilty at times. But I found the biggest need of the caregiver is for emotional support. Sure, I needed other types of help too, but what I craved most was a hug and someone saying, "How are you, Eloise? This must be rough on you."

Eloise M.

other person's eyes, even when you cannot count on her to see through your eyes. Speak calmly to prevent the discussion from getting over-heated or out of control. "A gentle answer turns away wrath, but a harsh word stirs up anger" (Proverbs 15:1 NIV).

Pray for wisdom. Remember to pray for God's wisdom and peace to superintend each meeting or discussion. If you are able to pray to-gether, do it often. Prayer unites hearts together in a common goal. If it is not possible to pray together, you can always pray personally. Look for God's light in the midst of tumultuous family dynamics. Know that the Lord will make a way. Keep a humble, prayerful atti-tude in every discussion. Remember, the welfare of your aging loved one is at stake.

Practical Helps to Cooperation

At family meetings or in conference calls, seek first to reach some de-gree of respect and trust between yourselves. Agree to some guidelines at the outset, such as taking turns talking, listening without interrupt-ing, and avoiding finger-pointing statements. Then follow this agenda:

- Include your elder if possible.
- Lay out the needs of your aging loved ones in black and white. Make a list of urgent needs (e.g., health care, housing arrange-ments) and a list of potential future needs (e.g., researching community services, organizing important documents). Rate the needs in order of priority as well as you can.
- Discuss which sibling is best equipped to handle which particu-lar need. One sibling may provide emotional support and feed-back to the family. Another may be gifted to articulate problems to a doctor, lawyer, or social-service representative. Another, to transport a loved one to the doctor or to cook extra meals occa-sionally.
- Your aging loved one should select one family member to have durable power of attorney in case he becomes incompetent. Ideally, this should be an adult child who lives nearby.
- Give each family member the opportunity to vocalize what kind

of help he or she might appreciate from the others. Although this may make some feel vulnerable or weak, it is worth it in the long run, especially when things get tough. Don't make others guess your needs. If you need something, say so.

- Appoint tasks and set goals for each sibling or relative as a caregiving team. Keep in touch often, being sensitive to how each is feeling about his or her role.
- Record solution options and any mutual decisions so nobody "forgets" what has been decided. Make sure everyone involved has a copy of the meeting notes, including solutions, valuable suggestions, and a list of delegated duties.

If you are the primary caregiver communicating with family, express your feelings and personal needs using simple terms and few words. Avoid accusing your siblings in any way. Just state your own needs and feelings, starting your phrases with the word *I* instead of *You*. If you are exhausted, say so. If you feel full of sadness, it will increase understanding if you willingly admit that. Don't play the martyr, listing all you do for your parent or relative and expecting your viewpoints to be validated or preferred. But do feel free to tell your siblings or supporters what they might do to ease your burden.

If one person is struggling with an inordinate share of the caregiving work, redistribute some duties to others.

If you are not the primary caregiver, or if you live at a distance from your aging loved one, consider volunteering to provide outside help for the person who is taking on the responsibilities. Perhaps you could offer to hire someone to do housecleaning, yard work, or babysitting, not just for the elder, but for the caregiver, too. If a sibling has cut his work hours to care for your elder, you could offer extra financial help or a larger share of the estate. Step in as often as possible. It may be helpful to shop by phone or Internet, shipping clothes or goods to your elder. Keep medications up-to-date by calling your loved one's local pharmacy when necessary. You might order and ship an occasional gift to the primary caregiver and let her know you appreciate her central role.

Within a few weeks or months, check back with family members to see how things are working and to reassess your aging loved one's needs. Agree to any necessary adjustments. For example, if one person is struggling with an inordinate share of the caregiving work, redistribute some duties to others.

DECISION-MAKING STEPS

When an acute problem or crisis arises, the family moves into the all-important decision-making process. It is important to keep your aging loved one centrally involved and to honor his preferences, but you also might need to plan one discussion without the presence of your aging loved one in order to discuss matters that might otherwise upset him. Now is the time to break down each caregiving issue into increments. Proceed step by step.

1. Present the facts specifically, addressing the practical implications of ignoring the problem. The conversation might start something like this: "Mom is unable to cook for herself. She burned her arm last week and scorched a tea towel that lay on the stove. A neighbor found the hot plate still turned on high when she dropped by to visit."
2. Next, generate ideas addressing the problem. Let each family member freely state possible solutions. You may want to appoint siblings to consult with local health services, agencies, or professionals in order to come up with more viable options.
3. Begin sorting through resolutions using these criteria: Which of the many ideas will give your aging loved one the most independence and still provide safety and security? Which will include most members of the family in the caregiving process so the burden does not fall on one person?

SIBLING SUPPORT

I have one sister, and we get along well. She is very supportive of me and we agree on almost everything concerning Mother. However, my sister does worry more than I do about leaving Mother alone; for that reason, it may be best that our mom lives with me. Because Mother no longer travels any distance, my sister does all the traveling to see us, so we split the cost. *Abigail C.*

DEALING WITH FAMILY CONFLICT

How does your family react to a caregiving crisis? See if you can find yourself, your siblings, or your other loved ones in one of these categories:

Avoiders of conflict retreat at the first hint of trouble because they just do not want to face it. Basic issues cannot be resolved because avoiders pacify and placate.

Exploders are provoked at the first hint of confrontation or disagreement. Basic issues cannot be resolved because exploders act as a conduit for a blowup.

Victors believe they must win. Basic issues cannot be resolved because victors argue about everything. They cannot tolerate the fact that another might be brighter, more educated, or more insightful.

Extinguishers deny that a conflict exists. Basic issues cannot be resolved because when a troublesome topic comes up, an extinguisher will change the subject.[1]

When family members cannot agree and you face these kinds of reactions, follow these guidelines:

- **Realize you may need more than one or two meetings.** Don't expect miracles and resolutions right away. Ask family members if they would be open to more dialogue. Say, "Let's stop for now and start again tomorrow (or next week)." Sometimes it just takes time and rubbing shoulders with each other to break down resistance. Sometimes a fresh new day makes a big difference.
- **Seek counseling from highly qualified professionals if you sense there is no movement toward agreement.** You can find contacts from fellow church members or a caregiving support group. Seek a competent counselor with experience working in family dynamics. "If it is possible, as much as depends on you, live peaceably with all men" (Romans 12:18 NKJV).
- **Admit it is not always possible to reach a satisfactory resolution.** If you have tried your best to resolve a conflict and do not seem to be getting anywhere, accept that reality without guilt. No one can change another

[1]Adapted from *You and Your Parents: Strategies for Building an Adult Relationship* by Harold Ivan Smith (Minneapolis: Augsburg, 1987), 14.

individual without his permission. Continue to pray for a resolution as you move on with your life.

- **Seek a support group for caregivers through your church or local Area Agency on Aging.** Local support groups can give you the emotional resilience you need under difficult family circumstances. They provide a place to express your thoughts and feelings, offer reassurance that you are not alone, and give you permission to be authentic. You might even make a friend or two.

4. List advantages and disadvantages of each option, taking into consideration your elderly loved one's wishes. You may say, "A live-in helper would help Mom to stay in her home and keep her company while watching over her. But it would be expensive and possibly difficult to find a quality person. Adult day care may be another option." Or, "Moving Mom into an adult foster home would get her away from the kitchen entirely and give her some social outlet. But she would have to sell the house, her furniture, her pet, and would have to deal with losing more of her identity as a homemaker."

5. Finally, boil down the options and put the two best ones in writing. Talk to your elder to find out which resolution would be most acceptable to her. (This might not be possible if your loved one is confused by dementia.) Agree beforehand to support the majority decision, and vote as a family on the most viable option—though it may seem a difficult choice.

6. Determine ways to transition into the necessary changes, dividing tasks and responsibilities among siblings or other relatives.

7. Set a date for follow-up meetings at regular intervals to reassess the results of your decisions. If there is conflict indicating historical issues that never were settled between siblings or between children and parents, seek the help of a professionally trained facilitator through your local Area Agency on Aging.

Do you feel like you are doing your share—and theirs? If you come up against a wall of resistance from a sibling, cousin, aunt, uncle, spouse, or parent who refuses to lend a hand in the caregiving process, do your best to stay calm. Remind your relatives that you are all in this together and that you need their assistance in order to do a good job.

Try to reach a consensus on major decisions, and welcome them to contribute to the care of your aging loved one in whatever way they can. For another perspective on the situation, consider seeking the insights of another caregiver.

PRACTICE EMPATHY

There is a paradox in the family dynamics of caregiving—the more you do, the less you may be appreciated by a dependent loved one, while the less your siblings do, the more they may be appreciated. A parent may be attempting to rationalize lack of attention from one child by picturing that person in a rosier light than is realistic. Try to put yourself in the shoes of your aging elder. Practice empathy. It is difficult to show consistent compassion and understanding in a family setting, but exercising those muscles is the key to strength and flexibility.

Regardless of how family dynamics manifest themselves in the caregiving process, work with what you have been given. Tap into your deepest reservoirs of strength by putting on the full armor of God each day and praying with all kinds of prayers and requests in the Spirit (Ephesians 6:10-18). Model love in action rather than mere feeling. Try to maintain a healthy balance between work and recreation, between time for your parents and time for your children, your spouse, your mental health, your spiritual health, and your physical health. Look for family to bring unique and wonderful gifts to the pro-

HOUSE OF CARDS

For the last 10 years of my parents' lives, I was aware that it was important to keep their social life alive. My dad loved playing cards, especially Sheepshead, and he usually won. So I encouraged my folks to invite my brother and sister-in-law and other local relatives to come over and play cards every Friday night. It became a standing thing; whoever wanted to come was welcome. That's also when my out-of-town cousin from Denver and my aunt from Kansas would call (or we'd call them), and we'd all talk by speakerphone. It was a fun time that kept my dad engaged in family life even after my mom died.   *Karen A.*

cess, and forgive family members and siblings when they do not live up to your expectations. You may need to be forgiven too.

Empathy and support take many forms, but sometimes you have to ask for them. Use e-mail, telephone calls, cards, letters, and personal visits to keep in consistent touch with siblings and other family members. Reach out to family and friends with a hug, a handshake, a helping hand. Don't be ashamed to ask favors from relatives, even if they seem busy—busyness can be a smoke screen for feelings of helplessness. People will often wait, wishing to be asked, wanted, or needed. Don't be too proud to receive support when offered. Allow others to share in the fulfillment of caregiving.

As you share responsibilities with family, share your common stories, too.

As you share responsibilities with family, share your common stories, too. Recall old times to yourself and to your brothers and sisters. Tell your children the lessons you learned from the hard times. Let the memories flow—both good and bad. Everything you have experienced together has made up your particular family history. That continuity between generations provides a context for an emotionally secure old age for the elderly.

Make joy your goal in the family dynamics of caregiving. Remember, joy never excludes sorrow, distress, or pain. Joy rises from a deeper place and permeates the saddest of times or grimmest of circumstances. Unlike happiness, joy is not dependent on circumstances; rather, it is a fruit of the Spirit (Galatians 5:22-23). Even in difficult caregiving situations or in weighty decisions that families must make, peace is possible when we let Christ be Lord of our concerns.

—⁘—

Lord, my heart is not haughty, nor my eyes lofty. Neither do I concern myself with great matters, nor with things too profound for me. Surely I have calmed and quieted my soul, like a weaned child with his mother; like a weaned child is my soul within me. PSALM 131:1-2 NKJV

Come to Me, all you who labor and are heavy laden, and I will give you rest. Take My yoke upon you and learn from Me, for I am gentle and lowly in heart, and you will find rest for your souls. For My yoke is easy and My burden is light.

MATTHEW 11:28-30 NKJV

Caring for Yourself
What You Need to Survive

WHEN Marlene's stepfather died, her mother needed someone to look after her, because she had mental illness and dementia similar to Alzheimer's disease. Marlene felt responsible to move her mother in with her family. After she talked it over and prayed with her husband and kids, they converted the back porch into an additional bedroom and bathroom for her mom.

Little did Marlene know how much her mother would disrupt their lives. In the middle of the night she would get up and dress herself in several layers of clothing, then wonder why the bus wasn't picking her up. During the day she'd complain about everything. "Dinnertimes were the worst," Marlene says. As the family ate together, her mother would jump into the conversation and start arguing. Marlene's husband and son learned to brush off the moody outbursts, but her daughter would argue back. "As they fought, my stomach would churn, and I'd get up from the dinner table and go out to our backyard, which bordered on some trolley tracks," Marlene says. "I'd look at those tracks and want to run away so badly!"

Friends would tell Marlene to take some time off, saying, "If you don't care for yourself, how can you care for your mom?" But it was hard to get away. Marlene cherished the occasional work conferences that took her out of town, especially a trip to the Rocky Mountains. "It wasn't vacation, because I was working, but I got there a day early in order to have some peace and quiet with God," she recalls. "I really needed that."

Despite the struggles and exhaustion, Marlene found hidden blessings along the way. "Sometimes I resented having to care for Mom, but then I would stop and think of the care she gave to me. And what better example is there to demonstrate the value of human life to our kids?" she says. "Also, in my five years as Mom's caregiver, she and I had a chance to heal some hurts. I now have a sense of healing and wholeness that I wouldn't have had otherwise."

Do you sometimes wonder, *When is it okay to take care of myself?* Or, *How long I can go on like this?* Do you find yourself exhausted, trying to balance raising a family and/or employment with caring for an elderly loved one? Perhaps you are an only child and must assume all the responsibilities for your parents. Or you may be one of the many who are experiencing so-called "boomerang children"—adult children who come home again due to a divorce or a job loss or for another reason. You already might serve as a substitute parent or babysitter for your children's children. When you add an elderly loved one to your home, or even the added burdens associated with caregiving at a distance, the situation calls for much patience, perseverance, and prayer. In addition to the physical overload on your time and energy, there is the psychological overload of meeting everyone's emotional needs.

Caring for an aging loved one is a labor of love, but it is labor. As your elder becomes more frail and needs more of your time and energy, you may find yourself giving up outside activities and vacations, saying no to friends, feeling distracted at work, and getting stressed at home. If you try to do everything, you risk neglecting your own health.

To stay afloat, you will need the help of friends; family members; relatives; local, community-based organizations; and hands-on resources. You will need wisdom, inspiration, and discernment, because your many responsibilities leave little time and energy for self-care. Most of all, you will need God's grace to help you stay faithful to fulfill your role as a caregiver effectively and compassionately.

CARING FOR MYSELF

I get so drained emotionally when Mom screams for long periods of time. I become drained physically as well when these incidents occur at night. The doctor has tried so many different medications, but there are times when nothing will calm my mother, who suffered a stroke last year that took her speech. Some of the medicines even make things worse instead of better.

Just recently the live-in caregiver we had for over a year went back to her family in Poland. In the last three weeks we've had three different people living with us. I discovered that the first one was here illegally, and the second one had back problems. So far the third one is staying, and she seems to be taking things in stride. But Mom is "acting out," because she can't verbally express her frustrations over the constant change.

I've been working at home as I've trained three different caregivers in the past month. It's been good the last few days to come back to work full-time.

I've learned to care for myself *mentally* by staying busy with my job, which I love. I even go on short business trips and vacations. When I'm gone, I let myself forget the circumstances at home, and I recharge. I try to stay *physically* fit by taking walks, eating well, and getting my sleep. When Mom has a bad night and has kept me awake, I try to spend the following day doing routine jobs that don't require a lot of hard thinking. I keep myself as *emotionally* stable as I can by staying in touch with friends through e-mail, by asking people to lift me up in prayer, and by looking for the humorous side of difficult situations. I work on staying *spiritually* fit by doing a daily devotional with a friend over the phone, by praying and singing songs of praise (alone and with Mom), and by reading Scripture—even if it's only a verse or two some days.

God has been good, providing me with the strength I need for each day. But I do get very tired, as does Mom's live-in caregiver. I can't help but wonder why God allows Mom to stay here so long when she would be happier in heaven, and I would have a much happier and more relaxed life if she were no longer suffering. But God is the Potter, and I am the clay. Right now He has called me to serve Him as I serve Mom. With His help, I know I'll be able to handle the situation for as long as I need to do it.

Betty F.

PRESERVING YOUR HEALTH AND WELL-BEING

As a caregiver, it is critical for you to take good care of yourself—even while you are taking care of your aging loved one. Finding that balance can be a challenge, but now is the time to establish some healthy goals and habits. If you already are nearing the point of burnout, it is time to identify the reasons and make some changes.

Do you find yourself becoming chronically irritable? too fatigued to eat right and exercise? often depressed or hopeless? feeling angry and guilty at the same time? These negative feelings are a signal that you need to take better care of yourself. Otherwise, your emotions will threaten your well-being, lower your resistance to disease, and make life miserable for you and your loved ones.

The physical demands of caregiving can also affect your health, aggravating osteoporosis or causing bursitis or damaged discs. Bathing or lifting an elderly person, for example, can be physically difficult for a caregiver to perform; carelessness can lead to injury, especially if you are pressed for time. You need to admit that there are limits to what one person can do and then seek some outside help.

Negative feelings are a signal that you need to take better care of yourself.

The challenges of caregiving may seem formidable, and the consequences—emotional, physical, economic, relational, and spiritual—overwhelming. However, not everything associated with caregiving is difficult or stressful. Many caregivers gain a sense of fulfillment and satisfaction from their role. Support and encouragement from others is also helpful. In fact, the caregiving pathway is lined with hidden blessings if you know how to look for them. Where you least expect it, hope appears. The Lord's grace is tucked into hard places.

OBSTACLES TO OVERCOME

What can hinder you from being an effective caregiver? Consider the following common obstacles and ways to overcome them:

Unrealistic Expectations

Are you expecting too much of yourself? Are others expecting more from you than you can give? If you answer yes to most of the following questions, you might have unrealistic expectations as a caregiver. If so,

CAREGIVER BURNOUT

It is important for caregivers to have a support network in place for assistance and relief. Those who do not have emotional support may suffer burnout. Consider these statistics from the National Family Caregivers Association:

- More elderly people enter nursing homes because of caregiver burnout than because of an exacerbation of their own condition.
- Sixty-one percent of "intense" family caregivers (those providing at least 21 hours of care a week) have suffered from depression.
- Three-fourths of all caregivers do not get consistent help from other family members.
- Eighty percent of all home care is provided by family caregivers.

The happier and healthier you are, the better your loved one will be served. Try these 11 ways to keep the threat of burnout at bay:

1. Determine services available in your area, and ask for the help you need.
2. Make healing habits of prayer, Bible and inspirational reading, music, and fellowship.
3. Model an attitude of respect for both children and the elderly in your family.
4. Plan your schedule around predictable mealtimes.
5. Look ahead and include fun family activities in your schedule.
6. Anticipate health concerns; keep nourishing snacks on hand, exercise consistently.
7. Don't major on the minors with family members. (Save your steam for big problems.)
8. Delegate household chores, but keep them simple.
9. Listen well and learn to read between the lines with children or elders.
10. Give yourself permission to enjoy hobbies. Take yourself out for a personal date.
11. Don't entertain "what-ifs" and "if-onlys." Say, "I am doing the best I can."

talk with a counselor or trusted friend and make adjustments for the sake of your own mental health.

1. Do you feel that if you do not do it all, you do not care enough about your loved one?
2. Do you feel you have to do it all, do it well, and see to it that others are happy, too?
3. Are you unable to set limits or boundaries in what you will or will not do?
4. Do you often go beyond the limits of your endurance?

Unrealistic expectations set you up for negative emotions and frustration. While you cannot control others' expectations of you, you can set priorities and realistic expectations for yourself. Start by treating yourself kindly, as you would a best friend.

In the ups and downs of caregiving, simply do the best you can in your particular circumstances. That means you must allow things you cannot change to be what they are. Don't agonize over them. Surprises will come. A caregiver named Karen was elated after her aging mother was given a clean bill of health as a result of experimental cancer treatments. When the cancer reappeared throughout her body six weeks later, it shocked her and the doctors. "I really struggled with that," Karen says. "I was angry and felt like God had played a dirty trick on us. Yet my mother did survive five years from the time of her first treat-

---

HUGS AND KISSES

As a caregiver, there were times when I could get away and shop for two or three hours while my mom was napping in bed. But toward the end—the last year—of her life, I didn't want to leave her. She needed help getting to the toilet. Her meals had to be brought to her. There were thousands of times I walked her somewhere. During that time, it would have been so nice just to have somebody hold me or hug me. A hug says something that words cannot say. (Sometimes I think we talk too much anyway.) Although I often felt too tired emotionally and physically to go to church, I knew I always could get a good hug there.   *Lois M.*

ment, even though her prognosis was only for two years. I was glad for the time we had."

It is possible to have unrealistic expectations of others, including your elder's medical team. Even with modern medicine, it is important to understand that there are limitations to what can be done as an elder's body gets older and breaks down.

Doubts and Fears

Whether male or female, the typical caregiver has a thousand irons in the fire and may be reading this book with many fears—or even tears. The role of caregiving is usually brought on by a state of crisis. You want the best for your aging loved one, but you recognize your lack of knowledge, time, and strength to carry out the responsibilities. Most likely, you feel your own mental and physical health is as much at risk as that of your elder. The more vulnerable he is, the more vulnerable you are. Some caregivers encounter physical illness, psychological wear, spiritual discouragement, or all three.

While you cannot control others' expectations of you, you can set priorities and realistic expectations for yourself.

Most caregivers have not planned for the role, and although many accept it with grace, others are forced to assume it. Most do not feel prepared to address the many issues ahead of them. You might be grieving the fact that the person you once looked to for advice and direction is now increasingly dependent on you. And if elderly parents become dependent on your money, you may worry about how you will make ends meet. You might feel anxious—especially when you are facing tough decisions such as nursing-home placement or end-of-life care for your elder. You may wonder where you will get the energy to assume caring for an elderly loved one in addition to your place in the labor market, your responsibilities to children, and your other personal roles.

As Karen's ailing mother (mentioned above) needed more personal care, Karen decided to travel down with her three young children to help take care of her. "It was really hard, because I left my husband, a full-time pastor, alone in the middle of a building program," says Karen, who stayed with her mom the last three months of her life. "At first, I was torn about my decision, but my husband kept saying, 'Karen, the building can go up without you, but five years from now, the only thing that will matter is that you were there for your mom.' It's been a few years now, and I have no regrets and a great peace."

Faith in our trustworthy God helps to dissolve our fear and personal insecurities. If, as the old hymn states, you are "cumbered with a load of care,"[1] tell the Lord about your worries. Follow this biblical advice: "Be anxious for nothing, but in everything by prayer and supplication with thanksgiving let your requests be made known to God. And the peace of God, which surpasses all comprehension, shall guard your hearts and your minds in Christ Jesus" (Philippians 4:6-7 NASB). Remember that God is able to handle your concerns. Peace is promised as you lean on Him and learn to turn every worry and need over to Him. As you do this, your doubts and fears will begin to subside, even when you do not understand everything.

Physical Fatigue and Emotional Exhaustion

Caregivers often feel exhausted and alone in their role, longing for some relief but lacking the energy to look for it. If you are feeling physically tired or emotionally overwhelmed, take a blank sheet of paper and write down your answer to this question: *What's heavy on my mind today?* Once you see your answers on paper, you can begin to address them one by one. *Which tasks do I have to get done today? What one first step can I take to accomplish this goal? Which responsibility can I postpone or delegate?* Giving your grocery list to a willing volunteer from your church, for example, would free you up to focus on a caregiving task only you can do.

If work, committees, or other outside activities are interfering with your ability to care for your aging loved one, it may be time to reevaluate your priorities and consider whether you should reduce your hours at work, take a leave of absence, or resign from an obligation. Or maybe the answer is to maintain your regular work schedule and learn about and use home-delivered services that meet some of the basic needs of your elder. You also might solicit the use of volunteers in your church to get involved, but it is not fair to expect their help on a long-term basis. Seek the advice of an expert in aging matters to look over your list of duties and responsibilities and help you think and pray through the issues. Sometimes it takes another person whom you respect to help you set realistic goals and come up with a workable schedule. Friends may be the best "recruiters," too, asking others to help.

In order for you to live a balanced life, your schedule needs to allow for crisis management as well as rest, recreation, and spiritual devotional times. Seek outside help from a doctor, pastor, support group, or one of the many organizations that offer assistance to the aging and to caregivers (see chapter 9: Finding Health, Medical, and Social Services).

Discouragement and Depression

Have you been working hard to appear diligent, selfless, and caring, while inside you are sinking in discouragement or depression? When a caregiver takes on the burdens of caring for elderly loved ones, it may be at a time when he or she was looking forward to other things. If your new role is initiated at retirement time, you may find that instead of enjoying grandchildren, travel, or hobbies, you face more mundane practical tasks. Perhaps you dreamed of turning your passions into profit with your own business. You may have been counting on extra money, a promotion at work, or the joy of writing that novel you have put together in your head. For some people, these unexpected consequences of caregiving are more difficult to accept than the actual care tasks.

Discouragement and depression are normal in caregiving. But God can use those times of discouragement to prepare us to be useful in His

MOTHER AND CHILD

I found being a caregiver much harder than raising children in some respects: It seemed the busier I was, the more my mom needed my attention. The week before my daughter's wedding, Mom needed me for everything, even though my older sister had come for the wedding. Then I noticed Mom was saying, "What?" every time my husband or I would say something. Often we would repeat what we said, but after a while we learned that was just another way to get attention. It's very tiring to repeat every statement you make two or three times. It's easier just not to say anything or to say, "Oh, never mind." If we paused and didn't repeat it again, she would often answer correctly anyway.

Bev S.

hands. Look for the hand of God in your situation. Author Gary Smalley calls it "treasure hunting" when you take a negative experience or trial and actively reverse the damage by turning it into something from which you can benefit.[2] It will help if you tell yourself, "I don't like this burden, but since it is here, I want to express appreciation to God. I'm grateful that He will bring good from this hardship." Treasure hunting allows us to thank God in the midst of a trial because we know that our suffering is producing good things like perseverance, character, and hope (Romans 5:3-4). Right now you may be called to love and serve God by loving and serving your elder. When you make God your primary concern, you can find satisfaction with your labors and joy in the mundane.

Simply be faithful to the task at hand. God sees your efforts even if no one else does. "For God is not unjust to forget your work and labor of love which you have shown toward His name, in that you have ministered to the saints, and do minister" (Hebrews 6:10 NKJV).

Anger and Bitterness

Some caregivers struggle with anger because they have so little time for themselves. At times, you may feel betrayed by the "system," by family or friends who do not do enough, or by the medical establishment if it fails to provide assistance as you expect it. You might get angry at your aging loved one for not cooperating in his care. Then you might feel guilty for being angry. You might be angry at yourself or even at God. If you are doing the majority of the caregiving without appreciation or help from other relatives, you might become bitter toward them. Down deep, you might resent your aging loved ones for getting older and frail.

When Jan and her brother got in an argument over how to care for their aging mother, who had early signs of dementia, it was not the best time to discuss the matter. Jan had left a rebellious teenage son back home and was weary from spending the whole day in her parents' house going through her mom's clothes. "Dad wanted me to clean, because Mom had stuff everywhere. There was no place to walk or even to put a suitcase," she says. She had made progress and was filling her car with clothes her mom no longer wore when her brother showed up. "What do you think you're doing with Mom's stuff?" he yelled. "You have an agenda, don't you?"

"Leave me alone," said Jan, who rarely got along with her brother. The two of them exchanged impatient words on and off until it was time for Jan to go home. The next week, she received an e-mail telling her to return the clothes because her mom wanted them back.

When your own family members become your adversaries, it makes caregiving more of a challenge—and it can cause relational and spiritual harm. In Jan's situation, there was rivalry between her and her brother, as well as a crisis in her own family. As the tensions mounted, it was increasingly difficult for the two to speak civilly to each other.

Unresolved anger leads to bitterness. Don't stuff down your anger, pretending it does not exist or hoping it will go away on its own. Deal with it before it turns to bitterness, which is simply anger that has been buried and given time to grow. When a root of bitterness has grown up, the best way to uproot it is with kindness. "Be kind to one another, tenderhearted, forgiving one another, just as God in Christ forgave you" (Ephesians 4:32 NKJV). Also, "if it is possible, as much as depends on you, live peaceably with all men" (Romans 12:18 NKJV).

Living peaceably means being harmless and inoffensive, not giving others occasion to quarrel with you and not taking occasion to quarrel with them. It means not seeking revenge but rather overcoming evil with good. The goal, if possible, is for a spirit of forgiveness and joy to

AFTER-SCHOOL SPECIAL

When I was ten years old my grandmother had a stroke. Each of my parents took a second job to help pay for Grandma's speech and physical therapy. Dad delivered propane part-time during the hours he was not on his job as a fireman. Mom worked at a water-bed factory by night and a bakery by day. For the next four years, every day after school Mom picked up my sister and me and drove us from Colorado Springs to Denver (about an hour away) where Grandma was in a nursing home. We would stay until about nine o'clock, doing our homework while visiting her. Then Mom would drive us back home. Next morning, we'd get up, go to school, and do it again. Every day.

My parents modeled love and commitment by doing that. I'm sure they were tired and sometimes discouraged. But watching them taught me that taking care of elderly people makes us stronger. *Emily G.*

prevail. (For more information, see "Communication in the Family Context" on pages 51-55.)

Enthusiasm in caregiving will waver as long as there are difficult realities to face. And God can seem very far away when you are exhausted and hurting. But that is the time to look up, to keep hope alive. When we lift our heads and look up, we are looking in the right direction, because—in Jesus' own words—our "redemption draws near" (Luke 21:28 NKJV).

Meanwhile, instead of allowing yourself to become overtired, discouraged, angry, or bitter, stop and ask for help when you need it. It is available. Keep a list of service-agency numbers near your phone, including the number of a friend whom you can call day or night. (For information on locating health, medical, and social services, see chapter 9.)

Preventing Guilt and Despair

Even though caregivers may set out to honor their aging loved ones, they still have weaknesses and are prone to failures and frustrations. The stress of trying to care for an aging loved one while neglecting your own needs can lead to negative feelings and a crushing load of guilt. You may resent having to "do all the work," then feel guilt or even depression over your anger. When guilt is an issue, it is useful to distinguish between misguided guilt and true guilt.

Misguided guilt. Suppose you are doing everything possible for your aging loved one, yet you feel it is not nearly good enough or often enough. Misguided guilt can be caused by others who are trying to make you feel guilty, or it may be self-imposed. To ward off such guilt, start by telling yourself the truth. Admit that you are doing your best and learning to do better. Give yourself credit for what you are able to do, knowing your needs are important in the caregiving process.

If you feel guilty about circumstances beyond your control, you may be imposing guilt on yourself. Sometimes employment restricts participation and presence with loved ones. Adult children who live a long distance from their elders often feel guilty for not being able to help at a moment's notice. Even when you live nearby and are available day and night, sooner or later you realize you cannot solve every problem. Yet if your elder falls and breaks a hip, you might blame yourself for not preventing the accident.

The remedy? Start by refusing to criticize yourself or dwell on your inadequacies. Dwell instead on what you can do, relying on the faithfulness and goodness of the God who created and redeemed you. "Take captive every thought to make it obedient to Christ" (2 Corinthians 10:5 NIV). Talk to a pastor or Christian counselor if the feelings of guilt are so strong that they are affecting your ability to live a normal life.

Self-imposed guilt also arises when a caregiver lacks feelings of love for aging parents. This may be due to a childhood history of abuse, neglect, or other kinds of offenses by a parent. When love, the number one motivating factor for caregiving, is absent, duties and tasks may be dull, monotonous, or even distasteful. Latent feelings of repulsion, anger, even hatred may rise to the surface, creating a fertile breeding ground for guilt. If you ignore or try to repress this guilt, your emotional state deteriorates. Everyone loses. Ask God to help you forgive your parents and to give you a new love for them that is not dependent on their feelings for you.

If you feel guilty for feeling resentful, try to separate your feelings from your commitment to your elder. Love is a choice and a commitment. You can choose to show affection even when you do not exactly feel like it. You can choose to treat another person honorably even when he does not deserve it. You affirm your willingness to help by re-

WHERE TO TURN?

I was single, working full-time, and had a part-time caregiver, a CNA (Certified Nurse Assistant) who came to our house two full days and three half days each week to help my parents. I was able to do much of my work at home, thanks to my laptop and a very understanding employer. Dad used diapers, a wheelchair, and a hospital bed. He was almost 95. One morning Mom, who was 90, got up and just made it to the foot of her bed when she fell and broke her hip. Less than a month later I had two parents in diapers, wheelchairs, and hospital beds. I wasn't sure where to turn. But God provided the help I needed through visiting nurses and church volunteers. Within another month Dad was home in heaven. Now it's just me and my mom.

Betty F.

minding your aging loved one, "I love you, and I am seeking to do what is best for you." God looks on your heart, knows your mind, and will help you. He wants you to be free from guilt. In fact, Christ died in our place so that we might have freedom from the guilt of our sin.

MAKING A LIST

Caregiving can seem burdensome if you are not prepared or supported by others. Make lists as a way to navigate the road ahead:

- Make a list of direct services that can be utilized to support caregiving. Seek help from your church and from your local Area Agency on Aging or your county's department of human services. (Check the front section of your phone book under Senior Citizen Services or Social Services.)
- Make a list of things you need help doing. Post it in your kitchen. This gives you an overview of your needs. It also gives visitors opportunities to see where you need help. If someone asks, "What can I do?" you have a ready list to read from.
- Make a list of your aging loved one's physical and emotional needs. Go to a medical library at your local hospital or via the Internet. You may also contact associations related to specific diseases. Gather information and knowledge that will help you understand, empathize, and make wise decisions.
- Make a list of simple pleasures. What might you do to revitalize and reenergize yourself? Perhaps you get recharged from taking an exhilarating walk. Maybe you like taking a break in a favorite coffee shop. Some people feel a sense of accomplishment simply by cleaning out a drawer or cupboard. "Getting away" for a few hours can calm the nervous system and reconnect you with a sense of control. Check one pleasurable thing off your list each day.
- Make a list of things for which you are grateful. Read it every day and express your appreciation to the Lord and to other people. Share some of your "grateful thoughts" with your aging loved one, and thank the Lord together.
- Make a list of questions that will help you find meaning in this new reality of caregiving. Ponder these questions: *What might I learn from this? How will I be a better person? How can I be more disciplined in managing my time? Where can I turn to find the love and support that is out there for me?* You will discover that positive changes start from the inside out.

More than anything, take time to give your burdens to the Lord. Do not wait until you "have your act together" before approaching God for help. "Draw near to God and He will draw near to you" (James 4:8 NASB).

True guilt. Real guilt, also to be faced and confronted, is a wake-up call from the Holy Spirit to listen, repent of your wrong attitude or behavior, and determine to change things for the better. You may have broken a promise or acted irresponsibly toward your elderly loved one. You may have intentionally harbored negative feelings against her. You may have been disrespectful or lost your temper. The good news is that true guilt was taken care of on the cross by Jesus, "who Himself bore our sins in His own body on the tree, that we, having died to sins, might live for righteousness" (1 Peter 2:24 NKJV). His blood applied to us cleanses us from the guilt of *all* sin, both original and committed sin (1 John 1:9, Isaiah 1:18). It is great to realize that if we confess our sins to God, He washes them "white as snow," declares us righteous in His sight, and gives us power to say no to sin more and more.

If you have offended your aging loved one, a relative, or someone else involved in your elder's care, first confess it to the Lord, then do your best to make amends with the one you offended. Admit your mistake and show empathy for the way you have hurt the person. Ask for forgiveness, and accept it if offered. "Therefore confess your sins to each other and pray for each other so that you may be healed" (James 5:16 NIV). If your elder does not offer forgiveness, be patient, and know that you receive it from God immediately.

SURVIVAL STRATEGIES

No mathematical equation can measure the appropriate ratio of time and allegiance you should give to children, a spouse, and dependent elders. You cannot be all things to all key family members. As a general principle, though, your own family needs come first.

"Feeling guilty, caregivers tend to give more than they should to the person in their care," say authors Wendy Lustbader and Nancy Hooyman. "When they then become overburdened and exhausted, they feel resentful. Responding to this resentment, they set limits on what they are willing to give. They maintain these limits for a while, but soon begin to feel guilty about all that they are not doing for their relative. Responding to their guilt, they start again giving more than they should. This dance between guilt and resentment goes round and round, until caregivers recognize this cyclic process and take steps to halt it."[3]

Finding balance and confidence in caring for an aging loved one is a gradual process, just like other kinds of learning experiences. You might proceed with a few blunders, detours, or occasions of failure. Be patient with yourself, with other people involved, and with your aging loved ones. To maintain order and balance in your life as a caregiver, consider these survival steps:

Don't Go It Alone

Maintain and nurture good friendships. If you are facing a draining or difficult family relationship, remember that the Lord knows and cares about the pain and frustration you are experiencing. But also keep in mind that your difficult sibling, parent, or spouse may be the one God is using to conform you more to Christ's likeness and make you dependent on Him. This may be your opportunity to persevere under trial, so that God can demonstrate His grace. Seek support from people who care about you, who love and encourage you, who model Christian charity in their own lives. Beyond value are friends, neighbors, or siblings who understand your efforts and problems, phone to hear how you are doing, pray with you, and help you clarify important issues and decisions. Social support is very important. Realize that you need to be close to someone. Although there will be times when you feel alone, God has designed you to connect with other people.

Ask for What You Need

Not only is it okay to ask for and receive help, but you will *need* help. You may have to dig for it. Keep digging. One contact will lead to another. If you network the resources, you will uncover more and more organizations, government agencies, and private individuals who are on your side, who understand, and who will go to bat for you.

Although you may be confused or frustrated in attempts to access services (each may have its own eligibility criteria), think of your attempts as a learning curve. Welcome the practical guidance of other caregivers or service providers. Look for services that meet the needs of your elder and relieve you of some stressful tasks. High on your list should be services for respite care that will provide opportunities for relief from day in, day out responsibility.

Welcome the practical guidance of other caregivers or service providers.

Expect Help from Your Family

Your family can be a source of emotional support, but learn what is reasonable to expect. Keep communication lines wide open. Hold family meetings to talk about the job ahead of you. Give your spouse reassurance of your presence and intentions, and let your children know the realities you face. Ask your family to hold you accountable to get enough sleep, eat healthfully, and take time for exercise. Let them know that you need time alone but also that you need their affection more than ever. Tell them how much you appreciate their help. Make sure they understand that you are in this for the long haul, and only God knows how long.

If you are raising children while taking care of an elderly loved one, try as often as possible to involve your children and your elder in one another's lives. Ask your older children to make it a priority to spend time with your loved one in a way that is meaningful for

HELPFUL BOOKS FOR YOU

Quiet Moments for Caregivers, by Betty Free (Wheaton, Ill.: Tyndale House Publishers, 2002).

Caregiver's Support Kit, Alzheimer's Project of the National Caregiving Foundation, 801 N. Pitt Street #116, Alexandria, VA 22314-1765; request a copy by calling 1-800-930-1357.

My Turn to Care: Encouragement for Caregivers of Aging Parents, compiled and edited by Marlene Bagnull (Ampelos Press, 1999; <www.writehisanswer.com>).

My Parents, My Children: Spiritual Help for Caregivers, by Cecil Murphey (Louisville, Ky.: Westminster John Knox Press, 2000).

The Final Mile: A Wife's Response to Her Husband's Terminal Illness, by Faye Landrum (Wheaton, Ill.: Tyndale House Publishers, 1999).

Wrinkled but Not Ruined: Counsel for the Elderly, by Jay E. Adams (Woodruff, S.C.: Timeless Texts, 1999).

them. It does not have to be the obligatory Sunday-afternoon visit to the retirement home. Even with busy schedules, there are many helpful things kids may initiate for their elders. Teens may bring their photographs, ribbons, and school awards and show them off. They might create a fruit basket or hide chocolate kisses around the room. Children who play an instrument might be willing to perform a solo or make a tape of music to give to their elders. If you have small children or grandchildren, play games as simple as "I Spy" or "Who's got the button?" Promote unity between the generations and reinforce the feeling of family, legacy, and heritage in your household.

Ask your family to hold you accountable to get enough sleep, eat healthfully, and take time for exercise.

Join a Support Group

Support groups for caregivers can be extremely beneficial. They enable overburdened caregivers to express their feelings in a supportive setting, as well as gain practical advice, understanding, and affirmation. By attending a support group, you will come to realize that you are not alone in the kinds of situations you face and the kinds of reactions you feel. Support groups can provide: 1) help in setting limits in how you care for an elderly loved one on an ongoing basis, 2) help in considering the effects of taking on or continuing caregiving responsibilities, and 3) help in making difficult decisions regarding the care of an elderly loved one.

VITAL ADVICE

I learned that a tremendous amount of adrenaline is required to live under the stress of caring for an aging parent. The body is in a constant state of alert, drawing heavily upon all reserves. As the caregiver, it's imperative that you give great attention to your own care. My husband and I walked two miles a day most days and took vitamin supplements. I also learned the importance of getting away from the house for extended times alone. However, it was difficult not to have my mother on my mind even when I was away. It was vitally important that I seek appropriate help from community resources. It was also important to spend time alone with God every morning to keep my perspective straight and focus on the One who is in control, the One who can give me grace to get through the day.

Terri H.

One resource is an organization called Children of Aging Parents (CAPS), a national, nonprofit organization for caregivers founded in 1977 by Mirca Liberti and Louise Fradkin. Caregiving was not considered a big issue back then, but it drew attention when CAPS was mentioned in a "Dear Abby" advice column in 1982. CAPS received 4,000 letters in response. Today CAPS answers questions on local, state, or federal aid and gives referrals and advice on products and services. CAPS also provides the training and ongoing support needed to start up a support group. (See appendix for contact information.)

Identify Your Strengths

As you realize you are going to be involved on an ongoing basis, identify your strengths. Are you good at administrative tasks? Do you do better at practical, hands-on help? Maybe you are a wonderful prayer partner. Build on your strengths toward meeting the challenges of being a caregiver. You may discover strengths you did not know you had. Even though Karen's brother lived closer to their ailing mother, there were things he couldn't do. Karen realized she was needed to provide the personal care, such as helping her mom get out of the bathtub and giving her suppositories for pain control when she could no longer swallow pills. "I never thought I'd have the physical or emotional strength to do some of those things," says Karen, "but it was important to preserve my mother's dignity." Her brother concentrated on the paperwork involved with being executor of their mother's will.

In addition to your own strengths, draw inspiration from God, the Bible, and fellow believers for the road ahead. As Joshua took over for Moses in leading the Israelites across the Jordan River into the Promised Land, he was commanded to be strong and of good courage, for the Lord God was with him (Joshua 1:9). You have the same promise today. Keep the faith, and count on the Lord to be with you as you are stretched spiritually.

Reevaluate Your Job

In 1940, only 25 percent of working-age women were employed outside the home. In 1995, that number had climbed to 80 percent. Today, more than half of all caregivers are employed outside the home. In one study, 35 percent of these caregivers rearranged work schedules, using flextime when available, to care for elderly parents; 23 percent took time off with no pay. Between 12 and 20 percent quit their jobs to be full-time caregivers. Women spend an average of 11 years out of the workforce caring for children and parents, while men spend a little more than one year (1.3) in such roles. Lost career opportunities for caregivers have consequences in determining social-security benefits, professional advancement, and pension income.

Women generally try to deal with multiple responsibilities by maintaining rigorous schedules, negotiating parent-care tasks around their work and family schedules, and giving up their own free time. They may take work home, skip lunch, or give up daytime phone calls of a personal nature, as well as experience physical and mental strain.

Corporations report reduced energy levels and chronic ailments among caregiving employees due to the drain of relentless responsibility. If possible, look for a job that includes benefits for caregivers such as flextime, sabbaticals, adult day care, and job sharing. Although many corporations do not yet offer such benefits, elder care is joining child care as a political issue that affects the United States as a whole. Many employees who are not helping an elderly family member today will likely do so in the not-too-distant future.

If possible, look for a job that includes benefits for caregivers such as flextime, sabbaticals, adult day care, and job sharing.

Because of the demands of caregiving, some adult children take a job just to pay the bills rather than to build a career they enjoy. Then when their elder dies, they may feel they have no real purpose anymore. In other cases, the death of their elder is the point at which they begin investing in their own future. Consider how you can provide care for your elder (including soliciting help from community services) and still fulfill some goals of your own.

Get Respite

Never feel guilty about getting away for respite—an evening at home without interruption or a drive to a different environment. To do this, you may need to hire a companion to watch your elder, ask a sibling or relative to assume your duties while you are gone, or enroll your loved one in an adult day-care program. Call your local Area Agency on Aging for referrals or information to help you.

Taking some time off for yourself is not a sign of weakness and will help you more than you may realize. Make time for hobbies and exercise. Call a friend and go out to dinner. Take a vacation every year and minivacations every season. Get out and go somewhere for a change of scenery at least once a month. Put something new in front of your eyes. Visual refreshment does wonders for the soul. Go for a drive in a new neighborhood, take off for a nearby beach on a Sunday afternoon, get away for a weekend to the mountains. Put some miles between you and your home (or place of work) just for a day.

For some, it might be helpful to write in a journal, writing whatever flows from your heart for a period of 10 to 20 minutes. Others may benefit from joining a Bible study. Still others may get a boost from reading an inspirational book. Rent a family video that makes you laugh or inspires you. These kinds of coping mechanisms are different for each caregiver. It sometimes takes a little experimenting to

REPEAT DIALING

The last six months before Mom died, I was her lifeline. Her son in Florida would call and visit occasionally, but I was only 10 minutes away from the retirement facility where she lived. If she needed something, I'd bring it. What changed was the number of phone calls she'd make. Every morning at 6:15 A.M., she'd call. I almost always had received three calls before I left for work at 8:15 A.M. Sometimes it wore on me. I'd think, *If I hear that phone ring one more time, I'm going to scream.* She'd call sometimes and say, "I'm sick as a dog." She wouldn't be, but she didn't sleep well. Sometimes I'd get a call at work during the day or at the end of the workday. She'd call and leave a weather report: "I just heard the weather is bad—you better go home early." She never stopped being a mom.

She just wanted to hear my voice. She'd say, "I'm such a bother, and I'm sorry I had to call you." I'd say, "No, no, you're not a bother. What bothers me is when you say you're a bother." One day, my sister-in-law said, "You have a life of your own. You shouldn't let her call you so much." But if a two-minute phone call was helping her cope, why not? I realized my frustration wouldn't last forever. Mom wasn't always going to be there to make those calls.

Marlene W.

Taking some time off for yourself is not a sign of weakness and will help you more than you may realize.

find the thing that, for you, is like a power nap: short but refreshing—and indispensable.

Think Realistically

Let go of false expectations and learn to think realistically and biblically. That means you should not expect circumstances in your life or in that of your aging loved one to stay the same as they were in the past. If your aging parent is suffering from Alzheimer's disease, for example, you need to shift your expectations, remembering that your loved one is not deliberately being stubborn or mean.

Change is inevitable, but it is also an opportunity to love and serve God in new ways. It can be an adventure with Christ, because "we know that God causes all things to work together for good to those who love God, to those who are called according to His purpose" (Romans 8:28 NASB). Although you may not know *how* the changes will turn out for good, you can trust that they will if you allow God to work in your life and conform you to His image.

Energize Yourself

Find out what makes you relish life, then do those things regularly and consistently. an hour reading on the porch? rearranging the living-room furniture? a game of golf? a symphony downtown? As a caregiver, you must budget for some of these activities and plan for them. Plug into resources that will stimulate, amuse, and regenerate your own soul

WHERE TO GO FOR HELP

For help with any area of caregiving, ranging from home-delivered meals and case-management services to residential repair and choices for long-term care, contact your local Area Agency on Aging. This aging network includes more than 57 state units, 680 area agencies, and about 25,000 supportive and nutrition service providers. Its basic purpose is to organize and deliver community-based services to all older Americans regardless of income. These agencies are listed in most telephone books, senior centers, city or county units of government, or senior-service agencies funded by an Area Agency on Aging.

and body. It might be helpful to keep a journal of all the things for which you can be grateful. Praise the Lord for His goodness and mercy in the past, in the present, and in the times yet to come. You will find your negative thoughts lifting.

Look for reasons to smile. When caregiving is difficult, humor can help to make it bearable. Even a brief chuckle can help you rise above a serious situation and see things from a different perspective. Cultivate an attitude of cheerfulness and thankfulness by reading books that focus on joy in the midst of pain, such as Christian author Barbara Johnson's *So Stick a Geranium in Your Hat and Be Happy* (Word, 1990). Make it a practice to look on the funny side of things and to laugh out loud. Your cheery outlook might even brighten your aging loved one's day.

Take time out for a few of these things too:

- Find someone with whom you can talk on a daily basis, not to voice complaints but to gain encouragement. Enlist a godly friend who is willing to pray with you regularly. Go to your pastor, get on the phone to a friend, join a support group, or start one. Leave a spiral notebook at your bedside to record your thoughts and prayers to God.
- Exercise daily (30 to 40 minutes, if possible). Participate in activities such as walking, doing aerobics, jogging, bicycling, or swimming. You need it, and you cannot afford *not* to take time for it. Exercise will keep you physically fit and will give you more energy to cope with the day's emotional demands.
- Schedule in some free hours every week to recharge. Use the time for napping, doing a hobby, running through the sprinkler with children or grandchildren, reading a favorite novel, visiting with friends, or doing something else you enjoy.

Reaffirm Your Faith and Calling

As you engage in the extraordinary task of caregiving, keep your eyes on God's perfect order. He has appointed a time and a place for everything. When discouragement, self-pity, fatigue, and complaining result from your caregiving tasks, rely on God's grace to get you through. Your sins have been forgiven through Christ. Your purpose now is simply to glo-

Change is inevitable, but it is also an opportunity to love and serve God in new ways.

When caregiving is difficult, humor can help to make it bearable.

rify the Lord by remaining faithful to the work He has called you to do. God will help you shoulder the load, because "He who has begun a good work in you will complete it until the day of Jesus Christ" (Philippians 1:6 NKJV). "Therefore, my beloved brethren, be steadfast, immovable, always abounding in the work of the Lord, knowing that your labor is not in vain in the Lord" (1 Corinthians 15:58 NKJV).

Meditate upon a Scripture verse in the morning, then call it to mind throughout the day. Prayer cannot be sacrificed—spend as much time as you can in the presence of God, even if you have to get up earlier than usual. As the saying goes, "A day hemmed with prayer rarely unravels." Worship consistently with other believers. Be willing to ask for encouragement, prayer, and support. Take Jesus' advice, who said, "Until now you have asked for nothing in My name; ask, and you will receive, that your joy may be made full" (John 16:24 NASB).

YOU ARE ON YOUR WAY

The caregiving road is crowded with millions just like you, but you may not always know it. Most likely, they are much too busy to notice you. You may walk this road for miles without feeling the support of a single

---

DID YOU KNOW?

- Prayer is the top coping mechanism used in caregiving, named by 74 percent of caregivers. Talking with friends is second (66 percent). Exercise and hobbies rank equally at third place.
- The average caregiver provides 18 hours of care each week. Over 4 million households provide 40 hours each of caregiving per week.
- Sixty-four percent of caregivers work full- or part-time. Absenteeism, interrupted workdays, and decreased productivity due to the demands of caregiving cost U.S. businesses between $11.4 and $29 billion a year.
- U.S. caregivers spend a total of about $2 billion per month on elders' needs. Half of these caregivers spend their own money for an elder's needs, at an average of $171 per month.
- Only 15 percent of caregivers report physical or mental-health problems due to caregiving.

soul. Other times, you will bump into people who offer to help just when you need it most. As a caregiver, you are going through an internal process that requires a great deal of change in the way you think and feel. Be patient with yourself, especially when you end up making decisions you wish you did not have to make. A great influence on the way you cope will be your attitude toward the hardships.

Know your limits. Your personal stress level may increase along with your aging loved one's needs. We all have breaking points, although some have more resilience than others. If you have little support from others or are coping with your own health problems, things may go from bad to worse. Recognize your personal warning signs of overload. For one caregiver, that warning may be that she suddenly flies off the handle. For another, it may be persistent colds and sniffles. For another, the warning may be the inability to sleep. Don't ignore the signals that tell you too much is *too much*. To preserve your sanity and health, follow the advice in this chapter, such as asking for help, arranging for a caregiving break, and doing things to energize yourself.

Meditate upon a Scripture verse in the morning, then call it to mind throughout the day.

Now, more than ever, trust in God's benevolence, providence, and omnipotence. This caregiving time of your life is a time to invest in the belief that you are exactly where you are supposed to be on your journey through life.

It has been said, "If there is an experience in front of you, go ahead—have it." Remember, you are being presented with challenges *and* opportunities. In caregiving, you will learn much from professionals. You will stretch toward greater knowledge and understanding. You will receive empathy from people who have walked in your shoes. You will discover that you have a lot to give. You are not just moving on a treadmill; you are on your way to a heavenly reward. And *you* make a difference.

———◈———

For you have need of endurance, so that after you have done the will of God, you may receive the promise: "For yet a little while, and He who is coming will come and will not tarry. Now the just shall live by faith." HEBREWS 10:36-38 NKJV

CHAPTER 5

Even to your old age and gray hairs I am he, I am he who

will sustain you. I have made you and I will carry you;

I will sustain you and I will rescue you. Isaiah 46:4 NIV

Physical Changes in Aging—Part I
Understanding and Caring for Common
Health Problems in the Elderly

KING Solomon, writing in Ecclesiastes 11 and 12, describes those years in a man's life when he trembles and stoops when he walks, when he has few teeth left, when his eyes grow dim, and when he is awakened by the sound of a bird but its songs are faint because of deaf ears. Solomon is describing some of the possible effects of growing old.

Not everyone who grows old suffers from deafness, bad eyesight, tremors, or insomnia, but eventually your aged loved one is likely to develop some illness, disability, or chronic health condition that will limit his capacity to function as in the past. Statistics show that 79 percent of noninstitutionalized persons 70 years of age and over have at least one chronic condition—a prolonged illness that is rarely cured completely. More than half suffer from arthritis, about one-third report they have hypertension (high blood pressure), more than one-fourth have heart disease, and 11 percent have diabetes.[1]

What does this mean to you and your elder? It means both of you may face some unique challenges—challenges not faced to the same degree by earlier generations. Because people are living longer, often with the help of medications and treatments unavailable even a few years ago, they have more time to develop illnesses that require care and medical expertise. But though the body deteriorates and loses physical strength with age, a person can gain wisdom with age. With a longer life, there are more opportunities for you to enjoy the company and wisdom of your aging loved one.

THE AGING PROCESS

Gerontologists have described aging in two ways: "Usual" aging includes changes caused by the aging process as well as the effects of diseases or unhealthy lifestyle and environmental factors. "Successful" aging is defined as changes due solely to the aging process, generally unaffected by disease, lifestyle, or environmental factors. An elder who has lived life basically free of disease has experienced successful aging.

Whether aging is successful or usual, it brings unique physical and mental challenges. Consider some of the most common changes seniors face as they age:

- A small percentage of elderly people are prone to experience fatigue, dizziness, and falls, in part because of emotional or physical stress. Their older regulatory systems cannot respond quickly to sudden movements or changes in position.
- Digestive and urinary functions slow down. Poor appetite is often the result. Saliva secretion—and its effectiveness in digesting carbohydrates—also declines. Taste buds atrophy and the amount of gastric secretions declines, reducing the ability of the stomach to properly absorb nutrients and ward off bacteria.
- Lungs begin to lose elasticity after age 40. In older patients, the lungs do not inflate or deflate as well.
- Trouble with constipation increases. The elderly also face dimin-

DID YOU KNOW?

A male who reaches age 65 is likely to survive at least fifteen more years. A 65-year-old female typically lives another nineteen years. Those who live to be 85 can expect to live five more years.

ished anal sphincter control and an increase in bladder-control problems.

• Aging skin becomes wrinkled, drier, thinner, and more fragile.

• Muscles deteriorate over time.

• Eyes are affected by aging. The lens of the eye becomes stiffer, compromising its ability to change shape for focusing. In addition, the lens protein gradually becomes blurry, causing a cataract. This makes the image on the retina less clear, causing decreasing visual acuity.

• The brain loses neurons (nerve cells) beginning at birth. By age 80, a person will have lost as much as 10 percent of her brain weight. Blood flow to the brain also decreases. Intellectual function can still remain intact, despite these changes.

• The elderly person's immune system becomes less efficient with age and less able to fight off microorganisms that cause infection. Stress may also weaken the immune system's ability to fight off invading germs by altering the body's ability to distinguish foreign invaders from one's own cells. Inactivity, inefficient swallowing, poor cough reflex, incomplete bladder emptying, immobility that causes skin changes, and other factors also can contribute to a person's inability to fight off bacteria or viruses.

Despite all of these changes, your elder's organ systems can continue to operate efficiently unless injury, illness, or intense stress pushes them beyond their limits. A health problem in one system can have a domino effect, leading to other health problems. A patient immobilized by a fractured hip, for example, can quickly develop problems with circulation, skin breakdown, pulmonary function, voiding (elimination of bodily wastes), and constipation. In addition, it is not unusual for individuals to die within one year of sustaining a hip fracture, due to secondary medical problems that develop.

The changes that occur with aging mean that your elder has a good chance of developing one or more acute or chronic conditions.

Chronic conditions. A chronic condition is one that is expected to be long-term and possibly permanent—such as heart disease, hearing loss, visual impairment, diabetes, arthritis, high blood pressure, stroke, and certain respiratory illnesses. While some of these conditions will not disable your elder, others may. The most common chronic conditions include arthritis, hypertension (high blood pressure), diabetes, hearing loss, heart disease, and cataracts.[2] Most visits to the doctor are for chronic conditions.

Acute conditions. An acute condition is one that is expected to be of limited duration. It may be mild or serious and can often exacerbate a chronic condition. Acute conditions can range from bruises and broken bones to pneumonia. Some diseases mix acute and chronic condi-

WHY DO WE AGE?

Though people are living longer, relatively few human beings live beyond 100 years. Aging is an inevitable but mysterious process. Modern scientists have many theories as to why we age. Some theories blame impaired cell function, a less effective immune system, or genetic factors as the causes of aging. One theory postulates that certain organs in the body—primarily the hypothalamus—are genetically programmed to run down with time. Another theory blames aging on normal cells that can reproduce only a finite number of times, while abnormal cells continue multiplying. Death is the final result.

Clearly, there are a variety of theories on why and how we age. But why must we age? From a spiritual viewpoint, the Bible teaches that we are born into a sinful and fallen world (Romans 3:23, Hebrews 9:27), and each one of us awaits an appointment with death. While researchers may extend life through medical breakthroughs—including cures for many infectious diseases, improved nutrition, and effective public-health practices—we all will eventually die. It is part of the human condition explained in Genesis chapter 3 and something we cannot avoid. Therefore, it is futile to place our faith in this life alone. As the days wear on while you care for your aging loved one, keep in mind that earth is a temporary home for believers of Jesus Christ; our victory lies beyond the grave. "For we know that if our earthly house, this tent, is destroyed, we have a building from God, a house not made with hands, eternal in the heavens" (2 Corinthians 5:1 NKJV). Jesus, whose crucified body did not undergo decay but was raised to life, promises eternal life in heaven to everyone who depends on Him alone for salvation.

tions, such as chronic heart disease that develops an acute heart attack, or chronic diabetes mellitus that develops acute hypoglycemia (low blood sugar), perhaps from taking too much insulin or from not eating enough or on time.

Whether acute or chronic, medical conditions may require some form of medical care involving one or more physicians, health-insurance companies, and hospital staffers. Your elder's health condition will also involve you—sometimes on a daily or weekly basis.

In consulting with your elder's physician, you may wish to find out if she routinely treats older patients or if she has had any geriatric training. A physician who has had geriatric training will have a clearer understanding of the unique needs of seniors. All internal-medicine physicians (and some family physicians) have a level of geriatric training. There are also some doctors who specialize in geriatric medicine. In most cases, your elder should be able to get very good medical care without having to see a geriatric specialist.

You are probably going to be working with a variety of physicians, each of whom will need to be informed about what the others are prescribing. To avoid dangerous drug combinations, it is a good idea to take along a list of the prescribed medicines, over-the-counter medications, herbs, vitamins, and supplements your elder is taking (or better yet, put them all in a plastic bag and bring them with you) to show each physician, nurse, and pharmacist. If possible, have your loved one's doctors jointly discuss the various illnesses your elder is facing. Or find out if the physician seeing your elder is sending a report of his assessment and recommendations to others involved. It is far better to overcommunicate than to undercommunicate when it comes to the health of your aging loved one.

As your loved one seeks medical treatment for various conditions that may develop, keep in mind that illnesses and drugs can both affect the elderly in different ways than they affect the middle-aged or young person. For example, hyperthyroidism in a young person results in tremors and hyperactivity, but in an elderly person this condition may result in lethargy, confusion, and heart failure. In a young diabetic, symptoms of blood sugar being too high or too low often can be sensed by the person. Extremes of blood sugar in an elderly person often are not apparent or may be attributed to fatigue or other chronic conditions, such as dementia or depression.

PHYSICAL CHANGES AND DISEASES

This section describes a number of diseases or physical changes that may take place in your aging loved one. Many of these are simply the natural results of aging; others are diseases that could directly threaten the life of your elder. You will also find tips for caring for common health problems of seniors. Once you understand what is normal and what is not, you will be better prepared to do everything you can to physically care for your aging loved one.

Body Frame and Senses

BONES, MUSCLES, AND JOINTS

Bones

More than 10 million older Americans have **osteoporosis,** or brittle bones, and 18 million more have **low bone density,** which may eventually deteriorate into osteoporosis if not treated.[3] **Osteopenia** is early bone degeneration and loss of calcium, particularly on the surface of the bone. Osteoporosis is a further degree of softening or breaking down of the bony matrix. A loved one with osteoporosis has an increased susceptibility to fractures, especially of the hip, spine, and wrist. One out of two women and one in eight men over age 50 will have an osteoporosis-related fracture during his or her lifetime.[4] Fractures from falls are a leading cause of disability among people over age 65. Confinement from a fracture often leads to other illnesses, such as pneumonia, which may be fatal.

It is far better to over-communicate with doctors than to under-communicate when it comes to the health of your aging loved one.

Over time, bones lose their density and mass, but there are often no physical symptoms except for loss of height and **kyphosis** (a curvature of the spine, causing stooped posture, back pain, and stiffness of the spine) to indicate that a person's skeletal structure is deteriorating. For this reason, women should be evaluated periodically after menopause by their doctor.

Bone-mineral density can be measured through a variety of painless tests. These **bone densitometry tests** can help you determine if your elder is at risk for (or already has) osteoporosis. **Dual-energy X-ray absorptiometry (DEXA)** is the most commonly used and preferred method today because of its low dose of radiation, its accuracy, and its ability to measure bone density in the hip as well as the spine. Other tests include **quantitative computerized tomography (QCT)**, which is used mainly for the spine; **single-energy X-ray absorptiometry (SXA)**, a screening technique used mainly for the hand and heel; and **ultrasound densitometry**, which is not as precise as DEXA. To have your elder screened for osteoporosis, contact a physician or your local hospital.

Certain people are more at risk than others for osteoporosis. They have one or more of the following risk factors:

- Went through menopause before age 45
- Have a family history of osteoporosis in the elderly
- Have a family history of fractures in the elderly
- Use certain medications, particularly corticosteroids, which treat arthritis or lung disease
- Have chronically low calcium intake

PREVENTING FALLS

An ounce of prevention is worth a pound of cure when it comes to protecting your elder from falls and injuries. Consider the following tips:

- Be careful to wipe up spills or wet places on the floor.
- Encourage your elder to have a physical-therapy evaluation to assess his gait and the potential need of assistive devices such as canes or walkers. (A walker is considered more protective than a cane because it helps to prevent both forward falls and falls sideways onto the hip.)
- Place night-lights in hallways, bathrooms, and bedrooms. Make sure stairs are well lit.
- Avoid throw rugs.
- When rising from a reclining position to a sitting and standing position, your elder should pause to make sure her equilibrium is okay before taking off.
- If your elder is living alone, consider getting an emergency-response device that can be worn around the neck and operated by pushing a button. That action by your loved one will connect him to a dispatch unit and/or medical facility via a remote transmitter. Although this device will not help prevent a fall, it can be helpful and a great comfort to caregivers.

- Have thin or small bones
- Are of Caucasian or Asian descent
- Have an inactive lifestyle
- Smoke cigarettes
- Engage in excessive use of alcohol
- Are 65 and older
- Are menopausal women not taking estrogen

Menopausal women are especially at risk for osteoporosis, so early diagnosis is important. The development of osteoporosis may be slowed with weight-bearing exercise (such as walking) and a diet containing adequate amounts of calcium and vitamin D (e.g., dairy products, calcium-fortified orange juice, kale, broccoli, salmon, sardines). The recommended daily dose of calcium (with vitamin D) for women is 500 milligrams a day between ages 40 and 50 and 1,200 milligrams a day after age 50. (Note: Soy contains **phytoestrogens** that may relieve menopausal symptoms but may not decrease cholesterol, plaque in arteries, or the risk of osteoporosis. Talk to your doctor before using soy.) Research shows that estrogen is required to

PAIN, PRAYERS, AND PEACE

The night Mom was admitted to the hospital because of a herniated disk, I felt myself becoming very angry at my dad because he had separated from my mom a few years earlier and wasn't there to help. But I prayed about it and gave it to God. The hardest thing for me was to sit there and see my mom in pain after back surgery and not be able to do anything. She was on morphine but in so much pain, and I would see her crying out to the Lord—that was heartbreaking! And knowing that the Lord could take away the pain but didn't—that was hard to accept. We prayed a lot together.

During that time I heard an eight-part series on Christian radio on the sufferings of Job. I listened every day and read the Word, getting comfort from it and crying out to God. It is God's peace and strength that helped me support my mom during her one-month hospital stay. One surprising thing that came out of her pain was that she lost the desire to smoke—a bad habit she'd had all her life. Today she's happy about all the extra money she saves from not having to buy cigarettes, and her back feels better too!

Debra W.

bind the calcium in the bones to prevent bone loss. To keep adequate calcium in the bones, women (even over age 65) often are advised to take **hormone replacement therapy (HRT).**

Women should carefully consider using HRT and discuss it with their physician. Some studies have suggested that **estrogen,** one of the hormones in HRT, can speed the growth of preexisting breast-cancer cells in women. Women who should *not* take HRT are those who have a history of blood clots or breast cancer. HRT has been thought to reduce the possibility of heart attacks in patients who do not have preexisting cardiovascular disease. Therefore, the advisability of using HRT depends in part on family history. If your elder is considering HRT, remember that an estimated 12 percent of women receiving HRT continue to lose bone despite adequate hormone levels. Also, there is a risk of **endometrial cancer** if a woman with an intact uterus takes unopposed estrogen (estrogen used alone). Therefore, if a woman still has a uterus (i.e., has not had a hysterectomy) and chooses to take HRT, it is recommended that she take one of the many regimens of **progesterone (progestins)** along with estrogen to prevent a buildup of tissue within the uterus. If a woman has had a hysterectomy, it is fine to use unopposed estrogen, because there is no uterus to be affected.

Selective estrogen receptor modulator (SERM) drugs are a new class of medicine available to prevent and treat osteoporosis, even in the elderly. The first drug of this class, raloxifene (Evista), is gaining popularity for women who want the benefits of estrogen on the bone but wish to avoid the potential side effects of HRT on the breast or uterus. It has some beneficial effect in preventing bone loss and also lowering cholesterol. Side effects of raloxifene include hot flashes and night sweats, which generally last for up to six months. Raloxifene does not provide all the benefits of estrogen. For example, there is no evidence that raloxifene decreases the risks of Alzheimer's disease or colon cancer as estrogen does.

Other classes of drugs that can help to prevent and treat osteoporosis include **bisphosphonates** (Actonel, Fosamax) and **calcitonin** (Miacalcin), which is used as a nose spray. These drugs can actually build new bone when combined with 1,200 to 1,500 milligrams of calcium per day, but they must be taken according to specific instructions. See your doctor for more information.

The development of osteoporosis may be slowed with weight-bearing exercise (such as walking) and a diet containing adequate amounts of calcium and vitamin D.

Muscles

Aging produces profound changes in a person's muscles, which decrease in size and flexibility over time. The good news is that a carefully devised exercise program can do wonders for your aging elder, increasing strength and helping to reduce high blood pressure too. Exercise may also improve the following conditions: problems with gait and balance, arthritis, type II diabetes, osteoporosis, obesity, depression, muscle weakness, and poor flexibility.

Studies have shown that exercise helps the elderly feel more relaxed, increases their sense of well-being, and increases self-sufficiency. Exercise also appears to enhance mental sharpness and improve sleep patterns. It may decrease the tendency to fall. (See "Exercise for Good Health!" on pages 102-103 for tips on exercise for the elderly.)

Joints/Arthritis

Half of all people over age 65 have arthritis. There are a number of varieties of this disease and several types of treatment. The most common form of arthritis is **osteoarthritis (OA)**, a degenerative joint disease that occurs as the result of an injury, obesity, joint overuse, or for no reason at all. Heredity is thought to be a factor. OA usually affects the spine, hands, knees, and hips. In the early stages of the disease, pain occurs after activity but is relieved when the person rests. In the later stages, pain and stiffness of the joints occur even with little or no bodily movements. Many people find that taking **glucosamine, chondroitin sulfate,** or a preparation that combines these two nonprescription products, results in less arthritic ache and better mobility after a three-month trial.

The second most common form of arthritis is **rheumatoid arthritis (RA),** which affects more than 2 million Americans, mostly women.[5] It is a more serious form of arthritis. No one knows what causes RA, but it is thought to be an autoimmune disease, where the immune system attacks the person's own tissues. Literally, the immune system turns against its body parts, mainly the joints. RA is not confined to the joints but is *systemic,* meaning it affects the entire body. For example, some eye problems are associated with RA. Symptoms of RA may include joint pain, fatigue, fever, rashes, and weight loss.

A third form of arthritis is **gout,** which occurs when uric acid crys-

CONTROLLING PAIN

Your elder may experience one of two kinds of pain: acute or chronic. Acute pain can be severe and last for a short period of time. It is typically the result of an injury, surgery, or medical illness. Acute pain will usually go away during the healing process. Chronic pain, on the other hand, continues for a longer period of time. It may be mild to severe. Arthritis and musculoskeletal disorders are two of the most common causes of pain in elderly patients. Treatment options may be different for acute and chronic pain.

Elderly adults are at risk of being undertreated for pain. They might be reluctant to complain of pain, or they may assume pain is a normal part of aging. Physicians also face barriers when it comes to properly managing pain in their patients. One barrier is their own doubt that the pain is real or that it is great enough to require treatment. Another barrier is a concern over the use of **opioids** (drugs like morphine). Some physicians have an unwarranted fear of introducing an addiction into the life of the patient; however addictions are extremely rare in patients who have pain associated with a terminal illness. They also may fear introducing another medication when a patient is already on a number of medications. Pain management for patients on multiple medications can be more complicated, but that does not mean it should not be done.

Uncontrolled pain can be devastating to a patient. Even if it is not that severe, it can significantly impair the person's level of functioning and quality of life. Sometimes confusion, agitation, or what appears to be dementia may be caused by uncontrolled pain. The truth is, pain beyond control should never happen. Since caregivers know their elders better than anyone else does, if any of these scenarios apply to your aging loved one, be sure to think of uncontrolled pain as a possible contributing factor.

In pain control, physicians can choose from two basic models of long-term use of pain medications for their patients:

- The first model is the **scheduled** or **continual model.** Short-acting medications are given at regular intervals, on schedule, to prevent exacerbation of pain. A variation on this model is to give long-acting pain medications for chronic pain. Both of these models provide an ongoing analgesic effect and attempt to help the patient avoid having any pain.
- The second model is the **"p.r.n." technique** (*p.r.n.* stands for *pro re nata,* or "as needed"). This technique uses short-acting medication on an as-needed basis for acute or breakthrough pain. The most appropriate use of the p.r.n.

technique is in situations where a patient who already is on regularly scheduled medications needs an additional dose to prevent breakthrough pain. Some patients notice more pain around 4 P.M. or near the supper hour. If your elder notices this pattern, it may be helpful to take a breakthrough dose at 3:30 P.M. or a half hour before the pain typically starts. The p.r.n. technique also is useful to prevent pain before a person needs to be repositioned or needs a wound dressing changed.

The p.r.n. model should not be used as the main method of pain control for treating chronic pain. If your elder has genuine chronic pain, it is best to get the person onto regular doses of some kind of analgesic first, so that the pain is being prevented rather than chased.

When discussing pain control with your elder's physician, ask the doctor about her philosophy of pain control. Ask her about the possible side effects of the medications she will prescribe. Inform her about the kinds of medicines, as well as any herbal remedies or nutritional supplements, that your loved one is already taking. Discuss the possibility of having your elder use a "pain-scale test" as a useful evaluation tool to determine the severity of the pain. This is a five- or ten-point scale—usually a ruler with markings between zero and five or ten, with zero representing "no pain" and five or ten representing "the worst pain imaginable." Patients rate their pain several times a day to have an objective measure of determining how bad the pain is and whether the treatment needs to be adjusted.

After your elder and the physician have decided on a philosophy of pain management, then it is time to determine together what may be appropriate at this point in time. Options may include the following:

- Nonprescription analgesics such as acetaminophen or ibuprofen
- Non-narcotic pain medications such as prescription anti-inflammatories
- Opioids such as morphine, hydromorphone, oxycodone, fentanyl patches, or Tylenol with codeine
- Antidepressants, which can be amazingly helpful in altering pain thresholds, even for people who are not depressed
- Steroids
- Anticonvulsants such as carbamazepine (Tegretol), which may be helpful in controlling certain types of pain

- Other treatment modalities, such as epidurals and nerve blocks, in particularly difficult cases

Depending on your loved one's circumstances, pills may be the best route of medication administration. Liquid medication may work better for some. For others prescription pain patches are wonderful and only have to be changed every 72 hours. There are other methods of medication administration that you could discuss with a pharmacist or a physician if the oral route is not working for your elder. Sometimes the use of rectal suppositories works the best.

A rule of thumb for giving analgesics to elderly patients is to start with low doses of short-acting analgesics and increase them gradually. No one should be given long-acting opioids until a stable dose of the short-acting opioid medications has been determined to control pain.

When a person can no longer get proper analgesia orally, a **patient-controlled analgesic (PCA)** pump can be preprogrammed to deliver a small, continuous dose of medication subcutaneously (under the skin). The pump allows your loved one to push a button for an additional dose when he perceives the need for pain relief. It also can be used on an intermittent basis for acute pain.

Another method of subcutaneous administration of medication is to use an indwelling butterfly needle (placed under the skin in the upper chest, arms, or abdomen) that has a rubber stopper on the other end and can be kept in for up to a week. Regular and breakthrough dosages of medication are injected through the stopper at regular intervals. If your elder is at home, a home health nurse or hospice worker can teach you or another family member to draw up the proper dosages and administer the medication. If you feel uncomfortable drawing up the dosages, a nurse can come in and do it, labeling each for use. This allows the same type of medication delivery without the necessity of the computerized pump, and the dosage of each medication can be adjusted independently for the patient.

In treating long-term chronic pain, it would be rare to deliver pain medication intravenously. If it is done intravenously, it should always be done as a continuous infusion, not on an intermittent basis. Intravenous medication is immediately available to the body, and when given intermittently, it leaves the patient without pain relief for extended periods of time. Also, there is almost never a place for intramuscular injections for palliative-care patients. The subcutaneous route is the preferred route, and in most cases, the medication is just as well absorbed.

Nondrug forms of pain control may include massages, manipulative techniques, application of ice or heat, correct positioning and frequent position changes, a comfortable chair, a special mattress, behavioral therapy, acupuncture, acupressure, and TENS (transcutaneous electrical nerve stimulation). Nonprescription topical products such as capsaicin (Zostrix) also are used for pain. A physical therapist may be helpful in suggesting stretching exercises, and an occupational therapist can help by assessing which home health aids are needed, such as bathtub rails and elevated toilet seats. Specialty pain clinics have proliferated in recent years to help people manage pain. Discuss with the family physician whether an assessment by a pain clinic would be reasonable or worthwhile, especially if your elder's pain management has not been completely successful.

If your elder is in pain, get assurances from the physician that he will do everything he can to effectively control the pain, including making appropriate referrals or seeking additional advice. It is unreasonable, though, to expect the doctor to fix your elder's pain overnight; controlling pain can be a matter of trial and error. Avoid an adversarial attitude, and assure the doctor that you are grateful for what he is trying to do to help your elder.

tals accumulate in the affected joint. This often strikes older men and affects their toes (usually at the base of the big toe), ankles, elbows, wrists, or hands. The joints are painful, will swell, and can turn red. Gout may be associated with excessive consumption of food and drink, but more often it occurs when people are on prescription medications that elevate their levels of uric acid. Sometimes it strikes for no apparent reason.

Another form of arthritis is **ankylosing spondylitis,** a chronic inflammatory disease of the spine. **Bursitis, tendinitis,** and **carpal tunnel syndrome** can cause pain in or around joints. Your elder may have arthritis if the following symptoms are present:

- Swelling in one or more joints
- Morning stiffness lasting 30 minutes or longer
- Joint pain that is constant or comes and goes
- Joints that will not move in a normal way
- Redness or warmth in a joint
- Weight loss, fever, or weakness and joint pain that cannot be explained

You can help your elder pursue treatment options in consultation with a doctor. These include diet, exercise, joint protection, prescription and over-the-counter medicines, vitamins or supplements, physical/occupational therapy, improved sleep, surgery, and heat and cold therapy.

Proper exercise on a daily basis is an important part of arthritis treatment. Exercise and weight loss can help lessen pressure on the joints and strengthen the muscles. For more information, contact the Arthritis Foundation (see appendix).

Feet

The foot is an amazing structure of 26 bones, 33 joints, and 126 muscles, ligaments, and nerves. The elderly face unique problems with their feet because a person's feet widen and flatten with age. The fat padding on the sole also wears down. Women are at higher risk for foot problems than men—primarily because of the practice of wearing high-heeled shoes.

Arthritis, including osteoarthritis and gout, can cause serious foot pain in the elderly. Diabetes is a major cause of foot pain, infection, and ulcers. Older adults who suffer from congestive heart failure, kidney problems, or hypothyroidism often experience swollen feet. A constant burning sensation in the feet is fairly common in people over age 65. It may be caused by nerve damage called neuropathy, by allergic reactions to socks, by athlete's foot, or even by inadeqate hygiene and nail trimming. Have your elder see a doctor for an accurate diagnosis and treatment.

To help relieve your elder's foot pain, suggest a warm foot bath for ten minutes.

Other causes of foot pain include decreased circulation, corns and calluses, ingrown toenails (typically with the big toe), bunions, flat feet, and hammertoe (a permanent deformity of the toe joint).

To help relieve your elder's foot pain, suggest a warm foot bath for 10 minutes at least two or three times a week. (Be careful not to burn the feet of diabetics; they may not feel heat adequately.) Also check to see what kind of shoes he is wearing. The shoes should be comfortable, with padding inside, a flexible sole, and a removable insole. There should be one-half inch of space between the toe and the front of the shoe. Advise against pointed shoes, tight shoes, or shoes with heels that exceed one inch in height. Moleskin or padding may help relieve the pressure of a bunion. If foot pain persists, ask a podiatrist or orthopedist about **orthotics,** insoles created from a plaster cast of the feet. Noncustom insoles, available at drug stores, may also provide relief.

Foot care is absolutely essential for the diabetic. Nerve damage from diabetes diminishes the ability to feel discomfort, so it is easy to overlook small injuries or the formation of skin ulcers until aggressive treatment is required. Meticulous daily foot care and early detection and treatment of skin ulcers may prevent up to 85 percent of amputations.[6] Feet should be washed carefully, using warm water and mild hand soap, and dried thoroughly with a soft, clean towel. Using a moisturizer is fine, but avoid hot-water soaks, heating pads, and harsh topical agents, such as hydrogen peroxide, iodine, and astringents. You or your elder need to inspect her feet daily to check for changes in color, texture, or odor and for firm or hardened areas. If your elder has diabetes, she should avoid wearing high heels, sandals, and thongs and should not go barefoot. She should wear soft, clean, absorbent socks and should avoid tight shoes, tight stockings, or any clothing that constricts the legs and feet. Diabetic patients also should have their feet examined at each doctor's appointment.

EXERCISE FOR GOOD HEALTH!

An elderly person who sits around all day will go downhill rapidly both physically and mentally. A sedentary lifestyle can contribute to loss of strength, weight gain, high blood pressure, depression, loss of sexual desire, and a loss of enthusiasm for life. Studies have shown that a regular exercise routine can reduce high blood pressure, benefit the lungs, help increase bone-mineral density, strengthen muscles, and sharpen mental acuity.[1] Daily walking, for example, has been found to reduce the risk of heart disease among elderly men.[2] Exercise helps improve mobility and functional strength, which might allow an elderly person to remain independent longer and postpone or avoid having to spend time in a nursing home.[3] Aerobic exercise can even increase the amount of sleep an elderly person gets each night and reduce the amount of time it takes to fall asleep.[4]

When beginning an exercise program, start by setting some achievable goals. Does your elder want to improve flexibility, strength, balance, and endurance? Does she wish to walk without becoming fatigued, carry grocery bags, or rise from a chair more easily? Encourage your aging loved one to review an exercise program with her doctor or get a referral from a physician for a qualified exercise specialist who can set up a realistic exercise program that will not exacerbate any current medical condition. After a thorough medical exam, the physician might refer your elder to a qualified exercise specialist who can design an individualized program that best addresses your loved one's needs. If your elder does not like the idea of exercising alone, it may be a good opportunity to join her in an exercise program that will benefit both of you.

The goal of an exercise program is to raise the heart rate and to expand the lungs. An ideal program of aerobic training (to increase the heart rate and breathing rate so that more oxygen goes to the muscles) is 20 to 30 minutes, three to five days a week. An older person who has been sedentary should begin with a 5-to-10-minute program one or more times per day and slowly increase the amount of exercise time. A good way to begin is by walking, which requires no special equipment and is ideal for people with osteoporosis.[5] Brisk walking, stair climbing, biking, and lifting small weights are good low-impact exercises that improve endurance and help keep bones strong. Weight-resistance training improves muscle strength and bone strength (or thickness) even in elderly people. Swimming and water aerobics are especially beneficial for people with arthritis or who have problems performing weight-bearing exercise. Gentle stretches should be used to warm up and cool down.

Exercising does not have to be boring. Depending on your elder's health or level of frailty, he may be able to walk, bicycle, swim, play tennis, work in a garden, or stroll through a shopping mall. Indoor exercise can include walking on a treadmill, riding a stationary bicycle, using a rowing machine, or lifting light weights (such as soup cans). If your elder is bedridden, she may be able to squeeze a ball or sponge, lift her legs up off the bed, flex her arms and ankles, and breathe deeply, exhaling completely several times. It is important for your loved one to warm up by stretching her muscles before exercising, to drink plenty of fluids to prevent dehydration, and to use a safety helmet, knee pads, eye goggles, or other protection when appropriate.

Your elder should consult a doctor before increasing physical activity if he has a chronic disease or illness, chest pain, shortness of breath, swollen joints, hernia, any new symptom, or is recovering from surgery.

[1]T. Hickey et al., "Exercise Participation in a Frail Elderly Population," *Journal of Health Care for the Poor and Underserved,* 7 no. 3 (1996), 219–231. [2]Amy A. Hakim et al., "Effects of Walking on Coronary Heart Disease in Elderly Men: The Honolulu Heart Program," *Circulation,* 100 (6 July 1999), 9–13. [3]R. J. Shephard, "Exercise and Aging: Extending Independence in Older Adults," *Geriatrics,* 48 no. 5 (1993), 61–65. [4]D. Buchner, "Physical Activity and Quality of Life in Older Adults," *The Journal of the American Medical Association,* 277 no. 1 (1997), 64–67. [5]Linda Pescatello and Loretta DiPietro, "Physical Activity in Older Adults: An Overview of Health Benefits," *Sports Medicine,* 15 no. 6 (1993), 353–361.

EYES, EARS, NOSE, MOUTH, AND TEETH
Eyes

Cataracts are a common age-related eye problem. As a person ages, the lens of the eye becomes cloudy. Vision becomes blurred, print seems faded, and car headlights may appear to have streaks of light radiating from them. Risk factors for cataracts include heredity, long-term use of corticosteroids, injury, long-term sun exposure, and health problems such as diabetes. Fortunately, surgery to correct this condition is now considered routine and has a very high success rate.

Macular degeneration is another condition associated with aging. The person with macular degeneration retains his side vision, but vision in the macula (the central portion of the retina that allows the eye to see fine details) is clouded. Macular degeneration sometimes can be treated with laser therapy, surgery, or photodynamic therapy. There is a caveat to this, though. It can be treated only if it is the "wet" type of macular degeneration, which accounts for a small percentage of the cases. For the "dry" kind of macular degeneration, there is no effective treatment to date. A person with macular degeneration can eventually lose all central vision. Some people recommend a daily multivitamin with lutein, but there is no proven benefit to this.

Glaucoma, another disease of the eye, affects about 3 percent of Americans over age 65—about 2 million people. Glaucoma causes a chronic optic neuropathy—that is, a slow loss of nerve fibers in the optic nerve. If untreated, glaucoma can lead to a gradual loss of peripheral vision—and eventual blindness. Glaucoma is treated with eye drops or, in some cases, laser treatment or surgery, but treatment will not reverse damage already done to the optic nerve. There are no early symptoms of glaucoma, so an annual eye exam is important for early detection.

"Floaters" are tiny spots or specks that float across the field of vision and may be accompanied by light flashes or the appearance of a curtain in the field of vision. New onset of floaters and flashes should prompt a visit to the ophthalmologist because they are occasionally accompanied by retinal detachment.

WHEN TO SEE AN EYE DOCTOR

Elderly people are sometimes reluctant to get an eye exam because they fear they will lose independence if visual changes are discovered. Other seniors believe it is normal for eyesight to worsen and that nothing can be done to slow the loss of sight.

The truth is, early recognition and prompt treatment of eye problems often can help to prevent blindness. Vision loss may be the result of retinal detachment, stroke, head injury, eye trauma, corneal disorders, glaucoma, or other problems that often can be treated. To prevent irreversible vision loss, the American Academy of Ophthalmology recommends a medical eye exam at least once every two years for people over 65. People at high risk for eye diseases, such as those who have diabetes or a family history of eye problems, should see an ophthalmologist more often.

Even elderly people who have dementia or a speech disorder should have eye checkups to ensure that no disease is present but also to see if they might benefit from eyeglasses, magnifiers, or other low-vision aids.

See an eye doctor *immediately* if your elder has any of the following symptoms:

- Sudden loss of vision in one or both eyes
- Sudden onset of double vision, lid droop, or enlarged pupil
- Severe pain in the eye

See an eye doctor *promptly* if your elder has any of these signs:

- Blurred or distorted vision
- Halos around lights
- Episodes of visual loss (lasting five or ten minutes)
- Sudden appearance of "floaters" and flashes

Financially disadvantaged people over age 65 who do not have access to an ophthalmologist (and who do not belong to an HMO or other managed-health-care plan) may be qualified to get a referral for a volunteer eye doctor through the National Eye Care Project, a public-service program of the American Academy of Ophthalmology (see appendix).

Diabetic retinopathy, a disease of the retina, is common in seniors with diabetes. High blood-sugar levels cause damage to blood vessels of the retina, resulting in blurred vision and gradual, progressive vision loss. Controlling blood-sugar and blood-pressure levels can help preserve vision. It is also important to see an eye doctor yearly for retina screen-

RESOURCES FOR LOW VISION

People with eye problems often find "low-vision" aids very helpful. These aids include special devices that are stronger than regular eyeglasses, such as telescopic glasses, lenses that filter light, and magnifying glasses. Some communities have low-vision clinics to help the elderly who have minimal or low vision—vision loss that cannot be corrected with medicine, surgery, or conventional prescription lenses. Check with your local eye doctor for recommendations.

To help your elder see in optimal lighting conditions, consider these sight-enhancing ideas:

- Use nonglare light bulbs and sheer curtains or blinds in the windows.
- Use dimmer switches and three-way bulbs.
- Arrange lamps and lighting fixtures to minimize shadows.
- Install bright lights at the top and bottom of stairs, use colored tape to identify each step indoors, and paint the edges of outdoor steps. Make sure the staircase has handrails.
- Put glow-in-the-dark tape on light switches and door handles or knobs.
- Request large-print type on medication bottles and on church worship bulletins.
- Keep a flashlight within reach of your elder's bed and chair—and perhaps in other locations.

Several organizations have resources for people with vision loss. For example, you can purchase the Bible in large print and on cassette from the American Bible Society. Lighthouse International, a not-for-profit organization, provides resources and information on the vision problems of the elderly. The Canadian National Institute for the Blind, a not-for-profit, national organization, offers free library services (braille books, talking books, and electronic and digital materials) to the 3 million Canadians who are blind, visually impaired, and print-disabled (see appendix).

ing. If diabetic retinopathy is detected at an early stage, laser treatment can often prevent major vision loss.

Ears

Twenty-five percent of people between 65 and 75 years of age and half of those over 75 have some form of hearing loss. The loss is usually very gradual but often gets worse over time. The person who is experiencing hearing loss typically loses the ability to hear high-pitched sounds and can eventually go deaf.

Presbycusis (from the Latin *presby,* meaning "old," and *cusis,* meaning "hearing") is the term given to hearing loss associated with the aging process. It occurs gradually and usually affects both ears. Beginning with a loss of the high tones (voices of women and children), it slowly progresses to involve the middle and lower tones. Age-related hearing loss is permanent and cannot be reversed surgically. A hearing aid can be helpful.

Conductive hearing loss results from a mechanical defect in the outer or middle ear. This keeps sound from reaching the inner ear. It can be

FAITH, NOT SIGHT

Despite her faith, my elderly mom worried about her sight as she became more feeble. "What's going to happen if I go blind?" she'd say. She had macular degeneration, and it affected everything. She'd call from the retirement home where she lived and say, "Something's wrong with the TV." If I couldn't drive over there to see what was wrong, I'd describe the location of the on/off switch, and eventually she would have the TV working again. Or she'd mistakenly hit the pause button on her tape recorder and think it was broken. So we put white tape on the buttons she shouldn't hit.

She wasn't one to give up, but when she got discouraged she would say, "I don't know why the Lord doesn't take me home." My daughter would reply, "He still has something for you to do, Grandma." When Mom would say, "Oh, I wish I were dead," I'd say, "When you talk like that it makes us feel bad." She'd say, "Oh, I know." She feared losing her sight, but at least she had no fear of dying—that was the positive thing.

Marlene W.

caused by infections, a rupture of the eardrum, arthritis in the ear, or simply wax buildup. It can also be caused by **otosclerosis,** a condition in which an abnormal bony growth replaces the bone of the inner ear. This disease seems to run in families.

Sensorineural hearing loss is caused by nerve damage or dysfunction. The damage may be due to birth defects, head injury, loud noise (prolonged exposure to noise at 90 decibels or louder), the aging process, or medications.

Tinnitus, a noise or ringing in the ear, is another problem common among the elderly. While tinnitus does not cause hearing disorders, it

BEFORE GETTING A HEARING AID

If your elder has recently experienced a hearing loss, you should take him to a physician for a medical evaluation. Hearing tests will determine the type and extent of hearing loss in your elder. He may need to be fitted for a hearing aid or simply have the wax in his ears cleaned out. If you are going to be involved in helping your loved one purchase a hearing aid, here are some precautions to take before buying:

- Consult with a physician before purchasing a product.
- Have your elder's hearing tested by an audiologist.
- Check your local library for magazines that rate products—including hearing aids.
- Ask for a 30- or 60-day trial period to test the hearing aid.
- Check with the American Association of Retired Persons for updated information on hearing aids. AARP has published a buyer's guide on purchasing hearing aids. Ask for "Product Report: Hearing Aids" from AARP (see appendix).

If your hearing-impaired elder often asks to have things repeated, here is a good coping strategy. Next time he hears only part of a sentence, suggest that he formulate a question that is designed to get the missing information, not just a simple repetition (which likely would be just as unintelligible). For example, if your elder hears, "We're having dinner at ???", instead of saying, "What?" or "Pardon?" he could reply, "When and where are we having dinner?"

can accompany decreased hearing and can include pressure, unsteadiness, or dizziness. An estimated 50 million Americans suffer from this annoyance. Many medications can cause tinnitus. To reduce the ringing, tinnitus sufferers have been advised to avoid nervous tension, fatigue, and stimulants. Another successful approach has been to distract the individual's attention from the ringing by introducing background noise. Wearing a hearing aid often helps mask the ringing sounds. Your elder's physician may also recommend the use of a tinnitus masking device, which is worn like a hearing aid. There are many clinics across the country that specialize in treating tinnitus. It is worth investigating to see if there is such a clinic in your loved one's area.

Vertigo, a sensation that you or the room is spinning, can occur when there is a problem in the semicircular canals—the portion of the inner ear that controls balance and equilibrium. This sensation may be triggered by a change in body position or the position of the head, such as lying on one side or tipping the head back. Benign positional vertigo usually ends quickly (in less than a minute) and is not medically dangerous. To prevent it, your elder should try to avoid head positions that cause vertigo. See a doctor if your elder suffers from persistent episodes of vertigo. There are a variety of positioning techniques that can be taught to the patient and/or performed by physical therapists to help stop vertigo when it stems from problems in the semicircular canals.

Nose
The sense of smell begins to decline after age 60. While loss of smell can be due to the aging process alone, it can also result from poor dental hygiene, infections, head trauma, and medications. Allergic rhinitis (hay fever) from exposure to pollen can impair the sense of smell temporarily. Other illnesses, as well as therapies (e.g., some chemotherapy) can change a person's sense of smell. A diminished sense of smell can have a devastating effect on an elder. Experts say that many flavors are sensed through smell, not simply through the taste buds. Taste and smell are inextricably linked to provide a person with an enjoyable eating experience. Consequently, loss of smell can affect an elder's ability to enjoy food, which in turn can affect her overall health. Losing the

ability to smell can also prove dangerous to the elderly if they are unable to smell gas leaks or smoke or are unable to tell if food has gone rancid.

A willingness to experiment with various spices to increase the flavor of foods can add to your elder's enjoyment of eating. However, if your elder begins adding more and more salt to food, he may increase the possibility of developing high blood pressure, which could lead to a stroke or heart attack. If there is a bacterial infection, treatment with antibiotics may help. Antihistamines often provide good relief for hayfever symptoms. In select situations, nasal surgery may be used to help repair smell disorders.

Mouth

The decline in taste begins around age 60 and becomes more pronounced by age 70. The 9,000 taste buds begin to decrease in number and size. If taste sensation is lost, it usually begins with a loss of salty and sweet tastes. Bitter and sour tastes remain longer. Losing the ability to taste, like the ability to smell, can frequently become a health threat. As elderly people lose the enjoyment of eating, they may eat less or reduce the variety of foods they eat—thus threatening their nutritional intake. If you find your elder losing interest in eating, encourage her to put extra spices or flavoring in her foods. Your elder can add texture to her food by eating crunchy foods. Products like cheese, bacon, and butter flavors can also enhance the tastes of foods. Your elder may benefit from certain supplements, too, such as zinc.

If you find your elder losing interest in eating, encourage her to put extra spices or flavoring in her foods.

Teeth and Gums

In the past, many people lost their teeth with age. But today, the use of fluoride, calcium, and vitamin D, along with better dental care, hygiene, and nutrition, have allowed people to keep their teeth longer. Many older people wear partial plates that contain one or more prosthetic teeth. About 25 percent of Americans over age 65 have lost all of their teeth, according to the Centers for Disease Control and Prevention. Women who take hormone-replacement therapy are less likely to lose their teeth. Tooth loss is more prevalent among people who smoke, have less than a high school education, and lack dental insurance.[7] Tooth loss is also the result of oral disease, not the aging process. Unfortunately, about one-half of all seniors fail to visit a dentist once a year for checkups. But with excellent, lifelong dental care and hygiene, the number of people needing dentures or partial plates can be significantly reduced.

Periodontal (gum) disease occurs if people are not eating correctly or have poor dental hygiene. This, in turn, can lead to heart disease and other diseases. Lack of vitamin C, for example, is associated with sore gums. Dental infections can be the beginning of infection throughout the body. Occasionally, they can be the underlying cause of a fever that has been difficult to identify.

Aging can affect the teeth, mouth, and gums in a number of ways. An elderly person's teeth may darken because of changes in dentin, a bone-like tissue underneath tooth enamel. The gums may recede, exposing tooth roots, and contributing to tooth decay. If your elder's gums are red, swollen, tender, bleed easily, or if he has pus between his gums and teeth, it could be a sign of gum disease. Your elder should get to the dentist as soon as possible. Regular visits to the dentist—at least once or twice a year—can help prevent tooth loss and gum disease. It is important to floss and to brush at least twice a day with a fluoride toothpaste. Using mouthwash is controversial; some dentists say this could actually upset the normal flora of the mouth and worsen dental hygiene. Patients should consult their dentist.

Malfunctioning salivary glands can cause mouth pain, affecting a person's ability to chew, taste, or speak. The elderly person may also

PROPER CARE OF DENTURES

If your elder has dentures, they should be taken care of properly. Dentures should soak in a container of water or denture-cleaning solution each night. (This will give the person's gums a period of time to rest.) Your elder should clean the dentures using a brush designed for dentures and a denture cleaner, not toothpaste. The dentures need attention if she notices looseness caused by tissue changes, if there is a bad odor, if there is a color change due to age or a reaction to mouth fluids, or if there are stains and calculus deposits. Your elder should brush and floss remaining natural teeth daily, as well as clean and massage her mouth and gums each day using a brush, cloth, or finger.

Regular visits to the dentist— at least once or twice a year—can help prevent tooth loss and gum disease.

develop "dry mouth" because of reduced saliva flow. Saliva serves as a cleaning agent in the mouth. When there is reduced saliva, plaque grows more freely, thus causing tooth decay. In addition, gum diseases develop more rapidly. Medications can also cause dryness in the mouth, which can result in abnormal healing and increased chance of infections. If your elder suffers from dry mouth, sugar-free candy can help to restore moisture to the mouth. Or the dentist or physician can recommend other ways to restore moisture, such as a commercially available artificial saliva substitute and other prescription medications.

SKIN AND NAILS
Skin

A person's skin begins a degenerative process in middle age, when it starts to lose elasticity and begins to wrinkle. It also loses fat, becomes thinner, and loses moisture. In addition, gravity is at work, causing it to sag. Lesions or skin growths become more common when a person ages. These can range from "liver spots" to skin cancers.

The most common skin change is the growth of **seborrheic keratoses**—waxy brown or black growths that appear stuck on the skin. Normally painless, they require no treatment unless they itch, irritate the person, or seem unsightly. The doctor usually can remove them easily in the office. The cause of seborrheic keratoses is unknown. Because these dark growths can look similar to malignant melanoma, your elder should see a doctor rather than assume they are seborrheic keratoses. Another common skin problem facing an elderly person is the appearance of white or red scaly spots on the face, scalp, and back of hands called **actinic keratoses.** These are caused by accumulated long-term exposure to the sun. If ignored, they can become skin cancers. **Basal-cell carcinoma** is the most common form of skin cancer. Appearance varies, but often it appears as a small, shiny, fleshy bump on the head, neck, or chest. When these are treated early, there is a 95-percent cure rate. **Malignant melanoma** is a serious form of skin cancer. Fair-skinned people and men over age 50 are at the highest risk of melanoma. It usually appears as a dark brown or black molelike growth with irregular borders. The most frequent sites are the upper back in both men and women, the chest and abdomen in men, and the lower legs of women. **Age** or **"liver" spots** are harmless, flat, brown spots called **lentigines,** which occur from overexposure to sun or from unknown causes. Very common after age 55, they are not dangerous and require no treatment.

The elderly may suffer from herpes zoster, also known as **shingles,** an inflammation of a nerve root. Shingles results in a painful, blistering rash on the skin. If your elder has shingles, he should see a doctor immediately for confirmation of diagnosis plus the addition of medication that can shorten the bout of shingles and lessen the odds of long-term pain in the involved nerve. Anyone who previously has had chicken pox (varicella) at any time in life can develop shingles. People who have shingles should stay away from AIDS patients, cancer patients, or anyone else whose ability to fight infection might not be normal. If your elder has never had chicken pox, consult her physician to discuss whether varicella vaccine might be right for her.

Your elder may also experience **bruising** (black-and-blue marks on

PREVENTING PRESSURE SORES

To prevent pressure sores in a bedridden senior, follow these tips:

- A person should not remain in any one position more than two hours at a time. As an alternative, there are special mattress pads that inject air and inflate in alternating parts of the pad; these eliminate the need to turn the patient every two hours.
- Watch for a persisting redness to the skin, which indicates there has been too much pressure on a bony prominence.
- Modesty is the enemy. It is important to regularly inspect the lower-back and tailbone area, the sides of the hips that get pressure when lying on the side, and the back and sides of ankles. Heels are common places of skin breakdown.

If your elder's skin appears damaged in any of these areas, seek urgent medical help.

his arms and legs). This is usually the result of thinning skin and sun damage. Loss of fat and connective tissue makes the skin more susceptible to bruising. Because bruising can also be caused by injury, medications, clotting disorders, or internal diseases, check with a doctor if your loved one is frequently bruised.

Skin Changes to Watch For

Most skin problems are harmless, but it is important to watch for changes in your elder's skin. Some may indicate a problem.

Most skin problems are harmless, but it is important to watch for changes in your elder's skin. Some may indicate a problem. People with light skin and hair, lifelong exposure to sunlight, and a family history of skin cancer have a higher risk of skin cancer. Contact a physician if any of the following symptoms appear:

- A scaly red spot
- A change in color, shape, or size of a mole
- Any new skin growth
- Bleeding in a mole or other growth
- Excessive dryness of skin or itchy skin lesions
- Shingles
- Bulging or tender veins
- A cut that fails to heal

Nails

A person's fingernails and toenails tend to harden with age. Curved, thick toenails are a common result of aging. Discolored nails or the development of ridges or pits in nails may signal an inadequate diet or an underlying disease. Consult a physician if you suspect a problem.

Many older people have one or more fungal toenails. Nail fungus can be hard to eliminate and may not be worth treating. You can ask your doctor about new therapies for the condition, but with few exceptions, fungal nails are simply a cosmetic nuisance that can be ignored. Besides, the cost of the medication may be high, the medication has to be used for months while the toenails slowly regrow, and certain antifungal drugs can interfere with other medications your elder may be taking.

Your loved one should take care when cutting her nails or, better yet, have someone else do it. Poor vision, unsteady hands, dull nail clippers, and hard-to-cut nails can all contribute to cuts, which can lead to infections, ulcers, and even amputation. The feet of diabetics are especially vulnerable if injured. Seek the help of a podiatrist for routine toenail care if there is any doubt about your loved one or you being able to do the job well.

Nails should be trimmed once every 2 to 3 weeks. If you are responsible for cutting your elder's nails, be careful not to cut them too short, and avoid cutting the cuticles, as this can lead to infection. Be sure to trim toenails straight across (not in a curve) to reduce the risk of an ingrown toenail.

Eating and Elimination

MALNUTRITION AND THE ELDERLY

The elderly are at risk for malnutrition, especially if they are living on their own. There are several reasons for this. Social isolation can result in loss of appetite and an unwillingness to prepare foods. People who are used to cooking for large crowds may feel it is not worth cooking just for themselves. Mobility problems may make it difficult for a senior to prepare food, and poor dental conditions inhibit chewing and limit food choices. Losing the ability to smell or taste can cause the elderly to eat less because food is not as tasty as it has been in the past. Prescription drugs can interfere with digestion, leading to nutrient deficiencies. As bodily-organ function decreases, so does the absorption, movement, and metabolism of food. People over age 65 can develop **atrophic gastritis,** the inability to produce adequate stomach acid. This can lead to pernicious anemia and occasionally stomach cancer.

In addition, the chronic health conditions that many elders have can affect their nutritional health. A person who is malnourished or dehydrated may become confused and disoriented. This is sometimes misdiagnosed as senility instead of a nutritional problem. If you suspect your elder is malnourished, pay attention to what he eats to make sure he is receiving enough nutrition.

Nutritional Care

If your elder lives with you, you will not have much trouble monitoring her nutrition. If your elder lives alone, however, or in a retirement home, it will take more effort to see that she has regular and healthful meals. The nurses at the retirement home can tell you if your elder is eating nutritious meals. Men are especially at risk for poor eating habits. If your loved one lives alone, check with your Area Agency on Aging for information on how to have a nutritious daily meal delivered to his home. These are usually available for free or at a greatly reduced price. Local senior centers may also provide meals and social companionship.

An elderly person has different nutritional needs than a younger person. Less muscle tissue and a lower expenditure of energy result in a need for reduced caloric intake. While elderly adults have a reduced need for calories, they quite often need more vitamins. Vitamin D, for example, is needed for proper calcium absorption. The elderly also need more vitamin B_6 (found in chicken, fish, eggs, oats, brown rice, and whole-wheat bread) to help form red blood cells, to assist in fighting infection, and to keep the skin healthy.

An elderly person's system removes vitamin A more slowly than that of a younger person, so there is a possibility of vitamin-A toxicity. A relationship has also been found between low vitamin-C intake and the development of cataracts. Diets high in antioxidants, such as vitamin C (found in citrus fruits and leafy green vegetables) and vitamin E

ENCOURAGEMENT FOR EATING WELL

To help an elderly person eat nutritious meals, try these tips:

- Invite your aging loved one to share a meal with you or arrange for him to eat with others.
- Bring over a home-cooked meal for your loved one's enjoyment.
- Buy food in smaller, more convenient packages.
- Eat out occasionally with your elder.
- Sign up your elder for a meals program at a senior center or Meals On Wheels.

The healthiest diet is one that is low in saturated fat, caffeine, alcohol, and sugar and high in fiber, fluids, fruits, and vegetables. If your elder wants help in maintaining a balanced diet, talk to a physician or dietitian about good nutrition. Or contact the American Dietetic Association (see appendix).

(found in vegetable oils, nuts, seeds, and leafy green vegetables) may help the immune system and prevent the development of age-related diseases. Before taking vitamin supplements, your elder should get the advice of her doctor.

While elderly adults have a reduced need for calories, they quite often need more vitamins.

DIGESTION

Older people have more illnesses of the digestive system than do younger people. Several changes occur in the digestive system with age. The swallowing motions of the esophagus become somewhat slower. Digested food also moves more slowly through the intestine. The flow of secretions from the stomach, liver, pancreas, and small intestine may decrease. These changes do not generally disrupt digestion. Nevertheless, if your elder experiences abdominal pain or unexplained weight loss, consult a physician.

Many medicines cause stomach distress. Consult a physician if you suspect your elder's medicines are causing stomach problems.

URINARY TRACT AND BOWELS
Urinary Tract

By the time your elder is seventy, she will have lost 50 percent of her bladder capacity. This is not a symptom of disease but just a normal part of aging. Most elderly people suffer from **nocturia,** the need to get up at night to go to the bathroom. With elderly people, the "micturition reflex" changes. This is the reflex that tells us when we have to urinate. With a young person, the micturition signal is sent when the bladder is half-full. In an elderly person, the signal is sent when the bladder is nearly full. This usually means there is not much time to get to the bathroom.

Incontinence

Some older people experience a problem with dribbling urine or incontinence. This involuntary leakage of urine may be caused by an underlying ailment or illness, but aging can be a contributor as well. For some women, pelvic changes can occur during childbirth that decrease the ability to control the bladder. This can last a lifetime if the pelvic muscles are not strengthened. Incontinence is divided into several types:

stress incontinence with leakage when coughing, straining, sneezing, or lifting; urge incontinence, which involves leaking urine with anxiety or with bladder fullness when the muscle wall goes into spasm, often not allowing the person to get to the bathroom before the bladder starts to empty; overflow incontinence, when the bladder is too full and, due to nerve damage, the person cannot fully empty the bladder (often called *neurogenic bladder*); and mixed stress and urge incontinence. Also, elderly men with an enlarged prostate may suffer from incontinence when the gland compresses the urethra, causing inadequate outflow of urine.

Incontinence can sometimes be treated with bladder training, called biofeedback. Pelvic-muscle exercises such as Kegel's exercises also can help to decrease leakage. Medication is only of benefit in women who have urge incontinence or mixed incontinence. These can be treated with prescription medications such as ditropan or detrol. The major side effect is dry mouth.

Urinary-control problems are complex. But under a doctor's care, most situations can be diagnosed and improved with treatment, if not cured.

If you are caring for an elder who suffers from incontinence, you can provide absorbent shields and undergarments to protect against accidents. These undergarments will help your elder avoid embarrassing situations when out in public. They come in both reusable and disposable forms. Reusable pads are often made of cloth, but have a plastic cover. Keep in mind that whether your elder uses a disposable or reusable undergarment, the urine cannot remain in contact with the skin for a long period of time. Once there is urine in the pad, the garment should be changed or cleaned and the skin should be thoroughly cleaned and dried.

In cases in which the cause of incontinence is from an overdistended, poorly functioning bladder, a catheter may need to be inserted through the urethra to drain the urine from the bladder several times a day. This is something that your loved one may be able to do for herself, or you may have to help her. Sometimes catheters are left in place and changed every 4 to 12 weeks. But chronic use of catheters does increase the risk of infection.

Urinary-control problems are complex. But under a doctor's care, most situations can be diagnosed and improved with treatment, if not cured. The urinary-control problem must be analyzed in the context of a complete medical history and physical examination by a physician. The problem can be as simple as a side effect of some medication that a person may be using (prescription or nonprescription), an asymptomatic urinary-tract infection, or unrecognized constipation. On the other hand, the problem could be as complex as nerve impairment from diabetes, a disc out of place in the back, a bladder tumor, multiple sclerosis, a pelvic mass, an ovarian cyst, a sagging bladder from previous childbirth, a head injury, bladder stones, or a host of other problems.

There are medications that can help, prostate operations, periurethral collagen injections, pelvic surgery, plus other techniques. Some women may have their stress or mixed incontinence corrected by surgery or by the placement of a **pessary,** a plastic device that fits into the vagina to help support and elevate the neck of the bladder. Biofeedback can teach some people how to control their urine better and use the toilet at the right time. Many prescription and nonprescription medications (including antihistamines and decongestants) can aggravate urinary-control problems. When dealing with urinary-control problems, be sure to discuss with the physician all medications and supplements your loved one is using.

Incontinence can be decreased by limiting the intake of caffeine and alcohol. Encourage your elder to continue drinking plenty of liquids despite incontinence. To prevent dehydration, seniors should drink enough liquids to maintain a good urine output and not be thirsty (about six cups of liquid daily). Inadequate fluids may trigger urinary infection, kidney stones, dizziness, weakness, and skin breakdown.

In some cases, your aging loved one may need help getting to the bathroom on a regular basis. Try to give him some privacy in the bath-

IT'S THE LITTLE THINGS

I learned lots of little tricks while taking care of my mom. For example, when she was no longer able to walk to the bathroom, I put a commode in her bedroom and poured a little water and Lysol in the bottom of it to eliminate any odor. I also kept some baby wipes there so that she could wash her hands after using the commode. She seemed to appreciate it.   *Fran H.*

room, and *do not rush him*. Be patient, and plan your schedule so that you can give him the time he needs. Treat your loved one with the utmost dignity, and never yell at him for being wet. Instead, assure him of your understanding and support.

Bowels: Constipation

Constipation is the abnormally delayed or infrequent passage of usually dry, hardened feces. In seniors it is often caused by a loss of muscle tone in the rectum and colon, where stool is formed. An inability to retain water as easily as in the past or a failure to take in adequate fluids and fiber also makes the stool drier and harder to pass. If your elder is concerned about his bowels, let him know it is not always necessary to empty the bowels each day. There is no "right" number of bowel movements to have each day or week. A regular schedule of movements may be twice a day for some or three times a week for others.

If your elder is constipated, a laxative or enema should be considered a temporary solution; they can be harmful if overused.

To determine if your elder is really constipated, ask the following questions:

1. Do you often have fewer than three bowel movements each week?
2. Do you often have a hard time passing stools? Are the stools hard or dry?
3. Is there pain?
4. Are there other problems such as bleeding?

If she answers yes to these questions, she is probably constipated. The cause is not always apparent. Misusing laxatives and medicines can cause constipation. Certain medications, a lack of exercise, and extended bed rest can also result in constipation. Some people are also constipated because of a blockage in their intestine. A variety of diseases can cause constipation, including multiple sclerosis, Parkinson's disease, stroke, diabetes, spinal-cord injuries, and thyroid problems.

Diet plays a role in constipation too. High-fat meats, dairy products, eggs, rich desserts, and other sweets high in refined sugars can result in constipation for some. A diet high in fresh fruits and vegetables, whole-grain cereals and other sources of fiber, and plenty of water can help to prevent constipation. Curiously, drinking a cup or more of hot water every morning helps many people to have a bowel movement.

Bulking agents such as bran fiber or psyllium can help the body produce softer, bulkier stools. Some daily exercise (even walking around the block a few times) often helps stimulate a bowel movement. Glycerin suppositories are also very helpful and have no harmful effects even if used repeatedly.

If your elder is constipated, a laxative or enema should be considered a temporary solution; they can be harmful if overused (see "Laxatives: How Much Is Too Much?" [below]). If the above methods are unable to overcome the constipation, your elder's bowels may be impacted. Seek help immediately if your elder has a painful, distended abdomen; is vomiting; or cannot pass gas.

Difficulty with bowel movements also can result in hemorrhoids and **anal fissures** (tears around the anus). Anal fissures can cause bleeding and require treatment. Sometimes straining can cause a small amount of the intestinal lining to push out from the anal opening. This is called **rectal prolapse** and may lead to secretion of mucus from the anus. **Rectocoele** (a bulging of the rectum into the vagina) can cause pressure and problems with defecation in women. For additional information on these and other topics related to constipation, contact the National Institute on Aging or the National Digestive Diseases Association (see appendix).

Bowels: Diarrhea

Diarrhea can lead to potassium imbalance. A few people experience di-

LAXATIVES: HOW MUCH IS TOO MUCH?

Most of the time, laxative abuse results when an elderly person is obsessed with having a stool every day. If she has trouble having a bowel movement, the person can become nervous and start laxatives, which can lead to dependence on them. Laxatives lose effectiveness if used daily for months or years and can cause changes in the bowels over time. They also interfere with absorption of nutrients such as vitamin D and calcium. If your elder needs a laxative more than three or four times per month, discuss the situation with a doctor. A change in bowel habits is significant, because it can be a warning sign of cancer. A change in bowel habits also can lead to bladder-control problems, or it may indicate a medication side effect, diverticulosis, bowel obstruction, or intestinal infection.

arrhea after having the gallbladder removed, but this can be helped with medication. Diarrhea can reflect an infection or problems in the pancreas, or parasites in the intestines. A change in a person's bowel habits can mirror changing health conditions in your elder's body. Because elderly people become dehydrated more easily than younger people, diarrhea can be a serious problem, especially if the elder is vomiting, too. If your elder experiences significant changes in bowel habits, he should consult his doctor.

Peptic Ulcers

Typically, people develop **peptic ulcers** (in the lining of the stomach or duodenum) between 55 and 70 years of age. The two major causes in the elderly are from *H. pylori* bacteria and nonsteroidal anti-inflammatory drugs (NSAIDS) such as ibuprofen. *H. pylori* bacteria can be treated with a special regimen of medications. Ulcers also may be caused by aspirin, arthritis medications or other medications, life stressors, alcohol, tobacco, caffeine, or the cause may be unknown. The symptoms of a peptic ulcer include burning, aching, gnawing, or hunger discomfort in the upper abdomen or lower chest (usually relieved by milk, food, or antacids); a bloated feeling after meals; nausea and vomiting; and black, tarry, foul-smelling stools. Most people with ulcers respond well to drugs that inhibit the production of acid in the stomach. The doctor will advise lifestyle or medical changes in your elder's situation, depending on the cause of her ulcer.

Diverticulosis

Diverticulosis, the development of tiny pockets in the colon that can trap waste material, affects up to half of all Americans by age 80. It often has no symptoms but can cause alternating constipation and diarrhea, abdominal cramping and bloating, or abdominal abscess. Diverticulosis may be caused by a low-fiber diet. Encourage your elder to eat more fiber—found in beans, certain fruits and vegetables, and whole grains—in order to lower his chances of developing this condition. If, however, he already has this condition, eating high-fiber foods can make him feel miserable. In that case, your elder may want to slowly start eating more fiber, but consult his physician if symptoms recur.

Glands and Hormones

HYPERTHERMIA, HYPOTHERMIA, THYROID CONDITIONS, DIABETES, AND PROSTATE

Hyperthermia

Hyperthermia is the name given to a variety of heat-related illnesses including cramps, heat stroke, and heat exhaustion. The elderly are especially at risk for hyperthermia. Why? Because their sweat glands do not cool the body as effectively as a younger person's do. An elderly person can easily overheat in hot weather and suffer symptoms of hyperthermia: lightheadedness, nausea, loss of consciousness, and even death. Your elder would benefit from being in an air-conditioned environment during hot spells. If air conditioning is not available, move him to a cooler location or rely on fans to cool his home. Encourage him to drink plenty of liquids, reduce activity, and wear light clothing. During times of extremely hot weather, try to check on your elder daily. If you suspect your loved one is suffering from hyperthermia, get him to the hospital as quickly as possible for treatment.

Hypothermia

Hypothermia is the opposite of hyperthermia. In this case, the elderly person's temperature falls below normal. A drop of only two degrees can threaten the health of your elder. Severe hypothermia can lead to excessive shivering, irregular heartbeat, heart failure, and death. Signs of hypothermia include: confusion or sleepiness; slowed, slurred speech; weak pulse; low blood pressure; a change in behavior during cold weather; excessive shivering; or poor control over body movements. Your elder probably has hypothermia if her temperature drops below 96 degrees. If you suspect hypothermia, remove any wet clothing and wrap your elder completely in blankets. If she is conscious, offer warm liquids to drink. Keep talking to her and get to a hospital as quickly as possible. You can protect your elder from hypothermia by setting the thermostat at 70 degrees or higher and making sure she has proper clothing to wear. Be aware that some confused elders may wander outdoors without proper clothing.

Thyroid Conditions

An elderly person may experience two common problems with the thyroid: **hyperthyroidism** or **hypothyroidism.** Hyperthyroidism is an overproduction of hormones in the thyroid gland while hypothyroidism is an insufficient production of the hormones. The thyroid controls metabolism.

In a younger person, hyperthyroidism results in symptoms of nervousness, sweating, tremors, weight loss, and heart-rhythm problems. People with hyperthyroidism from Graves' disease often have bulging of the eyeballs. But the disease may not cause typical symptoms in an elderly person, so it is difficult to diagnose. Doctors often use a treatment of radioactive iodine or oral medications to slow down hormone production.

Hypothyroidism is also difficult to recognize because its effect on an elderly person can be mistaken for normal aging: The person may have a hoarse throat, shaky walk, anemia, dry skin, muscle cramps, depression, and constipation. Physicians can look for clues, however, including changes in hair texture, or coarsening or thinning of the hair, harmless white skin spots, and patchy hair loss. Your elder can be easily treated for hypothyroidism by taking thyroid hormone supplements. If untreated, hypothyroidism can lead to coma and, ultimately, death. Talk with your elder's physician about screening for hypothyroidism at the time of health-maintenance exams.

For more information on thyroid problems, contact the Thyroid Foundation of America (see appendix).

Diabetes

Nearly 20 percent of Americans over the age of sixty-five have diabetes. The seventh leading cause of death in the U.S., diabetes is a group of diseases characterized by high levels of blood glucose (sugar) because of poor insulin secretion or action within the body.[8]

The two most common types of diabetes are Type I and Type II. Type I, formerly known as insulin-dependent diabetes or juvenile-onset diabetes, accounts for 5 to 10 percent of all diagnosed cases; Type II diabetes was formerly called non-insulin-dependent diabetes. This accounts for an estimated 90 to 95 percent of all diagnosed cases.

Hypothyroidism is difficult to recognize, because its effect on an elderly person can be mistaken for normal aging.

Old age, obesity, a family history of diabetes, physical inactivity, and certain racial and ethnic groups are all associated with an increased risk for diabetes. More than half of all women who have had gestational diabetes (elevated blood-glucose levels during pregnancy) end up developing diabetes later in life.

Diabetes is a serious health hazard to anyone who has it, including the elderly. The Centers for Disease Control have published the following sobering statistics:

- Adults with diabetes have heart-disease death rates 2 to 4 times higher than adults without diabetes.
- The risk of stroke is 2 to 4 times higher in diabetic people than in nondiabetics.
- Diabetes is a significant cause of blindness. (Good control of diabetes can reduce eye problems.)
- More than half of all lower-limb amputations in the U.S. occur in people with diabetes.
- Diabetics are more susceptible to infections and other illnesses, including pneumonia and influenza.

Type I diabetes is treated with strict diet, planned physical activity, insulin injections, and blood-glucose tests several times each day. Type

SYMPTOMS OF DIABETES

The symptoms of diabetes may include numbness or pain in the legs and hands, muscle weakness, leg cramps, vaginal itching, impotency, a need to go to the bathroom frequently, increased appetite and thirst, weight loss, nausea, vomiting, and tiredness. However, an older person may not show these classic signs. It is advisable to have your elder periodically undergo a blood-sugar test to see if he or she is developing or already has diabetes. Diabetes can result in nerve damage that lessens the ability to feel pain. This puts the person at risk of not noticing small injuries, especially in the feet, until aggressive treatment is needed. If untreated, diabetes can result in foot problems, amputation, gum disease, digestive problems, stroke, heart attack, visual loss, nerve damage, kidney failure, coma, and death. Good control of blood-sugar levels is important in minimizing many long-term effects of diabetes.

II diabetes is controlled through diet, exercise, blood-glucose tests, and oral medication and/or insulin. An estimated 40 percent of Type II patients must take insulin injections.

For updated information on diabetes, contact the American Diabetes Association (see appendix).

Prostate Gland Problems

The prostate gland, a walnut-sized organ that lies beneath a man's bladder and surrounds the urethra (urine tube), tends to enlarge with age. Four out of five American men develop an enlarged prostate (a condition called **benign prostatic hyperplasia** or **BPH**) by age 80. Although an enlarged prostate does not lead to prostate cancer, it may press on the urethra, causing difficulties with urination. Your elder may have difficulty starting the flow of urine, may need to urinate frequently—especially at night—and may feel his bladder has not completely emptied. Leftover urine that has not emptied can be a good breeding ground for bacteria and can promote infection in the urinary tract and prostate.

Prostatitis, an infected prostate, can be acute (causing frequent, painful urination; fever; chills; and pain in the lower back and in the area between the rectum and the testicles) or chronic (causing frequent, burning urination; pain in the pelvis or genital area; and painful ejaculation). If your elder has these symptoms, he should see a doctor promptly for evaluation and treatment.

Prostate cancer is the most common cause of death from cancer in men over age 75. It seems to run in some families and is more common among African-American men than it is among other ethnic groups in the United States. High levels of hormones, such as androgens (male hormones), may promote prostate cancer in some men. Smoking, alcohol abuse, and a high-fat diet also seem to increase susceptibility to the disease.

To aid diagnosis, many doctors recommend a yearly digital rectal exam and **prostate-specific antigen** (**PSA**) blood test yearly for men over age 50 who have a life expectancy of greater than ten years. If your elder's PSA level is high, his doctor may need to collect biopsy samples of tissue. If caught early, prostate cancer often can be cured. On the other hand, most prostate cancers grow slowly, without spreading for years, so some elderly men opt against treatment. In fact, men with slow-growing prostate cancer are likely to die *with* the disease, not *from* the disease.

Your elder has several options for treatment, all with risks and benefits, depending on your elder's age, general health, and other medical conditions. The stage of the cancer (how far it has spread) is an important factor in selecting a therapy and predicting prognosis. A grading system is used to show how fast the cancer is likely to grow or spread beyond the prostate. Treatment options include "watchful waiting" (monitoring the disease for possible spread), radical prostatectomy (surgery to remove the prostate gland), radiation methods, androgen-deprivation therapy, and newer treatments such as cryosurgery (freezing the tumor). Encourage your elder to get a second or third opinion before choosing a course of treatment. He may want to get opinions from a urologist and a radiation oncologist, for example. Questions your elder should ask a physician include:

- Is my cancer only in the prostate or has it spread?
- What is the stage and grade of my cancer?
- Should the cancer be treated, and if so, how?
- What are the likely side effects of each treatment?
- What are my chances of having a problem with urinating or with getting an erection?
- What is my expected survival rate? What is the likelihood of the cancer coming back after I have been treated?
- How will my condition be affected if I choose not to seek treatment?

Most prostate cancers grow slowly, without spreading for years, so some elderly men opt against treatment.

Because a high-fat diet may be linked to prostate cancer, your elder should eat a diet low in animal fat and high in fruits, vegetables, and grains. Tomatoes, watermelon, and grapefruit are rich in **lycopenes,** which help prevent damage to DNA and may help lower the risk of prostate cancer, according to the American Cancer Society.

For more information, contact the American Cancer Society, National Cancer Institute, or the American Foundation for Urologic Disease (see appendix).

My great Physician heals the sick—
The lost He came to save;
For me His precious blood He shed—
For me His life He gave.

I need no other argument,
I need no other plea;
It is enough that Jesus died,
And that He died for me.

Lidie H. Edmunds, from "My Faith Has Found a Resting Place"

See chapter 6 for more information on how to understand and care for common health problems in the elderly.

CHAPTER 6

My flesh and my heart fail; but God is the strength

of my heart and my portion forever. PSALM 73:26 NKJV

Physical Changes in Aging—Part 2
Understanding and Caring for Common Health Problems in the Elderly

AFTER Jack had his first open-heart surgery, his doctor sat down and had a heart-to-heart talk with him about making positive changes in his lifestyle. As a result, Jack knew he needed to start exercising and stop smoking. His wife, Bonnie, supported him by walking with him 40 minutes a day 4 to 5 times a week. She praised him when he quit smoking, but soon he started smoking again.

"I didn't even know about it, because he'd blow smoke out the window," Bonnie says. Jack finally admitted it was more difficult to quit smoking than it had been to quit drinking at age 35. But he kicked the habit for good after he broke out in a sweat during a business meeting and had shooting pain in his left arm.

"Jack's never had an actual heart attack," says Bonnie. "He's been fortunate to take preemptive actions, such as a quadruple bypass when he was 71." Now, at age 76, he's still able to work out five times a week on a treadmill and rowing machine, and he and Bonnie continue to enjoy walks together, which also keeps her in shape. Not only has Jack followed his doctor's orders and stayed active physically, but he also keeps his mind alert by writing travel articles and spending time with friends. "In spite of heart disease, my husband is working hard to stay healthy," says Bonnie. "And I'm proud of him."

———— ⌒℅ ————

Be careful not to nag or impose your lifestyle changes on your elderly loved one.

Few seniors are able to grow old without battling at least one chronic or acute medical problem. But it is possible to manage health problems and age successfully by paying close attention to the mind, body, and spirit. Whether your aging loved one is dealing with the effects of normal aging or poor lifestyle choices, your gracious support can have a positive impact on her attitude and willingness to do what is necessary to maintain good health. Make it a daily habit to pray for your elder's health and well-being as well as your relationship. Stay involved in your elder's life, offering information and encouragement that could help her tackle a medical condition, choose the best treatment, or live more healthfully. But be careful not to nag or impose your lifestyle changes on your elderly loved one. Try to strike a balance between your desire to give advice and your elder's freedom and ability to make her own decisions.

The Body's Vital Organs and Systems

THE HEART
Elderly people may be at risk for a variety of heart diseases. These may include aneurysm, angina pectoris, congestive heart failure, enlarged heart, chronic pulmonary disease, arrhythmias, heart murmurs, mitral valve prolapse, rheumatic heart disease, ventricular fibrillation, and others. Both lifestyle and heredity can contribute to heart disease.

Coronary heart (artery) disease is the single leading cause of death in the United States today. It almost always develops from **atherosclerosis,** a buildup of fatty deposits on the inside of the arteries that narrows the vessels and slows down blood flow. Larger deposits, called **plaques,** can cause recurring chest pain (**angina**), congestive heart failure (in which the heart fails to pump blood effectively), and heart attack (damaged heart-muscle tissue from obstructed blood flow).

After menopause, women have an increased risk of developing coronary heart disease and are more likely to die from it than from any other condition. The symptoms of coronary heart disease can be vague, especially in a woman with the disease. Also, another condition—

gastroesophageal reflux, or heartburn—can mimic symptoms of angina. Heart disease often is indicated by chest pain that worsens with stress or physical activity and improves with rest. When such pain or pressure lasts more than a few minutes, it could indicate a **heart attack (myocardial infarction).**

Signs of a heart attack may include tightness in the chest; chest pain that ranges from a dull ache to a heavy, crushing pain; pain radiating from the center of the chest to the shoulders, neck, or arms; lightheadedness with fainting, sweating, nausea, or shortness of breath; blue or pale skin, especially around the lips; rapid heartbeat; and unusual fatigue. If you suspect your elder is having a heart attack, get immediate medical attention.

Congestive heart failure (CHF) is common among elderly men and women. CHF occurs when the heart is unable to pump blood in a sufficient flow to meet the needs of the body's other organs. This can result from narrowed arteries that supply blood to the heart muscle, prolonged high blood pressure, weakened heart-muscle tissue from a previous heart attack, or damage or infection of the heart valves and/or muscle.

Failure of the left side of the heart can cause blood to back up into the lungs; failure to the right side of the heart can cause blood to back up into the legs and liver. Decreased blood flow to the kidneys can cause excess fluid and water to accumulate in the body.

Common signs of CHF include shortness of breath, early fatigue after physical exertion, swelling (edema), especially in the lower legs and ankles, and weight gain because of fluid buildup. It is important to monitor your loved one's weight. If an elder gains 3 to 5 pounds over a few days, it is a suspicious indicator of congestive heart failure.

There are a variety of diagnostic tests available for patients with chest pain or other heart-disease risk factors. An **electrocardiogram (ECG or EKG),** which prints a record of the heart's electrical activity while the patient is resting; an **echocardiogram** (ultrasound of the heart), which evaluates the size, shape, and function of the heart valves; and **cardiac magnetic resonance imaging (MRI),** a procedure that makes it possible to evaluate the heart's function and structure without using catheters, dyes, or radiation. The newest technology takes several

FOR A HEALTHY HEART

Whether your elder shows no signs of heart disease or has survived a heart attack, she would do well to control or avoid certain risk factors. Obesity, heavy drinking, tobacco use, high blood pressure, diabetes, kidney disease, physical inactivity, stress, and high cholesterol levels can all contribute to heart disease.

Exercise and good dietary habits are key factors in protecting your elder from heart problems. A recent study shows that elderly men who walk 1.5 miles a day cut their risk of developing coronary heart disease in half, compared to men who walk less than a quarter mile.[1]

Making healthful lifestyle changes, such as quitting smoking, cutting dietary saturated fat and cholesterol, eating more fresh fruits and vegetables, staying physically active, and losing weight, can help to control or prevent heart disease.

While the cardiovascular benefits of omega-3 fatty acids (found in cold-water fish) have been touted in recent years, the American Heart Association does not recommend taking fish-oil supplements. Instead, the AHA recommends eating fish at least two times per week. Similarly, garlic has been accorded miracle-food status by some, and numerous garlic supplements and preparations abound. At this point evidence suggests that garlic may indeed offer some health benefits, including cardiovascular benefits, but the interpretation of the data is hampered by the variability in the types of garlic preparations studied.

Although the evidence is not conclusive, some studies have suggested that vitamin-E supplements appear to reduce the risk of having a heart attack. Vitamin E serves as an antioxidant in the blood stream and seems to prevent oxygen in the blood from combining with low-density lipoproteins (LDL or bad cholesterol). However, the American Heart Association recommends that antioxidant vitamins and other nutrients be derived from foods.[2] Estrogen can lower bad cholesterol and may prevent atherosclerosis (hardening of the arteries) by decreasing plaque on the **intima (lining)** of arteries. And researchers are discovering that a person who takes a small dose of aspirin each day (baby aspirin or half an aspirin tablet) can greatly reduce her chances of a heart attack. Your elder should consult her doctor before beginning long-term, daily aspirin therapy.

For current information on heart disease, contact the American Heart Association (see appendix).

[1]Hakim et al., "Effects of Walking on Coronary Heart Disease in Elderly Men."   [2]American Heart Association, "Dietary Guidelines for Healthy Americans," *Circulation*, 94 (1996), 1795–1800.

X-ray pictures of the blood vessels, then reconstructs the pictures into a 3-D image. Physicians can rotate the image to see damaged blood vessels.

Other common, noninvasive tests include the **exercise stress test (exercise ECG),** in which a patient's heart is monitored while the patient is exercising. Even more precise information can be obtained by a nuclear treadmill. In this procedure, special tracers are injected into a vein, and after the treadmill part of the exam is done, the patient is painlessly scanned by special equipment to see how the exercising heart has been supplied by blood. If the arteries to the heart are narrowed or blocked, the test will reflect that.

For elders who cannot walk on a treadmill for a stress test, there are medications that can be injected in a vein in order to pharmacologically stress the heart as exercise would. Then, images of the heart can be studied under a scanner to get similar information. A newer, noninvasive technique called **ultrafast CT (computed tomography)** produces cross-sectional images of the heart to detect the amount of calcium, or calcium burden, in a patient's coronary arteries.

If further testing is needed, the next step is typically a **coronary catheterization,** which uses X-ray contrast, injected through a catheter, to examine the coronary arteries. If problems are identified using this invasive technique, the doctor may recommend **angioplasty** (a procedure that inflates a balloon inside a narrowed artery to reopen it), **stenting** (using a wire mesh tube to mechanically hold a blocked vessel open), or **bypass surgery** (using a blood vessel or artery from another part of the body to bypass the blockage in a coronary artery).

Routine physical examinations often include a blood test called a **lipid profile,** which measures the amount of lipids in the blood. Lipids are a group of fatlike substances that can affect heart health. Lipid profiles usually include measurements of triglycerides, total cholesterol, high-density lipoprotein (HDL—the "good" cholesterol), and a calculation of low-density lipoprotein (LDL—the "bad" cholesterol). Elevated levels of LDL and triglycerides have been correlated with coronary artery disease, while higher levels of HDL can have positive effects on the cardiovascular system.

Aside from the lipid profile, additional blood tests are sometimes performed to look for other heart-disease risk factors. These factors include **apolipoprotein B (apo B)**, **C-reactive protein (CRP)**, and **homocysteine.** Apo B is a protein found in LDL whose measurement can help physicians make a more accurate assessment of one's risk for heart disease. CRP is a sign of inflammation, a process that is believed to play a role in coronary artery disease. The detection of CRP in the blood signifies an increased likelihood of heart problems. Elevated blood levels of the amino acid homocysteine have also been correlated with increased chances of cardiovascular disease. Talk with your elder's doctor about whether testing for these risk factors might be beneficial for him.

The good news is that there are a number of ways for your elder to improve his lipid profile and reduce some of these risk factors. Homocysteine can be brought down by eating less meat and taking supplements of the B vitamins folic acid (folate), B_6, and B_{12}. Blood lipids can be lowered with proper diet, exercise, and niacin. Exercise can even serve to raise HDL. Certain drugs, including a class of medications called statins, may be prescribed to lower cholesterol levels. There is no consensus, however, about how far into aging one should continue these therapies. Should a 95-year-old with dementia be treated with cholesterol-lowering medications to reduce the odds of a heart attack? Some families and doctors say yes; others say no. It is important for you and your elder to discuss with the physician which choices for therapy might be most appropriate. Many older people with heart disease are conservatively treated with medications. Yet, many are excellent candidates for stents, angioplasty, and surgery.

BLOOD AND BLOOD VESSELS
Hypertension
Hypertension, popularly known as high blood pressure, is a common but controllable disorder in the elderly. If not treated properly, however, it can lead to stroke, heart disease, kidney failure, and other health problems. High blood pressure can speed up the shrinkage of the brain and memory loss in the elderly.

Research has linked hypertension with brain atrophy and memory loss.[1] High blood pressure can often be reduced by maintaining a healthy weight, exercising regularly, reducing or eliminating the use of alcohol and cigarettes, and modifying the diet to include less salt. High blood pressure may require daily treatment with antihypertensive medication.

Anemia

A simple definition for anemia is a condition in which the blood contains fewer red blood cells than normal, resulting in low levels of oxygen-carrying hemoglobin. Elderly people are prone to many types of anemia, and there are multiple causes of the disorder. Anemia can be the first warning sign of a serious problem.

Iron-deficiency anemia (iron-poor blood) is common in the elderly because of gastrointestinal bleeding, poor absorption of iron, or inadequate nutrition. Underlying causes of bleeding may include peptic ulcer, hemorrhoids, polyps, inflammatory bowel disease, cancer of the intestines or the stomach, or regular use of nonsteroidal anti-inflammatory drugs such as aspirin (which can cause bleeding in the gastrointestinal tract). The onset of anemia can be insidious. Your elder may have no symptoms or may feel tired and short of breath. Blood may appear bright red in stools or on toilet paper. In other cases, bowel movements look black and tarry. A fecal occult blood test can be performed to detect hidden blood loss from your elder's gastrointestinal tract.

To improve iron intake in cases of iron-deficiency anemia, encourage your elder to eat foods rich in iron, such as meats, eggs, legumes (peas and beans), and potatoes. Note that milk and tea decrease iron absorption. Be careful with iron supplements; too much iron in the body (**hemochromatosis**) can damage the liver or delay the diagnosis of a serious condition such as colon cancer and may also be associated with heart disease. In addition, constipation, diarrhea, ulcers, stomach irritation, and black stools often result from taking iron supplements.

Vitamin B$_{12}$ deficiency (pernicious) anemia is also common in older people. Although vitamin B$_{12}$ is found in meat and dairy products, deficiency cannot be corrected by taking vitamin B$_{12}$ orally, because the problem is not a lack of vitamin B$_{12}$ in the diet but results from the body's inability to absorb B$_{12}$ from the intestinal system. Severe deficiency can cause damage to the nervous system. Fatigue, shortness of breath, headaches, pale skin, and tingling or numbness in the hands and feet are some of the symptoms of this type of anemia. A

MANAGING MEDICATIONS

The Food and Drug Administration indicates that adults over age sixty-five buy 30 percent of all prescription drugs and 40 percent of all over-the-counter drugs.[1] In addition, the average older person sees more than one doctor and takes more than four prescription medications at once, plus two over-the-counter medications. If you are caring for an elderly person, you might have the responsibility of making sure your loved one takes her medications and takes them at the right time. Make sure each doctor is aware of what your elder's other physicians are prescribing. Drug interactions can be a serious problem and are more common if one physician is unaware of what another is prescribing. Drugs can inhibit or induce metabolism of other drugs, causing an interaction. Nonprescription drugs, grapefruit, vitamins, herbs, and supplements can also interact in strange ways with some prescription drugs, so doctors need to be aware of those as well.

The danger of drug interactions or side effects should not be underestimated. Consult a doctor if your elder experiences dizziness, upset stomach, blurred vision, sleep changes, constipation, diarrhea, incontinence, mood changes, or a rash after taking a drug.

The elderly not only face the dangers of drug interactions, they also frequently fail to take their medications or they take the wrong dosages. This noncompliance is worsened by poor eyesight, disability, memory lapses or mental illness, and the sheer volume of medicines an elderly person often must take.

Work with the physician to try to keep the elderly on as few medicines as possible and make the dosing instructions simple to understand. It is extremely important that elders go to only one pharmacy. That way, one pharmacist has records of all medications prescribed and is in a better position to spot medications that, if taken together, might have harmful interactions.

You may need to help your elderly loved one by consulting with his physician and then writing out explicit dosing instructions for yourself and for your elder. Ask about possible side effects, whether the medication should be taken with food or on an empty stomach, and what to do if a dose is missed. Pick up a pill box that contains compartments for each day of the week. If necessary, you can put your loved one's pills in these boxes every week and then remind him to take his medicines. You may have to purchase a separate box for nighttime doses. If your elder is mentally impaired, you may need to have someone give the medicines to him.

---

[1]U.S. Food and Drug Administration, *FDA Consumer* (September-October 1997).

physician can perform a complete blood-cell count and other tests to make a diagnosis. Pernicious-anemia sufferers are treated with monthly B_{12} injections for life, no matter how good their intake of foods and even dietary or vitamin supplements is. If your elder has poor nutritional habits, it may be reasonable for him to take a multiple-vitamin supplement as an "insurance policy" of sorts, but there is no need to take extra B_{12} supplements as a separate agent. And unless there is a specific deficiency of iron, the multiple-vitamin supplement should *not* contain iron.

LUNGS AND RESPIRATORY SYSTEM

Lungs can lose elasticity with age, but losing lung capacity is not an inevitable part of aging. Regular exercise can increase the ability of older lungs to work better. Nevertheless, the elderly are more prone to lung disease because of a poor cough and the tendency to aspirate secretions into the lungs.

Some of the most common lung diseases in the elderly are asthma, lung cancer, chronic bronchitis, emphysema, and pulmonary embolism. Congestive heart failure can cause the lungs to become congested with fluid, causing the sensation of breathlessness. A physician can help to diagnose these conditions in your elder and explain the treatments involved in each of these conditions.

Flu and Pneumonia

When an older person's immune system is weakened, influenza (a respiratory viral infection commonly called "the flu") can become a serious health threat. In older people it can lead to dangerous complications such as pneumonia. Flu and pneumonia combined rank as the fifth leading cause of death of Americans over age 65. Eighty percent of flu-related deaths are among the elderly.[2]

Your elder's best defense against infection is to wash her hands regularly with soap and water. If your aging loved one has the flu (characterized by chills, fever, muscle pain, sneezing, headache, sore throat, coughing, chest pain), encourage her to drink plenty of liquids, rest, and take cough and pain medication. There is a plethora of antiviral drugs that can be used to treat influenza and shorten the course of the illness if it is diagnosed promptly after the onset of symptoms. The type of influenza can be determined by laboratory testing. Certain medications can also be used to lessen the likelihood that people who have close contact with the ill person will get the influenza. (These medications have many side effects, though.)

If your elder has a fever, headache, dry cough, pain when breathing (even when lying down), increasing breathlessness, and/or coughs up blood in the sputum (mucus discharge), he may have viral pneumonia and should see a doctor promptly.

Antibiotics are ineffective against the flu and viral pneumonia, but may help fight a secondary bacterial infection if it occurs. Encourage your elder to get a flu shot each winter season. (Flu shots are tailored to fight the current year's flu strain.) A pneumonia vaccine is also recommended, and in special situations boosters are recommended every six years.

Pollution and Smoking: Two Threats to Older Lungs

Indoor Pollution. Aside from lung diseases that can be clearly diagnosed, one frequently undetected health threat to your elder's lungs is the breathing of indoor air that has not been properly filtered. The American Lung Association says most Americans spend more than 90 percent of their time indoors, and the levels of indoor pollution can be two to five or as many as one hundred times higher than outdoor pollution.[3] Because an elderly person will spend most of her time inside, you need to make sure her room or home has adequate ventilation and filtering. Be sure the furnace filter is changed often. Consider special filters that eliminate pollen, molds, and other pollutants. Research has shown that dust mites, molds, mildew, animal hair, insect waste, and tobacco smoke are strongly associated with respiratory problems. Asthma, for example, is on the rise and is currently the sixth-ranking chronic condition in the U.S., causing the highest death rate in those over age 85.[4]

Your elder may experience breathing problems as the result of a variety of pollutants, including: biological pollutants (molds, bacteria, pollen, etc.); radon, the second leading cause of lung cancer; carbon monoxide from heating systems; and formaldehyde, a chemical found in some carpets, upholstery, particle board, and plywood. This chemical can cause coughing, eye-nose-throat irritation, skin rashes, headaches, and dizziness.

Carbon monoxide (CO) poisoning is of particular concern for elderly people, especially during the wintertime when a home is typically closed up to avoid heat loss. Carbon monoxide is a colorless, odorless gas that is formed when hydrocarbons burn incompletely in wood-burning fireplaces and oil and gas appliances. It is easily absorbed by the lungs and as vapor through the skin. Carbon monoxide poisoning includes such symptoms as shortness of breath, rapid heartbeat, confusion, visual problems, chest or abdominal pain, and muscle cramps. Severe cases result in unconsciousness and death. Every winter more than 2,000 people die of CO poisoning and more than 10,000 become ill. You may wish to purchase a CO detector and install it in your elder's

HOW TO QUIT SMOKING

For the person trying to quit, try the following tips:

- Hide all matches.
- Throw away your cigarettes and ashtrays.
- Keep a supply of sugarless gum, carrot sticks, and other healthy snacks on hand.
- Drink lots of liquids, but avoid coffee and alcohol.
- Exercise to relieve tension.
- Tell everyone you are quitting and ask for prayers and reminders to hold you accountable.
- When the urge to smoke comes, take a deep breath, hold it for several seconds, and release it slowly. Take every thought "captive" and give it to God (2 Corinthians 10:5).
- Try the "buddy system" and get a friend to quit something too.

For more information on lung diseases and how to help your elder stop smoking, contact the following groups: American Cancer Society; National Cancer Institute; American Heart Association; Centers for Disease Control and Prevention's Office on Smoking and Health; American Lung Association; National Heart, Lung, and Blood Institute; Nicotine Anonymous (see appendix).

home or apartment. Nursing homes should already be equipped with these devices.

Smoking. If your elder smokes, he is probably aware of the dangers of smoking and the relationship between smoking and lung cancer, emphysema, chronic bronchitis, and other lung diseases. Smoking is also a major risk factor for heart attack, stroke, and other arterial diseases among older adults. A study by the American Academy of Neurology examined four European studies of more than 9,000 smokers.[5] The researchers discovered that smoking contributes to the loss of cognitive abilities such as remembering, thinking, and perceiving. They noted that smoking seems to damage cerebral functioning by causing small, silent strokes that cannot be detected in a clinical setting. In plain language, smoking may cause brain damage. Yet quitting the habit is beneficial at any age. For example, within one year of stopping smoking, excess risk of coronary heart disease is decreased to half that of a smoker, according to the American Lung Association. And from 5 to 15 years after quitting, stroke risk is reduced to that of people who have never smoked.[6] Lifelong smokers who quit the habit feel more in control and have fewer coughs and colds.[7]

Lifelong smokers who quit the habit feel more in control and have fewer coughs and colds.

Do not nag your elder, but if she wishes to stop smoking, offer to help her get nicotine-replacement therapy. The patch takes about eight weeks to lessen the tobacco desire. Gum therapy typically takes three months. There are also prescription medications available to help reduce addictive urges. The prescription medication bupropion (Zyban) has been approved for use in a smoking-cessation program. Other options that have been approved by the FDA for use are a nasal spray and a cigarette-shaped cartridge that delivers a small burst of nicotine when the user puffs on it like a cigarette. These therapies reduce the physical need for nicotine, but they have a higher success rate when combined with smoking-cessation classes. These classes address psychological components of smoking, such as the habits of smoking after eating or while talking on the phone.

If he has a serious problem that is not helped by nasal spray, gum, a patch, or nicotine inhalers, he may benefit from an intensive smoking-cessation program at a clinic or local hospital. The courses are usually 4 to 7 sessions over a two-week period.

THE BRAIN AND NERVOUS SYSTEM
Strokes

The risk of stroke is greatest for seniors. A stroke results from impaired blood flow to the brain. Without oxygen to the brain, the cells are either damaged or die within minutes or hours. An estimated half-million Americans suffer from strokes each year. During the past decade, improved diagnostic and treatment techniques have resulted in a 32 percent reduction in the number of stroke-related deaths each year. Still, an estimated 150,000 deaths occur each year from stroke. It is a leading cause of death and serious disability in the U.S., accounting for 11 percent of deaths among women and for 9 percent of deaths among men age 85 and older.[8] About 5 percent of people over age 65 have had at least one stroke.

Transient ischemic attack (TIA) is a temporary attack caused by reduced blood flow (**ischemia**) in a portion of the brain. It comes on suddenly and the symptoms usually last only a short time—from a few minutes to no more than 24 hours. During a TIA, the person may experience numbness or tingling, weakness on one side of the body, garbled or slurred speech or inability to talk, visual changes such as blindness in one eye or double vision, loss of balance, staggering, or a lack of coordination. These symptoms are short-term

GETTING ANOTHER OPINION

My mom used to run circles around my dad. She paid all the bills, packed all the suitcases when they traveled, did all the cooking and cleaning, everything. Then she started falling and had difficulty writing or holding things. The doctor took a CT scan of her brain but didn't find anything. It took me a year to convince my parents to change doctors or at least get a second opinion. I finally found a wonderful geriatric osteopath who looked at her year-old CT scan and said, "Are you aware that your mother has had some small strokes?" He did an MRI to confirm that she'd had vascular strokes in her cerebellum, which affects balance—hence the falling! It was a relief to finally get a diagnosis so that we could take the next step and discuss available treatment options. When in doubt, it pays to get a second opinion.   *Jill M.*

and reversible but should not be ignored; the episode is a warning that a "completed" stroke may be pending. A **completed stroke** is essentially a stroke with irreversible death of brain cells, but it may take a few weeks or a month to determine the extent of residual disability. The probability of a completed stroke occurring at some time after a TIA is 25 to 35 percent. A physical examination and testing are needed to make the diagnosis and rule out a stroke or other disorder.

Reversible ischemic neurologic deficit (RIND) is similar to a TIA except that the symptoms last from 24 hours up to a week. Recovery is complete or nearly complete, but as with a TIA, a RIND is a warning that the person is at high risk for a completed stroke.

Eighty percent of strokes are thought to be **thrombotic,** meaning they are brought on by a blood clot in the brain or arteries of the neck.

WARNING SIGNS OF STROKE

Signs and symptoms of stroke include:

- Sudden numbness or weakness in the face, arm, or leg, especially on one side of the body
- Sudden confusion, trouble speaking or understanding
- Sudden trouble seeing in one or both eyes
- Sudden trouble in walking, dizziness, loss of balance or coordination
- Sudden, severe headache with no known cause

If your loved one is exhibiting any of these symptoms and you suspect stroke, it is crucial that you get your elder to the hospital immediately. A person who suffers a stroke may be eligible for treatment that can help prevent irreversible brain damage, but he must be diagnosed and treated within three hours. New drug therapies can dissolve clots to the brain and save lives. In some cases, the injection of a blood thinning drug or **tissue plasminogen activator (tPA)** within three hours can greatly reduce the possibility of brain damage. However, tPA can cause further bleeding and is not to be used in the event of hemorrhagic stroke.

An **embolic stroke** is caused by a blood clot formed in another part of the body. It breaks loose and travels through the bloodstream, blocking an artery to the brain. Some strokes are called **hemorrhagic.** This results when an artery supplying blood bleeds into the brain.

After a stroke, your elder's mobility and mental abilities will be affected in a variety of ways, depending on where the stroke occurred. A cerebral stroke can cause dizziness, nausea, vomiting, and abnormal reflexes of the head and torso. A stroke in the right hemisphere of the brain will affect the left side of the body. Because the right side of the brain controls analytical and perceptual tasks, such as judging distance, size, speed, or position, right-hemisphere stroke survivors may have problems with space and perception. They may be unable to tie their shoes or pick up an object. They may also develop an impulsive behavioral style, which can endanger them.

A stroke in the left hemisphere of the brain will affect the right side of the body, which controls speech and language abilities. This stroke victim may develop speech and language problems. The victim may also develop a slow, cautious style, as well as memory problems. The

If you suspect stroke, it is crucial that you get your elder to the hospital immediately.

FROM BURDEN TO BLESSING

A few years ago, my wife had a stroke that affected her left leg and left arm. After the stroke, she was able to walk with a four-footed cane, though unsteadily. I helped her with bathing and other tasks and only left her alone for a few hours at a time while I taught part-time at a college.

Then one day I came home from teaching and found her prostrate on the floor by the bed, unable to get up. She'd fallen face forward and her forehead was all swollen. By the next day, her eyes were black. From then on, she was never left alone. I scheduled it so that two of our daughters and I took turns staying with her. Our second daughter's employer allowed her to work from home at that time so that she could take care of her mother. Even our two adult daughters in California were in constant contact by e-mail and phone, and both visited three or more times that year. It was good for us as a family. My wife enjoyed the company. Our family has always been close, but the experience of taking care of a sick mother bonded us even closer. No one thought it a burden; everyone did it very generously and willingly. *Paul G.*

person may not be able to form words, may have difficulty understanding words spoken to him, or may have difficulty speaking and understanding words.

A stroke in the cerebellum affects many of our reflexes, as well as balance and coordination.

A stroke in the brain stem can be especially devastating. This area of the brain controls involuntary life-support functions, including breathing, blood pressure, and heartbeat. It also controls eye movements, hearing, speech, and swallowing. Victims who suffer brain-stem stroke may also develop paralysis in one or both sides of the body.

Rehabilitation after a stroke is crucial to boost morale and help your elder regain as much function as possible. Besides the physical side effects, depression is a common response. A loving home environment can have a positive effect on a person who is recovering from a stroke. For more information on strokes, see chapter 7: Mental Change, Memory Loss, and Dementia, or contact the National Stroke Association (see appendix).

Preventing Stroke

Most strokes are related to high blood pressure and atherosclerosis (a condition in which fatty deposits accumulate in and under the lining of the artery walls, restricting blood flow). This means that most strokes are preventable. To help reduce the risk of stroke, consider these guidelines and talk them over with your aging loved one:

- Is your elder's blood pressure elevated? He should work with a doctor to keep it under control.
- If your elder has atrial fibrillation (an irregular heartbeat), the drug warfarin (Coumadin) may be indicated to decrease the risk of embolic stroke (stroke caused by a blood clot).
- If your elder smokes, encourage her to stop.
- If your elder drinks alcohol, he should do so in moderation or not at all.
- Find out if your elder has high cholesterol and, if so, seek treatment.

- If your elder is diabetic, encourage her to follow doctor's recommendations to carefully control the disease.
- Stress the importance of including exercise in a daily routine.
- Encourage your elder to eat a diet low in sodium and saturated fat.
- Encourage your loved one to seek treatment for any circulation problems.
- Ask the doctor about blood-thinning drugs, aspirin therapy, or other prescription drugs to reduce the risk of stroke.
- Discard any over-the-counter cough or cold medications that contain the active ingredient phenylpropanolamine (PPA). The FDA has asked firms that market pharmaceutical or drug

PRACTICAL HELPS FOR PARKINSON'S

A person with Parkinson's disease eventually may need assistance to complete daily tasks that involve smooth movements. You can help your elder remain as independent as possible by adapting your elder's living environment for ease of movement and support. Practical helps may include banisters along walls and handholds on beds and in bathtubs, elevated toilet seats, and hard-backed chairs with high arms that are easier to get up from. Remove thick carpets or rugs, because it is difficult for people with Parkinson's to lift their feet.

Your elder will benefit physically from doing exercises, such as stretching, circular arm movements, and raising the legs up and down while sitting. If your elder is resistant, offer to exercise with him. Physical- and occupational-therapy programs may help too.

It is also important for you to offer emotional and spiritual support to help your elder deal with the illness. Because depression is common in people with Parkinson's, encourage your loved one to be involved in church, volunteer activities, a Bible study, social get-togethers, or support groups, if at all possible. Contact local churches to find out about outreach ministries to older people. Cultivating contentment is important because stress, anxiety, and fatigue can make symptoms worse. You and your elder may want to meditate on Philippians 4:12-13: "I know what it is to be in need, and I know what it is to have plenty. I have learned the secret of being content in any and every situation, whether well fed or hungry, whether living in plenty or in want. I can do everything through him who gives me strength" (NIV).

products containing PPA to voluntarily discontinue marketing them because they appear to raise the risk of hemorrhagic strokes, especially in women. A Yale University study found the risk to be highest when taking more than 75 milligrams a day.[9]

- If your elder experiences any stroke symptoms, call 911 and seek immediate medical attention.

Parkinson's Disease

Parkinson's disease ordinarily begins in middle or late life and usually progresses very slowly. It is caused by a gradual deterioration of nerves in a region of the brain that controls muscle movements (the **substantia nigra**). As the nerve cells die, production of a neurotransmitter called **dopamine** is decreased. Dopamine is needed to regulate important brain functions. Low levels result in impaired walking, arm movement, and facial expression and may affect one or both sides of the body.

At first, your elder may sense stiffness in an arm or leg, the fingers of one hand may shake mildly, or one foot may drag slightly when walking. As the disease progresses, your elder may experience any of the following symptoms: tremor; stiff or rigid limbs; slowness of movement; an unsteady, shuffling gait; reduced ability to chew and swallow; sleep disturbances; a fixed facial expression; unblinking eyes; difficulty with writing; a stooped posture; episodes of being in a "frozen" position; and depression. In later stages, a person with Parkinson's may have some

KINDNESS IN MEMORY LOSS

When my son flew home to visit us recently, I told him to be prepared because my dad wasn't the same person (mentally or physically) he was two years ago. Dad suffers from dementia, as well as glaucoma, cataracts, and medication side effects. Living in an assisted-living facility would have been intolerable for Dad a couple years ago because he didn't need assistance with daily tasks, and he would have associated the wheelchairs and gray-haired people with a nursing home. But the geriatric social worker said something interesting. She said there's a kindness in the loss of memory. As an elderly person's universe gets smaller, it allows that person to be content. Despite his circumstances, my dad seems content.

Clara J.

memory loss and intellectual deterioration (see chapter 7: Mental Change, Memory Loss, and Dementia).

As yet there is no known cure for Parkinson's disease. Various medications are effective, at least temporarily, in helping the brain boost its production of dopamine, slowing the progression of the disease, and easing its symptoms. However, some medications given to treat Parkinson's can induce side effects such as depression. Ask your elder's physician to explain the benefits and side effects of various medications. Certain brain surgeries can also bring at least partial relief from symptoms.

Dementia and Alzheimer's

Senile dementia can be caused by more than 70 brain disorders of old age. It may be caused by vascular diseases, such as stroke or heart disease; metabolic diseases, such as thyroid or liver diseases; and other problems. The most common cause, Alzheimer's disease, progresses through a series of stages of deterioration.

More than 4 million Americans have Alzheimer's disease, a progressive, degenerative brain disease with, as yet, no known cause.[10] Symptoms of the disease typically develop slowly and cannot be reversed. Over time, the disease causes a severe decline in memory and a loss of mental functions such as abstract thinking and judgment. Although a definitive diagnosis is only possible upon autopsy, your elder's physician can do a thorough exam to rule out other possible causes.

For more information, see chapter 7: Mental Change, Memory Loss, and Dementia.

Is It Delirium, Dementia, or Depression?

Delirium. Elderly people are vulnerable to delirium, a sudden, transient state of confusion that is often accompanied by agitation, including an increased heart rate, sweating, trembling, and dilated pupils. Delirium may also cause restlessness, fear and suspiciousness, and slurred or incoherent speech. It often signals an acute illness, such as heart attack, infection (especially urinary-tract infection and pneumonia), or poorly controlled diabetes. Another common cause of delirium is noncompliance with prescription medication. Certain medications, such as indomethacin (a nonsteroidal anti-inflammatory drug) and steroids, can cause delirium even when taken properly. By treating the underlying medical condition, delirium can usually be reversed.

Dementia. This chronic brain disorder is usually irreversible in the elderly. But a person with senile dementia may also have delirium, which may be a signal of a serious underlying illness, such as pneumonia or urinary-tract infection. In that case, treating the underlying illness might clear up the delirium and lessen the dementia. Thyroid disease is also a common cause of dementia, which is lessened when the disease is treated. Other potential causes of dementia include: a progressive, degenerative brain disease, such as Alzheimer's disease; small strokes; metabolic disorders; head injury; and brain tumors. A person with dementia may have forgetfulness, disorientation, difficulty learning or retaining information, personality changes, and accident-prone behavior.

Depression. If your elder is withdrawn, apathetic, sleeping and eating poorly, or having trouble concentrating or remembering things, she may be depressed. Depression is a reversible cause of cognitive impairment that can be mistaken for, or mask, dementia. But when depressed elderly individuals have other medical problems, the depression often is not recognized, or the symptoms may be mistaken for dementia, such as Alzheimer's disease. There is no connection between the two, although a person with dementia may also be depressed. Contact a physician or mental-health professional to get a proper diagnosis.

DEPRESSION IN THE ELDERLY

Depression in the elderly is often the result of significant losses—loss of a spouse, job, home, or driver's license, frustration over memory loss, and deteriorating health. It usually is accompanied by symptoms of fatigue, loss of energy, and physical complaints. An elderly person who is depressed may dwell on the subject of death or think she is about to die.

You can help by being available and offering hope and spiritual support. Talk to your elder and be a *good listener.* If your loved one is overwhelmed by feelings of worthlessness and emptiness over the losses in her life, help her get pastoral or professional care. A physician should be alerted to the symptoms in order to rule out an illness or to treat an underlying cause.

Sleep Problems

Sleep is an important ingredient in maintaining a healthy immune system. Yet more than 50 percent of people older than sixty-five complain of regular problems getting to sleep and staying asleep. They complain of sleeping less, having to get up more often, waking up too early in the morning, and being sleepy during the day. Sleep deprivation can be caused by too much caffeine or alcohol, from medications that interrupt sleep, from physical pain that wakes the person, or from depression. But two primary reasons older people have trouble sleeping are changes in the **circadian rhythm** (sleep/wake cycle) and the presence of sleep disorders.

Older people have less deep sleep and less **rapid eye-movement (REM)** sleep. Their sleep efficiency at night is reduced and their need for naps during the day is increased. The circadian rhythm advances in old age, resulting in what is called advanced sleep-phase syndrome. The younger person can naturally sleep for 8 to 9 hours a night. The elderly person's sleep rhythm is advanced, so he goes to bed earlier and awakens earlier. Sunlight seems to be a stabilizer of circadian rhythms. An elderly person who is exposed to bright light in the early evening or late afternoon will tend to sleep longer. Encourage your elder to spend some time in afternoon sunshine; it may help him sleep longer. In addition, taking estrogen can help decrease insomnia and stabilize sleep patterns in menopausal women.

Restless Legs Syndrome (RLS), an achy restlessness of the legs that can disrupt sleep, is very common in elders. The primary cause for RLS is not known. Although many people worry about circulation, in reality, circulation problems are associated with cramping while *walking,* not cramping at night.

Leg cramps at night can be caused by low potassium, thyroid disease, pernicious anemia, folate deficiency, diabetes, neurologic conditions such as lumbar disc protrusion stretching a nerve, or spinal stenosis. These need to be excluded before RLS can be diagnosed. However, RLS is a very treatable symptom with medication such as Benadryl, clonazepam (Klonopin), or phenytoin (Dilantin).

Elderly people may experience an increase in the incidence of **sleep apnea.** This is a disorder that prevents a person from breathing and sleeping at the same time. Each stoppage of breathing lasts from ten sec-

RECOMMENDED CANCER SCREENING TESTS

Regular health-screening tests are a good way to identify cancer or precancerous conditions in your aging loved one while there is still time for effective treatment. But when is it reasonable for your elder to stop having the screening tests? Because people age differently, there are some physically "old" 50-year-olds and "young" 90-year-olds. Some patients and families push for the most aggressive screening at age 90 and are irritated with doctors if it is not done or offered. Other patients and families are offended by even the suggestion that Grandma have these tests at age 70. Be sure to discuss with your elder, family members, and physician what your elder's preferences are regarding screening. There is no absolute on these issues, although there are some guidelines (see below). In some cases, families show compassion by encouraging the screening; in others, they show compassion by *not* encouraging the screening. Screening recommendations tend to change often as advances in technology and medical research are made. Consult your elder's physician to determine the screening schedule that is best for him.

Tests for Women 65 and Older:

Mammogram: annually

Clinical breast exam: every one to two years by a doctor, or as part of regular health checkup

Breast self-exam: every month

Pelvic exam: yearly

Pap smear: may be discontinued or done less frequently in older women if they have two or three negative consecutive annual pap smears and there is no change in sexual partners, either for themselves or for their partner.

Digital rectal exam: every year or as part of regular health checkup

Fecal occult blood: yearly for low-risk individuals (without a family history in a first-degree relative—mother/father/son/daughter—of colon cancer and without a personal history of adenomatous colon polyps that are precancerous)

Flexible sigmoidoscopy: every five years OR colonoscopy every ten years (for low-risk individuals)

Skin exam: regularly and during routine physical exam

Tests for Men 65 and Older:

Rectal exam: yearly
PSA (prostate-specific antigen test): Consult with a doctor.
Fecal blood occult: yearly for low-risk individuals (without a family history in a first-degree relative—mother/father/son/daughter—of colon cancer and without a personal history of adenomatous colon polyps that are precancerous)
Flexible sigmoidoscopy: every five years OR colonoscopy every ten years (for low-risk individuals)
Skin exam: regularly and during routine physical exam

onds to one or two minutes. This can occur from 15 to 100 times in an hour. At middle age, 9 percent of men and 4 percent of women have sleep apnea. Among community-dwelling elderly, 27 percent of men and 19 percent of women have sleep apnea.

If your elder is experiencing sleep difficulties, consult a physician about possible causes and treatments. Sleep labs or sleep-disorder clinics may provide some help.

Cancer

Cancer, like heart disease, disproportionately affects the elderly. Researchers theorize that an older person may be more susceptible to cancer because of an immune system that is less capable of fighting off disease, as well as a lifetime of environmental assault. More than 50 percent of all new cases of cancer and 67 percent of all cancer deaths occur in people age 65 and older. During the past 20 years, lung, breast, and prostate cancer, melanoma, and non-Hodgkin's lymphoma have increased. In addition, lung cancer, common in elderly men, is becoming more common in women. In fact, in the U.S. lung cancer kills more women than does breast cancer.

Cancer occurs when a single cell begins to multiply in an abnormal fashion. The immune system sometimes tries to attack and kill the cancerous mass or tumor. However, tiny blood vessels can begin to nourish the cancer at the same time, causing it to grow.

Older people receive treatment for cancer less often than younger people, and when they do receive treatment it is frequently less aggres-

Aggressive treatment for cancer may not always be the best choice, depending on the condition of your elder.

THE GOLDEN RULE, REVISITED

They lie there, breathing heavy gasps, contracted into a fetal position. Ironic, that they should live 80 or 90 years, then return to the posture of their childhood. But they do. Sometimes their voices are mumbles and whispers like those of infants or toddlers. I have seen them, unaware of anything for decades, crying out for parents long since passed away.

I recall one who had begun to sleep excessively and told her daughter that a little girl slept with her each night. I don't know what she saw. Maybe an infant she lost, or a sibling, cousin, or friend from years long gone. But I do know what I see when I stand by the bedside of the infirm aged. Though their bodies are skin-covered sticks and their minds an inescapable labyrinth, I see something surprising. I see something beautiful and horrible, hopeful and hopeless. What I see is my children, long after I leave them, as they end their days.

This vision comes to me sometimes when I stand by the bedside in my emergency department and look over the ancient form that lies before me, barely aware of anything. Usually the feeling comes in those times when I am weary and frustrated from making too many decisions too fast, in the middle of the night. Into the midst of this comes a patient from a local nursing home, sent for reasons I can seldom discern.

I walk into the room and roll my cynical eyes at the nurse. She hands me the minimal data sent with the patient, and I begin the detective work. And just when I'm most annoyed, just when I want to do nothing and send them back, I look at them. And then I touch them. And then, as I imagine my sons, tears well up and I see the error of my thoughts. For one day, it may be them.

One day, my little boys, still young enough to kiss me and think me heroic, may lie before another cynical doctor, in the middle of the night of their dementia, and need care. More than medicine, they will need compassion. They will need someone to have the insight to look at them and say, "Here was once a child, cherished and loved, who played games in the nursery with his mother and father. Here was a child who put teeth under pillows and loved bedtime stories, crayons, and stuffed animals. Here was a treasure of love to a man and a woman long gone. How can I honor them? By treating their child with love and gentility. By seeing that their child has come full circle to infancy once more and will soon be born once more into forever."

This vision is frightful because I will not be there to comfort them or to say, "I am here" when they call out, unless God grants me the gift of speaking across forever. It is painful because I will not be there to serve them as I did in life and see that they are treated as what they are: unique and wonderful, made in the image of the Creator and of their mother and me. It is terrible because our society treats the aged as worse than a burden; it treats them as tragedies of time. It seems hopeless because when they contract and lie motionless, no one will touch them with the love I have for them or know the history of their scars, visible and invisible. I am the walking library of their lives, and I will be unavailable. All I can do is ask, while I live, for God's mercy on them as they grow older.

And yet, the image has beauty and hope as well. Because if I see my little boys as aged and infirm, I can dream that their lives were long and rich. I can dream that they filled their lucid years with greatness and love, that they knew God and served Him well and were men of honor and gentility. I can imagine that even if they live in their shadowland alone, somewhere children and grandchildren, even great-grandchildren, thrive. I can hope that their heirs come to see them, and care, and harass the staff of the nursing home to treat Grandpa better. I can hope that they dare not allow my boys to suffer but that they hold no illusions about physical immortality and will let them come to their mother and me when the time arrives. And best, I can know that their age and illness will only bring the day of that reunion closer.

My career as an emergency physician has taught me something very important about dealing with the sick and injured, whether young or old. It has taught me that the Golden Rule also can be stated this way: "Do unto others as you would have others do unto your children." I think that this is a powerful way to improve our interactions with others, not just in medicine but in every action of our lives. And it is certainly a unique way to view our treatment of the elderly. For one day all our children will be old. And only if this lesson has been applied will they be treated with anything approaching the love that only we, their parents, hope for them to always have.

Dr. Edwin Leap, "The Golden Rule, Revisited," Emergency Medicine News *(October 2000): 18.*
Used with permission from Lippincott, Williams, and Wilkins, Baltimore, MD.
See <www.lww.com>.

sive. It is noteworthy that cancer itself is often less aggressive in older people. Aggressive treatment may not always be the best choice, depending on the condition of the patient. Due to debilitated states, after receiving informed consent, many elders and their families opt for less aggressive treatment regimens as they weigh potential benefits against side effects of treatment.

What does this mean for you and your elder? It means your elder should receive frequent checkups and diagnostic tests to locate early signs of cancer (see "Recommended Cancer Screening Tests" [at left]). If cancer is diagnosed you should expect thorough discussion of treatment options from the physician. It is strongly recommended that your elder seek a second opinion to confirm the diagnosis or treatment options. For more information on cancer and the elderly, contact the American Cancer Society (see appendix).

MAINTAINING OPTIMAL HEALTH

Good medical care is important, but so is the positive feedback you give your elder. Research has shown that when elderly people are told that they are old and decrepit, their bodies will begin to behave that way.[11] But if they receive positive messages about embracing the wisdom and benefits of aging, they will continue to lead active lives. Engaging in regular physical activity can help lengthen a senior's life and reduce the chances of heart disease, stroke, osteoporosis, and other medical problems.

To foster a healthy attitude toward aging, praise your aging loved one even for small accomplishments. Take whatever steps you can to help her avoid settling into a sedentary or solitary lifestyle. A person who lacks physical and mental stimulation, a purpose for living, and an interest in others can deteriorate physically, emotionally, and spiritually.

To foster a healthy attitude toward aging, praise your aging loved one even for small accomplishments.

Social Contact. To keep your elder from becoming inactive and even reclusive, try to include your loved one in family activities. Invite your elder to accompany you on shopping trips or frequent outings to add variety to life. Suggest volunteer activities you could do together. Many communities have a registry of volunteer opportunities. Seniors often find renewed energy and vigor by serving others. They can volunteer as teachers' helpers, as surrogate grandparents, or as readers to children in public libraries. They can teach English as a second language, serve hot meals at a rescue mission, or share their professional expertise in a class at a senior center.

Physical Activity. Many apparent symptoms of aging are simply the result of a lack of exercise. Regardless of age, people who exercise regularly can increase their stamina, muscle size, and joint mobility. Exercise can spur feelings of well-being and help keep your elder's mind alert. Whether your elder lives with you, in his own home, or in a retirement community, encourage regular exercise.

Religious Life. A growing body of research has been published, showing that religious belief has a positive impact both on the physical and the mental health of older people.[12] For example, a recent study of nearly 4,000 older adults showed that the risk of having high blood pressure ranked 40 percent lower in those who both attended religious services at least weekly and spent daily time in prayer or Bible study.[13] Another study indicated that frequent church attenders not only tend to live longer, but they also are more likely to make healthier lifestyle choices, such as quitting smoking, exercising more, and having more social contacts.[14]

Pray for your elder's spiritual health. If your elder is a Christian, pray that she will continue to grow in the knowledge of God, bearing fruit in her old age (Psalm 92:14). Encourage your loved one to get involved in a church activity or ministry if she is ambulatory. She may want to teach a Bible class, work in the tape ministry or church library, or greet people as they come into church. If she cannot get out to church, bring the church to her through audiotapes, videotapes, music, and personal visits. See if your elder is interested in doing a Bible study or praying with you each week. An active faith is good for your elder's— and your—health!

Beloved, I pray that you may prosper in all things and be in health, just as your soul prospers. 3 JOHN 1:2 NKJV

CHAPTER 7

When anxiety was great within me, your consolation

brought joy to my soul. Psalm 94:19 NIV

Mental Change, Memory Loss, and Dementia

Understanding Brain Changes in Aging

ONE morning, Ruth awoke early to find her mom in the kitchen getting ready to use the stove. "I want to cook breakfast for the boys who are out milking," she explained.

"Mom, we don't have any cows," replied Ruth, who grew up on a dairy farm with her parents and three brothers.

"Well, that's good," her mother said, sitting down. "I didn't know what to make anyway."

Ruth's 93-year-old mother had been living on her own in a California retirement village until she was diagnosed with dementia a year ago. She moved into an assisted-living facility but didn't seem happy, so Ruth and her husband took her into their home.

Even though Ruth feels privileged to care for her mom, it has been a big adjustment. She gets tired of continually having to repeat herself. "My mother will forget what I just told her 15 minutes ago," Ruth says. "She also seems to be living in the world of 50 years ago."

Trying to reason with her mother is pointless. "My mother used to be a very reasonable person. Now she insists that her mother is still alive, even though that would make her mom 120 years old! I used to try to convince her logically, but now I just say, 'It's okay if that's what you think.'"

Because of the memory loss, her mother no longer recognizes Ruth and can't be left alone or allowed to use the stove. It is also a challenge to find things for her mother to do all day. "She likes to be helpful, but usually the task is beyond her capability," says Ruth. "Right now she's dusting the living room. She also enjoys taking a cloth and cleaning the tile grout in our kitchen. We probably have the cleanest grout in the county!"

Although her mother dislikes crowds, she doesn't seem to mind being transported by bus to an adult day-care facility twice a week. Ruth appreciates the breaks and the occasional help from her relatives. Still, like many caregivers, she's reluctant to ask for more help. "We're getting ready to put carpet down, and it would be nice if one of my brothers could take Mom for the day," she says. "I know I just have to ask, but sometimes I wish I wouldn't have to ask. Then I feel guilty for resenting them, because it's my fault for not asking."

Providing care for an aging loved one who is losing the ability to function mentally can be a tremendous challenge. It requires compassion and patience as you deal with an elder's repeated questions and changes in behavior. Dementia—usually diagnosed when two or more brain functions are impaired—may affect language, memory, visual/spatial perception, personality or emotional behavior, and cognitive skills. You may wonder whether your loved one has Alzheimer's disease or is just getting old, although age by itself does not cause brain dysfunction. Your own tangled emotions fluctuate as you try to meet your own family's needs as well as those of your elder.

Many brain dementias, such as Alzheimer's disease, are progressive, irreversible, and disabling, and the prognosis is often less hopeful than with other diseases. Dementia usually starts as forgetfulness, then slowly progresses from decreased problem solving to difficulty with daily activities of living to severe memory loss and social withdrawal. It is difficult to see the person you used to know—and who used to recognize you—gradually change. Nevertheless, this is not a time to despair. There are ways to help preserve normal brain function and even help slow the progression of dementia. Plus, the more you learn about your aging loved one's cognitive deterioration and functional limitations, the better care you will be able to provide. Resources are available that can help you in that task, so there is no reason to "go it alone." Besides community services, you might enlist a friend, family member, or people from your local church to give you some assistance or a reprieve from caregiving. Your heavenly Father also invites you to cast your cares and burdens upon Him, for He cares for you (1 Peter 5:7). Psalm 145:18 (NIV) says, "The Lord is near to all who call on him, to all who call on him in truth."

WHAT IS NORMAL AGING?

In years gone by, memory loss during old age was considered a given. Today, however, researchers are discovering that healthy elderly individuals experience only slight losses of memory function as they age. It is true that our minds, like our bodies, begin to slow down and work less efficiently as we get older. Even a healthy brain shrinks with age, and its neurotransmitters—chemical messengers that cross the synapse between brain cells—become less active. But this does not perceptibly affect the ability of most seniors to think, perceive, and remember. For the healthy elderly person, what is lost is merely speed in retrieving a memory.

Intelligence

How does aging affect intelligence? Researchers distinguish between two kinds of intelligence in a person: **crystallized intelligence** and **fluid intelligence.** Crystallized intelligence refers to intellectual abilities and education. Fluid intelligence is a person's innate intellectual analytical abilities, independent of education and experience. Although fluid intelligence does seem to decline with age, a person's overall intelligence can remain stable into his eighties and beyond.

Not long ago, researchers at the University of California, Davis School of Medicine and Medical Center released the results of a 10-year study of 5,888 community-dwelling senior citizens. Their findings, reported in the *Journal of the American Medical Association,* revealed that 70 percent of the participants showed no significant decline in cognitive function over the study period.[1] Cognitive function refers to a person's intellectual ability to reason and think—to become aware of, perceive, or comprehend ideas. It involves all aspects of perception, thinking, reasoning, and remembering.

A separate study concluded that decreases in intelligence are modest in certain categories of cognitive function. Research done by K. W. Schaie showed that mental ability declines only slightly, even by the age of 80, if the person is not suffering from a debilitating disease like Alzheimer's.[2] In comparing an 80-year-old with a 25-year-old, there was virtually no decline in verbal ability, but there was a slight decline in inductive reasoning, verbal memory, spatial orientation, and numeric abilities. In short, the brain's processor is slowing down.

USE IT OR LOSE IT

Your elder's memory can be improved by using the brain! Studies have found that higher levels of education are associated with lower rates of dementia. But "education" does not necessarily mean a university degree. Mental activity, including learning a new hobby or skill, is what counts; it seems that using the brain increases neuron connections and activates processes that keep the neurons and their circuits alive and well. If brain cells are not used regularly, they and their connections will deteriorate.

Memory and the ability to think clearly can be boosted by mental exercises and/or training programs. Working crossword puzzles or playing chess, checkers, or card games with friends can help stimulate the thinking process. Visiting new places or learning a new skill, such as the piano or computer, can also help sharpen the mind. Elderhostel's educational programs offer seniors short-term learning excursions throughout the United States and the world. Trips range from studying historic lighthouses in New England to exploring a rain forest in Costa Rica. (See appendix for information on Elderhostel, Inc.) Many colleges offer courses specifically geared for the older learner. Elder-care facilities that provide game rooms and interesting training programs can help your elder retain or even improve her mental acuity.

As a caregiver, you can jog your loved one's memory by singing familiar hymns and songs together; musical ability is often retained longer than other skills in patients with Alzheimer's. If possible, memorizing and meditating on Scripture is an excellent way to exercise the brain and also to grow spiritually. Distant caregivers can help stimulate their elder's thinking by exchanging daily e-mails; playing chess together by computer; sending books, magazines, tapes, and CDs to their loved one; and reciting Scriptures to each other by phone.

The good news is that there is considerable elasticity in cognitive functioning; therefore, many elderly people can benefit from participating in education programs to keep their minds sharp and active. In fact, Schaie's research suggests that the slight intellectual decline in the elderly can even be reversed by programs and exercises to stimulate the brain. An 88-year-old who is in good health, is mentally active, and has some formal education will probably show minimal, if any, decline in verbal ability. Daily physical activity is also beneficial in preserving and protecting the brain.[3] Walking, gardening, and going up and down stairs are a few ways to help maintain cognitive function.

It is worth noting that intelligence is not as valuable as wisdom. An intelligent person can lack wisdom, and a person suffering from intellectual decline can still be wise. "Who is wise and understanding among you? Let him show it by his good life, by deeds done in the humility that comes from wisdom" (James 3:13 NIV).

Many elderly people can benefit from participating in education programs to keep their minds sharp and active.

Personality

A person's core personality tends to remain consistent throughout life—unless he suffers from a disease or mental illness. Research has shown that someone who is cheerful and optimistic when young remains so throughout life, while a person who is grouchy and pessimistic in early life typically keeps the same personality characteristics in later life.

Mental disorders can drastically alter a personality. But a change in the way your elder deals with a particular challenge does not mean he is suffering from a mental illness. It may simply indicate that he has discovered a different method of coping. Older adults tend to rely more often on passive, emotion-focused forms of coping, rather than active, problem-solving approaches. Because the elderly frequently see their personal situations as unchangeable, they often deal with distressing feelings by withdrawing or lashing out rather than by trying to alter the situation.

Memory Loss

Regardless of age, everyone has an occasional lapse in memory, misplacing the car keys or forgetting someone's name. Most of us learn to work around these annoyances as they come. But there are some significant differences between normal memory lapses and memory loss due to disease or brain injury. How can you tell whether your elder's fading memory is due to more than normal aging? Here is a checklist of some possible signs and symptoms to look for:

1. Confusion about how to perform simple, familiar tasks
2. Increasing loss or misplacement of everyday objects
3. Changes in personal care—wearing shirts backwards or wearing dirty or ripped clothing
4. Trouble doing simple arithmetic
5. Changes in eating habits—food left out, meals uneaten, evidence of burned food
6. A proliferation of reminder notes and lists throughout the house
7. Changes in how your loved one manages her home. She may use the air conditioner in the winter or leave the windows open when it is raining.
8. Confusion about the month or season

TREATING MEMORY LOSS

Although diminishing neural function can cause some short-term memory loss in old age, long-term memory generally remains intact. If memory loss is significant, especially short-term memory loss, it can be a sign of a disease, such as Alzheimer's disease (AD), that results in dementia.

There are several prescription drugs that are currently being used to treat age-related memory loss, including donezepil (Aricept) and rivastigmine (Exelon). Discuss with your elder's physician whether the potential benefits for your loved one might be worth giving one of these drugs a try. The medications are costly, and potential side effects, such as gastrointestinal upset, need to be balanced against the benefits.

Research on new memory-restoring drugs is ongoing. Richard Wurtman, a neuroscientist at the Massachusetts Institute of Technology, has shown that citicoline, which increases brain levels of the neurotransmitter acetylocholine, can partially restore memory function in older people.[1] Other researchers are looking into the uses of vitamin E, estrogen, and antioxidants to help minimize memory loss.

[1]P. A. Spiers et al., "Citicoline Improves Verbal Memory in Aging," *Archives of Neurology,* 53 (1966), 441.

9. Difficulty completing sentences or understanding the meaning of words
10. Changes related to the use of the phone. Conversations become vague as memory fades. He may call at inappropriate hours.
11. Handwriting deteriorates
12. Wandering. You may find your loved one wandering the streets, not knowing where she is going.

When a few of these signs occur, take your loved one to the doctor for a thorough evaluation. The doctor will perform tests to rule out other potential causes of these symptoms and to make a diagnosis.

According to the U.S. Department of Health and Human Services, diseases that affect mental functioning or cause dementia increase with age. These diseases are devastating to their victims and their victims' families, and they place an enormous burden on our nation's health-care system. Nevertheless, there are coping strategies that can help you and your loved one deal with a debilitating mental disease. Also, some promising treatments are being developed to give hope for the future.

REVERSIBLE CAUSES OF DEMENTIA

There are many medical conditions that can show up as dementia. That is why it is important for an elder to have a thorough evaluation to look for any possible reversible cause for the dementia. Occasionally a medical problem or psychiatric problem can present as dementia, and with appropriate treatment, the apparent dementia improves.

Depression

Depression can mimic dementia or Alzheimer's disease with symptoms of confusion, passivity, helplessness, and hopelessness. However, the onset of depression is usually more rapid than that of Alzheimer's and may be triggered by a traumatic event, such as the death of a spouse. Treating the depression may clear up or lessen the other symptoms. In some cases, however, a person with Alzheimer's disease may also have undiagnosed depression. If your elder is showing signs of memory loss, be sure to consider the possibility of depression. (For more information on depression, see chapter 8: Emotional Changes in Aging.)

Delirium and Confusion

Delirium is characterized by a reduced ability to pay attention. A person with delirium experiences disorganized thinking and rambling, irrelevant, or incoherent speech. Delirium, an acute state of confusion, differs from dementia in that it comes on rapidly, fluctuates in its development, and usually has a short duration. There often is a reduced state of consciousness, hallucinations, sleep-wake cycle disturbances with insomnia, or daytime sleepiness. In addition, the person becomes disoriented to time, place, and person. He may also have memory impairment.

Delirium is potentially reversible, while progressive dementia usually is not. Delirium can be brought on by toxic substances within the body (such as wrong dosage or wrong medication), metabolic disorders, infectious diseases, and structural changes within the brain. Surgery and certain medications (including some nonprescription drugs) can cause delirium in elderly people. Severe constipation caused by opioids can occasionally cause delirium. Alcohol intoxication can cause dementialike symptoms such as confusion in an older adult.

Delirium is often the only signal of a serious underlying illness—such as pneumonia or a heart attack—in a person with dementialike symptoms. Treating the cause may reverse the delirium. If you think your elder may be suffering from delirium, get her to a physician immediately for a diagnosis. (For more information, see "Is it Delirium, Dementia, or Depression?" on pages 147-148.)

IRREVERSIBLE/PROGRESSIVE DEMENTIA

Senile dementia is the umbrella term for a number of diseases that involve nerve-cell deterioration and afflict the elderly. The term *senile* simply refers to old age, while dementia means a loss of brain function resulting from persistent physical, neurological damage to the brain. Senile dementia is also referred to as **organic brain syndrome** or **chronic brain syndrome.** A senior with true dementia displays evidence of a progressive global decline in cognitive function (thinking and memory).

Dementia affects language, perception, visual/spatial functioning, calculation, judgment, abstraction, and problem-solving skills. It develops slowly and usually cannot be reversed. Alzheimer's disease is the most common type of irreversible dementia; it is responsible for up to 85 percent of cases of dementia in seniors. Vascular disorders such as strokes and ministrokes are the second most common cause of dementia after Alzheimer's disease.

Vascular or Multi-Infarct Dementia

Vascular or multi-infarct dementia is a deterioration of mental capabilities caused by multiple, minor strokes that reduce blood flow to the brain and cause an **infarction** (an area of dead tissue resulting from blockage of blood supply). Oxygen deprivation quickly leads to destruction of brain tissue, which is why early intervention is important. Consider any symptoms of a "brain attack" (or stroke) as an emergency and seek urgent medical attention. (See "Warning Signs of Stroke" on page 142.) Multi-infarct dementia causes 15 to 20 percent of all dementia and occurs most frequently between the ages of 60 and 75. Not all strokes lead to dementia, but those that do affect memory and the ability to think clearly. Once-simple tasks, such as tying a shoe, may become too complicated.

Though this type of dementia is not reversible or curable, controlling an underlying condition or risk factor (e.g., hypertension, diabetes, smoking) may slow its progression or cut the risk of another stroke. (For more information on strokes, see chapter 5: Physical Changes in Aging—Part 1, or contact the National Stroke Association [see appendix].)

Mild Cognitive Impairment

Mild Cognitive Impairment (MCI) is used to describe a state of memory loss somewhere between that of normal aging and that of Alzheimer's disease. This intermediate stage of memory loss was discovered as a result of a study on aging and dementia funded by the National Institute on Aging. In this study, researchers observed 76 patients who experienced memory loss beyond what was typical for their age-group yet were not significantly impaired.[4] This study provided researchers with the first quantitative data for a distinct kind of memory loss. It showed

Alzheimer's disease is the most common type of irreversible dementia; it is responsible for up to 85 percent of cases of dementia in seniors.

that people with MCI appear to be at increased risk of developing Alzheimer's disease at a rate of 10 to 15 percent per year. This compares to only 1 to 2 percent of the general population who develop Alzheimer's without going through MCI. Researchers speculate that 80 percent of those with MCI will eventually develop Alzheimer's. They hope this study will help researchers identify people with MCI and then will help them to develop treatments to slow down the progression into Alzheimer's.

Alzheimer's Disease

Alzheimer's disease has been described as the "death of the mind before the death of the body."[5] It is a major cause of organic brain disease and was first described by the German physician Alois Alzheimer in 1906. Currently the seventh leading cause of death among adult Americans age 65 and older, Alzheimer's is a progressive, degenerative, and, so far, irreversible brain disease.[6] It affects more than 4 million people in the U.S. Symptoms of Alzheimer's disease first appear after age 60 (although occasionally the disease strikes persons in their forties and fifties), and the prevalance doubles every five years beyond the age of 65. The cost of caring for an AD patient at home is $12,500 per year, while the cost of nursing-home care is estimated at $42,000 per year.[7] For a disease that can span from 3 to 20 years after diagnosis, the overall cost of AD to families and to society is staggering. The annual economic toll in the United States in terms of health-care expenses and lost wages for both patients and their caregivers is estimated between $80 and $100 billion.

WHAT CAUSES ALZHEIMER'S DISEASE?

The exact cause of Alzheimer's Disease (AD) is not known. It is a disease that methodically destroys brain cells, leaving a person incoherent and unable to care for himself. Researchers have targeted two abnormal structures as hallmarks of AD: **amyloid plaques** and **neurofibrillary tangles.** Amyloid plaques are patches of the sticky protein **beta amyloid** that occur in the brains of people with symptoms of AD. Neurofibrillary tangles are twisted and tangled nerve-cell fibers that also show up significantly in people with AD. These specific patterns are defined microscopically in brain tissue and can be determined only through postmortem examination of brain tissue. Therefore, the clinical diagnosis of Alzheimer's disease can only be definitively confirmed after death.

It is not yet known if amyloid plaques actually cause AD or are a side effect of the disease, but autopsies of AD victims show lesions (plaques or neurofibrillary tangles) inside the **hippocampus** and **cerebral cortex** of the brain. The hippocampus is the center of thought, language, and memory. It connects with sites in the cerebral cortex, which is responsible for higher brain function, including sensation and voluntary muscle movement.

Two types of AD are known to exist: **familial AD (FAD),** a rare form found in families where AD follows a certain inheritance pattern called **autosomal dominant,** and **sporadic (seemingly random) AD,** where no obvious inheritance pattern is seen. AD is also described as either **early-onset** (younger than 65 years of age) or **late-onset** (65 years and older). Early-onset is relatively rare but can affect people as young as 30. Early-onset AD progresses faster than late-onset AD.

Alzheimer's is thought to have a genetic origin (familial AD) in less than 10 percent of cases. In this form, all offspring in the same generation have a 50-50 chance of developing AD if one of their parents had it.[8] The remaining 90 percent of Alzheimer's cases have a random or sporadic origin. Researchers have found a genetic link to **ApoE (apolipoprotein E),** a protein that carries cholesterol through the blood. Several years ago scientists studied a German family with 21 members who had AD. It appears that people who inherit a form of the

REST AND RELIEF

My mother was very difficult after she had her stroke. In addition to the dementia, she became combative and easily annoyed with me. Of course, the primary caregiver is often the bad guy in the mind of the care receiver. But the doctor understood geriatrics. He said, "Maybe she isn't sleeping well." So he put her on Prozac. She was a changed woman! She was sweet, and she thanked me for doing things for her. I don't know if her lack of sleep had caused her to become depressed or if she had been depressed and couldn't sleep, but the medication really helped. It made taking care of her a much easier task.   *Francie H.*

protein ApoE-4 have an increased risk of developing AD. Other scientists are researching the link between declining estrogen in the brain and AD. Hormone-replacement therapy does not appear to reduce Alzheimer's symptoms, nor is there yet any good evidence that estrogen itself prevents the disease.[9]

SIGNS OF ALZHEIMER'S DISEASE

Alzheimer's has several stages and it is important for you to recognize each stage. Keep in mind, however, that the progression of the disease varies widely depending upon the patient. In some cases the disease progresses rapidly; in other cases it is a slow process. In addition, the progression often plateaus for a time. Some patients do not go through each stage. Here are the basic stages:

- **Early Stage.** The person cannot remember things that happened recently and is unable to recall a major aspect of his current life (such as a longtime address or telephone number). He has impaired language ability, mood swings, and personality changes. The patient may have problems balancing his checkbook, finding his way around, identifying the season or day of the week, or remembering where he put things. He may respond to this loss of memory with irritability, hostility, and agitation.

- **Intermediate Stage.** The elderly person is unable to learn anything new or to recall new information. She may have trouble remembering past events. She may require help in eating, bathing, dressing, or toileting. She may wander and be agitated, uncooperative, anxious, and violent. Obsessive symptoms may appear, such as continually repeating simple cleaning activities. She has lost all sense of time and space. She is at a significant risk for falls and accidents.

- **Severe or Terminal Stage.** At this stage, the person is unable to walk, may be totally incontinent, and cannot perform any daily activity. He has lost all or most of his memory and may not even be able to swallow. He is at risk for malnutrition and pneumonia. At this point, he must be confined to an institution or have 24-hour-a-day care. He will eventually become mute and unable to describe any of his symptoms. The end stage of AD is coma and death.

A definitive diagnosis of Alzheimer's can only be made by examining the brain after death (in an autopsy). But physicians can make a probable diagnosis while your elder is still alive by doing a thorough evaluation that includes a physical exam, a mental assessment, and neurological tests. Additional tests, such as blood and urine analysis, electrocardiogram, CT (computed tomography) scan, MRI (magnetic resonance imaging) scan, and X rays may also be done to help rule out other potential causes of dementia, such as problems with medications, vitamin B_{12} deficiency, thyroid disease, or altered body chemistry.

For more information, contact the Alzheimer's Association. In addition to free booklets, they have a Web site that contains a helpful series of articles and a section explaining how to spot the warning signs of AD as well as other mental illnesses (see appendix).

HOW YOU CAN HELP

Caring for a loved one with dementia or Alzheimer's disease has its meaningful moments. For example, you may find it meaningful to gently brush your loved one's hair or to witness his contented smile. Some caregivers are thrilled to watch the spiritual aspects of their elder's life continue to blossom, despite the dementia. "Even when my mother could no longer put sentences together, she had no problem praying the Lord's Prayer and asking God to cleanse her and purify her," says one caregiver. Single or childless caregivers may find particular meaning in the parenting role, cherishing the opportunity to nurture their aging loved one.

Nevertheless, caring for someone with dementia can take a toll on you and your family. At times you may feel stress symptoms, such as fatigue, stomach distress, headaches, and difficulty sleeping. The long hours and energy required can leave you feeling angry, guilty, depressed, and overwhelmed. If your loved one lashes out at you or no longer recognizes you, you may feel grief and sadness. Your own marital relationship may suffer and your financial reserves may be depleted due to the expense of caregiving and loss of work time. As your loved one's disease progresses, you may have less time for yourself.

It is important to have a plan of action to help you manage the needs of your loved one and still have some time for yourself. Here are some suggested steps to take:

1. **Get a diagnosis.** The sooner you know whether your elder has dementia that is treatable or untreatable, the better you will be able to manage the situation. Although Alzheimer's disease cannot be cured, certain drugs may be able to ease the symptoms. You will be able to understand and cope with the challenges of caregiving for an AD patient if you know what you are dealing with.

2. **Write a daily schedule.** A structured day of planned activities helps to promote a sense of routine and stability for your elder. If you are the primary caregiver, set aside time for respite (brief breaks from caregiving responsibilities) by having a home health aide or visiting nurse come in for a few hours; a trained helper can assist your elder with bathing, toileting, preparing meals, and taking medication. Adult day-care facilities offer a way for your elder to spend time with others and engage in simple activities while you have time for your own activities. Some nursing homes, hospitals, and residential-care facilities offer short-term stays to give caregivers a break. Find out if your church offers respite care or other services.

3. **Locate available resources.** Take advantage of the services and information available from county and state health or social-service agencies. Contact national nonprofit organizations that specialize in Alzheimer's disease for resources (see appendix). Let family and friends know specific ways in which they can help. Ask for help in a way that expects a positive response. Instead of complaining that no one offers to help, make a list of things others could do. Perhaps you could delegate tasks such as handling bills, making phone calls, providing occasional meals, or finding out what support services are available locally. See if a relative would be willing to make a daily call to chat with your loved one.

4. **Seek financial and legal advice.** Prepare for the future by discussing your elder's needs, such as wills, trusts, and durable power of attorney, with a professional financial adviser or an attorney. (For

more information, see chapter 10: Financial Care, and chapter 11: Legal Care and Estate Planning.)

5. **Be realistic about your loved one's changing capabilities.** Many caregivers expect too much and get frustrated when their elder cannot remember or perform as in the past. It is best to concentrate on your loved one's remaining strengths to help him feel valued and to give him a sense of accomplishment. For example, if you are cooking, your elder may not be able to help you measure ingredients, but he may be able to stir the mixture. As abilities deteriorate, look for activities that your elder is still able to do, such as browsing through birthday cards or old photographs; pushing a child on a swing; folding laundry; emptying wastebaskets; taking a ride in the car; or listening to familiar hymns, books, Scriptures, and sermons on audiocassette or CD. Stop an activity if it causes your elder frustration at not being able to remember.

6. **Ask your pastor to come over to visit your aging loved one.** This is a good opportunity to pray together, sing favorite hymns and choruses, and give your elder Communion. Your pastor may be able to recruit others to visit as well.

7. **Cope with change.** Try to recognize what you can and cannot do. Ask reliable friends (perhaps from your church) to take turns staying with your loved one for a few hours on a designated morning, giving you some free time. Join a support group. The Alzheimer's Association has about 200 chapters nationwide and also offers referrals to local services, a help line, and information on caregiving. Support groups provide a safe place to vent frustrations and feelings; share experiences; and receive support, feedback, and information.

DAUGHTER'S HELPER

Mother wants to be helpful, just as she always has been. One of the things she still can do at age 92 is dry dishes, so we don't use the dishwasher very much. However, once in a while, Mother doesn't even remember how to do that simple task. She will take the towel and try to wrap the dish in it. Then she cries and says, "I want to help, but I don't know how."

Dorothy F.

8. **Keep up with personal devotions.** Make it your prayer each morning to present your body as a living sacrifice, holy and acceptable to God, which is your reasonable service (Romans 12:1 NKJV). Allow the Word of God and the power of the Holy Spirit to renew your mind, replacing discontentment or self-pity with praise and a fresh commitment to serve the Lord by serving your aging loved one.

9. **Do not rush your elder.** Plan accordingly, allotting enough time to accomplish daily tasks, get to doctor's visits, etc.

Communicating with Your AD Loved One

If your loved one has been diagnosed with Alzheimer's disease, you will need to develop strategies to communicate with him. The guidelines listed below can also be used in dealing with other mental disorders.

- Don't assume your elder cannot understand you.
- Address your elder by name.
- Keep your sentences short and simple.
- Be specific. Instead of saying, "Here it is," say, "Here is your coat."
- Your discussion should center around actual events, things, and people—not abstract ideas.
- Position yourself at eye level with your elder.
- Give your elder time to listen, comprehend, and respond.
- Eliminate background noise if at all possible.

TAKE A BREAK

My best advice to other caregivers is to get some respite care. It was very stressful for me to be working two jobs, finishing my bachelor's degree on weekends, and having a couple young people at home when my mother needed care. We were responsible for her total care for five years. My brother and sister-in-law never offered to help, and I didn't feel comfortable asking them. I had home health aides two or three times a week for about a six-hour stint, and adult day care from about 9 A.M. to 4 P.M. And through one program, we had a live-in caregiver for three days, which provided a needed break.

Sarah H.

- Ask only one question or give one instruction at a time. Coach your elder through each step of a task.
- Repeat yourself if necessary.
- Reassure your elder you will take time to listen to her.
- Avoid becoming overexcited, using wild gestures, or being overly demonstrative.
- Provide cues and help your loved one find a "lost" word when he is talking.
- Pay attention to the words and emotional messages being conveyed.
- If your elder loses the thread of a story or is unable to complete a sentence, repeat the last phrase she said to prompt her memory or ask questions based on the last thought your elder expressed.
- Help your elder become tolerant of his communication difficulties.
- Offer encouragement and treat your elder with respect and dignity.

A structured day of planned activities helps to promote a sense of routine and stability for your elder.

Safety Concerns

If your elder has dementia and lives with you or is still coherent enough to live on his own, you have some important modifications to make to your home or his. Alzheimers.com, a Web site devoted to providing caregivers with advice on how to care for a loved one with dementia, has provided a helpful list of household modifications. Here are some of the suggestions from that list:

- Keep the outside of the home free of debris. Have the area well-lighted and equip stairs with handrails. Paint the edges of the stairs to make them more visible.
- Keep emergency-contact information in pockets of clothing or sewn into clothing.
- Fill uneven ground areas in the yard, remove thorny bushes, etc.
- If you have a swimming pool, make sure it has a security fence around it. Keep it locked.
- Lower the temperature of your water heater to avoid scalds.
- Use rubber underpadding on area rugs or remove the rugs completely.
- Avoid having glass-topped coffee tables or kitchen tables.

MY MOTHER'S MIND

Mom fell and broke her hip a month before Dad died. Physically she came through surgery just fine, but mentally she did not. She had already been experiencing memory loss due to hardening of the arteries. Her ability to think had been clouded for some time. The surgery caused her to "blow a few fuses in her brain," as our family doctor said.

When Dad was dying, I wanted Mom to see him one more time. I wanted to try to help her understand that he could not stay. A neighbor who had a van with a wheelchair lift took us to the nursing home. Mom was very frightened, for she thought she was being kidnapped—until I wheeled her into Dad's room. She saw him lying there, eyes closed, not responding to us. She looked at him for a moment, this strong farmer from Sweden to whom she had been married for 62 years. She sat up straight and told him: "Now you say, 'Jesus, kom snart!'" (Jesus, come soon). He died two days later.

At the funeral home Mom talked to Dad in the coffin. She said, "I'll be coming too—sooner than you think." Everyone thought she would join him within the week. She developed a fever and breathing difficulties that week, but she rallied. Because she seldom remembered that Dad was gone, she didn't lose her desire to live. I told her often that we had each other, and that always brought a smile to her face.

Much of the time Mom cannot say the words she wants to say. She doesn't hear well either. So we don't converse a lot. We smile at each other, hug each other, and say, "I love you" a lot. But there are times when Mom says the most memorable things. One time she was like a giggly schoolgirl. Wanting to help me dry dishes but not knowing how to move her wheelchair, she said, "My feet can't think, so I can't come to you." One evening she talked about how Dad will be waiting for us in heaven. She said, "When you can't jump around, you can jump into heaven."

During the Christmas holidays, I experienced many emotional ups and downs. One of the nicest gifts I received was Mom wishing me a Merry Christmas first thing in the morning on both Christmas Eve and Christmas Day. (Usually she has no idea what day of the week it is—or even what season of the year.)

In fact, Mom often talks to me as if I'm a stranger. She has no idea who I am. One Sunday afternoon this got on my nerves and I yelled at her. Then I sobbed in her arms, and she prayed for me. She asked Jesus to forgive her for making me suffer so much. I looked at her, my teary eyes filled with love. She said, "Oh, those eyes." I asked Jesus to forgive me for losing my temper. I asked for the Holy Spirit's gift of self-control, and Mom said, "Your Savior has heard you. He says, 'I have made you whole.'"

Sitting in her electric recliner in the family room one afternoon, Mom was worried about whether or not she would get "the Jesus crown" someday. I assured her that she will and had her look at some psalms from a children's Bible. She slowly read the large print, reading Psalms 23, 46, 61, and 71. When she read from Psalm 71:5—"I have trusted you since I was young"—she stopped, smiled, and said, "Yes!" Then she asked me to read more from the Bible. As I read Romans 8 she said, "That's beautiful. That's wonderful. Everything but Jesus is gone from our poor minds. We're worse than babies." I told her that having Jesus is all that matters. He wants us to love him and depend on him like babies. "That's right," she agreed.

I can get so upset with Mom when she asks me the same questions over and over again or when she won't stop worrying about me. Then she prays for me and my heart melts. One day she prayed, "Thank you, Jesus, for this dear, precious child. We'll be together forever when we meet in heaven. Thank you, Jesus."   *Betty F.*

- Make sure all curtains, upholstery, and linens are flame-retardant.
- Keep matches well hidden.
- Consider using plastic dishes, not ceramic dishes, for meals.
- Use childproofing latches on the refrigerator. (Alzheimer's patients often hide food in drawers, pockets, and other strange places.)
- Install handrails in bathtub enclosures.
- Lock your medicine cabinet.

As Alzheimer's disease progresses, your elder may walk more slowly and require assistance. You may need to replace low, stuffed living-room chairs with office-style chairs that are easier to manage. There are comfortable, upholstered chairs available that have an electric "lift" in the seat to help a person to stand. A cane or walker usually is not helpful because it requires learning a new skill. Instead, have your elder take hold of your arm for balance, and don't rush him. You may have to remind him how to raise his foot for the first step. A wheelchair may also be worth acquiring—even if your elder can still walk—because it will allow you to take him on longer excursions, such as trips to the store, zoo, or church.

If your memory-impaired elder loses or hides things, she may not remember where she hid them or even that she had them in the first place. To prevent the loss of keys, dentures, eyeglasses, and other items, keep essentials and valuables locked up or out of sight when not in use. Keep spares when possible and always check wastebaskets before emptying them.

Develop strategies to communicate. Be specific. Instead of saying, "Here it is," say, "Here is your coat."

When a person with Alzheimer's no longer recognizes familiar people or places and feels confused, he may be prone to wander away and become lost. Wandering may also occur when he is trying to escape the stress of a noisy or crowded environment or fulfill former obligations, such as going to work. He may wander off when he feels isolated, fearful, or restless (due to lack of exercise or a side effect of certain medications).

To guard against such incidents, structure each day to include pleasant activities (e.g., folding towels with you or sweeping the floor), physical activity (e.g., taking walks together), and familiar music. If your elder is trying to leave, find out if he is hungry, needs to use the bathroom, or feels uncomfortable. Remind him that he is in the right place. To keep your loved one from leaving unnoticed, consider camouflaging doors with wall hangings or screens, or use double-bolt door locks that are positioned out of sight or out of reach (very high or very low). Keep an extra key handy for yourself.

Alert the neighbors and police that you are caring for a person with dementia, and keep a list of names and phone numbers. Make copies of a recent close-up photograph of your loved one to show others in case she gets lost. Check into the Safe Return program, a national, 24-hour, toll-free number to contact when someone is lost or found (see Alzheimer's Association in appendix).

As your loved one deteriorates mentally, you will have to make the decision as to what is the optimum living situation for him. It may be that you will be able to cope with him in your home, as long as you have plenty of help. On the other hand, he may be more comfortable in a stable place with a steady routine. This type of patient typically deteriorates to the point where the family caregiver, even with help, can no longer cope with the effects of this progressive disease. This is when a nursing-home placement becomes vital. If there is real evidence that your elder is becoming dangerous to himself or to those around him, you should immediately find a nursing facility whose staff has expertise and experience in dealing with those types of disorders.

You will need to seek the advice of your physician, social worker, or a wise counselor (some pastors are experienced in this way) to determine what the best course of action is for you to take to protect your loved one. What do you do if your elder objects to being placed in a facility? If she still has her mental faculties, you should make every effort to allow her to remain in her home as long as possible. If she is living with you, make whatever home modifications are reasonable to accommodate her. You do not want to come across as paternalistic or authoritarian if she is still mentally alert. On the other hand, if she has been

FORGET ME NOT

Valentine's Day was always special at our house because that was the day in 1948 that Muriel accepted my marriage proposal. On the eve of Valentine's Day in 1995, I read a statement by some specialist that Alzheimer's is the most cruel disease of all, but the victim is actually the caregiver. I wonder why I have never felt like a victim. . . .

That Valentine's Day eve, as I thought about victimhood, I recalled a time when I was changing her clothes. Instead of the usual scowl reserved for such occasions, she smiled warmly, triggering a happy thought.

"You are a lucky girl," I said. "You don't have a worry in the world; you're well loved and well cared for. Why, you don't even have any sin to repent of!"

That evening I bathed Muriel on her bed, kissed her goodnight, and whispered a prayer over her. "Dear Jesus, you love sweet Muriel more than I, so please keep my beloved through the night. . . ."

The next morning I was pedaling on my Exercycle at the foot of her bed and, while Muriel emerged from sleep, I dipped into memories of some of the happy Lovers' Days long ago. Finally she popped awake and smiled at me. Then, for the first time in months, she spoke, calling out to me, "Love . . . love . . . love. . . ."

I jumped from my cycle and ran to embrace her. "Honey, you really do love me, don't you?"

Holding me with her eyes and patting my back, she responded with the only words she could find to express agreement. "I'm nice," she said.

Those may prove to be the last words she ever spoke.

Excerpted from A Promise Kept *by Robertson McQuilkin. Copyright © 1998.*
Used by permission of Tyndale House Publishers, Inc. All rights reserved.

clearly diagnosed as having a mental disease, you must begin assuming control of her affairs. In effect, you will have to overrule her and assume the role of parent in her life. As painful as this may be, it may be the only way you can protect her from hurting herself or others.

Pray about the various options open to you and don't let your decision be guided by feelings of guilt. You and your family may be at risk if your elder becomes violent or totally unpredictable in his behavior. When the safety of your family is on the line, you should err on the side of safety, not sentimentality or guilt.

Late-Stage Care

To prevent the loss of keys, dentures, eyeglasses, and other items, keep essentials and valuables locked up or out of sight when not in use.

A person with late-stage Alzheimer's usually requires round-the-clock care. This stage may last from several weeks to several years. If you are the primary caregiver, you will need considerable support and help to provide for your loved one's basic needs. More typically, your elder will need round-the-clock support offered by a nursing facility that specializes in Alzheimer's disease and related disorders. Such facilities, thankfully, are becoming more available across the nation.

Eating and swallowing can be difficult in late stages of the disease. Pneumonia is also common. You will need to educate yourself and weigh the pros and cons of using, withdrawing, or refusing medical treatments. Talk with the doctor about whether a treatment will improve your elder's condition and for how long. Ask about the treatment's risks, burdens, and discomforts to your loved one. Talk with family members, the health-care team, and pastors or spiritual advisors to develop a care plan that respects your elder's wishes. (For more information, see chapter 18: End-of-Life Issues.)

Be Compassionate

Dealing with your elder's emotional issues, such as high anxiety, calls for insight and compassion. A person who taught you always to be kind to people and never to say something hurtful may now say insensitive things in a helper's presence. "Why doesn't she go home?" your anxious elder may say. "I don't trust her." Or she may tell a caregiver directly, "You're mean. I don't like you."

Recognize that anxiety or brain-disease processes may be affecting your elder's attitude and discernment. If he says something that is untrue or that does not make sense, try not to make him feel foolish or confused. Pay attention to your loved one's feelings and keep your answers simple and understandable. If your elder accuses you of never visiting her, even though you were just there yesterday, try not to take it personally. It might help to leave a guest registry in which you and other visitors can write down your names, the date, and a few highlights of your conversation. When you visit, read the notes to your elder to cheer her.

People with dementia often experience anxiety in the evening—sometimes called sundown syndrome. That may be a good time to engage in some singing and storytelling. Some people with Alzheimer's can still remember songs, dates, and details from long ago. Since Alzheimer's patients may become confused in the dark, you may wish to keep a low-wattage light on at night, in or near your elder's room.

Quite often, elderly people are not very interested in what is going

LOVING GRAMMY, LOVING LIFE

When I started college, Grammy was becoming confused. She parked her car and couldn't find it. She stopped balancing her checkbook. She gave lots of money away and had none left to buy groceries. She couldn't remember words for things and eventually lost her ability to reason and understand. She was less steady on her feet and needed assistance to go to the bathroom. So at age 18, I agreed to be the primary caregiver for my grandmother, who lived downstairs in my family's duplex-style house.

For the next four-and-a-half years I enjoyed taking care of my grandmother. She was a lot of fun and took great pleasure in life. She'd watch the squirrels, and although she couldn't remember what they were called, she thought they were cute. I drove her everywhere. I'd take her to church and carry her up the stairs if I had to. I'd push her in her wheelchair and occasionally take her along to one of my college classes. Sometimes I'd ask her if she knew who I was. She'd say, "Yes, you're my favorite."

One night, after Grandma had gone to bed, I left for a Bible study and told a friend that I really loved my life and wouldn't change anything about it. That night my grandmother died and went to be with the Lord. I still miss her, but I have fond memories that I'll always treasure.

Lauran H.

on in the outside world. They prefer to get back in touch with the world they remember. That often includes religious upbringing. If your elderly loved one grew up with the King James Version of the Bible, for example, consider reading aloud from that version. Your elder may recall verses he memorized years ago. The familiar words might bring comfort in a way that a contemporary version could never do.

As you draw on God's strength, draw also on the strength of others in your church and community. There is no reason to go this alone—and many reasons not to! Access one of the many organizations ready with specific types of help. The wisdom is in knowing when and how to tap into the person or group you need at the right time. As you become more acquainted with the issues your loved one is facing, you will know better what kind of assistance you need.

Final Thoughts

Caring for a loved one with Alzheimer's disease involves a host of emotional, financial, physical, spiritual, and lifestyle issues that can challenge the strongest faith. Perhaps you are feeling anger or resentment at God for allowing your aging loved one to develop a disease that has robbed her of the ability to think and function. You have painful questions about whether you are doing enough or making the best decisions for your elder. You pray daily—or may not even know how to pray about the situation anymore. You may wonder if God has abandoned your elder—and you.

Try engaging in some singing and storytelling. Some people with Alzheimer's can still remember songs, dates, and details from long ago.

It may comfort you to consider that your loved one was created in the image of God. Although that image is now sadly disguised in confusion and loneliness, it remains His image. And when earthly measures to restore your elder's mental health and vitality have been exhausted, remember that Earth is not the final destination. Here, pain and suffering are commonplace. Yet your loved one's suffering is not meaningless to our heavenly Father; He is the Potter who shapes vessels from marred clay (Jeremiah 18:4). He is also the One who, according to the psalmist, collects your tears in a bottle; not one of them is ignored (Psalm 56:8). It is because He sent His Son to suffer the agony of the Cross on our behalf that He can sympathize with us. As you allow God to meet you in the midst of your circumstances, He can help you to grow spiritually and can even give you joy. Your faith will deepen as you depend on Him.

It may seem a long way off, but Christians await eternal blessings that are promised to far outweigh the troubles down here. So do your work heartily, knowing that you will receive an inheritance from the Lord as a reward (Colossians 3:23-24 NIV). Our hope, then, is not in what is seen but in what is unseen. For what is seen (e.g., Alzheimer's) is temporary, but what is unseen (e.g., full restoration with God) is eternal (2 Corinthians 4:18 NIV).

One day the groaning will end and your loved one will be clothed in immortality. For believers, the promise of full healing will take place in heaven, where there will be no pain or decay. The Lord Jesus Himself will transform our lowly bodies to be like His glorious body. Until then, take heart as you entrust your loved one to the God whose mercies are new every morning (Lamentations 3:22 KJV).

——— ∾ ———

We know that if the earthly tent we live in is destroyed, we have a building from God, an eternal house in heaven, not built by human hands. Meanwhile we groan, longing to be clothed with our heavenly dwelling. 2 CORINTHIANS 5:1-2 NIV

For God has not given us a spirit of fear, but of power and of love and of a sound mind. 2 TIMOTHY 1:7 NKJV

Emotional Changes in Aging
Helping Your Elder Cope

Frank had always been a very strong, almost domineering person. Before he retired, he had been an executive managing a large department and big budgets. He was also a leader in his church, teaching the adult Sunday school class and chairing the board of elders. Others often came to him for advice about both financial and spiritual matters. His dominant personality made him the focus of family gatherings, where he would hold court, regaling aunts and uncles, nieces and nephews with stories from his childhood. But a few years into retirement, his natural confidence seemed to fade. He resigned from his leadership positions in the church and became more and more withdrawn. He began to worry over financial decisions and major purchases. He lost interest in the outside world and spent much of his time reading books about theology. His natural tendency toward pessimism deepened.

"He was the same person but not the same person," observes his daughter, Jan. "Some of his personality characteristics seemed to be accentuated with age, while others seemed to change. He developed tendencies toward anxiety and depression that may have been there before but weren't apparent until he got older. On the other hand, he became more sensitive in his relationships, especially with his children. And toward the end of his days, he seemed to take stock of his entire life and find satisfaction in it—even though he had been through many hardships and difficulties. He wasn't looking forward to the process of dying, but he was at peace with his life."

———— ⌦ ————

Like Frank, many seniors go through a series of emotional changes as they age. How a person responds, however, depends on the individual's core personality, life situation, and spiritual health.

DEALING WITH LIFE CHANGES

The physical changes your loved one experiences as she ages—discomfort, illness, frailty—are simply the most visible of a host of other changes. You may notice psychological fluctuations such as confusion, anxiety, or sadness. Aging may intensify these emotions, and it may be up to you to help your aging loved one cope. You might be surprised at the way she responds to aging—with anger or self-pity, for example. But it is important to remember that this is often an expression of inner turmoil. You as a caregiver need to make allowances for this and may even need to lovingly confront your loved one concerning her behavior.

No matter what our age, each of us walks a balance beam straddled between the stresses of life and the personal resources that enable us to handle them. Any imbalance can affect our emotional health. Even positive changes—marriage, the birth of a child, or a windfall of money—can create stress. As we grow older, our amount of stress often increases while our ability to deal with it decreases. This can happen at differing rates, depending on individual genetic makeup and the spiritual and emotional resources a person brings into old age.

Growing old gracefully occurs when one has made peace with her past and present life and has hope for the future. Successful aging is based on the capacity to master life changes and stresses.

LOSSES IN AGING

A major cause of stress at any age is loss—and losses are usually multiple as people grow older. If your aging loved one talks incessantly about anxieties, tells the same stories over and over, or becomes argumentative, it may be because he realizes he is losing someone he hope he would never lose—himself. He may be fighting the realization that the capabilities he spent a lifetime honing are no longer sharp. The person he relied on most (himself) is failing. A normal reaction is to attempt to regain control. One person may become demanding. Another may withdraw for a while. Both reactions are probably different ways of asking the same important questions: *Who was I? Who am I? Who am I becoming?* The aging individual who successfully grapples with these questions will eventually find new responsibilities or expectations to focus on and new reasons to be thankful.

One of the most significant losses in later life occurs when friends and family members from the same generation begin to die. An older person may experience extreme sadness as her peers and close friends pass away one by one. These were people with whom she swapped stories, photographs, secrets, laughter, and tears. These were people on whom she counted when times were rough. These were people who came around to give her a pat on the back, a generous hug, words of encouragement or admonition, maybe even spiritual support.

The loss of younger loved ones is also traumatic. A son or daughter may suffer a terminal illness in midlife, a grandchild may be killed in an accident. These losses are unexpected and considered unnatural, and

EMOTIONAL TOLL

After my mom suffered some ministrokes and could no longer do basic housekeeping tasks, my sister and I began delivering meals to their condo an hour away. Dad heated the meals, took over doing laundry, washed dishes, and made breakfast. It was all new to him. Although Dad was still physically strong, the emotional adjustments, as well as the loss of life as he'd known it, were very hard on him. He never complained, but eventually my dad began hallucinating because of the unrelenting psychological and emotional pressures of caregiving. He'd always been able to fix things, but this was a situation he couldn't fix. He lost the stamina to play golf with his buddies and focused all his attention on his wife's care.

My siblings and I had a meeting to assess the situation and to consider how we might encourage them to move closer. We knew moving would be emotionally difficult, not because they were so attached to their condo but because they feared losing any independence. Soon after that, Mom fell down the stairs at their condo. She didn't break anything—praise God—but she and Dad were finally willing to move to a one-floor apartment nearby where we could be of more help to them. *Jill M.*

therefore it is harder to cope with them. A parent typically wishes he could go in a child or grandchild's place. The irony and senselessness of losing a younger person is keenly felt into old age—one more factor in a personal sphere that is spinning out of control.

Grief is a universal—and divine—process. We are *supposed* to hurt when death takes someone from us. To be able to cry is a gift. Our bodies are designed with tear ducts for a purpose. Research shows that crying actually releases **endorphins**—"feel good" hormones—and leaves the sorrowing person feeling more peaceful. When you know your loved one is hurting, give permission to cry. Look for opportunities to give biblical comfort too. Although the Bible does not promise immunity from sorrows or grief, it does remind us that we do not have to grieve as those who have no hope (1 Thessalonians 4:13). For Christians, there is hope in Jesus' resurrection. As the old country song goes, "I'll fly away—oh glory!" This material world is not meant to be permanent; loss merely uncovers the tug in our hearts to be home in heaven with God.

> *A major cause of stress at any age is loss—and losses are usually multiple as people grow older.*

There are many different ways to grieve, but grieving must not be denied or minimized. Your loved one will need to adjust to each loss and incorporate the necessary changes into her lifestyle. If your elder seems angry and turns hostile feelings toward you, it is likely that she simply feels you are the safest person in her world. This is common, although it may be hard to take. You should not accept blame-shifting or take personal responsibility for something you did not do, but you need to recognize that your loved one is grieving. Anger is often masked grief, born out of frustration when a person feels she is losing control.

Here are some of the other losses that may contribute to your elderly loved one's changing emotions:

- **Loss of intimacy.** Research shows that sexual intimacy remains important for older people and enhances self-esteem. But loss of a spouse or poor health may preclude lovemaking. The loss of intimacy, both physical and emotional, found in sex, touch, and physical closeness is often underrated. One 77-year-old man said, "Sex isn't as important when you're older, but in a way you need it more." Men, especially, feel intimidated by losing some degree of "masculinity" and competence.

- **Loss of respect.** Moral standards and traditional virtues are being de-emphasized. Young people may adopt negative stereotypes of older people, who in turn may become alienated from youth culture, world events, trends, and modern values. With all these changes, the elderly may feel invisible, outdated, marginalized.
- **Loss of the standard of living and meaning found in one's life work.** Some experts think the hardest adjustments to retirement are not financial but psychological, especially for those whose identities are tied to their life's work. Elderly people may feel disposable and disregarded when they are no longer economically productive. Many elderly people feel disengaged from today's fast-paced, high-tech culture.
- **Loss of health or well-being.** With increasing age, the likelihood of health problems increases. Heart conditions, arthritis, diminishing eyesight, and a host of other problems can reduce elderly people's ability to do things they used to enjoy. Health problems are a burden because they take up so much of an elder's time (e.g., doctor visits, medications). An elderly person may wonder, "Why am I always sick?" Feelings of anger and resentment may follow.
- **Loss of a future.** The old saying goes, "Everyone wants to go to heaven, but just not today." As an older person grapples with the reality of death and dying, spiritual growth may or may not occur. Looking back on life, your elder may become introspective, depressed, or insecure as she considers what she has or has not accomplished. Layers of worry and indistinguishable fears may be entangled in the trauma of aging. If professionals, religious leaders, or family members treat elders in a patronizing way, this only increases their feelings of worthlessness. It is not enough to focus on correcting physical problems; we all need supportive environments where we can learn to constructively handle fearful or disappointing changes in life from a strong spiritual framework.

If an aging person becomes preoccupied with the losses in life, there can be an emotional toll. For some, the result may be an emotional disorder such as anxiety or depression.

ANXIETY

As the losses associated with aging mount, anxiety may begin to build. Hidden fears may rise to the surface: *Will the cost of a nursing home empty my life's savings? What happens then? Can I afford the repairs my house requires? Will insurance cover the cost of my surgery?*

In youth and midlife, we may talk about fears or deal with them by engaging in familiar activities with predictable outcomes. But some older adults spend much time inactive and unfocused. If they do not have a plan for the day, their thoughts can wander and they begin to dwell on their fears or the latest newspaper headlines. They may worry compulsively about seemingly minor things—like a grandchild driving around the block.

In addition to excessive worrying, anxiety is often accompanied by physical symptoms and can include diarrhea, palpitations, headaches, dizziness, loss of memory, difficulty sleeping, trembling, problems with concentration, irritability, frequent urination, a feeling of a "lump in the throat," and a short attention span. Some elderly people have panic attacks—accompanied by hyperventilation or hysterics. Although these may seem like an overreaction, it is important that you take these symptoms seriously. Panic attacks and other forms of anxiety are telling signs that an elderly person's capacity to handle stress is on overload.

If your elder is extremely anxious, it is important to see a physician about treatment with specific kinds of therapy, which may include medication. One behavioral therapy technique, for example, teaches a special breathing exercise to reduce anxiety.

Whether or not formal treatment is needed, you can be a great help to your anxious loved one. Use comforting words and caring body language to soothe and calm your elder. Sit close to her when talking about a concern. Even if you cannot relate to all her circumstances, ask God to give you sensitivity and a heart of compassion for her. Put your arm

WONDERFUL PEACE

My mother has to take medicine for anxiety. But she knows the true source of peace is Jesus. One day she said, "Jesus has a way of taking you in his arms and keeping you forever, and it's wonderful—more than wonderful!"   *Betty F.*

around her and show your love with a hug or a kiss. This need not be patronizing; true empathy reaches deep and works hard to understand what another person is feeling.

Be a good listener and allow your elder to air his troubles as he chooses. No matter what is causing your loved one to be anxious, remind him that God has a perfect plan and is designing a resolution that can be trusted. Take time to pray with (or for) your loved one, asking God to calm your elder's heart and strengthen his spirit. Not only is there power in prayer, but it shows the anxious person that you care. Perhaps a bigger challenge is to help your loved one take the advice of the apostle Paul, who wrote, "Give thanks in all circumstances" (1 Thessalonians 5:18 NIV). Thank God together with your loved one for everyday blessings, including each other. Name the blessings in your lives, including the promise of the day when the Lord will wipe away every tear (Revelation 7:17). Don't try to minimize the pain your elder is experiencing, but in every loss, look for grace.

Use comforting words and caring body language to soothe and calm an anxious elder.

Depression

While the Bible is clear that the presence of God and the joys of heaven await the Christian, depression still sets in for some people, including the elderly. Life for the elderly person is not easy. Physical incapacity, increasing dependence, chronic pain, loss, and fear of death may bring about depression, a condition that goes beyond temporary sadness. De-

A PURPOSE UNDER HEAVEN

My father squeezed some nerves in his neck, causing his right hand to wither. He just has no strength in it. He also has cancer and some hearing loss. He has shut himself off from other people and doesn't talk on the phone. He kind of has the attitude, "Well, I guess God wants me around today, but I don't know why." He becomes quite depressed. That adds a depressive atmosphere to the whole household. It is hard to know what to do to help or please him, so we start avoiding him. Several years when we could have done things together are gone, so we have missed some opportunities, and that hurts. I guess I should start praying for our relationship and for my father to find a purpose for living.

Carl N.

pression is a disorder that affects thoughts, feelings, behavior, and physical health. If your loved one is depressed, it may seem as if a cloud is covering his world. He may have trouble thinking clearly, cry for no apparent reason, and express vague complaints. He may have feelings of self-recrimination or unfounded guilt; he may say he is tired of living

GOOD COUNSEL

How can you be a good friend and help an aging loved one who is down in the dumps or emotionally distressed? First, it is important to seek medical help if your elder is depressed. Depression is sometimes biochemical in nature and often can be treated effectively with medication. Second, examine your own heart and acknowledge your own shortcomings to God before trying to get your elder to cheer up. Once you have experienced the humbling, regenerating, and comforting power of God's Word in your own heart, you will be better equipped to bring its healing and consoling message to your loved one (2 Corinthians 1:3-4). It was not until after Peter had become thoroughly aware of his own weakness (after denying Christ) that Jesus entrusted him with the burden to feed his lambs and sheep.

Third, be a compassionate listener. Give your aging loved one an opportunity to speak of himself and his affliction. A hopeless or dreary outlook on life often brightens when there is someone else who cares.

Fourth, offer healing words. As you listen carefully, a pertinent Bible verse may come to mind that is appropriate to your loved one's situation (2 Timothy 3:16). Passages that are somewhat familiar may be more likely to strike a responsive chord in an aging loved one's heart. Psalm 23, for example, allows a hurting individual to join in the devotion, to pour out her soul and speak comfort to her own heart. A short, meaningful verse like 1 Peter 5:7—"Cast all your anxiety on him because he cares for you" (NIV)—permits your loved one to release her troubles to God. Be careful, though, not to get "preachy" and not to sound judgmental.

Speaking the promises of God reminds an aging person that he still possesses spiritual resources on which he can draw in times of loneliness or worry. Singing spiritual songs and familiar hymns can also calm the wounded soul (Colossians 3:16). Ask how you might pray for your loved one, then lift up a prayer based on the words and promises of God. Keep in mind that someone who is deeply depressed may need more support than you can offer as a caring family member or friend. In that case, seek professional help.

because he is useless and forgotten. Depression is at times the result of anger turned inward.

The most common signs of depression include:

- A flat or sad-looking facial expression
- An "empty" feeling, ongoing sadness, anxiety
- Tiredness, lack of energy
- Loss of interest or pleasure in everyday activities
- Sleep problems, including very early morning waking
- Problems with eating and weight gain or loss
- Frequent crying
- Aches and pains that will not go away
- A hard time focusing, remembering, or making decisions
- Feeling that the future looks grim; feeling guilty, helpless, or worthless
- Irritability
- Recurrent thoughts of death or suicide; a suicide attempt

Depression in the elderly can also be characterized by memory problems, confusion, social withdrawal, loss of appetite, and even delusions and hallucinations.

It is important that you recognize the symptoms of depression in your loved one, because older people are less likely than younger people to seek help. Today's elderly grew up in the years during and following the Great Depression, when hard work was valued more than feelings. Sharing intimate and personal matters was considered inappropriate. Even today, seniors tend to hide their emotions, especially negative ones, and keep problems to themselves. Emotions that are stifled may begin to fester inside.

Types and Causes of Depression

Major depression is a mood disturbance that persists more than two weeks and includes such symptoms as overwhelming sadness and loss of interest in activities that normally bring pleasure. If it is not treated, major depression can endure up to 18 months—or even longer. Early treatment is important to keep the depression from becoming more severe

It is important that you recognize the symptoms of depression in your loved one, because older people are less likely than younger people to seek help.

THE MOST SERIOUS RISK OF DEPRESSION: SUICIDE

Mentally healthy people of any age bounce back and adapt to limitations. If you are afraid your loved one is not recovering as she should from a stressful situation, talk with her physician about diagnostic and treatment options. Suicide occurs more often among the elderly than among persons of any other age group. About 25 percent of all suicides occur in people 65 years of age and older.[1] Passive suicide is also a reality; older people sometimes try to end their lives indirectly by refusing to eat, overexercising to cause a heart attack, or not taking medicine as it was prescribed. (Note: Sometimes an elder's actions, such as wandering off during bad weather or neglecting medical attention, may be a matter of confusion rather than passive suicidal behavior.)

Warning signs that your elder may be thinking about taking his own life include:

- Suicidal threats or talk of death
- Withdrawal from activities and relationships
- Sudden improvement in mood after a period of deep depression (he may have decided to commit suicide and is feeling relieved at having made the decision)
- Self-destructive behavior
- Pacing, agitated behavior, frequent mood changes, and sleeplessness for several nights
- Unusually risky behavior
- Giving away possessions or "putting things in order" (not necessarily a risk unless combined with at least one other warning sign)

If you notice one or more of these signs that your loved one may be contemplating suicide, call a physician or your local community mental-health center; many offer crisis intervention at reasonable cost. Your Area Agency on Aging can also supply a list of agencies and specialists in geriatric mental-health issues. In a crisis—if your elder is threatening suicide and has the means to carry out the threat—call emergency personnel immediately and stay with her until help arrives. If possible, remove large amounts of medications (which could be used to commit suicide), firearms, or other means of self-harm.

[1]National Center for Health Statistics 1988; Meehan, Saltzman, and Sattin 1991; Koenig and Blazer 1992.

and to prevent the risk of suicide (see sidebar on facing page for more information about suicide risk).

Dysthymia is a less severe form of depression. Although the symptoms of dysthymia are not as disabling, elders with this condition have an increased risk of developing major depression.

Bipolar disorder is a third kind of depression that afflicts some people. People with bipolar disorder have recurrent cycles of depression and elation (mania). Bipolar disorder affects judgment and can cause behavior problems, such as spending money wildly or taking unwise risks. The disorder can be treated with mood-stabilizing medications.

Depression can be a side effect of various prescription drugs.

Seasonal affective disorder (SAD) is a form of depression that afflicts some individuals when winter approaches and the days grow shorter. It is thought that reduced exposure to sunlight during winter days may affect the level of serotonin—a mood-controlling hormone—in the brain. Some therapists are finding success in using "light therapy" to help reduce feelings of depression.

Other possible causes of depression include stressful life events and illnesses such as diabetes, hypothyroidism, Parkinson's disease, and Alzheimer's disease. If your elder has a chronic illness such as heart disease or cancer, she is at higher risk of developing depression. Depression can also be a side effect of various prescription drugs. Some medications even mimic depression or aggravate depressive symptoms. These can include drugs used to treat heart disease (propranolol, methyldopa, reserpine), hormones (cortisone and anabolic steroids), and Parkinson's disease medication (levodopa). Herbal remedies may interact with other medications to cause depression. If you suspect that your elder is depressed, it is important to see a physician to rule out a medical condition that may be causing or mimicking depressive symptoms.

Treating Depression

Depression should never be considered normal, even late in life. It is not a natural outcome of getting old. It can and should be treated. If depression appears to linger, call a professional. Although some older people distrust mental-health professionals, early therapeutic treatment is important to prevent further, more serious problems. Most people who are treated for depression, including seniors, show improvement within a few weeks.

The most common treatments for depression include antidepressant medications, counseling, or a combination of both. Although medications cannot fix spiritual problems that may be involved, they can help to effectively alleviate the chemical imbalances in the brain so that the patient can work on problems facing him.

Some of the most commonly prescribed antidepressant medications are the so-called "selective serotonin reuptake inhibitors" (SSRIs). These include fluoxetine (Prozac), venlafaxine (Effexor), citalopram (Celexa), zertraline (Zoloft), paroxetine (Paxil), and others. Your elder should not drink alcohol when taking any SSRI. In some elderly patients, SSRIs can affect sleep patterns and energy levels. Your doctor and pharmacist can discuss side effects, temporary discomforts, and precautions for various medications. Your elder may increase his own endogenous serotonin levels naturally with diet (orange juice, bananas, turkey, ham, green leafy vegetables), exercise, and laughter.

Mental-health professionals available for counseling include biblical counselors, psychiatrists, psychologists, clinical social workers, and li-

DEPRESSION OR NORMAL AGING?

Be aware that not all withdrawal is depression. Some studies show that as people reach old age, "interiority" can occur, in which elders lose interest in outside events and become preoccupied with themselves. "Interiority" is accepted by gerontologists as a process by which the elderly accept their losses and limitations. It can be disconcerting, however, for an adult child who has known and respected a parent for his life passion, outgoing personality, and many interests. If your elderly loved one begins to draw the shades down on the windows to his former world, don't panic. It may be a natural preparation for leaving this life and entering the world to come, part of our God-given instincts for moving on into the eternal. If your loved one's withdrawal is accompanied by chronic sadness and an inability to feel pleasure in any realm, seek advice from a doctor.

censed counselors. Counseling for the elderly could also take the form of a close friend or minister. Elders and/or caregivers should get references and recommendations before agreeing to see one of these professionals. For depressed seniors who resist therapy, it may help to say, "You deserve to feel better than you do." In cases of serious depression, counseling plus medication is generally more effective than either therapy alone.

Some elderly people who are suffering from mild depression may not need drugs or formal counseling. They may just need friends who will spend time with them. They need someone who is a good listener—someone who will listen to them relive their past as well as talk about their cares, fears, and hopes. Many short visits from family and friends are better than one long visit. As you spend time with your loved one, you will grow to better understand his particular anxieties and needs. You may be able to offer an appropriate verse of Scripture, or perhaps the comforting words of a beautiful hymn, that suits your elder's situation.

It can be helpful for your elder to have a guest book, in which visitors can write a greeting. That way, elders can reread the greetings and gain encouragement. Guest books can also serve patients with dementia, reminding them who has come to visit and perhaps what they talked about.

Another thing you can do for your depressed elderly loved one is to

PEARL OF GREAT PRAYER

One day, while I was ministering in a California nursing home, Pearl called me to her room saying, "Come see my new ministry." When we reached her room she smiled a gigantic smile and pointed to the wall beside her bed. I looked up to see a large corkboard with a bunch of children's pictures on it. Pearl said one of the nursing assistants asked her to pray for her son. Pearl said of course she would pray but that she was a little forgetful. If the woman could just bring her a picture of the boy to hang on her wall she would pray every day. The other workers heard about Pearl's praying and one after another the pictures and requests came piling in. Now Pearl has about 30 kids she prays for every day. She says, "Now I know why God allowed me to be here in this nursing home. He brought me here to pray for these children. I am so grateful to God for using me in this way."

Sam P.

encourage her to reminisce about years gone by. Remembering events and people from the past with a loved one can help draw her out of her depressed state. Just knowing someone cares enough to listen to her can bring about the healing she needs. Share your pets with your elder or help her to keep hers. Pets are extremely important in supporting an elder's health. Some nursing homes and hospitals use "pet therapy" to give elderly people an incentive to laugh at a puppy's antics, to use arthritic fingers to pet or cuddle a furry animal, and to reminisce about pets of their own.

It is also important to help your loved one move on and look for-

GRIEVING BUT NOT DEPRESSED

Paul and Sue were active missionaries in Columbia; besides raising eight children, Sue ran an orphanage in their home and Paul pastored a church made up of students from the university where he taught. In 1994 Sue's rheumatoid arthritis grew severe, forcing them to move back to the States. The weaker and more dependent she became physically, the more passive she seemed to become as well. "This concerned me, but I had to learn not to insist that she try to do things for herself, because she would get very defensive about it," says Paul. "Her father had been an invalid for many years before his death and had been the same way." Although Sue was very sweet—never demanding—whatever Paul didn't do for her didn't get done. "If she was hungry for a snack, I wouldn't know it unless I asked."

Although he never resented her growing dependence and passivity, he was sorry she gave up. She had been such an active person. Now she wouldn't exercise except when the physical therapist was with her. She spent the day reading books and Paul spent more time caring for her.

Faith kept Paul and Sue from being in despair. "We both had to grieve the loss of her strength, mobility, and complete health, but we didn't get depressed," says Paul. "The whole family knew she was dying, and that was cause for grief but not despair. We had the hope that what awaits the Lord's people after physical death is infinitely better than anything we could imagine or ever experience here."

Paul and Sue didn't talk about the future too often, but it soothed their emotions when they did. "One day I told her I was going to miss her so intensely," says Paul, "and she told me a hymn she wanted sung at her memorial service. It's taken from a passage in the book of Lamentations: 'Great Is Thy Faithfulness.'"

ward to the future. Take time to plan future events for and with your elder. Give her something to look forward to. Very often a person without a goal will sink into a depressed state. If your loved one is able to take interest in your life or in the lives of other family members, be willing to share struggles and personal concerns. Often an elderly parent will "imagine the worst" if events in the extended family are not honestly shared. The elderly person may feel shut out, left out, and unable to be helpful to the rest of the family. If she is physically or mentally able, encourage her to volunteer to help someone else. Helping others is a wonderful way for elders to help themselves. If your aging loved one focuses her attention on helping the poor or needy rather than dwelling on herself, she may find that her depression is soon alleviated.

HELPING YOUR ELDER COPE WITH LOSS

You can help to reduce the likelihood that your loved one will succumb to severe anxiety or depression by helping him cope with the inevitable losses of aging.

Aging people must eventually come to terms with loss—even the loss of the person they used to be—and find consolation in the new person they are becoming. This generally happens for each of us throughout life as we change, moving from childhood to adolescence to young adulthood. We grow up; perhaps marry, start a family, and learn to be parents; change jobs or juggle home and career; cope with midlife's distractions and turbulence; and move into the empty-nest stage. Eventually retirement and old age roll our way. Each of these stages is, in its own way, another new beginning. People find their way to acceptance at different paces, and some struggle more than others.

Entering old age is crossing a threshold of major proportions. Watch for signs of adjustment in your loved one. Often a caregiver may be the best one to help unravel the tangled ball of emotions inside an elderly person, to articulate hope and promise, and to remind a loved one that the end of life as we know it is never the end of life. Those who believe the Bible's message of redemption and resurrection through Jesus Christ have faith in life beyond the grave. They also have a purpose for living that transcends their own problems and circumstances. If these things are true for your loved one, be sure to tell

Some elderly people who are suffering from mild depression may not need drugs. They may just need friends who will spend time with them.

her how much you admire the wisdom she has gained, her deepened faith and godliness, and the experience through which she may still help others.

Encourage your loved one's enthusiasm about things he believes in. Spend time talking about his area of expertise. Ask him about how he solved certain problems or faced difficult decisions in a career. As often as possible, validate your elder's knowledge and contribution to life. Suggest ways he still may contribute to society. Even if your elder is suffering from chronic health problems or a serious loss, a positive attitude can improve his ability to cope. To extend vitality and inhibit deterioration of body and soul, encourage your loved one to spend time with people of all ages, to be active in meaningful activity (such as prayer or volunteer service), and to exercise physically.

Think of creative little ways to encourage your elder's emotional health. Can your loved one walk across the room? If so, make the most of it. Have a conversation as you walk, slow dance to her favorite music, time how quickly you move to the other side of the room. Does your el-

EXERCISE FOR POSITIVE FEELINGS

For caregivers and aging people alike, there will be bumps in the road ahead. Do you want to get over them easily? Do you want to have a good journey? Physical exercise stimulates the feel-good, "happy" hormones in your body. Released into the bloodstream throughout the entire day, those hormones, called endorphins, help you and your loved one feel uplifted for hours.

Scientists tell us that a sedentary life leads to isolation, lethargy, and loss of interest in life. The less active a person is, the less she *wants* to be active. That is because the body becomes accustomed to the level of activity offered. When the body gets sluggish, it is harder to get going. So keep whatever muscles are still working working!

The more daily exercise a person gets, the more bounce there is in the body, mind, and spirit. Even people who cannot stand or walk may be able to clap their hands, wave their arms to music, and bob their heads to rhythm. Draw your elder into physical interaction—preferably with others doing the same thing. And by the way, don't forget to smile. Researchers have proven that even forcing a smile releases those same "happy" hormones by contracting the muscles associated with pleasant experiences. When you give a smile away, you usually get one back, helping someone else to feel good.

der have a sibling across the country? Do you know of missionaries supported by your church? Buy a box of stationery, an assortment of pretty stamps, and some colored pens. Help your elder write notes of encouragement to others; you can preaddress the envelopes and take pictures to include in the letters. To counteract occasional periods of downheartedness, take your elderly loved one for a ride in the countryside, a stroll through a rose garden, a visit to a museum, or involve her in any activity she likes.

Many seniors try to ignore or minimize any signs of weakness. If your elder downplays physical symptoms or emotions, you may need to pay closer attention to his health. Worry and fear may prevent him from telling you, as caregiver, what you need to know. Watch your loved one's behavior and listen to what he says. Caregivers who continue to offer appreciation and admiration for older people, as well as admit their own mistakes and times of weakness, will create an environment where it is acceptable to admit weakness and to hint when something may be wrong.

Look for Others to Join Your Team

Preventive programs are the best form of treatment for emotional issues of aging people. Go to your community senior center and ask questions. Talk to the older people there and ask what activities they like and why. As you talk to friends and neighbors, obtain referrals to government and private agencies for special elderly problems. Call your Area Agency on Aging for information on local health services that could help your elder. Search the Internet for national Web sites that will refer you to local addresses (see appendix). If your elder is still mobile, encourage him to join a senior club at church, or help him start one.

Take note of nonprofessionals who might be willing to befriend your elder. Look for good listeners and people who understand the elderly or are curious about life in the old days. Consider these ideas:

- Teenagers sometimes volunteer community-service hours through high school clubs.
- Children may have school assignments involving a need to interview people who lived during world events like World War II.

To counteract periods of downheartedness, take your elder for a ride in the countryside or a visit to a museum.

Neighborhood kids could be invited to bring their small pets or pictures they have drawn to share with your elder.

- Ask the pastor at your church about teens or adults who might be willing to befriend your loved one. Or perhaps your elder would enjoy being a foster grandparent, mentor, or tutor for a teen at church or through a community program.
- Midlife volunteers in churches, clubs, and local service programs are available for the asking. Or invite neighborhood adults to celebrate a birthday with your loved one.
- Encourage an aging loved one to reach out to others. Buy a few gifts like bath oils, soaps, stuffed animals, books, or candies. Wrap them and let her give them to a neighborhood child, friend, or charity.
- Consider a day-care center that is geared toward intergenerational care. Some, such as the St. Ann Center in Milwaukee, Wisconsin, operate on the philosophy that elderly people fare better if they have contact with children.

Encourage Friendships

Spending time with peers is important for the elderly. Few things are as meaningful or pleasurable as having good companions (people with whom you can do things) and confidants (dependable people with whom you can share). Friends support each other, build a common history, and help maintain independence. Friends are often the main source of keeping loneliness at bay. Friends are people we *choose*. Therefore, friends, possibly even more than family, are tied to an elder's sense of well-being.

Growing old successfully is to a great extent dependent on remembering who we are in Christ. So when your elder's friends share the bond of Christian faith, they can be a tremendous encouragement during challenging times. They can offer comfort, guidance, advice, acceptance, respect, and joy.

Emotions that one feels with friends include fun, fellowship, anticipation, mutual understanding, and human warmth. These are important as people age. Friendships help the elderly maintain these emotions on an ongoing basis. When going through major changes like retirement or moving into an assisted-living facility, friends new and old can make the adjustment easier because they share experiences and feelings from their own lives.

As old friends are lost through death or relocation, it is vital that your elder make new ones. This may not be easy, depending on her living environment and personality. But elderly people usually develop friends among the people with whom they come into daily contact: their service providers, apartment managers, local senior center, and next-door neighbors. Caregivers should do whatever they can to nurture such friendships. Many people are willing to go beyond the responsibilities their jobs normally require in order to befriend the elderly.

Support Your Loved One's Faith

In our culture, happiness is often based on being rich, successful, and young. But what is more important is contentment and optimism. Those who are content with what they have and are optimistic about the future feel more in control of their own lives. This, in turn, leads to better health.

People who are strongly religious—exhibiting contentment and faith, a kind of optimism—tend to respond positively under stress. With faith, a person expects that *good* will ultimately come out of bad situations. Faith puts one in touch with the love of God, even in the face of great loss. It is tied to group activities such as worship and volunteer service, putting one in touch with other faithful people. If happiness, then, is tied to qualities like these, the elderly, too, can be happy.

Religious beliefs, along with prayer and church attendance, contribute to both physical and mental health. The International Center for the Integration of Health & Spirituality (formerly the National Institute for Healthcare Research) has shown a close connection between spiritual well-being and physical and emotional well-being. In one study, elderly nursing-home residents who had a strong faith and a cohesive family structure were less depressed than those without faith or family ties.[1] In another study, elderly people who attended religious services reduced their hospital stays by more than half, compared to elderly people who were not religious. Researchers noted that religious affiliation may help elderly people cope, which also lowers the proba-

Elderly people usually develop friends among the people with whom they come into daily contact: their service providers, local senior center, next-door neighbors, and others.

bility of being hospitalized.[2] Church attendance was also linked with smoking less and quitting or avoiding the habit altogether.[3] In addition, churchgoing seniors have little fear of dying, and those who attend services more than once a week may extend their life by seven years or more.[4] (For more information about research on the connection between faith and well-being, check out the Web site for the International Center for the Integration of Health & Spirituality [see appendix].)

You cannot force your elderly loved one to seek God or to pray, but you may be able to encourage interaction with other believers. You can also pray diligently for her while giving her freedom to pursue God at her own pace. Keep in mind that when an elderly person's religious activity declines as a result of physical limitations or decreasing mental capacity, it does not mean that the person is less religious or devout. Positive personal and emotional expressions of faith can continue. Some elderly people find it easier to tune in to religious television or radio programs than to attend church. Research has indicated that a decline in church attendance may also be a sign of an older person's shift from an outward to a more inward focus on life.[5]

Whether a person has a lifelong history of knowing God or no belief at all, God's Word still rings true. James 4:8 encourages us to draw

LOOKING UP

Dad was a happy, healthy farmer who enjoyed his retirement. But eventually he became incontinent due to prostate cancer that returned and was inoperable. He also developed macular degeneration plus glaucoma and was almost totally blind.

He suffered like Job the last couple years. The physical pain that he experienced from polymyalgia rheumatica required medication that often caused him to be depressed. But his first thoughts were always about Jesus. He would pray over and over again, "Cleanse me, purify me, make me ready to meet you." Worthy as we might have thought him to be, he was aware of his unworthiness and was preparing to meet his holy Creator-God.

In spite of all this, he would sing and pray and talk about all the happy memories he had. He'd lie on the sofa for hours, "seeing" many wonderful things in his mind. His favorite line from the old hymn "Turn Your Eyes Upon Jesus" during that time was "Turn your eyes upon Jesus . . . and the things of earth will grow strangely dim in the light of his glory and grace." The joy of the Lord was evident on his face. *Betty F.*

near to God, with God's promise that He will draw near to us, even in our imperfect faith. The vulnerabilities of aging will test your loved one's spiritual foundations, yet times of suffering and pain can result in spiritual growth (James 1:2-4). If your loved one can no longer see well enough to read, see if he would like you to read the Bible to him. Perhaps he would appreciate listening to the Bible on audiocassette or CD. (You could even record a cassette tape of favorite passages for him.) Find ways to keep the Bible, prayer, worship, sermon tapes, and fellowship with other Christians a consistent and vital element in your elder's life—and yours! Speak of the joys of heaven, too, where there will no longer be suffering or pain. You might lack answers for the worst anxieties, but you can always say, "Let's take it to the Lord," or "I'm praying for you." Dealing with anxiety and other emotional issues of aging requires a view to the whole person: body, soul, and spirit. Maintaining or restoring balance requires treating all three of those parts at the same time and in sync with one another:

- Keep in touch with your elder's doctor to monitor physical health.
- Encourage the local church or chaplain and friends and family to be personally involved in your aging loved one's life; this is an important part of maintaining emotional health and spiritual well-being.
- Stir your elder's spiritual faith by the Word of God and your faithful prayers.

People who are strongly religious—exhibiting contentment and faith—tend to respond positively under stress.

Use Good Communication Skills

Your ability to coax conversation and empathize may be a lifeline for an aging loved one. If your elder is anxious and worried, the following communication skills may be helpful:

- Give your loved one your full attention; maintain eye contact when she is talking.
- Encourage him to share by a nod of your head or short affirmative and validating statements.
- Notice tone of voice, body language, and mood changes to really *hear* what she is saying.
- When speaking, reflect your loved one's feelings by using the same words and phrases.

- When expressing your own feelings, use "I" words instead of "You" words. Say, "I would like to hear from you more often." Don't say, "You never call me."
- Understand that there is a time for everything; don't hurry or force issues. Try to sense when it is appropriate to talk about your own specific problems or concerns.
- Before speaking, consider how your loved one may be feeling. Ask yourself, "How would I feel in his place?"
- "Let no unwholesome word proceed from your mouth, but only such a word as is good for edification according to the need of the moment, that it may give grace to those who hear." (Ephesians 4:29 NASB)

PROMOTING EMOTIONAL HEALTH IN YOUR ELDER

It has been said that in middle adulthood one of our tasks is to make a commitment to leaving a better world for the next generation. In older adulthood, the task is to take stock of one's life and experience, arriving at some degree of satisfaction. For Christians, it is amazing to look back and recount the ways God has worked in and through our lives. But what about the less-than-satisfying aspects—the regrets, mistakes, and disappointments of the past? If your elder still bears the weight and burden of past failures, the place to drop those failures is at the foot of the cross. No matter what our age, having the proper perspective of ourself—that Christ died for sins once for all, the just for the unjust, to bring us to God—can help us give up the baggage that keeps us bound to the past. Each day is a new day to "fix our eyes on Jesus, the author and perfecter of our faith" (Hebrews 12:2 NIV), so that we will not grow weary or lose heart. "This I recall to my mind, therefore I have hope. The Lord's lovingkindnesses indeed never cease, for His compassions never fail. They are new every morning; great is Thy faithfulness" (Lamentations 3:21-23 NASB).

Perhaps then, one of the developmental tasks for your elderly loved one is to integrate his emotions into a new attitude that influences the way he will live the rest of his days on earth. Many elders are uncertain of the roles they are to play in old age. You (or another family member or friend) may be able to help your loved one reaffirm his God-given value and purpose—especially if he is feeling useless or limited by his infirmities. Carrying on a ministry of prayer can be vital and effective at any age. As you show respect for the experiences of your elder; reinforce positive and biblical attitudes; and take a wholistic approach that emphasizes the body, mind, and spirit, you will be helping your elder to achieve that task.

When considering your elder's emotional stability, pay attention to spiritual needs. An older loved one who feels worthless may benefit from the reminder that she is a child of God by faith. An older person who is depressed needs your compassion, which might include thinking of ways to encourage faith and a knowledge of God's presence. Your physical presence and support is valuable, and so are your prayers. If your loved one feels excessively guilty, it may be an opportunity to share the forgiveness and grace of God in Christ. If he feels deprived of earthly comforts or afraid of the future, it may help him to look past the temporal and on to the eternal. Compile a list of Scripture verses that are important to your elder. Favorite hymns on tape are helpful too.

When considering your elder's emotional stability, pay attention to spiritual needs.

Your loved one's emotional stability will likely fluctuate in the midst of crises and losses, but encourage your elder to endure to the end. Yes, "outwardly we are wasting away, yet inwardly we are being renewed day by day. For our light and momentary troubles are achieving for us an eternal glory that far outweighs them all" (2 Corinthians 4:16-17 NIV).

Strengthen the feeble hands, steady the knees that give way; say to those with fearful hearts, "Be strong, do not fear; your God will come." ISAIAH 35:3-4 NIV

CHAPTER 9

Let the wise listen and add to their learning, and

let the discerning get guidance. PROVERBS 1:5 NIV

Getting Help:

Finding Health, Medical, and Social Services

AFTER her mom suffered a paralyzing stroke, Rachel and her husband, Ron, and their two sons chose to take her into their home to live with them, even though they knew it would be a difficult move for all of them. That was the beginning of a nine-year journey, as the family found itself maneuvering through a maze of health-care services.

Before she could move her mother from the rehabilitation hospital, Rachel did some research to find medical services, home health care, and senior programs within her community. She worked with a medical-equipment mail-order company to obtain the lift chair, commode, and special recliner they needed to make their home accessible. She and her oldest son spent three afternoons with a physical therapist to learn how to safely transfer Rachel's mother from wheelchair to car and vice versa. "It was extensive training but worth it so that we wouldn't hurt ourselves," Rachel says. When her mom was discharged from the hospital, the doctors set up a program to have visiting nurses come over to help with bathing and other physical needs.

Once her mother had moved in, Rachel found she also needed to take advantage of the hospital's respite-care program, local adult day-care center, and discounted cab services for seniors. The amount of paperwork involved in caring for her mom was nearly overwhelming. Eligibility requirements, time schedules, and insurance forms were tough to keep track of, but social workers and discharge planners offered helpful suggestions. "I learned a lot about caregiving each time Mom was in the hospital for various reasons," Rachel says. "There were so many services out there that I didn't know about until my mom needed them."

—— ✲ ——

Most people who become caregivers have no medical or legal background. And many are unaware of the wide variety of resources that are available to them. Most often it is this lack of information that prevents people from receiving the help they need.

Perhaps your aging loved one needs to find a good doctor, a home health nurse, or new housing. Maybe you could use a few days of respite care or someone to transport your elder to a doctor's appointment so that you will not miss work. Perhaps you are not sure of your elder's eligibility requirements for various programs and services. Where do you turn for help?

There are myriad agencies and resources available that are devoted to providing supportive services and information to caregivers like you. Spend some time investigating what is available in your community. The more you know about how the system operates, the better chance you will have of providing the best care for your elder.

TRACKING DOWN HELP

When it comes to finding available services for your aging loved one, it helps to be a good sleuth. A good place to start is your local Area Agency on Aging (AAA), a government-funded agency that coordinates senior programs and services in your region. (Check the government white pages or information pages of your phone book under "Senior Citizen's Services.")

In addition, the nonprofit National Council on the Aging (NCOA) and America Online, Inc. have recently partnered with several sponsors to begin an on-line service that identifies all federal and state assistance programs designed for older persons. This is a *free* program called Benefits CheckUp—reached through the Internet at www.benefitscheckup.org—

that readily and easily helps individuals determine what benefits they qualify for and how to get them in their area.

Assistance through this free service includes health care, transportation, income support, legal services, housing, meals, and other important services. More than 5 million older Americans are currently missing out on the benefits of available assistance programs. Benefits CheckUp may help change that.

You can also find valuable help in the yellow pages and your local newspaper. Talk to others in your community who have cared for elderly relatives. Sometimes word of mouth is the best resource. Ask your doctor to recommend services and support groups specifically targeted to specific needs. Often, hospital- or community-sponsored senior health fairs and caregiver seminars provide a wealth of information.

One of the greatest motivators to finding information is *need*. When you know that a loved one is in desperate need, you are willing to search everywhere. That can mean calling several places and following leads until you finally track down the help you need.

Even if the need exists, some elderly people find it hard to ask their family and friends for help. Talk to your loved one (preferably *before* a medical crisis thrusts you into the role of caregiver). Ask how he would like you to be involved with his health care. Ask your elder to name two or three specific things you might do for him. And then, as time goes on, continue to ask how you can best help. This will reassure your elder that he is not a burden on you and that he occupies a central place in your heart and on your schedule.

One of the best ways you can help your loved one is to be informed about the resources and services that are available to seniors.

If your elder desires your presence more often than you can be available, let her know that you will help her get the help she needs whenever she needs it. Anticipate future needs and think about how you might be involved as time passes or as your elder's health deteriorates. Keep in mind that caring for our elderly is something we do not just for our elders but for ourselves as well. It is also something we need to model for our kids. As we commit ourselves to the care of our aging loved ones and help to bear their burdens, we not only fulfill the law of Christ (Galatians 6:2), but we also demonstrate to the next generation the principle of Christian charity.

One of the best ways you can help your loved one is to be informed about the resources and services that are available to seniors, to identify the ones that can be helpful, and to try to get your elder to accept these services. Identifying and mobilizing services for your elder will not only help your loved one but will go a long way toward helping you survive as a caregiver.

CHOOSING A PHYSICIAN

In addition to doctors and nurses, it is not uncommon for an elderly person to be seen by technicians, therapists, and medical assistants. Ideally, your elder should have one primary physician (usually an internist, geriatric specialist, or family physician) who manages the total care of your loved one, including prescribing medications and directing him to specialists if needed. Many elderly patients become confused when several different doctors are giving orders and writing prescriptions.

If your elder goes to more than one doctor, it is important that each one know what the other is prescribing.

If your elder has a longtime relationship with a physician, you can come alongside both of them to assist them in any way you can. A trusting relationship, even a friendship between your loved one and the doctor, can go a long way in giving you some peace of mind. This does not mean, however, that you must put blind faith in the doctor's diagnoses. Work to develop a rapport with the doctor (and her office staff) so that you feel comfortable talking with her if you are uncertain about a treatment option. In many instances, it might be helpful to ask for a second opinion. Most doctors are not offended by this. If your elder goes to more than one doctor, it is important that each one know what the other is prescribing. Drug interactions can be dangerous, especially in the elderly, which is why it is important to go to the same pharmacy for all medications.

So what types of medical practitioners treat older people? Consider the following:

- **Doctors of medicine (M.D.)** treat diseases and injuries, do checkups, prescribe drugs, and do some surgery. They have completed medical school plus 1 to 7 years of graduate medical training and must be licensed by the state.
- **Doctors of osteopathic medicine (D.O.)** have similar training to

that of M.D.s but also have training in treating problems of muscles, joints, and bones with manipulation (in addition to drugs and surgery). They have completed osteopathic medical school plus 2 to 7 years of graduate training and must be licensed by the state.

- **Family physicians or general practitioners (M.D. or D.O.)** provide comprehensive health care for all ages.
- **Geriatricians** are doctors with special training in diagnosing, treating, and preventing disorders in older people.
- **Internists (M.D. or D.O.)** have specialized medical training for adults.
- **Surgeons** operate on the body to treat diseases and injuries. Many surgeons specialize in one area of the body. For example, thoracic surgeons treat disorders of the chest; neurosurgeons treat problems of the nervous system, spinal cord, and brain; and orthopedic surgeons are concerned with bones and joints.

Many older people have had the same trustworthy doctor for years. But when that doctor retires, or when an elder relocates or has a medical condition that requires more expertise, it may be necessary to choose a new physician. If your aging loved one has the option of choosing a new physician or specialist, you can help by contacting your county medical society or Area Agency on Aging for some recommendations. A medical school or university medical center can also provide reliable information. There are several steps to take when making a choice.

Find a doctor who understands aging. The first issue to consider is whether a doctor is skilled in dealing with an elderly patient. Ideally, your loved one's physician will be a geriatric specialist, who is specially trained to spot the often complex illnesses of the elderly. Some internists and family-practice physicians have extended experience in treating elderly patients. Having a doctor with training and experience in geriatrics will minimize the need to send your loved one to different specialists for tests. When a doctor is trained to treat the elderly, he can more readily distinguish the symptoms of a disease from the normal process of aging. He can also treat acute diseases that occur on top of chronic diseases and is aware of the implications of multiple prescription drugs. It is becoming somewhat easier to find a geriatric doctor since geriatrics is a medical specialty that is expanding. If, however, you cannot find one in your area, consider an internist, a family-practice physician, or a general practitioner who has extensive training in adult medicine. In finding a doctor, it can be helpful to ask people you trust who have experience or contacts with physicians.

Here are some suggested questions to consider as you look for a physician:

Having a doctor with training and experience in geriatrics will minimize the need to send your loved one to different specialists for tests.

- Does she have training or experience working with older people?
- Is he willing to work with other specialists?
- Is she open to second or third opinions?
- Does he appreciate the importance of treating the whole person and not just symptoms?
- Does she have a good understanding of community-based elder-care programs?
- Do you and your elder like and/or trust the doctor?
- Does the doctor treat you and your loved one with respect and invite open communication?

Find a doctor with a good "bedside manner." In most cases, it is good to accompany your elder to the doctor's office to make sure the right questions are asked of the doctor and to note the answers to the questions, along with specific directions, so they can be followed properly. During your visit you can also monitor the way the doctor treats your elder. A good doctor will be patient, thorough, and compassionate toward an elderly patient. You do not want to put your elder under the care of someone who is in a hurry or who seems distracted. The ideal doctor will:

- Communicate well, listening to concerns and answering your questions.
- Emphasize prevention and healthful lifestyle changes to help prevent future medical problems.
- Present a range of treatment options, including risks and benefits.

- Explain the reason for ordering certain tests and report results promptly.
- Refer your elder to specialists when necessary.
- Describe possible symptoms and side effects of treatment.
- Schedule follow-up exams and regular checkups.
- Be willing to recognize and value your spiritual beliefs.

Of course, this is the ideal physician. In the real world, nobody is always ideal. What is important is medical expertise delivered in as humane a way as possible, given the realities of the current pressures on doctors. Also, a good doctor does best with a good patient. It is the patient's responsibility to be honest and to communicate openly with the doctor, as well as to follow the doctor's specific plan.

Find a doctor who views you and your loved one as part of the health-care team. One thing you should convey to your elder's physician is that you are a team player and that you want to work with her to achieve the best results. The doctor should understand that you are not an adversary—although there may be times when you wish to discuss her diagnoses or treatment plans or seek a second opinion. More than anything else, work hard to build a sense of mutual trust and respect between you.

Doctors are often pressed for time, so make the most of your time with the doctor. Have a list of questions prepared beforehand and take

---

A CARING CALL

I took my mother to her doctor for the first time in a year because she was basically not eating (only drinking Ensure) and in a sleeping state most of the time, whether in her bedroom or sitting in the living room. It was a typical visit (not a thorough exam): updating information and asking questions. The doctor gave Mother a prescription for Prozac. That evening he called me at home and said he had looked over a brochure for the one medication she was taking for high blood pressure. He told me not to fill the Prozac prescription and to stop the medication because he wanted to see if possible side effects might be affecting her appetite and mental alertness. I was glad to know that he continued to think about her after we left the office and that he decided to take a different approach at least temporarily.

Jean S.

notes as needed. If a treatment does not seem to be working, discuss it with the doctor and ask for alternatives.

Find out about insurance coverage. Choosing a doctor usually is not dependent on the health-insurance coverage your aging loved one has. Most doctors accept Medicare as a primary payer (the insurance carrier that pays the bills first). Contact Medicare for a handbook that covers Medicare benefits (see appendix). In some instances, it may be helpful to ask the physician how he bills patients and whether he accepts Medicare claims. (Some doctors do not participate in some or all medical managed-care plans, such as health-maintenance organizations [HMOs], preferred-provider organizations [PPOs], and Point of Service plans [POSs], because the insurance companies have decreased payments for services provided under the umbrella of these plans. Choosing such a doctor will mean your elder will have to assume personal financial responsibility for bills.)

Make the most of your time with the doctor. Have a list of questions prepared beforehand and take notes as needed.

Beware of buying specific disease insurance, which can be a waste of money. Policies that are restricted to a single disease, such as cancer, may not be a wise choice simply because your elder could develop a disease or condition that is not covered, such as arthritis or diabetes.

Also, ask which hospital your elder's primary doctor is affiliated with. If your elder needs hospitalization, he will need to be admitted to the hospital where his primary doctor works or has admitting privileges. When choosing your elder's primary physician, investigate whether the doctor takes care of her patients when they are hospitalized. It is often best to have the same primary physician see your elder both in and out of the hospital to maintain the best continuity of care. (For more information, see chapter 10: Financial Care.)

Assess technical skills. If your elder is trying to decide on a surgeon, she should choose one who has a good reputation for technical skill. Encourage your loved one to get a referral from her primary-care physician. If your elder is comfortable with her primary-care physician, she should rely on the doctor's recommendation. Make an appointment with the surgeon and come with a list of questions. Your elder should ask about alternative treatments as well as the possible consequences of waiting.

The American College of Surgeons can tell you whether a surgeon you are considering is a member or fellow of the college (see appendix). A fellow has passed a peer-review evaluation; an associate fellow has undergone less scrutiny.

Consider the doctor's team. There are many types of training for various allied health professionals to be part of the health-care team for your elder. The primary physician chooses what type of support staff she wants to employ. Some hire registered nurses, others hire licensed practical nurses; some hire nurse practitioners, others hire physician's assistants. There is no right or wrong way to do this. But you should discuss with the potential primary-care doctor what role these other allied health professionals might play in the care of your elder, either in the home, office, hospital, or nursing-home setting. How that question is answered may help you and your elder to decide on a primary doctor. Consider some of the health professionals who may be involved in your elder's care:

Licensed practical nurses (L.P.N.) care for the sick, injured, convalescing, and handicapped under the direction of physicians and registered nurses. Typical tasks include taking vital signs, collecting samples from patients for testing, performing routine laboratory tests, and assisting patients with bathing, dressing, and personal hygiene. Requirements vary widely; L.P.N.s need specialized training, which may include an associate degree, and they must pass a licensing exam.

Registered nurses (R.N.) administer treatments, educate patients, and give medicine that has been prescribed by a doctor. They have 2 to 4 years of nursing training and usually work in a doctor's office, clinic, hospital, or community health agency.

Nurse practitioners (N.P.) have additional nursing training, sometimes including gerontological nursing; they do physical exams and diagnostic tests as well as counsel and treat patients. In most states, N.P.s can sometimes prescribe medication under the supervision of a doctor. They may work in a rural clinic, hospital, or other health facility.

Physician assistants (P.A.) take medical histories, do physical exams, and write prescriptions. They must always be under the supervision of a doctor, but they can make house calls or go to nursing homes and hospitals to check on patients and report back to the physician. They usually work in a physician's office, hospital, health clinic, nursing home, or home-health-care agency. Their education includes four years in a university, plus a two- or three-year period of specialized training. Because the P.A. works under the supervision of a doctor, the fees charged usually will reflect the doctor's office fees.

When a Specialist Is Needed

Your elder may need the help of a specialist from time to time. Usually your loved one's primary-care doctor will make the referral to a specialist. To get the best possible care you can for your loved one, you may want to consider a board-certified physician. A board-certified doctor is one who has been certified in a specialized field by one of 24 boards recognized by medical-oversight groups like the American Medical Association. The board-certified doctor has gone through years of specialty training and passed a set of rigorous exams to earn certification. If you want to find out if the specialist is board certified to practice in his field, you can contact the American Board of Medical Specialties (see appendix). ABMS offers the "Certified Doctor Verification Service," a searchable database of board-certified physicians, on their Web site. By entering the physician's name and location, you can find out if he is certified, discover what hospital affiliations he has and what health plans he serves, as well as access links to a home page if he has one. The American Medical Association also has a physician-search service on its Web site (see appendix).

Familiarize yourself with this listing and description of some of the specialists your elder might need:

- **Cardiologist.** An internist who specializes in problems of the heart
- **Cardiac surgeon.** A specialist in heart surgery
- **Dermatologist.** A skin specialist
- **Endocrinologist.** A specialist in disorders of the glands of internal secretion, dealing with issues such as diabetes and thyroid problems

- **Gastroenterologist.** A specialist in diseases of the digestive system
- **General surgeon**
- **Geriatrician.** A specialist in medicine for older people
- **Gynecologist.** A specialist in the female reproductive system
- **Hematologist.** A specialist in disorders of the blood
- **Internist.** A specialist in adult medicine
- **Nephrologist.** A specialist in the function and diseases of the kidneys
- **Neurologist.** A specialist in disorders of the nervous system
- **Oncologist.** A cancer specialist
- **Ophthalmologist.** An eye specialist
- **Orthopedic surgeon.** A specialist in problems of the musculoskeletal system, including bones and spine
- **Otolaryngologist.** A specialist in diseases of the ear, nose, and throat
- **Physiatrist.** A specialist in physical medicine and rehabilitation
- **Psychiatrist.** A specialist in mental health
- **Pulmonologist.** A physician who treats disorders of the lungs and chest
- **Rheumatologist.** A specialist in arthritis and rheumatism
- **Urologist.** A specialist in male and female urinary systems and the male reproductive system

Seeking a Second Opinion

There may be instances in which you will want to get a second opinion on a treatment recommended by your elder's physician. Most doctors have no objection to a second opinion; many welcome it. The American Medical Association's guidelines on second opinions read simply: "A physician should seek consultation upon request; in doubtful or difficult cases; or whenever it appears that the quality of medical care may be enhanced thereby."

Patients have a right to a second opinion (insurance companies may require this) and even a third opinion if the opinion of the patient's doctor and the second-opinion doctor disagree. You may want to seek a second opinion if: surgery is recommended in order to treat a problem or aid in diagnosis; the doctor has no explanation for persistent symptoms; the diagnosis is of a rare, disabling, or potentially fatal illness; the diagnostic tests seem too complex or expensive; or you or your elder feel uncertain about the physician's ability to carry out treatment. When seeking a second opinion, ask your elder's physician to send X rays, medical records, and lab tests to the second-opinion doctor to avoid having duplicate tests.

Medicare pays for a second opinion just as it does for any doctor's service—80 percent of the allowable charge. If your elder is paying out-of-pocket doctor fees, he can choose any doctor to give a second opinion or he can ask for the physician's advice to obtain another doctor's

FINDING GOOD MEDICAL INFORMATION ON THE INTERNET

There are numerous sites that offer good medical information on the Internet. However, health-care consumers should be very cautious. Many Web sites offer information that is accurate but perhaps not complete in scope. There is also, unfortunately, much misinformation, quackery, and even outright medical fraud on the Internet. The best medical-information sites are usually operated under the editorial oversight of a panel of health-care experts or under the auspices of a highly reputable and trusted medical organization (e.g., the American Heart Association).

Regardless of how much good information a particular Web site might offer, it can never replace the care provided by a physician. While some people are tempted to compare their problems with those on a symptom list found on a Web site and then make a self-diagnosis, this can be hazardous. The physician who knows your elder best is in a much better position to provide a careful examination, perform appropriate tests, make an accurate diagnosis, and map out a proper course of treatment.

Many people will diagnose their own problems with information from the Internet then take reams of printouts to the doctor to try to get her to validate their self-diagnoses. Resist this temptation! For many conditions, an accurate diagnosis requires the careful evaluation of a number of different factors. The expertise and information required to make such evaluations cannot always be obtained simply by perusing the Internet. Likewise, while a good medical Web site can give information that might prompt frank discussion about your elder's medical condition with his doctor, it is unrealistic to carry huge volumes of information to your loved one's doctor and expect her to be able to spend an hour talking through it all.

opinion. If your elder belongs to a health-maintenance organization (HMO), however, he may be required to go directly through his primary-care doctor to get a second opinion. If your loved one's physician seems overly hostile or resistant to the request for a second opinion, you and your elder may need to consider finding another primary doctor. Most HMOs allow you to change physicians if you are dissatisfied with the one you are using. On the other hand, HMOs have been dropping Medicare patients in certain categories, such as the elderly. If your elder belongs to a preferred-provider organization (PPO), he will need to choose from a list of doctors within the plan in order to receive optimal insurance coverage. If possible, ask friends or other patients who belong to the same PPO to tell you which physicians they would recommend.

Regardless of how much good information a particular Web site might offer, it can never replace the care provided by your physician.

Ask the Right Questions

Questions are keys when working with the medical caregiving team. Use questions as tools to get the information you need. Before appointments, put your questions in writing, listing primary concerns first. Know what you want to understand when you walk out of the office, and take notes. Be efficient in asking questions.

- Ask questions using the words *how, what,* and *when,* instead of questions that can be answered with a yes or no.
- Always ask about alternative treatments and options.
- When you get answers using the words *probably, may,* or *usually,* ask for explanations.
- Summarize the information you gained, repeating it back at the end of your conversation.
- Ask for corrections and clarification before you leave the appointment.
- If you must telephone, briefly describe the reason for your call and ask when you can expect the doctor to return it.

What if you need information that your aging loved one will not give you? If you seek it directly from the medical professionals, you place them in an awkward position. Their patient has a right to confidentiality. In this situation, you will need to explain to your loved one,

without intimidating her, that you cannot help without her cooperation. Ask for permission to contact her doctor. You may also gain information from:

- The hospital medical library
- National Institutes of Health (see appendix)
- Specialty clinics across the country or organizations related to a
  specific illness (e.g., Alzheimer's Association or American Heart
  Association)
- Your local health department
- A social worker

OTHER HEALTH PROFESSIONALS

Your elder may require medical attention from a number of health professionals. Here are the main categories to keep in mind when coordinating for your elder's care.

Dental Care

Dental care is just as important in old age as it is at younger ages.

Dentists (D.D.S. or D.M.D.) treat oral gum disease and tooth decay, do
checkups, fill cavities, remove teeth, provide dentures, and do oral surgery. For difficult tooth removals, the dentist might refer your loved
one to an oral surgeon.

Endodontists perform root canals and other specialized treatments.

Periodontists treat gum diseases.

Eye Care

Ophthalmologists (M.D. or D.O.) diagnose and treat eye diseases, prescribe glasses and contact lenses, and can prescribe drugs and perform
surgery. They typically treat or perform surgery for cataracts, glaucoma,
and macular degeneration, which are widespread among older people.

Optometrists (O.D.) can diagnose some eye abnormalities but will refer
patients to an ophthalmologist if surgery or medical treatment is

needed. Optometrists also prescribe glasses and contact lenses. Medicare does not cover routine eye examinations or eyeglasses, except prosthetic lenses, if needed, for cataract surgery.

Rehabilitative Care

If your elder has been impaired by an accident, illness, or other disability, she will need rehabilitative care.

Occupational therapists (O.T.) use special activities and assistance to help promote independence in cooking, eating, bathing, dressing, and homemaking. Medicare pays for these services if your elder is in a hospital or skilled nursing facility or is receiving home health care. If your elder has impaired strength, movement, or sensation, her doctor may refer her to a **physical therapist (P.T.)**. Medicare (Part B) covers medically necessary physical therapy and occupational therapy in a doctor's office, as an outpatient, or in the home.

Speech therapists deal with speech and language problems, such as difficulties due to strokes or head injuries. Speech therapists also help determine the safest techniques for consuming foods or liquids to prevent the aspiration of these items into the lungs.

Audiologists test and treat patients for hearing disorders. They dispense hearing aids when needed. Medicare covers speech-language pathology services in a doctor's office, as an outpatient, or in the home but will not cover routine hearing-loss exams or hearing-aid services.

General Care

Pharmacists fill prescriptions and dispense medications as instructed by physicians, dentists, or podiatrists. They have a wealth of knowledge about the uses and side effects of medicines, including nonprescription products. It is important to go to the same pharmacy for all medications to minimize the risk of drug interactions. Outpatient prescription drugs are not covered by Medicare, but this policy may be modified in the future by Congress and the president, depending on the priorities of national politics.

Podiatrists (D.P.M.) diagnose and treat foot diseases and injuries. They also can provide toenail care, make orthotic devices to correct or treat foot problems, do surgery, and prescribe certain drugs. Medicare does not cover routine foot care except when a medical condition affecting the lower limbs (such as diabetes) requires care by a medical professional.

Registered dietitians (R.D.) provide nutrition services and help patients plan a well-balanced diet. Most R.D.s work in hospitals, public-health agencies, doctor's offices, or nursing homes.

Social workers help patients and caregivers find community services and often coordinate care for an individual, such as planning discharge from the hospital. Medicare covers these services in hospitals, home-health-care agencies, and health-maintenance organizations.

What about Alternative Medicine?

This is a sticky question. First, alternative (or complementary) medicine is a broad term that covers things such as acupuncture and certain nutritional supplements that may have various benefits. It can also include practices that are based solely on Eastern philosophies (such as Ayurveda) as well as practices that are controversial from a scientific standpoint (such as homeopathy). In fact, some unscrupulous practitioners offer alternative therapies that are fraudulent and have no demonstrated benefit.

Second, some naturopaths, chiropractors, and practioners of alternative medicine are good at recognizing their limitations and will collaborate with and refer to conventional physicians when appropriate. Others are openly hostile to conventional medicine and medical practitioners.

If you or your elder wish to seek alternative medical care, you should investigate the treatment plan carefully to ensure that it is not rooted in the occult or in a false religion (e.g., crystal therapy, transcendental meditation). Also make sure it has some merit for a particular problem and does not, in fact, harm your elder. Consult your physician beforehand to make sure it will not pose any physical danger. Also, coordinate with your doctor so that he is aware of any herbal or nutritional supplements that your elder might be taking. (Certain supplements can have dangerous side effects when taken in conjunction with various prescription medications. Some herbs can lead to excessive bleeding in patients undergoing surgery.)

Feel free to discuss with a physician any specific illness your elder has to see if an alternative treatment would be appropriate. Too many people assume physicians are against methods such as chiropractic and acupuncture and might be surprised to find that for specific problems that is not necessarily the case.

IF YOUR ELDER MUST BE HOSPITALIZED

Finding a Good Hospital

If you have a choice of hospitals in your area, keep in mind that you will need to choose a hospital where your elder's primary doctor or specialist has admitting privileges. To make sure you are comfortable with the hospital and trust its reputation, consider asking these questions:

- Is the hospital accredited by the Joint Commission on Accreditation of Healthcare Organizations? (See appendix.)
- Does the hospital often treat people with your elder's condition?
- Are the majority of the hospital staff physicians board certified? (About 85 percent of all U.S. doctors are board certified.)
- Does a clinical pharmacist review physician orders?

Preparing for a Hospital Stay

Before your elder checks in to a hospital, he should discuss any concerns, upcoming tests, and treatment plans with his doctor, if possible. It may be helpful for you to accompany him; then you can help him remember or record answers and ask follow-up questions if necessary. To avoid medication mistakes in the hospital, always carry a list of all prescription and nonprescription medications, plus any vitamin supplements, herbal and natural remedies, aspirin, antacids, or bowel products that your elder uses routinely or occasionally. The list should include the name, dosage, and purpose of the drugs.

If you are helping your loved one pack, be sure she brings a bathrobe, nightclothes, slippers, clothes to wear home, personal hygiene items, her health-insurance card or policy number, and a list of names and telephone numbers of family members to contact. Aside from a little money for magazines or sundry items from the gift shop, she should leave cash, credit cards, checkbooks, jewelry, and expensive watches at home or with a trusted friend. Otherwise, ask if there is a hospital safe in which to keep them.

When your elder checks in, the information on his wristband should include his name plus any drug allergies. He also should be visited by a discharge planner or admissions counselor at check-in to discuss payment methods. To prevent mix-ups in doctors' orders, make sure the primary-care physician is coordinating your elder's treatment, especially if multiple doctors and specialists are involved in his care. If

HOSPITAL HELPER

When my mom was admitted to the hospital for back surgery, I rearranged my work schedule so that I could spend some time with her every day. When that became exhausting, I took a two-week leave of absence. My being there was a good thing. I'd come in before noon and stay until after dinner, so that I could help motivate Mom to eat. The nurses didn't have a lot of time to stay and help that much, so I would also wash her up at the sink or in bed, comb her hair, and brush her teeth. I noticed how important it was to her to be clean. These are little things we take for granted, but it was the star of her day to be clean, to have some powder and deodorant on and her teeth brushed.

Mom was in too much pain to ask questions or to understand everything that was going on. She had five or more different doctors—a surgeon, a resident, her primary-care doctor, an anesthesiologist, and specialists. I was glad I could ask the doctors what her condition was, what the surgery would entail, how long the recovery period would be, and what other problems she had and how they were being treated. I answered their questions too. That way my mom didn't have the stress of having to remember everything. Sometimes I needed them to explain procedures in simpler terms. If they seemed in a rush and I felt a little intimidated, I would still ask, because I needed to know what was going on in case something happened to my mom. I prayed a lot for wisdom and the strength to do what I needed to do to help her through that time.

Debra W.

you have questions about a certain test or the risks and benefits of treatment for your elder, ask the doctor or nurse. And if your elder has an advance directive, such as a living will or durable power of attorney for health-care decisions (DPAHCD), the primary physician should have a copy in the patient's medical file.

Planning for Surgery

Usually, your elder should avoid aspirin and any nonsteroidal anti-inflammatory drugs (such as ibuprofen) for one to two weeks before surgery if possible. She also should not take dietary supplements or herbal remedies for two weeks before surgery. Such drugs and supplements may increase the risk of blood loss during and after surgery. Be aware that if your elder is undergoing abdominal surgery, a bowel preparation may be necessary. This is intended to purge the bowels, and it often requires drinking a substantial amount of a liquid preparation, such as Colyte, GoLYTELY, or NuLYTELY (and possibly taking other medications), that induces frequent, watery stools soon after ingestion. Talk with the surgeon about the protocol for receiving preventive antibiotics, transfusions, or pain control if needed. Also, discuss fears and questions your loved one may have.

To avoid medication mistakes in the hospital, always carry a list of your elder's prescription and nonprescription medications, plus any supplements.

Planning for Recovery

If possible, it could be helpful to try to arrange for your elder's postoperative care *before* surgery. Ask the hospital discharge planner or social worker for a list of the medications or assistive-living devices your elder may need at home, information on how to acquire them, and instructions on how to use them. Ask for complete information about convalescing at home. Will any follow-up care be needed? Will your loved one need physical therapy or home health care? Will he need to curtail his regular activities for a while? What course of action should be taken if your loved one has a medical crisis or concern, particularly over a weekend?

The hospital discharge planner is usually a good source of information about rehabilitative services, transportation needs and handicapped-parking designations, senior centers, adult day care, alternative living arrangements, emergency-response systems, home-delivered meals for homebound seniors, and other support services. Even if you do not need it yet, take whatever information is offered and keep it on file for future reference.

Above all, don't neglect prayer before, during, and after your aging loved one's surgery. Pray with your elder, asking the Lord to bless her with His peace, protection, and healing. Ask her pastor and other praying Christians to intercede for your elder, ultimately committing everything to God's perfect will. "The effective, fervent prayer of a righteous man avails much" (James 5:16 NKJV).

The hospital discharge planner is usually a good source of information about rehabilitative services, transportation needs, adult day care, and other support services.

Going Home

Due to insurance requirements, it is common for today's patients to leave the hospital much earlier than in the past. If your elder's discharge seems premature, make a firm objection. A hospital discharge planner or social worker will be responsible for helping your elder make the transition to recover at home.

Pain Control

Be sure to keep your elder's physician informed about any significant pain he may be experiencing. If the pain is severe or chronic, the doctor may need to refer your loved one for additional help. Many hospitals have pain centers directed by physicians who specialize in pain management.

There are also a number of organizations dedicated to promoting pain management. The American Academy of Pain Management (AAPM), for example, can provide a listing of physicians in your area who are skilled in pain management. The AAPM Web site contains a searchable database for you to use in locating a pain manager in your community. All you have to do is enter your zip code in a search window and you will be provided with a list you can download and print.

In addition, the American Pain Society provides information on pain control plus a listing of other resources designed to help a patient deal with a specific illness or ailment. The American Chronic Pain Association is a network of 800 peer-support groups. Other good resources include the American Academy of Hospice and Palliative Medicine and the American Society of Pain Management Nurses. (For more information on pain control, see the appendix for addresses and Web site information. Also see "Controlling Pain" on pages 97-100.)

COMMUNITY-BASED RESOURCES

Throughout your caregiving journey, whether you are just beginning to provide minimal help or are deeply involved with intensive care, it is always important to seek out community services; they can spell the difference between surviving and not surviving as a caregiver. Some programs and services are free or based on ability to pay; others can be costly. They may be funded by client fees, Medicare, Medicaid, government funds, managed-care plans, employers, nonprofit organizations, or private health insurance. They can be found in many communities of the nation.

If your elder is reluctant to use outside assistance, you might suggest getting help for the sake of the caregiver. An aging mother or father might be more willing to accept help if he or she knows it will benefit you. Programs that may be of interest to you and your elder are discussed below.

Access to Services

• **Area Agency on Aging.** To get access to senior services, your best bet is to contact the Area Agency on Aging (AAA) that serves your community. More than 600 AAAs nationwide have been established to coordinate the services needed by older people in their areas. (The State Units on Aging, which are overseen by the federal Administration on Aging, can also be a resource.) To reach your AAA, look in the white pages of your phone book under "Community Services" or in the yellow pages under a heading such as "Social Service Organizations." Or call the Eldercare Locator's toll-free number (1-800-677-1116) to identify the AAA nearest you. The AAA should be able to help you or your elder locate medical services, financial-planning aid, and other valuable resources—or at least point you in the right direction. For a state-by-state listing of the most current commissions on aging, see "Current Commissions on Aging" at the back of this book.

- **Eldercare Locator.** The National Association of Agencies on Aging has established an Eldercare Locator service. This program taps into a nationwide network of organizations specializing in elder care. It can provide referrals on a variety of topics, including Alzheimer's hot lines, adult day care, nursing-home assistance, Meals On Wheels, fraud, in-home-care complaints, elder abuse/protective services, and more. (Call toll-free 1-800-677-1116, or see appendix for contact information.)
- **Crisis and emergency.** Humanitarian organizations, such as the American Red Cross, provide emergency relief to victims of disaster, such as vouchers to purchase food, clothing, medicine, eyeglasses, and other essentials, and financial assistance for rent and medical bills.
- **Medical attention.** Call 911 or go to the nearest hospital for immediate emergency treatment.

Financial and Legal Assistance

- **Economic assistance agencies.** Eligible seniors can find needed help for health care and community services by contacting their local Area Agency on Aging or the Eldercare Locator (see appendix).
- **Legal services.** Seniors seeking legal help regarding advance directives, government benefits, landlord/tenant disputes, and other issues can check with their local Area Agency on Aging for information. The AAA can also refer seniors to legal-aid offices that provide free legal counseling for low-income elderly. Your county's senior services might provide names of attorneys who

ACCEPTING HELP

It was hard for my dad to accept help. He had always done everything himself. It took all our urging to get him to call and get some help. I think it was a sign of defeat for him, admitting that Mother wasn't going to get better. It required a change of habit just to have other people helping. It was a difficult process for him, but once he got used to people being there he really appreciated it.

Chris M.

will prepare wills at reduced cost. For more information, see chapter 11.

• **Low-income home-energy assistance.** This is a governmental plan for financially eligible seniors. For help with energy bills, check with the local social-service agency in your county.

• **Social security district offices.** To contact social security, look in the white pages of the phone book or check the Internet at <www.ssa.gov>.

General Assistance

• **Information and referral agencies.** Professionally trained staff help to identify individual needs and link seniors with available resources (e.g., social-service agencies, churches, government bodies, civic groups, legal and medical organizations, and case managers). Contact your county's department of human resources or your local Area Agency on Aging. The Eldercare Locator also offers referrals for senior services (see appendix).

• **Social-services agencies.** Sponsored by government, churches, or associations, these agencies provide many services for elderly people.

• **Private, nationally based, nonprofit organizations.** You can obtain a lot of helpful information about specific diseases or health care from specialty organizations that deal with those matters, such as the American Diabetes Association, the Alzheimer's Association, or the National Cancer Institute (see appendix). The American Association of Retired Persons (AARP) has state offices and offers free publications on a range of critical issues for older persons and their caregivers. Call 1-800-424-3410 for guides to these publications. AARP's services include information about insurance, financial matters, tax assistance, legal and disability issues, Legal Services Network, AARP motoring plan, on-line services, pharmacy service, health-care options, driver education, grandparent information center, outreach support, and caregiving. The Christian Association of PrimeTimers (CAP) offers special rates on insurance, health-care discounts, interstate-

To get access to senior services, your best bet is to contact the Area Agency on Aging that serves your community.

moving discounts, a bed-and-breakfast travel club, Christian cruises and tours, senior conferences, and ministry opportunities (see appendix).

Health or Medical Needs

- **Hospitals.** Most hospitals have a variety of services for seniors. See your local hospital's Web site or call the public-relations office for more information.
- **Illness and disability associations or treatment centers.** These offer various services, rehabilitation, and support groups.
- **Low-income medical care.** Some community clinics provide primary-care services for seniors enrolled in Medicaid or who have low incomes and no medical insurance, including no Medicare. Contact your department of public aid to inquire about eligibility requirements and availability.
- **Medical-equipment suppliers.** Talk to your elder's doctor or a hospital social worker to get information on home medical equipment/supplies, such as canes, wheelchairs, oxygen tanks, and products for diabetes management. Or pick up a claim form from your medical-appliance supplier or doctor. For more information, see chapter 15.
- **Visiting nurses.** Public-health nurses may make telephone assessments, then home visits, if necessary, to assess a senior's situation and to make referrals to community resources. Call your local public-health department for help. Visiting Nurse Association is a national home health agency that provides skilled nursing, rehabilitation services, IV therapy, wound care, and other medical and social services in the home.
- **Visiting in-home physicians.** Some communities and private organizations provide in-home medical care (non-life-threatening) for homebound and elderly patients who cannot be transported to a physician's office or an urgent-care center. Call your local Area Agency on Aging for more information.
- **Screenings and immunizations.** Blood-pressure screenings and wellness-promotion services may be held periodically at public-health centers, senior centers, adult day-care centers,

congregate meal sites, senior housing and retirement communities, churches, and health fairs at malls. Breast- and cervical-cancer screening may be provided by your public-health department. Flu clinics are held in the fall to protect seniors from the influenza virus. Check your local newspaper for locations and schedules.

- **Private, nationally based, nonprofit organizations.** You can obtain a lot of helpful information about specific diseases or health care from specialty organizations that deal with those matters, such as the American Diabetes Association, the National Cancer Institute, or the Alzheimer Society (see appendix). Note: Use caution with advice from the Internet; sometimes it is useful, but in many cases it is not accurate or comprehensive.

Home Support Services

- **In-house or out-of-home respite care.** For short-term relief from constant caregiving, contact your local Area Agency on Aging, a nursing home, or church for referrals.
- **Homemaker services.** Cooking, shopping, laundry, and light housekeeping services are performed in the elder's home for a fee. Contact your senior center or local Area Agency on Aging for a list of referrals.
- **Home-delivered meals.** This service is provided for homebound

---

RELATIVELY SPEAKING

There was an elderly couple I was providing some nursing care for. The husband wasn't able to mow the lawn anymore and he finally allowed his wife to call a local senior-service organization and get some help. The organization contacted a person who had just signed up to help and it ended up being the couple's son-in-law. The son-in-law knew by the address that it was his in-laws, but they didn't know it until he showed up. They laughed about it for weeks, saying they finally got up the nerve to call senior services when what they should have done was call their relatives—namely, their daughter and son-in-law.

Sharon N.

seniors who are unable to shop, prepare meals, or attend a senior dining center. Check with local senior centers, Meals On Wheels, or your local Area Agency on Aging.

- **Home-health-care services.** Check into an accredited home health agency for certified care. It may include rehabilitation therapy, food and nutritional help, and other services. See chapter 15 for more information.
- **Geriatric-care manager.** This person may be a registered nurse or social worker within a home-health-care agency. He or she does assessments and can help to coordinate the care of an elder, especially if you live far away from your loved one. Contact the National Association of Professional Geriatric Care Managers (see appendix).
- **Home repair and renovation.** Some programs offer financial assistance to help seniors install door locks, grab bars, and other safety features so that they can remain in the home environment as long as possible. Check with your county's senior services.
- **Senior-citizen's services.** From case-management services and personal care to help with filling out paperwork and weatherizing your elder's home, myriad senior services can be found through your local Area Agency on Aging.
- **Stores that deliver.** Homebound seniors may be able to get their medications, groceries, and other goods delivered. Contact a pharmacy, social worker, or Area Agency on Aging for more information.
- **Monitoring programs.** Some senior centers, churches, and community agencies offer telephone check-in services, in which a volunteer calls your aging loved one to make social contact and check on health status. Some geriatric-care service organizations will arrange to visit your loved one on a daily, weekly, or monthly basis for a fee, serving as a surrogate family member to the elder. This service is especially comforting to long-distance caregivers and family members who are out of state.
- **Hospice.** For pain control and supportive home care in the final stages of life, hospice care is available. For more information, see chapter 18.

Housing

Where an older person lives has tremendous impact on his life. Most older people want to stay in their own home as long as possible. But sometimes this is not possible. Listed below are a few examples of housing for older people that can assist in meeting their needs. A more complete description of housing is found in chapter 16.

- **Rental assistance.** Limited funding is available for subsidized rental housing to income-eligible elderly through the government's Section 8 rental-assistance program. Some apartment complexes also offer subsidized housing. Contact your county's housing authority or senior services for more information.
- **Shared housing.** Some communities have programs to match unrelated seniors who are seeking to share a home with a compatible roommate. Contact your local Area Agency on Aging for information, or see chapter 16.
- **Continuing care retirement community (CCRC).** This living arrangement guarantees older adults will have a continuum of care, including independent living, assisted living, and nursing care if necessary. Sometimes called a "life-care community," CCRCs require an entrance fee and monthly maintenance fees. For more information, see chapter 16.
- **Congregate housing.** This is frequently a private home unit (room or apartment) within a residential facility that provides shared activities and services (formerly called "home for the aged," "retirement home," "old people's home," and "sheltered housing"). Congregate living is a bridge between independent living and the kind of care a senior may eventually need in a full-service nursing home. For more information, see chapter 16.
- **Assisted-living communities.** This type of housing is for people who do not require round-the-clock skilled nursing care but are typically too frail to live alone. For more information, see chapter 16.
- **Nursing facilities.** A nursing home provides skilled care, intermediate care, and sheltered care for people who need medical,

nursing, dietary, and rehabilitative services or supervision and personal care. For more information, see chapter 17.

Insurance

- **Medicare.** This federal health-insurance program is the primary insurance for hospital and medical expenses for seniors. For more information, obtain a Medicare handbook; to apply, visit your local Social Security Administration office. There are programs that can help Medicare beneficiaries with very low incomes and few assets to pay their Medicare premiums. Supplemental policies can also be purchased to supplement gaps in Medicare insurance coverage, such as prescription drugs. (For more information, see chapter 10: Financial Care, or contact your county or local senior-services department.)
- **Medicaid.** This national health-care program for the poor is partially funded by the federal government but administered by state governments. (See chapter 10: Financial Care, or contact your state's public-aid office or human-services department.)
- **"Medigap" (Medicare Supplemental) insurance.** This can be purchased to cover some of the costs not paid by traditional Medicare, such as the coinsurance payments for doctors' and hospital services. Private insurance companies sell Medigap insurance to people on Medicare. They offer ten standardized

TRACKING DOWN SERVICES

The frustration for me was knowing that services exist but not being able to easily track them down. For example, someone told me about a free service for stroke victims that my mother probably qualified for. It took me a lot of digging and several phone calls to locate the program and get my mother signed up. It was a time-consuming search but worth the effort; three days a week my mom was able to talk with other people who'd had strokes during a half-hour phone conference call. They would discuss their symptoms and encourage each other's progress in rehabilitation.

Fran H.

policies, each varying in price and benefits. Contact your state's insurance department to find out which insurance companies in your state offer the plan your elder prefers. Then compare the premiums and see whether the Medigap insurer will arrange for Medicare to file your elder's Medigap claims automatically, which can save time.

- **Qualified Medicare Beneficiary (QMB) program.** In this program, state governments pay the Medicare premiums, copayments, and deductibles for very low-income elderly people who cannot afford to pay them. Those who receive Supplemental Security Income (SSI) are usually eligible for the QMB program.

Long-Distance Caregiving

- **Case manager or geriatric-care manager.** This could be a registered nurse or social worker within a home-health-care agency or other agency serving older people. The case manager does assessments and can help to coordinate the most appropriate and cost-effective care of an elder. This service is especially helpful if you live far away from your loved one. In some areas of the nation, case-management services are offered on a nonprofit or low-cost basis to help keep elderly people out of institutions as long as possible. For more information, see chapter 15. Also, contact the Eldercare Locator, a federal, nationwide telephone referral service (see appendix) or the National Association of Professional Geriatric Care Managers (see appendix).

Long-Term Care

- **Ombudsman services.** Funded by the Older Americans Act, these organizations receive, investigate, and resolve complaints made by elderly residents of long-term-care facilities or by their loved ones. For more information, see chapter 17.
- **Hospice.** For pain control and supportive care in homes and institutions in the final stages of life, hospice care is widely available. For more information, see chapter 18.

Nutrition

- **Home-delivered meals.** This service is provided for homebound seniors five days a week. Check with local senior centers, Meals On Wheels, or your Area Agency on Aging.
- **Congregate meals.** Balanced meals and opportunities to socialize may be provided in senior centers, community centers, churches, and group housing.
- **Grocery delivery.** For a fee, your elder can have groceries delivered to the door. Contact your local Area Agency on Aging for more information.

Recreation and Social Programs

- **Adult day-care programs.** Less expensive than institutional care, these services are for seniors who need daytime supervision, social interaction, and assistance with more than one activity of daily living, such as eating, walking, toileting, bathing, or dressing. Look for adult day-care centers in the phone book or call a hospital, church, or your local senior-services agency.
- **Senior centers.** These government/private-funded centers offer a range of services such as congregate meals, nutrition programs, adult day care, legal and income counseling, health screening, housing assistance, and group activities. Most are available at low cost or free of charge to seniors.
- **Volunteer programs.** These can include transportation, home-delivered meals, church programs, and other helpful services. Contact the local Area Agency on Aging, a senior center, or a church for more information.
- **Foster-grandparent programs.** Funded through the Area Agencies on Aging, this program provides companionship to the elderly by making them foster grandparents.

Transportation

- **Transportation services that have wheelchair-accessible vehicles.** Transportation primarily to doctor appointments, medical facilities, or local government offices is provided by a variety of agencies and public or private organizations, including the

American Red Cross and the Department of Transportation. Many senior centers, day-care centers, and churches provide their own transportation for seniors. Some counties provide subsidized taxi services to low-income residents. See chapter 15 for more information. Or contact your municipality, park district, township, or county to find out about subsidized transportation programs.

DEVELOP YOUR PLAN

Whether you are new at the caregiving role or have been involved with caring for an aging loved one for years, it is never too late to make a plan as you seek out services for your loved one.

Pick up the phone. The phone can be your best friend in finding help. Besides calling your local Area Agency on Aging for referrals, call your local senior center and ask them what services are available. Or make an appointment to visit the center and have your questions answered. Be persistent. It may take a lot of phone calls and a lot of questions to find the answers and help you need.

Practice good organization. In her book *The Aging Parent Handbook* (HarperCollins, 1997), Virginia Schomp recommends keeping a notebook or a file box for a resource system. Have a page or a card for each organization you call and jot down the name of the person you talked to and what services are offered. Organize your thoughts before you call. Jot down an introductory sentence. Write down the questions you would like to ask and leave space for the answers.

Schomp offers this list of potential questions:

- What services does the agency provide?
- What are the qualifications and training of the staff?
- What are the eligibility requirements?
- What is the application process?
- Is there a waiting period?
- What are the fees?
- Is financial aid available?
- Are there brochures or other literature describing the program?

Photocopy paperwork. If you are coordinating your elder's health-care expenses, keep photocopies of all receipts, bills, check stubs, and communication relating to health care in case a question about a bill or benefit arises. If you are told that your prescription receipts never reached the public-aid office, for example, your copies may help prove your elder has met her monthly deductible.

Pursue advice from people you know. Ask advice of the professionals you already know. Your doctor may be aware of special services or may refer you to the best health-care workers in your community. Your minister may be familiar with area nursing homes that have good reputations or retirement communities occupied by older, satisfied Christians. Your attorney may be able to refer you to experts in elder law. Pray for wisdom and ask questions of your friends, coworkers, and church members. So many people are in caregiving situations; you should be able to find someone going through similar experiences.

Ask, and it will be given to you; seek, and you will find; knock, and it will be opened to you. MATTHEW 7:7 NKJV

CHAPTER 10

Buy the truth and do not sell it; get wisdom,
discipline and understanding. PROVERBS 23:23 NIV

Getting Help:
Financial Care

B efore Donna's father died, her mother was hospitalized with two bad bouts of pneumonia and the bills were piling up—literally. "She would just keep them," says Donna. "She didn't give them to my dad; she didn't give them to me. She just held on to them." So after Donna's dad died, collection agencies began calling.

Because Donna had spent several years as a visiting nurse, she knew about a program that allows Colorado residents who are not eligible for Medicaid and cannot afford medical care to get help at a reduced rate. The Colorado Indigent Care Program allows those in need to pay according to a sliding scale. The state then provides partial reimbursement to participating hospitals and clinics. Donna organized her mom's unpaid bills and took all the paperwork down to the hospital. Because of the indigent care program, she was able to work out a copayment plan.

"Financial help is out there, but getting it takes a tremendous amount of time, because you have to have all kinds of records and cut through piles of red tape," says Donna. "Unless older people have someone to help them, it is really hard to take advantage of programs like these."

———— ✧ ————

Like Donna, you may be concerned about your aging loved one's financial security. You may wonder if he will outlive his retirement savings—

and possibly will need to dip into yours. Other questions also arise: Are the bills being paid? Which ones are covered by Medicare? Does your elder need supplemental health insurance? Perhaps the biggest financial question you face as a caregiver is knowing how and when to get involved with managing your elder's money matters.

These concerns are not unique. Some seniors, due to infirmity or age, find it increasingly difficult to manage their own affairs. Others may be able to cover their regular living expenses but would find it impossible to afford a lengthy stay in a long-term-care facility. Although many seniors with limited incomes are eligible for certain benefit and assistance programs, many may not know how to participate. Lengthy, complex forms, uncertainty about where to apply, and varying eligibility requirements are just a few of the obstacles that keep seniors from getting government benefits. Consequently, it often falls on caregivers to ensure that their loved ones are getting available services and benefits. Evaluating your loved one's medical coverage and finances in light of available resources and rising costs will help you and your elder to prepare for the future.

RISING COST OF RETIREMENT

Your aging loved one may be facing a financial dilemma as she moves into her later years. She may have carefully planned for her retirement, using pension funds, stock-market investments, social security, home equity, or other sources of income to help her maintain a comfortable standard of living. Yet, your elder may be caught in what is called the "longevity-inflation" squeeze. Medical science and improved diet have extended the lives of many older Americans. But the longer a person lives, the more likely she will be to deal with reduced income and chronic health problems. (Women, in particular, live longer and may outlive their money.)

Inflation, stock-market downturns, and medical expenses may have eroded your loved one's retirement dollars. The ever-increasing cost of living means some retired seniors have an ever-shrinking income and diminishing assets. The money your loved one has saved may not pay for current or future needs. Inflation can decrease the real value of assets such as bonds, checking accounts, savings accounts, and some insurance policies. Pensions, as well as the earning levels of employed older persons, may lag behind inflation. Social security increases with inflation, but with fewer younger people paying into the system, there is political pressure to put a cap on these increases. The inflated cost of health care can devastate an elderly person's budget. Some elderly people simply run out of money.

The cost of health care is a big concern for the elderly. In 1997, older persons averaged $2,855 in out-of-pocket health-care expenses, compared to $1,576 in out-of-pocket costs for those under age sixty-five. The elderly go to the doctor more than twice as often as younger people (11.7 visits versus 4.9 visits as of 1997) and have hospital stays averaging 6.8 days, as opposed to 5.5 days for people under sixty-five.[1]

The single largest economic threat to the elderly today is the potential need for long-term nursing-home care. Costs range between $36,000 and $60,000 a year or higher. The principal government program available for long-term care is Medicaid, but older Americans are required to "spend down" into poverty to qualify for it. For 70 percent of single older Americans, this "spend down" occurs within 13 weeks of being admitted to an institution. This is humiliating after working a lifetime to pay bills, raise children, support social institutions, pay taxes, and maintain a fair standard of living.

Families, not institutions, provide 80 to 90 percent of the personal care needed by the elderly.

It is clear, however, that adult children do not routinely simply turn aging family members over to an institution. Two-thirds of older people who require help with activities of daily living get no paid assistance. Families, not institutions, provide 80 to 90 percent of the personal care needed by the elderly, according to the U.S. Census Bureau. This is due to government cuts in the early 1980s that reduced entitlements and downsized services by 20 percent. Even so, Americans have typically been willing to do what is best for their aging loved ones.

PLANNING FOR THE FUTURE

If you are concerned that your loved one may be facing financial trouble, it is important to assess the situation. First, make sure your elder is comfortable sharing personal information with you. If not, you may need to consider using a financial advisor, accountant, or attorney as a neutral third party to help you talk about finances with your loved one.

WHO IS POOR AMONG THE ELDERLY?

The overall poverty rate has declined among the elderly since the late 1950s, yet many older Americans remain at risk—especially older women, minority elderly, the less educated, those living alone, the oldest-old (age 85 and up), and those without housing equity.

The U.S. Census Bureau in 1998 estimated that there are 3.4 million seniors who live below the poverty line—10.5 percent of the senior population. The federal poverty line is adjusted yearly for annual cost-of-living increases and family size. In 2000, for example, the poverty line was $17,050 for a family of four. (This figure excludes noncash public assistance and the Earned Income Tax Credit program.) For all older persons reporting income in 1998, 36 percent reported less than $10,000.

Women. Among the poorest people in America are single elderly women, including widowed and divorced women. In fact, the loss of a husband often marks the point of economic reversal for the surviving wife. At that point, many women experience near-poverty for the first time in their lives. Single elderly women derive 51 percent of their income from social security (compared to 39 percent for unmarried men) and have smaller pensions than men, because they generally earned lower wages and were in the workforce for fewer years. (Elderly married women fare better; social security contributes 36 percent of their income.)[1] Minority women and those 85 and older are cause for particular concern, because their income and assets are often insufficient to meet their normal needs and completely inadequate to handle the expenses of a catastrophic illness or long-term care.

Minorities. Elderly African-Americans are at more risk of being in poverty than whites, according to the Social Security Administration. In 1990, for example, they were more than three times more likely to be poor than whites. Elderly Latinos also face serious financial hardships. Among elderly Latinos, 33.5 percent were poor or near poor, compared with 16.4 percent of elderly whites.

Oldest-old. Those age 85 and up are at greater risk of poverty than people who are more recently retired. In 1990, for example, 20.2 percent of the oldest-old were classified as poor. When those who are "near poor" (income between poverty level and 125 percent of this level) are added to this group, the figure goes up to 24.9 percent.

Women and Retirement Security, a report prepared by the National Economic Council Interagency Working Group on Social Security, Social Security Administration, Office of Policy (October 1998).

Once you have the go-ahead, begin by helping your loved one calculate the total value of all his assets, such as savings, investments, and real estate. Then subtract all debts and outstanding loans. (You may want to get the names and phone numbers of your elder's financial professionals, in case of an emergency.) Next, calculate your elder's income, including pension, social security, and income from investments and retirement accounts. Then add up the monthly expenses, including housing, food, utilities, insurance premiums, property taxes, federal and state taxes, clothing, transportation, medical bills, and other costs. (You may find it helpful to review past entries in his checkbook.)

Now ask questions to see what kind of financial shape your loved one is in. How much of his savings, if any, is being spent each month? Can he eliminate any expenses? Are there other sources of money available (e.g., cashing in a life-insurance policy, selling items or properties)? What about health coverage? Does your loved one have Medicare or Medicaid and any supplemental insurance coverage? Keep in mind that too little insurance can put your loved one at great financial risk. But the older your loved one gets, the more likely he will be to become ineligible or unable to afford the premiums for certain types of insurance.

To locate local professional agencies that can help your elder resolve a financial matter, you can contact the Eldercare Locator, a free, nationwide directory-assistance service (see appendix). Local government and nonprofit agencies can provide information and referrals without charge. For state and county organizations, check the government section of the white pages under Aging, or go to the National Association of Area Agencies on Aging's Web site (see appendix).

FINANCIAL PLANNING

After having to put my mom in a nursing home, I realized I needed to think about selling her home and having a garage sale to liquidate her assets. I was doing the financial planning for her and knew about how long we had before the money ran out. I had to estimate what it was going to cost us for medicine and care at the nursing facility. As it turned out, she ended up passing away probably eighteen months before she would have run out of her funds.

Jim B.

Sources of Income for the Elderly

Typical sources of income for elderly persons may include social security, Supplemental Security Income, pensions, savings and investments, reverse mortgage, and work.

Social security. According to the Social Security Administration (SSA), as many as 9 out of 10 retired people receive social-security benefit payments each month. Nearly 45 million receive old-age, survivors', and disability benefits from the system. Social security was not designed to provide all the resources an older person needs in retirement, yet it is the only source of income for 18 percent of beneficiaries.[2]

If your aging loved one is signing up for social-security benefits, he should visit the local social-security office or call their toll-free national telephone number. (It can all be done by phone. See appendix for social-security information.) They will need your elder's social-security card or number, the most recent W-2 form from work, and a birth certificate or other proof of age and U.S. citizenship or eligible noncitizen status. Checks are deposited directly into your elder's bank account, so he will also need to provide the name of the bank and the account number in which to deposit the checks.

Supplemental Security Income (SSI). This program, funded by general taxes (not social-security taxes), provides cash assistance for old, disabled, or blind persons who have little or no income. A person must meet income and asset tests before being admitted into this program.

Pensions. Five categories of pension plans cover less than half of all American retirees and workers: 1) Private pensions; 2) State and local public-employee pensions; 3) Federal civilian-employee pensions; 4) Military retirement pensions; 5) the Railroad Retirement System.

Private pension plans, which are the most common category, are undergoing significant changes. Up until the mid-1980s, the typical pension was a "defined-benefit" plan. Under this pension plan, the worker is guaranteed specific retirement benefits from the employer. A new approach has now been introduced called the "defined-contribution" plan. This type of plan places the responsibility for retirement funding on the employee. It allows the employee to set aside part of her wages in 401(k) accounts for her retirement. Employees can contribute to these plans but are not required to do so. In some instances, employers match or partially match employee contributions. More than 10 million workers are covered by 401(k)s.

Savings and investments. Income from investments in stocks, bonds, mutual funds, or property is a major source of funds for the elderly. Two-thirds of the elderly receive such income, according to the National Academy of Social Insurance. The elderly person who "saves" does so by investing his funds into savings bonds, annuities, medical savings accounts, and regular savings accounts.

Reverse mortgage. If your aging loved one is a homeowner and needs extra income to be able to remain in her home, she may qualify for a reverse mortgage or home-equity conversion mortgage. By securing a loan from a banking institution against the equity in her home, minus what is still owed on the house, the senior homeowner receives the loan in the form of monthly checks, a lump sum, a line of credit, or a combination of these options. The loan is due for repayment when your elder permanently moves out or dies. At that time, the home is sold and the profits from the sale are used to pay off the loan. (For more information on reverse mortgages, see chapter 15: Helping Your Elder Remain at Home.)

Work. In 1999, 28 percent of men and 18.4 percent of women 65 to 69 had income from work. For those 70 and older, only 11.7 percent of men and 5.5 percent of women had any income from work. In the U.S. there used to be a trend toward earlier retirement among men; this was due to many factors, including dropping eligibility for social-security benefits from age 65 to age 62 in the early 1960s. For many, pensions began to be a major factor leading to early retirement. This is changing as employers provide fewer and fewer pension benefits.

The more recent trend to continue employment has been due to the elimination of mandatory retirement laws, liberalization of—and for those over 65 the elimination of—the social-security "earnings test," and the need for many to supplement their incomes. There are significant financial benefits for a senior who continues to work full-time. Working even part-time can improve an older adult's quality of life. But an older person who retires early and works part-time may face financial penalties. For those ages 62 through 64, the Social Security Administration reduces benefits by one dollar for every two dollars of wage and salary income above $10,080 per year. Fortunately, a new law eliminates that rule for people between 65 and 69 who used to lose one dollar in benefits for every three dollars in wages above $17,000 a year. Now people who are age 65 and older may earn as much as they like and not lose any social-security benefits.

Now people who are age 65 and older may earn as much as they like and not lose any social-security benefits.

Tax-relief programs for older homeowners. These programs help elderly persons stay in their own homes. "Circuit-breaker programs," for example, provide tax cuts or refunds for elderly people when property taxes rise above a certain percentage of their household income. Homestead exemption programs allow a fixed-percentage reduction in the assessed valuation of an older person's residence. Contact a tax accountant or your local Area Agency on Aging to find out more about tax-relief programs in your state.

INVESTMENT OPTIONS

In order to do financial planning for your aging loved one, you will need to have a basic understanding of the various kinds of investments available. You likely will need more information than we can provide in this book before making investment choices.

Stocks or equity securities are ownership shares in a company and the right to share in its profits. Stocks sometimes pay their shareholders dividends, which are a partial distribution of earnings. Over the long term, stocks have had the highest return on investment, but their value can fluctuate greatly, putting that part of a person's nest egg at risk.

Bonds are fixed-income securities. When you purchase a bond, you are lending your money to a company or government entity for a year or more in return for interest payments. When the bond matures at the end of a set period of time (up to 30 years or more), the borrower returns your original investment to you. With a bond, you do not receive future profits from the company or government agency. An investment in high-grade or government bonds can provide your parent with a steady income with little risk if held to maturity. Nevertheless, caution needs to be exercised in investing in bonds that are considered "junk bonds" or whose ratings suggest there is significant risk involved. Also, keep in mind that bond funds and individual bonds that are sold before maturity will fluctuate in value just like stocks and stock funds.

Short-term fixed-income products include money market, U.S. Treasury bills, and Certificates of Deposit (CDs). These are relatively low-risk investments that preserve the principal while generating a modest return.

A mutual fund is a collection of stocks, bonds, or other investments owned by a group of investors and managed by a professional investment company. The risk level is proportionate to the type of investment that is in the fund and the management style.

Fixed annuities are tax-deferred savings-and-investment income vehicles for individuals. Until you begin distributions, the principal is secure and the insurance company determines how much interest it pays each year. Once it is annuitized, you typically receive monthly guaranteed income for as long as you live, but the payout can actually be structured to provide anything from a lump-sum payment to monthly income payable for different periods of time. Annuities are popular among elders because they are age specific and the payout is higher the older you begin distributions. You can also buy them when you are

MONEY CHALLENGES

I was faced with the financial responsibility of handling my mother's affairs when she passed away. My mother was working on a revised will and estate plan at the time. The will wasn't signed so I had to get another lawyer and then another to get it taken care of. You just don't know what the right decision is in a situation like that.... My folks have a little duplex, and rentals can be a problem—a real problem. I was concerned about cash-flow problems for my dad. I finally put the rental up for sale because it's a real headache dealing with tenants who don't pay their rent. And then there was the problem of getting funeral expenses paid. Getting that paid off was a challenge.

Sharon W.

younger and let the principal grow tax-deferred until you need it or you can buy them at the time you actually want distributions. There are several important issues to consider, such as age limitations for the initial purchase, the financial strength of the insurance company that issues the annuity, and the tax implications of when and how you take distributions, so working with a competent and trustworthy insurance agent or financial planner is important.

Variable annuities are similar in many regards to fixed annuities. The main difference is that, as the name implies, a variable annuity's investment returns are variable and dependent on the returns of a portfolio of stocks and bonds. The owner selects the investments from among the options within the annuity and can change the portfolio selections as his needs change. Variable annuities are subject to market risk and possible principal loss. They also may have surrender charges and carry higher internal costs that require you to hold the annuity for 10 or more years before the benefit is greater than simply investing in a mutual fund outside of a tax-deferred variable annuity. For these reasons a variable annuity may not be suitable for an elder and it is important to work with a trustworthy advisor who is not dependent on selling you an annuity for his income.

A charitable-gift annuity provides the greatest financial benefit to older donors, who receive the highest rates of return.

A charitable-gift annuity is similar to an annuity, except that when the term is complete, usually at death, the balance goes to a charity. With this option, the client transfers assets to the foundation. In exchange, the foundation agrees to pay a specified annuity amount for life. There are favorable tax incentives for setting up a charitable-gift annuity. Because it is age sensitive, it provides the greatest financial benefit to older donors, who receive the highest rates of return.

Individual retirement accounts (IRA and Roth IRA) are privately-funded retirement plans that provide a tax-deferred shelter. Money withdrawn from a normal IRA is taxed. With a normal IRA, your parent can deduct the contributions from taxable income, and any earnings can be tax deferred. Your loved one begins paying taxes on the money when it is removed from the IRA. For all IRAs, there is a 10 percent penalty if the funds are removed before the age of 59½.

In a Roth IRA, your elder cannot deduct her contributions, but all money removed is tax free. Because funds from the Roth IRA are tax free, your loved one can end up in a lower tax bracket when she collects, thus lowering taxes on other retirement income. There may be significant state-tax benefits for your elder to convert to a Roth IRA. Check with your tax advisor.

What is the best way for your elder to begin withdrawing funds from his retirement accounts? Some financial experts suggest that it is better to first withdraw money from taxable accounts and postpone withdrawing money from tax-deferred accounts. That way, an IRA investment, for example, can continue to compound tax free and earn him more money to live on. (If your elder has a traditional IRA, he must begin making withdrawals by age 70½; a Roth IRA has no such restriction.)

Investment Planning

To continue a standard of living many middle-class workers are accustomed to, the average retiree today has to provide about 60 percent of his living expenses, while social security pays for the rest.[3] This brings questions to mind:

- Does your loved one have enough money to last his lifetime, based on pensions, assets, savings, and social security?
- Does your elder have enough insurance or cash to carry him through a medical or other emergency?
- Will there be anything to leave for your elder's heirs?
- Will your elder need to keep working past age 65 to amass enough money to retire comfortably?
- Is a pension available? Is there any adjustment for inflation? Will it continue to pay the surviving spouse if the pension holder dies?

Now is the time for your elder to evaluate her retirement portfolio and consider the best way to diversify her investments if investments are a major part of retirement income. Remember that your elder is probably past her earning years, and the amount of savings and investments is, more than likely, all there will be. Investing is personal. It doesn't matter what your neighbors are doing. Invest according to your elder's needs, circumstances, and temperament. The less your elder is dependent on any one investment growing as she hopes or providing the income she expects, the more likely she will be to maintain her financial independence.

Use a Financial Planner

If you do not feel competent enough to help your aging loved one on your own, you can contact a financial planner, who will work with you to design the best financial plan. Where do you begin? Ask friends for recommendations; try to get three referrals, and contact each planner before deciding. Look for a reputable financial advisor with integrity and a good track record. It is important to find an individual or company that shares your values. Consider the following principles when seeking advice:

- Seek godly counsel from other believers who live out biblical principles.
- Use multiple advisors. The Bible says, "Without consultation, plans are frustrated, but with many counselors they succeed" (Proverbs 15:22 NASB).
- Weigh all counsel. "The naïve believes everything, but the

PORTRAIT OF TWO GRANDMOTHERS

When my husband's grandfather died five years ago, his grandmother was really overwhelmed. She had never paid bills, never balanced her checkbook, never even set foot in a bank. Although we tried to teach her how to track her finances, she still doesn't have a real clear understanding of money matters. When she received her husband's life insurance money, she deposited the entire amount in her checking account, saying she wanted "easy access" to her money at all times. Although we've tried to help her invest the money wisely so that it will last into her future, she's very leary of CDs, mutual funds, or anything of that nature.

My grandmother, on the other hand, has always been very careful with her money. Soon after her husband died, my grandma sat down with her banker and set up a financial program that allows her to live off the interest of her investments. "I never dip into that principal," she says. "I know the day will come when I'll really need that and I'd rather live simply now than not have enough when I really need it."

Lisa J.

prudent man considers his steps" (Proverbs 14:15 NASB). Do not be naïve. There are plenty of scam artists out there, ready to take your elder's funds. How should you weigh counsel? Check on an advisor's track record and get references from others. If there is a topic in which you ought to share common knowledge, ask the advisor about it. If she is wrong about the topic, reluctant to divulge information, or does not return calls in a timely manner, avoid her counsel.

To find a financial planner to help you with your aging loved one's affairs, you can contact the Christian Financial Planning Institute for a reputable referral. The National Association of Personal Financial Advisors provides referrals for fee-only financial advisors. Or consider contacting the Certified Financial Planner Board of Standards (see appendix). They also provide a searchable database for you to use in locating a certified, reputable financial planner in your area. Here are 10 questions they recommend you ask a planner before working with him:

1. What experience do you have?
2. What are your qualifications?
3. What services do you offer?
4. What is your approach to financial planning?
5. Will you be the only person working with me?
6. How will I pay for your services?
7. How much do you typically charge?
8. Will you act in my best interest or could anyone besides me benefit from your recommendations?
9. Have you ever been publicly disciplined for any unlawful or unethical actions in your professional career?
10. Can I have it in writing? (Get a written agreement that details the services that will be provided and the cost of those services.)

Financial planners are paid in three ways: fee only, commissions only, or a combination of fees and commissions (sometimes referred to as fee based). Various government agencies and professional organizations or associations oversee and regulate these professionals. For example, lawyers are regulated by state bar or disciplinary agencies and

BIBLICAL MONEY MANAGEMENT

At some point you may be called on to manage your elder's financial resources. Even if your loved one is advanced in years and living on a fixed income, some basic principles of stewardship still apply. To become a wise and prudent money manager, it is important to know what the Bible has to say about managing money. In fact, the New Testament alone has more to say about money than it does about heaven and hell combined. There are over 2,000 verses dealing with money and possessions, including the dangers of debt, the importance of honesty in financial dealings, and the faithfulness of God to supply all our needs. The parable of the talents found in Matthew 25:14-30, which speaks primarily of Christ's return, reveals four basic biblical principles regarding money and money management, according to financial advisor and author Ron Blue:

1. God owns it all. Matthew 25:14 says, "For the kingdom of heaven is like a man traveling to a far country, who called his own servants and delivered his goods to them" (NKJV). We are stewards of what God has entrusted to us, but all that we have belongs to Him. "If I really believe that God owns it all, then when I lose any possession, for whatever reason, my emotions may cry out, but my mind and spirit have not the slightest question as to the right of God to take whatever He wants whenever He wants it," writes Ron Blue in *Master Your Money* (Thomas Nelson, 1986). Knowing this should free us to give generously of God's resources to His purposes and people. Many elderly people, however, tend to fear running out of money or not having enough for their needs. And even if they were regular givers in the past, they may start to grow less generous. They may need to be gently reminded that God still owns it all and they are still stewards of His gifts. This should also influence our spending decisions. Chances are, your checkbook is a good indicator of what you believe about stewardship. Someday we each will give an accounting of how we used God's resources.

2. We are in a growth process. In the parable of the talents, a master entrusted his possessions to three servants before leaving on a journey. While the master was gone, he expected each to work according to his ability. When the master returned, he discovered that two of the three were diligent in putting their money to work and even doubling it. The master individually commended the two good stewards for their faithfulness: "Well done, good and faithful servant; you have been faithful over a few things, I will make you ruler over many things. Enter into the joy of your lord" (Matthew 25:23 NKJV). Whether we have an abundance of wealth or an apparent lack of financial resources, the Lord uses the money we have to test us and to train us in faithfulness. That training process continues right up until the day we die. Our elderly loved ones need to remember that God never stops being concerned about how they respond to the challenge of faith. For the caregiver, how you handle your elder's finances will be part of God's training program for you, whether you operate with much faith and integrity or a lack thereof.

3. The amount is not important. The master used the same words to commend the servant who had been given two talents and the one with the five talents (Matthew 25:21, 23). God does not condemn wealth nor does He advocate poverty, or vice versa. It is how you handle what God has entrusted to you that is most important. "Whoever can be trusted with very little can also be trusted with much, and whoever is dishonest with very little will also be dishonest with much" (Luke 16:10 NIV).

4. Faith requires action. What about the third servant who buried the talent he had been given? He had not embezzled it or squandered it; he simply had buried it so that it could do no good for anybody. He knew better, but he neglected his talent and did nothing. In the end, the master condemned the slothful servant and gave his talent to the most faithful servant. A person who has an estate and does not use any of it for works of charity or to advance the gospel is like the unfaithful servant who sought his own interests more than Christ's. Some people take no action because they fear making a financial mistake or are confused by worldly advice. Instead of being paralyzed by emotions, consider biblical principles in light of your elder's financial plan, then sit down and discuss with your loved one how best he can continue to support God's work and make the most faith-affirming use of His resources.

insurance agents by state regulatory commissions. Inquiries can be made to the appropriate agency.

If you want to check the disciplinary history of a stockbroker, you can contact the Securities and Exchange Commission or the National Association of Securities Dealers (see appendix).

In addition, you may wish to check with a local senior center to see if they have a list of reputable financial planners for the elderly. Your elder's church may have its own financial-planning ministry as well. If your community has a Christian yellow pages, check the listings of financial planners. But keep in mind that listing oneself as a Christian financial planner does not necessarily mean the planner is competent or trustworthy.

Here's another thought: If things don't turn out financially the way

Look for a reputable financial advisor with integrity and a good track record.

you expected, you may feel tremendous guilt and your elder may be angry with you. Using a professional will help protect you from this. You can always fire an advisor; your elder may not want to fire you.

HOW TO FIND THE RIGHT BANK FOR YOUR ELDER

As you work with your elderly loved one on his finances, you may want to investigate whether it is time for him to change banks. He may have stayed at the same bank for decades, assuming he was getting good service and a good return on his savings. He may also have developed a friendship with those in the bank, but with frequent bank mergers and personnel changes, this is less likely. Your elder may not be getting the best service by staying with the same bank. You will have to take a good look at what he is receiving from his bank and do some comparison shopping before moving to a new one.

The Better Business Bureau's (BBB) Web site has published a helpful series of tips on choosing a good bank. Here are some things to consider:

- **Location.** Just because a bank is located nearby does not mean it offers the best possible service for your loved one. If she is ambulatory, it may be good to consider shopping around for other deals. If you are going to be doing her banking, it might be helpful to set up an account with your own bank and do all of your banking at the same location.
- **"Relationship Banking" vs. Shopping Around.** Some banks encourage a person to have all of his accounts at the same bank. There is added convenience to this—which may be more important to you or your loved one than getting a better deal. This also may make it easier for a trustee or power of attorney to serve you effectively. Compare what other banks are offering in the way of savings accounts, free checking, and other services.
- **ATMs.** Using automatic teller machines provides a convenient way of banking, but check the bank's policy to make sure your elder is not incurring unwanted fees over time.
- **Minimum balances and maintenance fees.** Find out the mini-

mum amount the bank requires a patron to keep in an account at all times to get free checking. Compare how much more you might earn in interest if you placed your loved one's funds in a savings account or Certificate of Deposit (CD).

- **Interest-bearing checking accounts.** Compare interest rates paid on CDs, savings accounts, or interest-bearing checking accounts.
- **Special accounts.** Many banks have special accounts specifically designed for elderly people. See what your loved one's bank is offering and do some comparison shopping.
- **Fees for special services.** Does the bank charge for canceled checks returned to your elder? What kind of charge is there for overdraft protection? Is direct deposit available?
- **Charges per transaction.** Some banks charge per transaction, along with other charges. Find out exactly what your loved one will be charged for.

If your elder is still mentally competent, you should begin discussing her financial situation as soon as possible—but this must be done with your elder's permission and a respectful attitude. You need to find out how much money she has in various accounts; if she has stocks, bonds, dividend payments, pension funds, real-estate investments, safe-deposit boxes, etc. You should be aware of exactly how much income she has so you can help her carefully manage her assets. (See "Getting Affairs in Order" on pages 485-488 for a listing of financial and legal records to gather.)

Automatic deposit/payments. One way of simplifying the entire process is to see if you can arrange to have your elder's utility bills, health insurance, mortgage, and other commitments paid directly from his checking account. You should check with the various companies to be notified if the payments are not made. Many utilities and other agencies have third-party notification procedures to notify a family member or caregiver if the elder's bills have not been paid. You might also consider setting up direct deposit for benefit checks or income from stocks, bonds, and other sources.

Joint accounts. If you are going to regularly help your aging loved one pay her bills, you might suggest opening a joint checking account. This

Arrange to have your elder's utility bills, health insurance, mortgage, and other commitments paid directly from his checking account.

will allow you access to her funds. A "joint account with right of survivorship" means that when one owner dies, the account automatically belongs to the survivor.

PAYING FOR HEALTH CARE

To pay for high health-care costs, insurance is a necessity for most older adults. Supplemental insurance is important because Medicare does not reimburse for some services; the nonreimbursed costs can amount to thousands of dollars. In addition, some doctors refuse to accept direct Medicare payments because the fees assigned by Medicare are inadequate. Hence, the patient is liable to pay in advance and assume responsibility for the charges that are not reimbursed by Medicare.

If possible, help your loved one find a supplemental insurance policy that covers all charges above what Medicare reimburses. There are 10 standard Medicare supplement plans from which to choose. Legislation to standardize Medigap policies went into effect in 1992. Other options might include employer or union coverage, private fee-for-service insurance plans, or religious fraternal benefit plans. Contact your state insurance department to find out which companies offer health plans, as well as the availability of state programs or protections for your aging loved one. The National Association of Insurance Commissioners (NAIC) Web site has links to each state's insurance department (see appendix).

BUSINESS BURDEN

When my dad suddenly died, he still owned his business. He had employees and died two days before payroll was due. Fortunately, I had some business experience so I could help out. My mom didn't have a clue about what to do. I managed my dad's business for a year and a half before we were finally able to sell it. Working full time and having four teenagers at the time, it wasn't long before I hit the wall with burnout. My younger brother has picked up the pieces to make sure our mom's tax returns get filed, and he's managing a bigger part of the financial burden now—and I'm grateful for that.

Jan S.

Medicare

Medicare insurance was introduced in the 1960s to make health care available to the elderly. Although it was originally designed to help those 65 or older, it now also covers those who are permanently and totally disabled and those who have end-stage renal disease (kidney failure).

To qualify for Medicare coverage, your elder must be entitled to payments under social security or the Railroad Retirement Act. Medicare has two parts. Part A—which helps pay for care in a hospital, care in a skilled nursing facility, hospice, and for some home health care—does not require a premium if your loved one (or a spouse) paid Medicare taxes while employed. Part B (medical insurance) does require a small monthly premium that is usually withheld from participants' social-security checks. Your loved one can sign up for Part B anytime during a seven-month period that begins three months before she turns 65. If your elder is late and does not take Part B when she is

Help your loved one find a supplemental insurance policy that covers all charges above what Medicare reimburses.

MANAGING MOM'S MONEY

One of the more challenging things for me has been managing my mother's finances. My father handled this entirely before his death, and Mom wasn't interested in assuming responsibility for this area. She simply wanted to know that there was enough money in her checking account to pay her bills. For the first few years, that wasn't a problem.

However, a couple years ago, she received a balloon payment from the sale of her house. Since part of her income was from the interest on that sale, she needed a vehicle for investing that lump sum and continuing to earn income. I felt very inadequate for this responsibility.

I was able to retain an investment consultant to review my mother's situation and recommend a conservative portfolio that was supposed to earn her about $600 to $800 per month. That, plus her social security, should meet her needs. However, the chosen funds made no gain for the next nine months. During that time, Mom depleted her other savings. I had to research and make a complete change on her portfolio. While it is not guaranteed to earn quite as much as before, it also will not be susceptible to the ups and downs of the stock market. However, I still have to keep close watch on this area.   *Joan K.*

first eligible, she may sign up during a general enrollment period (between January 1 and March 31), but the cost of Part B may go up 10 percent for each 12-month period that she could have had it but did not sign up for it, except in special cases. Her premiums would be 10 percent higher for the rest of her life. A special penalty-free enrollment period is reserved for those seniors who did not take Part B when they were first eligible because they (or their spouse) were working and had group health coverage.

In recent years, many HMOs have dropped older persons who are on Medicare, affecting millions across the country.

If your loved one is not automatically entitled to Medicare, he may purchase it just like a private insurance policy. If you are not sure if your elder has Parts A and B, look at the lower left corner of his Medicare card; it will show "Hospital Insurance (Part A)" and "Medical Insurance (Part B)." Or call your local social-security office.

Here is what Medicare covers as of publication; verify current coverage and costs through your local Medicare or social-security office.

MEDICARE PART A (HOSPITAL INSURANCE) COVERS:
- **Hospital stays,** including a semiprivate room, meals, general nursing, and other hospital services and supplies. This includes care you get in critical-access hospitals and inpatient mental-health care. This does not include private-duty nursing or a television or telephone in your room. It also does not include a private room, unless medically necessary.
- **Skilled nursing facility care,** including a semiprivate room, meals, skilled nursing and rehabilitative services, and other services and supplies (after a related three-day hospital stay).
- **Home health care,** including part-time skilled nursing care, physical therapy, occupational therapy, speech-language therapy, home-health-aide services, medical social services, durable medical equipment and medical supplies (such as a wheelchair, a hospital bed, oxygen, and a walker), and other services.
- **Hospice care,** including medical and support services from a Medicare-approved hospice for people with a terminal illness (probably less than six months to live), drugs for symptom control and pain relief, and other services not otherwise covered by Medicare. Hospice care is given in your home. However, short-term hospital and inpatient respite care (care given to a

hospice patient by another caregiver so that the usual caregiver can rest) are covered when needed.

MEDICARE PART B (MEDICAL INSURANCE) COVERS:

- **Medical and other services,** including: doctors' visits (except for routine physical exams); outpatient treatment; emergency care; ambulance service; durable medical equipment (such as wheelchairs, hospital beds, oxygen, and walkers); second surgical opinions; diabetes-monitoring supplies; and blood services (80 percent after the cost of the first three pints of blood, unless you or someone else donates blood to replace what you use). Medicare Part B also helps pay for immunosuppressive drug therapy (limited), some anticancer medications, medications/ nebulizer for breathing problems, prosthetic devices, transplants, X rays, and some other diagnostic tests.
- **Preventive services,** including: mammograms, bone-mass measurements, colorectal cancer screenings, diabetes services and supplies, glaucoma screening, and prostate cancer screenings once every 12 months; pap smears once every 36 months in most cases; and flu and pneumococcal pneumonia shots.
- **Intermittent home health care** through a Medicare-approved agency if a physician determines that skilled medical care is needed in the patient's home. Care must involve a skilled professional and the patient must be homebound.

HERE ARE SOME HEALTH-CARE COSTS *NOT* COVERED CURRENTLY BY MEDICARE:

- Most prescription drugs, vitamins, routine or yearly physical exams, acupuncture, dental care and dentures (in most cases), hearing aids and hearing exams, eyeglasses except after cataract surgery, elective cosmetic surgery, routine foot care, orthopedic shoes, health care outside of the United States, and personal custodial care (help with bathing, dressing, using the bathroom, and eating) at home or in a nursing home.

Until the passage of the Balanced Budget Act of 1997 (BBA), Medicare gave the elderly two options for coverage: (1) original fee-for-service coverage offered by the federal government, or (2) managed care through a health maintenance organization (HMO). With passage of the BBA, the elderly now have what is called the Medicare+Choice program, which allows more private insurance companies to offer coverage to people in Medicare. The elderly can choose what are called "coordinated-care plans," such as HMOs with point-of-service (POS) plans or preferred provider organizations (PPOs).

A health maintenance organization (HMO) is a managed-care plan offering health-care services (including preventive care) for a monthly fee and sometimes a small copayment. Members must choose their primary-care physician from the HMO-provided list of doctors in order to get insurance coverage. A person who sees a doctor outside the HMO must pay the whole bill. A word of caution: In recent years, many HMOs have dropped older persons who are on Medicare, affecting millions across the country.

An HMO with a point-of-service (POS) option allows your elder to go to other doctors and hospitals that are not a part of the HMO and still get some coverage. This option tends to cost more, but it gives more choices.

A preferred provider organization (PPO) lets members choose from a list of doctors, hospitals, and other health-care providers who have agreed to accept lower fees from the insurer for their services. A copayment is usually required for those lower-priced services—say $10 for a doctor visit or prescription. Members who go outside the plan must meet a deductible and pay coinsurance based on higher fees.

The private fee-for-service plan is an option in which Medicare pays a set amount of money to the private insurance company each month, providing health-care coverage on a pay-per-visit basis. Private fee-for-service plans allow the elderly to go to any doctor or hospital they choose and may provide extra benefits that the original Medicare plan does not cover; however, the plans may differ in the amount charged for premiums, deductions, and copayments. Fee-for-service care usually requires you to pay more out-of-pocket costs. The Balanced Budget Act (BBA) also allows for medical savings accounts (at the time of publication, no private insurance companies were offering these).

These new Medicare programs may not necessarily be available in your community. To find out which plans are offered where your loved one lives, call Medicare (1-800-MEDICARE) and ask for a free, up-to-date list of available plans, plus cost and benefit comparisons. Or check their Web site (www.medicare.gov). Or check with your local Council on Aging or physician to find out if Medicare+Choice is an option for your aging loved one.

If your aging loved one appeals a denial of payment, it is quite possible that it will be reversed.

When choosing a Medicare health plan, consider what your out-of-pocket costs will be, whether you can see the doctors you want to see, whether there are "prenotification" requirements (such as notifying the plan of any planned inpatient admissions), and whether you will need coverage for extra benefits and services, such as prescription drugs or hearing aids. Also keep in mind that your loved one can ask for a second opinion under Medicare policy. Many times the elderly hesitate to consider getting a second opinion because they do not want to offend their physician—especially if she has been a longtime friend. If the doctor resists your getting a second opinion, consider getting one anyway. Medicare pays for 80 percent of the cost of a second opinion whenever nonemergency surgery is recommended or when no surgery is involved, as long as the Part B annual deductible has been met.

On occasion, a Medicare claim is denied. What can the person do? The claim can be appealed to a higher authority. Statistics collected by the Health Care Financing Administration (now the Centers for

GOING ON A CHAIR HUNT

As a caregiver for my mom I thought I might have a nervous breakdown. I would send in an application for a wheelchair and a high-rise chair through Medicare and the claim would come back denied. I could have the wheelchair or the high-rise chair, but not both. After the third denial, I requested a hearing and took Mom in a wheelchair before a Medicare judge. He took one look at her, saw that she couldn't get out of her chair without assistance, and granted the request for both chairs. That was after eight months of frustration.

The record keeping is enough to drive you out of your mind. I finally bought a copy machine so that I could keep copies of everything. *Fran H.*

Medicare and Medicaid Services) indicate that fewer than one percent of Medicare Part B claims were appealed in 1995, yet 77 percent of appealed claims were paid after the first appeal and 43 percent were paid after a second appeal.[4] The point is clear: If your aging loved one appeals a denial of payment, it is quite possible that it will be reversed.

Medicaid

Medicaid is a joint federal and state program designed to provide medical insurance assistance to people with low incomes and limited assets. Today, Medicaid pays for about two-thirds of all nursing-home care in the U.S. Medicaid coverage and eligibility vary from state to state, but the typical coverage includes: physician services, in- and outpatient services at a hospital, diagnostic tests/screening, laboratory/X-ray services, nursing-home care, medical transportation, and in-home health care. In addition, many Medicaid programs cover: dental/foot/eye care, prescription drugs, social workers, private-duty nurses, rehab, dentures, eyeglasses, case management, prosthetic devices, and hospice care.

A person who qualifies for Medicaid can use a variety of health-care facilities if these facilities participate in the Medicaid program. Many health-care groups, however, are beginning to drop out of Medicare and Medicaid programs due to financial losses, slow reimbursements, and a staggering paperwork load to comply with federal law governing these programs. Only 30 percent of the elderly poor get Medicaid benefits.

PAYING A PRICE

My dad is close to 75 years old and has lived a very hard life—alcoholic—the whole thing. He and Mom divorced in about 1979. In 1986 he had a massive heart attack. He was living on his own at the time and had to have quadruple bypass surgery. All he lives on is social security, which is about $800 a month. Before he was in an assisted-living home, we had to step in and help him because his medicine prescription costs were going up. Now that he's in a nursing home, he's on Medicaid. My sister takes care of his financial affairs.

John T.

To qualify for Medicaid, your aging loved one must have a low income and low personal savings (the amount varies from state to state). In many cases, an elderly person must "spend down" his income in order to qualify for Medicaid and nursing-home care. States have differing rules on what limitations they place on the assets your loved one can possess. In general, he can own a home, personal belongings, a car, and have a prepaid burial fund. Check with the Department of Social Services or your Area Agency on Aging for a list of limitations in your elder's state.

When a person applies for Medicaid, the officials will review all of her personal financial transactions during the past 36 months to determine if assets have been given away in order to qualify for coverage. If the officials discover there has been a transfer of assets, the applicant may be

LEARNING ON THE JOB

I had power of attorney over my grandmother's finances and took care of all her bookkeeping from the time she sold her home and moved to a senior center, then to assisted living, and finally to a nursing home. I learned as I went along, but I was glad I could be her advocate because all the paperwork would have confused her. Bills would come from the provider that said, "Don't pay," because Medicare coverage was still pending, but then they would keep billing her. I was pretty organized, so I avoided paying doctors twice for the same bill. And when Medicare denied coverage of a medical claim, I called her doctor to find out why. He realized his coding was incorrect and fixed it so that it would be covered. After my grandma developed diabetes and needed insulin, a pharmacist told me about a state-run prescription drug program for low-income seniors; it required a copayment rather than the full amount for prescriptions.

When Grandma had nearly used up her funds to pay for nursing home care, we bought her a TV set and a bathrobe to "spend down" the rest of her income so that she'd qualify for Medicaid. These were allowable expenses because the items were purchased for her. It took six months for Grandma to get approved for Medicaid. She got down to $500 in the bank. That was stressful, because I never knew at what point I might have to kick in to pay her monthly nursing-home bill. But it worked out. She had Medicaid coverage for just two months before she passed on.   *Mike H.*

required to wait on benefits for the period of time those assets would have paid for nursing-home care. Assets of married couples, however, usually receive special treatment so that the spouse who still lives at home will not become impoverished. The noninstitutionalized spouse may be permitted to keep a percentage of all their assets up to a certain limit as well as a large portion of the couple's income.

To apply for Medicaid for your loved one, contact your local social-service agency or Area Agency on Aging. Your local library or senior center can probably help you as well.

Medigap

Many elderly people purchase what is called a "Medigap" health-insurance policy. This insurance is offered by private companies to fill the "gaps" in the original Medicare plan coverage. It provides coverage for items *not covered* under Medicare.

Insurance companies in most states offer 10 kinds of Medigap insurance programs: Plans A through J. Each plan offers a slightly different kind of coverage to deal with copayments, skilled nursing care, prescription-drug copayments, and other benefits. Plans C through J, for example, offer coverage for emergencies encountered in foreign travel. Plans H, I, and J cover a limited amount of prescription-drug costs after meeting an annual deductible. Check with your elder's insurance agent for a detailed description of each Medigap program to find one that best fits your loved one's specific needs.

There are precautions you must take when purchasing Medigap insurance, however. Prices can vary from as little as $444 a year to more than a $1,000 a year. Some insurance companies raise premiums each year; others do not. Before buying a Medigap policy, consider how much your elder is spending on health care and what the money is spent on, which benefits are needed, and how much he can afford to spend on premiums.

For updated news on Medigap insurance, you can access ElderWeb on the Internet. This site deals with all aspects of elder health care, insurance challenges, funeral plans, social security, reverse mortgages, etc. (see appendix). Or, to find out about Medigap policies in your state, call 1-800-MEDICARE for the most updated phone number of whom to contact.

Religious Fraternal Benefit Society Plans

Health plans offered by a religious fraternal benefit society, such as the Aid Association for Lutherans, are for its members. The society must meet Internal Revenue Service (IRS) and Medicare requirements for this type of organization.

Long-Term-Care Insurance

Although many older people rely on Medicaid to help pay for nursing-home care, out-of-pocket expenditures by patients and their families can account for nearly half the cost. With the soaring costs of long-term care, some people believe the answer is found in long-term care (LTC) insurance. Most of the policies sold today cover various community-based options, such as nursing-home placements, home health care, adult day care, and respite-care services. Such insurance can help to preserve income and savings, since neither employer health insurance nor Medicare pay for long-term care. But it is generally not available once a disabling long-term illness has struck. And the premiums are typically very expensive for people older than 70 years of age.

According to one government-contracted study of 700 community-dwelling, disabled seniors who had private LTC insurance, the average monthly insurance benefit paid to claimants was $1,527. This compares to an average public-insurance benefit (Medicaid waiver) for home care of $450. Having private LTC insurance allowed many of the claimants to remain in their homes and rely less on adult children for care. Without it, about half of the claimants and informal (unpaid) caregivers said they would have to seek institutional alternatives, such as nursing-home care or assisted living.

While purchasing a LTC insurance policy can give you and your loved one some peace of mind, great care must be taken to avoid possible pitfalls of policies, such as lack of increases in benefits to cover inflation, tricky ways in which the policy is written or confusing language in the policy, the possibility for large rate increases, and questions as to whether claims will be paid. LTC insurance is often too expensive for elderly people to purchase. A good rule of thumb is that no more than 7 percent of your elder's annual income should go to paying premiums. Because LTC insurance is expensive, it may not be beneficial unless there are substantial assets to protect. Some experts say a senior is a good candidate for LTC insurance if he has assets of at least $75,000 (excluding home and car) and retirement income of at least $35,000 a year. Also, keep in mind that LTC insurance is still in its relative infancy. Insurance companies are on the learning curve regarding setting the premium and benefits on these policy contracts. And unlike life insurance, it is difficult to compare long-term-care policies.

In looking for LTC insurance, find an agent with extensive expertise on the subject. Be sure the policy approximates the difference between your loved one's daily income and the daily cost of a nursing home. Coverage also should include all levels of care, from custodial to skilled, as well as care for dementia and Alzheimer's disease. Read the fine print to make sure in-home care is covered. The policy should *not* require that your loved one be hospitalized before becoming eligible for benefits. It should also include inflation protection and be guaranteed renewable, so the company cannot cancel the policy. If your elder plans to purchase a long-term-care insurance policy, she should do so as early in life as possible to assure that she will be able to get coverage at a reasonable cost. Because of the complexities of LTC insurance, a trusted, competent insurance advisor is crucial. (For more information, see "Long-Term-Care Insurance" on pages 442-446.)

FINDING SUPPLEMENTAL HEALTH INSURANCE

When my mother moved to Colorado, we found a nice supplemental program to go with her Medicare and Medicaid. It worked very well for several years, until the company she was using announced that as of December 31st that year, it would discontinue this program.

This was traumatic for Mom because she relied on the security of the program. I asked her to do some research. She did ask some of the residents what they used. But she wouldn't make any calls. Finally, my wife made calls, got the information, and we were able to find a nice replacement for her lapsing plan. *Luis C.*

FINDING HELP WHEN THE MONEY DWINDLES

There may come a time when your loved one's assets, savings, pension plan, and other sources of income are insufficient to cover expenses. As you see this situation approaching, you should turn to other family members, your church, and local elder agencies for whatever assistance they can provide. You might hold a family meeting (if there are siblings) to brainstorm ideas and to pray together. Some may be able to give money and others, time or assistance. Local, state, and federal agencies can also direct you to the kinds of resources you may need to care for your loved one. Eventually you may want to pay some of the costs. Local, state, and federal agencies can help you find assistance in caring for your loved one. Local support groups can be of great value to you as you struggle with the complexities of caring for an elderly loved one.

The Internet can also provide you with a wide array of resources. You can also be a source of insight and encouragement to others. You may discover you have a new ministry opportunity when you join a forum or a formal caregiver support group in your area.

Try not to give in to worries about your elder's finances. Maintain a prayerful, positive attitude and keep in mind that being financially prepared is only part of the picture. What matters long-term is that we "lay up for ourselves treasures in heaven" and make it a priority to share our spiritual heritage—our beliefs, memories, time, talents, and wealth—with our loved ones on earth.

———— ⚭ ————

Whoever robs his father or his mother, and says, "It is no transgression," the same is companion to a destroyer. Proverbs 28:24 NKJV

CHAPTER 11

Blessed is the man that walketh not in the counsel of the

ungodly. . . . But his delight is in the law of the Lord.

PSALM 1:1-2 KJV

Getting Help:

Legal Care and Estate Planning

After Linda's dad died, her mom sold the home and had her will up-dated. She also asked the lawyer to give Linda access to her bank accounts in case of an emergency. No problem—she could simply add her daughter's name to her bank accounts and avoid probate, although she would still have the tax liability. So they opened a joint-tenancy bank account, and Linda eventually took responsibility for writing checks and paying the bills.

After her mom died and Linda went to settle the estate, she saw a new attorney, who said Linda had indeed avoided probate because her mom's money had automatically become her money as the surviving joint tenant. But even though the will specified to divide the inheri-tance—about $200,000—between Linda and the other three siblings, Linda was not legally bound to do so. That is because a joint-tenancy account inherently includes the right to survivorship. In other words, upon the death of a joint tenant, the surviving joint tenant becomes sole owner of the property. Therefore, it overrides a will, which covers assets that are in the deceased person's name alone.

"At that point I was legally giving a gift to my siblings," Linda says. She kept her siblings updated regularly as the attorney worked out the tax liability. "I didn't want them to think I might pull a fast one on them and keep the money," she explains. Fortunately, they trusted her and even told her she did not need to keep calling with every detail. "I guess it helped that we're all Christians."

As it turns out, Linda did pay a state tax but no federal estate tax because the estate was below one million dollars—the maximum amount sheltered from federal estate taxes upon death. (That amount is subject to increase gradually in years to come.) Linda went to an accountant to fill out a gift tax return that showed she had divided the money between her siblings. When Linda asked her lawyer what would have been the best way to handle her mom's money, he said the best way is determined by family circumstances. "It worked out fine for your mom and for you and your siblings." What's most important, he said, is to get a lawyer who is knowledgeable about elder law and estate planning.

As a caregiver, it is important to learn about your aging loved one's legal affairs. Does your elder have an updated will or trust? A will is valuable because it covers unexpected assets and ensures that your elder's belongings will be allocated according to his wishes. A trust is valuable because it controls the distribution of assets without going through probate. Has your loved one planned ahead to minimize taxes on his possessions and property when he dies? What if your parent becomes incapacitated? Has she signed a durable power of attorney and named an agent to make property and financial decisions if she is not able to do so? Encouraging your loved one to take care of legal matters now can help your family avoid lengthy legal proceedings and potential arguments down the road.

WHEN TO GET INVOLVED

Most caregivers struggle with knowing how and when to get involved in managing an elder's money and assets. If your elder is displaying signs of dementia, he will need to authorize someone to make his financial and health-care decisions. You may be called on to help if your loved one runs into problems with Medicare, needs Medicaid coverage, or is exploited in some way. In time, you may be needed as an intermediary between your aging loved one and a host of businesses, health-care professionals, and insurance and governmental agencies.

Of course, it is best to sit down with your aging loved one to review her will, trust, health-care wishes, or other arrangements before she is incapable of participating. Choose a time when you and your elder are both rested and calm. Chances are, your elder will appreciate some help sorting through complex legal matters. If your elder resists your help, back off, and try again another time. For example, if your elder is going away on a trip, this is a natural time to obtain power of attorney to help with paying bills. That way, it is in place for later when needed. There will be times when you do not fully understand the legal terms or feel qualified to act on behalf of your elder. But with the assistance of a trusted attorney or financial planner, your efforts can bring positive results and peace of mind.

Most caregivers struggle with knowing how and when to get involved in managing an elder's money and assets.

ELDER LAW

In response to the growing aging population in the U.S., a new, specialized area of law has emerged in the past decade—elder law. Seniors have unique needs and may need legal assistance for a variety of issues: guardianships and conservatorships, estate planning, probate, advance directives, mental-health decisions, Medicaid issues, Medicare appeals, assisted-living/nursing-home contracts, HMOs, age discrimination in employment, elder abuse and fraud recovery, and other legal matters.

Elder-law lawyers are a relatively new specialty of attorneys who concentrate on handling the often complicated legal affairs of seniors. They deal with financial matters but also with family dynamics, doctors, geriatric-care managers, and others. The goal of their practice is not just legal planning but life planning. Elder-law attorneys handle general estate planning and help clients to prepare for the future with alternative decision-making documents. They can also help plan for possible long-term-care needs, such as nursing-home care. An elder-law attorney must be well versed in a variety of fields: medicine, ethics, ageism, real estate, abuse, and more.

The National Academy of Elder Law Attorneys (NAELA) is an organization that is growing steadily in membership. NAELA maintains a

Web site that includes a series of "Law & Aging" brochures addressing various elder-law topics (see appendix). The organization also sells a listing of several hundred attorneys nationwide (free on its Web site). University law schools are beginning to see the importance of elder law as a growing field—especially with millions of baby boomers entering the "senior citizen" status during the next few years. Wake Forest University School of Law, for example, has an elder-law clinic that provides free legal advice for low-income seniors in North Carolina. The service is provided by law-school students under the supervision of an attorney from the law school.

Affliated with NAELA is the National Elder Law Foundation, which certifies those who have gone through a testing process. Various state bar associations also certify elder-law attorneys as proficient in that specialty.

Fee Schedules

Attorneys may provide an initial consultation for free and then offer one of a number of fee arrangements. The attorney may first ask for a **retainer fee,** which acts as a down payment to cover some initial attorney's fees and costs when more involved or protracted legal proceedings or work are required (e.g., for complex or large estates). You will also be responsible for court costs and filing fees. There are **flat fees** or **set fees**. This method is used for simple transactions. An **hourly fee** is used when the issue is more complex and there is no way of telling how much work it will take. There are also **percentage** or **contingency fees**. These are used by some attorneys to collect a percentage of the amount you get as the result of a settlement or judgment. Typically this arrangement is used only in cases of personal injury, disability, damage to property, or a lawsuit to get back payments of pensions. If your aging loved one is involved in a dispute with his employer over pension payments, for example, his attorney might charge a contingency fee. If you and your siblings end up in a legal battle over your elder's estate, the lawyer who defends your rights usually charges on an hourly basis, after payment of a retainer fee.

Elder-law attorneys can be expensive, but there is help available from a variety of services. We will discuss those options below.

Free or Reduced-Cost Legal Advice

Under the Older Americans Act (OAA), the law requires that your state agency on aging fund free legal counseling programs for seniors through local Area Agencies on Aging. In some states, the agency contracts with the federal Legal Services Corporation to provide legal services. The agencies may also contract with private attorneys to provide these services for seniors. While there are no income guidelines that a senior must meet to qualify for services, agencies have the authority to prioritize the kinds of free counsel they will provide to seniors.

The Legal Services Corporation (LSC) also has a network of legal-aid offices that provide help for low-income persons. Many of these offices have staff who are skilled in elder-law issues. There are eligibility requirements for these services. One requirement is that the person's income be no higher than 125 percent of the federal poverty level guideline. In some cases, however, the income guidelines can be waived. The National Legal Aid and Defender Association publishes an updated list of LSC-funded services nationwide.

Some legal-aid offices and state bar associations have established "pro bono panels" of attorneys who will provide free legal help as a public service. Some private attorneys are also willing to work for reduced fees for low-income clients. Your state bar association may have a listing of attorneys who are willing to do pro bono work or reduced-fee work for you and your elder.

The American Association of Retired Persons (AARP) has also developed the Legal Counsel for the Elderly (LCE), which educates legal professionals, advocates, and consumers on the legal rights and benefits of the elderly. The LCE produces educational materials to show how you can find the help you need. LCE will provide you with a list of its publications when you write them (see appendix).

The Administration on Aging also sponsors statewide legal-advice hot lines for those needing counsel. These provide advice to anyone over 60, regardless of income or the nature of the problem. The hot lines are staffed by attorneys who are well versed in elder-law issues. To find out more about these hot lines, call your Area Agency on Aging.

Your local senior-center director may also be a good source of information on elder-law concerns. He or she can probably refer you to

Some legal-aid offices and state bar associations have established "pro bono panels" of attorneys who will provide free legal help.

other agencies or private attorneys who can help you sort out the complications of your elder's financial and health concerns.

You can also call the Christian Legal Society for a referral for a Christian elder-law attorney in your area (see appendix).

FreeAdvice.com is a legal Web site that can provide you with a wealth of information on elder law and other legal issues. The site contains articles on asset protection, elder law, estate planning, probate law, trusts, and wills. It also contains a section on "Estates Legalese" to help you understand the dozens of obscure legal terms used by lawyers who deal with estate planning and elder concerns. The site is well written and easy to understand (see appendix). The more you understand, the less time you will need to spend in the lawyer's office, and the less money you will spend.

When selecting an attorney, find out what percentage of her practice is devoted to elder law.

When selecting an attorney, find out how long she has been in practice and what percentage of her practice is devoted to elder law. Ask whether the lawyer specializes in a particular area of law. Since many elder-law attorneys do not specialize in every area, you will want to make sure you hire the attorney who emphasizes the area of law that concerns your loved one (such as disability planning) but who also has a broad understanding of laws that could affect your loved one in other areas (such as Medicaid).

ESTATE PLANNING AND LEGAL ARRANGEMENTS

Many Americans worry about inflation eating into their retirement income. Yet despite this concern, some of them are not saving enough to produce the level of income they would like to have when they retire. A survey conducted by U.S. Trust Company indicated that among affluent Americans over fifty years old, only 58 percent will have the amount of income they desire when they retire.[1] The amount a person saves for retirement depends to a great extent on pension amounts and social security.

Many experts say estate planning should begin early—as early as age 45, and perhaps as early as age 30. (For example, young couples with children need to do estate planning to cover who will be the guardian of their children and their estates if both parents are killed.)

While this advice may benefit you as you look ahead to retirement, it will be of little consolation to your elderly loved one if she has not planned ahead. However, it is not too late to help your loved one get her affairs in order.

Consider the following strategies for estate planning:

- Hold a family meeting with your elder to discuss how property and money will be allocated upon his death.
- Make certain your elder has a trust or will and has named an executor, with successors named if the first-named executor is unable to serve.
- Discuss the possibility of your aging loved one disbursing her assets to family members while she is still alive. As of the year 2002, up to one million dollars of a person's assets (and double that amount for couples) are sheltered from federal estate taxes upon death. (This amount will increase gradually in future years, but it is subject to change by Congress.) A person can also give away $10,000 per year ($20,000 per married couple) to one or more persons or organizations, free of gift and income taxes. This can be a good way of passing on an inheritance while your loved one is still alive. The goal is not to "spend down" your elder's estate so he can qualify for Medicaid; the goal is to take advantage of tax-shelter laws to benefit his children. However, monetary gifts should be given at least three years before your elder needs Medicaid to avoid a delay in Medicaid coverage. There currently is a 36-month "look-back" period for such transfers if the transferor is attempting to qualify for Medicaid benefits for long-term nursing-home care. This area of Medicaid planning is fraught with perils, so get professional advice before making such gifts.
- If your elderly loved one owns a business, seek advice and plan now for ownership succession.
- Talk to your elder about setting up trust funds and life-insurance policies for her heirs.
- Encourage your elder to meet with qualified professionals to discuss a good estate plan—tailored to your aging loved one's specific needs and financial situation. If your elder is not capable

of discussing, planning, or deciding on his estate, you may have to go to guardianship court and get permission from the judge to have the guardian do some estate planning on behalf of your elder. State laws may differ on this subject.

Importance of Mutual Decisions

As you work with your loved one on her estate planning, an important goal is to minimize the amount of friction and animosity that may occur if siblings begin battling over property and money from an inheritance (if any remains after long-term-care expenses). Remind your aging loved one of the benefits of planning ahead. Let her know that as she plans ahead, she can be assured that she will be the one who can choose who takes care of her business; she will be the one to describe what kinds of health-care decisions she wants made; she will be able to handle her own financial affairs until she becomes incapacitated; she can also name the person who will be authorized to act on her behalf once she is incapable of making decisions on her own.

Do-It-Yourself Estate Planning

For somewhat simple situations, such as creating a basic will for $100,000 worth of assets, you might consider using one or more of the various software programs on the market that encourage people to do their own estate planning. If you are good with figures and a computer, there are a variety of products available. At the FindLaw.com Web site, you will discover a number of companies producing estate-planning software. These include: Brentmark Software, Cowles Legal Systems, InsMark, ProBATE Software, Zane & Associates. Each name is linked to the company Web site (see appendix).

Another source you will find helpful is Nolo.com, a major publisher of law books (see appendix). Nolo has a series of articles on its site dealing with elder law, wills, and estate planning. It also markets WillMaker and LivingTrust Maker on CD.

Keep in mind that "do-it-yourself" estate planning can be a very risky venture if not done properly. Self-help estate planning often goes awry, resulting in substantial legal costs to straighten out the estate. For estates beyond a minimum size, for any estate designed to avoid probate, and when there are other complicated issues such as business interests, there is no substitute for seeking professional estate-planning advice.

How Do You Begin?

An estate plan is a written expression of how you want your assets to be owned, managed, and preserved during your lifetime and how you want them disposed of upon your death. The purpose of estate planning is to make sure those assets are transferred quickly and efficiently to your beneficiaries after your death—with minimal tax consequences. The process includes making an inventory of assets and establishing a will or trust.

To plan your elder's estate, take a complete inventory of everything your aging loved one has and then assign a value to each asset. Assets include:

- Real estate (including residence and any other real estate)
- Savings and checking accounts
- Investments
- 401(k), IRA, pension, and other retirement accounts
- Life-insurance policies and annuities
- Ownership interest in a business
- Motor vehicles
- Jewelry
- Collectibles (e.g., coins, stamps, antiques)
- Other personal property

The goal of estate planning is not to "beat the system" or to avoid legitimate taxes. Rather, it is a way to provide the best possible protection for your loved one's assets—and to minimize the tax liability that results from poor planning. What are the elements of a good estate-planning program? According to Lorin Castleman, a California estate-planning attorney, a proper estate plan requires the following elements:

- Supervision of assets until your elder's death
- A business exit strategy for your elder if he owns a business
- Instructions for the care and management of your elder's assets if he becomes incompetent

- Instructions for the care of your elder if he is unable to make medical decisions on his own behalf
- A plan of distribution that will give your loved one control over who gets the money, when, and with whatever controls he wants
- A savings of the greatest amount in taxes and postdeath administrative costs

Castleman says many estate plans do not work because of the "3 Fs": failure to fund, failure to maintain, and failure to administer the plan after death. In other words, any estate plan needs to be funded, actively maintained, and faithfully administered after the person dies. To neglect any of these elements is to risk losing everything.[2]

Choosing an Estate Planner

If you are already an accountant, a lawyer, or a business operater, you may have the skills needed to do estate planning. If you do not fit into one of those categories or if you need professional advice, you should hire an estate planner. Estate-planning attorneys are trained to handle wills, trusts, powers of attorney, and the intricacies of estate taxes. Some insurance vendors, accountants, and financial planners also do estate planning, but sometimes they are selling a type of product or service.

How do you locate a good planner? One of the best places to get referrals is from people you know and trust. Talk to someone in your church who is involved in estate planning or who can recommend a planner. Be careful, though. That person may expect you to choose his services and may be hurt if you choose a different planner. Your local senior center can also be a good source for advice.

The Christian Legal Society is a reputable source for locating a lawyer (see appendix). It is a good idea to seek an attorney who specializes in estate planning, so you can be more assured that he will be knowledgeable about current laws and the finer legal details that may benefit your elderly loved one. Many states have a board certification process for attorneys that specialize in estate planning.

Use caution in working with an estate planner. When you call the planner, discuss your needs and the initial consulting arrangements. If you are satisfied, schedule an appointment. If you schedule a meeting with an attorney and end up meeting with a paralegal, you should probably look elsewhere for help. Many estate planners will send you a questionnaire to fill out and return before you come in for the initial consultation. This will enable the planner to prepare adequately for the interview. Ask how long the meeting will take. Even with advanced preparation, a thorough consultation often will take two hours or longer, although planning for small estates should not take as long.

Be a smart consumer. Before proceeding, have a clear understanding—in writing—of the work to be done, the fee, and other costs. Try to work out a fixed-charge arrangement.

After the interview is completed, the planner will prepare a series of documents for your aging loved one to review. These should include: a standard will and a revocable living trust with companion pour-over will (that "pours over" into the trust any assets that may not have been transferred into the trust during the trust creator's life), a certificate of trust, a durable power of attorney for asset management, a health-care power of attorney, and a physician's directive. What will this cost? An estate-planning program—without tax planning—will range from $1,000 to $2,000. If tax planning is also involved, the price could range from $1,500 to $3,000. These plans do not include life-insurance trusts, charitable trusts, or planning for generation skipping. The plans are optional, depending on your elder's wishes. Planning for larger estates will

UPDATING AN OLD WILL

When my grandmother was in a nursing home, we hired a lawyer to make sure her will was drawn up properly. She'd had one done in Colorado about 50 years earlier, but the attorney recommended updating it now that she was a resident of Illinois. Plus, the original will had left some of her inheritance to a brother who was no longer living. Having an attorney who was a friend of mine and who was familiar with senior citizens was invaluable. He put together a simple draft and she signed it (she still had the mental capacity to do so). After she died, he also directed me to sign a "small-estate affidavit," which showed that she had limited assets; that way we avoided probate.

Mike H.

be more expensive. Prices will vary, depending upon what state or community you are in as well as the size of the estate and its complexity.

PROTECTING YOUR LOVED ONE'S ASSETS

Understanding Legal Terms

So what is the best way for your loved one to legally preserve his assets? What is the difference between a will and a trust? Taking time now to learn some basics about proper estate planning will help your elder avoid improper distribution of his property and higher levels of taxation when he dies.

There are pitfalls involved in all of these scenarios. An adult child who gains control over her parent's assets, for example, faces financial liabilities as well. In addition, a person who obtains power of attorney may alienate her other siblings during the process. An agent active under a power of attorney has a duty, called a fiduciary duty, to act in the best interest of the person giving the power of attorney; the agent cannot benefit financially at the expense of her elder. If there is a business partnership involved, this can also complicate matters within a family. Elder-law attorneys are seeing a rise in the number of serious disputes between siblings over control of a parent's property and money.

An elder-law lawyer can help you clarify the pros and cons of obtaining a power of attorney, a trust, conservatorship, guardianship, and other legal documents. You need to be aware of both your rights and obligations as you enter into any of these binding agreements.

Will. Every person should have a will. This is a legal document that describes how the person wants her property distributed after her death. A will can contain the name of an executor or personal representative who will handle the person's affairs after she has died. It can contain lists of individuals who will receive property. The will can also name a guardian for surviving minor children. With supplementary documents, the person making out a will can provide instructions for burial and whether or not she wants her organs donated. Unless a will has been drawn up, the state will decide how to divide the person's possessions and property according to its own guidelines.

When writing up a will, suggest that your elder—*with the help of a good attorney*—address the following:

- Who should receive your assets (property, money, etc.)? If children are to receive them, at what age?
- Should a trust be created for your spouse, children, or others? How will this benefit them?
- Should charitable gifts be made and how frequently?
- Who should be named executor or personal representative of your estate?

Each state has varying laws on how wills are drawn up and what can and cannot be done in a will. You will have to contact a local elder-law or estate-planning attorney in your area for specifics on what your state approves or prohibits in a will. You can also find helpful resources in your local library or on the Internet. If you do a simple Internet search using the keywords *estate planning* and *elder law,* you will discover hundreds of useful resources.

A living will is different than a regular will. We will discuss living wills in the section entitled "Medical Decisions and Disability Planning," later in this chapter.

Trust. A trust is a document that gives a person the right to manage another person's money and property. It is an agreement between your elderly loved one (the settlor or trustor) and the individual (the trustee) appointed during your elder's lifetime or to succeed your elder upon his death. Unlike a durable power of attorney, the trust is a long and detailed document that outlines specifically how money and property should be handled. In addition, the trust can remain in effect after the person dies. The trust will continue to be managed by the person placed in charge of it. A trust is created to avoid costly probate processes and probate expenses after your loved one dies. It is typically used to save on estate and income taxes, to provide support for a dependent after a person dies or becomes incapacitated, to distribute property after death, to protect land from development, and to make gifts to charity.

A trust can be *revocable* or *irrevocable.* With a revocable trust, your loved one can manage and change the trust at will until he dies. An irrevocable trust prohibits a person from changing it—although often an irrevocable trust can be abolished as long as both grantor and the beneficiaries agree. The irrevocable trust is frequently set up to manage money given to minors and to charities.

A trust is created to avoid costly probate processes and probate expenses after your loved one dies.

There are several different kinds of trusts, depending on how your loved one wants to arrange the protection and disbursement of his inheritance. You will need a lawyer to set up a trust for your aging loved one. Here are two of the most common types of trusts:

- **Living trust.** This legal document provides for the management of your elder's assets during her lifetime and provides for someone to assume responsibility for these assets once your loved one becomes incapable of making decisions. Unlike a will, the trust allows your elder's estate to avoid probate by going through trust administration. This usually is a quicker and more private process. Some feel that revocable living trusts (which can be changed while your elder is still alive) have been oversold to elderly people, because most estates are simple enough that they do not need a living trust. Also, property and bank accounts have to be retitled in the name of the living trust, and most people will not keep up with the maintenance of it. In general, a living trust makes sense if privacy is an issue, if swift, orderly transfer of assets to your elder's heirs is desired, or to provide an entity for the efficient management of estate assets during your elder's life and after her death. Consult competent legal counsel before deciding to implement this type of trust.

- **Charitable remainder trust.** This reduces the amount of your elder's estate, thereby reducing your loved one's exposure to estate taxes. This type of trust grants a church or charity a remainder interest in your loved one's assets, such as the right to receive your elder's property at the time of his death. Your loved one would reserve the right to enjoy the property while still alive and may receive income from the trust.

Letter of instruction. This is a document prepared by your aging loved one and her lawyer. It should contain the names of the individuals to be notified upon death, funeral arrangements, directions for disposal of personal property, numbers of bank accounts, information on insurance policies, anatomical-gift information, etc. This is not a legal document; it is just a listing of personal requests to be followed along with the will.

Family limited partnership. This estate-planning tool allows the parent or elder to reduce the value of his business for tax purposes and to adjust the cash flow received by children who are "limited partners" in the business. This is often used to protect assets from irresponsible offspring, failed marriages, or claims of creditors. With a family limited partnership, the elder (business owner) is the general partner and his spouse or offspring are limited partners. This combines personal tax planning, transfer of family wealth, and business succession planning all under one plan. This is a way for a businessperson to protect his business and provide for his surviving relatives. It is ethical to create family limited partnerships for business-planning, estate-planning, and asset-protection purposes. But it is not ethical or legal to create one as a fraud against existing creditors. It can be a violation of state fraudulent conveyance laws.

Joint tenancy. Husbands and wives quite often have common ownership of their money, property, and other possessions. One form of common ownership is called "joint tenancy with a right of survivorship." This means that if one spouse dies, the other automatically inherits everything. Other joint-tenancy agreements add an adult child to the agreement. Joint tenancy can help your loved one avoid probate, but it has its drawbacks. It is certainly no substitute for a will. Joint tenancy can lead to problems in states that have a community property law. The surviving spouse can lose important tax benefits. The joint tenant may also be liable for the debts or liabilities of the other spouse. In addition, the person who dies may unintentionally leave all of her assets to her spouse—instead of dividing them up among her spouse and children. This is a complicated area of estate planning; make certain you get adequate legal advice on the pros and cons of joint tenancy.

Probate. This is the process by which legal title to property is transferred from the deceased's estate to his beneficiaries. If the person dies with a will (also called dying "testate"), the probate court determines if the will is valid, orders that creditors be paid, and makes sure the will is executed properly. If a person does not have a will (dies "intestate"), the probate court appoints a person to receive all claims against the estate, to pay creditors, and to distribute all remaining property in accordance with the laws of the state. The cost of probate is set by state law or by custom in your community. In some states, it can cost from 3 to 7 percent of the entire value of the estate.

A will can be contested during probate for a variety of reasons: if it was not properly executed; if the elder was not mentally stable when the will was written; or if the elder was unduly influenced by a relative, friend, spouse, or offspring. These matters must be judged during probate hearings and can drag on for years.

If your elder's estate contains only a small amount of probate property, he may qualify for a quicker version of probate, called **small-estate administration** or **summary administration.** In that case, a court order or affidavit directs the transfer of assets, which takes no more than a few months to complete. Talk to an experienced local attorney for help.

Power of attorney. Your loved one may wish to give you power of attorney over her affairs. You can have either *general* or *special* power of attorney. General power of attorney grants you power to take care of any financial transactions. A special power of attorney authorizes you to do a limited number of actions for your elder. A power of attorney is usually granted for a specific period of time. If you have a properly drafted power of attorney, it can help you and your loved one avoid court action and save substantial legal expense. In most jurisdictions, however, powers of attorney are not reviewed or regulated by any agency. Therefore, there is potential for abuse by an agent under a power of attorney. Consult a competent professional before executing such a powerful document.

Durable power of attorney. This is a document you and your aging loved one create (with the help of a skilled elder-law or estate-planning lawyer) to give a trusted friend or relative the power to make either financial or medical decisions for your elder when necessary. A durable power of attorney does not terminate if the person granting the power becomes mentally incompetent. It can be either general or special. Every state allows some form of durable power of attorney. Some states, however, have restrictions on what kind of health-care decisions can be made by one who has power of attorney. You will have to check with your attorney to find out what restrictions your state imposes.

Conservatorship. If your aging loved one becomes totally incapacitated, you can go to a probate court and ask that you be appointed a conservator over his money and property. This can be done against the will of your loved one and can cause friction between siblings, especially if there are significant amounts of money and property involved. Use extreme caution, and be sure to communicate with other family members.

Guardianship. If the court determines your loved one is incapacitated and unable to make her own decisions because of physical or mental disability, you can be named her guardian. She becomes your "ward,"

MAKING DURABLE POWER OF ATTORNEY DECISIONS

One of the hardest decisions for me was knowing when to exercise my durable power of attorney privilege to make decisions for my grandmother, such as when to move her out of her own home or take away her driver's license. That's the number one critical decision for many caregivers. I suggest that you make decisions early, and *not too late*. When my very independent and active grandmother was 76 years old and her driver's license came up for renewal, I said, "Gram, you're not driving anymore; it's not safe." She agreed but said, "You're not selling my car." So I let it sit in the driveway for two years, and her neighbor would use the car to take her to the bank and the store. That's how I weaned her off of driving. At that time her insurance rates were $1,800 a year. I told her, "You can take a lot of taxi rides for $1,800 a year." That decision was worth it, though, for her sake and for the safety of others on the road.

She also volunteered part-time in the Crime Watch division of the local police department. After she gave up her driver's license, I told her to ask the police department to make arrangements for her transportation. As a courtesy, the Crime Watch department had one of the lady officers pick her up each week for volunteer duty, and for many more years she continued to volunteer.　　　　　　　　　　　　　　　　　　　　　　　　　　　*George T.*

and you have authority to manage her money or property and in many states can sell real estate with court approval. As a guardian, you also can determine where your loved one will live and what medical treatment she will or will not receive. A knowledgeable attorney can advise you about possible alternatives to guardianship, such as durable powers of attorney or living trusts. Guardianship or conservatorship can be an involved and expensive legal proceeding.

Representative payee. If your aging loved one has a disability and is unable to manage a pension or public-benefit income, you may consider becoming a representative payee. Social security, Veterans Affairs, and other public agencies can appoint you to disburse the funds. You should contact each specific agency for an application form.

Questions to Ask

The Colorado Bar Association has published on its Web site a detailed description of what is involved in estate planning (see appendix). On this site, the CBA lists a series of questions you and your aging loved one need to ask an elder-law attorney as you plan for the future. These include the following:

- Does your elder need a will?
- Is a revocable living trust more appropriate than a will?
- Should your elder's spouse have a will or revocable trust if there is no property in the spouse's name?

IS A LIVING TRUST A SUBSTITUTE FOR A WILL?

A living trust is not really a "substitute will," as some people suppose. Although both a trust and a will dictate how assets will be distributed, it is almost impossible to include all assets of an estate in a trust. Therefore a will is necessary to manage assets that are not in the trust. Even if your loved one has a living trust, he also should have a pour-over will, as well as carefully selected health-care and property durable power of attorney—someone to manage those assets and to handle other legal and financial matters if he becomes incapacitated. Ultimately, the decision to have a will and a trust is one that must be made by your elder with the advice of a good elder-law attorney.

- Is joint tenancy a good substitute for a will or trust?
- If your elder does not have a will, trust, or joint tenancy, who will distribute her property?
- Should your elder leave all of her assets to her spouse?
- Will creating a trust save taxes?
- Should your elder place her life-insurance policy in a trust?
- Can life insurance be taxed as part of your elder's estate?
- What can your elder do to reduce her death taxes?[3]

Reducing Strife

If you and your elder do not work out some reasonable agreements on how the inheritance will be divided, you may face lengthy lawsuits, court battles, and family splits. Unfortunately, when it comes to money, family loyalty sometimes goes out the window and siblings become people dividing money. This can lead to major family strife. Second marriages, for example, can be financial disasters waiting to happen.

Lawyers who specialize in estate planning say there are a number of ways you can help reduce the potential for family strife. By working with your aging loved one, you can discuss the following:

- Prepare for how you and your elder handle second marriages. There are numerous stories about children being disenfranchised by second wives or husbands who inherit the deceased's assets and fail to pass on any inheritance to the deceased's biological children.
- Your elder may wish to leave an inheritance to his grandchildren through his child. This can prove difficult if his biological child dies, leaving the assets to a spouse—who does not pass anything on to the grandchildren. Elder-law lawyers can help you and your elder devise a **generation-skipping trust** that will ensure the inheritance goes to the grandchildren once they reach a specific age.
- If you or any other relative were loaned a large sum of money by your elder, make sure this information is included in your loved one's will. This should include the amount of the loan, interest charged, and when it was to be repaid. You and your elder should work out details describing who gets the family business (if there is one).

Unfortunately, when it comes to money, family loyalty sometimes goes out the window and siblings become people dividing money.

LEAVING AN INHERITANCE

In estate planning, the question to ponder and pray over is, "What is God's plan of stewardship for my estate?" Consider what the Bible has to say about leaving an inheritance:

First, the Bible teaches that an inheritance is a good thing. "A good man leaves an inheritance to his children's children" (Proverbs 13:22 NKJV). In other words, the person who properly manages his assets will be able to leave an inheritance to both his children and his grandchildren. In the Old Testament, God provided for each succeeding generation through an inheritance. "You shall inherit according to the tribes of your fathers" (Numbers 33:54 NKJV). Typically, the father would give the estate to his eldest son during his lifetime, then train him to manage it, says Kenneth Frenke, founder and president of Kenneth Frenke & Co., a fee-only wealth-management company based in Asheville, North Carolina. "That way, the father was able to oversee the stewardship of his assets while he was still alive." Christian parents do well to teach their children by word, deed, and example to manage money, to be generous, and to give tithes and offerings to further God's work. Then, when the children receive their inheritance, there is a better chance that they will use and invest the money wisely.

Second, our financial inheritance is secondary to our spiritual inheritance, says Frenke. As you're discussing plans for a will or other legal documents with your elderly loved one, encourage him to think not just in monetary terms but also in terms of the spiritual legacy that will be left behind and what still can be done to foster and pass on his faith to the family. For example, your elder may wish to write out his spiritual history, or story of God's faithfulness through the years, for the edification of loved ones. He may need to think about what can be done to repair damaged relationships or reconcile with family members, asking for or offering any needed forgiveness while there is still time. He may benefit from a reminder that his continued Christian work is valuable and appreciated, even if it is "just" being a prayer warrior from bed, as an example to family and friends. Consider Proverbs 14:26 NASB: "In the fear of the Lord there is strong confidence, and his children will have refuge."

When preparing a will or trust, consider the following ways to practice biblical stewardship (and share them with your elder):

1. Use the document to proclaim your spiritual faith and purpose. Reading God's word is powerful, and having a Scripture passage read by the judge, executor, or others can be meaningful. In addition to what is mentioned in the will or trust, you also are "writing" a testament with your life, so it is important to honor and mirror Christ in all you do and say.

2. Tithe 10 percent (or more) off the top to your local church or favorite ministry. Because all our money belongs to God (Haggai 2:8), it is reasonable to give a portion back to the Lord for His work.

3. Leave your children enough so they can be a little more secure or comfortable in the life that they have made for themselves, but not so much that they are tempted to make radical changes or think that they do not have to work. This is a good rule of thumb, says Frenke, particularly if you have a wealthy estate. How much you give to your children will depend on your financial situation. If you have a small estate and every cent is crucial, you may need to give more to your heirs. If you have a wealthy estate, a higher percentage of the estate can be donated to the church or other charitable organizations. Luke 12:48 says, "And from everyone who has been given much shall much be required; and to whom they entrusted much, of him they will ask all the more" (NASB).

• Your elder may want to disinherit one of her children, particularly if the child is irresponsible even in adulthood. However, completely disinheriting a family member may not be the wisest decision in a strained relationship between elder and child. A son or daughter who perceives, however incorrectly, that he is not loved by his parents may see this as the final proof that they didn't love him. It also can result in lawsuits and family disputes, but it is up to your elder to decide. One possible alternative is for your elder to attempt restoration and affirmation by providing a small direct inheritance and then setting up an incentive trust fund for the wayward child. This type of trust allows your elder to determine the circumstances under which the child receives an inheritance. The money becomes available to the child only when he has conformed to the deceased's wishes. The qualifications for receiving the money, such as going to college or remaining married, can be spelled out in detail in the trust papers and can be as broad or as narrow as the elder deems best.

Routinely Review the Plan

Review the estate plan every two years or so to keep up-to-date on changes in your elder's financial condition.

Estate planners suggest that you and your aging loved one make it a habit to review the estate plan every two years or so to keep up-to-date on changes in your elder's financial condition. There may have been a change in the family dynamic as well. Siblings die, get divorced, etc. These and other changes may result in the need to alter specifics within the will or trust. You and your elder should review the plan if the value of your loved one's assets has changed considerably, there has been a divorce or remarriage, your elder moves to another state, the executor of the will dies, one of the heirs dies or has a change in health, or the laws affecting the estate change.

MEDICAL DECISIONS AND DISABILITY PLANNING

Your aging loved one would do well to set up directives now for medical decision making and disability planning. For one thing, this enables your elder to explain *in advance* medical instructions that are consistent with his values and religious beliefs and to designate someone to make treatment decisions in his stead, if necessary. It also frees others from having to guess (and potentially disagree) about your loved one's wishes if he is too ill or confused to communicate his preferences during a medical crisis. An **advance medical directive** is a legal document that provides guidance for medical professionals and loved ones if a situation arises when a patient cannot speak for himself.

If your elder is entering a hospital, the staff will ask about an advance directive. Suppose, for example, your loved one is diagnosed with a terminal illness (generally defined as an incurable disease with a prognosis of six months or less to live). Would she want to receive all medical care available to prolong her life, or would she want to forgo life-sustaining treatment, including or except for assisted nutrition and hydration? To whom does your loved one wish to delegate the decision-making authority should she become incompetent or incapacitated? These are some of the questions your elder should take time to think through and get in writing *before* a crisis hits.

Advance Directives

The **living will** has been popularized in our culture as a way of permitting the patient to determine end-of-life decisions. The living will is one of two major advance directives for controlling end-of-life decisions. The other, and often preferable, advance directive is the **Durable Power of Attorney for Health-Care Decisions** (DPAHCD). There are also hybrid documents that combine elements of both of these.

The living will is a signed and witnessed document that provides a list of things the doctor can and cannot do if your loved one is in a terminal condition. It generally is a declaration of end-of-life preferences that rightly gives authority about medical decisions to the patient while she is lucid. However, a living will is limited in use and can be of benefit only when a person is terminal (which usually means having six months or less to live). Some find it troubling because the word *terminal* and the phrase "unable to make medical decisions" are vague and can be broadly interpreted. It is not always easy to tell if a loved one is in a terminal condition. Furthermore, some worry that in your absence, the attending physician on duty could make a decision you, your loved one, or your primary doctor would not agree with. (For more information, see "Advance Medical Directives" on pages 458-462.)

The Durable Power of Attorney for Health-Care Decisions is a document that designates an agent who will make health-care decisions when the patient is unable to do so. The DPAHCD appoints an agent in any crisis, not just terminal illness. Your loved one should use care in choosing an agent, because the agent will have authority to make decisions about providing, withholding, or withdrawing medical treatment from your elder if your elder is unable to make these decisions himself. This document holds significant authority. Only a court can take away the powers of the agent if it finds the agent has abused her authority.

The International Task Force on Euthanasia and Assisted Suicide urges everyone to have some form of advance directive: "It is important that all adults consider who will make medical decisions for them if they are temporarily or permanently unable to make them for themselves. Unless a person has an advance directive, many health-care providers and institutions will be forced to make critical decisions for him, or a court may appoint a guardian who is unfamilar with the person's values and wishes."

Your aging loved one would do well to set up directives now for medical decision making and disability planning.

The International Task Force has produced its own advance directive, the **Protective Medical Decisions Document (PMDD),** which may be attached to the advance directive form(s) approved by your state legislature. It is a protective Durable Power of Attorney for Health-Care Decisions that specifically prohibits assisted suicide and euthanasia.

Below are stories of two families and how they handled the question of assisted nutrition and hydration (AN&H) and their loved one's wishes. For more information on AN&H, see chapter 18: End-of-Life Issues.

"YOU'LL KNOW WHAT TO DO"

My folks never made out a living will, but they did sign papers giving me power of attorney over their property and health care. As Dad went in and out of the hospital a number of times during his last year, I learned to carry the health-care legal documents with me. Otherwise I had to go home to get the papers before the hospital would do anything for him.

Dad had always told me that whatever decisions would need to be made, I would "know what to do." Well, I always did seem to know until the doctor advised me to list my father as a DNR (Do Not Resuscitate) patient. I agonized over that one a long time, waking up in the middle of the night after I had said yes, wondering if the hospital staff would refuse to save my dad's life if he had difficulty breathing. It took a while before I really understood the meaning of DNR. The reassurance the doctor gave me was that they would do everything they could to keep him breathing, but if the breathing stopped they would not break ribs on his fragile body only to save him for another day or two.

Another decision I had to make at the end was whether or not to insert a feeding tube. After Dad's final stroke, he was in a nursing home for five days. When he first arrived, the nurses said I'd have to insert a tube because he wasn't eating or taking medicines. I didn't know what to do. Since I have no siblings, I called our pastor as well as a Christian visiting nurse who had been coming to see my dad for several months at home. Both advised me not to have a tube inserted. They reminded me that my father had been asking for a long time why God didn't take him home. He would not want the extra days a feeding tube would give him. He had already closed out this world by refusing to eat or open his eyes. His time had come. He was ready. And after talking with these two wise counselors, I was ready to let him go.

Betty F.

"DO NO HARM"

Before going through quadruple-bypass surgery, my mother let us know that she did not want any heroic measures to prolong her life should something go wrong. At the hospital's request, she filled out some advance-directive forms that stipulated her wishes. But when complications developed after surgery and it became apparent that she would starve to death unless the doctors inserted a central line in her chest so she could receive nutrition, it was hard to know what exactly constituted "heroic measures" in this situation. Feeding an individual seemed like a basic need, not an extraordinary measure. But my mother's prognosis was uncertain at that point. She would definitely die if she didn't have the central line, but the doctors hadn't been able to diagnose the cause of the complications—so it wasn't clear if assisted nutrition would get her over a temporary hump or if it would just artificially prolong her life by a few weeks.

Mom was still conscious, so we were able to discuss the decision with her—she opted to receive the assisted nutrition—but being confronted with the dilemma made me aware of the nuances that go into these decisions. I became convinced that, while it is very important to find out a loved one's wishes about medical care before a crisis, it's also important to leave some room for judgment calls based on the facts at the time of crisis. Above all, we should heed the principal ethic of the Hippocratic Oath and "do no harm."   *Jan H.*

The PMDD makes it clear that your loved one's agent (who could be a spouse, family member, or close friend) does not have authority to approve the direct and intentional ending of your elder's life. It forbids the agent from authorizing a lethal injection or drug overdose. It also prohibits him from directing that your loved one be denied food or fluids for the purpose of causing death from starvation or dehydration. It also states that Do Not Resuscitate (DNR) decisions and other such decisions are to be made *only* by your elder's agent if your loved one is not able to make those decisions. The agent should be an adult who shares your loved one's values and who will be comfortable asserting her rights. This is especially important for Christians who want an advance directive that reflects a pro-life/anti-euthansia position. For information on ordering a PMDD kit, get in touch with the International Task Force on Euthanasia and Assisted Suicide (see appendix).

Before an advance directive is signed, it should be discussed with the entire family, so that nothing comes as a shock during a crisis. Once it is signed, a copy should be given to your loved one's primary doctor. You and your elder should keep copies and review the document annually (perhaps at income-tax time) or anytime there is a significant change in your aging loved one's life, relationships, or location. (For more detailed information on advance directives, see chapter 18: End-of-Life Issues.)

Medicare and Medicaid

Medicare, the main source of medical-care coverage for older Americans, can be a confusing program. When mistakes are made or claims are denied, you have the right to make an appeal. An experienced elder-law attorney may be able to assist with such appeals. But be sure to ask about her experience with Medicare, because few lawyers are familiar with the program. For advice and literature on Medicare benefits, Medigap insurance policies, Medicare HMOs, and other related issues, you can contact Medicare itself or your local Area Agency on Aging. (Also see chapter 10: Financial Care.)

Medicaid, which helps to pay for the medical needs and long-term care of seniors who have low income and limited assets, is one of the most complex laws of the United States. Medicaid coverage and eligibility vary from state to state. Many elder-law attorneys have studied the statutes and regulations governing Medicaid and can assist you in helping assure your loved one's rights under the law. A reputable attorney can help you plan for the expenses of your loved one's long-term care as well as the protection of resources for family members. (For more information on Medicaid, see chapter 10: Financial Care.)

Legal expertise is expensive, but it is usually worth it, considering the complexity and costs of long-term care. You can also seek assistance or referrals from local agencies, such as the Department of Social Services or the Area Agency on Aging in your loved one's community.

Dealing with Abuse

Abuse, neglect, and exploitation of the elderly are major problems. However, such abuse may be difficult to detect and prove, especially if the victim is disabled or inarticulate and unable to describe what happened. An unexplained bruise, for example, may be blamed on an elder's unsteady feet and dementia. If your loved one appears to have been neglected or deprived of necessities, most states require you to show that the wrongdoer had a duty to provide for your loved one. Nevertheless, if you suspect abuse, contact your regional ombudsman program, the local Area Agency on Aging, or a protective agency in your loved one's state. They may refer you to an attorney who is knowledgeable about issues of the elderly and who can protect your loved one from further abuse or neglect. A lawyer also can take steps to recover damages for any injuries caused by abuse and may be able to secure the return of belongings or assets taken by an exploiter. (For more information, see chapter 13: Elder Abuse.)

A FEW MORE WORDS

This is complicated material. And terminology of estate-planning documents and procedures can vary from state to state. That is why you need all the legal advice you can get. It is a good idea to find a lawyer or financial planner through contacts you may have in your church, your family, or your work—someone who has proved competent and trustworthy, someone who generally shares your values.

Find a lawyer or financial planner through contacts you may have in your church, your family, or your work.

Pray continually that the Lord will clearly guide you through this legal maze. "The fear of the Lord is the beginning of wisdom," according to Proverbs (111:10 KJV), so that is a good posture to begin with when considering legal decisions. This job is bigger than any one person can handle without divine intervention. Always keep in mind the following truth: If you are a follower of Jesus Christ, you have the resources of the Creator available to you. You need only ask—but ask believing you will receive the wisdom you need (Matthew 21:22).

If any of you lacks wisdom, he should ask God, who gives generously to all without finding fault, and it will be given to him. JAMES 1:5 NIV

CHAPTER 12

Those who are planted in the house of the Lord . . .

shall still bear fruit in old age. PSALM 92:13-14 NKJV

Church, Religious Activity, and Spiritual Life

How to Encourage and Support Your Elder's Faith

When Olivia's 73-year-old mom needed help because of Parkinson's disease and mild dementia, Olivia and her husband invited her to move across state to live with them and their four children. "I felt called to care for her and to be a Christian witness to her," Olivia says. But the noise of the household made her mother anxious and confused, so she moved into a nearby assisted-living facility. Olivia regularly brought two of her sons to play piano (whatever they were practicing at the time) for the residents, and on special occasions, she handed out treat bags containing candy, shampoos and lotions donated by hotels, and a Bible verse. She also brought her mom to church events such as a children's musical she directed.

Olivia, whose mother has since moved to a nursing home to receive care for diabetes, says, "I always thought I had to make sure my mom became a Christian. But God has brought me to a place where I realize it's not my job to convert my mom. He's calling me to love her, to honor her, to tell her about Jesus—and to let Him take care of their relationship."

That realization has helped Olivia to relax in her conversations with her mom, and it has helped her mom to see that Olivia is not being kind only in order to convert her. "We don't pressure her to become a Christian; we just love her," says Olivia. "One day I was changing her Depends diaper, and she said, 'You shouldn't have to do this.' I told her, 'It's okay, Mom. You did it for me the first few years of my life. It's the least I can do.'"

What if her mom never becomes a Christian? "I hope she will," Olivia says, "but either way, it is still my job to share God's love with her now while I can."

———— ✺ ————

One area that provides room for continuing growth in the senior years is the spiritual domain. The body may break down, but the spirit is still capable of growth, renewal, or even new birth in old age. Those who are "spiritually dead" can find spiritual life through a new or renewed faith commitment in Christ. The new believer can grow toward spiritual maturity. The spiritually mature person can keep growing in wisdom, love, joy, and other spiritual gifts. In fact, many of this world's greatest prayer warriors are senior citizens. In spite of changes, losses, and chronic health conditions, elderly people can continue to cultivate their relationship with God.

Too often, however, elderly people encounter obstacles to spiritual support systems. Some are too feeble to get to church or to participate in religious activities with other believers. As their friends die or move away, they may lose their connections to the community of faith. Others feel alienated in churches that focus most of their energy on attracting a younger crowd. Failing eyesight can make it hard to read the Bible, and hardness of hearing can make it difficult to hear sermons. Seniors may be affected by negative stereotypes and myths that project old people as unteachable, useless, unproductive, or dependent on others. Like all Christians, seniors need the fellowship and encouragement of other believers. Faith that is not nourished stagnates.

Your sensitivity to your aging loved one's spiritual needs can give comfort and stability in a time of change and uncertainty.

What can be done to foster an elder's faith? As a caregiver, you have a special opportunity to demonstrate the love of God to your elder. Your sensitivity to your aging loved one's spiritual needs can give comfort and stability in a time of change and uncertainty. Looking up to your elder spiritually is very affirming to him. A minister or chaplain can keep in contact with your elder too. Despite the obstacles, spiritual growth is both possible and desirable for the continued well-being of elderly people.

FAITH AND SPIRITUAL GROWTH

Growing old is a long process that typically includes illnesses, losses, and time for reflection. One spiritual task of late life is to draw meaning and purpose out of why and how one has lived. For some, the experiences of life and aging produce negative attitudes: bitterness, self-centeredness, despair. Others are able to find significance in the past, meaning in the present, and hope for the future. A senior adult on the pilgrimage of the Christian life might honestly confess, "I'm not yet what I ought to be, but I'm grateful to God that I'm not what I used to be." An elder whose faith has been tested and tried through life's experiences usually has a stronger, more mature faith as a result—and a testimony to share with others.

But in order to have spiritual growth, there must be a starting point. Just as our physical life has a beginning, so also the Christian life has a beginning. Faith is a gift of the Holy Spirit, who enables an individual to repent and believe the message that Jesus Christ has come from God as Savior. A person is never too old to receive this gift, but it can be a spiritual struggle for one who has spent the majority of her life depending on something other than Christ.

Some elderly people find it upsetting if great importance is placed on an exact moment of conversion. This may be because the "conversion moment" tends to play up the dramatic testimonies of those who were saved out of an immoral life and tends to play down the process toward conversion experienced by those who were raised in Christian homes and came to Christ at a fairly young age. Others are not very vocal about their faith, but that does not necessarily mean they are not Christians. The important thing to remember is that being a Christian is demonstrated by our continuing love for the Savior and obedience to the Word of God. And just as physical growth involves a process, so also spiritual growth is a process. When a person exercises faith, spiritual growth takes place.

More or Less Religious

Gallup polls have shown that three-fourths of Americans past age 65 consider religion to be very important. A 1997 study found that people tend to pray more as they age; nearly 75 percent of the study's oldest respondents prayed at least once a day.[1] And although Bible reading has declined since the 1980s, half of all Americans over the age of 65 read the Bible at least weekly, compared to 27 percent of people between the ages of 18 and 29.[2]

But do we become more religious as we grow older? It seems logical to think that people who have more free time and who are nearing the end of life would become more religious in their later years. Yet research indicates that this is not true for most older people. Religious behavior is related to previous religious activity, the period or time in which a person was raised and lived most of his life, and whether he has chronic health problems.[3]

A person's faith and religious activity generally follows a steady pattern. The range of a person's religious involvement before retirement is a reasonable indicator of her religious commitment after retirement. If your elder was religious in earlier years, she is likely to be religious as a senior. If your elder was not very religious in younger years, she will tend to follow the same pattern in old age.

Keep in mind that being religious is no guarantee that one is a Christian. While good works done in the name of Christ may be evidence of spiritual fruit, Christianity is based on a personal relationship with Jesus Christ (who saves sinners through His finished work alone). In fact, God has prepared good works for us to do *as a result of*—not to merit—our salvation (Ephesians 2:8-10).

The range of a person's religious involvement before retirement is a reasonable indicator of her religious commitment after retirement.

If your aging parent or elder is not a Christian, you can intercede on his behalf in prayer. There is no point in life at which a person is beyond the power of our prayers and the transforming work of God (James 5:16; Luke 18:27). Do your best to "let your light so shine" before your elder that he "may see your good works and glorify your Father in heaven" (Matthew 5:16 NKJV). Show concern for the total person, which includes their safety, practical needs, health, and well-being. Some elderly people find it hard to trust others. But if your elder is able to trust you as his caregiver, he will be more apt to one day trust the "Shepherd and Guardian" of his soul (1 Peter 2:25 NASB).

God is patient, "not wanting anyone to perish, but everyone to come to repentance" (2 Peter 3:9 NIV). He does not force anyone to accept the gift of salvation, but He offers it freely to those who believe.

Losing to Gain

One of the most difficult problems we endure in later life is chronic illness, which can lead to total life changes and loss of independence. This may cause a real sense of loss that can be alleviated by helping your elder develop a renewed purpose to serve God even in these difficult circumstances. Chronic physical troubles, ongoing losses, or impending death are some circumstances that might lead to an even closer contact with, and dependence on, God's grace.

Having faith in God can help a senior to cope with losses and health problems as well as to find new meaning in life. True faith is active; it involves exercising belief and living with new enthusiasm. Highly spiritual people—those who agreed that "my religious faith is the most important influence in my life"—are twice as likely to say they are "very happy," according to one study.[4] Another study showed that elderly hospital patients who wondered whether God had abandoned them or questioned God's love were significantly more likely to be dead two years later than those who held fast to faith.[5] The content and object of our faith is what matters in the end. When soul-searching leads an el-

FERVENT PRAYERS FOR A FATHER

A few months ago it became evident that God was drawing my dad back to Himself. This, after my father walked away from God and the church 30 years ago and never looked back. Well, in January my husband and I and my sister were privileged to attend a service at a nearby Christian church during which my dad made a public profession of faith and was received into membership. (Yes, I'm serious!) It was significant to me that this service took place within a few days of being *exactly* 20 years after I committed my life to Christ and began praying for Dad.

The story doesn't end there. This past weekend, my dad was over for dinner with my husband and me, and he shared a concern that he wanted us to pray with him about. We took time while he was there to pray together, and he prayed right along with us. I got tears in my eyes. I can never remember praying with my father before that. I can't wait to see what further miracles God is planning to work in these situations.

Kathy O.

derly person to depend on Jesus Christ as his Savior, abiding peace is the result (Romans 5:1). The lure of this world loses its power and losses seem less devastating. In fact, the losses can become a means for spiritual gain.

When the apostle Paul reviewed his life before and after he had become a Christian, he concluded, "I consider everything a loss compared to the surpassing greatness of knowing Christ Jesus my Lord, for whose sake I have lost all things. I consider them rubbish, that I may gain Christ" (Philippians 3:8 NIV). Second Corinthians 4 also presents a good perspective for Christians to embrace: "Therefore we do not lose heart. Though outwardly we are wasting away, yet inwardly we are being renewed day by day. For our light and momentary troubles are achieving for us an eternal glory that far outweighs them all" (2 Corinthians 4:16-17 NIV).

But what happens if your elder does not depend on Christ and instead grows angry or bitter? How can you help your elder see her losses from God's perspective? The key is to find ways to show God's love through your actions. Your consistent love will open doors of opportunity to speak truth. Consider these tips:

- Be a listening friend. Allow your aging loved one to relive past stories and talk about her losses.
- Offer hope and encouragement. A loving hug and tender words can go a long way toward bringing healing to a grieving heart.
- Look for ways to help. If your elder's health problems prevent him from getting to church, try to find ways to bring church to him, such as reading a daily devotional book together or singing familiar hymns. Sermon tapes as well as music tapes and CDs are available from most churches.
- Remember days that are special to your elder, such as the anniversary of her spouse's death. When you care about what matters to your aging loved one, she will notice.
- Encourage new friendships and activities. If your loved one has lost a spouse and is lonely, it is important that he make some new friends with whom he can share his intimate concerns. Is he willing (and able) to attend a senior-adult function or choir concert at church, join you in some volunteer activity, or take

part in religious/spiritual support opportunities in a support-services facility? As his health allows, encourage him to become involved in reaching out to others in some capacity.

• Suggest a pastoral visit. If your aging loved one has spiritual concerns, would she be open to a consultation with a pastor, chaplain, or counselor who could address some of her concerns and perhaps offer to pray with her and give her communion?

• Do not rush recovery. Getting over losses takes time—and may take a lifetime! Instead, be patient, model a joyful spirit, and pray for your aging loved one.

Looking on the Bright Side

An older person who has optimism—a positive outlook on life events—is better able to cope with major changes than a person with a negative outlook. Research shows that older people who use their religious faith to cope with life are more optimistic than less religious people.[6] Optimistic people feel more in control of their lives, and this tends to lead to better health.

If your aging loved one frets about his circumstances or dwells on the disappointments of getting old, be sensitive to his feelings, but try to maintain an optimistic attitude. Let your aging loved one know that you are thankful for him. Give him a hug, and share with him a promise of God. For example, we can cast all our cares upon Him, because He cares for us (1 Peter 5:7 KJV). "God is our refuge and strength, a

AN ENCOURAGING WORD

A caregiver named Tara observed her mom grieving loss after loss, including her health, her home in California, and her memory. When Tara's mom was working on a scrapbook and realized too late that she had cut up a special photo collage she had been given for her 70th birthday, she felt terrible. "I just can't remember things anymore!" her mom cried. Tara comforted her and said, "Mom, this is not who you are. God loves you for who you are *inside*—you're His creation. We love you too, not because of what you do or don't do." Her mom soaked up the encouraging words, and Tara was able to share some Scripture with her too.

A senior who is bedridden can still be a powerful intercessor.

very present help in trouble" (Psalm 46:1 KJV). Sometimes, just reading a comforting Psalm or singing a hymn can brighten a gloomy outlook.

Leaving a Legacy

Every person on earth undoubtedly has a story to tell about his life, his passions, his beliefs, his successes, and his failures. As a person ages, he often begins to recount what he has done as a way of keeping connected to his past. It is also a way for an elderly person to look back on his life to remember what he has accomplished—or what God has accomplished through him—and what kind of legacy he has left for the future. Telling his story will help him gain a renewed sense of worth and hope for the future. It gives him an opportunity to recount how his life has influenced the lives of others.

If your elder is a Christian, ask how the Lord has been faithful in leading her through life. When did she encounter trials that tested her faith? In what way did God comfort or provide for her and her loved ones? Does your elder have a favorite verse from the Bible that carries special meaning? What is her favorite hymn? Encourage your loved one to tell her life story—not only to you, but to her grandchildren, too. This will give those children a sense of connectedness with the past and hope for the future. They will realize that they are part of a family continuum that stretches back for generations. Recording the occasion could leave a wonderful legacy for your family in years to come.

WHERE'S DAD?

"Where's Dad?" my mother, who suffers from dementia, asked over and over each evening. "Is he sleeping on the sofa? Is he coming to bed soon?"

"No, Dad's not here," I would tell her.

"He's dead, isn't he?"

"Yes, but he's more alive than he's ever been," I'd say, smiling. "He's living with Jesus in heaven."

"That's a good place to be," she'd say with a smile.

Betty F.

IMPACT OF A CHANGING CHURCH AND POPULATION

America's changing demographics should send an urgent wake-up call to the church. The population of the United States is growing older. The elderly population is expected to continue to grow tremendously, with the oldest-old (85 and older) as the fastest-growing sector.[7] For the last quarter century, the birth rate has fallen while the senior population is exploding. Yet most American churches continue to focus on youth programs and reaching out to the next generation while neglecting the fastest-growing sector of society. We certainly need youth ministries, but we also need equally passionate plans to integrate older people into the life of the church and to reach out to those who are too frail to attend.

There are benefits to remaining active in a religious community. Church attenders are not only more likely to avoid unhealthy actions, such as drunkenness or smoking, but they also have a stronger social network to call on for advice or help—important for both caregivers and elders. Frequent church attenders develop close ties with friends,

SACRIFICE AND SERVICE

I'll never forget the time I accompanied a 79-year-old friend from my church to a nursing home to see his wife. She was in the advanced stages of Alzheimer's disease. She was bedridden and didn't recognize anyone. We came in, and I watched as her husband fed her cantaloupe and banana, chopped up in bite-size pieces. He lovingly prayed with her, recited the 23rd Psalm, kissed her, and said good-bye. She gave him no indication that she knew who he was, yet he would do this without fail three times a week. Even though her mind was gone, there was real ministry happening to her (Matthew 25:40). But more than that was the impact it had on me. It changed my outlook on the meaning of commitment to marriage and to our loved ones; it changed my whole idea of faithfulness, service, and sacrifice—those virtues we extol. The lesson I got from that visit, which rattled me for days, was that God allows things like suffering, disabilities, and disease, not because of anything our loved one did, but so that *we* might change as we respond properly to them.

Pastor Bryan B.

neighbors, and relatives, and these have a positive impact on their health.[8]

While many elderly people do attend services, for others church attendance is a negative experience. One reason is that many churches and denominations have undergone dramatic changes in recent years, such as reexamining their doctrinal stances regarding the role of women in the pulpit, contemporary music styles, homosexuality, and other issues. The result is a church very different from the church of years gone by.

For older persons there is a sense of security in the traditional ways and a feeling of loss when these ways are abandoned. The switch from traditional hymns to contemporary songs, the incorporation of drums, and the use of drama and dance in some churches makes many older people uncomfortable. While some adapt to the changes or tolerate them because they do not want to leave their church, others slack off in attendance. Those who stop attending church might feel guilty for "for-

MORE FAITH, LESS CHURCH?

My parents were rooted in faith and were very active in the church all their lives. Church was their life; it was their social life too. But once they reached their late 80s and early 90s, their church became less relevant to their lives. They became more isolated and their religious expression more interior. Yes, the church was still important, but they felt like strangers to the church because they were unable to attend regularly and they sometimes felt nobody they knew was still alive. When they were able to attend, the order of service and music had become more contemporary.

The people who became important to my parents were the church pastor to some extent—he would come to visit and give them communion—and the chaplain in their retirement village. The chaplain became very important to my parents, even though he was from a different denomination. That didn't seem to matter at all. And their personal relationship to Jesus Christ continued to be the most important aspect of their lives. They felt close to God and really didn't need anybody else, other than their children, near the end. The last year of his life (age 97) my dad read no books but the Bible. He became a fountainhead and wealth of spirituality to his children and grandchildren.   *Robert R.*

saking the assembling" of believers together (Hebrews 10:25 NKJV), but they may not feel up to looking for a new church that is more traditional. In that case, consider checking around for a church with a worship style that suits your elder, then offer to attend with her. If poor eyesight keeps your elder from driving to church (a common problem for evening or midweek services, when it is dark), offer to arrange transportation.

Decreasing mental capacities also can make church an overwhelming or negative experience for a senior. Research shows that people with dementia (such as Alzheimer's disease) experience too much stimulation from attending religious services. Many people in this situation find it less stressful to watch religious television or listen to radio programs.[9]

In addition to Christian radio or television programs, chaplains and some parachurch ministries can offer valuable alternatives to "in-church" services. Services geared to seniors in nursing homes and retirement communities are often led by a chaplain or by a team from a neighborhood church. If your elder lives in a long-term-care facility, ask about in-house worship services and Bible studies. Plan to attend

GENUINE CHRISTIANITY

When I was growing up, there was a man in our church named Mr. Wiedman. He had always been an old man in my estimation. Looking back he was probably in his 60s or 70s. He had many health problems, but his daughter brought him to church every Sunday. We'd have sharing time often in the evening service and he could quote large sections of Scripture. He would ask for prayer for his neighbors and actively witness to them.

One time he told me about the difficulty he had had with his in-laws when he was first married. They didn't accept him and thought their daughter had made a mistake in marrying him. He said he always treated them with respect and kindness and made sure he was a good husband and father. In time, they came to love him as a son. And his daughter, in turn, became a faithful caregiver to him in his old age. That example helped me respond with kindness when people treated me badly later in life. He and his caring daughter were examples of genuine Christianity, an inspiration to me.

Nancy H.

services with your loved one if possible, or if your elder is bedridden, see whether a pastor or chaplain is making regular visits.

THE CHURCH NEEDS OLDER PEOPLE

A congregation can learn much from the spiritual maturity, wisdom, and humility of older, seasoned believers. In fact, older people play a key role in the life of a healthy church. Psalm 71:17-18 (NIV) says, "Since my youth, O God, you have taught me, and to this day I declare your marvelous deeds. Even when I am old and gray, do not forsake me, O God, till I declare your power to the next generation, your might to all who are to come." These verses outline the contribution the elderly can make to a church body.

Worship and Witness

I declare your marvelous deeds. The praise and thanksgiving offered by elderly church members is important to the health and life of the church. Older adult Christians bring a depth of experience and a lifetime of answered prayers to their worship and witness. When they say, "Great is Thy faithfulness," they speak from experience.

Personal Testimony

I declare your power to the next generation. Some people are not as open about spiritual things as others, but even quiet individuals might share their faith or personal testimony in the course of conversation in the nursing home or in the context of a Sunday school class discussion. One well-placed comment from someone who has been a believer for generations can have a profound impact on a group of growing Christians.

When seniors are able to give an honest, unsanitized recounting of their life and share a testimony of God's faithfulness, it adds meaning to their own lives and leaves a spiritual legacy for others to follow. It inspires us to show the same diligence in helping God's people as we "imitate those who through faith and patience inherit what has been promised" (Hebrews 6:12 NIV). One retirement center chaplain said, "It's important to seniors to be able to say, 'I left some of my important treasures—my inner drive, my love of Christ—to my children, grandchildren, and to the world.'"

Service or Ministry

With years of real-world experience and a wealth of wisdom, older saints who have "walked with God" throughout their life have a mature perspective that younger believers rarely possess. Seniors have much to offer as pastors, elders, financial counselors, lay leaders, and church volunteers. Churches do well to periodically recognize the elderly workers among them. If your elder has been serving in the church, encourage her to continue in some capacity, such as helping with children. The church is blessed when it recognizes and utilizes the special gifts and talents of its seniors. Elders who are too ill or frail to get to church services or to join service organizations may be able to serve others through prayer and role modeling.

Prayer

A key contribution of seniors is prayer. One Michigan pastor has a monthly consultation with four church members over 90 years of age, all active in church and in their faith. When he asks them why they are different from many of the other folks their age, they say, "Well, prayer is important to us." Their prayer life has changed over the years, they add. "My prayers used to be 'Gimme, gimme, gimme,'" says one senior. "Now they're 'Thank You, thank You, thank You!'" Another one acknowledges, "We can't do all the things we used to do." Yet another says, "But look at all the things we *can* do!"

Many older persons, including those who are not able to attend church services, find prayer a significant part of their spiritual life. A senior who is bedridden can still be a powerful intercessor. If your elder is a believer but cannot get to church, make sure specific prayer requests—and answers to prayer—are being delivered to him on a regular basis. Encourage seniors to pray for their own pastor, children, unsaved family members and relatives, as well as for leaders and all those in authority (1 Timothy 2:1-4). Your elder may want to become part of a church prayer chain or may choose to pray for one country or people group every day. Find your elder a book that gives information on missions in countries around the world. Schedule time to pray with your loved one on behalf of others. "For where two or three have gathered together in My name, there I am in their midst" (Matthew 18:20 NASB).

Encourage your loved one to tell her life story—not only to you, but to her grandchildren, too.

Finances

Many elderly people contribute to their local church financially. Be careful, though, about giving to unregulated parachurch groups and TV ministries; unfortunately, some scam the elderly for their money. (For more information, see "Safety and Sense of Community" on facing page. Also, see chapter 13: Elder Abuse.)

YOUR ELDER NEEDS THE CHURCH

Just as a healthy church benefits from the presence of older people, older people truly need the church body to support and defend them. The church that addresses the needs of seniors can add meaning and purpose to your elder's remaining years.

STILL TEACHING FOR GOD

Nelson Cowen, 91, has a passion, and it is not money. His passion is to teach the Bible to children in Sunday school—something he has been doing at Park Avenue Baptist Church in Mount Vernon, Illinois, since 1945. Still active, he and co-teacher Patsy Reeves use visual aids—maps, posters, games, and illustrations—to draw third- and fourth-graders into the weekly lesson.

While some older adults fear they cannot be effective teachers because they wear hearing aids or have physical limitations, Nelson doesn't let the effects of aging stop him. When his eyes grow weary from reading the Bible to the kids, he asks Patsy to continue reading. His weaknesses remind him that God will receive all the credit for any spiritual victories.

"It's my privilege to teach for God," he says.

Sometimes an adult will remind him that he or she became a Christian in his class. Some of his former Sunday school students have grown up and entered the ministry.

"I'm not going to give up as long as they let me teach one child," Nelson says. "It's a joy when you're doing what God wants you to do."

Patsy is glad to teach with him. "He loves the Lord. It just wouldn't be Sunday school without Nelson."

Adapted from Michael Leathers, "Retirement's Not an Option,"
Illinois Baptist *(6 September 2000). Used by permission.*

Safety and Sense of Community

An article in *Modern Maturity* reported the following: "Respect your elders; cults certainly do. They respect elders' retirement incomes, investment portfolios, and paid-for homes. No longer satisfied with recruiting wide-eyed and penniless youths, the cults have shifted their focus to older people—even those who have little more to offer them than their social-security checks or small pensions."[10]

Cults try to recruit people who are the most vulnerable and looking for answers—those who are asking why they have lost a spouse or a child or who are trying to find spiritual answers about their own death and the afterlife. Elderly people are perfect targets because they may be lonely, have time to talk, and are usually at home. Some cults are centered around better health, longevity, and physical well-being, all of which are important to many seniors. Televangelist scams and publications that are heretical or misleading pose the biggest threats.

To prevent cults from reaching your elder, stay involved in her life. If you suspect she may be getting involved in a cult or giving excessive amounts of money to televangelists, encourage her to find out more in-

PRAYING ACROSS THE MAP

One of my father's favorite things to do as a Christian was to pray and intercede for others—at church, with family, and alone. He wanted God's blessings for everyone. And the greatest desire of his heart was for all his family and friends to know Jesus as Savior.

When my dad grew older and couldn't do much all day other than lie on the sofa, he spent more time praying for those he knew and loved. He told me that his mind's eye followed a path across a map so that he wouldn't forget to pray for people he knew in many different places. He started by praying for neighbors, relatives, and friends in our local area. Then he moved on to people he knew in other states, and finally to those he knew in other countries.

A former pastor would often stop by for a cup of coffee and ask my father to pray for individuals and families in need of a special touch from God. How wonderful it was for my father that through prayer he was able to continue serving God and the church until the day he died.

Betty F.

formation about the organization's finances, programs, and doctrinal beliefs and to guard her autonomy. The Evangelical Council for Financial Accountability (ECFA) serves as a "Christian Better Business Bureau," assessing the financial integrity of Christian organizations. The ECFA's Web site includes a member directory, "donor's bill of rights," and "seven standards of responsible stewardship." The equivalent in Canada, the Canadian Council of Christian Charities, also certifies Christian organizations that meet established standards of management, stewardship, and accountability. (See appendix for contact information.)

Also encourage your elder to participate in religious activities that are available locally or where he lives. In addition to spiritual care, a congregation can provide your elder with a sense of connection and community. Churches provide worship opportunities, social networks, and, in many instances, support systems for older people. This is especially true for elders who have close ties to a particular church, typically rooted in earlier times when they were able to be active members of the church.

Spiritual Involvement

Church involvement also can keep elderly people growing spiritually. Other church members can encourage your loved one to grow in faith and finish strong. Praying—especially for missions—helps seniors get their eyes off themselves and gives them a vision for what is happening around the world. It also gives them a way to participate in what God is doing.

Some retired seniors bear fruit by yielding to the call of missionary service or church planting. Others take part in church projects that involve Christians of all ages working together. The seniors and teens at a Christian church in Grand Rapids, Michigan, built a one-third-mile prayer pathway around the church, complete with benches, bird feeders, and wildflowers. Another seniors group chipped in to pay for musical instruments for its church's praise-and-worship team.

If possible, encourage your elder to serve by participating in the educational or spiritual-growth programs of the congregation, or by comforting depressed or grieving folks of all ages.

WHAT CHURCHES CAN DO FOR YOUR LOVED ONE (AND YOU)

The church's ministry to the elderly can be both spiritual and practical, and ministry can be conducted both within the church and in homes— wherever home may be for your loved one. The church can be a source of help for caregivers, too.

Spiritual Help

Ministry to shut-ins. The church can provide a vital function in caring for people who are "shut in" and cannot attend church. Pastors can make regular visits to talk with individual seniors, pray with them, and offer the Lord's Supper. Ask someone at church to recruit church volunteers to send birthday cards to your aging loved one or to drop by for a visit. This not only makes the older people feel special, it makes the younger people aware of their presence.

Senior-adult pastors. In the 1960s and 1970s, churches began adding the position of youth pastor to reach young people. Now, with the growing aging population, some churches are adding staff members and pastors who focus particularly on seniors.

One church gave this role to their retiring pastor. As he stepped down from the position of senior pastor, he stayed on staff part-time as the church's pastor to seniors. This enabled him to continue serving the people he had built relationships with over the previous 20 years.

Counseling. In addition to pastors, there are churches—especially larger congregations—that have counselors on staff. These professionals can help elderly members and caregivers deal with interpersonal problems, stress, or unresolved guilt or anger. In addition, staff members might assist church members in planning funerals and assist families through the grieving process when a loved one dies.

Telephone assurance networks. Ask your church to recruit a few dependable members to take turns calling your elder once a day to say hello, to ask about any health concerns, and to chat a bit. A Sunday school class or care group could take on this kind of ministry, which provides natural opportunities to pray with an elder who has prayer requests, as well as share prayer requests with the elder. This service helps elderly people feel secure, knowing someone cared enough to check on them. It is also especially reassuring to long-distance caregivers.

Caregiver support groups. As a caregiver, it may be hard for you to ask for help. But the reality is, you need the support of others. There may be caregivers in your church who also would benefit from a Christian support group. Many people find great comfort in talking and praying about their frustrations and problems. They feel as if a burden is lifted. Simply listening to a group discussion and learning from each other can prove beneficial. Also, most professionals see support groups as effective ways to cope with isolation—a condition that tends to make all other problems seem worse. Just the sight of others who are in a similar situation can make your burdens more bearable.

Form a congregational support group for caregivers and relatives of aging loved ones. If finding a meeting time is difficult, you could make your group into a Sunday school class. Or, meeting directly before or after other scheduled activities may enable caregivers to simply extend the amount of time they have someone staying with their aging loved one rather than having to schedule a separate time. Put together a caregiver phone or e-mail list so you can reach each other.

Stephen's Ministry. A six-month training program equips lay people to provide one-on-one Christian support to individuals dealing with emotional, physical, or spiritual problems. A Stephen's minister can help a person sort out feelings and thoughts as they reflect the love of Jesus Christ. Stephen's ministers help the hospitalized, the homebound, the terminally ill and their families, those who are depressed or grieving a death or loss, those who are in spiritual crisis, and others. Thousands of congregations, representing 90 denominations, are enrolled in the St. Louis-based Stephen's Ministry program. If you or your elder need a Stephen's minister, call local churches to see if they offer the program. Or see appendix for contact information.

Practical Help

There are numerous practical services churches can offer seniors and their families, such as help with insurance or other paperwork, housekeeping support, provision of meals, and biblical guidance on end-of-life issues. Ask your church to organize a volunteer network of people to respond to these most frequently cited needs. Helping with practical needs often opens the door to sharing the Word of God and praying with caregiving families.

Respite care. If you care for an aging loved one in your home, try to find someone to relieve you regularly so you have time for yourself. This kind of relief—respite care—is essential for your own well-being. Your church family should be available to offer you that kind of support, but you need to speak up and make your needs known. If no one in your immediate circle of friends is able to help, ask for a few minutes to address adult Sunday school classes or Bible study groups and tell them about your needs.

It's important to ask for help in a specific way so that volunteers will not be overwhelmed. For example, you might say, "I need a helper for two hours three times a week. It could be six different volunteers, who would only have to come once every two weeks. I will need this help for two months, and then we will reevaluate." That way, someone can try it for a limited time and can get out if it does not work; people are leery of committing for an unlimited period of time.

If you find someone who is interested in staying with your aging loved one for a few hours, offer him some informal "training." Invite him to come spend an afternoon with you in your home. Ask what he is comfortable doing and introduce him to the tasks he might need to do, such as bringing your elder something to drink or simply sitting next to your loved one. Allow your elder and your friend to become acquainted so the time of respite care becomes more comfortable for both parties.

Adult day care. Some Christian churches are beginning to offer daytime care and activities for aging adults. For example, the Harlingen Reformed Church of Belle Mead, New Jersey, operates an adult day-care ministry that provides a safe, protective, Christian environment for seniors. The center, which has been open for 15 years, welcomes all sorts of elderly people, including relatives who are no longer safe at home alone, elderly single people who are lonely, and physically disabled people who need mental stimulation or a place where they can feel at home.

Helping with practical needs often opens the door to sharing the Word of God and praying with caregiving families.

About a dozen clients enjoy memory-stimulating games and activities, armchair exercises, crafts and flower arranging, Bible study, occasional theme parties and field trips, and a homemade lunch prepared by church volunteers. Expenses are paid through donations.

Call churches in your area to see if any of them offer this kind of service. Start by calling older, mainline denominational churches, which tend to have a larger population of seniors.

Transportation. Many older people depend on public transportation or other services to take them to the grocery store, doctor's appointments, hospitals, worship services, and wherever they need to go. If an elderly person disengages from church services, the reason may be a simple lack of transportation. In a random survey of two hundred Christians age 60 and older in Worcester, Massachusetts, almost one-third of those questioned cited lack of transportation as the principal reason for not attending church more frequently.[11]

> *If an elderly person disengages from church services, the reason may be a simple lack of transportation.*

Churches have a unique opportunity to assemble a core of volunteers to visit elderly people, pray with them, and give them sermon tapes. For elders who are still active, volunteers could invite them to church and related events, providing transportation and using the drive time to minister to their emotional and spiritual needs. If your elder's church does not have a plan in place, talk to the leadership about starting a visitation program and a bus ministry or a sign-up sheet for car pools and volunteers.

Clean-up and repair services. A single house call from a plumber can cost from $40 to $100. The cost of a professional oil change is about $30. Many elderly individuals do not have the resources to hire professionals for all repairs. Simple fix-it jobs can usually be handled by a church member who is handy with tools. For bigger jobs, the church could take a collection once a month to provide benevolent help to elderly members who need repair services.

An Illinois church youth group designates one Saturday in the spring and again in the fall to wash windows, repair fences, rake leaves, and flip mattresses. They work in the homes of their own church people and also arrange to work in a nursing home. Some of the elderly people give the young people a few dollars toward the group's missions trips.

Others receive the service free as a ministry of the church. The elderly are encouraged when they see young people doing something worthwhile, and the teenagers benefit spiritually from doing something helpful for their elders.

Parish nurses. Parish nurses represent a return to the historic role of churches involving themselves in health concerns. They do not offer hands-on nursing care—these activities are provided by visiting nurses or private agencies. Instead, parish nurses are registered nurses who provide education and counsel, and who act as referral agents for the health care of a church congregation. There are more than 3,000 practicing parish nurses in the United States today.

Most often the parish nurse works with both a church staff and a medical facility such as a hospital or hospice. Some parish nurses are paid staff members, others are volunteers.

Parish nurses have the training to discern things that the pastor might not recognize, such as signs of depression or hypertension. The parish nurse might also address the fears of elderly people in the congregation. For example, one parish nurse learned that her elderly patients were afraid of riding the motorized carts in big grocery stores, so she had some carts brought to the church for some private lessons.[12]

In another situation, a caregiver told her church's parish nurse that her disabled parents could not afford a wheelchair ramp they needed to be built at their home. When the nurse took the request to the congregation, a retired carpenter in his 70s volunteered to build it, even providing the materials and labor free of charge. In the process, he became friends with the couple, and his wife called the church to thank them for keeping her husband busy and useful.

Equipment loan program. Some church members may have canes, wheelchairs, commodes, or other home-care equipment that they no longer need and could donate or loan to others. Ask the church to post a list of available equipment and a contact person for each item.

Social and educational events. Seniors benefit from social time together. See if your church offers lunch outings, day tours to local sites or religious organizations, or ministry-related events that you and your aging loved one could attend. Perhaps your church could host an edu-

Parish nurses have the training to discern things that the pastor might not recognize, such as signs of depression or hypertension.

cational program on end-of-life issues or financial planning to address caregiving issues from a Christian perspective.

Housing. Some churches help with senior housing needs by purchasing an old home and developing it into a shared-housing unit. For example, North Branch Reformed Church of Bridgewater, New Jersey, bought an old home next to the church and named it Kirkside, which means "a house next to the church." Kirkside's stated purpose is "to provide a shared living arrangement in a Christian setting for seniors capable of self care, and to fill the gap between private homes and health-care facilities." A part-time social worker oversees the residents' needs, and a cook/housekeeper provides one hot meal a day Monday through Friday. Residents pay a modest monthly fee, but church fund-raisers help subsidize the cost of running the home.

How Do I Get Something Started?

It is all well and good to detail the reasons why the church and the elderly need each other. But what if your church has little yet to offer?

WHEELCHAIRS WELCOME

Our church was having a picnic. Mother lived with us, but because she was in a wheelchair she rarely consented to go anywhere, but that day she did. I took her up to where the church was having the picnic and while everyone played volleyball and did all the fun things, we sat in the shade and watched. People would come over and just talk with her. Then we ended up staying for a service there at a chapel and I wheeled her in. She got such a positive impression of the church.

It reminded me of years ago when my husband and I would pick up a lady and take her to church with us. She lived with her children and was in a wheelchair, but her kids wouldn't take her to church. It meant so much for her to be there, hearing the Word of God, that she would sit there and cry.

It's important for disabled elderly people to feel included in the Christian community. Others can say, "I'm so glad you got to come today," or "I'm glad you're feeling well enough to be here." That's simple social caring.   *MaryLynn B.*

What if your church leadership is unaware of the need for a senior ministry?

It takes just one person and a lot of prayer to get a seniors ministry started. "Our group started with one woman who was motivated by God to do something about helping the widows," says a widow who belongs to a large church in California. Responding to James 1:27, which says that pure and faultless religion is to look after orphans and widows, "she prayed, told God she was available, and asked him to lead her. She invited four other widows to have lunch at her house to discuss the possibility of starting a widows' group. They prayed and decided to get the

FOUR WAYS THE CHURCH LOVED MY PARENTS

1. A choir director in our church always enjoyed talking to my parents. He headed to their pew to chat as soon as they walked into the sanctuary each Sunday morning. He was a good listener, too, and he liked to hear about "the good old days." He always made Mom and Dad feel wanted and needed and loved.

2. A little girl named Stephanie adopted my parents as her grandparents. She wrote them notes when they could not be in church or when they had a birthday or anniversary. She came to their house sometimes to play her piano pieces for them. She liked to climb into my dad's lap to hug and be hugged. When my dad died, Stephanie's mother brought a red rose to the funeral, and we placed it inside Dad's coffin.

3. On Saturdays, four women from our church take turns coming to stay with Mom so I can do errands. They never complain or make me feel as if I'm intruding on their time. They seem to truly enjoy spending this time sharing a cup of coffee with Mom, listening when she wants to talk, or sitting quietly when she needs to sleep.

4. Our pastor brings communion to Mom once a month around the kitchen table. He pours a little grape juice into a juice glass so Mom can handle it herself. She sometimes sings with us and repeats the Lord's Prayer along with us. She usually prays beautiful prayers aloud, too, even though most of the rest of the time she can't say the words she wants to say. She asks Jesus to forgive her sins and thanks Him for all He has done for her. There is no doubt that Mom knows what communion is all about.

Betty F.

names and phone numbers of as many widows in the church as possible and invite them to a luncheon.

"The first luncheon was held at the home of one of the widows and 25 women attended. They were very enthusiastic about meeting regularly. As the church became more aware of the number of widows in the church and the needs they had, an elder was appointed to be in charge of this area. From this developed a service group within the church to take care of various needs of the widows such as repairs, cleaning, and transportation.

"With the Lord's leading, this group developed into a rewarding and worthwhile ministry, helping meet some of the needs of the widows in our church."

To start a seniors ministry, there first must be someone willing to devote time to it. The person must promote it, offer interesting programs, and be flexible. This is an ideal ministry for a caregiver whose loved one has died. If your elder's church needs a seniors ministry, call the church and see if there is interest. If possible, sit down with the church staff and explain what such a program could accomplish.

It takes just one person and a lot of prayer to get a seniors ministry started.

The Community Reformed Church in Whiting, New Jersey, holds Bible studies and other programs specifically for older people. One event the church offers is Vacation Bible School for seniors. "We advertise in the community and welcome all older adults to participate," says Rev. Peter Berry, the church's senior pastor. "About 50 or more seniors come out for our morning VBS program, which includes opening worship, Bible study, and crafts."

Three times a week the church is the site for a community-run nutritional program for more than 100 people who arrive for a congregate meal. "Many of our church members volunteer to serve as well as socialize with those who participate in the meal, 90 percent of whom are unchurched," says Rev. Berry. "When we have an upcoming activity at church, we invite them."

Be Faithful

As you take care of your aging loved one, don't neglect your own times of prayer and personal Bible study. When you allow the Holy Spirit to enlighten the eyes of your own heart to know the hope to which He has called you, you become better equipped to encourage your elder's faith and spiritual growth. No matter what happens, take the apostle Paul's advice, who, while a prisoner, said, "Rejoice in the Lord always. I will say it again: Rejoice!" (Philippians 4:4 NIV). Then commend your aging loved one to the Lord's sovereign plan and tender mercies, trusting God to be faithful.

As you take care of your aging loved one, don't neglect your own times of prayer and personal Bible study.

———ᴄⅣᴐ———

For it is by grace you have been saved, through faith—and this not from yourselves, it is the gift of God—not by works, so that no one can boast. Ephesians 2:8-9 NIV

Rise in the presence of the aged, show respect for the elderly and revere your God. I am the Lord. LEVITICUS 19:32 NIV

Protecting Aging Loved Ones from

Elder Abuse

Marcia, a single woman in her 50s, had a part-time caregiver for her mother during the week. But on the weekends Marcia was on her own—and that's usually when her mother was at her worst. Much of the time she didn't recognize Marcia or her surroundings. She would become agitated, wanting to go "home." She would try to get her wheelchair over to the telephone so she could call someone to come and rescue her.

Even though Marcia knew there was no point in trying to reason with her mother, she would try. And the less sleep she had received the night before, the more frustrated Marcia would become. Sometimes she would try to get her mother to "come to" by shaking her and yelling at her. "Can't you understand anything?" she would scream. Seeing how frightened her mother looked made Marcia feel terrible. She would hug her mother and pray that the incident would be forgotten.

Marcia soon realized she needed extra help so that she could get some time to herself and collect her thoughts. "One time, while a volunteer from church watched Mom, I just went and sat at the school playground to pray," Marcia says. "Having that freedom to spend a few moments outside with God helped me to think rationally and to adjust my attitude about my mom." Eventually, Marcia opted to hire a live-in caregiver—someone who was less emotionally involved and could help care for her mother. If funds ran out, a move to a nursing home that accepted Medicaid payments would be necessary.

Her mom has loving, round-the-clock care now, and Marcia has more freedom to come and go. When she's with her mother, they are happy, sharing hugs and smiles. Marcia thanks God every day for His provision.

———— ✿ ————

No one should be abused. And it makes us shudder to think we are capable of hurting someone we love. But the truth is, even Christian caregivers can be stretched to the point of abusing an aging loved one, especially when juggling many responsibilities on top of dealing with an elder who is needy or uncooperative. Sadly, abuse can also occur at the hands of others, including those who are paid to care for your loved one.

Abuse of the elderly—often underrecognized and unreported—is widespread in the United States. Nearly a half million seniors in domestic settings are abused and/or neglected or experience self-neglect—the loss of ability or will to care for oneself—according to a recent government study. Yet only one in five of those cases is ever reported.[1]

The American Medical Association's Council on Scientific Affairs has defined **elder abuse** as an act or omission that results in harm or threatened harm to the health or welfare of an elderly person.[2] Elder abuse takes place in domestic or institutional settings. It may be perpetuated by attitudes that consider old people, women, or the disabled as inferior. It may occur when a caregiver reaches the point of exhaustion and loses control. Greed and easy access to money may be motivating factors in cases where an elder is taken advantage of financially. Abuse may include:

- Physical mistreatment by force or rough handling that results in bodily injury, pain, or impairment (e.g., shaking, slapping, hitting, and striking with objects)
- Verbal mistreatment by demeaning language, threats, name-calling, or manipulating types of conversation
- Mental or emotional anguish caused by insults, endangering behavior, humiliation, intimidation, and threats (e.g., threats of abandonment or institutionalization)

- Failure by the caregiver to fulfill obligations or duties to meet the needs of a dependent elderly person (intentionally or unintentionally) and neglect resulting in injury, illness, or anxiety
- Nonconsensual sexual contact of any kind
- Unauthorized, dishonest, or exploitive use of an older person's funds, property, or resources (e.g., stealing social security or pension checks)
- Mistreatment or neglect of oneself including refusal to eat and to maintain one's own well-being by staying clean, clothed, and sheltered

WHO ARE THE VICTIMS OF ABUSE?

Among the elderly, older women are usually the most vulnerable to abuse and neglect, especially those who are confused, extremely frail, and 80 years or older. While abuse and neglect do occur in institutional settings, most of the research to date has focused on abuse that is committed in residential settings—in the elder's home or the home of the person caring for the elder. Sadly, the most common culprits are family members: adult children, spouses, siblings, and other relatives.[3] Yet elder abuse is difficult to detect, in part because of the social isolation of some elderly people who live alone or with family members and see very few outsiders.

Studies show that rates of elder abuse are similar for minority races and whites, and there are no significant differences based on religion, economic status, retirement, or education.[4] However, cultural expectations about what constitutes abuse sometimes vary.

Some elderly people abuse themselves by neglecting their own care. This self-neglect is most likely to occur among the oldest-old (those 85 and older). Typically, such people are confused, at least somewhat unable to care for themselves, and likely to be socially isolated. Loss of ability or will to care for oneself may cause an older person to wander outside without a coat in winter or ignore good hygiene. An elder who is suffering from depression may skip meals or get dehydrated from not drinking enough water. Also, lack of exercise or mental stimulation may result in physical deterioration. Emotional deterioration can set in when an aging person has too little interpersonal interaction. Once feel-

Older women are usually the most vulnerable to abuse and neglect, especially those who are confused, extremely frail, and 80 years or older.

ings start to become numb from loneliness, it is easy to let go of hope. At that point, self-neglect may become chronic.

When an elder lives alone, regular interaction with neighbors and friends is essential. Outsiders may be able to monitor whether or not the elder is maintaining healthy daily habits. Although the state is usually careful to consider a person's right to refuse protective services such as establishing legal guardianship, a last resort to prevent self-abuse may include court action to place the elder in a long-term-care institution.

CONDITIONS LEADING TO ELDER ABUSE

In shared living situations, elder abuse is complex because of the many social, family, financial, emotional, and health factors. Daily pressures or conflicts sometimes create an environment where mistreatment can occur.

Caregiver Stress and Fatigue

An elderly person, especially one who is needy, disabled, or in poor health, can be a direct source of stress to the caregiver. Often the caregiver herself is older and is caring for an even older and very frail person—a parent, spouse, sibling, or other relative. Many caregivers just do not have the strength to continue the job unassisted. Still, they keep on keeping on as they have done throughout life—and that can lead to danger. Even when an elder is not willfully or compulsively difficult— as is usually true—the demands or monotony of the work may put the caregiver over the edge of physical exhaustion or emotional fatigue.

A caregiving spouse, for example, may not realize how desperately tired or lonely he feels. Then in a weak moment, he may start yelling at his wife. A caregiving daughter who is also trying to hold down a job and raise a teenager may begin neglecting her parent a little more each day—not consciously, but because her emotional energy is depleted. Running on empty is no way to care for an aging loved one. Unfortunately, others are not likely to encourage, inspire, or motivate a caregiver to take care of herself. When the human spirit is discouraged, physical energy goes next. Forms of neglect such as refusal to bring a glass of water before bedtime, frequent scolding, or an angry slap are, more often than not, signs of desperation on the part of the caregiver. Don't excuse such behavior; seek help early if you have neglected your elder in even subtle ways. (For more information, read "Showing Empathy in Caregiving" on pages 337-339.)

Studies show that in cases of domestic abuse, adult children commit harmful acts against their parents twice as often as spouses abuse spouses. While spousal abuse was found to be primarily physical, abuse from adult children was more psychological or material.[5] Unfortunately, when the caregiver is as isolated and vulnerable as the care receiver, abuse is rarely detected.

Personal Problems

Sometimes the stress of caregiving is an additional burden, added to personal problems the caregiver already has. If a caregiver is deeply in debt or struggling with an addiction, caring for another person can be overwhelming. The stress of trying to balance everything can easily lead to abuse, such as using demeaning language, taking an elder's money, or teasing his loved one needlessly.

Elder abuse often results when a caregiver feels inadequate to handle the task of caring for a loved one. Small aggravations may trigger inappropriate responses. If a caregiver lacks practical know-how or coping skills, he might turn to alcohol or to prescription or illegal drugs to quell his anxieties and forget his worries. These coping mechanisms can lead to neglect of the elderly, accidents, and a lack of discernment when the caregiver is called upon to make judgment calls.

Unresolved Family Issues

Past family conflicts, difficult care needs, and current life stress can merge into an abusive situation. In some homes where elder abuse occurs, parents may have failed early on to develop intimate, caring relationships with their children. The adult children, in turn, often lack nurturing feelings toward their aging parents. Caregivers may be carrying childhood issues of shame that have never been admitted or resolved. If necessary ingredients like love and friendship are missing, a caregiving situation may become threatening.

Adult children with unresolved resentments may consciously or unwittingly use predicaments to get back at the aging loved one or at

The demands or monotony of the work may put the caregiver over the edge of physical exhaustion or emotional fatigue.

other family members. Caregivers who want to triumph over previously dominant siblings may try to control their siblings' access to information about a parent's care. Assuming control of the parents' financial resources is a particularly potent weapon in sibling battles of this nature. In cases where a caregiver is a drug addict, there is even more chance that valuables or money may disappear in order to support the habit. For the addict, providing care becomes a way to get what she needs.

Financial abuse is difficult to detect by outsiders or even other family members. Since there are numerous ways to abscond with funds, the theft is rarely discovered until it is too late. Sometimes an elderly person will find himself destitute and wonder how his savings disappeared. This is a cruel blow from which it is difficult to recover.

Increased Dependency of Elders

Those who become victims of elder abuse tend to be people who cannot speak for themselves. Often they cannot even get out of bed. In fact, older people in poor health are three to four times more likely to be abused than those in good health.[6] In some cases they see no one but their caregiver all day long. Despite the mistreatment, dependent elders are reluctant to report abuse because they fear what will happen to them if they lose their caregiver.

An adult who spends the majority of his time caring for a needy elder may resent the loss of freedom and feel a sense of unfairness, powerlessness, and a consequent loss of self-esteem. To gain power over the situation, the caregiver might vent his frustration on the elder or withhold needed care. Even emotionally stable, healthy individuals can find it a challenge to handle the ongoing responsibilities and demands of caring for a needy, elderly adult. But if the caregiver himself is weak, needy, and ill prepared, his aging loved one may pay the price.

Caregivers who do not allow professionals to be alone with the older person usually have something to conceal. Forms of abuse such as leaving a dependent senior alone for long periods of time or yelling at her for spilling foods or wetting the bed may emerge only after a professional conducts a careful series of interviews and checks on the potential abuse. A shrewd professional will convey an attitude of gathering information for the sake of improving care, rather than seeking to uncover weakness or to blame the caregiver for malicious intent.

Learned Violence

While some families take advantage of weaker elders through manipulation or neglect, others routinely use violence. In such homes, abuse is usually not questioned because it has become a way of life. It may be passed down from generation to generation.

Many victims will not report such violence because of shame and fears of abandonment or retaliation. If an elder does complain to a friend or neighbor, he may not be taken seriously. In fact, if you listen to the complaints of an elderly person, it may be difficult to discern whether his fears are a result of some degree of dementia or whether there is a real problem. The situation calls for close observation, compassionate listening, reading between the lines, and the willingness to take action if necessary. If you are not the primary caregiver and you have misgivings about a situation, you may want to become more closely involved and spend more time alone with your loved one on a consistent basis. It may be helpful to partner with another sibling or the elder's doctor.

Other Causes

Although unintentional mistreatment is often the rule, it is still abuse. And there are a few other potential causes for domestic elder abuse. They include:

- The subtle acceptance of aggression and violence as an American way of life
- Lack of financial resources and/or community support resources
- A history of mental problems or disabling conditions in the caregiver

The important thing for anyone in a caregiving situation is to hone and improve skills that enable you to cope with ongoing stress and multilayered responsibilities. Recognize when your temper is flaring and take time to calm down. Learn all you can about your loved one's condition so that you are not surprised by challenging

Don't wait until you reach the point of sleep deprivation and nervous exhaustion before you seek help from support services or other family members.

RECOGNIZING ELDER ABUSE

Be on guard for warning signs of abuse or neglect. Note: Please determine that these symptoms occur over a period of time before assuming them as evidence of abusive conditions. If you suspect abuse, alert the Adult Protective Services agency in your county.

Possible Signs of Physical Abuse:
- Unexplained bruises, welts, sprains, fractures, lacerations, or abrasions
- Patchy hair loss, redness of the scalp, or hemorrhaging below the scalp line (from excessive hair pulling)
- Evidence of past injuries on the skull, face, ears, neck, or nose—or tenderness, swelling, or pain
- Injuries to the abdomen, buttocks, or upper thighs—or parallel injuries, such as bruising on both upper arms, which suggests shaking or forceful restraining
- Injuries shaped like an object, such as a hand or a belt buckle
- Burns, possibly caused by cigarettes, caustics, or friction from ropes (resulting from being tied up or restrained for long periods)

Possible Signs of Physical Neglect:
- Consistent complaints of hunger or thirst, unexplained weight loss
- Poor hygiene or excessive dirt or odor
- Inappropriate clothing
- Persistent listlessness, fatigue, increasing confusion, or immobility
- Unattended urine burns or pressure sores
- Presence of fleas or lice
- Missing or nonfunctioning hearing aids, walking devices, glasses, dentures, or wheelchairs
- Isolation of elder by caregiver
- Over- or undermedication, especially oversedation

Possible Signals of Sexual Abuse:
- Difficulty walking or sitting
- Torn, stained, or bloody underclothing
- Pain or itching in genital area
- Bruises or bleeding in external genitalia, vaginal, or anal areas

- Extreme reluctance to cooperate with bathing, the toilet, or physical examination

Possible Signs of Emotional Mistreatment:
- Hesitation to talk openly
- Fear, withdrawal, or depression
- Implausible or conflicting accounts of incidents by family, caregiver, or elder
- Antisocial behavior, destructive conduct
- Sleep or speech disorders
- Hysteria, obsessive or compulsive thoughts, behaviors, phobias, hypochondria
- Habitual sucking, biting, rocking, etc.

Possible Signs of Financial Exploitation:
- Transfer of assets from a sole account to a joint account or from one holder to another
- Large cash withdrawals
- Suspicious signatures on checks and other documents (e.g., signatures do not resemble the elder's handwriting)
- Eviction notices or utility cutoff threats when there should be adequate funds
- Elder does not understand legal documents or financial arrangements that were made, or documentation is absent
- Unauthorized trust or property-ownership changes
- Reluctance on the part of the caregiver to pay bills or to spend money on the elder's care
- Lack of amenities, such as appropriate clothing and personal grooming tools, when funds should be available
- Missing jewelry, silverware, or other personal belongings
- Caregiver isolates the elder and/or gives strange explanations of finances

behavior and can respond with compassion. Also, it is never good to attempt to care for an aging loved one without help or relief from duties. Declining health makes elderly people vulnerable, diminishing their ability to defend themselves, to escape, or even to call for help. As caregiver, don't wait until you reach the point of sleep deprivation and nervous exhaustion before you seek help from support services or other family members.

IDENTIFY ABUSIVE CONDITIONS

If you are a part-time or secondary caregiver, and you are suspicious of abusive behavior toward your elderly loved one, you will need to be willing to confront it. The easiest way to begin is to ask the person you suspect of mistreating your loved one, "Can I help you?" or "Do you need some rest?" If nothing else, such a question acts as a warning and a reminder to the abuser that things are not as they should be. Remember, most abusers are not viciously or maliciously mistreating elders. If a caregiver is feeling overwhelmed and tired, he may confide in you. Or he may recognize that he needs sleep, recreation, or relief—and begin to seek it.

The people who provide services for the elderly are usually the first to suspect and report abuse. These include housekeepers, gardeners, home health-care workers, and social workers. Home health-care workers are trained to recognize the symptoms of abuse, as are doctors and nurses. They may win the confidence of their patient and indirectly encourage her to talk about abusive situations or the potential for danger. Usually trained to ask subtle but valuable questions, health professionals may probe elderly patients' fears, the satisfaction level of their relationships, and the possibility of self-neglect. Encourage your elderly loved one not to be put off by doctors' questions. These are often just a way to screen for abuse with people who may never raise the subject themselves.

It is rare for an elderly person's friends and neighbors to report abuse. This is probably due to a reluctance to get involved in someone's private business. People care but do not want to appear nosy. It is also difficult to separate the signs of elder abuse from the normal experiences of older persons who bruise easily, fall and break bones more frequently, and are generally more discontent or fearful. Many older people are reluctant to talk about private situations. They may be afraid it will only create further loss of care, food, home, independence, or money. They may have been threatened in some way to keep quiet.

In other cases, elderly people may not even realize they are being exploited or neglected. They may have grown accustomed to being left for long periods of time, to meals gradually diminishing in nutritional content, to being handled roughly or spoken to harshly. They may be unaware their financial resources are being drained by a caregiver.

If an elderly friend of yours moves away, try to keep in touch. Go and visit, and find a way to talk with him privately to make sure he is safe and happy in his new surroundings. You may have reason to be suspicious of distant relatives who suddenly invite an elder to move in with them—especially if the elder is well off financially. Don't attribute an elder's complaints, confusion, or lack of communication to "normal aging." It could be a sign of medical problems or a potentially abusive situation.

When making judgments about abuse, carefully consider your elder's total environment and living context. As one of many caring people in the life of your aging loved one, learn to discern patterns of control. Unfortunately, not all people are as committed to the welfare of the elderly as you may be. Balance kindness and courtesy with awareness and discernment. Look at things from a broad perspective and think deeply about them. If you have a sense that "something is wrong with this picture," then it may be. It is perfectly all right to confront the people who are responsible for your loved ones. Ask when and how an injury happened, how much time passed before medical attention was sought, and whether this type of injury has happened before.

If you suspect your loved one has been abused, try to speak to her alone in a safe, private spot (away from her primary caregiver or potential abuser). Ask questions that allow your elder to feel free to open up, such as: "Injuries like this usually don't happen by accident. Perhaps someone else was involved. Did someone hurt you?" If your elder is distressed, you might say, "You seem a little upset today. Has anyone called you names or put you down or made you feel bad recently?" If your elder seems reluctant to talk, ask whether she is afraid of the person who cares for her. Remind your loved one that abuse can happen to anyone and even nice people can be abusive. Ask if anyone has forced her to do things she did not want to do or taken something that belongs to her without her permission. Assure her that if she has been mistreated or abused, you will do all you can to protect her from future abuse.

Don't attribute an elder's complaints, confusion, or lack of communication to "normal aging." It could be a sign of medical problems or potential abuse.

HOW I MISSED THE SIGNS OF ELDER ABUSE

My involvement with Katherine began when my 12-year-old son wanted to do some volunteer work by making regular visits to an elder. As an elder law attorney, I easily connected him with a local aging coalition, which in turn matched him with Katherine. Though well over 90 years old, she lived in a second-floor apartment with her two cats. Widowed, she had only a few distant cousins who visited fairly regularly. My son quickly became friends with Katherine, talking about her travels, playing with her cats, playing board games. She joined our family for some holidays and at least a once-a-month dinner.

One day she fell and was taken to a hospital for a hip fracture. She considered moving into an assisted-living facility near her church but instead chose to move in with her relatives 60 miles away. My son tried to keep in touch but finally stopped calling. "She doesn't sound the same and she can't understand me and it's just weird," he said.

Why didn't I call her myself? She had never sounded "weird" before or had trouble communicating. Did I ascribe the change to the move, the fall, and/or the hospitalization, or, worse yet, her advanced age?

One Saturday, several months later, I received a call from the parish nurse at Katherine's church, who told me Katherine was in a hospital and had come in dehydrated, confused, and, it appeared, malnourished. As the hospital straightened out her medications and got her eating and drinking, Katherine had remembered the phone number of her parish nurse and told her story. Evidently, her cousin's wife, Fern, had been berating her whenever the husband was out of the house. Fern wouldn't let Katherine nap, gave her small portions of food, and accused her of being lazy and useless. Since Fern was named on Katherine's power of attorney, Fern assumed (incorrectly) that she had the authority to place her in a nursing home—and threatened that she would.

When I immediately called Katherine, she told me she wanted to leave the cousins. Within two days, the parish nurse, the local elder-abuse office, the hospital social worker, and I arranged for Katherine to enter the assisted-living facility that she'd originally considered. I prepared documents to revoke the health-care and financial powers of attorney that had appointed the cousins, and I contacted the banks to cancel her old accounts. A volunteer drove her to the facility, where I met Katherine with some fresh clothes. The elder-abuse coordinator arranged for her property to be picked up and put into storage. A few weeks later, I arranged for another elder law attorney to meet with her to draft a new will and powers of attorney and also hired a paralegal to investigate the status of her assets.

A social worker, Katherine, and I then met with the cousins, who handed over the contents of a safety-deposit box, revealing that Katherine was in excellent financial shape. When the husband reiterated that his wife could have put Katherine in a nursing home, I pointed out that Katherine was perfectly competent; therefore her health-care power of attorney was not activated. I added that she'd revoked both of her powers of attorney.

Katherine is now doing very well. She's gaining weight, catching up on doctor's appointments, and enjoying the renewed visits from my son and me. Each week she says, "I thank the Lord for the day you people came into my life."

Betsy Abramson, former director of Coalition of Wisconsin Aging Groups (CWAG) Elder Law Center. Adapted from CWAG Advocate, Summer 2000. Used by permission.

WHEN YOUR ELDER IS THE ABUSER

In some situations, the one who is receiving care becomes the abuser. Studies show that greater degrees of dementia may lead to disruptive behavior and abusive demands. A bedridden husband may complain, then belittle his wife, causing her to blame herself. She may not know how to keep from internalizing her husband's lies and accusations. Her caregiving may be faultless, yet it is typical for a woman in such a situation to think, *If I were a better wife, he wouldn't yell so much.*

In another case, a frail older person may take advantage of a son- or daughter-in-law's willingness to be kind and helpful. The elder may consume hours of attention above and beyond the call of duty. People who used manipulation to get what they wanted as younger people often use that power later in life to control an unassuming caregiver. Because there are endless configurations of this kind of abuse, a caregiver may not recognize mistreatment even when he is right in the middle of it. He may work harder, longer, and more diligently to please the elder.

If you wonder whether your aging loved one is manipulating you by abusive behavior, ask yourself, *Does my elderly loved one . . .*

- find fault in any and every situation?
- feign symptoms to get attention?

- berate me or yell at me for innocent mistakes?
- talk nonstop, prolonging caregiving hours?
- wake me at night unnecessarily?
- push, scratch, bite, hit?
- make excessive long-distance phone calls but refuse to spend money on essential services?
- make unreasonable demands for alcohol or drugs?
- give away resources irresponsibly to other family members or friends?

If you recognize your situation in any of these scenarios, it might be wise to consult a counselor who can help you to define your role and personal boundaries. A counselor will help you to articulate and to announce these to the elderly person for whom you are caring. You should also realize that a pause in caregiving may be in order. Find alternative care for a few days and assess the situation from a distance. Talk it over with your elder's doctor or another sibling. Seek feedback from others who are related to or acquainted with your aging loved one. Pray for wisdom in order to protect yourself from further abuse and to respond correctly to your elder's behavior, not returning evil for evil. Determine to speak the truth in love and to honor God in your own behavior.

ELDER WATCH

Do you wonder whether an elderly friend or neighbor is being abused or neglected? The best way to protect the elderly citizens in your community is to have regular contact with them. One way is to keep a log of the unmarried elderly people in your neighborhood, call them once a month, and take them out to lunch or dinner for their birthday each year. Or make a point to greet each elderly couple after the worship services at church. Ask if they need anything—and listen well. You could double a recipe and deliver a home-cooked meal to an elderly neighbor who is "shut in." If you or your spouse have handyman skills, you could volunteer to help with home repairs. The occasional contact would give you a chance to encourage the person and watch out for signs of mistreatment or failing health.

SHOWING EMPATHY IN CAREGIVING

Today's oldest Americans grew up in a more trusting era and were taught to accept and obey authority figures without question. When the elderly become ill or are in pain, they are often grateful for any care they get. They may be unable to articulate what they need or to think to ask for a more comfortable bed or a gentler touch.

Conscientious caregivers try to practice empathy consistently. Imagine yourself in the shoes of your elderly loved one. What small changes in the living environment might bring comfort? How would

WHEN THE UNTHINKABLE HAPPENED

My mom had just returned to the nursing home after having a breast tumor removed when I was called in to the administrator's office. There I was informed that my mother, who couldn't communicate due to dementia, had been raped by Joel, one of the male aides. I almost couldn't believe what I was hearing. I had known this man for almost two years. I'd given him presents when his wife had a baby. I knew he had some problems in his marriage, but he had told me he had found a good church with supportive people. Yet Joel had admitted to a therapist that he'd had sexual contact with my mom a few months earlier. Some of the other aides who cared for Mom indicated there were days she acted differently and stiffened up.

I wondered when Joel would have been able to abuse Mom sexually. I'm not sure, but I do know that Joel, who was taking college classes, had been allowed to come to work early in the morning when there were few other staff members there. While the skeleton crew was busy writing reports, he would have had ample time with no one observing him.

Joel was fired, but the nursing home, which is owned by a hospital, didn't want the story to spread, so the administrator tried to keep it from the staff. Yet I was assured that Joel wouldn't be hired at any other nursing home. Later a friend of mine saw him wheeling an older person outside a nursing home in another part of town! I worried about whether nursing homes do sufficient background checks on their employees. I dug out my mom's nursing-home contract and saw that they emphasized security and safety and caring. My husband and I finally called a lawyer and met with the hospital's lawyer for arbitration. That didn't go well, so we're considering a lawsuit against the nursing home.

you wish to be held? Where might you find unexpected but simple enjoyment?

On days when you feel stressed and overtaxed as a caregiver, stop and reflect before you interact with your aging loved one. Do you cry easily? Does your temper flare with the slightest provocation? Physically, are you exhausted? Is it hard to get up in the morning or make it through the day until bedtime? Subtle distress may cause problems when you are with a vulnerable and possibly irritable elderly individual. When your own tension or negative attitude filters through, even innocent comments you make can sound offensive to your aging loved one.

To gain perspective on your own potential for abusing a loved one, ask the following questions (or, if applicable, modify them to address a primary caregiver you oversee):

- How many personal sacrifices am I making in order to be a caregiver?
- Am I getting enough sleep and rest?
- Am I neglecting my own health in any way?
- Is constant surveillance required as part of my caregiving task?
- Has my elder's personality changed drastically due to illness?

NURSING-HOME NEGLIGENCE

Cindy's 89-year-old great aunt, Crystal, had a stroke that left her paralyzed on her left side. One day the nursing-home attendant seated her on the bed to dress her when someone knocked on the door. Forgetting Crystal couldn't sit up on her own, the attendant let go and headed for the door. "My aunt fell over and hit the floor head first," says Cindy.

Some days later, sore and bruised, she was taken to her room and left alone in her wheelchair. There she began sliding down, but the belt caught her and caused the wheelchair to flip forward. When Cindy visited her aunt in the hospital, she found her once again sliding out of her chair and calling for help. "No one anywhere seemed to understand her inability to hold herself upright alone," Cindy says.

Crystal's family responded by moving her to a different nursing home that seems to expect more concern and compassion from its staff.

- Do I use alcohol or drugs as a coping mechanism? Has substance abuse been a lifelong problem for me?
- Am I overwhelmed by demands from several dependent people in my life?
- Do I have financial constraints that interfere with following medical advice for my loved one?
- Do I have a family history of problems or issues that could be contributing to the mistreatment of my loved one?[7]

To curb any potential abusive tendencies you might have, get acquainted with your limitations. Offer a disclaimer before you start a visit or task: "I am really tired today, so please forgive me if I say the wrong thing in the wrong way. I'm really glad to see you." Or take a breather before you begin—get a fruit smoothie, a cup of tea, or any healthful refreshment that helps calm you. Learn to monitor your own inner resources. Make boundaries for yourself so that you begin to recognize when you need sleep, food, or recreation in order not to offend or mistreat the people around you. Get community support and regular periods of respite. Call a friend with whom you can talk and pray, bearing one another's burdens (Galatians 6:2). You might be stressed because you are alone!

Scripture can be a great benefit when you notice the frustration level rising within. Meditate on the verse "Love is patient, love is kind" (1 Corinthians 13:4 NASB).

Scripture can be a great benefit when you notice the frustration level rising within. Consider meditating on the verse "Love is patient, love is kind" (1 Corinthians 13:4 NASB), or memorize another verse that helps you maintain a positive perspective and a servant's heart. Hold firmly to the faith you profess. It may comfort you to know that Jesus Christ is able to sympathize with your weaknesses, because He was tempted in every way—yet was without sin. His triumph over sin means that you can approach the throne of grace with confidence to receive mercy and find grace to help in your time of need (Hebrews 4:15-16). Do what is good for your own physical health and spiritual well-being, and you will do what is good for your aging loved one.

INSTITUTIONAL ABUSE

It seems reasonable to expect the trained workers in long-term-care facilities to treat their elderly patients with care and dignity. After all, these institutions are state licensed, which means the facility operator promises to comply with a variety of laws, including health, safety, and quality of care regulations. Yet research indicates that 36 percent of community nursing-home staff members have observed physical abuse by other staff, such as use of excessive restraints. Eighty-one percent of staff reported they have seen psychological abuse such as shouting and name-calling, and 40 percent admit to having committed such an act. Ten percent admit to physically abusing patients.[8]

The elderly may complain, "I don't like that nurse," but inside they may be trying to communicate a deeper problem. Take it seriously.

Since at least half of all nursing-facility residents suffer from some form of dementia or mental impairment, these patients are particularly vulnerable to abuse—and highly unlikely to report instances of it.

Although there are many good nursing homes, nursing homes are generally notorious for offering inferior care. And recent news stories showing violent acts against nursing-home patients are enough to make caregivers think twice about placing their elders there. Forms of abuse vary: Patients might be yelled at, handled roughly, oversedated, denied clean linen, denied assistance with feeding or in reaching the bathroom, not checked for bedsores, or isolated for long periods in their rooms.

The stressful working environment and difficult or unpleasant tasks required in nursing homes contribute to reports of dissatisfaction—even burnout—among staff. This is often compounded by lack of staff, training, or understanding of patient behavior. Low wages and inadequate supervision by superiors make it even worse. Such conditions can be a setup for abuse. But be careful not to jump to conclusions about abuse just because less than optimal conditions exist. Many nurs-

---

FORGETTING MOTHER

When my mother was in the nursing home, the staff forgot they had left her on the toilet. The aide just didn't get back to her. Mother decided, *Well, I can't sit here all day.* She got up herself then fell and broke her hip into shards. The only thing the staff could do was to keep Mother on complete bed rest. Eventually she died from pneumonia. I understand the young aide didn't mean to injure my mom, but it was not what should have happened. *Sally B.*

ing homes are run by highly competent administrators and staffed by compassionate people trained to be patient and understanding.

Keep a Watchful Eye

A great deal of discernment is called for when confronting institutional abuse. A seasoned eye will observe undue distress by a patient or an unacceptable tone of voice from a staff member. If you visit a loved one in a nursing home, you will come in contact with numerous patients. You may witness many kinds of interaction between them and staff. Be liberal with praise when it is appropriate. Be watchful if something makes you feel uneasy. Sometimes you need to follow your hunches and report suspicious activity to the administration or your local advocacy group. It may be necessary to photograph wounds or injuries, the condition of a room or bed, etc.

Many nursing-home residents do not have regular visitors who can monitor their care. Vision and hearing impairments can cause misunderstandings or a sense of confusion on the part of the elderly. After years in such a center, the elderly may acquire a learned helplessness and acquiesce to inferior and inadequate care. They may complain, "I don't like that nurse," but inside they may be trying to communicate a deeper problem. Perhaps the nurse has been degrading them verbally, not allowing them to eat their fill, or pushing their wheelchair in a

HELP FOR ABUSE VICTIMS

If you suspect abuse, call your local Area Agency on Aging or a local hospital or health clinic. Or contact one of the following (see appendix for contact information):

- The National Center on Elder Abuse (NCEA) provides information, technical assistance, and a list of publications on request.
- The Clearinghouse on Abuse and Neglect of the Elderly (operated by the NCEA) collects materials and resources dealing with elder abuse.
- The National Citizens Coalition for Nursing Home Reform is a consumer/ citizen action coalition in behalf of older people. It defines quality care and promotes the best practices. A list of publications is also available on request.
- Contact Adult Protective Services in your county.

rough manner. Take seriously any problem that diminishes your aging loved one's quality of life.

Sometimes the problem is not mistreatment but sheer neglect. The staff may socialize with each other while residents sit alone staring vacantly into space. Perhaps a resident cannot get to the toilet on time because the employees are too busy and the home understaffed. At times a patient may cry for help but be ignored because "she cries all the time anyway." There are sometimes fine lines between neglect and normal tolerance. Keep the lines of communication open with staff, asking frequently about the welfare of your elder. Ask your loved one if she is comfortable between your visits. Look for a consistent level of service and care. Document signs of neglect so you can refer to them later.

When choosing a nursing home, look beyond the marketing people and get to know the staff and administrators. Are they caring? Are they competent? If they are, they will welcome your questions and concerns. Observe residents: Choose a home where they appear to be engaged in conversations and activities, are neatly dressed and clean, and where many visitors come and go. Volunteer to help with activities. Pray earnestly for the employees who care for your loved one. As people get involved in the nursing-home care of an aging loved one, abuse and neglect will be reduced and maybe even eradicated.

WHEN MOM TURNS MEAN

Sweet, gentle, innocent Mom. She never wanted to hurt anyone's feelings. She taught me to always be careful about the way I talked to people. Being kind was one of the most important things to her in life. When dementia began to take its toll on my mom, I hired a highly recommended Christian caregiver who could care for her while I worked in another room. Yet Mom would say to me in front of her, "Why doesn't she go home? I don't trust her." Or she'd say directly to the caregiver, "You're mean. I don't like you." I listened to her interaction with Mom through a hidden nursery monitor, so I knew the caregiver had done nothing to provoke her. If my mom had known what she was saying, she would have felt terrible.

Betty F.

Ask Good Questions

Be aware and alert. Because abuse is often an invisible problem, you may need to ask your aging loved one frequently about the kind of care he believes he is getting. Is he often hungry between meals or unsatisfied after a meal? Is he sometimes forced to eat things he does not like? Are certain staff members consistently unkind or harsh? Mix in questions like these with positive conversation and other more constructive kinds of questions. They may open a crack in the door for your loved one to confess a fear or concern. If you don't do this, he may not wish to bother you and you will never know.

Sometimes the problem is not mistreatment but sheer neglect. Look for a consistent level of service and care.

Take Preventive Steps

Encourage your aging loved one to stay sociable and to develop a "buddy system," a network of friends. If you are unable to visit your elder regularly, ask a friend outside the nursing home or within the institution to check in with your elder by phone or by visiting several times a week. Keep your loved one active in church and family activities as long as possible. To prevent financial abuse, arrange to have his social-security or pension checks deposited directly to a bank account. Review his will with him periodically. Remind him to ask for financial, physical, or emotional help when it is needed. Keep valuables stored safely in a safe-deposit box or safe. Familiarize yourself with emergency-response agencies and services available in case of sudden need.

Encourage your aging loved one to stay sociable and to develop a "buddy system," a network of friends.

Seek Help If You Suspect Institutional Abuse

If you suspect any form of institutional abuse, there is help. The Long-Term Care Ombudsman programs found around the nation are excellent sources. Funded by the Older Americans Act, they receive, investigate, and resolve complaints made by residents of long-term-care facilities or by others acting for them. In most states, Adult Protective Services (APS) are also responsible for receiving reports, investigating, and substantiating or refuting them. The APS also provides emergency services, administers assessments, and does evaluations. They may prepare legal procedures, refer cases to programs, remove victims or abusers from the abusive environment, and provide advocacy, volunteers, and education—the most common and effective form of prevention. You may also call the licensing and certification agency in your state (a list of such state agencies is maintained at the federal Health Care Financing Administration) or contact the National Citizens' Coalition for Nursing Home Reform (see appendix). You may need to find a lawyer for assistance if you choose to prosecute for damages for abuse and neglect of an elder, or to enforce the elder's rights in an institutional setting.

Before making an official complaint, work with your nursing-home staff first. Attempt to sort out and settle the matter, coming up with a resolution for any abuse you may document. Address the supervisors in a nonadversarial way. If they are not cooperative, contact one of the programs or associations mentioned in the sidebar "Help for Abuse Victims" with any suspicions you have. Discuss your doubts about the nursing-home facility where your loved one resides. They may be able to relieve your fears or suggest other things to look for, listen for, or ask about. In the context of elder abuse, it is better to be safe than sorry.

PROMOTING ELDER RESPECT

To effectively deal with the issue of elder abuse, it is important to be aware of the warning signs and indicators of abuse and neglect as well as

SUPPLEMENTAL MEDIA MATERIAL

- If you wish to be equipped with effective intervention strategies for defusing volatile abusive or potentially abusive situations, read *Abuse, Neglect, and Exploitation of Older Persons: Strategies for Assessment and Intervention*, edited by Lorin A. Baumhover and S. Colleen Beall (Health Professions Press, 1996).
- For a bimonthly bulletin providing updates on new ideas and programs, "Victimization of the Elderly and Disabled," write to: Civic Research Institute, PO Box 585, Kingston, NJ 08528.
- Videos that examine how to spot and prevent institutional abuse or financial abuse are available for rent or purchase from Terra Nova Films: *Financial Exploitation of the Elderly* or *Institutional Abuse: Everyone's Responsibility*. Call 1-800-779-8491 or order from Terra Nova Films at 9848 S. Winchester Ave., Chicago, IL 60643 or at www.terranova.org.

protective and support services that are available. But the best way to prevent our elders from being mistreated is to view them as valuable individuals who are made in God's image and worthy of honor and respect.

Keep in mind that the condition and limitations of your elder's body do not reflect the character of her spirit. Gray hair, stiff joints, and fading short-term memory do not signal the loss of worth or humanity. Proverbs 16:31 NIV says, "Gray hair is a crown of splendor." We can be a good example to others by respecting our elders, rising in their presence, and making them a part of our personal worlds and our community. The frequency of abuse will change only when we as members of society change our thinking about aging and determine to value aging people. Check your own attitude about the elderly by applying the Golden Rule. Are you treating your aging loved ones as you would want to be treated? After all, if you live to the age of your elders, one day you will be as they are. (See "The Golden Rule, Revisited," on pages 152-153.)

The best way to prevent elders from being mistreated is to view them as valuable individuals who are made in God's image.

Beloved, let us love one another, for love is of God. 1 JOHN 4:7 NKJV

CHAPTER 14

Therefore be as shrewd as snakes and as innocent as doves.

MATTHEW 10:16 NIV

Protecting Aging Loved Ones from

Fraud, Scams, and Greed

A senior citizen in suburban Washington, D.C., had her purse stolen from her car in the parking lot of a gym. While she was inside, she received a phone call from a calm, professional-sounding "bank manager" who said the thief had just been caught trying unsuccessfully to use her bank cards. He said he would cancel the bank cards immediately if she could provide her PIN numbers. The woman rattled off the digits, and subsequently had $900 stolen from her accounts.

"It was a terrible, terrible thing, and I just felt so stupid," said the woman. "He was just so smooth-talking."[1]

Another elderly woman with arthritis spent $100 for a three-ounce bag of "Moon Dust," guaranteed to cure her painful joints. Turns out, it was plain old sand.

A 69-year-old retired carpenter thought he was investing $15,000 in a conservative, high-yield mutual fund. Instead, it was a high-risk junk bond. He lost a third of his money. . . .

———◦∿◦———

Phony telemarketing ploys . . . bogus health cures . . . get-rich-quick investments. . . . These are just a few of the vast assortment of scams designed to cheat elderly people out of hard-earned savings and retirement income. To protect your aging loved one's resources from such scams, it is imperative that you have a working knowledge of the deceitful world of consumer fraud.

Through your awareness and consumer savvy, you may be able to safeguard your elder's lifelong, conscientious efforts at working, saving, and investing. In cases of medical quackery, for example, you may be able to protect your elder's health and pocketbook by alerting him to the unproven effectiveness of a particular health product or treatment. Part of your role as a caregiver is to increase your loved one's awareness of his own rights and of the dangerous risks of fraudulent business.

WHY SENIORS ARE TARGETS

People age 65 and older make up less than 14 percent of the population of the United States, yet more than 30 percent of consumer fraud is directed toward them.[2] In some schemes, older people—typically women living alone and seniors who are 65 to 79 years old—are the only target. Why? Some elderly people tend to have more disposable income than younger people. Plus, they are often at home, more likely to take phone calls from strangers, and more willing to allow a salesperson into their homes because they welcome someone to talk to. They may be lonely or restless after losing a spouse or retiring from employment. Some seniors are lured into entering sweepstakes or gambling because they are concerned about having more money for retirement. The lure of big money puts them at risk of making bad financial choices.

Some seniors are lured into entering sweepstakes or gambling because they are concerned about having more money for retirement.

Predators look for the most vulnerable older people to victimize. They intentionally pervert the truth in order to persuade seniors to part with their money. Predators sound convincing as they try to wear them down, playing on their fears, needs, insecurities, and helplessness—and the games become more sophisticated all the time. Many fraudulent ploys are effective because they rely upon the mental deterioration and resulting defenselessness of elderly people.

TYPES OF FRAUD

Fraud primarily falls into the following categories: identity theft, home maintenance, telemarketing, mail, sweepstakes/lottery (including gambling), health/medical, and financial (including banking, investments, living trusts, and misuse of guardianships). Most of these scams have at least one thing in common: they prey upon the fears and insecurities of elderly people.

The best way to combat fraud and scams is to make sure your aging loved ones have a comprehensive financial plan for their personal investments, insurance, and estate. A reputable planner can help. Then it should be easy and automatic to say no to all solicitations.

Identity Theft

"A good name is more desirable than great riches," according to Proverbs 22:1 (NIV)—but a host of scam artists specialize in getting a victim's identity in order to obtain more riches for themselves. According to the FBI, identity fraud is one of the fastest-growing white-collar crimes in the nation.[3] Every identifying number your elder possesses—social security, credit card, driver's license, telephone—is a key that unlocks some storage of money or goods. The social-security number, originally meant only for benefit and tax purposes, has become the universal identifier. A thief can hijack it from a senior by simply asking for it over the phone on an invented pretext. It may also be stolen from an aging loved one's wallet, found on mail taken from the mailbox, or seen on receipts found in the trash.

But seniors need not fall victim to this type of deception. Seniors who use credit cards can protect themselves against identity theft. Remind your aging loved one of the following precautions:

> *The best way to combat fraud and scams is to make sure your aging loved ones have a comprehensive financial plan.*

MY PARENTS' DESERT PROPERTY

It was the free flight out to Lake Havasu, Arizona, that got my aging parents' attention. With the real-estate agency's assurances that the undeveloped land they looked at would soon be equipped with water, sewer, and street lighting, my parents thought they were getting a great deal. They invested a lot of money into the property and property taxes and expected to either retire there or sell it for a good-sized profit. The land never was developed, however, and they were forced to sell it for far less than they paid for it.

David P.

- Never carry your social-security card with you. Keep it in a secure place, such as a locked box in the house.
- To minimize the work involved to cancel cards if your wallet is lost or stolen, carry around no more than one credit card, or leave it at home.
- Never give social-security or credit-card numbers over the phone unless *you* make the call and know who you are calling.
- Never give someone—even a bank manager or police officer—your personal identification number (PIN). That information would never be requested under legitimate circumstances.
- Verify if a caller is legitimate by asking the person for her name, organization, and telephone number. Hang up and look in the phone book for the agency she says she represents. Use the number in the phone directory to call and ask for the person by name. If she answers the line, she is probably who she says she is.
- Keep all receipts, and never leave them on countertops or in the hands of employees in stores or businesses.
- Keep a record of credit-card charges and watch monthly statements for discrepancies.
- Never leave your purse or wallet in your car.
- Report all suspicious calls to the police.
- Tear or shred your charge receipts, copies of credit applications, insurance forms, physician statements, bank checks and statements that you are discarding, expired charge cards, and credit offers you get in the mail.
- Keep a list of your credit-card numbers (and each company's toll-free number) in a safe place so that you know whom to call in case your credit cards are stolen.

If your elder's wallet was stolen or he suspects he is a victim of identity theft, the Federal Trade Commission (FTC) recommends taking the following steps:

First, contact the fraud departments of each of the three major credit bureaus—Equifax, Experian, and Trans Union (see appendix). A "fraud alert" should be placed in his file, as well as a victim's statement asking that creditors call him before opening any new accounts or changing his existing accounts. This can help prevent an impostor from opening additional accounts in your elder's name. Also, call the credit reporting agencies if you suspect someone is using a deceased loved one's credit cards or social-security number. (See appendix for contact information.)

Second, contact the creditors for any accounts that have been tampered with or opened fraudulently. Your elder should immediately close accounts that have been tampered with. Open new accounts with new personal identification numbers (PINs) and passwords.

Third, file a report with the local police or the police in the jurisdiction where the identity theft took place. Request a copy of the police report in case the bank, credit-card company, or others need proof of the crime. This proves to credit providers that your elder was diligent and is a first step toward an investigation (if there ever is one).

Finally, file a complaint with the Federal Trade Commission (see appendix) by contacting their Identity Theft Hotline. And ask for a copy of *ID Theft: When Bad Things Happen to Your Good Name,* a free booklet to help guard against and recover from identity theft. (Or check their Web site for a listing of over 400 free brochures on such consumer topics as identity theft, consumer fraud, and telemarketing; see appendix for contact information.)

Every identifying number your elder possesses— social security, credit card, driver's license, telephone—is a key that unlocks some storage of money or goods.

Home-Maintenance Fraud

Usually, this type of fraud involves a prepaid improvement or repair that is offered at greatly reduced prices. The most frequent schemes involve siding, roofing, driveways, and sidewalks. After receiving payment, the con artist disappears or finishes the job with inferior materials. If a victim complains about the workmanship, the crook may pressure her to accept a new, more expensive contract for additional work. Often the work is never completed. He may try to get the victim to take out a home-equity loan or sign a balloon payment, putting the elder in danger of losing her home. Unscrupulous contractors sometimes work in concert with predatory lenders, who may pressure victims into signing contracts they do not understand or into putting up their home as collateral. Some simply overcharge.

To prevent your loved one from being taken in by a home-improvement scam, find out how long the contractor has been licensed to do business. Ask about affiliations with professional trade associations and check with local consumer agencies to see if there are any outstanding complaints on record. It is a good idea to avoid hiring workers who solicit door-to-door; they often are not reputable. Encourage your elder to comparison shop at several established lenders before agreeing to a loan and never to sign under pressure. Once repair work is agreed upon, make sure the payment schedule is spelled out in detail in the job contract. Rather than prepay on repairs, your elderly loved one should agree to make a modest initial payment, additional payments as the work is being completed, and a modest final payment when all the work is done.

Telemarketing Fraud

Although some states now have tougher restrictions on telemarketers, consumer advocates say telemarketers are making more calls than ever. In what amounts to a new type of organized crime, 14,000 of the esti-

HOME-REPAIR IMPOSTOR

A car drove up the alley behind my mom's house when she was in her backyard. A man got out and told her he was a neighbor who lived up the street. He said he had put the roof on her house and needed to check it out.

Mom said, "No, my husband put the roof on."

He said, "But I sold him the materials."

Lying like this, the man managed to convince Mom to let him and his "wife" into her home to see if there were spots indicating leaks. When the woman asked for a glass of water, Mom got it for her, and the man walked through Mom's house. Almost as quickly as they'd arrived, the man and woman left.

Mom called me a few hours later. We called the police, who told us similar things had happened recently in the neighborhood.

When Mom was younger, she would not have let strangers into her home. She would have thought of a reason to send them away. She's not as mentally sharp as she used to be. Thankfully, no cash or jewelry was missing from Mom's house, but it's easy to see why con artists target the elderly.   *Robin J.*

mated 140,000 telemarketing operations in the United States are illegal, according to the FBI. Top telemarketers make up to 560 calls per second with the help of computerized automatic dialers. Callers dial constantly to make connections from lists of newly retired or widowed elderly.

Many elderly people are scammed when they are convinced to buy goods and services they do not need, especially over the phone. They are usually pressured to place an order immediately using a credit card, because the offer is "limited." One version sells basic items such as lightbulbs and trash bags then delivers inferior product at high prices. Another version is the "guaranteed prize," where cheap trips, luxurious items, or vacation housing are promised. The caller will be friendly, smooth, solicitous; then she will ask for a checking-account number, ordering a "demand draft." (This functions like a check but does not require signatures.)

Many elderly people are scammed when they are convinced to buy goods and services they do not need, especially over the phone.

Mail Fraud

Postal fraud happens every day. People are lured by a glossy, mail-order advertisement picturing a toolbox and tools for "only $40." Once payment is received, just the box is delivered. Ads are often vague and loosely phrased, promising lofty products like a "solar clothes dryer for only $39" that turns out to be a clothesline and clothespins. A free personal stereo that is "great for road trips" may turn out to be a tiny transistor radio.

Sweepstakes and Lottery Fraud

Sweepstakes letters come with all kinds of "bells and whistles." Some envelopes are totally plain, but the window shows what is obviously a check. In this way, the recipient is lured to open the envelope and fall for the gimmick. Envelopes may come special delivery with handwritten return addresses or may be colorfully packaged and replete with official-looking seals, stars, and addresses. Help your elder recognize such "wolves in sheep's clothing." Use a paper shredder to dispose of them. Avoid dumping them in public trash containers because con artists can dig them up, using names and numbers for further scams.

In another form of mail fraud, the senior receives notification of having won a "guaranteed" prize. The letter encourages the winner to call a 900 number to find out how to claim the prize. In one woman's case, the cost of the call was about $40, exceeding the value of the prize—$1. In lottery fraud, someone may ask for a minimal payment to do a computer search verifying winnings. Encourage your elder to beware of all such offers. If it sounds too good to be true, it is.

Gambling

Although it may not seem like a scam in the classic sense, marketers of gambling are hard at work targeting senior citizens. Casino tour buses, for example, make regular stops at convalescent homes to pick up bored or lonely retirees. Many seniors join "players' clubs" to get perks like discounted meals or hotel rooms in exchange for filling out a demographic questionnaire with personal information. With data ranging from wedding-anniversary dates to monthly mortgage payments, the gambling operators have a computer profile of each gambler and can tailor their marketing efforts to attract them back again. State-sanctioned gambling also entices older people to gamble who normally would not gamble at all. States promote lotteries in almost every corner store; in 1997, state lotteries spent more than $400 million to advertise their get-rich-quick fantasies.[4]

The result? A growing number of seniors are gambling with religious zeal. They are losing their retirement savings, pensions, and meager social-security checks at a time in life when that money cannot be recouped. Some run up thousands of dollars in credit-card debt to feed their addiction. They face financial ruin and can become suicidal. Understandably, many caregivers are concerned.

For some seniors, gambling is a chance to have some excitement while craving a big win. For others, it is a way to fill a lonely day or escape unpleasant situations in life. Those who are going through major transitions, such as retirement, moving, health problems, or the loss of a loved one, are particularly vulnerable. Statistics indicate that within the first year after a spouse's death, the surviving senior is at greater risk of developing a compulsive gambling problem.

How can you tell if your aging loved one has a problem with gambling? Consider these warning signs in your elder:

- Preoccupation with gambling and related activities
- Less interest in activities with family, friends, or church
- A change in relationship with spouse
- A change in attitude and personality, such as depression, guilt, remorse, or anxiety that worsens by gambling
- A sudden need for money, including borrowing from friends or taking out loans
- Unexplained absences for blocks of time
- Secrecy and avoidance when asked about use of time and money
- Increased use of alcohol
- Neglect of personal needs (e.g., cutting food budget or not purchasing medication to save money for gambling)
- Stress-related physical disorders
- Continued gambling despite warnings from family or friends
- Hiding evidence of gambling (e.g., lottery tickets, betting slips, sweepstakes entries)

If you suspect your elder is addicted to gambling, help is available. Contact Gamblers Anonymous and the National Coalition Against Legalized Gambling (see appendix) for help and resources. Confronting a person with a gambling problem can be difficult, so pray for wisdom and the right timing in order to confront your loved one in a nonthreatening way. Let your elder know you care, then explain your specific concerns. When a compulsive gambler is willing to admit to having a problem and has a desire to stop gambling, change is possible. Volunteer your support to help your loved one make needed changes. Also, set a good example for your elder. It is hard to expect your loved one not to gamble if you yourself play the lottery or go to casinos.

State-sanctioned gambling entices older people to gamble who normally would not gamble at all.

Health and Medical Fraud

Gone are the nineteenth-century salesmen selling snake oil and "vigor-restoring formulas" spiked with cocaine or other ingredients. But health-care deception is still rampant, taking millions of dollars annually from its victims, most of whom are elderly Americans. Two-thirds of the generated money in health fraud comes from nutritional remedies targeted to address the needs of aging people. Products come with promises to cure everything from arthritis and diabetes to cancer and other serious diseases.

Health-care imposters distort the truth, take advantage of seniors' fears, and offer false hope. Unfortunately, some of these frauds claim to be Christians. Misleading or false claims are often attached to promotions in magazines, tabloids, and direct mail flyers. They can be found on TV and radio infomercials and the Internet and in presentations by telemarketers. Common sales gimmicks include claiming a miracle drug or product can cure a wide range of ailments (often while accusing the medical profession, government, or research scientists of suppressing their "breakthrough" product). Instead of scientific research, the product makers rely on personal and hard-to-prove testimonials

---

THE WORD ON GAMBLING

If you or your aging loved one think the Bible has nothing to say about gambling, think again. While no direct commands declare it a sin, gambling may violate several Scriptural principles. It can promote covetousness and greed instead of contentment, luck instead of trusting the sovereignty of God, irresponsibility instead of good stewardship, and the love of money and self instead of the love of one's neighbor. Consider these verses:

- Whoever loves money never has money enough; whoever loves wealth is never satisfied with his income. (Ecclesiastes 5:10 NIV)
- No servant can serve two masters. Either he will hate the one and love the other, or he will be devoted to the one and despise the other. You cannot serve both God and Money. (Luke 16:13 NIV)
- People who want to get rich fall into temptation and a trap and into many foolish and harmful desires that plunge men into ruin and destruction. For the love of money is a root of all kinds of evil. Some people, eager for money, have wandered from the faith and pierced themselves with many griefs. (1 Timothy 6:9-10 NIV)
- You shall not covet. (Exodus 20:17 NIV)
- Keep your lives free from the love of money and be content with what you have, because God has said, "Never will I leave you; never will I forsake you." (Hebrews 13:5 NIV)

from "satisfied customers" as the only evidence that the product works. A Federal Trade Commission (FTC) investigation found that over 400 Web sites made questionable claims that their organic and natural products are useful to treat serious diseases and other health claims.

People with chronic, cyclical ailments such as arthritis are especially vulnerable to medical scams. With these diseases, there are often natural periods when the affliction flares up, then temporarily subsides. Sooner or later a natural remission will often occur. It is then easy for the product makers to claim effective treatment. When the symptoms come back, makers claim the victim should increase the dosage or "just wait." The FTC estimates that consumers spend $2 billion a year on unproven arthritis remedies, ranging from mussel extract and desiccated liver pills to shark cartilage.

To check out a product or treatment, encourage your elder to:

- talk to a doctor, pharmacist, or other health professional. If the treatment or product is unproven or unfamiliar, it is always beneficial to get a second opinion from a medical specialist.
- get advice from family members and friends. Be on your guard if the people offering a drug or treatment try to discourage you from talking to others about their "secret treatment" or "cure."
- check with the Better Business Bureau, your state attorney general's office, state department of health, or local consumer protection agency to see whether other consumers have submitted complaints about the product or its marketer. Or contact your local Food and Drug Administration (FDA) office (look in the blue pages of the phone book under U.S. Government, Health and Human Services). The FDA can tell you whether the agency has taken action against the product or its marketer. (See the appendix for their Web site.)
- check with a health-professional group, such as the American Heart Association, the American Diabetes Association, or the National Arthritis Foundation for products that are promoted for heart disease, diabetes, or arthritis. Ask about local chapters that can provide you with resource materials about a given disease.

• call your local FDA office to report a company for falsely labeling its products. To report an adverse reaction or illness that you think is related to the use of a supplement, call a doctor or other health-care provider immediately.

Financial Fraud

Several forms of financial fraud are especially aimed at elderly people. Consider the following examples:

THE "BANK EXAMINER" SCHEME

There are variations of this scheme, but in the classic scam, swindlers pose as bank or police officials, again targeting the elderly. The "bank examiner" calls the senior and reports that his checking or savings account has had some unusual withdrawals. Explaining that the bank is attempting to catch an embezzler, the con artist requests that the victim withdraw anywhere from five hundred to several thousand dollars for marking and recording serial numbers. The "official" comes to the senior's home, provides a receipt for the cash, and promises that the money will be returned when the suspect has been caught. The victim never sees that money again.

INVESTMENT FRAUD

Fraudulent investors make use of computer-generated lists of newly retired employees or elderly people who have just sold a home. Sophisticated investment con artists try to sell shares in gold, gemstones, or rare coins that are legal but not appropriate for the elderly because the risks are too high. Elderly people may be promised cheap land in beautiful places. Many of the investments lose their value rapidly and are not marketable shortly after purchase. The best advice here: don't.

LIVING TRUST SCAMS

These have emerged out of the need for an estate-planning device that avoids probate. Living Trust scams take advantage of older adults who want to make financial arrangements relating to their death. While a living trust—in which a person's assets are transferred during his lifetime and distributed at the time of death—can be legitimate, disreputable attorneys misrepresent the costs and benefits of trusts versus wills. They charge fees far above fair (ranging from $150 to $1000 regardless of the size of the estate), even though elders with annual incomes of $25,000 or less are the least likely to benefit from sophisticated estate-planning services. The attorney issues living trusts that are often defective or riddled with mistakes. Afterwards, you or your elder may have a hard time reaching him. In some cases, the offer of help in estate planning is a ploy to gain access to a consumer's financial information and to sell other financial products, such as insurance annuities. Great care needs to be part of any "living trust" agreement or negotiation. Compare costs. Get referrals for reputable attorneys. Pay for a second opinion or evaluation. (For more information, read "Protecting Your Loved One's Assets" on pages 280-290.)

PYRAMID SCHEMES

Be skeptical of any program that promises quick money for recruiting new members. Although some multilevel or "network" marketing plans are legitimate ways of selling goods or services through distributors, others are illegal pyramid schemes. In pyramids, commissions are based on the number of distributors recruited. Most of the products are sold to these distributors—not to the public at large. Your elder should beware of plans that promise enormous earnings, sell "miracle" products, or ask new distributors to spend money on costly inventory and marketing materials. The plan's promoter might pay false references to lie about their earnings through the plan. The vast majority of participants end up losing money to pay for the lucky few. If your elder is considering a multilevel marketing opportunity, suggest she call the local Better Business Bureau and state Attorney General about the plan. For more information, contact the Federal Trade Commission (see appendix).

DISPOSABLE INCOME

The most difficult caregiving circumstance I have dealt with so far involved two people who probably viewed Mother as someone with money. As a Christian, she wanted to meet the couple's needs, so she paid some of their monthly expenses. She also made it possible for them to get a dependable car. Within a year, the car was traded for drugs.

Jeremy W.

FRAUD BY FRIENDS AND GUARDIANS

Financial exploitation is common by court-ordered guardians who are appointed to manage the banking of elderly people. This kind of fraud is not easy to detect and even harder to prove. Most states do not require much accountability because proving it is complicated. It involves examination of savings accounts and items of deposit and retrieval of canceled checks. It also mandates following the flow of the victim's and the victimizer's funds. An aging person may be physically or mentally impaired (even dead) while a fraudulent guardian uses his money to acquire luxuries such as land and fancy cars.

FRAUDULENT ASSOCIATIONS

A common form of financial fraud involves groups that solicit donations using names similar to authentic charity or religious organizations. These con artists prey upon an elderly person's altruism and community spirit. Help your elder investigate the credentials of any group that is soliciting money. Remind him it is not wise to give to a group just because he hears trusted words or phrases such as *American* or *Christian.*

Your loved one also may be approached by so-called government-service officials (with titles that include legitimate-sounding words such as *social security*) who offer "required" or "critically needed" items such as plastic-coated ID cards. Try to make sure your parents or older loved ones refuse such services.

Other warnings to the elderly about financial fraud:

- Be careful if children you do not recognize come to the door and want to sell magazine subscriptions. They may be putting the money into their own pockets.
- Travel clubs offer bargain packages, but look and listen for hidden conditions.
- Work-at-home schemes promise big bucks for simple tasks, but they generally are not worth it. For example, after paying a fee to a mail-in ad, the victim may receive instructions on how to circulate the same ad, victimizing others.
- Do not give money to anyone you do not know.
- Do not buy into mail-order lab tests—they often yield phony results.

RELIGIOUS PREYING

My grandmother, Grace, was a kind, generous woman—the kind of woman who would always drop pennies into the "Help the Children" boxes in grocery stores. When she was 74, she got a birthday gift that she thought was extravagant: a "colored TV." She'd always said that a black-and-white was good enough for her, since it had been good enough for her husband, Sander, who had died nine years earlier. But with the arrival of that colored TV, she sat entranced, hour after hour. She became especially hooked on "evangelistic programming." When she was asked to give to help the station reach more people for Jesus Christ, she gave. And then she gave some more.

We had no idea how much money she was giving these "religious" organizations until one day when my father was there and happened upon my grandmother's checkbook. He was stunned. In less than six months, she'd given more than $4,500 of her income, which was only $13,000 a year, to one of these "needy" religious stations! My father was intensely angry. Although he's a Christian himself and generous to those in need, he knew that particular religious organization had been charged for misusing funds. And yet the group was still allowed to "market" itself over the air! To make it worse, my grandmother admitted, when asked, that people from the station—and other "kind souls" from myriad organizations somehow associated with the television station—had been calling her house weekly to solicit donations for other projects, including needy children. Plus, she'd already sent in six of the dozen $100 payments required to take a "trip to Israel" with a supposedly Christian group that only had a post-office box for an address.

Appalled, my father made immediate phone calls to the station, directing them to take my grandmother's name off their mailing list, phone-calling list, and any lists that they sold to other organizations. Then he followed up with a letter to the station that same day, documenting his actions and saying that he had an attorney standing by to pursue the case, should they continue to contact my grandmother. Regarding the trip to Israel, my father found out that there was no such group. The individual who'd rented the box had used an assumed name and then left town.

After that, my father convinced my grandmother, who felt horrible when she found out her money hadn't really been helping the needy, to talk with him before writing a check to any organization.   *Ramona S.*

HELP YOUR AGING LOVED ONES ELUDE SCAMS

The National Consumers League warns senior citizens that fraudulent businesspeople are criminals, not shrewd people who have simply outfoxed them. Some salespeople are brilliant manipulators who continue to prey upon victims again and again. Experts agree that the best way to help an elderly person combat fraud is to remind her to:

- get your feedback on any transaction over an amount you two agree on.
- realize no one is too smart to be outwitted by a scam—clever criminals find ways to exploit people's blind spots.
- answer the telephone as carefully as he answers the door. Tell him to just say, "No" or "I don't take sales calls" and hang up.
- have a message recorder on the telephone—scam artists do not leave messages.
- never give social-security, bank-account, or credit-card numbers over the phone.
- get an unlisted phone number in the event of consistent soliciting phone calls.
- get Caller ID in order to screen calls.
- request that her phone number be put on the "Do Not Call" list from the Direct Marketing Association's Telephone Preference Service. Your elder may also opt out of direct-mail marketing and e-mail marketing solicitations from many national companies. To remove her name from many national direct-mail lists, write to DMA Mail Preference Service (see appendix).
- forgo filling out a product-warranty card or entering a sweepstakes. (Phone numbers may be sold to other lists, increasing the amount of calls from solicitors. Besides, the warranty is in effect even if the card is not sent in.)
- remember this: if you have to pay even a small amount for something you have won, you have not won!
- hang up on telephone solicitors, shut the door on intruders, and walk away from pushy salespeople.
- seek advice before investing any money in anything, even giving to charities. Check with the Better Business Bureau first. Ask for verified financial statements before giving. Require in writing a statement of each charity's name, address, and phone number, as well as a breakdown of where the proceeds will go. Contact the Evangelical Council for Financial Accountability, or, in Canada, the Canadian Council of Christian Chartities for an assessment

of the spiritual and financial integrity of certain Christian organizations (see appendix).

- get all estimates for home repairs, and any promises, in writing. Do not prepay.
- avoid loaning or giving cash to strangers or panhandlers.
- read every form before signing. Do business only with those whose references, licenses, and credentials you have checked.
- consider purchasing *From Victim to Victor*, a guide on how to regain credit, written by victim of identity fraud and attorney Mari J. Frank. Published by Porpoise Press (1998), the book can be purchased in a local bookstore as part of an Identity Theft Survival Kit. This includes a computer diskette with attorney-composed letters to write to financial and governmental agencies in order to restore credit.

HOW TO STOP FRAUD

Contact Organizations That Can Help

Some communities have formed Triad/S.A.L.T. (Seniors and Lawmen Working Together) organizations that work with senior citizens to prevent victimization of the elderly. They cooperate with local sheriffs and police departments to determine the needs and concerns of older people in various regions. They also help form neighborhood-watch groups, distribute information about current trendy scams, and offer victim assistance. In some areas, representatives make daily phone calls to older people who are housebound. Volunteers can "adopt a senior" in their community and make frequent visits. Regularly scheduled transportation may be offered to local groceries and clinics. Some public-service organizations teach safe ways to carry money and store valuables, with a focus to enhance the quality of life for elderly citizens. Contact your local Area Agency on Aging for the phone numbers and addresses. Have a S.A.L.T. group make a presentation at your church or senior center; that way, the information comes from "experts," not just from the caregiver. If there is no S.A.L.T. program in your area, talk to your local law-enforcement agency, district attorney's office, or the Better Business Bureau for suggestions (see appendix).

Be Discerning and Open

Older adults may be embarrassed about being "taken" in a scam and would prefer not to let anyone know, especially if large amounts of money are involved. Con artists are not only aware of this, they bank on it! More than anything else, to prevent fraud, openness is called for by both you and your elderly loved one. It may be a challenge to monitor your parents' or older loved one's affairs without appearing to patronize or "parent" them. And your loved one may not want to admit or believe that a seemingly nice person could be a lying, stealing, scheming con artist. The main goal is to encourage your aging loved one not to be in denial about fraud—it is out there full force. Standing together against fraud makes it easier to admit the reality of this wide world of schemers. If your elder does not have a comprehensive financial plan, look into finding a reputable planner who can help make arrangements for his estate, insurance, investments, and giving. That way he will be less prone to entertaining fraudulent schemes. (For more information, read "Use a Financial Planner" on pages 250-254.)

The main goal is to encourage your aging loved one not to be in denial about fraud— it is out there full force.

Look for Warning Signs

Neither you nor your aging loved one should have to end up in a position to ask, "Who could have known?" Look for the following warning signs that your elder may be involved in some kind of scam. Does your aging loved one:

- receive large stacks of mail each day?
- not want to go out, because she is afraid she will miss a prize delivery (or does she leave notes for the postal worker)?
- act frustrated and confused when the bank statement has mysterious debits?
- receive many magazine subscriptions, especially ones that are inappropriate to his age-group, interests, or lifestyle?
- tally 900 numbers on her phone bill?
- accumulate a large number of "prizes" such as tapes, CDs, jewelry, videos?
- ask you frequently to help him decide which vehicle or prize he should choose?

Be in tune with the needs, wants, and concerns of your aging loved one. Put her in contact with a reputable attorney, doctor, and counselor or pastor who can give consistent, grounded advice. Ask your loved one to talk to friends about the possibilities of fraud and how to avoid it. Pray for your elder's protection and discernment so that he is not taken in by a con artist's schemes.

Keep the Faith

No matter what kinds of schemes and scams are out there, we do not have to become cynical and cold. Helen Keller, the blind and deaf woman whose life demonstrated how light overcomes darkness, said, "The world is full of suffering, but it is also full of overcoming it." Just because evil preys on weakness does not mean your loved one has to succumb to it or be overcome by it. Keep your elder informed of new and old scams. Take the initiative to see if your elder has a complete financial plan in place for his investments, assets, and charitable giving. The more prepared your loved one is, the less vulnerable he will be to fraud and scams. When possible, read Proverbs or study the Bible with your loved one in order to "be wise in the way you act toward outsiders" (Colossians 4:5 NIV). If your elder is defrauded, pray for God's provision of wisdom, offer comfort, and seek help for your loved one.

Be very careful, then, how you live—not as unwise but as wise, making the most of every opportunity, because the days are evil. Ephesians 5:15-16 NIV

But if a widow has children or grandchildren, these should learn first of all to put their religion into practice by caring for their own family and so repaying their parents and grandparents, for this is pleasing to God. 1 TIMOTHY 5:4 NIV

Helping Your Elder Remain at Home
Plus, Community-Based Resources

Judy's elderly mom was not eating her meals on time and often was distracted while cooking food on the stove. When Judy dropped by and smelled burnt food on several occasions, she knew it was unsafe for her mother to continue living alone. Her mother made it clear that she did not want to move out of her condo, so Judy and her sister began contacting home health agencies to find a part-time homemaker/companion who could stay with their mother during the day. "We went through several helpers, including an older woman who didn't seem to know what to do and an Eastern European teenager who could barely speak English," Judy says. Finally they found the right woman—a friendly companion who makes meals, does light housekeeping, and takes their mother to the store and fitness center. The agency supplies an alternate helper during vacation days in the summer. "Mother loves the companionship and help, and I have peace of mind that she's not going to burn the building down!" Judy says.

———— ✼ ————

Despite the health problems that accompany old age, most seniors prefer to grow old at home, where they feel most comfortable. For a generation raised on the principles of independence and hard work, nothing is quite as devastating to seniors as realizing they are losing their independence and perhaps even the home they worked so hard to purchase. As a caregiver, your sensitivity to these concerns is important when it comes time to evaluate your elder's living situation.

Although nursing homes used to be the option of choice for housing elderly Americans, they may not be the most appropriate or the most cost-effective option for seniors who need less care. In-home and community-based long-term-care services are becoming more available to help your aging loved one remain in his own home. Careful

ELDERLY INDEPENDENCE

Most elderly Americans feel capable of caring for themselves, according to recent surveys. One survey of 896 adults age sixty-five and older found that 70 percent did not receive social services to help them remain independent. Furthermore, 67 percent did not think they needed services at the time of the survey.[1]

Two-thirds of the older adults had not talked with their children about independent living, but 56 percent felt it would be "very easy" to discuss it. One in three adult children said they did not know what type of information to give their parents and did not know where to find that information.

According to another survey, more than half of adult children think their parents will need their help but only 27 percent of older parents agree.[2]

In short, seniors wish to remain independent as long as they can, while adult children are willing to give information on independent living to their elderly parents but do not know where to start. As a result, the American Association of Retired Persons (AARP) has established what it calls "Connections for Independent Living"—a Web site that provides a wide variety of educational resources describing ways elderly people can enhance their ability to continue living independently (see appendix).

[1]Linda L. Barrett, *Independent Living: Do Older Parents and Adult Children See It the Same Way?* (Connections for Independent Living Research Team, AARP Research Group, Excel Omnibus Survey, International Communications Research [ICR] of Media, Pennsylvania, November 1998).   [2]Linda L. Barrett, *Can We Talk? Families Discuss Older Parents' Ability to Live Independently . . . or Do They?* (Connections for Independent Living Research Team, AARP Research Group, International Communications Research [ICR], April 2001).

thought must be given to safety issues; the cost of maintaining your elder's home (including repairs and modifications); and proximity to shopping, family, and community support systems.

NO PLACE LIKE HOME

Almost 95 percent of the elderly live in some form of independent household. According to Census Bureau figures, 83.8 percent of people ages 70 to 74 are homeowners, as are 77.7 percent of Americans age 75 and older.[1] Home ownership was a major goal after World War II, and millions achieved this goal. Many have remained in their homes and have paid off their mortgages with hard work and thrift.

Ideally, your aging loved one will be able to "age in place" in the comfort of his own home. Most Americans age 45 and over say they would like to remain in their current residence for as long as possible.[2] Having to move can be very traumatic when it tears an older person out of a familiar neighborhood where she has well-developed social relationships. On the other hand, many elderly people who wish to "age in place" face the prospect of social isolation, high home-repair costs, deteriorating neighborhoods, rising property taxes, and transportation concerns.

If your elder lives in an urban neighborhood, for example, he has access to public-transportation systems but may be unclear about how to use them or may be unable to afford the cost. Stores and churches may be within walking distance, but the threat of crime, pollution, and traffic can make the city less than ideal at times. The suburbs are attractive to many seniors, because they provide more peace and quiet, yet the scarcity of public transportation is a hardship for older people who no longer drive. As suburbs continue to grow, the social problems plaguing urban centers tend to move out as well, threatening the safety of the elderly. Small towns (communities with fewer than 2,500 residents) may offer a neighborly environment but lack some of the social support networks available in metropolitan areas.

No matter what neighborhood they live in, many older persons who own a home may face special challenges. As they become older and more frail, they may need help in maintaining and repairing their home, such as installing grab bars in bathrooms or ramps at doorways.

An elderly person's home often represents a wealth of past memories as well as ties to the community and friends.

They may need someone to transport them to doctors and dentists or help them with personal care. They may need hot meals and groceries delivered at home. These are just a few of the issues and concerns that affect an elder's ability to remain at home.

CAN YOUR ELDER REMAIN AT HOME?

As you and your loved one evaluate her housing situation, ask the following questions:

- How determined is your elder to stay in her own private residence?
- Is the home itself safe for your elder to live in? Are many household repairs needed?
- Has the neighborhood deteriorated? If so, how badly?
- What are the public-transportation options? Some cities, for example, provide van transportation exclusively for seniors and disabled people who need a ride to the doctor or other appointments.
- Is quality medical care available in the area?
- Can your elder afford to continue living in her own home?
- How frail is your elder's mental and physical health? How much help does she need performing activities of daily living (e.g., cooking, bathing, vacuuming, doing laundry, taking care of pets)?
- What health-care and community services (e.g., chore services, home-delivered meals, day care) can assist your elder so that she can continue living at home?
- What social supports are available? Are friends, other family members, and church members willing and able to help care for your elder?
- Is there a supportive church nearby?
- What cultural and recreational opportunities are available?
- Is your elder's home clean and tidy? (A messy, cluttered home increases the chance of injury and infection.)
- What other housing options have you and your elder considered if and when the time comes to move?

A major factor influencing where an elderly person lives is his financial status. Keeping a roof over his head often becomes his main struggle in life. The elderly person is frequently caught in a "catch-22" situation: He may have his mortgage paid off yet worry about property-tax increases and inflation. In addition, his home may be deteriorating, and he may not have the resources to keep it repaired. Plus, if his neighborhood is going downhill, it reduces the value of his home for resale. Brainstorm together about possible solutions. Chapter 10 addresses financial care in more detail, but here are two financial strategies for helping your elderly homeowner remain at home:

Tax-Relief Programs for Older Homeowners

Almost all the states have some form of property-tax relief program to help older persons stay in their own homes. Circuit-breaker programs, for example, provide tax cuts or refunds when property taxes rise above a certain percentage of their household income. There are also homestead exemption programs, which allow a fixed-percentage reduction in the assessed valuation of an older person's residence. Community agencies in some areas will help elderly homeowners fill out the paperwork to get the benefits of these programs. Contact your county's senior services department or your state's department of revenue for assistance.

Reverse Mortgage Creates Monthly Income

One of the most creative programs to be developed in recent years is the reverse mortgage or home-equity conversion mortgage, which may enable your aging loved one to stay in her home.

In a reverse mortgage, your elder can get a loan from a banking institution against the equity in the home, minus what is still owed on the house. The homeowner gets the loan in the form of monthly checks for as long as she lives. When she dies, the home is sold and the profits from the sale are used to pay off the loan. To qualify for a reverse mortgage, the person must be 62 or older, have a low mortgage balance, or own the home free and clear.

Recent changes in federal and state rules on reverse mortgages require elderly homeowners to receive professional advice before taking out one of these loans. Professor Flora Williams, an expert on family and consumer economics at Purdue University, published a study on the economic benefits of reverse mortgages in a 1998 issue of the *Journal of the Association for Financial Counseling and Planning Education*. She analyzed the potential income of 639 seniors with an average age of seventy-two who owned their homes free and clear. These homes had an average payoff value of $88,587. She found that a reverse mortgage could increase a senior's income between 13 percent and 19 percent. If seniors in the study had borrowed on a fixed, 10-year reverse mortgage, they would have increased their monthly income by $427.[3]

Williams says reverse mortgages have both good and bad points. The pluses: No repayment is due as long as the borrower stays in the home, and the homeowner cannot be forced to vacate; income payments are tax free; payments are not counted as earnings for social-security or Medicaid purposes; and payment can continue for the lifetime of the homeowner or spouse. Among the negatives: a reverse mortgage means leaving less to survivors; depending on your elder's state of residence, a reverse mortgage may affect welfare benefits, such as food

HOME-CARE SHUFFLE

After being widowed for the second time in her life, Mom was living alone and doing fairly well, despite occasional memory lapses. When she had a stroke while we were shopping one day, I knew she needed extra care, but I lived an hour and a half away. Mom refused to admit that she could not live in her own home, so I commenced my power of attorney and lined up visiting nurses and other agencies, and for more than two years I shuffled between our home and hers to oversee her care and doctor appointments. I was physically exhausted and cried out to my heavenly Father for help. Within a week, my phone rang and Judie, a lady from our church, called to offer her services. She'd just started her own elderly-care service after having been an RN and then a nursing home administrator! The Lord is so good. Judie's services were reasonably priced, and not only did she come over to take Mom to appointments and clean her home, but she also scouted out nursing facilities in the area and sent her recommendations to me in case I'd need them down the road. That was such a blessing and relief. It would have taken me much longer to research them.   *Linda L.*

stamps; and it can be an expensive way to generate cash income, especially during periods of high interest rates.

The Federal Housing Administration offers several reverse mortgage programs through Fannie Mae. One is called the "Home Keeper Mortgage." This program allows the person to borrow on the value of the home. Eligible properties include one-unit, single-family homes; condominiums; planned-unit developments; and properties held in trust. A second program is "Home Keeper for Home Purchase." Under this plan, the senior can purchase a new home by utilizing a reverse mortgage on his previous home. A third plan is the "Home Equity Conversion Mortgage," which does not impose any limits on income. The maximum mortgage amount insured by the Federal Housing Administration is based upon local FHA loan limits. For additional information on reverse mortgages, check out the AgeNet Web site: <http://www.agenet.com>.

HELPING YOUR ELDER LIVE IN HIS OWN HOME

Living at home in familiar surroundings is always a plus if it can be done safely and within personal and financial constraints. If possible, spend a few days with your aging loved one to see what adjustments need to be made. There are several things you can do to adapt a home to fit your elder's changing needs and to help him "age in place" for as long as possible:

Making Home Safe

With decreased mobility, oncoming deafness, or diminished eyesight, the elderly person gradually begins to face certain threats at home that would be of no great concern to most younger people. Home can become a hazard if the lighting is inadequate, stairs are too hard to climb, or doorknobs and faucets are too difficult to use. But some simple changes and minor remodeling can make a big difference in home safety, comfort, and convenience. Go over the following tips with your elder, then make any necessary changes:

- Use swing-back hinges to widen doorways.
- Install ramps over doorsills or remove sills altogether for wheelchair accessibility.

- Elevate toilet seats.
- Replace or convert faucets and round doorknobs to lever-action closures; they are easier for arthritic hands to use.
- Install handrails on both sides of stairs or hallways.
- Install sturdy grab bars in the bathroom by the toilet, shower stall, and bathtub. Observe how your elder will use the grab bars and install them at his natural reaching point. For safety, consider having a professional install them.
- Equip bathtubs and shower stalls with nonskid mats.
- Lower the setting on the hot-water heater to "low" or 120 degrees to reduce the chances of getting scalded.
- Install night-lights in bedrooms, bathrooms, and hallways.
- Mount motion-sensitive lights near all outside doors, including the garage.
- Place flashlights near your elder's favorite chair, beside the bed, and in other convenient places.
- Check stairways to make sure they are well lighted and equipped with nonslip strips.
- Use rocker wall light switches rather than standard toggle switches.
- Use higher-wattage lightbulbs and lamps that turn on with a touch rather than a switch.
- Make sure a telephone and lamp are within reach of the bed.
- Add a bed rail for help in getting in and out of bed.
- To avoid tripping, remove area rugs and runners that slide.
- Use rugs with slip-resistant backing.
- Eliminate low furniture such as coffee tables and footstools.
- Make sure all lamp, extension, and telephone cords are out of the flow of traffic.
- Remove cords from under furniture or carpeting.
- Replace damaged or frayed cords.
- Post emergency phone numbers on or near the telephone.
- Make sure the home has working smoke detectors and carbon-monoxide detectors. Check them at least twice a year.
- Obtain a small fire extinguisher and teach your elderly loved one to use it.

- Keep a container of baking soda by the stove; it makes an excellent fire extinguisher.
- Check electrical outlets and switches to see if they are in working order.
- Make sure space heaters have safety shut-off switches.
- Develop an emergency escape plan. Practice evacuating the home.
- Remove towels from the stove.
- When cooking, wear short- or close-fitting sleeves to prevent a clothing fire.
- Teach proper use of the microwave, which is often safer than a stove.
- Replace heavy dishes and glasses with lightweight, nonbreakable dishware.
- Make sure the chimney is clean.
- Check small appliances to see if they are in working order.
- Check the expiration dates on all medications and discard those with expired dates.
- Store any flammable liquids properly.

For more details on how to provide a safe environment for your elderly parent, read *Elder Design: Designing and Furnishing a Home for Your Later Years* by Rosemary Bakker (Penguin Books, 1997). Or contact the U.S. Consumer Product Safety Commission; their Web site includes a document entitled "Safety for Older Consumers: Home Safety Checklist" to assist you as you help safety-proof your elder's home (see appendix).

If the person you are caring for is living in a two-story home, you might want to consider rearranging the living environment to allow your elder to live on the first floor. Above all, there should be a bathroom on the first floor. The second floor can be used for storage—or perhaps your elder would want to rent out a room to a student or single working person. Sometimes more extensive changes must be made in the home to accommodate a wheelchair-bound elderly person. Perhaps a kitchen must be remodeled, light switches lowered, and shag carpeting removed. Also, a stair lift or "stair glide" elevator may be within

Home can become a hazard if the lighting is inadequate, stairs are too hard to climb, or doorknobs and faucets are too difficult to use.

your elder's price range. Get several estimates in writing. If you need financial assistance in order to renovate an aging loved one's home for safety, check with your local Area Agency on Aging to find out about low-interest loans for remodeling.

Home Medical Supplies and Assistive Devices

Home medical equipment and supplies include canes, walkers, crutches, wheelchairs and scooters, elevated toilet seats, bathroom grab bars, shower chairs, oxygen tanks and respiratory care equipment, urinary incontinence products, ostomy and wound-care products, and glucometers and other diabetes-management products. Under physician orders, these and other products and services may be covered by Medicare, Medicaid, or private insurance.

Contact the Arthritis Society or the National Institute of Arthritis and Musculoskeletal and Skin Diseases for suggestions on helpful assistive devices, such as nonslip doorknob covers, large-handled garden tools, and hands-free book holders (see appendix).

Nutritional Care

Poor vision, physical frailty, or a simple lack of knowledge make cooking tasks difficult for some elderly people. An elderly person—especially one living alone—will be less likely to prepare nutritious foods than if he were living with a spouse or sharing a meal with someone. As a result, he may experience nutritional deficiencies that can affect his physical and mental health.

Sometimes arthritis or other disabling problems can make it difficult for an elderly person to prepare meals. Suggest the use of clamps,

UPLIFTING DEVICE

My mom has a basement in her home, but she had a chairlift installed that works really well for her. She still walks up and down the stairs unless she's really not feeling well at all. But anything she has to carry, including laundry, she puts on the chairlift. She has used her going up and down the stairs as her exercise for the day, which is good.

Jan S.

table vices, and spring clips (like those that hold food bags closed) to help hold items that require two hands. A piece of nonslip plastic or rubber can make it easier to open jars. If your elder has low vision, try using contrasting colors, such as a dark tablecloth beneath white plates.

If your elder is having trouble maintaining a healthful diet, ask whether he would like help planning a weekly menu. Be careful not to force an older person to change his diet or eating habits. If he is open to your assistance, offer to go shopping with him to pick out foods that will provide well-balanced meals. Good choices include a wide variety of vegetables, fish, meat, poultry, eggs, and low-fat dairy products. Leafy green salads are especially healthful; for convenience, many stores sell packages of ready-to-eat salad. An occasional TV dinner can help ease the burden of daily food preparation. Prunes, peaches, apricots, bran cereals, and multigrain breads are good sources of dietary fiber, which helps with bowel function. To utilize fiber and avoid dehydra-

HELP! I'VE FALLEN AND I CAN'T GET UP!

Remember the old television commercial? It pictured an elderly woman lying on the floor, speaking into a message system. It became the target of many jokes, but it really was not a laughing matter.

The commercial was advertising an Emergency Response System (ERS). ERSs enable elderly people who live alone to signal for help in an emergency. The medical alarm system involves an electronic device worn as a pendant or wristband or clipped to clothing. By pressing a button on that device, a person can signal a central monitoring station. Services differ, but essentially the monitoring station will dispatch the help this person needs. Some models allow the wearer to speak through a device to the monitoring station. Other services will try to call the person on the phone and if she cannot be reached, another person is called to go check on her.

The ERS services generally are not "community services" because they are businesses. You pay for what they offer. But the service is worthwhile to help enable an elderly loved one to remain independent at home and have peace of mind, especially if your elder is recovering from surgery and is alone for periods of time. Make sure the device is waterproof and can be worn in the bath or shower. If your elder is reluctant to use such a device, it may help to suggest that doing so would give you, the caregiver, more peace of mind; a loved one will often accept it when she is doing it for you.

tion, seniors should drink plenty of liquids, especially water (about six cups a day is a good rule of thumb). Check with a physician for information on the best vitamin and mineral supplements for your elder.

Some supermarkets or grocery stores accept telephone orders and deliver food and household supplies to the homes of frail older people who are unable to go out and shop. Groceries-on-wheels programs transport and sell groceries at or near the residences of older individuals.

You may also want to consult with your local senior center to see if you can arrange for a Meals On Wheels delivery five days a week for the person you care for. (Frozen meals are often provided for the senior to heat and eat over the weekend, too.) These are available to homebound seniors for free or for a minimal charge or donation. Meals On Wheels guarantees at least one nutritious, hot meal a day—and it will lessen the burden of food preparation.

Another option for seniors is to have lunch at a neighborhood meal

PREPARING FOOD SAFELY

Consider the following checklist when you work with your elder on food preparation. (The entire checklist, "To Your Health! Food Safety for Seniors," is provided by the U.S. Department of Agriculture's Food Safety and Inspection Service. See appendix for Web site.)

- To keep food safe, refrigerate or freeze it.
- Never thaw food at room temperature. Allow meat to thaw in a refrigerator or in a pan of cold water, or defrost it in the microwave.
- Wash hands with warm, soapy water before preparing food. Immediately wash hands, utensils, cutting boards, and other work surfaces after contact with raw meat or poultry.
- Never leave perishable foods out of refrigeration for more than two hours. Discard food left out longer than two hours.
- Thoroughly cook raw meat, poultry, and fish. Set the oven at 325 degrees when cooking.

For more tips on nutrition for the elderly, contact the American Dietetic Association (see appendix).

site or "dining center." The centers provide inexpensive, hot, nutritious noon meals for older people who cannot afford to eat adequately, as well as for those who no longer prepare meals because of loneliness and isolation. (An elderly person does not have to be poor to participate.) These are often located in senior centers. For a listing of congregate meal sites in your county, contact your county aging unit or your local Area Agency on Aging.

Assistance in this one area enables many seniors to stay in their own homes. Check your yellow pages for organizations that may offer nutritional services. And if one organization says no, ask them if they know of a local organization that does deliver meals. This is also a great ministry opportunity for a church. Find out if there is a system in place in your loved one's church that could provide meals regularly or as needed. A small group—such as a Sunday school class or Bible study group—could take on this ministry. (You may need to make deliveries only three times a week, since leftovers often stretch a meal over two days.)

Preventing Isolation

It is crucial for you to stay in touch with your aging loved one, particularly if she is living in her own home. Loneliness can be a seriously debilitating condition for an elderly person.

Make a concerted effort to visit your loved one on a regular basis. When visits are regular, the elder often relaxes and waits more patiently until the next scheduled visit, instead of "bugging" you all the time. Offer to do chores or just sit down for a chat. What elderly parents may want from their adult children more than any assistance or advice is close contact. Even if your relationship has been strained in the past, act in a loving way *and the feelings may follow.* If your family has never been a "touching" family, see if you can break that pattern. Give your aging loved one a hug and a kiss when you arrive and when you leave. All of us need the touch of people who love us.

Remember birthdays, anniversaries, and holidays. Throw a small birthday party for your older loved one, including cake and ice cream. Even if your elder feels fine being alone much of the time, he may be lonely if he is by himself on a holiday. A widowed adult may feel espe-

What elderly parents may want from their adult children more than any assistance or advice is close contact.

cially lonely on a wedding anniversary. Alternate where the person will spend holidays and special celebrations. An elderly parent may want to spend Thanksgiving with one sibling and Christmas Eve at your home. If your sister or brother lives in another state, you might agree to split the cost of a plane ticket with your sibling to allow your parent to spend a holiday season there. Involve as many family members as you can, and share the caregiving whenever possible.

If you live out of town, seek out one or more friends or relatives in your loved one's community or church who will agree to keep an eye on your elder and give you regular updates. Make contact with the local senior center or adult day-care center for activities tailored to the elderly. Talk often by phone and send letters, family photos, and gifts to show your love.

Neighborhood Safety

The elderly are often targets of crime. Even the fear of crime is enough to keep some seniors from venturing out of their homes. See if there are Neighborhood Watch groups in your elder's own community that are working to safeguard the neighborhood. If need be, remind older loved ones to keep their doors and windows locked. (Three-quarters of the burglaries committed against the elderly involve unlocked doors and windows.) Also remind them not to put keys under mats or in mailboxes. Install motion-activated outdoor lighting, double-bolt locks, and a home

---

ON HIS OWN, BUT NOT ALONE

After my mom died, my brother and sister-in-law invited my dad to live with them. But he really wanted to stay in his own house as long as possible. Even though he wanted to be independent, he got very lonely, so I would invite him to stay overnight at our house once or twice a week. I'd also try to include him in as many of our kids' activities as possible, given that he lived almost an hour away. We'd bring Dad to their piano recitals and soccer games—any little thing that was going on. He loved little kids, so when he couldn't be with us, I'd have my son, who was in kindergarten at the time, call him almost every day. My dad loved hearing from him and my son loved the attention from an adoring adult.

Becky G.

alarm system to thwart potential burglars. Suggest that your elder keep an inventory, with serial numbers and photographs, of appliances, antiques, furniture, and jewelry. You can also do a home-video survey of your elder's home while having your elder describe the important belongings. Leave copies in a safety deposit box. Seniors are also prime targets for consumer fraud and scams. For more information on protecting your elder from fraud, scams, and greed, see chapter 14.

To Drive or Not to Drive?

Most adults hope to keep driving as long as they live. However, age-related factors such as vision problems—a loss of central or peripheral vision—and/or cognitive impairment can make driving a hazard for your loved one and for other drivers, passengers, and pedestrians. Older drivers have higher rates of traffic violations, collisions, and fatalities per mile than younger drivers. They also tend to have more serious injuries when they get in an accident.

Senior citizens naturally (and understandably) feel threatened when told it is time to give up their driving privileges. Getting a driver's license was a significant rite of passage when they were young, and after driving for decades, it is traumatic to relinquish the right. It can also be a hardship. Without a car, it is much more difficult for an elderly person to get groceries and run errands, visit family and friends regularly, participate in church or social activities, perform volunteer service, and seek sufficient medical attention. Transportation is particularly critical given the Medicare system of "diagnosis-related groups" or DRGs. Because of DRGs, Medicare patients are released from hospitals earlier and require more follow-up care. For some patients, a lack of transportation makes follow-up appointments difficult to attend.

The ideal, then, is for your elder to be able to drive as long as possible—but without jeopardizing anyone's life. If your loved one has trouble seeing at night, it may only mean limiting driving to daylight hours. If your elder has hearing loss, the frequent use of mirrors (and perhaps larger side mirrors) will help compensate for the loss of sound coming from various directions, such as the approach of an emergency vehicle from behind. If you suspect the person is having problems paying attention while driving, consider having a physician give her a "Mini Mental

Install motion-activated outdoor lighting, double-bolt locks, and a home alarm system to thwart potential burglars.

State Examination" to measure her cognitive awareness. Ask her doctor or a pharmacist whether your elder's medications may be interacting with each other to impair her cognitive abilities. It is a good idea to start talking about your elder's safety on the road early and hypothetically—before it affects her—so that it will be easier to discuss the issue later.

If you are convinced that the person you care for is dangerous on the road, discuss with her the importance of getting off the road. If she resists, you may need to ask her physician, pastor, friends, or other relatives to talk to her. If she continues to resist, you have an obligation to report her. Failure to report someone who is impaired may result in your being held criminally liable for any accident she causes while driving. Some states have laws protecting the anonymity of a person who reports such drivers.

To increase safety on the road, the National Highway Traffic Safety Administration and the American Association of Motor Vehicle Administrators have sponsored research and proposed some changes in how states deal with elderly drivers. For example, they suggest that states use graded and restricted driver's licenses for the elderly—just as they do for teenagers. Some states are also working on policies that deal with "impaired skills" for determining who will drive, rather than an age-based criterion.

Some groups are designing programs to actually improve the mental acuity of elderly drivers. In Florida, for example, the Getting in Gear program helps retrain elderly drivers. For a national program, the American Association of Retired Persons (AARP) offers 55 ALIVE, a two-day driver improvement course designed for motorists age 50 and older. (For a class near you, call AARP; see appendix.)

Transportation Options

If your aging loved one can no longer drive an automobile, investigate alternatives in the community. Some options may include: walking, carpooling with family and friends, shuttle buses or vans, public buses, trains, subways, taxicabs, as well as special bus programs offered by local senior centers, churches, or agencies on aging. Make arrangements with siblings or friends to take turns transporting your elder to the doctor, store, church, and other places.

Lack of mobility is a problem that can lead to premature institutionalization, so states can save money by helping elderly people find transportation. Hence, a number of states and private groups are working on policies and programs that will make it easier for an elderly person to get around town. In Portland, Maine, for example, a privately run group, Independent Transportation Network, is operating a 24-hour-a-day reduced-fare taxi service specifically for the elderly. ITN operates with volunteer drivers and charges less than half of what a regular taxi would charge for transportation. The service uses the volunteers' cars or one of their own cars to transport the elderly wherever they wish to go. ITN has caught the attention of Congress, and several foundations are considering funding similar programs in other states. The program features "gift packages" of rides that can be purchased by children for their parents. This helps reduce the personal costs to the elderly.

Two federal departments assist older persons with transportation: the Department of Health and Human Services (HHS) and the Department of Transportation (DOT). The HHS administers a number of programs, including a service under Medicaid to transport the elderly poor to medical facilities. The DOT assists with basic transportation services, including 50-percent fare reductions for elderly and handicapped persons.

In some places, American Red Cross volunteers transport older people to physician appointments. The community bus services may offer help and information to teach new bus passengers how to read passenger schedules, transfer to other buses, and reach convenient bus stops. Check the phone book under Senior Citizens Services for other transportation possibilities.

If you are in a quandary about finding transportation help for your aging loved one, you can use the Eldercare Locator, operated by the federal Administration on Aging. The locator is a directory-assistance program that will provide the telephone numbers for agencies offering transportation services and other elder-care programs in your loved one's community or county (see appendix). You will need to give your elder's county, city name, or zip code and then describe the service or assistance you are seeking. Call the Eldercare Locator at 1-800-677-1116.

USING COMMUNITY AND PROFESSIONAL SERVICES

As the population ages, health-care services for seniors continue to adapt and change. Today, a number of community-based services are available to make it easier for your aging loved one to get needs met while remaining at home.

WHO PROVIDES HELP?

Family and friends make up beween 75 and 90 percent of those who provide long-term care to the elderly in the U.S., according to the federal Administration on Aging. Another 20 percent are cared for by both informal (unpaid) and formal caregiving services. Less than 5 percent of seniors age sixty-five and older are cared for in formal caregiving settings, such as nursing homes. An increase in the use of home health services (stimulated by changes in the government's policy regarding home health reimbursement) has helped to produce a drop in nursing-home use.[1]

You may need to do some homework to sort through the services available to help your elder remain at home. Each state has designed its own network of resources and institutions to provide long-term care options for the elderly. New York State, for example, has developed a variety of programs including:

- Expanded In-Home Services for the Elderly Program (EISEP). This provides case-management services (someone who will work with the elderly person), housekeeping/chores, homemaking/personal care, and respite services.
- Senior centers. These provide myriad services, such as congregate or home-delivered meals, nutrition programs, adult day care, health screening, and group activities.
- Supplemental Nutrition Assistance Program. Targeted to high-risk elderly, this program provides home-delivered meals and nutrition services.
- Home care for a variety of services within the home.
- Certified home health care, available through an accredited home health agency.
- Adult day health care, available through nursing homes. This includes medical services, rehabilitation therapy, food and nutritional help, and other services.

[1]Kenneth G. Manton and XiLiang Gu, "Changes in the Prevalence of Chronic Disability in the United States Black and Nonblack Population above Age 65 from 1982 to 1999," *Proceedings of the National Academy of Sciences USA* 98, no. 11 (22 May 2001), 6354–6359.

Case-Management Services

Case- (or care-) management services help people assess what kind of help they need. An outside professional, usually a nurse or a social worker, is invited into the home to overview the entire caregiving process; this person helps the caregiver determine what types of services are needed, who can help with these services, and the financial benefits to which your aging loved one is entitled.

There is no obligation after the initial assessment. In some areas of the nation, case-management services are offered on a nonprofit or low-cost basis to help keep elderly people out of institutions as long as possible. In other instances the service is offered for a fee, which should be discussed ahead of time.

The case manager's job may involve establishing eligibility, unraveling red tape, and negotiating with agencies. It may also include identifying personal preferences of the elder and managing potential conflicts of interest. Case managers are also trained to report suspected abuse.

Although you may be able to do these kinds of tasks yourself, those who live far away, especially, are turning to this relatively new type of managing coordinator. In many instances, case-management services provide long-distance caregivers with the opportunity to help directly in the care of their elderly loved ones without moving near them. Such professionals often locate rehabilitation facilities, make sure insurance and other paperwork is done, and counsel the family.

Case managers are good at picking battles wisely—and even being the "bad guy" sometimes. But caregivers should check carefully before contracting with one. Get referrals from a trusted source such as a doctor, attorney, or friend. Also, know what you are getting into financially: Some case managers may charge between $50 and $150 an hour, while many nonprofit agencies provide case management at low or no cost. Contact the Eldercare Locator, a federal, nationwide telephone referral service (see appendix).

Case-management services can provide long-distance caregivers with the opportunity to help directly in the care of their elderly loved ones without moving near them.

Multipurpose Senior Centers

Senior centers provide a range of resources and services for people age 60 and older. These services can include recreation and education, such as crafts, music, lectures, and movies, as well as services such as lunchtime meals, legal and income counseling, and health-screening clinics. The local senior center is also a comfortable, familiar place for older people to meet and interact with other seniors. Sometimes transportation to the center and to grocery stores is provided. Senior centers may be run by the city, the park district, private organizations, charities, or churches.

Thanks to funding from the Older Americans Act and to state and local funds, many services are offered to seniors free of charge. Donations are accepted to offset operational expenses.

Adult Day-Care Services

What do you do with an aging loved one who cannot be left alone while you go to work? One solution is to take your elder to an adult day-care center. These centers offer a variety of health, social, and related support services to senior adults who need a structured, protective environment due to a decrease in physical, mental, and social functioning. Since most centers are geared toward people who need limited assistance and some medical supervision, these centers delay the need for nursing-home care because they allow seniors to stay longer in their own homes. The people who benefit most are those who need supervision, social interaction, and assistance with more than one activity of daily living, such as eating, walking, toileting, bathing, or dressing. Adult day-care services are generally offered five days a week, with seniors going a certain number of days per week on an eight-hour basis.

Adult day care is a popular option for caregivers who live within reach of their aging loved one. It works well for caregivers employed outside the home and as a relief for at-home caregiving spouses. Day care counteracts isolation and meets elders' needs to socialize with peers. It may be available in an independent facility, a senior center, a neighborhood center, a hospital, or a church.

Adult day-care centers typically offer some or all of the following services:

- Health monitoring by a registered nurse
- Preventive medical care, such as flu shots
- Podiatry care
- Physical, occupational, and speech therapy

- Care for people with Alzheimer's Disease or related disorders
- Personal care, such as handicapped-accessible bathing, hair care, and nail clipping
- Transportation
- Meals
- Crafts
- Cooking
- Gardening
- Pet therapy
- Music therapy
- Field trips
- Reminiscing
- Exercise programs
- Games and activities
- Holiday parties

Adult day-care services are less expensive than institutional care, ranging from a few dollars to $100 a day (based on the services included). Many centers operate on a nonprofit basis. Funding for this type of program can come from Medicaid, Social Services Block Grants, Title III of the Older Americans Act, and fees paid by the recipients and their families. Some centers may be able to offer low-income persons a reduced fee based on ability to pay. Medicaid and Veteran's Administration Benefits may pick up part of the cost of adult day care if the client would otherwise need nursing-home care and if the site is approved by the federal government. Some have scholarships to help defray the cost of day care.

If you are considering using an adult day-care center, get references from others. Then visit the center and ask yourself the following questions:

- Is the staff caring and kind?
- Has the staff been trained to care for the special needs of my loved one? Are there other people in the center with similar kinds of needs?
- Does the staff allow seniors to do as much as they can for themselves?

Adult day-care centers delay the need for nursing-home care because they allow seniors to stay longer in their own homes.

• Are activities varied and interesting?
• Do the clients seem to be enjoying themselves?

In addition, ask questions about staffing, programming, and transportation. Some adult day-care centers provide transportation.

Check with your local senior center to find out what adult day-care options are available in your area. Your state's Agency on Aging is also a good resource.

In-Home Services

Whether your elder needs caregiving assistance long-term or on a temporary basis, such as after surgery or when you are on vacation, you may want to look for and employ in-home help. Such caregiver substitutes make it possible for an aging loved one to remain in the comfort of his own home. This service is available on a limited, hourly basis or, if your elder needs considerable help, on a "live-in" basis, offering 24-hour supervision. Either way, you will be involved to overview the care of your elder, hire and fire the helpers, and manage the finances.

In-home services can be divided into three basic categories: **intensive** or **skilled care, personal care,** and **homemaker services.**

Intensive or skilled services are those ordered by the attending physi-

---

DAY CARE FOR OLD AND YOUNG

Some specialists have found that elders fare better in environments where they have contact with children. Based on that philosophy, some day-care centers are intergenerational—opening their doors to seniors and children. While mixing the old and young is nothing new in family settings, it is a novel concept in institutional care. The St. Ann Center in Milwaukee, for example, serves 150 senior adults and 84 children in day care with special interactive programs. The center features stores that offer used toys and clothes, an indoor park, and a patio, all with an intergenerational theme. The interaction is energizing to elderly people, who often look forward to holding children in their laps and working on activities together. This has been borne out in studies at the University of Pittsburgh showing higher levels of cognitive functioning in older people who spend time with children.

cian, usually upon hospital discharge, and supervised by a nurse. Professional care may include nursing; speech, physical, and occupational therapy; and medical services, such as treatment for heart patients and for people with broken bones, open wounds, or illnesses requiring catheters, tube feedings, and other services. Home health-care agencies often make arrangements for this type of care.

Personal care or intermediate services are for those who are generally healthy but need help with functional impairments that affect daily activities such as bathing, dressing, eating, exercise, and taking medications. Custodial care is generally arranged by the patient or family.

Homemaker/companion services may include light housekeeping, meal preparation, laundry, transportation, and other activities. They may be provided through community, religious, civic, or service organizations.

These categories are not mutually exclusive—any of these services can be provided in conjunction with the others. For example, the person who needs skilled nursing care may also need personal care and other services in order to sustain independent living in a clean, safe, and healthful home environment.

How to Contact In-Home Services

Several state- and community-based agencies provide in-home services. These include:

THE GOOD NIGHT NURSE

I worked as a temp nurse through a home health agency for an elderly woman who was very ill. Her husband hired me to stay in their home at night so that he could get some sleep. I would check her IV, clean her room, and change the sheets. While she slept I'd sit in a chair in her room and read a book or just pray. It was wonderful, because her husband would wake refreshed and have energy to take care of her during the day. And just the fact that I was there at night gave his wife comfort. If she couldn't sleep, I'd talk with her. I would always call her by her name, because our names are so important. She wasn't "just another patient." *Joni V.*

- Home-care units of community hospitals
- Departments of social services
- Private, nonprofit community agencies such as the Visiting Nurses Association
- Community health centers
- For-profit agencies, which offer services for a fee.

The recipient pays for most in-home services. Medicare can be used for health-related services if your elder meets eligibility requirements based on need and financial resources. Title III of the Older Americans Act provides some limited funds for in-home services through your local Area Agency on Aging. These funds are intended to avoid putting people in long-term care institutions. They provide for preinstitution evaluation and screening, homemaker services, shopping, escort services, reader and letter-writing services. To be eligible, a person must be at least 60 years of age. Like other OAA services, there are no income restrictions, but efforts are made to target the low-income elderly.

Your doctor or a case-management team can help you decide what kind of in-home help is needed. They may ask you questions along these lines: Will your elder need nursing services including medical therapies, or will you simply need some hands-on help with your elder's personal hygiene or with simple housekeeping and errands?

Make a list of what your aging loved one can and cannot do. Also decide what you will be involved in and how often you will be in the home to supervise and confer with the helper.

Ask the hospital discharge planner or your Area Agency on Aging for a list of in-home-care agencies that provide helpers, along with a list of independent helpers. The center may also give you tips on the interviewing and hiring process or suggest books with information on this process. Check out the applicant's references thoroughly, or go through a licensed agency that runs a criminal check on all applicants. You can phone the Eldercare Locator for assistance (see appendix). If you are looking for live-in help and the agency's applicant is from a foreign country, make sure he has a social-security number and a working visa. As you take a potential helper through an interview, ask what he does best, what he prefers not to do, and what he will not do. Talk to your insurance representative about coverage and to a certified public accountant about your tax responsibilities as an employer. Make sure you are aware of deductible expenses.

This initial footwork may seem complicated, but once you have made a selection, show the helper around the house and explain tasks in detail or demonstrate the way you would like things done. Show where to find emergency numbers. Give instructions about your elder's routines, peculiar behaviors, and lifestyle preferences. Be available for questions, and allow whatever time is needed for your loved one to feel comfortable.

You will be working out the kinks in the system and in relationships while supervising the practical and financial end of it. And since you will be dealing with another personality, you will find his ways of doing things will sometimes differ from yours. In addition, your aging loved one will be coping with the emotional transition of accepting a new person in the home. An in-home helper may shed light on things you did not notice. Hopefully, your helper will offer friendship while keeping things running smoothly.

Have a trial period for both employer and employee to review if the contract should be extended three to six months. Don't take it personally if things do not work out; there is a high turnover rate among in-home helpers because the work demands are emotionally and physically draining. Hours are usually long. Your helper may be working for someone else, too, and, of course, must often deal with unexpected things on his own. As you keep problems centered on *what*, not *who*, you can maintain a friendly but professional manner.

As a safeguard, don't tempt an in-home helper by leaving money, jewelry, and other valuables accessible. Remove financial records, checkbooks, credit cards, and your loved one's social-security number from the home. Give the helper cash for anything he must purchase—such as food and supplies—then ask for receipts. Double-check expenses by reviewing statements promptly.

If you are a long-distance caregiver and need to arrange in-home services for your aging loved one, call the department of aging or senior services in your elder's county to get referrals and eligibility requirements for home-support services. They can help you arrange for a case

LIFE AT THE FARM

Just after losing her older sister to brain cancer, Susan faced the task of helping her frail, 88-year-old father take care of her mother, who was suffering from diabetes, congestive heart failure, Alzheimer's, and a broken hip she'd incurred while in the hospital. Rather than put her mother in a nursing home, she and her four siblings agreed to take turns caring for their aging parents at the big country farmhouse where they all grew up.

Twice weekly, Susan left her husband and three sons to drive an hour and a half to reach the farm, where she'd clean house, make dinner, and take care of her mother's needs, such as dressing her and helping her in the bathroom. She'd read the Bible aloud and pray with her mom, who often apologized for being a burden. "I'd tell Mom how glad I was to have this opportunity to care for her," Susan says. She also used Scripture to console her father, who'd become bitter and distraught after the double blow of losing his daughter and having a newly disabled wife. Susan's sister and a niece also did caregiving shifts, and her brothers came over to mow the grass, pick apples from the farm's orchard, and visit.

While lifting her mother one day, Susan injured her back (despite wearing a protective belt). Her dad intended to contact a nursing home, but the rest of the family urged him to consent to live-in help, which he had resisted in the past. "I don't want a strange woman in my house," he had said. This time he softened and agreed to give it a try. Susan's sister interviewed a number of female caregivers, checked every reference, and brought individuals to the farm to let Dad give his approval. Nevertheless, her dad fired the first helper after one day because he thought she charged too much to "sit around and eat my food."

After trying a couple more live-in helpers, he found one he really liked. She worked out well until she injured her back and had to quit. The family finally agreed to move their increasingly frail mother to a nursing home, where she could get more help. Family members visited her daily until her death several months later.

"We don't feel guilty, because we did all we could to care for our parents in their home," says Susan, who still goes out to the farmhouse regularly to spend time with her dad. "We're just a big farm family that was raised to rally around our loved ones. Loving our parents has been a way to honor the Lord."

manager to make an outreach visit to assess your loved one's needs and to locate the most appropriate and cost-effective resources.

Respite Care

Respite is defined as a "temporary period of relief or rest." In the context of caregiving, respite care is when someone else watches over your loved one for a short time—anywhere from a few hours to a couple weeks. This short-term relief is intended to give you a break from the constant care of an impaired elderly person, so that you can continue providing care over the long term. Respite care is a modification of the adult day-care option. Sometimes the care is provided in a temporary, substitute living environment, such as a center, hospital, group home, or nursing home; other times a qualified person will come into the elder's home for a short period of time so that the primary caregiver can get some rest or go away for a conference, vacation, or other occasion.

There may be people in your church willing to offer respite. And, as always, check the yellow pages under *senior citizens* or contact your Area Agency on Aging. A list is at <http://www.aoa.dhhs.gov/agingsites/state.html>.

Employer-Supported Services

A few American employers are now realizing that elder care is an important concern among employees. The toll that elder care can take on employees includes increased absenteeism, tardiness, stress, increased telephone calls at work, and shortened hours. One study estimated that the cost to employers for workers who had to lose days at work to attend to aging parents was up to $29 billion a year.

Some companies sponsor lunchtime lectures and "care fairs" in association with local social-service organizations. Others offer flexible hours, knowing that elderly parents at home need regular care at particular hours.

A few companies are combining day care for children and elderly people in the same building. Financial support is also offered through some employee-benefit plans.

Check with your company's human-resource department to see if they offer this kind of support. If not, encourage your employer to investigate the need for such services among your coworkers.

THE CONSIDERATE CAREGIVER

Many older Americans have lived in the same house for many years and desire to remain there for the rest of their lives. With some modifications, it often is possible to make a house or other independent dwelling place safe and functional for seniors. And with the increased availability of in-home and community support services, many elderly people can receive assistance with daily activities of living and other needs in their own home.

Whenever possible, to whatever degree, involve your aging loved one in every lifestyle decision. Seek to understand your elder's thoughts and feelings alongside his practical needs. Think about how your loved one's feelings and needs may change in the near or distant future. Seek to make decisions *with* your loved one, not *for* him.

Consider how you and other family members can help your elder live the life of her choosing. When your aging loved one sees her ideas or wishes incorporated into the decision—such as whether to remain at home or move into a relative's home or a care facility—she has a vested interest in making the decision work. Pray for wisdom, and seek counsel from doctors, discharge planners, family members, or friends who have experience in caregiving. The goal is to help your elder "age in place" for as long as possible. Much of the time, the right place is home.

With some modifications, it often is possible to make a house or other independent dwelling place safe and functional for seniors.

———— ∽ ————

If anyone does not provide for his relatives, and especially for his immediate family, he has denied the faith and is worse than an unbeliever. 1 TIMOTHY 5:8 NIV

Your decrees are the theme of my song wherever I lodge. In the night I remember your name, O Lord, and I will keep your law.

PSALM 119:54-55 NIV

When It's Time to Move

Independent and Assisted-Living Options

One day Alice Stock received a long-distance call from someone who lived near her mother, Irene, in Nebraska. "I'm concerned your mom isn't eating right," said the caller. Around the same time, Alice's sister, Mary, heard from a friend of her mother's who had seen Irene wandering around in a grocery store. "Your mom seemed confused and didn't know where to find the meat department," the caller reported. Alice, who lives in Minnesota, and Mary, who lives in Texas, agreed to fly to Nebraska to check on their mom.

At age 87, their mother had recently sold the jewelry business she had run for 22 years after her husband died. When the daughters arrived, they discovered their mom seemed less energetic and lacked purpose. "She was very tired and wanted to rest a lot," Alice recalls. "We found piles of mail on the dining-room table that hadn't been dealt with. She needed a haircut; before that, she had been so fastidious about her appearance."

The daughters wondered if their mother would resist giving up her independence and moving closer to one of them, but she actually seemed relieved to close up her two-story home and receive their help. The three of them discussed some possible options, such as living with Mary in Texas or moving into an assisted-living facility near Alice in Minnesota. Irene wanted Alice and Mary to advise her on what was best, so they began the task of searching for alternative living arrangements for their mother.

Whether your aging loved one lives in another state or just across town, there may come a time when it is no longer wise for your elder to live in his own home. The house may involve too much upkeep or it may not be feasible to renovate for safety. Your elder may be lonely and may want to consider moving closer to family—or to a place where he can have more social contact with peers. Your elder may become disabled, forgetful, or chronically ill and in need of assistance. The strain on both the caregiver and the care receiver may force you to reevaluate the living arrangements.

For seniors who have enjoyed their independence and the privacy of their own home, it is tough to contemplate a move, and you may have fears about broaching the subject. In addition, there are a variety of living options to consider. Should you bring your elder into your own home or locate another home where your loved one will receive an appropriate level of care? If your elder has been living with you and the care is becoming too taxing, what are your options? It could be that you need more emotional or physical support and times of respite from caregiving. In other cases your loved one will be better off in another environment with the care of professionals who can monitor and treat her as needed. Pray for wisdom as you weigh the decision. By talking sensitively with your elder about her health-care needs, discussing her preferences, and examining cost and safety issues, you have a good chance of coming to an agreement on the best living arrangement.

The Decision to Move Your Loved One

How do you know when it is time for your aging loved one to move? Reasons are varied, but here are some common issues to consider when determining whether to seek alternative care and housing for your elder:

Safety. Has the neighborhood deteriorated or become less safe? Is it difficult for your elder to climb stairs in his present residence? Does your elder no longer drive, and is available transportation inadequate?

Is your aging loved one too frail, ill, or impaired to cook or take care of himself? Is there no relative or family member nearby to provide caregiving services or support? (For more information, see chapter 15: Helping Your Elder Remain at Home.)

Finances. Is your aging loved one's home too costly to maintain or renovate? Are assets tied up in the home at a time when your elder needs cash? Selling a home can free up equity that can then supplement your elder's income. Or, consider a loan for a reverse mortgage or home equity conversion mortgage, which would allow your elder to remain in her home. (See "Reverse Mortgage Creates Monthly Income" on pages 371-373 for more information.)

Caregiver burnout. If you are the primary caregiver, is it becoming difficult for you to continue hands-on care for your loved one? Are you emotionally drained or chronically tired? Does your loved one need specialized supervision or rehabilitation?

Your elder's wishes. Is your aging loved one hoping to relocate closer to adult children or other relatives, looking for a new lifestyle with other retired seniors, or wondering if it is time to downsize to a place with less maintenance? When it comes to your elder's health and well-being, it is important to weigh the value of living in one place over another. Even if mobility is challenged and cognitive ability fades, most seniors prefer to maintain their independence for as long as possible.

Even if mobility is challenged and cognitive ability fades, it is not unusual for an older adult to resist moving away from the familiarity of home.

INDEPENDENT LIVING OPTIONS

Depending on the health, mobility, and financial condition of your aging loved one, there are a variety of independent housing options from which to choose.

The first thing to consider is whether your elder wants to live in an environment with people his own age (age-restricted or age-segregated) or in an environment where all ages live in proximity to each other (age-integrated or intergenerational). Older people often prefer age-restricted housing because it fosters companionship with peers, safety, convenience, and a quiet environment. Some seniors especially prefer quiet, age-restricted housing when it involves close living quarters, such as an apartment complex or mobile-home park. Others miss having young people around and feel energized by interacting with them. In short, your aging loved one's choice is just a matter of personal preference.

Apartments. If your elder is still active, relatively healthy, and wants to downsize from home ownership, apartment living can be a great option. An apartment can relieve your aging loved one of the many obligations of property ownership. Although there is always the possibility that rents will go up annually, senior housing in your community might have restrictions on how often and how high rents can go. A yearly lease can provide your elder with a sense of stability, the means to budget effectively, and the knowledge that he can eventually move if he becomes dissatisfied with the way the complex is operated. Check with your local senior center for apartment options in your community. Internet ser-

MIDNIGHT NURSING

When taking care of the yard and their home became difficult, my husband's parents moved into a two-bedroom apartment with an elevator. That worked quite well for about six years. Then my father-in-law began having bad spells with his heart and diabetes, especially in the middle of the night. By the time he underwent a triple-bypass operation, my mother-in-law was in bad shape. She felt it was up to her to nurse him around the clock.

The nighttime crises were the most difficult. My mother-in-law was unable to sleep well, always listening for a sigh or a moan that would signal her husband needed medical attention. So we found them a one-bedroom apartment in a health retirement facility that provided a nurse around the clock. At first my father-in-law wasn't too happy about making a move. He felt he was doing just fine; he didn't like to adjust and to let go of furniture and possessions.

After about the second nighttime episode, my father-in-law realized what a good move it had been and what a comfort it was to his wife to have a nurse evaluate the situation and call the doctor if needed. Because of increasing care needs, he has since moved into a nursing facility in a complex with the same company. They give my mother-in-law a ride to see him every weekday, and despite her own aches and pains, she is able to sleep better now. *Kathy E.*

vices that offer guidance in housing options include Senior Resource and the American Association of Homes and Services for the Aging (see appendix).

Condominiums. Condominiums are a form of real-estate ownership. They come in various forms: detached single units, apartments in high-rise buildings, renovated hotels, and more. The outside property is commonly owned by the residents. The person owning the unit typically has to pay an association fee to the group maintaining the complex in addition to a mortgage payment. This can become a hassle when there is mismanagement of the complex or when maintenance fees rise. It is important that you consult with an attorney familiar with the laws governing condominiums. Ask about the master deed or the declaration that spells out how the condo is governed. You should also find out about the powers and responsibilities of the board of directors and how grievances are handled. Will your aging loved one have access to the association's financial records to make sure it is being run properly? You will need to know if there are limitations on how high the fees can be raised and what rights the condo owners possess.

Mobile- or manufactured-home parks. These are very appealing for some senior citizens. The cost of a mobile home is inexpensive compared to that of a single-family dwelling. It is possible that your loved one could sell her own home, purchase a mobile home, and have a good amount of money left over for living expenses. Usually a mobile-home purchase does not include the land it is on. The total cost may include extensive setup expenses, monthly rental rates, and extra fees such as water and sewage charges. Rising rental fees are a major concern in mobile-home parks. However, some senior mobile-home parks have restrictions in place that limit rent increases. Another drawback of mobile-home living involves rising real-estate values. The company owning the park may eventually decide the property is more valuable as a strip mall or a new housing development. It is often difficult, if not impossible, to move a mobile home from one park to another.

A wise variation of the mobile-home park is a cooperatively owned park where the residents actually own the lot on which their home sits. A cooperative consisting of all the property owners runs the park, just as in a condo complex. The elderly residents participate directly in decisions regarding the park's operation, there is no rent to pay beyond minimal service charges, and the park cannot be sold unless there is a cooperative decision by the resident owners. A park run by the residents affords more security for those living there.

Public housing. For some seniors, subsidized housing may be the least appealing prospect for a housing choice, but it may be the most economical. Persons who demonstrate economic need can receive federal assistance to help them with rent. For example, a government program called Section 202 provides housing to low-income senior citizens and usually includes meals, transportation, and special features such as nonskid flooring, grab bars, and ramps. Not surprisingly, there are long waiting lists for government-funded housing programs. Preference is usually given to seniors who pay more than 50 percent of their monthly income in housing costs, are being involuntarily displaced from their present residence, or live in substandard housing. (The average resident is a frail, single woman in her mid-70s with an annual income of less than $10,000.) Some of these facilities are new and very nice. In fact, many churches have developed senior housing

REMODELING FOR MOM

When my mom moved in with us, the house needed renovating. The carpeting threw my mom off balance, so we replaced it with wood floors. The bedrooms were on the second floor, so we installed a chairlift. The hallway door was too narrow, so we unhinged it. We bought a toilet extension and a special recliner. We took advantage of adult day-care services as well as senior services that provided local bus and cab rides for seniors. A home health nurse came in when Mom had a stomach ulcer and taught me how to bathe her.

When my mom had another major stroke, a case manager came in to assess her situation. Mom qualified for public aid, so we chose to move her into a convalescent center. She enjoyed the programs, because they kept her mind busy so she wouldn't feel sorry for herself.

Maria C.

with federal funding. Contact the National Resource and Policy Center on Housing and Long Term Care for highlights about government-funded housing programs (see appendix). Or contact your local housing authority or Area Agency on Aging for a list of Section 202 complexes in your elder's area. Then contact apartment managers to place your elder's name on a list. (Being on more than one waiting list is allowed.)

Single room occupancy (SRO). This refers to a single room in a city hotel or rooming house. It is usually a room of less than 100 square feet that is designed to accommodate only one person. The bathroom, kitchen, or common areas are shared by others in the hotel or building. A larger form of the SRO was introduced several years ago. It is called the microefficiency unit and it features a kitchenette and bathroom with sink, toilet, and shower stall.

The SRO is usually created from one of three different kinds of building structures. Rehabilitated SRO hotels are turn-of-the-century hotels originally built for inner-city workers. A second kind is the "adaptive reuse building," which was designed for another purpose but has been renovated into SROs. A third kind is a "purpose-built house," which is specifically designed as an SRO housing unit.

One of the pioneers in new SRO developments is the Tom Hom Group, based in San Diego. This organization designs apartments for working-class individuals on a limited income. To ensure safety, each complex has a front desk, special lock systems, and security monitors and cameras. (See appendix to contact the Tom Hom Group.)

Shared housing. This is also called "homesharing," in which two or more unrelated people live together in the same home or boarding house, where meals and bathroom facilities are shared. Expenses for food, utilities, housing costs, and transportation are also shared. (The costs typically range from $200 to $500 a month.) This can be a good way to help an elderly homeowner to remain independent while still having someone available to help in times of need. It is important to make sure the homesharers have the same basic values and tastes. Your local senior center or Area Agency on Aging can provide you with more details on the pros and cons of homesharing.

Accessory apartments. These are "in-law" apartments that are created in basements, other areas of the home, or in separate buildings on the premises. This can provide a very workable situation for the elderly person and his landlord (which may be you). It provides the elder with the privacy he needs and helps you maintain your sense of privacy as well. If you are thinking about creating an accessory apartment within your home or in a separate building on your property, be sure to check with the city zoning office to see what kind of restrictions are in place. If your loved one is simply living in one room in your house, there is no need to contact the zoning department.

Elder Cottage Housing Opportunity (ECHO). ECHO describes a small, freestanding, removable housing unit that can be placed on the side or backyard of your single-family home. The ECHO concept, which originated in Australia, provides your elder with private and independent living but enables you to be nearby in case of emergencies. Zoning can be a problem for ECHO housing. The American Association of Retired Persons has several publications on ECHO homes and zoning laws (see appendix).

Cooperative housing. Usually in the form of an apartment building, this provides a living environment in which the residents actually own and control the facility. They are shareholders and govern its operation, including setting rent and developing a budget. Residents might share meals and chores, as well as common space, with their housemates. By owning the cooperative, the seniors gain the same benefits they would

SWEET DREAMS

What my mother did faithfully for me many years ago, I now do each night for her. Our routine is simple but sweet. Tucking her into bed brings a sense of satisfaction. The nightlight is turned on, the wheelchair set aside. I wind up the music box and sit on the side of her bed. We listen together to the melody "Amazing Grace" while tiny angels turn to the tune. I smooth Mother's hair back, rub in the touches of night cream on her cheeks, and kiss her good night. I say, "I love you." Her closed eyes flutter as she mumbles what I know is a repeat of that message back to me.   *Sandee S.*

from owning a single-family dwelling, but they also enjoy safety, social interaction, and less maintenance.

LIVING WITH YOU

Having your elderly loved one come to live with you should involve serious discussion, analysis, and prayer. On the plus side, a wise elder can have a positive influence on children in your household, and children have a natural opportunity to learn to treat their elders with respect and honor. Also, it may be easier to look after an aging loved one if and when she needs assistance.

But be sure to look closely at everyone's expectations before taking your elder in, especially if it creates a multiple-generation home. Two consecutive generations may tolerate each other fairly well. When a third generation enters the picture, however, the family dynamic changes. Tensions arise if an elderly parent moves in and expects the middle-aged child to revert to a dependency relationship as in childhood days. This is unreasonable to expect, yet many elders do. Another difficult aspect of caring for an elderly parent involves role reversal—having to parent your parent. And when caregivers are caught between caring for their children and an elderly parent, emotions can turn negative. It is important to discuss these scenarios with your aging loved one before he moves in. Since it is your home, you are ultimately in charge of what happens there.

Having your elderly loved one come to live with you should involve serious discussion, analysis, and prayer.

The more you talk openly, plan thoroughly, and pray for direction and wisdom, the more likely you will be to come to a mutually beneficial decision.

Should Your Elder Live With You?

Here are some questions to ask when considering having your aging loved one live with you:

- Can you tolerate each other's lifestyle?
- Do you have similar values and beliefs?
- Can you relate to each other as mature adults?
- Would living together give a non-Christian elder the opportunity to see your Christian values and lifestyle?

- How do your elder and other household members feel about sharing a home?
- Does your home have adequate space?
- How will you handle errands and appointments?
- How does your elder interact with your children?
- Will there be privacy?
- If your elder is mentally incompetent, will she endanger the safety of your family?
- Is she in danger of wandering away?
- Does your elder need specialized medical care?
- Will caring for your elder require you or your spouse to quit a job?
- Do you see this as an interim solution until around-the-clock care is needed?
- Can you establish guidelines up front about how your loved one will interact with your children?
- Will your elder eat meals with your family every night, or will he have his own space to eat and store food?
- Will your elder be bothered by your family's dog or cat? Is there room for your elder's pet?
- What effect will the move have on your elder's and your own income?

WHAT I LEARNED FROM GRANDMA

My grandmother lived with my parents while I was in college. I was living there too. We didn't have extra bedrooms so Grandma slept in the living room. None of us had much privacy. She was hard of hearing and kind of delusional. There was a lot of stress. This changed the feel of our home.

Although it seemed like an eternity at the time, my brother and I decided we needed to look at this as though it was not going to last long. We decided we were going to be glad for the memories. I have a strong sense of roots that grew out of that. I became more aware of my heritage. Caring for my aging grandmother helped me mature. I learned you need to keep a positive perspective on aging because for one thing, you might get there someday yourself.

Elise R.

- Can your aging loved one help pay for renovations or an addition to your home if extra space is needed to accommodate her?

As you begin to think about the answers to these questions, others will come to mind. Be sure to consider the actual and hidden costs of having your elderly loved one live with you. Unless your elder has independent income to contribute to your home, you may find that your disposable income will be decreased considerably. In many home-care situations, a working woman will give up her job to care for an older loved one. This can further reduce the overall income of the family. On the other hand, eliminating an outside job also reduces the need to pay for extra clothing for work, gas for daily commutes, and lunches out. If your elder is still relatively independent, he may actually be an asset—driving children to after-school activities, shopping, going to the post office, or being home while you are gone. It may be wise to consult other siblings or relatives to see if they would be willing to share the financial costs as well as certain tasks of caregiving. This issue should be worked through before your elder is brought into your home. There are numerous tax-reform proposals being floated in Congress that would provide taxpayers with a tax exemption to help those who provide long-term, in-home care for a family member.

An important consideration is whether or not your home has adequate space for you, your children, and your elder. You do not need an exceptionally large home or an accessory apartment in the back of your home, but all of you must have privacy and personal space if the arrangement is to work. Each of you must have the ability to "get away" from the rest of the family. Some remodeling may be in order to accomplish this.

Don't Be Motivated by Guilt

Many people feel obligated to take their aging parent into their home. Although certain ethnic groups traditionally have had intergenerational households, this has not necessarily been the standard in recent American history.

Even in colonial days, the three-generation family was an exception. Instead, groups of two or more related families lived in a single community, not a single house. These kinship groups were dependent upon each other but did not share the same quarters. It is similar in our culture. Most elderly people desire some independence but are still dependent upon their children. The elder is close by but does not live with the children unless it is absolutely necessary. Keep in mind that arranging for an independent-living situation for your parents is not abandoning them. Often it is the best choice for both the adult child and the elderly parent.

Most elderly people desire some independence but are still dependent upon their children.

Nevertheless, widowed older people are much more likely to live with a child, and daughters outnumber sons four to one in sharing their households with an aging relative. About 13 percent of older, widowed persons live with children, siblings, or other relatives.[1] But this proportion decreases with age. Especially due to increased care needs, a majority of people who live past age 85 spend their remaining period of life in a long-term-care facility.

Safe and Sound

Before moving an aging loved one into your home, you will need to check it for safety and mobility. See chapter 15 for suggestions on how to make your home safe and accessible to an elderly person. Also, let your elder have some regular responsibilities in your home, in keeping

---

DREAMS AND REALITY

My mother does not recognize the difference between dreams and reality. One day I found her groping around in the dark garage, trying to find her way outside. She had dreamed that someone called me on the phone and because she knew I was outside, she was trying to find me.

She frequently dreams that I am calling her or knocking on her bedroom door. She quickly gets out of bed to answer me, which could result in a serious fall.

Before going to work one morning, I told her a health assistant would be coming over in case Mother needed her while she took a shower. She did not remember what I told her, even when the person arrived. When I came home at noon, Mother accused me of putting something over on her. Now I leave a note telling her what is going to happen in case she forgets.

Ellen J.

with his mental and physical capabilities. An elderly person who has lost the ability to do certain things may still be able to fold laundry or help with the dishes. (To make it easier for your elder to help in the kitchen, replace heavy, breakable dishware with lightweight, nonbreakable plates and cups.) By doing jobs around the house, your loved one will feel useful and cooperative. Pray daily for wisdom and a gentle spirit as you work through the relational challenges of having your elder live with you.

An elderly person who has lost the ability to do certain things may still be able to fold laundry or help with the dishes.

CONGREGATE HOUSING

Congregate housing takes many forms and has many definitions. It is typically a multi-unit housing arrangement containing private rooms or full apartments. Somewhat like a dormitory for the elderly, this type of facility offers housing units with a common dining room for meals, as well as access to social, recreational, and spiritual programs. Congregate-living facilities usually provide a senior with some assistance in daily living but do not provide around-the-clock medical or nursing care.

Generally restricted to persons over a specified age, congregate-living arrangements have been called "retirement homes," "old people's homes," "sheltered housing," and "homes for the aged." Many of them were originally developed and operated as nonprofit homes by religious institutions and fraternal or social organizations. To change the perception among some elderly people that homes for the aged are dismal places (and to attract more affluent older people), entrepreneurs are developing new approaches to congregate living, with sparkling surroundings and upscale services. Typically, congregate-living facilities have social directors to arrange social and recreational activities, linen and housekeeping services, and some medical assistance, with a nurse who can monitor medications.

Experts see congregate living as a bridge between independent living and the kind of care a senior may eventually need in a full-service nursing home. If your elder is looking at congregate living, these factors should be considered before making a decision:

1. Who owns the facility, and is the management competent? If it is a new facility, who can recommend the management?

Entrepreneurs are developing some new approaches to congregate living, with sparkling surroundings and upscale services.

2. Is it not-for-profit? If so, how much money is behind the facility to ensure its long-term financial stability? If it is for-profit, is there enough financial stability to prevent large monthly rate increases?

3. Is there an entry fee, and if so, what happens to it if your elder changes his mind before or after moving in?

4. What services are included in the monthly fees? What costs are extra?

5. What are the other residents like? Do they seem happy, or do they have lots of complaints?

6. What are the facility's rules? For example, can residents decorate or furnish their rooms as they wish?

7. What food choices are offered? Can the facility accommodate special diets?

8. How are medical emergencies handled?

9. What, if any, are the spiritual activities and opportunities for ministry?

10. What happens if your parent becomes physically disabled?

Costs generally range from $1,200 to $2,000 a month or more. Fees are lower for residents of federally sponsored programs, who only pay a percentage of their incomes.

Retirement Communities

A form of congregate living, a retirement community is where older people move after they can no longer maintain their independent living unit—houses, condos, etc. For example, a senior who develops macular degenerative blindness may move into a retirement care facility because she can no longer cook her own meals. Usually age-segregated and located in the Sun Belt, retirement communities can take the form of high-rise senior-housing complexes and leisure villages. These communities—which can be expensive—offer a variety of services, leisure activities, and avocational opportunities in one setting, which can include continuum of care (providing housing, services, and nursing care over the long term). If an aging resident needs nursing care, it may be necessary to move to a long-term-care facility.

Adult Group Homes

In these larger congregate facilities, care is provided for up to 16 unrelated senior citizens who split the monthly cost of rent, housekeeping services, utilities, and meals. Residents in group homes often suffer from cognitive difficulties. Federal and state Supplemental Security Income (SSI) funding may be available to help seniors with limited income and assets, including those who have never been employed. Contact your local social-security office for more information.

CONTINUING CARE RETIREMENT COMMUNITIES

One of the more popular and growing trends in the U.S. is the spread of continuing care retirement communities (CCRCs), a concept that started among religious groups in Pennsylvania and in Grand Rapids, Michigan, more than 100 years ago. Sometimes called a Lifecare community, this type of organization starts with independent living and progresses to more intensive care services as needed. It offers active seniors an independent lifestyle and a private living space, regardless of

---

ON THE MOVE

Since 1970, my parents have gone through several housing changes. After they moved out of the home I grew up in, the sequence has been my father's dream house in another state, a retirement community in another state, and a third move to the state where I lived.

My father died two months after the last move. A year later my mother decided to move to a retirement community, and a year after that, my mother purchased the townhouse that adjoined mine. We were able (legally) to put an opening in the common basement wall so we could go back and forth without going outside. More recently we purchased a house where we live together.

The shared housing has been beneficial financially for both of us. It is more convenient because I don't have to pick her up for things like grocery shopping. (My mother never drove.) Also, I see how she is changing gradually and can give my sister in Minnesota an accurate picture.

Ruth W.

future medical needs. In some cases, your elder must be able to walk in unassisted in order to move in. When a senior enters a CCRC, he will sign a long-term contract, pay a sizable entry fee, and then pay a monthly fee that will guarantee he will be cared for during the rest of his life. These are expensive facilities, but the senior can rest assured he will have a continuum of care. The number of CCRCs has grown tremendously in the last twenty years, from 100 to 2,500.

What Is Offered?

CCRCs provide a full range of housing, residential services, and health care (usually all in one location) in order to serve their older residents as their needs change over time. This includes all services typically included by an assisted-living facility, but it also provides a complete range of medical care. In the continuum of care for an elderly person, a CCRC goes from independent living to complete nursing-home care. A CCRC offers some or all of the following services: meals, grounds maintenance, local transportation, security systems, and on-site physician services. Most offer housekeeping, laundry, and the processing of Medicare and Medicaid reimbursement forms.

A growing number of CCRCs are wooing clients with a variety of special amenities—putting greens, 24-hour snack bars, ice-cream parlors, computer centers, and beauty salons. Diverse activities might include art, music, theater, lectures, knitting gatherings, writing workshops, health-education programs, and visits to local museums and parks.

LONELY NO MORE

My pastor's wife was alone 17 years after her husband died. When she came to live at the continuing care retirement village where I work, she said she never realized how lonely she'd been. Now she has all kinds of friends and companions, plus guaranteed meals and health care. We've found that people tend to live three to seven years longer in a retirement community than they would on their own because they have less stress and more social interaction.

Julie M.

Praises and Pitfalls

There are benefits and drawbacks to CCRCs. Although group living can be difficult for some elderly who have been accustomed to living on their own, this can be an ideal environment for the elderly person who is still mobile, sociable, and healthy enough to make new friends. A well-run facility will encourage activities that foster friendships. And because this type of facility makes available multiple levels of care, your elder should not have to wonder where he will live when more care is needed.

Those entering a CCRC will sign a "life contract," which is a kind of housing insurance. The contract may cover the duration of the resident's life and provide unlimited nursing care or cover a limited amount of nursing care. There are potential pitfalls in purchasing a life contract, however. There is the possibility of fraud, mismanagement, lack of capital, underoccupied units, rising medical costs, and unclear contracts.

The financial stability of CCRCs is also a concern, and it is important to see if they are financially sound. Look for well-respected, Christian-based, nonprofit CCRCs, such as Covenant Retirement Communities (Evangelical Covenant denomination) and Holland Homes (Reformed). Check with your denomination for information about Christian senior-housing options.

Paying for Life Care

Typically, CCRCs provide housing and care for residents under three basic financial arrangements: Extensive Agreement, Modified Agreement, and Fee-for-Service Agreement. The Extensive Agreement includes housing, residential services, and unlimited long-term care without major increases in payments—except for inflation adjustments. It provides for prepayment of medical expenses. The Modified Agreement covers the same things, but care is limited to a certain number of days each year. When the limit is reached, the person must pay a daily charge. The Fee-for-Service Agreement is becoming the most commonly used one by CCRCs. Under this arrangement, the elderly person pays only for the services he uses. This benefits both the CCRC and the senior. The CCRC can more easily predict its costs and the resident does not have to pay for services he may never use. However, keep in mind that the charge for daily care adds up quickly when paid out of pocket. If your elder has long-term-care insurance to help with such fees, make certain the policy includes assisted-living coverage (some only cover skilled nursing-home care). The policy should also increase its amount of coverage annually to keep up with cost increases in the industry.

The price of lifetime care? CCRCs can be expensive. Entrance fees range from $10,000 for a small apartment up to $300,000 for a two- or three-bedroom model, depending on the basic fee structure outlined above. Entrance fees also vary depending on the level of care desired. Monthly fees can range widely from a few hundred dollars to thousands of dollars depending on the CCRC. When an elderly resident leaves or dies, most plans refund a percentage of the entrance fee to his estate if he purchased an apartment.

If your elder is considering a CCRC, encourage or help him to do the following:

- Check the contract carefully with the help of an elder-law lawyer.
- Analyze the organization's financial condition.
- Talk to the residents.
- Evaluate the meals if they are included.
- Assess the nursing facility for quality and staff training.
- Check the facility's accreditation.
- Evaluate the community's lifestyle. Will it fit your aging loved one's lifestyle?

Check with your local senior center for information on retirement communities in your area. There can be long waiting lists to get into a CCRC. If your aging loved one is considering a CCRC, make sure her name is on a list as soon as she has made a CCRC choice.

ASSISTED LIVING

Although nursing homes were once one of the few places for seniors to go when they needed ongoing care, there are now many other options available. One popular option is assisted living. Although definitions are not uniform, assisted living generally refers to a caregiving model that provides more care than independent living but less care than a nursing home. More seniors are embracing this concept because it allows them to remain somewhat independent yet still receive necessary services. There are now an estimated 25,000 assisted-living facilities in the United States, serving more than a million seniors.

Assisted-living facilities come in a variety of shapes and sizes. They may be freestanding, part of a retirement community or nursing home, or within a continuing care retirement community that provides independent living, assisted living, and nursing care. The residences may house as few as two older people in a homelike setting or may hold up to

ASSISTED LIVING: STATISTICS AND TRENDS

The Assisted Living Federation of America cites the following statistics and trends in this growing industry:

- The average assisted-living resident is a woman in her mid-80s who is mobile but needs assistance with some personal activities; men account for 29 percent of the residents.
- Two in five assisted-living residents have a cognitive impairment, while one-third use a wheelchair or walker and one-fifth suffer from incontinence. One-quarter were hospitalized before moving into an assisted-living residence.
- The average stay is 3.3 years. Of those who leave due to death or other reasons, 44 percent move to a nursing home, 10 percent to a hospital, 4 percent to a relative's home, and 4 percent to another assisted-living facility.
- Average per-day rate of assisted living in a private/studio room is $66 as compared to $125 per day for nursing-home care and $83 per visit for a home health-care nurse.
- The median annual income of residents is $25,000 with median assets of $100,000.
- Three-quarters of assisted-living residents need help with medication dispensing, 60 percent with bathing, half need medication reminders, and 25 percent need assistance with toileting.[1]

[1]Assisted Living Federation of America, *Typical Assisted Living Resident—ALFA's 1998 Overview of the Assisted Living Industry.* See <http://www.alfa.org>.

HELPING GRANDMA

For most of my life I grew up in a single-parent family. As a child I would spend many summers in Boca Raton, under my grandma and grandpa's care and authority. They helped to raise me. Therefore, when my grandma became a widow in 1979, I felt a biblical and moral obligation to care for her as a widow. Aside from my mother and my sister, she's my only living relative. Grandma lived on her own until she was 88½ years old; she spent 20 of those years as a widow.

When I found out she was putting the kettle on and forgetting about it until it was melting into the stove, I had her come up north to live here with us, but after 12 very long days, she didn't want to stay with us, so we sent her home again. Several times we tried having my mother and then my wife stay with her in her own house, in her own surroundings. If it worked, we were planning to make it a permanent situation and move back to Florida to be with Grandma. However, she became very combative, hitting them with her cane. She even chased them with a knife. Needless to say, my mother and my wife were afraid of this behavior. Because of her deteriorating condition and dementia, she had become paranoid and abusive toward the very people who loved and cared for her—and potentially abusive to herself. We realized we could not handle her in this condition.

I made it a point to establish a good relationship with her primary-care physician. Occasionally I'd fly down, take Grandma for her monthly office visit, and meet personally with the doctor. One day her doctor called me and said, "George, your grandmother can no longer live on her own. I have diagnosed her with mild senile dementia and recommend she have daily personal care in an assisted-living facility. In six months, she will likely need full-time care."

I asked the doctor to put his words in a letter to show that this was not my opinion but rather a medical necessity; then I copied the letter for my mother and sister. I also contacted Grandma's neurologist, who tested her and concurred with her primary doctor. After many family conferences, we reached a consensus. It was time to move Grandma out of her house. We knew she would object, so we also agreed that it would have to be a "capture."

We had Grandma pack her bags for a two-week trip to Tampa to visit my mother for Mother's Day, then later broke the news to her that she would not be returning to her house. I said, "Grandma, if you're not living with us, then you will be living in adult congregate living." She was angry and tried to make us feel guilty, but even with her gnashing of teeth, we were determined to follow through with the plan. She has been in a nursing home for 18 months now, where she has a beautiful private bedroom, a common dining room, and a stable routine. We visit her regularly; however, her condition has progressed to the point that she does not recognize her family.

A lot of people, especially Christians, think you're somehow shirking your responsibility if you move a loved one into a long-term-care home. But when you've made your good-faith effort, have done everything else you possibly could do, and you've had good counsel, it's probably not a matter of *if* but *when* you're going to have to take that step. In that case, you have to be steadfast and not look back.   *George T.*

200 in an institutional environment. Assisted-living facilities are described by different names, including *board-and-care homes, adult foster-care homes, personal-care homes, sheltered-care facilities, residential-care facilities,* or *dormitory-care facilities.* Many of the new facilities are upscale apartments operated by corporations.

What Is Offered?

Assisted living combines housing, personal services, and some health-care services in an environment that promotes individual independence, privacy, and choice. While residents in assisted-living facilities do not require round-the-clock skilled nursing care, they typically need help with at least two or three activities of daily living (ADLs) that many younger people take for granted: eating, bathing, dressing, toileting, and walking. Some assisted-living communities also have special units for individuals with Alzheimer's disease or dementia. The staff is geared toward helping residents function as independently as possible.

While the size of the residence varies, all assisted-living facilities typically offer the following services: assistance with ADL deficiencies, 24-hour security, three meals a day in a common dining room, medication dispensing or reminders, housekeeping, laundry, social and recreational activities, and an emergency call system. These may be included in the basic-care package or may be offered for additional fees.

The fees your elder will pay depend upon the kind of housing he desires (private vs. shared room) and the kind of services he wishes to have. Some of these services can be purchased "à la carte." Although fees for assisted living are normally two-thirds the cost of a nursing home, most assisted-living facilities accept private pay only. The price of rent and assistance costs between $1,000 and $4,000 a month, depending on the size and design of the unit and the amount of personal amenities included.

How to Choose an Assisted-Living Facility

The first step in choosing a facility is to be honest and forthright about your aging loved one's physical, financial, and lifestyle needs. If your elder seems like a good candidate for assisted living, your next task is to shop for a facility with well-trained, reliable staff and quality care. Your elder's hospital-discharge planner, physician, case manager, clergy, social worker, financial planner, and friends may be able to recommend area facilities. Or contact the local social-services department to find out which assisted-living facilities are available in your elder's area.

Visit as many facilities as you can to get a sense of the kind of choices you will have. Note whether you are greeted warmly by staff and whether the administrator and staff call residents by name as you tour the facility. Ask about staff training and turnover. Find out how the facility will accommodate your elder's current needs and what will happen if the needs increase. Who decides when a resident must leave for health reasons?

Consider how close you live to the facility. Residents who have frequent visitors tend to get better care, so proximity is a plus. Look at the physical surroundings—the presence of handrails, easy-to-reach cupboard space, accessibility to the dining room, color-coded hallways. A new trend is to incorporate skylights into the facility design of common areas, such as dining rooms and corridors; this brings in more natural light and creates a friendlier, less "institutional" environment. Ask about special amenities. For example, some assisted-living facilities have beauty salons with shampoo bowls that elevate several inches to accommodate people in wheelchairs.

When you have narrowed your selection to the top three, return to the facilities with your elder for a more in-depth look. Visit at different times of the day and on a weekend to observe the routines and activities. Make surprise visits to the places you are seriously considering, and arrange for an overnight stay before making a final decision. Eat a meal at the facility. Is the food tasty? Do the residents socialize and appear happy? Chat with the residents about their experiences. Ask them questions like these:

- Do you have a choice of main courses? Do you help decide the menu?
- How long do you have to wait for services?
- What happens if you have a problem?
- Does the staff smile and respond to you as individuals?
- Is there an active residents' council?
- Are pets allowed?
- Can residents' grandchildren spend the night?
- What kinds of things do you do on a typical day?
- Are you very glad to be living here?
- What happens if someone dies?
- What special observances (secular and Christian) are recognized here?

Ask the administrator for a copy of the rules and the contract and read them carefully at home. Then ask a lawyer (preferably one who specializes in elder law) to review the contract for you. If you do not know an elder-law attorney, search for "elder law" on the Internet and you will find dozens of sites—including some that have searchable databases of attorneys in your area. Ask to see the facility's licensing inspection report. Your local long-term-care ombudsman can advise you and provide you with a recent listing of complaints. (For more information, see chapter 11 on legal care.)

The Consumer Consortium on Assisted Living (CCAL) has developed a lengthy questionnaire you can take with you when you meet with the director of the assisted-living facility. You can download the entire document free of charge from the CCAL Web site or send for a printed booklet (see appendix). Here are some questions excerpted from the questionnaire:

- What services are provided in the fee?
- What happens if funds run out? Is there any financial assistance?

- Does the contract clearly describe a refund policy in cases of transfers, discharges, changes in ownership, or closing?
- If a resident displays a difficult behavior, what steps will the facility take?
- Is there special training for staff about dementia and Alzheimer's disease?
- Is there a separate area specifically for people with dementia, and if so, how do services differ from services in the rest of the facility?
- What kind of emergencies are staff expected to handle and how are they trained for them?
- To what extent will the facility monitor your elder's health?
- What safeguards are in place to see that your loved one receives his medications on schedule?
- Is transportation to health appointments available, is it wheelchair-accessible, and what are the fees?
- How are religious/spiritual needs met? Is there transportation to church? Are there arrangements and room for worship programs in the facility?
- If your elder does not like a meal, what alternatives are there?
- Are background checks made on all staff?

Residents who have frequent visitors tend to get better care.

How to Pay for Assisted Living

Assisted-living residents or their families generally pay the cost of care out of their own funds. Medicare does not pay for assisted-living services. Medicare pays the bills only for a limited number of days when a more intensive form of care, called skilled nursing care, is needed and provided in certified facilities. Some facilities offer subsidies and financial aid on a limited basis, although a waiting list typically exists. A growing number of private insurance companies are beginning to offer assisted-living coverage as part of their insurance package, but services covered under these policies vary widely, and many elderly people do not have long-term-care insurance.

Most facilities accept only private pay, although some states offer limited assistance through Medicaid or Supplemental Security Income. Thirty-seven states reimburse or plan to reimburse for assisted-living services as a Medicaid service. Check with your state Medicaid office for more information.

Fees for assisted-living services can mount quickly, depending on amenities, level of care offered, and additional services. Ask about what is covered under the monthly payment (e.g., room and board and meals) and what is an additional fee. Facilities generally charge for services in one of these ways: **flat** or **bundled rate** (in which everyone pays the same rate for personal-care services that are adjusted in the basic rent); **tiered rate** (in which residents may choose from several tiers or price levels, depending on the level of care needed); **flat rate plus an hourly charge for personal assistance** (which may include walking a resident to the dining room or even tying shoes); **one-time entry** or **community fees** (which can equal a month's rent). Because of the labor-intensive work, be aware that rate increases of 3 to 5 percent per year are not uncommon.

At present, the industry is attracting seniors who are age 75 or older and who meet the entry criteria of at least $25,000 in annual net income, have no combative or disruptive behaviors, and can pay monthly fees of $2,000 or more. At the low end, assisted living can cost between $985 and $1,500 per month with basic amenities included. For more information, contact the American Health Care Association (see appendix).

Is Assisted Living the Best Option?

To determine if your elder is a good match for assisted living, consider your loved one's personality and health needs. If your aging loved one is losing some function but is a sociable person, it may be the ideal choice. If your elder is not fond of congregate living, a better option may be to arrange for help through adult day-care programs and/or home care. (For more information on adult day care/home care, see chapter 15.) Following a hospital stay, extended care/subacute care hospital rooms are offered by some hospitals on a temporary basis for those who cannot go home but do not want to move into an assisted-living or continuing-care facility.

Consider your elder's financial stability, too. Will your elder's income and assets be enough to cover assisted-living expenses for the next few years, including possible increases in monthly charges and additional fees if more services are needed?

A continuing problem with assisted-living facilities is what happens to the elder when she needs care beyond the levels provided by assisted living. She may end up transfering to a nursing home if the assisted-living facility is not licensed or equipped to handle her increasing medical needs. After spending much of her savings on the assisted-living facil-

---

MAKING A SPIRITUAL MOVE

At age 74 Linda's mother stopped writing checks to pay her bills and seemed very confused at times. Linda and her brother were concerned that their mom was no longer safe living alone. When she had a natural-gas leak under the kitchen and refused to leave the house for the fire chief, they decided the time had come to move their mother from her home. They contacted the facilities recommended by a friend and soon found a room available at a nursing facility. "Because Mom didn't go willingly, it was an extremely difficult day when we moved her," Linda says. "I began to wonder if we should have taken more time to consider our options and find something that better suited Mom."

Linda did more research, and eventually God graciously opened up a room in a smaller, homier facility only three miles from Linda's door. "It's operated by a wonderful Christian family, and Mom has settled in beautifully," she says. Linda and her brother visit their mother often and take her on afternoon outings or to their homes for dinner.

When Linda started this ordeal, she was overwhelmed and faltered along the way, but God upheld her and guided her steps with Scriptures such as Isaiah 41:10 and Proverbs 20:24. She recommends the following four tips if you're considering a move for your elder:

1. Pray about every move, take as much time as you can, and pour out your fears, hurts, and frustrations to the Lord (Philippians 4:6-7). Your own strength cannot sustain you when emotionally charged issues overtake you, but God's can.
2. Ask God to make correct moves obvious and to close doors tightly to any wrong moves.
3. Ask God to bring a trustworthy friend to help you and to listen to you (Hebrews 10:24-25).
4. Seek godly counsel from people and agencies with experience who can help you in concrete ways. Talk with people in your church who have gone through this with their parents or aging loved ones. Maybe you can start a support group at church for other caregivers.

ity, the elder may be asked to leave with no guarantee of where to go. Many seniors have been left "high and dry" by the assisted-living industry when they needed more care. That is why the continuum of care offered by continuing care retirement communities appeals to many.

If assisted living seems to be the most appropriate and welcomed kind of care for your aging loved one, the best time to talk about it is before it is needed. Try to anticipate the day when in-home care combined with community services and family help is no longer viable.

Stay in Touch with Your Elder

It will take time for your loved one to become adjusted to living in an entirely new environment. He may have come from living in your home, condo, apartment, or his own home. In any case, he is in unfamiliar territory. In the beginning he will need as much emotional and spiritual support as you can muster. Loneliness can be a seriously debilitating condition for an elderly person. He can be just as lonely in an assisted-living facility as he is at home if his emotional and social needs are neglected by his loved ones.

Encourage your siblings to help you during this adjustment period. You can take turns visiting. You and your siblings may wish to plan for occasional family reunions so that your elder can enjoy time with relatives. Old friends can also come by to visit and talk.

NURSING HOMES

For an elder who has multiple medical problems and is disabled to the point of requiring daily nursing care and other support services, nursing homes provide comprehensive care in one setting. A CCRC also provides this care for its residents. (For more information on nursing homes, see chapter 17: Nursing-Home Care.)

MAKING A GOOD MOVE

Moving is traumatic for an older person, especially when it involves leaving a longtime residence and neighborhood. It is hard to say goodbye to a house full of memories, that familiar face at the drugstore, and next-door neighbors. When a move makes it necessary to find a new

Moving is traumatic for an older person, especially when it involves leaving a longtime residence and neighborhood.

church, that too is a difficult adjustment. If it seems time for your aging loved one to consider moving, discuss the issue with your elder. Talk through each concern, and try not to rush making a decision. Pray for clear guidance, and allow time to weigh the options, if at all possible. If moving becomes a reality, consider making a video of your elder's old home and neighborhood so he can watch it and share the memories with new friends. Photo albums are also helpful.

Whether your aging loved one comes to live in a retirement community, some type of assisted-living facility, or with you, you can support your elder in his spiritual walk. To help ease the transition, spend a few weekends with your elder to explore the new area, meet neighbors, and visit churches. Once your loved one is settled in, accompany him to worship services if possible and to lunch afterward. Bring Christian literature, books, and sermon tapes. If your elder cannot venture out to church, listen to a sermon tape together, or consider reading a devotional book or the Bible to him. Take time to pray with your aging loved one. You might also consider giving him the entire Bible on audio tape or CD so he can listen to it at his leisure. If your elder has a VCR, he might enjoy watching videos with a Christian viewpoint or at least ones that have a positive, life-affirming message.

Old age does not mean your elder is too old to have a ministry of her own.

Old age does not mean your elder is too old to have a ministry of her own. Prayer, for example, should be an avocation of all Christians. Even elderly people who are homebound should be encouraged to pray for others—it is the best thing a Christian can do! "The effectual fervent prayer of a righteous man availeth much" (James 5:16 KJV). In addition, your aging loved one might be able to help to mentor or to disciple a new Christian; to help with simple tasks at church, such as folding church bulletins; to offer gospel tracts to other residents or acquaintances; or to be a surrogate grandparent to a young person. (For more information on spiritual care, see chapter 12: Church, Religious Activity, and Spiritual Life.)

If your elder is discouraged by failing health or a new, unfamilar living environment, it may help to remind him that this really is not the end of the line. While bodies deteriorate and retirement homes can crumble, there is something permanent to look forward to. Besides the promise of a new, glorified, sinless body after we die, Christians have the assurance that a home is being prepared for them in heaven by the Son of God Himself (John 14:1-3). That home will be eternal and will not cost a dime, because the price to get us there has already been paid in full by the shed blood of our Savior, Jesus Christ.

———— ⌇ ————

But our citizenship is in heaven. And we eagerly await a Savior from there, the Lord Jesus Christ, who, by the power that enables him to bring everything under his control, will transform our lowly bodies so that they will be like his glorious body. PHILIPPIANS 3:20-21 NIV

CHAPTER 17

Should I not try to find a home for you,
where you will be well provided for? Ruth 3:1 NIV

Nursing-Home Care

What You Need to Know

After a house fire forced Marilyn, her family, and her disabled mother out of their house, she found herself in a dilemma. Marilyn needed time to be with her son, who had suffered burns in the fire. And the high-rise apartment they were temporarily staying in was not conducive to wheelchairs. So who would care for her mom?

Marilyn called the senior-services agency in her county and asked for help. A case manager came out to assess Marilyn's mom, who needed full-time care, and said she was a good candidate for public aid to pay for nursing-home care. The case manager explained the rules and helped her complete the paperwork. Within a week, Marilyn was able to move her mother into a nearby, highly rated convalescence center that had space available for Medicaid patients.

"I would have done that sooner if I'd thought she'd have a good experience in a nursing home," says Marilyn. "I mistakenly thought she'd have no will to live and would shrivel up and die." Although her mother was depressed at first and asked, "When can I come home?" soon she began to thrive. She especially enjoyed going to Bible studies, visiting with Marilyn, and taking monthly outings to special restaurants or shopping malls with friends.

———— ⁓ ————

No one looks forward to the day when an aging loved one may need to be placed into a nursing home. Usually the decision is made when all other options have been exhausted and relatives or siblings have agonized over their choices. Depending on an elder's need for care and other issues, a nursing home is sometimes the most practical solution to the caregiving question. If you are weighing this decision or already coping with a loved one in a nursing home, your involvement and ongoing encouragement in your elder's life will make a big difference in his or her satisfaction and well-being—and in your own sense of peace.

WHEN A LOVED ONE NEEDS LONG-TERM CARE

Long-term care describes a combination of health care and other services that assist older people who, because of chronic illness, disabilities, or reduced intellectual function, need help with basic "activities of daily living" (ADLs), such as eating, getting in and out of bed, bathing, or using the toilet, and "instrumental activities of daily living" (IADLs), such as shopping, cooking, cleaning, and taking medications.

Long-term care is geared toward the person who suffers from a chronic health condition, such as dementia, that will remain until death.

The goal of long-term care is not the same as that of acute care. The goal of medical care is to provide short-term help to heal your elder of an illness. Long-term care, however, is geared toward the person who suffers from a chronic health condition, such as dementia or incontinence, that will remain until death. Long-term care is designed to slow mental or physical decline or create small improvements in the person's life.

In recent years the health-care system has expanded to include a wide variety of long-term care options, including home health-care services, home meal delivery, transportation services, live-in caregivers, respite services, adult day care, continuing care retirement communities, assisted-living facilities, and nursing homes. Skilled nursing facilities may be freestanding or may be part of a senior community offering congregate living and assisted living, all comprising a continuum of care. In today's diverse market, it is important to determine the appropriate level of care, activity, and social group to suit your elderly loved one's level of need. Too much or too little care can result in unneccessary stress and suffering for your elder, whereas the appropriate environment can mean peace and satisfaction for you both.

Less than 5 percent of all Americans sixty-five and older live in nursing homes. Yet that percentage increases to 19 percent for those eighty-five and older.[1] Many states, as well as the federal government, are working to provide alternatives based in home, faith, and community. But when a loved one needs round-the-clock assistance, the most appropriate long-term care is often the custodial and skilled care associated with nursing homes, which is the emphasis of this chapter.

Too much or too little care can result in unneccessary stress and suffering for your elder.

Nursing-Home Services

If your loved one is disabled or has multiple medical problems that require services in addition to daily nursing care, nursing homes provide comprehensive-care services in one setting. Three levels of care are offered in a nursing home: **basic care,** involving personal care (e.g., bathing and dressing), mobility (e.g., help getting in and out of chairs or bed), and supervision by a nurse assistant; **skilled care** for treatments that require the services of a registered nurse, doctors, or therapists; and **subacute care** for a patient who needs frequent care and assessment after an acute illness or injury. Some nursing homes have special care units dedicated to specific needs or diagnoses, such as Alzheimer's disease, ventilator/pulmonary care, rehabilitation, or hospice care. It is not uncommon for people to move from an assisted-living facility to a nursing home to accommodate their increasing medical needs.

How do you know when your aging loved one needs long-term care? The reasons usually fall into two categories: 1) the continually deteriorating condition of the elderly person and 2) the ongoing strain and eventual exhaustion of the caregiver.

Elderly people who have been cared for by their families usually have four health problems per person by the time they finally enter a nursing home.[2] At least one or more of the following factors may indicate that nursing assistance is needed to manage an elder's health:

- **Multiple health problems.** An elder has reduced physical ability and needs assistance when eating, moving from a bed to a chair, bathing, taking medications, dressing, and using a toilet (e.g., help with transferring on and off the toilet, reminders to use the bathroom, or help with bathroom hygiene). Many caregivers are unable to deal with an elderly loved one's loss of bladder or bowel control (incontinence). Some nursing assistance may be needed, such as changing wound dressings, giving injections, or monitoring vital signs. Because of your elder's reduced physical ability, someone must be present to help him accomplish self-care tasks. More than four-fifths (83 percent) of nursing-home residents require assistance with three or more activities of daily living.[3]

- **Reduced intellectual ability.** The aging person suffers from mental disabilities that prevent her from accomplishing routine tasks. A person must be present to help her and to protect her from injuring herself or wandering off. Sixty percent of nursing home residents over age 65 have some form of loss in either short-term memory, long-term memory, or both.[4] When an elderly loved one has a combination of physical and mental problems, it often leads to the careful consideration of a nursing-home placement.

- **Skill level and intensity of care.** The medical skill level required to care for an aging loved one exceeds the caregiver's understanding, or the amount of care needed grows to 15 or more hours of care each day. In those cases, other arrangements need to be made to ensure quality care and to prevent caregiver burn-out.

- **Other needs.** An elder needs round-the-clock assistance for a number of other reasons, including medical care, socialization, spiritual affirmation, or personal growth. Family demands, employment needs, lack of space and privacy, financial costs of caregiving, and other tensions also compete with a caregiver's ability to be the primary caregiver.

To accurately assess when and if your elder needs long-term nursing care, you will need to work with his physician, social worker, or an adviser with a local senior center. Make sure you explore all possible options, such as hiring a live-in caregiver or having visiting nurses provide care in your loved one's home.

Making the Decision

The decision to move an aging loved one into a nursing home may be one of the most difficult you will ever make. In fact, it is common for adult children to promise themselves they will never subject a parent to "that kind of place." They may be sincere, but that kind of promise is based on unpredictable circumstances. Life, especially with the elderly, is fluid and changing. Promises that include the word *never* or *always* are unrealistic. Not one of us knows what the future will bring. So give yourself grace in making the decision for a nursing home. Heart-searching goes with the territory, but don't torment yourself with guilt.

Start the decision-making process by asking these questions:

1. Are you finding it difficult to continue hands-on care for your loved one?
2. Do you feel emotionally drained or chronically tired?
3. Does your elder need rehabilitation or specialized supervision?

Caring for an aging parent or spouse is tough work. As an elderly person requires more and more care, the tired caregiver often scolds himself for not loving more, for not working harder, and for not having more energy. Yet it is difficult to give the type of constant loving care that many elders need. At times, an aging person can make your job even harder by being irritable, demanding, or angry. If you do not get enough rest and help, you yourself might feel angry, depressed, anxious, and resentful.

It is helpful to discuss your situation with a friend or in a support group for caregivers. Besides having the comfort of a listening ear, you might come up with some practical answers to your elder's specific situation. You also might find new ways to cope with your weaknesses and limitations.

Acknowledge your limitations. Caregiver burnout is one of the main reasons a family eventually places an elderly loved one in a 24-hour-a-day nursing facility. While the average caregiver provides care for 18 hours per week, one in five provides "constant care," or at least 40 hours per week caring for an elderly loved one.[5] More than seven in ten caregivers are women, although 27 percent of caregivers are men. Because many caregivers also work outside the home—an estimated 14.4 million full- and part-time workers balance caregiving and job responsibilities[6]—perpetual weariness is a common problem. Many are discovering they cannot do it all. Some have to reduce their hours at work or quit a job, which also reduces their income during key wage-earning years. Caregivers grow weary of being on call all the time. Unless they can find someone to help them, they tend to neglect their own lives, their health, their marriages, and their children in order to care for the ailing elder.

Caregivers often feel isolated and overextended. A 1997 survey by the National Alliance for Caregiving found that one in three caregivers who provide care for at least 40 hours a week says that no one else helps.[7] As caregivers struggle to survive a difficult situation, they may not recognize their own changing needs. Those without a support system are more prone to emotional strain and physical and mental problems (such as depression, sleeplessness, back pain, and other health conditions) and are less apt to wade through the complex health-care and social-service systems for help.

Acknowledge the impact caregiving is having on you and get support and good counsel about available resources.

If you have been trying to go it alone in caring for an elderly loved one, remember that burnout is a very real possibility. It is important to acknowledge the impact caregiving is having on you and to get support and good counsel about available services and resources. You need the help of friends, relatives, siblings, your church, and local community-based organizations to assist you. If your aging loved one needs round-the-clock specialized care and is not satisfied with home and community-based services, it may be time to discuss the possibility of nursing-home placement.

Consult your elder. If at all possible, be sure to involve your loved one in the decision. Even those who are ill or suffering from memory problems should know about considered changes in a living situation. A recent study by the Family Caregiver Alliance indicated that people with mild to moderate cognitive impairment are able to state consistent preferences and choices for their care, participate in care decisions, and express lifelong values and wishes regarding their care in the future.[8] So it is important to include your elder's wishes in the discussion and process of planning. There may be heartache and anger, but your loved one will be at risk for much greater pain if she is not included in the family discussion. And it could also put you at risk for losing her trust.

Allow your loved one to express negative feelings, but don't take them personally. Be ready for any kind of reaction from raging bitterness to passive resignation. You will likely encounter feelings of anger, anxiety, depression, and hopelessness. As you communicate, take into consideration the significance of such a move for her. She will lose familiar surroundings, people, sounds, foods, routine, a certain degree of independence, and privacy. There also might be adjustments to having strangers as roommates, caregivers, and companions. The more your elder is able to participate at the planning stage, the better her chances of adjusting to leaving home and living in a new environment.

The more your elder is able to participate at the planning stage, the better her chances of adjusting to a new environment.

Delegate duties. In a family meeting with siblings and trusted counselors or friends, discuss what tasks each is willing and capable of doing to support your aging loved one through this transition. Don't be afraid to ask for the help you need. Who will offer practical assistance? Who is best at emotional support? Before the meeting, gather information about your loved one's special medical needs. Bring the financial options, personal preferences, and family values into the decision-making process. Most of all, pour out your heart to the Lord and rely on His strength and wisdom as you work through the complexities of obtaining appropriate long-term care for your loved one.

FINDING THE RIGHT PLACE

As you begin your search for a nursing home, you will need to know what kinds of facilities are available in your area. Ask your elder's doctor for a good recommendation or contact your local Area Agency on Aging for a list. Call local churches for the names of reputable facilities that are associated with a particular denomination. Ask your friends if they know people who have stayed in local nursing homes. In the selection process, consider whether your loved one needs personal care only or skilled nursing care, too. Try to choose a place that maximizes independence and morale while providing safety, comfort, and the right level of care for her health needs.

It is best to visit several facilities and compare them. This takes time, but in the long run, it is well worth the effort. Call administrators and ask basic questions about what they consider strengths and weaknesses at their facility. Make visits at different times of day or evening, and walk around long enough to be able to make a judgment about both emotional environment and orderliness. Interact with res-

CARING FROM A DISTANCE

My experience of caregiving was as the out-of-town adult child. My brother and I had become concerned that my mother was drinking secretly. (This was a shock, since our father had been an alcoholic, while she had not been a drinker.) By the time we confirmed our suspicions, she was in bad shape. I flew home, and my brother and I took her to the doctor, who immediately hospitalized her. He informed us she needed to be in a nursing home with round-the-clock care. We tried an alcohol-treatment program first, but her mind had been so affected that she couldn't benefit from the program. Neither of us was able to provide round-the-clock care, so we began the grueling ordeal of finding a good nursing home.

One of the hardest days of my life was going from nursing home to nursing home, crying between each one, and calling on God to be to me what I'd always believed He was—my comforter, guide, and loving Father. He answered that prayer. We ended up choosing a nursing home my brother's doctor recommended and were so pleased with it. Most people are in a nursing home only a few years. Our mother lived in hers eleven years—from age 76 to 87.

Over the years of traveling out to spend a week each year with my mom, my initial view of her nursing home changed. Rather than viewing it with horror and fear, I began to see it as a haven for helpless people. I am most thankful my mother had good care and the same loving attendant assigned to her throughout her stay. The ironic thing is that my mother, a dyed-in-the-wool Southerner and very prejudiced (although she didn't think so), was cared for by a very special African-American lady whom my mother came to love.

I have many poignant memories. I would encourage anyone in the situation of visiting a parent in a nursing home to look for God's blessings. Take along a family picture album to look at. Photos trigger memories even in those with dementia. There were times when my mother didn't know me, but she knew me as a child in the album's pictures.

Bev H.

idents and their family members, if possible. Observe and reflect. Make notes.

Ask to see one of the living units and take a close look at its characteristics. For example, does the bathroom have grab bars, cabinetry adapted for wheelchairs, and nonslip flooring? To help you evaluate a nursing home, take along a checklist of questions to consider:

- Is the facility licensed? Is it not-for-profit or for-profit? Is it part of a chain? Is it supported by or affiliated with a religious organization? Does it appear to be a stable operation that will exist for a long time?
- Who owns and manages the facility? Is the administrator licensed and friendly? Who is in charge when the administrator is away?
- Are Medicaid and Medicare accepted? Does the home have Medicaid residents, or is it restricted to private-pay patients? If it is restricted, what happens to private-pay residents when their funds run out?
- What are the basic costs, and what do they include? Are there additional charges for special diets, walkers or canes, reserving a bed while the resident is in the hospital, etc.?
- What physician services are included? Which ones are extra? Are private physicians allowed?
- Who provides eye care and dental care?
- Are private rooms available? How much privacy does each resident have?
- What are the rules concerning personal possessions and furniture?
- Is the facility's location close to family?
- Are religious services held weekly? Is there a chapel or prayer room in the facility? Does the facility support the residents' religious needs?
- Are there handrails along the walls?
- Is the floor kept dry and free of litter?
- How does the facility smell? Are there lingering odors of urine or feces? If so, the residents' diapers may not be changed often enough, which can lead to life-threatening illnesses such as urinary-tract infections or bedsores.

- Do the faucets, call buttons, telephones, and television sets work?
- Is the atmosphere pleasant and cheerful?
- Does the staff appear to care about and respect residents?
- Is there a recreation staff, and is there a social worker on staff?
- What is the ratio of staff to patients?
- Are staff members courteous to the residents, family members, and visitors?
- Does the facility work with a local hospital? How ill must a resident become before being hospitalized?
- Is the food hot, attractive, and tasty? Do residents have any choice? Are special diets accommodated?
- Have fees increased significantly in the past few years?
- Does a resident advisory council exist? What are the rights of the council, and how are suggestions and complaints handled?
- Are community organizations (libraries, church groups, volunteers) involved?
- Is the facility in good standing with state inspectors?
- Does the facility specialize in certain types of care (e.g., Alzheimer's disease)?

Choose a facility that maximizes independence and morale while providing safety, comfort, and the right level of care for your elder.

While these questions should be answered before you make a decision about what nursing home to use, you should also be aware that each state has an ombudsman program to oversee the quality of care provided in nursing homes throughout the state. (See "Ombudsman Programs" on page 446.)

You may request a copy of the inspection report, available by decree of federal guidelines. Also, ask for a copy of the facility's policies and procedures. Ask which social services are available through the facility, what recreational activities are offered, how often the menus change, and about daily and weekly routines. As you visit the nursing home, ask yourself the all-important questions: Are staff members cordial and friendly? Is the administration accessible?

Word of mouth can be a good source of information about a nursing home's reputation. To help you narrow your list or decide on a particular nursing home, it might be helpful to consult a hospital-discharge planner or social worker, pastors, physicians who serve the elderly, or volunteer groups that work with seniors.

Minimizing "Transfer Trauma"

When an elderly person moves from an independent-living situation into a facility where he needs either custodial or continuing care, he may experience what sociologists call "transfer trauma." It was once thought that transfer trauma could actually result in the death of the person, but more recent studies have shown that it is not as serious a condition as once believed. If you do any gardening, you can liken transfer trauma to "root shock" experienced by plants when you trans-

---

DAD'S FINAL DAYS

When we were contemplating moving my 91-year-old dad to a nursing home, there really wasn't any other choice to make. He was in the hospital after hip-replacement surgery and was incontinent and bleeding from advanced prostate cancer. But for Mom, being asked, "When am I going home?" made the decision very hard on her. She called the church for prayer, but the pastors were out of town at a pastors' retreat. Evidently, the church secretary let them know, because one of the pastors and his wife left early to come to the hospital and pray with Mom. At that moment, I saw my mom's countenance change to one of relief.

The hospice people (who had been caring for Dad for the previous three or four months) also came and helped us finalize the decision. We didn't have a clue because we'd never been through this before, but they had, so they literally took charge—making all the necessary calls and arrangements for the nursing home. Because Dad was dying, he was placed in what's called a hospice room, and the hospice workers still continued to bathe and care for him. The nursing-home staff was great too.

Dad really never fussed or begged to leave. If he had gone down the hall and seen the people in wheelchairs who'd lost their minds, I think it would have gotten to him because he was sharper than a tack up to the day he died. But he was in the last room down the hall and never got out of bed. It was a good option because Dad finally had good pain control and we were able to drive there in five minutes. After 30 days, I was there when, at the age of 91, my dad took his last labored breath and went to be with the Lord.

Paul M.

plant them from a pot to a permanent place in your yard. The plant's system must readjust to a new environment and to new soil. It must also begin taking in nourishment immediately if it is to survive. It must be watered, fertilized, and carefully nurtured during those first few weeks after being transplanted. The same is true for anyone who relocates—and especially for an elderly person who is being moved from a familiar environment to one that could be potentially unfriendly and confusing.

In order to minimize transfer trauma, take your aging loved one with you as you visit various long-term-care facilities in your community. (If your elder is too feeble, get literature and photos of the facility to show to your loved one. Perhaps you can get permission to videotape the foyer and a typical room where your elder would be staying.) Bring along a list of questions to ask the directors of these facilities. Take time to visit with those who live there as well as the aides who will be furnishing care. Visit the facility several times with your elder before having her make the final move. Let her know that she will be with

ON THE MOVE

My mom always talked about a certain nonprofit nursing home she wanted to go to. She was on a waiting list to get in. Finally I moved her in. It used to be outstanding; my grandparents had stayed there. But it was not so outstanding anymore. She couldn't dress herself and needed assistance with everything, yet she was not getting adequate care. She couldn't open and close the bathroom door, so she'd get trapped and couldn't get out. She was really upset that first week, but when I went to see her, she said, "I'm going to stay. I just have to get used to it." When I went to see her the second week, I wouldn't have recognized her—not physically but mentally. She wasn't herself. I said, "Mom, tomorrow I'm getting you out of here and taking you home to live with me. We'll figure something out." She said, "Okay." When I took her out, I was open with the management about my reasons, and they said, "You're right. We do fine with Alzheimers' patients, but your mom needs constant attention 24 hours a day, and we can't give that."

Nursing homes are supposed to be able to provide constant care, but they aren't all up to par. I learned that you have to be selective and monitor the care.   *Jacqueline S.*

others who also have limitations and that they can help one another. Emphasize the fact that this can be a time of great service to others who may be in more serious physical or mental need. Ministry opportunities will abound in a nursing-home facility. If your elder is a Christian, this could become one of her most productive times in life to share her faith in Christ.

If your elder wishes he were still in an independent-living environment, help him to understand that because of his physical or mental needs, he must have the care of professionals who can best serve him.

Once you have agreed on a nursing home, give the staff some information about your aging loved one's background, interests, and preferences. Consider writing a little "book" about your elder's life, including photos, for the staff. If they operate a credible facility, they will welcome the information as valuable and helpful and will support your role as advocate for your loved one's care.

WHAT DO LONG-TERM-CARE SERVICES COST?

The costs of different types of long-term care will vary by state or region and can change rapidly. One year of care in a nursing home can range anywhere from $35,000 to $80,000, but averages range from around $35,000 to more than $50,000. Here are some estimated prices for other long-term-care services:

- Adult Home: $15,000 a year
- Registered Nurse Home Visit: $80-$121 a visit
- Physical/Speech Therapy: $80-$100 a visit
- Home Health Aide: $40-$50 a visit
- Personal Care: $12 an hour
- Housekeeper/Chore: $12 an hour
- Home-Delivered Meals: $5 a meal; $2 suggested donation
- Adult Day Care: $30-$40 a day
- Adult Day Health Care: $100 a day

Long-term costs can quickly wipe out a family nest egg. And these expenses are expected to skyrocket in years to come. In 1996, the average annual expenditure for health care was $5,864 for noninstitutionalized people age 65 to 69 but rose to $9,414 for people age 75 to 79 and $16,465 among those age 85 and older.[9] (People age 85 and above are in the fastest-growing segment of the population and are the most likely to need nursing-home care.[10]) By the year 2020, people sixty-five and older will grow to 16.5 percent of the population, and the share of gross domestic product devoted to elder care will double to 10 percent. Annual health-care spending per senior will jump to nearly $25,000 (in 1995 dollars) by 2020.[11] This will strain the resources of state and federal governments as well as the seniors themselves, who currently cover the cost of about one-third of their own medical bills.

Meeting long-term-care needs will continue to be a challenge in the future as more Americans enter their senior years. Working toward so-

FINDING A HOME FOR MY MOTHER

A few months after my father died, I decided to take a job that required us to move from Oregon to Colorado. My mother agreed to move with us. However, shortly before the move was scheduled, she became very sick. She was hospitalized with pneumonia and the doctors said she could not move for a few weeks. Neither would she be able to continue living in her apartment; for the short term, she would need some nursing care. I had two days to find such a place.

While cost was a factor, my primary concern was the care my mother would receive. It happened to be a weekend when I did most of my looking. That was an excellent time to do this, because during regular business hours, there is the chance that someone will put the best possible spin on a facility. During the weekend, you'll have different staff, and you may find quite a different picture.

I visited several facilities on a Saturday evening. At one moderately priced facility, the manager on duty showed me around. I asked to see a room. The man took me down a hall, unlocked a door, and opened it. I looked in and found myself staring into the face of an elderly woman sitting up in bed. The man did not apologize or say, "Excuse me." So I immediately ended the tour, eliminating this facility from any further consideration.

I use this example to show that when I was looking for a place for my mother, an important consideration was how the staff treated the residents. The manager of that one facility never seemed to consider that these were real people. *Joyce P.*

lutions now for your own elder, such as meeting with an elder-law attorney or shopping around for long-term-care insurance, will also be a way for you to begin preparing for the future when *you* might need long-term care.

PAYING FOR LONG-TERM CARE

Paying for nursing-home care is an expensive proposition—and one of the most serious problems facing our nation in the 21st century. Yet only 6 percent of elderly people and a very small number of baby boomers have purchased long-term-care insurance as a means for funding extended nursing-home care if needed.[12] In addition, two-thirds of single seniors and one-third of couples with a spouse in a nursing home fall into poverty after being in a nursing home just 13 weeks. The average older person has enough personal resources to pay for only seven months in a nursing home. What payment options are available to help?

Private Resources

At present, an estimated 48 percent of nursing-home costs are paid for by individuals in the form of out-of-pocket expenses. **Private long-term-care insurance** is one option to help pay for care (see section below for more information). Another option is a **viatical settlement**. A viatical settlement is a way of financing long-term care if the person cannot qualify for long-term insurance. This allows a terminally ill person to sell his life-insurance policy to a settlement company. The company pays the person a lump-sum death benefit in exchange for being named as the beneficiary of the person's life-insurance policy. In order to be most effective, the life-insurance policy should have a death benefit of at least $100,000. **Reverse-annuity mortgage** is another way of personally financing long-term care. Older homeowners can use this to convert home equity into a monthly cash stipend to pay for nursing-home care. (For more information, see chapter 15.) **Help from relatives:** The elderly may have to rely on financial assistance from their children or other relatives. Offering financial help is implied in the biblical admonition to honor our fathers and mothers and take care of older relatives (1 Timothy 5:8, 16). Showing generosity to your elders

One year of care in a nursing home averages around $35,000 to $40,000.

The average older person has enough personal resources to pay for only seven months in a nursing home.

also sets a good example for your children, who may end up helping you someday.

Public Funding

Medicare is one option, but it only pays for approximately 2 percent of nursing-home care in the U.S. It does not pay for the custodial, chronic, or continual care of elderly persons. It does, however, pay for short periods of skilled care—daily attention from a licensed health professional such as a registered nurse or respiratory therapist who is working under the orders of a physician. Medicare also pays for acute or curative care. Acute care involves the costs associated with an illness or injury that requires hospitalization. Curative care refers to treatments prescribed by a physician and performed by a health professional that are intended to improve a patient's condition.

To receive care in a nursing home under Medicare, your elder must have had a three-day hospital stay prior to admission, must be admitted within 30 days of hospital release, must enter the nursing home for treatment of the same condition for which she was hospitalized, must need skilled care on a daily basis, must have a condition that is able to be improved, must be in a Medicare-certified facility, and must have a care plan that is written by a physician and carried out by the facility. (For more information on Medicare, see Financial Care, chapter 10.)

Medicaid, a joint federal-state program, does provide health-insurance assistance to seniors who are impoverished by high medical expenses or whose low income and limited assets will not cover the cost of nursing-home care.

To become eligible for Medicaid, a person must be nearly impoverished. However, an elderly recipient usually can still retain some assets, such as term life insurance, life insurance with a face value of less than $1,000, a car, a burial account not to exceed $1,500 in most states, a home if it is the person's primary residence (in some states), and cash—the amount is contingent upon state rules. Depending on the state in which your elder resides, he may be able to retain his home. Keep in mind that these rules could change rapidly, depending on what happens in Congress. Contact Medicaid (see appendix) or your local Area Agency on Aging for more information.

Medicaid estate planning is a questionable phenomenon that has developed in recent years. It involves the person giving away most of her assets to her relatives in order to artificially reduce her income level to the point where she can qualify for Medicaid coverage. Some elderly people establish a trust fund to remove assets from the hands of the nursing home and result in Medicaid picking up more of the bill. Medicaid estate planning has become so common that new rules were put in place in 1991 to review all transfers of assets during a 36-month period prior to applying for Medicaid assistance. If the person has given away her assets to qualify, she will not be eligible for coverage until a period of time passes—during which time those assets would have paid for coverage. In addition, a more recent law passed by Congress in 1997 makes it a federal crime for someone to "knowingly and willfully dispose of assets" in order to become eligible for Medicaid. If the person gives away her assets three years before applying for assistance, she will not be prosecuted.

HELPING IN-LAWS

When my father-in-law recently had a stroke, my mother-in-law could no longer care for him. He'd already been blind for four years and now he also needs insulin injections for diabetes. Mom was a wreck, so I flew out to Arizona (where they've been retired for 16 years) to help her pick a nursing home for him. First we met with an elder-law attorney to help her apply for Medicaid. The law allowed her to keep her home, some IRA money, and cash. Next we looked at four nursing homes, based on location. However, the closest nursing home had an odor. It may have been a bad day, but first impressions are lasting, so we chose a different one. Dad did not want to be in a nursing home, but they didn't have much choice because Mom just couldn't handle him anymore. She hasn't been happy paying $4,000 a month, either. So my husband and I are now renovating our home in Illinois in order to move both of them in with us soon. Neither of my in-laws are Christians, but my husband and I are, so we hope to have a good, calming influence on them.   *Pat L.*

Long-Term-Care Insurance

Long-term health-care insurance is becoming more popular as a viable way to pay for nursing-home expenses. The interest in this kind of insurance has been fueled by several factors: the increasing costs of long-term care, the increasing longevity rate, the loss of the extended family, the rising costs of getting old, the number of women who are going from primary caregivers to workers, and the rising number of single-parent households.

Long-term-care insurance can provide an elderly person with some measure of peace as she faces the possibility of needing long-term care in a nursing home or other facility. Like other types of insurance, long-term-care insurance allows a senior to pay a known premium that offsets the risk of much larger out-of-pocket expenses. Policies vary; they may cover care in a nursing home, in the home, or in adult day care or some other community setting. Most policies are "indemnity" policies, meaning they pay a fixed dollar amount—for example, $100 a day for each day a person receives a specified type of care. No policy will cover all expenses fully.

At present, more than 100 companies offer long-term-care policies. The National Academy of Elder Law Attorneys (NAELA) says that long-term-care insurance is expensive but is usually worth the cost if there are substantial assets to be protected. (Some experts say a senior is a good candidate for long-term-care insurance if he has at least $75,000 in assets, excluding home and car, and retirement income of at least $35,000 a year.) A person age sixty-five who is applying for long-term-care insurance will pay $2,000 to $3,000 a year. A younger person will pay less. Costs will vary, depending on what kind of coverage your elder is seeking. Applying for long-term-care insurance requires that the elder undergo rigorous physical and mental evaluation. Be aware that applicants can be turned down.

Look for the following features in any long-term-care insurance policy:

1. A basic policy should cover the differences between one's daily income and the daily cost of nursing-home care. If one's income is $30 a day and the cost of a nursing home is $100 a day, insure for at least $70.

2. Make sure the policy has an inflation-protection feature. It should add 5 percent each year to the value of the policy.
3. While a person is collecting benefits, the waiver of premium should continue coverage with no added costs.
4. Coverage should include all levels of care, from custodial to intermediate to skilled.
5. There should be no requirement that a beneficiary be hospitalized before becoming eligible for benefits.
6. The policy should cover Alzheimer's and other mental disorders.
7. A reasonable waiting period before collecting benefits (such as 100 days) can lower the premium costs.
8. The policy should be guaranteed renewable, so the company cannot cancel the policy.[13]

The National Academy of Elder Law Attorneys suggests you get answers to the following questions when considering a plan:

- Is the insurance company highly rated—an A or A+ with A.M. Best Company's rating service? (See appendix.) Companies with ratings of B or lower tend to be higher risk to their insureds.
- Are the premiums competitive? Do the premiums go up when you get older?
- Is there a grace period for late payments?
- What is the deductible?
- What is the maximum benefit period?
- What services are covered? registered nursing? physical therapy? home health aides, homemakers, personal care?
- When does the insurance go into effect?

What should you avoid? We have already listed what you should look for as you consider a long-term-care insurance plan. It will also help if you understand what *not* to accept in a policy. Beware of these undesirable features found in some insurance plans:

- Insurance premiums *increase with age.*
- Home health benefits are *not* provided or provided only after receiving nursing-home care.
- Hospitalization or skilled care must occur before benefits are paid.

Long-term-care insurance can provide an elderly person with some measure of peace as she faces the possibility of needing long-term care.

- A clause specifies that the policy is renewable only under certain conditions.
- Maximum benefit period is *less than two years.*
- The deductible or waiting period (called the policy-elimination period) *exceeds 100 days.*
- Policy does not include all three types of nursing care: skilled, intermediate, and custodial.
- Policy excludes coverage for *mental or nervous disorders,* including Alzheimer's disease.
- The "preexisting-condition clause" is *longer than six months.*

How can you get the best policy? The National Center on Women & Aging suggests that you check with your state insurance commissioner regarding advisories on purchasing long-term-care insurance. To get the best policy, you should also shop around and do careful comparison pricing. Guard against being bullied into having your loved one purchase a policy. Ignore promotional brochures, which can be misleading. Don't believe what a salesperson tells you about the policy, either; instead, only believe what you read and understand in the policy. If you do not understand the policy's terms, hire someone (e.g., an elder-law attorney or a financial planner) who can help you make an informed decision. Consult with a reputable financial planner before signing up after a free review period. And never pay in cash.

If you want more information on long-term-care insurance, go to your local library and look through copies of *Consumer Reports.* This magazine has published several articles on the pros and cons of obtaining long-term-care insurance. You will also find it helpful to read through a lengthy analysis of long-term-care insurance written by San Jose attorney Richard Alexander. His paper, "Avoiding Fraud When Buying Long-Term Care Insurance" is posted on his law firm's Web site (see Alexander, Hawes, and Audet, LLP in appendix). At more than 60 pages in length, it is one of the most extensive reports on the pitfalls of purchasing certain long-term-care insurance policies. Here are some highlights from Alexander's report:

1. Seniors are primary targets of scam artists who try to sell them unneeded or overly expensive policies. Very often the scammer will

return the following year and offer a "new and improved" policy. This is known as "turning," "turning to earn," or "churning."

2. Seniors are told that premiums will not increase. Insurance companies cannot raise premiums on individual policies, but they can petition the state to have rates increased on all policies.
3. Seniors frequently misunderstand the extent of the restrictions on the policy. These become obvious only when the care is needed.
4. Seniors also can get into trouble when they file claims. You should make sure you understand how and when to file claims—and what benefits are provided.
5. Seniors frequently provide a medical history that is incomplete or inaccurate. This can result in the insurance company canceling the policy. A thoroughly filled-out application will reduce the likelihood of your elder being canceled.
6. Seniors should purchase policies only from a reputable insurance company. Several companies provide ratings of insurance companies. Here are just a few: A.M. Best Company; Moody's Investor Service, Inc.; and Weiss Research, Inc. (see appendix).

To understand fully what long-term-care insurance policies offer in your community, contact your state insurance commissioner, your local Area Agency on Aging, a senior center, or a qualified elder-law attorney. The Center for Long-Term Care Financing in Bellevue, Washington, can provide you with additional helpful guidance (see appendix).

Watch Congress. For an update on the various legislative proposals in Congress, access the Library of Congress Web site at <http://www.loc.gov>. This site allows you to do a word search on any legislation dealing with long-term-care insurance. In addition, you can read the Congressional Record to see how the issue is being debated. You can also contact your district's U.S. Representative or two U.S. Senators for updates.

Plan ahead. If your elder is under 65, you will probably discover that a policy will be less expensive than it will be after 65 and certainly after 75 or 85, when the premiums will be out of reach. It may seem like an unneeded expense right now, but careful planning now will help provide your elder with security in the future if and when her health declines and she needs long-term care. Nevertheless, you must weigh the cost of insurance against your elder's ability to pay the premiums. If your elder is older and indigent, for example, she may be eligible for care through Medicaid tax dollars.

Last, but certainly not least, *pray* for God's guidance and wisdom every step of the way as you shop for a long-term-care insurance policy for your aging loved one. If you make prayer your primary effort during this process, you can live in peace with your decisions.

MONITORING NURSING HOMES

Ombudsman Programs

The ombudsman program was established as a result of passage of the Older Americans Act (OAA) in 1965. The ombudsman is a public official appointed to investigate complaints against those who may be violating the rights of the elderly in nursing homes or other care facilities. The ombudsman also works with a group of volunteers who visit nursing homes to investigate elder abuse, fraud, and waste. See page 523 for a list of ombudsman programs for each state.

Resolving Disputes

Community-based mediation is being widely used to resolve disputes between two or more parties in elderly-housing situations both in traditional neighborhoods and in various assisted-living or congregate-living facilities. The goal in mediation is to avoid going through a costly legal process to resolve disagreements. The parties attempt to reach a "win-win" situation—not a situation where one party loses and the other wins. The American Association of Retired Persons has a Standing Committee on Dispute Resolution that helps resolve disputes involving criminal activity—not just personal disagreements. There are more than 450 mediation centers nationwide that resolve nursing-home disputes over such issues as food, stolen belongings, visiting hours, cleanliness, and family or roommate disputes.

With dozens of elderly people living in proximity with one another, it is essential that a facility have some form of dispute-resolution forum as a way of peacefully resolving disagreements. As you are considering a nursing home for your aging parent, find out if the facility has a dispute-resolution committee in place. If they do not have one, ask how they deal with disputes among their residents.

NEW TRENDS IN NURSING HOMES

Eden Alternative

Until just a few years ago, the term *nursing home* conjured up a picture of a sterile environment filled with stern health-care workers and elderly patients who simply lay in their beds or sat in wheelchairs waiting to die. Today that image is being radically challenged by the introduction of a concept called the Eden Alternative. It was pioneered by Dr. Bill Thomas in 1991 as a response to much-needed changes in how the elderly were treated in nursing-home environments. Thomas was a nursing-home director in Sherburne, New York, at the time. He became discouraged by the lives led by staff workers and by the elderly in nursing homes, so he decided to begin promoting a unique alternative. Two years after he instituted the Eden Alternative at his own nursing home, researchers who studied the program found that the death rate had dropped by 25 percent, infections had fallen by 50 percent, and there had been decreases in medication costs, resident agitation, and depression.

The Eden Alternative, which now is being used by an estimated 130 nursing homes nationwide, introduces plants, companion animals, and children into the nursing-home environment. Staff members are encouraged to bring their children to work with them. Other Eden nursing homes actually have established child-care centers in tandem with the nursing home. The plan also introduces gardens, and the elderly residents and children are encouraged to take care of the plants and animals. In addition, nursing homes adopting the Eden plan institute a complete management-style overhaul. Eden Alternative homes change rigid, hierarchical management structures to self-governing "care teams" that work consistently with one resident.

One Eden Alternative nursing home is the Arboretum in San Marcos, Texas. At the Arboretum, there are 105 elderly and children,

The Eden Alternative introduces plants, companion animals, and children into the nursing-home environment.

HEAVEN'S WAITING ROOM

He's in heaven's waiting room." I had heard this expression many times by the time I met my husband more than 60 years ago. I knew it referred to someone who might not have long to live. But I didn't think it would ever apply to Jack, whose active life had been spent as a missionary.

Yet here Jack is now, tucked up in a bed in a nursing home. He didn't know what it meant to quit. Years ago he'd developed diabetes but kept on ministering. Even when neuropathy in his legs worsened, no alarm bells sounded. After all, hadn't he recovered from open-heart surgery? But Jack's memory was failing, and as his mental capacities deteriorated, his personality underwent a subtle change. I found it difficult to adjust to this new, often-belligerent, stubborn husband. Jack had always been so sharp. Before going to the mission field, he had been a banker. I had trusted him to make decisions. He could be depended on to show good judgment. Now everything was turning around. I was the one who made the plans. I took care of finances. I did the driving.

Then Jack began falling down. I'd try to lift him off the floor, then call security, and finally dial 911.

Eventually, following a two-week stay in the hospital, a social worker took me aside. "I'm not telling you what to do," she said kindly, "but congestive heart failure and years of diabetes are taking their toll on your husband. He can't get out of a chair or stand without help. You aren't able to care for him, so you need to think about placing him in a nursing home. That's where he belongs now."

I felt as though a pail of cold water had been dumped over me. A nursing home? How could I subject Jack to existence in one of *those* places? You know the kind of pictures that came across my mind: patients slumped in wheelchairs, hopeless-looking men and women with their mouths hanging open, bedridden people calling over and over, "I want to go home!" How could I do that to my beloved partner? How could I live with the guilt? I struggled to be willing to do what appeared to be God's will for our lives. It was an emotional nightmare.

And what about expenses? How could I ever pay what a nursing home would charge? When a hospital social worker in Phoenix offered to set up an appointment with representatives from the Arizona Health Care Cost Containment System and Medicaid, I agreed to talk to them.

This signaled the beginning of endless interviews, trips to the bank to "spend down" our modest savings, letters to and from our mission board, psychiatric evaluations for Jack, and the securing of various documents, the most important of which was Jack's health-care power of attorney and living will.

Finally I braced myself to tell my husband that I was admitting him to a nursing home. How would he take it? Would he be able to accept my decision . . . or would he sink into one of his deep depressions? "Oh, dear Lord," I prayed, "please don't let Jack feel I'm abandoning him." There was that feeling of guilt again.

Our daughter had urged me to call her anytime, day or night. "Feel free to cry on my shoulder, Mom," she said. "I'm here for you." She reminded me that God had led us thus far. He wouldn't fail us now. "Leave it with the Lord."

To my relief, Jack took the news without crumpling. "It's okay, honey," he said. "I'm sure you know what's best for me, so let's do it."

I found the people who worked on our case to be sympathetic and understanding. To arrive at the amount I needed to live separately, they added together Jack's and my social security and our modest pension. Then they figured my expenses, electricity, home insurance, rent, and personal needs, such as food. Finally, they came up with the amount of Jack's "share of cost" for the medical center where he now lives. I feel they have been very fair.

My friends had warned me this nursing-home experience would be traumatic and that I should find a support group to turn to for encouragement. I am so thankful I have found one—right there at the nursing home. The nurses, assistants, therapists, and even the young ladies who clean patients' rooms never make me feel like I'm imposing when I ask questions or need to talk. They treat Jack as if he were their own grandpa, and they are generous with hugs for me, too.

When Jack was being wheeled out to a van that would take him to the hospital to have a leg amputated, one of the nursing assistants, with tears in her eyes, kissed him good-bye and assured me, "Now, don't you worry, Sally. He's going to be all right. Jack will be back before you know it."

Yes, this place looks, smells, and sounds like a nursing home, but with a great difference: Here there are enough loving pats, care, and concern to go around. For me, this nursing home has given new meaning to the timeworn expression "It's heaven's waiting room."

Sally Hawthorne

Editor's note: After several months in the nursing home, Jack was ushered out of the "waiting room" and into the presence of his Lord.

Adapted from Today's Christian Senior, *volume 4, number 1.* Used with permission. For a free subscription, call 1-800-723-0210.

plus 50 birds, 7 cats, 4 dogs, and 3 hamsters. The plan has helped to alleviate not only physical problems but loneliness, helplessness, and boredom, too. After instituting the program at the Arboretum, the director found that the use of psychotropic drugs on the elderly dropped significantly. In addition, there were fewer behavorial problems among the elderly, and staff turnover decreased too.

To learn more about the Eden Alternative, contact them by phone or Web site (see appendix).

"Nursing Home without Walls"

As an alternative to institutionalized long-term care, this state program provides a level of care equivalent to that of a nursing home to persons in their own homes or apartments. Seniors in New York state, for example, are eligible for the Long Term Home Health Care program if an assessment indicates that they are nursing-home eligible and the services required will cost no more than a specified percentage of what those same services would cost if provided in a nursing home. To see if there is such a program in your area, contact your local Area Agency on Aging or your county's department of social services or the health department.

A SMOOTH MOVE AND TRANSITION

When it is time for your aging loved one to move into a nursing home, there are some things you can do to make the transition easier. For example, have your elder take her most cherished possessions with her. (Be careful of theft.) This will help her remain connected with her past. If she is associated with a church, ask the pastor or a close friend to greet her at the nursing home when she arrives.

Once she is settled in, encourage your elder to get involved in the various activities planned at the facility. A well-run facility will have a variety of activities to meet the many needs of the elderly. Perhaps you can attend with her at the beginning. Let her know how important it is for her to remain active and alert if she is to live out her life with dignity and vigor.

Try to stay aware of how your loved one is eating, feeling, and doing once the move takes place. Are appropriate therapies and medications being provided? Discuss the facility's rules for taking your loved one out to dinner, church, or other activities. As you get to know the staff, build a positive relationship so that when problems come up, a solid foundation is laid for the best care possible under the circumstances. Bring treats and flowers for them. Send notes of thanks when they go out of their way to help. Participate in family-care conferences. If you must investigate mishaps, try to understand all sides.

It will be important to establish realistic expectations about visits with your aging loved one. Plan for times with other family members and friends as well as personal times when you can visit alone. When are the best times to come by, based on your elder's schedule and yours? Are drop-in visits welcomed? What amount of time is about right for you to stay? It may take a little time to work out how frequently you should visit and what works best.

Plan for times with other family members and friends as well as personal times when you can visit alone.

Your Changed Role as a Caregiver

You may feel overwhelmed by the task ahead of you. There are so many decisions to be made, so many people to consult. But remember that there is wisdom in many counselors. Seek wise counsel and pray to receive wisdom. God gives wisdom generously to those who ask for it.

If you must do something you had hoped would never be necessary, such as placing your loved one in a long-term-care facility, it does not mean you are abandoning him. It means your role has changed and the challenges will be different. Pray about each step and ask, *How might I make my loved one more comfortable from this new perspective?* Look for the life-giving elements in each step forward, even when it seems like a backward step. God's grace shows up as you ask for it.

You may experience feelings of guilt and distress because you personally cannot provide the care your aging loved one needs. These are common reactions to placing a loved one in a nursing home. Yet you can continue to be a caregiver by visiting your elder regularly and monitoring his care. Don't try to relieve your own possible guilt feelings by becoming too demanding of the nursing-home staff. The employees are usually underpaid and work under difficult, tense conditions. Try to show appreciation and praise for the care given to your elder. If there is a problem, try to talk to the individual first. If the problem is not resolved, go to the person who has the authority to do something about a situation, such as an attending staff person, supervisor, or administrator.

It may take your loved one a while to become adjusted to living in a congregate-care facility—an entirely new environment. In the beginning she will need as much emotional and spiritual support as you can muster. Encourage your siblings, your children, and your elder's friends and church to help you during this adjustment period. You can take turns visiting her on a regular basis.

Before you show up, think about things to talk about. Don't just run in, make small talk, and leave. Adult children and grandchildren need enough time to make the visit worthwhile. Have your children or familiar friends come in with flowers, magazines, chocolates, a book or puzzle, a stuffed animal, or a new CD. Everyone enjoys receiving presents—no matter how small they may be.

Greet your loved one with a hug and a kiss. Plan pleasurable times reading together, listening to music, or drinking tea from a favorite china cup and saucer with homemade cookies. Your elder may appreciate your special touch brushing her hair, giving a manicure, or dancing a waltz. When you cannot be there at an appointed time, make a call, drop off a note or a small gift, or ask a friend to step in. Volunteers may be available from local agencies to visit or take your loved one out for a drive.

Pray about each step and ask, How might I make my loved one more comfortable from this new perspective?

You certainly are not obligated to include your aging loved one in every social event in your home, but remember to invite your elder to special occasions such as birthdays, holidays, and family reunions. An elderly parent, in particular, benefits from feeling connected to family, friends, and activities. This is a way of paying honor to your elders for their sacrifices—even if you had a strained relationship with them as a child. It may be wise to bring your elder to your home for special "low-key" times that include fewer people and are quieter and less chaotic. Elderly (especially hearing-impaired) people often find large, boisterous gatherings too stressful.

Make arrangements to get your loved one to a worship service each week if he is physically able and wishes to attend. Some churches operate a bus program to transport seniors to church. Often, the long-term-care facility provides worship services, which you can encourage your loved one to attend. Some residents are not up to this and prefer individual spiritual attention, which is typically provided by a chaplain from the facility. Above all, let your elder know you will be praying daily that God will use his life and talents to glorify Him during his remaining time on the earth.

As you enter the home, give it your greeting. If the home is deserving, let your peace rest on it; if it is not, let your peace return to you. Matthew 10:12-13 NIV

You guide me with your counsel, and afterward you will

take me into glory. Whom have I in heaven but you?

And earth has nothing I desire besides you.

P<small>SALM</small> 73:24-25 NIV

End-of-Life Issues
Facing Medical Decisions

Afer my father's heart surgery, he lay in intensive care with a tube in his throat," says Joan. "He could communicate only by pointing to letters on a spelling card." Joan and her sister were visiting him when he spelled out, "How long?" Joan's sister said, "We don't know, Daddy. We'll just have to wait and see what the nurses say." Their dad just shook his head and looked away. "I think my sister assumed he was asking how long he'd have to have the tube in his throat or how long he'd be in intensive care. But I think he wanted to know how much longer he had to wait to die," says Joan. "He was ready to go home to his Savior."

People who have placed their faith in Jesus Christ for salvation face the end of life differently than those who have no assurance about where they will spend eternity. Believers view death as a great beginning, exchanging a life of pain or sorrow for eternal life in the wondrous presence of God.

But that does not mean dying is easy. Many of us do not fear death itself but rather the dying process. We worry about the possibility of a long illness, of being hooked up to tubes, of having uncontrolled pain, of being kept alive artificially by machines. Some of us worry that we will leave our loved ones with large medical bills and financial losses. Many worry about dying alone.

Many of us do not fear death itself but rather the dying process.

For most people, however, these fears are never realized. Many people die in their sleep, without pain, and with family and friends nearby. For those who have pain, sophisticated options in pain control are available when simpler remedies fall short. High-technology pain-treatment interventions, such as patient-controlled analgesia and epidural catheters, can bring great relief. Well-trained clinicians can provide some level of pain relief for all patients. In occasional cases, sedatives may be required to relieve symptoms in the last days of life.

If your aging loved one expresses some of these concerns about the end of life, talk with her about her fears and remind her that most people do not die in uncontrolled pain or suffer long illnesses. The fact that you are involved in your elder's life should reassure her that she will not die alone.

MAKING ETHICAL TREATMENT DECISIONS

Americans are living longer, and with that longevity comes the increased likelihood of living with chronic health conditions or a terminal illness. At the same time, recent advances in medicine can prolong life in otherwise dire situations. Medical technology has extended people's lives, but that also means that elderly people and their families face end-of-life decisions their grandparents did not have to make. Some people want to take advantage of every possible treatment available; others do not. The option of a life-sustaining intervention may be considered a blessing to one patient and a burden to another.

The decisions your elderly loved one may face at the end of life can be complicated and daunting. If your elder is suffering from dementia, you might find yourself having to make medical decisions for him in the future. Ideally, you will have the chance to discuss end-of-life preferences with your elder and mutually plan the desired care before there is a crisis. Talking through the following discussion questions may help your elder to clarify his personal medical desires and help you to understand his wishes:

1. How does your aging loved one generally view the use of life-sustaining technologies, such as kidney dialysis, pacemakers, and ventilators? What does your elder think about using such interventions for patients who are nearing the end of life?
2. Does your elder view such interventions as a moral responsibility in order to preserve life at any cost? What kind of medical intervention does your loved one want toward the end?
3. If your loved one faced a terminal illness (a life expectancy of six months or less to live) with no expected hope of recovery, how would he feel about attempts to extend his life through the use of heroic measures such as cardiopulmonary resuscitation or chemotherapy?
4. Whom does your elder want to make medical-care decisions for him when he cannot?
5. What would help your elder to feel more comfortable when he is dying?

In Ecclesiastes 3:1-2 (NASB), the Bible states that "there is a time for every event under heaven—a time to give birth, and a time to die." While Christians need not fear death, today's medical advances can place believers in a moral dilemma as we ask the question, "When is it time to allow nature to take its course and let my loved one go home?" Here are some guidelines to consider in these circumstances:

- We are created in God's image. Therefore, all human life is sacred and valuable, regardless of a person's health or quality of life. This viewpoint should help us to make decisions based on faith, not human reason alone.
- Any medical treatment, intervention, or procedure that is expected to *improve* a patient's condition, prognosis, or comfort level should be given serious consideration.
- The existence of a medical treatment, intervention, or procedure does not require you to utilize it if it is not expected to benefit the patient's condition, prognosis, or comfort. Each medical situation contains its own unique circumstances. The patient's prognosis for improvement should be considered along with her potential burden of suffering with or without the medical intervention.

- If the patient's condition is irreversibly terminal, the patient (or family) need not feel morally obligated to utilize all available medical technologies. At this point, the patient moves from the category of receiving **acute care** (where the goal is to cure the patient) to that of **palliative care** (where the goal is to make the patient comfortable and meet his physical, spiritual, and psychological needs).

- A particular medical treatment, intervention, or procedure may qualify as both acute care and palliative care. Such treatments may include antibiotics, oxygen, pain medication, feeding tubes, and surgery. (However, there is some disagreement about what constitutes medical treatment versus ordinary, routine care.) An action that may be curative (acute) for one patient may also be palliative (comfort) for another. The question should be, "Does it benefit the patient?"

- Competent adults have the legal right to refuse or have withdrawn any unwanted medical treatment. If an adult patient is not mentally competent to make her own medical decisions, a proxy decision-maker or surrogate, usually a close family member, is generally recognized to make decisions for the patient. The mission of the medical surrogate or contacted family member is to convey what the patient would want in a particular circumstance (within reasonable ethical boundaries), and not necessarily what the surrogate or the family wants for the patient.

All human life is sacred and valuable, regardless of a person's health or quality of life.

ADVANCE MEDICAL DIRECTIVES

Advance Medical Directives provide guidance for medical professionals and loved ones if a situation arises when a patient cannot speak for himself. There are two primary legal documents that fall into this category: the living will and the Durable Power of Attorney for Health Care Decisions (DPAHCD). Although they both rightly give authority about medical decisions to the patient while he is lucid, they differ about who has decision-making authority when an elder is unable to make those decisions. The living will has been popularized in the media, but the DPAHCD has distinct advantages. According to some, including

UNDYING LOVE

When Vince's 69-year-old wife, Annie, had a heart attack and went into a coma, it was just the beginning of a tug-of-war to save her life. She came out of the coma but had to have kidney dialysis, a feeding tube, and a tracheotomy. After being in intensive care for nearly a month, her heart stopped but was revived.

Vince knew Annie needed a pacemaker and requested it in a meeting with about 25 people who were involved in her care—doctors, cardiologists, pulmonologists, as well as her pastor and deacons. Considering her medical condition, the professionals recommended withdrawing Annie's life support, but Vince wanted to give her more time. When he remained firm about wanting the pacemaker put in, the chairman of the deacons stood up and said, "Are you trying to force God?"

Vince replied, "What are doctors and hospitals for?"

Annie got the pacemaker and began to improve, but some of the doctors and nurses were reluctant to do more to promote her recovery. When two nurses suggested hastening her death by no longer feeding her, Vince refused. "I told them that if she just lies in bed and smiles at me until we're both gone, that's enough for me."

Soon, Annie was transferred to a long-term-care hospital where she was weaned off the dialysis within a month and also started breathing on her own again. She had to learn to swallow and talk again, but after eight months she returned home and received therapy from there. After a several months, she also got off the feeding tube. Two years later, she hardly uses her walker and has the doctors mystified.

Vince concludes that in today's health-care environment, it is important to be your loved one's advocate. He's grateful for the support he received from a few of the doctors as well as many people in his church—including meals delivered to the hospital waiting room and countless prayers. "There was a chapel in the hospital, and I was in it every day, praying," Vince says. "My wife had so many visitors from our church. The waiting room was often full of friends and family members who cared for her." Today their church calls Annie their "miracle girl."

Please note: Annie's story is unusual. Each case is individual—what is best in one situation may not be best in another. Utilizing all available life-sustaining interventions is not always appropriate or loving. As your loved one's advocate, your role is to make the best decision you can with the information you have been given. Also, this anecdote is not meant to disparage all medical professionals. It is simply meant to point out that they are not always correct; there are times when we must speak up in defense of our relatives and friends.

CitizenLink[1], a Web site of Focus on the Family, the DPAHCD is preferred over the living will for the following reasons:

The Living Will

- is a vague statement saying a physician may withhold or withdraw treatment if you are terminally ill.
- is a piece of paper medical professionals may ignore or misinterpret.
- gives authority to a doctor you may or may not know; this is a serious concern in these days of cost containment and managed care.
- generally exempts doctors from liability, regardless of directions from the medical surrogate.
- presumes nontreatment, regardless of the medical situation.
- does not guarantee your wishes will be carried out.
- allows "treatment" to be defined by state law. (In many states, assisted nutrition and hydration are considered medical treatment, not ordinary care.)

The Durable Power of Attorney for Health Care Decisions (DPAHCD)

- appoints someone to make your medical decisions in any crisis, such as losing consciousness, not just terminal illness.
- names a *person* who will be your legal surrogate.
- generally exempts doctors from liability *if* they are following the surrogate's directions.
- may include an addendum in which you outline your specific wishes about medical care (life support, feeding tubes, etc.). This document provides written guidance for your surrogate, in addition to talking about your wishes. As with any advance directive, an addendum may be updated or deleted at any time.
- defers to the surrogate and your written wishes.

Other Information to Consider

- The Patient Self-Determination Act of 1990 requires health-care facilities receiving federal funds to ask patients upon admission if they have or want to sign an Advance Medical Directive. However, the best time to consider and sign such a document is *before* you are hospitalized, ill, or injured.

- The first living will was devised in 1967 by members of the Euthanasia Society of America, later known as Choice in Dying and now called Partnership for Caring. This original connection to euthanasia should cause some concern.

- If you sign a DPAHCD, consider adding an addendum or letter to your surrogate outlining your wishes in specific situations. This may include when you would desire tube feeding, the use of a ventilator, and cardiopulmonary resuscitation (CPR), as well as your views regarding the beginning, withholding, and/or withdrawing of medical treatment. This may also include your wishes regarding where you want to die (hospital, nursing home, at home) and whether you want your age, physical condition, finances, or other circumstances to play a role in decision making. For help in making ethical decisions from a Christian perspective, contact the Center for Bioethics and Human Dignity, the International Task Force on Euthanasia and Assisted Suicide, the Christian Medical & Dental Associations, the Christian Legal Society, or Focus on the Family (see appendix).

The Protective Medical Decisions Document (PMDD) is a general Durable Power of Attorney that defines and prohibits euthanasia.

- Always name a successor to your surrogate in case your surrogate is deceased or cannot be reached by medical professionals.

- Update your document on a regular basis to ensure it reflects your current wishes and desires.

- Copies of your Advance Medical Directive should be provided to your family, primary physician, local hospital, and attorney (if you have one).

- Don't just designate a medical surrogate without talking with loved ones. No document can replace open and honest communication with your family and friends before a time of crisis.

How to Obtain an Advance Medical Directive

All states have statutes allowing Advance Medical Directives. Copies of the document(s) approved in your state can be obtained through an attorney.

However, you may also locate these documents through other sources such as stationery stores, your state legislature, or probate court. You do not have to hire an attorney in order to sign these legal documents.

However, not everyone is comfortable with the standard Advance Medical Directive language provided in a state statute. For individuals who want to ensure that their Advance Medical Directive reflects a pro-life/anti-euthanasia position, we recommend a document created by the International Task Force on Euthanasia and Assisted Suicide. This document, entitled the Protective Medical Decisions Document (PMDD), defines and prohibits euthanasia, as well as stating that "ordinary nursing and medical care and pain relief appropriate to your condition" be provided. The PMDD is a general Durable Power of Attorney which allows the signer to name a trusted family member or friend to make medical decisions in the event the signer is incapacitated for any reason, not just terminal illness. The PMDD may be used in any state and may be attached to the Advance Medical Directive form(s) approved by your state legislature. For copies, contact the International Task Force on Euthanasia and Assisted Suicide (see appendix).

(For more information on Advance Medical Directives, see chapter 11: Legal Care and Estate Planning.)

FREQUENTLY ASKED QUESTIONS ABOUT MEDICAL INTERVENTIONS

The following section discusses several types of medical interventions you may need to understand in order to make an informed decision for your loved one. Ideally, these are decisions that should be made by the patient. When that is not possible, the proxy or surrogate should make the decision, which is why having an advance directive and a discussion with the patient is so important.

What Is Assisted Nutrition and Hydration?

Also called tube feeding, this medical intervention provides hydration and nutrients to patients who cannot swallow food and water. Assisted nutrition and hydration (AN&H) may be provided intravenously (I.V.) by needle or catheter, administered by a tube inserted through the nose into the stomach, or delivered through the skin directly into the stomach. (Ask your loved one's doctor which of these three delivery methods would be best for your loved one.) AN&H may be used to stabilize a patient with a short-term medical need, such as care during recovery from an accident or surgery, or to sustain a patient in a long-term situation. If your loved one is mentally competent, he or she should make the decision about whether or not to utilize AN&H. If you are making decisions regarding AN&H for your elder, here are some questions to answer:

- Did your elderly loved one indicate a preference for or against AN&H in an Advance Medical Directive or in conversation?
- Have you discussed the possible physical benefits and burdens of AN&H with your loved one's physician? For example, some potential benefits might include: allowing a restful healing time for a diseased or damaged gastrointestinal (GI) tract; providing nutrition/hydration when normal oral feeding would cause choking or is not possible; or reversing malnutrition and dehydration. Some possible risks of AN&H could include: pain, discomfort, or infection; dependency on that delivery method of receiving food and water, and subsequent loss of the ability to swallow; aspiration of fluid into the lungs and potential pneumonia; or fluid overload causing shortness of breath, need for suctioning, swelling of extremities, and other symptoms.
- Is AN&H being considered for medical reasons or for the convenience of the caregiver? In other words, is it being considered because it would really benefit the patient or only because the caregiver does not want to take the time to feed the elder orally?

One of the most difficult decisions to make for your aging loved one is whether to begin, withhold, or withdraw AN&H. When weighing the decision, it is important to consider the goal of the intervention. As a general rule, AN&H should be provided to patients who are unable to swallow food and water, for without it they will die. Up until 1986, the provision of food and fluids through a tube was considered ordinary care. Then the American Medical Association changed the definition of AN&H from *ordinary care* to *medical treatment,* which meant it was optional and could be withheld or withdrawn. This change concerns many in the Christian community. For example, the concern of the Christian Medical & Dental Associations pertains to individuals in a coma or with dementia who could live for an extended period of time with a feeding tube but who are increasingly viewed as "useless mouths."[2]

For patients who are in a debilitated state (i.e., comatose or with dementia) and are medically dependent but who are *not* dying, pulling the feeding tube is sometimes seen as a way to help them along toward death. However, when a person is not in the active process of dying, the lack of hydration and nutrition is immoral and causes a painful death.[3]

On the other hand, if the person is in the active process of dying and her body is shutting down, hydrating with a feeding tube can actually make the dying process more burdensome. It can cause such symptoms as difficulty breathing, swelling (edema), and bloating. Studies of dying hospice patients showed that dehydration was not uncomfortable as long as the patient's mouth was kept moist.[4]

AN&H should never be withheld or withdrawn by a surrogate for the sole purpose of ending the patient's life. However, there are times when it may be appropriate to withhold or withdraw AN&H:

1. Patients who are imminently dying due to an advanced disease state will experience a slowing down and an eventual stopping of their body systems, including the digestive system. AN&H during this end-stage of dying can cause additional pain and suffering to the patient. During this time, the patient's need for hydration should be met through mouth care and whatever fluid he or she can take orally.

2. The wishes of patients who have clearly indicated through an Advance Medical Directive that they do not want their lives sustained through AN&H should be respected. As a surrogate decision maker for your loved one, you may have no legal choice but to follow an Advance Medical Directive that refuses AN&H. Mentally competent patients have the legal, though not necessarily ethical, right to refuse such feeding; it can also be withheld in incompetent patients who have earlier stated that wish in an Advance Medical Directive. Such directives are legal documents and should be carefully and prayerfully considered prior to signing.

What Is a Do-Not-Resuscitate Order?

A Do-Not-Resuscitate order (or DNR) states that, in the case of cardiopulmonary arrest (when a patient stops breathing because his or her heart has stopped), the patient (or proxy) does not want any intervention to restart the heart. The DNR prevents any aggressive medical interventions, including cardiopulmonary resuscitation (CPR), should the patient stop breathing or suffer a cardiac arrest. A DNR order is appropriate in cases where the patient has an Advance Medical Directive stating that CPR should not be provided. It may be appropriate in cases where CPR cannot be performed. For example, CPR in older patients poses a risk of breaking brittle bones, including ribs. A DNR order may be appropriate for patients who are terminally ill and in the process of dying.

What Is a Ventilator?

A ventilator (or respirator) is a machine that pumps air in and out of the patient's lungs, effectively breathing for the patient. The air can be pumped either through tubes inserted in the patient's mouth, nose, or trachea, or through a mask over the patient's face. Ventilators will breathe for the patient but will not cure the situation that is causing the patient to need assistance in breathing.

A ventilator may be used on a long- or short-term basis. For example, there are many disabled individuals who are permanently dependent on a ventilator, while others may need ventilation only until their bodies recover from a temporary illness or injury. Often, the doctor will not be able to predict who will be on a ventilator for a short time and who will require more long-term or permanent support for their breathing. Additionally, in an emergency-room scenario, the surrogate or any other family member who can be reached promptly may have only one or two minutes—or less—to help to decide if the elder should be placed on a ventilator.

The ethics of withholding or stopping use of a ventilator are the subject of much debate. If a person does not want CPR or aggressive medical management, it is easiest not to use the ventilator in the first place unless the physicians feel the condition has a high likelihood of being reversible (e.g., anaphylactic allergic reaction to antibiotics).

PHYSICIAN-ASSISTED SUICIDE AND EUTHANASIA

Proposals to legalize physician-assisted suicide have triggered intense legal, medical, and social debate throughout the world. Legalized euthanasia and physician-assisted suicide are both dangerous and unnecessary. For some Americans, the debate is fueled by their fear that medical technology may someday keep them alive past the time of natural death. However, this concern is unfounded for mentally competent adults who have a legal right to refuse or stop *any* medical treatment at *any* time. It is also important to consider that, in general, today's health-care climate may lend itself more to undertreatment than to overtreatment.

Proposals to legalize physician-assisted suicide have triggered intense legal, medical, and social debate.

However, the present debate is not about refusing treatment or taking extraordinary measures. The issue is whether physicians should be allowed to intentionally kill their patients, either by providing the means of death or by ending the patient's life by the doctor's hands. There is a tremendous distinction between allowing someone to die naturally when medical technology cannot stop the dying process and causing someone to die through assisted suicide or euthanasia. The question is one of intent: Is the intention to cause the death of the patient?

The act of physician-assisted suicide involves a medical doctor who provides a patient with the means to kill himself. Euthanasia in the true sense of the word involves the intentional killing of a patient by the direct intervention of a physician or another party. Euthanasia can be voluntary (at the patient's request) or involuntary (without the knowledge or consent of the patient and possibly against her wishes).

The nation with the longest-running experiment with euthanasia and physician-assisted suicide is the Netherlands. There, both physician-assisted suicide and euthanasia are legal. Nonetheless, the Dutch government's own studies document that the practice of euthanasia is 10 times more common than physician-assisted suicide. What is even more disturbing in the Dutch studies is that among all euthanasia deaths in 1990 and in 1995, approximately one-quarter involved patients who were killed without their knowledge or explicit consent.[5]

Could the abuses witnessed in Holland be repeated in the U.S.? Escalating health-care costs coupled with a growing elderly and disabled population set the stage for an American culture eager to embrace alternatives to expensive, long-term medical care. The move toward managed care also threatens to promote euthanasia, as more and more doctors are offered financial incentives to decrease the number of health-care dollars spent per patient. The so-called "right to die" may soon become the "duty to die," as our senior, disabled, or depressed family members are pressured or coerced into ending their lives. In Oregon, where physician-assisted suicide is legal, the Oregon Health Division's annual reports have revealed that one reason cited by patients in Oregon who committed suicide is fear of becoming a burden on their families, friends, and caregivers.[6] Many people do not want to impose a burden on their loved ones, whether it be a financial burden or the loss of time and freedom. The question remains: Is the fear based on reality, or could the fear be lessened or eliminated by hospice care and family and community support?

Another concern among opponents of physician-assisted suicide is that legalizing the practice will make patients vulnerable to coercion by family members who are motivated by fear or greed. Physician-assisted suicide also threatens the doctor-patient relationship by endangering the trust patients have in their physicians.

A consistent, time-tested medical ethic based on the Hippocratic Oath calls health professionals to heal illness, to alleviate suffering, and to provide comfort to sick and dying patients. At times, some patients with severe illnesses may feel fearful, isolated, depressed, and hopeless. Some of them might seek assisted suicide as a "solution" to life's problems.[7] Yet depression is often treatable, and treatment can lessen or even eliminate suicidal wishes in terminally ill individuals. People who request assisted suicide because of fear of abandonment or fear of becoming a burden need our reassurance that their life is valued.

Reassurance about pain control throughout the dying process is also beneficial. Terminally ill patients need not suffer a painful death. Physicians who specialize in treating patients who are in pain report that today's pain- and symptom-management techniques can provide

Today's pain-management techniques are so effective that patients often change their minds about seeking assisted suicide.

substantial relief for the vast majority of patients treated. For the remaining patients, these techniques can lessen the effects of pain and other symptoms. When applied correctly to relieve pain and depression, today's pain-management techniques are so effective that patients often change their minds about seeking assisted suicide. Dr. William Wood, clinical director of the Winship Cancer Center at Emory University in Atlanta, has said, "If we treat their depression and we treat their pain, I've never had a patient who wanted to die."[8] (For more information, see "Controlling Pain" on pages 97-100.)

People living with terminal illnesses deserve more than the offer of a physician or other practitioner to expedite death. They merit effective pain relief along with real compassion. For true dignity in dying, dying must be kept separate from killing. The best defense against any consideration of euthanasia is good medical care, including hospice and expert palliative care—treating the symptoms and making the patient as comfortable as possible during the natural dying process. Hospice programs and pain-control efforts are strong deterrents for those considering euthanasia and physician-assisted suicide. But once killing is accepted as an answer, there may be less motivation to offer hospice programs or research new pain-control methods.

(For more information, contact the International Task Force on Euthanasia and Assisted Suicide or the American Academy of Hospice and Palliative Medicine [see appendix].)

THE WORD ON EUTHANASIA

The Bible states that God is the giver and taker of life (Job 1:21). We are created by Him, and He alone has the authority to end a life. Euthanasia wrongly empowers us—mere mortals—to determine the end of life, based on subjective or situational reasons. While euthanasia and physician-assisted suicide are often defended on the assumption that death ends suffering, the biblical truth is that death is not the end; it is rather the beginning of eternal life for believers in Christ[1] or eternal torment for those who reject Him.[2]

[1]John 5:24, 6:47; 2 Corinthians 5:8.   [2]Mark 9:47-48; Luke 12:5, 16:23; Hebrews 9:27; 2 Peter 2:4, 9.

HOSPICE CARE: HELP IN THE FINAL STAGES OF LIFE

In 1967 in London, Dr. Cicely Saunders founded St. Christopher's Hospice, a special treatment center for the dying. She emphasized pain control and provided the dying with sympathetic support staff. She recognized the dying person and his family as the unit of care so the patient did not feel that he was dying alone. The patient's pain was controlled, but he was not too sedated to relate to family members and friends. This center became the model for the present-day hospice.

The goal of the hospice movement is to maximize the quality of life for the dying patient and his family and to make the most of the time remaining. There is an emphasis on the comfort of the patient, including

DYING NATURALLY

About six months after Mom, who had cancer, moved in with me, she started talking about her death, saying she didn't want any heroic measures, but she wanted to make sure her needs were met. She was concerned about euthanasia and didn't want someone to say, "Well, it's your time," and come and finish her off. After looking for information at the library, I said, "Why don't we call a lawyer?" So I called someone who had been recommended to me, and he came to our house and sat down and talked to Mom. He said, "Well, tell me what you're thinking." She said, "I want to die a natural death. But I don't want anyone hastening my death." He seemed a little surprised by her forthrightness and candor. He talked about who should have power of attorney, and she said, "I trust all my kids, but since Linda's here, I'd like to give her that authority." So we arranged an Advance Medical Directive and Durable Power of Attorney.

Mom did die at home with minimal intervention. The day after her death, I went to see her lawyer to settle her estate. I said, "I don't know if you remember me, but you came to our house one day to talk to me and my mom." The lawyer said, "I sure do remember you and your mom. I have never spoken to an elderly woman so clear on her wishes and so well informed and able to articulate her ideas about death and dying. I always tell others about your mom."

Death isn't an easy passage, but I'm glad my mom got her wish to die at home.

Linda H.

The goal of the hospice movement is to maximize the quality of life for the dying patient.

appropriate use of medication for control of pain and other symptoms. Hospice uses a team approach, incorporating professionals and volunteers. It also seeks to serve the patient's family, helping them cope with the illness and death of their loved one.

While the nation's hospice programs are filled with professionals dedicated to helping terminally ill patients die a comfortable, natural death, this is not to say that all hospice programs or employees necessarily embrace a life-affirming philosophy. Also, the very nature of hospice (providing an environment in which to die) can lend itself to the restriction of medical treatments and procedures, which may make some families uncomfortable. Try to find out if the ethical views of a hospice you are considering align with yours; if not, ask if they would be willing to work with you with respect to your ethical views.

What Hospices Can Offer

Most hospices offer home care supported by a team of doctors, nurses, physical and occupational therapists, health aides, dietitians, pastoral-care professionals, social workers, and volunteers. Some hospice pro-

RECOMMENDED RESOURCES

1. *Dignity and Dying: A Christian Appraisal,* ed. by John F. Kilner et al. (Grand Rapids, MI: Eerdmans; and United Kingdom: Paternoster, 1996).
2. *Suicide: A Christian Response,* ed. by Timothy J. Demy and Gary P. Stewart (Grand Rapids, MI: Kregel, 1998).
3. *Basic Questions on End of Life Decisions: How Do We Know What's Right?* Gary P. Stewart et al. (Grand Rapids, MI: Kregel, 1998).
4. *Basic Questions on Suicide and Euthanasia: Are They Ever Right?* Gary P. Stewart et al. (Grand Rapids, MI: Kregel, 1998).
5. *Forced Exit: The Slippery Slope from Assisted Suicide to Legalized Murder,* Wesley J. Smith (New York: Times Books, 1997).
6. *Culture of Death: The Assault on Medical Ethics in America,* Wesley J. Smith (San Francisco: Encounter Books, 2001).
7. *Assisted Suicide and Euthanasia: Past and Present,* J. C. Willke (Cincinnati, OH: Hayes Publishing, 1998; revised 2000).

grams have their own on-site facilities where dying people can spend the final days or months of life. Other times hospice workers will go into a nursing home to supplement the care received there. Many hospice workers talk with family members about death and dying and spend time at the patient's bedside. Hospice is a comforting choice and can be a good option when you do not live near your dying loved one. Consider these examples:

One family turned to hospice care because none of the children lived near their parents. "My father had hospice care when he was dying of cancer," one of the daughters related. "He had been hospitalized, and finally the doctor said there was nothing more they could do. So Dad decided he wanted to go home with Mom. The hospital assigned a hospice worker to him. She was wonderful. She really came to love them. She was also a great resource. She knew how to get Dad in touch with someone who would bring him oxygen. When he died, she came out to the house and sat with my mom. They had already made all the funeral arrangements but she was available for whatever they wanted her to do. So it was really nice for me to know that this person was loving him and holding his hand and kind of taking our place."

One woman told how a hospice volunteer supported her parents with "nonmedical" care as her father endured the end stages of cancer. "A lot of times she would just come and sit with them. Once when I was there she came over just to see how they were doing. She asked about them and told them about her life. Her father had died of cancer and that was what got her involved. She was someone who cared, someone they could talk to. My parents didn't have to treat her like company; mom didn't clean house before she came. They talked openly about death and dying. She talked to people at the church about coordinating meals. She walked with Dad in the garden. She was like a companion for both of them."

Hospices can also offer "tune-up" services to make patients more comfortable. A patient may be admitted to a hospice to get her pain and other symptoms under control, to get help finding a hospital bed for her home, or to get nutritional help or home help in order to get her back into her own home again.

How and When to Qualify for Hospice Care

To receive hospice services, the patient, family, and doctors must agree that the patient probably has six months or less to live. Families often feel it is "too soon" to begin hospice care and wait until death is very near. A better approach is to begin some level of professional care before a crisis exists. Arrange introductory home meetings or hospice visits before you need services so that a support network is in place.

Paying for Hospice Care

Medicare coverage of hospice care is available under Medicare Part A hospital insurance. (States may also offer hospice services under Medicaid for eligible seniors.) Medicare helps pay for:

- physicians' services
- nursing care
- medical appliances and supplies related to the terminal illness (such as wheelchairs, bandages, and catheters)
- drugs for symptom control and pain relief
- short-term acute inpatient care, including respite care
- home health aide and homemaker services
- physical and occupational therapy
- speech therapy
- social-worker services
- counseling, including dietary and spiritual counseling

To receive Medicare payment, the agency must be approved by Medicare to provide hospice services. Be sure to ask your doctor or the organization if they are approved by Medicare for hospice services.

The patient will be responsible for paying a copayment for outpatient drugs and part of the Medicare-approved payment for inpatient respite care.

A Medicare beneficiary may elect to receive hospice care for two 90-day periods, followed by an unlimited number of 60-day periods. These may be used consecutively or at intervals. In some cases, a terminally ill patient's health improves or his illness goes into remission, and hospice care is no longer needed. Either way, the patient must be certified as terminally ill at the beginning of each period.

For more information, contact Medicare (request the booklet *Medicare Hospice Benefits*), or contact the National Hospice & Palliative Care Organization (see appendix).

Hospice Checklist

When checking out hospice programs, competency in making patients comfortable should be the top priority. A hospice's values and beliefs regarding life, death, and the afterlife are also important. To help determine if you are comfortable with the hospice's principles, you might ask them to send you their "mission statement" or "statement of faith" for consideration. In *The Aging Parent Handbook* (HarperCollins, 1997), Virginia Schomp recommends you ask the following questions when looking for an agency:

1. What area does the hospice serve? Many programs accept only patients from within a specific geographic area.
2. Does the hospice specialize in dealing with certain types of illness? Some hospices, for example, provide care only for people with AIDS.
3. Will the hospice develop a professional plan of care? You and your loved one are entitled to a written copy of the care plan, which should spell out the hospice's duties and work schedule.
4. Who will be on the hospice-care team? Will the team include your elder's current physician? If not, who will provide medical direction?
5. What are the qualifications of the staff and volunteers? Ask if nurses, social workers, clergy, and volunteers have any special training in working with the dying.
6. What are the responsibilities of the family caregiver? What duties will you be expected to perform?
7. What resources are available to assist you?
8. Does the hospice provide bereavement counseling and support for the family?

9. What happens if there is an emergency in the middle of the night? You will want to know if after-hours calls are answered by a hospice staff member or an answering service, and how quickly help is available.

10. Is the hospice Medicare-certified? Medicare covers only care provided by an approved hospice program. Find out what out-of-pocket expenses Medicare patients are expected to pay.

11. What are the fees and how are they applied—per day, per visit, or some other rate? If your aging loved one has private insurance, ask whether the hospice will accept whatever the insurance company pays as payment in full.

12. Will the hospice handle the billing with Medicare or private insurance carriers? If not, find out if someone from the hospice can help you with insurance forms.

13. Does the hospice meet state licensing requirements? Your state

---

PAYING ATTENTION

My mom had hospice care for the last seven weeks of her life. She had a hospital bed set up in her bedroom. The hospice workers were wonderful, not only to my mother but also to me. In fact, they paid as much attention to me as they did to my mom! That's not typical. Most people pay attention to the patient, which is good, but the caregiver also needs support. My siblings would come over to the house occasionally and say, "How's Mom?" I'd answer, "Well, go in and see." In contrast, the hospice personnel would sit down with me and genuinely ask how I was doing. They assumed I would be tired and overloaded. And they followed up. "How are you now?" They even helped me cope with my sister, who differed with me on my caregiving decisions. She was suspicious of hospice care and wanted my mom fed even when she didn't want to eat anymore. My sister would bring over nourishing food to help Mom put on weight, but who cared about that when Mom was dying?

One morning I walked into the bedroom and saw my mother lying on the bed after she'd just been bathed. The workers were talking in whispers, and everything seemed so light and bright. I knew Mom was going to die soon and she was so ready to go to heaven. It was such a tender, special moment. The hospice workers were right there with me. They held me and let me cry.

Diana F.

department of health will provide information on applicable regulations. Also ask if the program has any kind of outside review or accreditation.

13. Will the hospice provide references from professionals such as hospital staff or a social worker with a community agency? Also check with the local Better Business Bureau for the hospice's complaint record.

WHAT IS GOD'S WILL?

When making decisions about the appropriateness of initiating or withdrawing life support or other medical interventions, the Christian caregiver asks, *What is God's will regarding the treatment of my loved*

WE CAN DO IT TOGETHER

When Mom had lymphoma 25 years ago and a bowel obstruction 20 years ago, I saw her suffer so much from being jabbed, stabbed, and poked. Tiny veins that roll and break make I.V.s sheer torture for her. It didn't make sense to put her through that again after she'd suffered a major stroke at age 92, so I called in a hospice group connected to a local Catholic hospital.

The hospice staff put to rest all the fears I had. They told me they would keep Mom comfortable, providing liquid medication or suppositories for pain and anxiety. They would not give I.V.s; doing so would simply force fluids into her tissues as her kidneys began to shut down. They would give me sponge swabs to keep Mom's mouth moist. I would continue to pay Josephine, our live-in Polish caregiver, but all other expenses would be taken care of by hospice. A nurse would visit three times every week, then every day as Mom's pilgrimage on this earth began leading her to her permanent home in heaven.

Within a few days a chaplain came out to read Scripture to Mom. Then a social worker came to see how she could help meet my emotional needs, advise me regarding finances, and arrange for volunteer relief for Josephine and me. Every person I've met from hospice, whether paid staff or volunteer worker, has a vibrant, joyful, we-can-do-it-together attitude. They help me have the confidence and peace I need to know that Mom is getting the best care on her final journey.   *Betty F.*

one? No two situations are identical. There are always circumstances to weigh and consider in every person's illness and death. But we can also consider the Creator's point of view. Imagine how God would treat your aging loved one in a given situation. The way we treat ourselves and our elders actually reflects the way we treat God.

In our Maker's eyes, human life is sacred, created in His image, and of inestimable value—at every stage, from conception/fertilization to natural death. He knew the number of our days before one of them had come to be (Psalm 139:16), and He has appointed the time to die (Hebrews 9:27). He has not given Christians a spirit of fear, but of power and of love and of a sound mind (2 Timothy 1:7).

The way we treat ourselves and our elders actually reflects the way we treat God.

Medical technology can be a marvelous tool God uses to bring healing. But it is not a cure-all. When a treatment is invasive but ineffective, causes extended suffering, and creates an excessive burden in terms of physical function and pain, it may be time to allow treatment to be stopped and/or withheld. There is no requirement to continue treatment that has no benefit or which may cause a burden to a terminally ill patient. Ultimately, whatever questions you face, such as when to use or withdraw life-prolonging procedures, should be answered in light of God's perspective and with the wisdom He supplies (James 1:5). It is also vital to seek wise counsel and support from others—family members, friends, pastors with experience in these matters, hospital chaplains, and support groups.

The mouth of the righteous brings forth wisdom. PROVERBS 10:31 NKJV

CHAPTER 19

But when this perishable will have put on the imperishable, and

this mortal will have put on immortality, then will come about the

saying that is written, "Death is swallowed up in victory."

1 CORINTHIANS 15:54 NASB

When It's Time to Let Go

Facing Your Loved One's Death

When Linda's mom knew she was dying of cancer, she talked to her daughter about her death. "If I'm dying and seem restless, would you sing hymns to me?"

Linda agreed, knowing that a big part of her mother's devotional life included singing with a hymnbook. "She always liked hymns that contained a lot of doctrine," Linda says.

It had been three years since her mother—who also suffered from severe osteoporosis and compression fractures of the spine—had moved in with her daughter, a single woman. Linda had arranged for home health care during the day while she taught school, but the nights were long. Her mom needed help getting to the bathroom three or four times a night. Or she would be so restless and uncomfortable that she would call Linda to come into her bedroom and sit with her. Linda was always tired. She would pray, "Lord, please give me the heart of a servant!"

Always conscientious, her mom felt bad about needing so much of Linda's help. "This has to end; this is too hard for you!" she would say in tears. But Linda would reply, "It's okay, Mom."

When her mom went into a coma and seemed near death, Linda's brother, Dan, came over. For the next five days, the two of them fulfilled their mother's wish by taking turns singing hymns to her. On a Friday evening, when neither of them felt like singing anymore, they got something to eat and read the paper, checking on their mom every 10 minutes. Finally they went into the bedroom and sat down. Soon, their mother's breathing slowed down, grew farther apart, and then just stopped.

It was over, but the relief Linda expected quickly turned to grief. "The last week of Mom's life, I was praying, 'Please, God, let it end. No more pain. Please let it end.' And the moment she died, I was kicking myself for wanting it to end!"

There comes a point when, despite numerous prayers for healing and the efforts of doctors and modern medicine, it becomes clear that a loved one will not recover. The idea that he or she will not be around much longer is hard to swallow. How can this person, who has been part of your life for so long, really go away? It is common for caregivers to have guilt and conflicting emotions—wanting the suffering to be over (and being exhausted from caregiving), yet not wanting the loved one to die. You might spend all your energy taking care of your elder and postpone talking about death, avoiding words like *terminal* or *dying*. Your elder might also avoid the subject.

Even if your elder is too sick or mentally impaired to respond, you can still talk, touch, and show affection.

But the reality is that it is important to broach the subject of death, including your loved one's preferences for end-of-life care and funeral arrangements, while your elder is still living. This may be your only chance to talk about your fears, make any apologies, express your love and appreciation, and recall special shared memories. It also may be your last opportunity to help your elder prepare to meet the Lord. The words of Scripture often take on special meaning to one who is dying. Even if your elder is too sick or mentally impaired to respond, you can still talk, touch, and show affection, reassuring your loved one of your ongoing love and care.

The Dying Process

If your loved one fears the dying process, it is understandable. Some people are afraid because they have no assurance of what is on the other side.

Others may be certain of their final destiny but not feel ready to leave this present world. The greatest fear people report is having to undergo the dying process itself, the one thing that is not possible to escape.

Older people sometimes worry that they will die alone, in considerable pain, or become a burden on their loved ones. Yet one study involving 1,000 persons over age sixty-five found that most died peacefully and more than half were in good health a year before they died.[1] Although death in American society tends to be hidden in hospitals and nursing homes, most elderly people are able to see various members of their families before they die.[2]

In the late 1960s, Elisabeth Kubler-Ross defined five emotional stages of dying which have become well known and widely accepted. Not all people go through every stage or experience them in the same order, but it should prove helpful to realize some of the common reactions of those facing death. Also, these stages can be experienced cyclically, over and over with each subsequent loss (e.g., loss of bladder control, loss of mobility, loss of independence, etc.). The stages are: 1) shock and denial, 2) anger, 3) bargaining, 4) depression, and 5) acceptance.[3]

In the first stage, your aging loved one may not believe he has a terminal illness. He may go beyond seeking a second doctor's opinion, asking for a third or fourth. He may refuse to talk about death and claim that he will beat the disease. He may claim that his faith is so strong that God will heal him.

When your loved one can no longer deny the reality of his illness he may become angry. This anger may be directed toward God, family members, doctors, or life in general. He may feel God has been unfair, vindictive, or punitive. Often the anger will be directed at those closest to him.

If your elder works through his anger, he may go on to the stage of bargaining. He may promise God that if he can get well he will devote the rest of his life to religious work, or never smoke again, or be a better husband. He will make apologies for past mistakes and try to start again.

Once it is clear bargaining will not work, your loved one might become depressed. This could take the form of a sorrow over leaving loved ones or not being able to support or assist the family.

Finally, your dying loved one will probably come to accept his death. Acceptance does not mean he is necessarily happy about dying but that he no longer denies it will happen. He attempts to make peace with God, himself, and others.

Even the Christian who is anticipating the home awaiting her in heaven knows that she must leave this familiar time and space to get there. That includes leaving those people and things she has loved here on earth. It is hard to feel ready for heaven when there is so much to keep us here! We first must be weaned from the pull of this present life. Even when a loved one knows death will relieve pain and suffering, it is natural not to feel ready to depart from this life. One older woman who was painfully ill asked her husband to pray that God would take her in death. The obedient husband, a faithful Christian, started to kneel by her bed to pray. The wife quickly responded, "Maybe not yet!"[4]

Although a dying person might feel some tug-and-pull about leaving what is familiar, you can assure your loved one that there is a great

LIVING IN DENIAL

My husband, Bob, had chronic multiple sclerosis the last 14 years of his life, but as his disease progressed, he remained in a state of denial, never admitting how helpless he was. He went from needing a cane to using a walker to a three-wheeled cart to a wheelchair, and each step of the way I had to force. Finally he was unable to move any part of his body.

His MS was much worse the last four years, and Bob was in and out of the hospital a lot. He had chronic infections and required a feeding tube and catheter. Even with a live-in caregiver, I was exhausted, so I prayed frequently that the Lord would take him home. But when the doctor said it was time to put Bob in hospice care, I completely lost it and cried and cried. I wasn't ready to let him go; I just thought I was!

After we brought him home, I said, "Honey, do you realize that hospice means the doctor signed a statement saying he thinks you have no more than six months to live?" Predictably, Bob said, "I don't feel that sick." Just two days before he died, the hospice nurse came over and asked him how he was doing. He said, "Fine." That's a chuckle for me now because that was his pat answer. He never complained or said he felt crummy.

Nena T.

welcome planned beyond the grave for those who trust in Christ. "For so an entrance will be supplied to you abundantly into the everlasting kingdom of our Lord and Savior Jesus Christ" (2 Peter 1:11 NKJV).

MAKING PREPARATIONS FOR DEATH

While it may seem morbid or unpleasant, it is important to talk to your loved one about what to do with his body after death. There are a few options, and it will help you not to have to make these kinds of decisions in the midst of grief.

Organ Donation

Federal law now requires hospitals to inform patients and family members about organ donations, so the topic should come up if your loved one is hospitalized toward the end of life. Generally, organs are more suitable if they come from people under 70 years of age. Plus, the organs of most cancer patients or of patients with infections or other serious diseases are not suitable for donation, although corneas often can be donated without a problem.

Some people hesitate to consider donating their organs, fearing it will interfere with their care. However, doctors are more interested in providing their patients with proper care than they are in obtaining organs. Organ donation is considered only after all attempts have been made to save a life.

The most common organ and tissue transplants are skin, lungs, heart, liver, kidneys, corneas, certain bones, pancreas, and middle ear. Eyes, bone, skin, and other tissues can be obtained from 6 to 24 hours after breathing and heartbeat have stopped.

NEARER TO JESUS

Having both of my parents live with me and watching them become more detached from the world around them as they became more closely attached to Jesus has been an inspiring experience for me. One day Mom was trying to read the alarm clock but was having difficulty seeing the numbers. Then she said, "It doesn't matter what time it is when you love one another and you love Jesus."

Betty F.

The body will not be disfigured by organ donation. After the removal of the donated organs, the surgical team will leave the body intact for funeral or burial arrangements.

Medical Science

When one man became ill with cancer and rheumatoid arthritis, he arranged for his body to be donated to medical research. He told his family, "I've got two diseases for which there is no cure. Maybe this can be used to help someone else."

If this is your loved one's desire, have her write it down for verification. Also, notify your doctor of this when your elder becomes seriously ill so your doctor will know how to handle the body upon death.

Cremation

Cremation—the process of reducing human remains to ashes by burning—is becoming more and more common. The number of cremations doubled in the United States between 1980 and 1990. One reason for the popularity of cremation is that it is only about one-eighth of the cost of a traditional burial.

Cremation also offers more flexibility in planning memorial services. The funeral home can help with the cremation and death certifi-

---

EARLY FUNERAL ARRANGEMENTS

Long before she needed it, my mother preplanned her funeral. She decided she wanted to be cremated and prepaid for that. That made it so much easier on us because none of us had to make those tough decisions at a time when it would have been really difficult to do so. Preplanning was so nice because that way you don't have one person saying, "Oh, I'm sure she wanted to be buried," and someone else saying, "I'm sure she wanted to be cremated," and arguing about the whole thing. We didn't have any of that because Mom made it clear. And if you don't go into funeral plans with some idea of what you want, the funeral director can talk you into something you don't want or need. Plus, after Mom's stroke she couldn't communicate, so it was wonderful that she had taken time to plan these things long before she needed them.

Jennifer O.

cates, but you can plan the service according to the time schedule that works best for you. For example, when relatives are coming in from out of town, it may work better to postpone the memorial for a couple weeks.

Many people are hesitant about cremating a loved one's body, however, because it seems disrespectful to destroy the body intentionally. Also, viewing the body in the casket provides a sense of closure for many.

Some oppose cremation on biblical grounds. Whereas cremation has pagan roots, ground burial has been the established custom among Jews and Christians since early church history. For example, in the Old Testament, Abraham purchased a burial site (Genesis 23:9), Joseph comanded that his bones be carried out of Egypt (Genesis 50:25), and the Lord Himself buried Moses (Deuteronomy 34:5-6). The practice continued in the New Testament with the burial of John the Baptist (Mark 6:29), the Rich Man (Luke 16:22), Lazarus (John 11:17-19), Ananias and Sapphira (Acts 5:6-10), and Jesus Christ (Mark 15:46). There are no recorded cremations in the New Testament. In addition, since God used fire to destroy Sodom and Gomorrah and will one day judge the world by fire, some find it inconsistent for Christians, who have been saved from the coming judgment of fire, to have their bodies cremated. After all, the body is the temple of the Holy Spirit; it belongs to the Lord.

One reason for cremation's popularity is that it is only about one-eighth of the cost of a traditional burial.

Christians look forward to the bodily resurrection of the dead as promised in Scripture (1 Corinthians 15:42-57). It is true that our bodies on this earth will eventually turn to dust (Genesis 3:19). Whether the process takes place through prolonged decay in the grave or cremation, the end result is the same. The God who holds us in life does not need our specific ashes and chemical components to bring about resurrection, because the resurrected body is a new creation. Therefore, cremation does not hinder resurrection. In the end, the choice should be what your elder and family feel comfortable with.

Traditional Burial and Funeral

Many people prefer that their bodies be embalmed and buried in a casket, even though it is the most expensive option. The reasons vary (see

"Cremation" above). For many families, funeral costs become the third most expensive venture they encounter—behind purchasing a home and purchasing a car. Some estimates place funeral costs between $7,000 and $10,000, including a burial plot, vault, and monument.

The funeral industry has been charged with taking advantage of people who are in a state of shock after the death of a loved one. Undoubtedly some funeral directors have overcharged clients and sold unnecessary items and services, but there are ethical funeral directors who are very helpful during a difficult time. Your minister is probably familiar with various funeral homes in your community. Ask for advice from your pastor or other Christian friends in choosing a reputable, caring service provider.

If possible, try to make funeral arrangements before the shock of death. If you do not, you will be making decisions during a period of intense grief. You can be at a distinct disadvantage if you wait until the last minute to make funeral arrangements.

Some people feel that they need to have an elaborate funeral for their loved one in order to show how much the deceased was loved or

WALKING AND LEAPING

The day before my disabled husband died, he was in a coma and the family gathered around his bed to say our good-byes. We read Scripture verses and I told him, "You can let go, darling. When you get home, you'll be able to walk again." I'd moved the piano into the bedroom, so I played hymns while our children sang. And we sang him that cute little chorus about the lame man, which goes, "He went walking and leaping and praising God . . ." My granddaughter kept wiping tears from my husband's eyes.

The next day, my son Greg was reading the 23rd Psalm and got to the part about lying down in green pastures. My husband had been a sod producer, so Greg said, "Just think, Dad—that will be the prettiest sod you ever saw." That's when Bob quit breathing. His breathing had been very gaspy, but it slowed down and stopped. I've heard of other dying people who really struggled at the end, but when Bob died, it was a very quiet, peaceful thing. We think it was because he knew exactly where he was going.

Nena B.

respected. Others feel their families must maintain their social status by arranging for an expensive funeral. Try not to be drawn into either trap. A funeral is for the benefit of the family, and whatever suffices for the family will work best.

Many older people are buying preburial agreements and prepaying their funeral years before death. People can purchase a cemetery plot, a casket, and indicate what type of funeral they prefer. Buyer beware, though. Some people have lost some or all of the money when their plans changed, they moved to another state, or the company selling the contract went out of business. Another alternative might be to set up a small joint savings account containing funds to pay for the funeral, with the principal caregiver as a cosigner.

It would also be helpful for your loved one to make a record of the information needed to prepare an accurate obituary. Some newspapers require families to write the obituary themselves while others will write it for you if you provide them the essential information. Encourage your loved one to show you a sample of an obituary he likes and then be sure you have the information on hand to produce a similar article.

Now is also a good time to find out what favorite hymns and Bible verses your elder would prefer at the funeral. Ask for photos or picture albums, from which you can put together a photo montage of your loved one's life on poster board. If it is your loved one's desire to include a message about salvation in his service, be sure to engage a minister or speaker who is prepared to make such a presentation. A funeral service is an opportunity for mourners to express their love and grief. But it is also a chance for the love of Jesus Christ to be shared with people who may never be more open.

A funeral is for the benefit of the family, and whatever suffices for the family will work best.

GETTING AFFAIRS IN ORDER

Don't wait until your loved one has died to find out if his financial and personal records are in order. It is better to organize papers and vital information beforehand to avoid the inconvenience later. If you are a wife or husband caring for an aging spouse and your spouse normally handles the finances, try to handle all financial matters (e.g., bills, car repairs, investments) for one month a year while your loved one is still alive and can help you. Or your loved one might want to designate a friend or family member to help manage or gradually assume responsibility for her records. Keep detailed files, and make sure the information is reviewed and updated regularly. In some cases, rather than list the information, the files will indicate where the information can be found.

Financial and Legal Information
- Last Will and Testament (identify location and executor)
- Durable Power of Attorney for Financial Matters (identify location and individual)
- Bank accounts
- Insurance policies (including policy number, beneficiary, and type of insurance)
- Investments

WHAT A DAY THAT WILL BE

My wife had some precious moments with my dad during his final days in the nursing home. One day, he asked her, "Shirley, when am I going home?" She said, "Daddy, you probably won't be going home to the condo. You'll be going home to heaven." He smiled and said, "Shirley, that's great!" Then she asked him, "Daddy, who do you want to see most when you get to heaven?" That was probably a setup question because his first wife had passed away in their third year of marriage, and Shirley wondered if he'd want to see her most. But he said, "My Lord Jesus Christ."

The thing that was neat for me was his clear focus on heaven. There was no sense of despair. Yeah, he occasionally asked when he was going home to his condo, but usually that meant he had a desire to be in his own bed or he was tired of institutional food. He was ready to be with Jesus.

On another day, Shirley was there with him when he sighed, "What a day."

She said, "Daddy, that's the name of a hymn," and she started to sing it. "What a day that will be—"

He interrupted her and continued the song: ". . . when my Jesus I shall see, when I look upon His face, the One who saved me by His grace, when He takes me by the hand, leads me to the promised land, glorious day, glorious day that will be."

Not long after that, my dad's pastor sang that same hymn at his funeral. *Paul M.*

- All sources of income
- Trusts
- Mutual-fund and IRA holdings
- Deferred annuities
- Pensions/retirement benefits
- Veterans benefits
- Social-security benefits
- Medicare information
- Medigap insurance
- Safe-deposit box (location, key, list of contents, who has access)
- Home mortgages
- Loans
- Liabilities
- Credit-card names and numbers
- Property taxes
- Titles/deeds/leases to all property, including vehicle, home, and other real estate
- Location of recent income-tax returns (including name of accountant or tax preparer, if applicable; save seven years back to be safe)
- Warranties for equipment and appliances
- Location of all personal items such as jewelry

Personal "Vital Statistics"
- Full legal name*
- Date of birth*
- Place of birth*
- Social-security number*
- Address
- Citizenship*
- Marital status*
- Full legal names and addresses of spouse and children (or location of death certificate if any are deceased)
- Father's legal name and birthplace*
- Mother's maiden name and birthplace*
- Location of will or trust

• Location of birth certificate
• Location of certificates of marriage, divorce, or separation
• Military history, including rank and branch of service, dates, discharge papers, and military serial number*
• Information/authorization for organ/tissue/eye/whole-body donation
• Funeral and burial arrangements
(* needed for death certificate)

(For more information on financial and legal matters, see chapter 10: Financial Care and chapter 11: Legal Care and Estate Planning.)

A Time to Die

Caring for a dying loved one is a physically and mentally demanding task. All your energy and attention are focused on your aging loved one as you try to help him feel comfortable physically, help him deal with any unfinished business, and prepare him to meet the Lord. It is important to have emotional and caregiving support to help you. As death draws nigh, consider following these steps:

Saying Good-bye

If your loved one is approaching death, don't wait until it is too late! Take the time now to say good-bye.

If your loved one is approaching death, don't wait until it is too late! Take the time now to say good-bye. Sometimes a dying person lingers because she is worried about her spouse or children and how they will cope without her. This is the time to express sentiments of love and thankfulness to your elder and to give her permission to let go. One couple took the opportunity to say good-bye to a terminally ill loved one in a special place and time, then said, "Whatever happens, we've said our formal good-byes." The end did not come for another six weeks, but they were glad they had been able to choose when to say good-bye.

Just as Jesus made provision for His mother by entrusting her care to the disciple John, let your loved one know that the surviving family members will be taken care of. Don't be embarrassed if you cry. Tears are a natural part of saying good-bye and can help you to let go, too.

In That Final Hour

When the soul is about to return to God, it is a moment of great awe. If you have the opportunity to be there when your elderly loved one takes that final breath, be there. But let your words be few and meaningful. If any sounds can reach the ear now, if any words can touch the heart, God's words can. Speak to your loved one slowly and distinctly, not in a whisper or in a loud voice but clearly and gently. Singing your elder's favorite hymn or praying the Lord's Prayer (Matthew 6:9-13) and speaking the comforting promises of God in short sentences should take priority. Psalm 23 is especially comforting to Christians. Also consider the following Bible verses:

- We wait in hope for the Lord; he is our help and our shield. (Psalm 33:20 NIV)
- Fear not, for I am with you; be not dismayed, for I am your God. I will strengthen you, yes, I will help you, I will uphold you with My righteous right hand. (Isaiah 41:10 NKJV)
- "Come now, let us reason together," says the Lord. "Though your sins are like scarlet, they shall be as white as snow; though they are red as crimson, they shall be like wool." (Isaiah 1:18 NIV)
- Come to me, all you who are weary and burdened, and I will give you rest. Take my yoke upon you and learn from me, for I am gentle and humble in heart, and you will find rest for your souls. (Matthew 11:28-29 NIV)
- Christ was offered once to bear the sins of many. To those who

FAITH AND FUNERALS

Dad was a very committed Christian but a quiet man who didn't talk about his faith a great deal. Our minister knew Dad very well; at Dad's funeral he said, "Leroy regretted the fact that he didn't speak out about his faith more often. So if he could stand before you today I'm sure he would say, 'What are you going to do about Jesus?'" Dad's coworkers, neighbors, and other friends were there. Not one of them left without having to confront the question of their relationship to Jesus Christ. That would have pleased my father immensely. *Sara P.*

CARING DECISIONS

The doctor was running late. Anxiety hung thickly over his sterile white office. To fill the time, my mother-in-law and I chatted about nothing, then fell silent. Finally he breezed in, apologized for the delay, and took a deep breath.

"Is it cancer?" she asked, cutting him short before he could launch into the little speech he'd prepared.

"Yes," he said, after a split-second hesitation. The breast cancer we'd hoped was a thing of the past had returned to invade her lungs.

The eyes of this stoic, no-nonsense woman widened, but she didn't flinch.

One question led to another. And then, "No, you won't be able to move into an assisted-living facility," the doctor said. "Your breathing will have to be monitored."

"You're welcome to come and live with us," I said.

Long ago, my husband and I had decided that when the time came, his mother should move in with us. But now that time had come, and I wasn't ready. My mother-in-law and I have many differing views, which could make sharing a home a challenge.

As a writer, I work at home. My husband understands that I'm working even when I appear not to be. I curl up with a book or leaf through a magazine or stare silently at the computer screen. My mother-in-law believes that idle hands are the devil's workshop.

I'm the world's lousiest nurse. When my children were little and I took them in for vaccinations, I couldn't bear to watch the needle go in. When a student had a seizure in my classroom, I ran for help. I certainly wasn't ready for oxygen tanks, loss of privacy, and watching someone I love suffer.

Ready or not, my husband and I were preparing to join the ranks of the one out of every four American families providing care for an elderly person in their homes. But in our case, my mother-in-law decided she wanted to die in her own home. So during her last weeks, with the help of a hospice program, we cared for her there, taking turns with my husband's brother and his sister-in-law, a nurse with 20 years of elder-care experience.

There is no one option that's right for every family. For some, the hospital offers crucial medical attention that's needed at the end. For others, a nursing home is the best solution for long-term care beyond what a family can provide at home.

For our family, we will always be grateful for those last weeks in my mother-in-law's home. What I had dreaded turned out to be a precious time of final bonding. Our son flew home from Seattle to spend a few days with his grandmother. He encouraged her to reminisce about the old days. Together, we went through a cedar chest full of old photographs, and we heard stories from her that we'd never heard before. I played all her favorite hymns on the piano. We laughed and cried. Friends stopped in to say their farewells, and she sent each of them home with a little memento from her shelves of bric-a-brac.

When our son kissed her good-bye, he said, "Save me a chair in heaven, Grandma."

Later, at the airport, he said, "I'm so glad I came. It's been good for me to see how this is done." He knew—as I did—that one day I could be in Grandma's place and he in mine.

Adapted from Sharon Sheppard, "When Roles Are Reversed,"
Sunday/Monday Woman *(January/February 2001).*

eagerly wait for Him He will appear a second time, apart from sin, for salvation. (Hebrews 9:28 NKJV)

- Then he said, "Jesus, remember me when you come into your kingdom." Jesus answered him, "I tell you the truth, today you will be with me in paradise." (Luke 23:42-43 NIV)
- For whosoever shall call upon the name of the Lord shall be saved. (Romans 10:13 KJV)
- Let not your heart be troubled; you believe in God, believe also in Me. In My Father's house are many mansions; if it were not so, I would have told you. I go to prepare a place for you. And if I go and prepare a place for you, I will come again and receive you to Myself; that where I am, there you may be also. (John 14:1-3 NKJV)
- So do not throw away your confidence; it will be richly rewarded. You need to persevere so that when you have done the will of God, you will receive what he has promised. (Hebrews 10:35-36 NIV)
- Let us hold unswervingly to the hope we profess, for he who promised is faithful. (Hebrews 10:23 NIV)
- For I am persuaded, that neither death, nor life, nor angels, nor principalities, nor powers, nor things present, nor things to come, nor height, nor depth, nor any other creature, shall be

able to separate us from the love of God, which is in Christ Jesus our Lord. (Romans 8:38-39 KJV)

Signs of Approaching Death

What are the signs that your aging loved one is close to death? The signs vary greatly from person to person but may include skin that is increasingly cool to the touch, increased time sleeping, less responsiveness, and irregular breathing. In reality, it is incredibly difficult to predict when someone is about to die.

Identify yourself by name but speak quietly to your loved one as you normally would, even though there may be no response. Don't assume your elder cannot hear you; hearing is often preserved when other senses are lost. Your loved one may have incontinence as the muscles begin to relax. She also may have congestion that sounds like loud, gurgling sounds coming from her chest, or something that sounds like deep snoring, and her regular breathing pattern may change its pace. These changes often are not distressing to the patient. If the dying person has a decreased appetite, don't force food or fluids into her mouth. Small chips of ice or frozen juice may be refreshing, but only if the person is conscious enough to swallow them properly. Glycerine swabs or artificial saliva preparations also can be used at any time to help keep the mouth and lips moist and comfortable. The person may seem unresponsive, withdrawn, or comatose. Death comes when the physical systems have shut down and cease to function. For more detailed information, contact a local hospice organization.

Don't assume your elder cannot hear you; hearing is often preserved when other senses are lost.

Keep in mind that there is nothing magical about being there at the last moment. Many people are wracked with guilt because they were not there for their loved one's final breath. But loved ones would be better served if you focused on their last years more than their last seconds.

O Death, Where Is Your Sting?

We can expect to grieve the loss of a loved one. Your reaction may be immediate or delayed, and you are likely to feel both relief that the suffering is ended and guilt for feeling that way. You will likely grieve that your loved one is gone and wonder who you are now that you are not a caregiver. You will need to give yourself time to refuel and time to reflect.

Nevertheless, grief is different for the Christian. We grieve, but not as those who have no hope of the resurrection of the dead (1 Thessalonians 4:13). "For if we believe that Jesus died and rose again, even so God will bring with Him those who have fallen asleep in Jesus" (1 Thessalonians 4:14 NASB). Christians await Resurrection Day, when the souls and bodies of the saints who have died shall be reunited and gathered to Christ, that He may present them to the Father: "Behold, I and the children whom God has given me" (Hebrews 2:13 NASB). A loved one whose body was ravaged by cancer will be raised with a glorious body like Christ's (Philippians 3:21). The Christian who suffered from Alzheimer's in this life will be able to look on his Lord with full cognition and joy in heaven. Grief is different when you know a person is absent from the body but present with the Lord in heaven. Your tears are not for that person but for yourself (which is a totally appropriate response).

Grief is different when you know a person is absent from the body but present with the Lord in heaven.

If you do not know whether your dying loved one has accepted the Lord, consider praying that God will give you wisdom and a door of opportunity to share the mystery of Jesus Christ while your elder is still alive (Colossians 4:3; 1 Corinthians 15:1-4). Even a person in a coma may be able to hear words of Scripture. Pray that your loved one will be receptive to the message. Then leave the matter in God's hands. Your elder may trust in Christ on her deathbed with or without your knowledge. Either way, the decision for or against Christ is a matter of personal responsibility. God will judge fairly, for those who come to Him He will by no means cast out (John 6:37). Genesis 18:25 (KJV) says, "Shall not the Judge of all the earth do right?"

(For more information on the grief process, see chapter 20: Moving Forward.)

PARTING WORDS

One woman offered this advice to families facing the death of a loved one: "Say what needs to be said. This is your chance to tell your loved one all the things you want him to know."

In the same vein, encourage your loved one to say the things that need to be said. This will help her feel more prepared for the end of her life. And it may help comfort the people left behind. Granted, some people find it difficult to talk about their feelings, so don't press the issue. Simply make a suggestion and offer to tape-record or write down your elder's thoughts if desired.

One woman told about a letter her father wrote: "Years before my father's death, he penned a letter to his children. He encouraged us to put the Lord first and seek God's will for our lives. He expressed some regret for not spending more time with us. And he simply said, 'I love you.' The letter, read at his funeral, helped us say good-bye to Dad because it was, in a way, him saying good-bye to us."

Another man used a letter to say the things he could not say in life. He was an alcoholic and was not the kind of father his children needed. In a couple paragraphs he simply apologized, saying that he was sorry for the way he had lived his life, and that he was proud of how his children had turned out—in spite of him. He apologized for the way he had treated their mother. The letter helped his adult children forgive him for his years of neglect and abuse and then move on with their own lives.

A man who was diagnosed with colon cancer took advantage of the final days of his life to gather his family around him and give them a

---

THE DAY OF SMALL THINGS

When my dad got sick, someone told me to look for the small things God would do to show His love and comfort. It was amazing all the things I saw. It was as if the Lord said, "I'm not going to take the illness away, but I want you to know that I do care."

The night he died I kept thinking of John 14:1-6: "In My Father's house are many mansions . . ." (NKJV). The next day I was sitting with my sister and my mom and I said, "I've been thinking about that passage where the Lord says He's going to prepare a place for us." Mom said that they had just watched a video where the teacher was talking about that very passage. Then when we were planning the memorial service the pastor said, "Your dad asked for John 14:1-6 to be used at his funeral." It was like a gift from God, as if God said, "See! I brought this passage to all of you as a comfort." It meant so much that in the middle of a difficult time, God would do little things like that.

If that woman hadn't told me to look for those things, I might not have seen that God was reaching down. I think sometimes we look for God to answer our prayer the way we want it answered—which for me, of course, would have been to have my dad longer.

Carol C.

parting spiritual lesson. "Before he died he wanted to lead us in a devotional," says his caregiving daughter. "The theme of it was 'When you grow weary with the world, remember the spiritual shade of the cross.'

"He told about when he was a boy and, since they had no air conditioning, the best thing he could do was find a big tree with lots of shade. After he'd been working in the fields there was nothing he enjoyed more than relaxing, exhausted, under that cool tree, where even the ground was cool.

"He said the cross was like that shade tree. When you're weary and tired, go to the foot of the cross. Rest there, cool off there, and be revived there. As he said all this he knew he was facing death. He wanted to tell us all one more time of his love for the Lord."

So be sure to talk. If possible, don't wait until the very end. Talk while your elder is still lucid. The disease, medications, and organ failure can all lead to confusion or unconsciousness. Don't delay! Tell your loved one about the common stages of death so she is better able to face them. Ask what her desires are regarding life-support measures. Find out what your loved one wants to do with his body after he dies. Talk about what to include in the funeral service. Hold hands and pray with your loved one. And say all those things you have been meaning to say. There is never a better day than today.

Say all those things you have been meaning to say. There is never a better day than today.

———— ⌘ ————

I'll love Thee in life, I will love Thee in death,
And praise Thee as long as Thou lendest me breath;
And say when the death-dew lies cold on my brow,
"If ever I loved Thee, my Jesus, 'tis now."

In mansions of glory and endless delight,
I'll ever adore Thee in heaven so bright;
I'll sing with the glittering crown on my brow,
"If ever I loved Thee, my Jesus, 'tis now."

—FROM "MY JESUS, I LOVE THEE," BY WILLIAM RALPH FEATHERSTON

CHAPTER 20

Blessed are those who mourn, for they shall be comforted.

MATTHEW 5:4 NKJV

Moving Forward
Dealing with Grief

A month after her husband's funeral, Elsie knew the numbness of losing him had worn off when waves of grief began to hit her at unexpected times. One day she was eating a pickle and choked on it. "It hurt!" she recalls. "I began to cry because Bill choked a lot on food toward the end of his life, and I never realized how much it hurt him." She also wept when she thought about things they had enjoyed doing together, such as watching her grandson's football games. "I'd push Bill's wheelchair right onto the 50–yard line," she says. A friend whose spouse had died a few years earlier e-mailed her with this advice: "Don't expect to get over your husband's death quickly. Allow at least a year, but then again, you may never get over it."

Starting over after 47 years of marriage is difficult, and Elsie finds it hard to concentrate. "I'm an avid reader, and I don't think I've even finished a book since his death," she says. Nevertheless, she is in the process of remodeling the master bedroom to match her personal tastes and is planning a three-week trip to her aunt's beach house in Hawaii to spend some quiet time with the Lord. "I'm no longer a wife or a caregiver or an actively involved mother, so I need to find out who I am," she says. "I'm really being prayerful about that. God has plans for me, so I have a sense of anticipation. I say, 'Lord, what is it we're going to do?'"

—⟨∿⟩—

Grieving the death of a loved one is an individual process. Some caregivers initially feel numb and disoriented, then endure pangs of yearning for the person who has died. Others feel anxious and have trouble sleeping, perhaps dwelling on old arguments or words they wish they had expressed. Sudden outbursts of tears are common in grief, triggered by memories or reminders of the loved one. Even those who are confident that their loved one is with the Lord struggle with sadness over their loss. Not all people grieve the same way or for the same length of time, but dealing with grief is essential in order to come to terms with the loss of your loved one and move on with your life. To do that, you need to be honest in your grieving and ask God the tough questions. He is big enough to handle them! And wrestling with tough questions helps us mature. (Read Lamentations 3.)

The circumstances of your elder's death can affect how you grieve. If a loved one suffered with a long illness, death is often considered a blessing. For the families of Alzheimer's patients, mourning begins with the onset of the disease, long before death occurs. Because of the time spent in anticipating death, this kind of bereavement differs from the intense grief over someone who dies following a brief illness, surgery, or accident.

Keep in mind that the weight of grief is lighter when shared.

Over time, the intensity of your grief will likely subside, but do not try to rush the grieving process. And do not expect your feelings and emotions to be like anyone else's. God made you unique, and your grieving process will be a personal journey. But keep in mind that the weight of grief is lighter when shared. Support from others can help you to handle the aftermath of your loss. God also offers comfort in times of bereavement. Jesus said, "I will not leave you comfortless: I will come to you" (John 14:18 KJV).

AFTER LOSING YOUR ELDERLY LOVED ONE

When the funeral is a memory and your relatives and friends have returned to their busy lives, you may wonder how you are going to cope. If grief threatens to overwhelm you, try saying with the psalmist, "My soul is weary with sorrow; strengthen me according to your word"

(Psalm 119:28 NIV). Cling to God's promises as you work through your grief. "He gives power to the weak, and to those who have no might He increases strength" (Isaiah 40:29 NKJV).

But how does a person "get over" the death of a loved one? How long after a loss should one still be grieving? It is generally agreed that there are four "tasks of mourning" every bereaved person must accomplish to be able to effectively deal with the death of a loved one:

1. Accept the reality of the loss.
2. Experience the pain of grief.
3. Adjust to an environment in which the deceased is missing.
4. Take the emotional energy you would have spent on the one who died and reinvest it in another relationship.[1]

The first task, **accepting the reality of the loss,** involves overcoming the natural denial response and realizing that the person is physically dead. This can be facilitated by viewing the body after death, attending funeral and burial services, and visiting the place where the body is laid to rest. In addition, talking about the deceased person or the circumstances surrounding the death can be very helpful.

It is necessary to grieve the physical finality of losing a loved one and come to grips with the fact that you will not see your elder again in this life. But the spiritual life goes on. If your loved one was a professing Christian, not only will you see her again in the life to come, but she is now in an immeasurably better place—in the Lord's presence, with no more pain or fear or sorrow. This is true for all those who die in the

EVIDENCE OF AN ELDER'S LIFE

I remember when my gramma died, I couldn't get out to her house in Oregon till two days later. I was so relieved (unexpectedly so) that absolutely nothing of hers had been touched or moved—not even her wig or water glass or lipstick-blotted tissue from the bathroom! (I kept that tissue.) In my opinion, perhaps the worst thing people can do when someone dies is "get rid of the evidence" of that person's life. Some of the people left behind may want to literally touch the last things their loved one touched or used—even a dirty dish!   *Norma B.*

Lord. "'And God will wipe away every tear from their eyes; there shall be no more death, nor sorrow, nor crying. There shall be no more pain, for the former things have passed away.' Then He who sat on the throne said, 'Behold, I make all things new'" (Revelation 21:4-5 NKJV). Therefore, we mourn for ourselves, not for our Christian loved ones. They are where we yearn to be.

When 33-year-old Susan's mother died of liver cancer a few months after her dad died in a farming accident, Susan was still writing thank-you notes to guests who had attended her dad's funeral. "When my mom was dying, I couldn't help out as much as my other three siblings, because I was pregnant with my first child and sick all the time," she says. "None of us are depressed, though, because both of our parents were strong Christians. In fact, they had planned to move to the headquarters of an evangelistic mission agency this year, so everyone was expecting them to move. Instead, they moved to heaven."

"For our citizenship is in heaven, from which we also eagerly wait for the Savior, the Lord Jesus Christ, who will transform our lowly body that it may be conformed to His glorious body" (Philippians 3:20-21 NKJV).

WISH YOU WERE HERE

Mom died three years ago, which doesn't seem that long ago. I'm still pretty raw at times. Knowing we have the assurance of heaven helps, but grief is so miserable. And I was ready for her death. Her death was prolonged, and I welcomed it, but it was still so hard!

Mom talked about her death a lot before she died. She would say to me, "I'm concerned that you'll fall apart. This is going to be harder on you than you think." She was right. I grieved for her in a different way than my siblings. She was my best friend, and I feel that loss. Sometimes I think I just can't stand it if I can't talk to Mom. At those times I say, "Well, you don't get to talk to Mom." Instead I get productive and do something, or I cry.

My grief reminds me of how my grandpa grieved for his mom and dad. He'd say, "See that picture of my parents? They've been dead 60 years, and every day I wish they were here." I can understand what he meant.

Linda H.

The second task, **experiencing the pain of grief,** also confronts the denial so common in grieving persons. Many people try to avoid pain by bottling up their emotions or rejecting the feelings they are having. They may avoid places and circumstances that remind them of their loved one. They may try to take shortcuts through the grieving process, not admitting to the feelings of anger or denial that usually exist. However, the only way to move through grief is to *move through it.* It is impossible to escape the pain associated with mourning. The person who avoids grieving will eventually suffer from some form of depression or even from physical problems. Fully experiencing the pain—most often through tears—provides relief. Jesus wept over the loss of his friend Lazarus, even though He knew He was about to raise him from the dead, and we, too, have permission to weep.

We all experience pain in this life, and the only thing worse than the pain of losing a loved one is the pain of never loving or being loved in the first place. In a way, the pain of grief is a gift to us because it demonstrates love.

The third task, **adjusting to an environment in which the deceased is missing,** requires the grieving individual to assume some of the social roles performed by the deceased, or find others who will. For example, a grieving spouse may need help with household chores and cooking. Someone who never learned to drive must either learn how to drive or find other forms of transportation. The alternative is social withdrawal and sitting home alone. A person who dreads coming home to an empty house may find comfort in taking in a friendly pet.

The final task is **taking the emotional energy you would have spent on the one who died and reinvesting it in another relationship or relationships.** Many people feel disloyal or unfaithful if they withdraw emotionally from their deceased loved one. But the goal is not to forget the person who has died; it is to finally reach the point where you can remember your loved one without experiencing disabling grief. Some find it impossible to invest in new relationships because they are unwilling to take the risk of feeling another loss. Others were so immersed in caregiving that, now that their loved one has died, they are not sure what to do. Yet investing time in friendships is important for different reasons. Old friends can reminisce about your loved one but also give you encouragement and permission to rebuild your life. New friendships allow you to begin again as a person with a future, not just as a widow, widower, or survivor. For some, getting involved in a volunteer ministry gives structure, a sense of purpose, and built-in companionship. Others swap phone numbers with new friends they make in grief-recovery groups. Do not feel like you have to hurry to this stage. If attending a lighthearted party seems incongruous with your current state of mind, perhaps having coffee and conversation with a good friend would be a refreshing change of pace. Many surviving spouses enjoy focusing more time and energy on children, grandchildren, and great grandchildren.

Do not rush into making major decisions or changes that could add stress to your life. Give yourself time and space to grieve. If at all possible, do not move for at least one year. You might benefit from setting aside an hour every day or two to "work" on grieving, especially if your loved one's death was recent. To do this, turn to caring family members or friends for support. Read a good devotional book, such as *Streams in the Desert* by L. B. Cowman (Zondervan, 1997) or *Quiet Moments for Caregivers* by Betty Free (Tyndale, 2002). Or look in a Bible concordance for words like *comfort* or *hope*. As you look up the verses, meditate on each one, recording them in a prayer journal. Allow God's healing words to sink in. Psalm 94:19 says, "In the multitude of my anxieties within me, your comforts delight my soul" (NKJV).

GRIEF FROM A DISTANCE

One woman observed, "I lived far from my parents during the last years of my dad's life, while my two sisters lived in their same town. When Dad died, they felt his loss in their everyday lives. And as their everyday lives adjusted to Dad's absence, they were able to grieve and move on. I, on the other hand, may not have felt Dad's absence as acutely because I had lived away from him for a time, but I also had a harder time getting over it. Every time I would go visit my mother I had to face Dad's death all over again. So my mother's and my sisters' experience was very different from mine. Not harder or easier, just different. Neither one was easy."

Tanya J.

WIDOWHOOD

Grief over the death of a spouse occurs whether or not the marriage was happy. But the grief may be even greater if the relationship was not a happy one. Whether you recently lost your spouse or are caring for a loved one who has lost a spouse, understanding the grief process involved can be helpful.

When Your Spouse Dies

The loss of a spouse is unique among deaths. It is one of the most painful and disorienting experiences in life. This is the person with whom you probably spent more time than anyone else in your life. You shared a history together. You were together through ups and downs, in sickness and in health, in the mundane and in memorable times. Perhaps you raised children together. If you were your spouse's caregiver, you might feel a mixture of relief, sadness, and guilt when the caregiving comes to an end. Without your spouse, loneliness and anger about being alone are typical. Sleepless nights and sudden responsibilities can take their toll. Routine things seem to take more effort. Spiritual questions may trouble you. The intensity of grief often peaks at 3 months

---

A SHOVELFUL OF DIRT

When my wife's mom died eight months before my dad died, I didn't grieve because I didn't have a close relationship with her. So I worried that I wouldn't feel emotional at my dad's funeral. Well, I worried needlessly, because at the funeral, I couldn't keep from weeping during the message. My brothers and sister and I sang a hymn together at the service and could barely get through it. We were too choked up. But we all grieve differently. My older brother and I felt open to weep, but I didn't see my mom weep other than when the funeral director gave her Dad's wedding ring.

After the funeral, we gathered at the cemetery in the cold air, and I felt almost peaceful at the finality of it. As the casket was lowered into the grave, I stayed around so that I could take a shovelful of dirt and toss it in the hole. It was almost surreal. The rest of the family had already left for the luncheon at church. I'd said good-bye to Dad at his bedside the night he died, but this was a way for me to say my final good-bye.

Alan H.

and 12 months following the death of a loved one, and it may be as strong as when your spouse first died.

"It's been two years since my husband died, and the grief still comes in waves," says one woman who was married nearly 50 years. "I will hear something on the news, and in the back of my mind, I'll think, *I've got to tell Frank.* Or something will need to be fixed, and I'll have that feeling of not being able to discuss it with him. He was a take-charge kind of man, so after we discussed something, he would always see that it was done. Now if I need a new car or wisdom in financial matters, I have to 'borrow a brain' to help me. It can be frustrating, but I have to learn to adapt and be productive, because otherwise, at the end of the day, I have nothing to feel satisfied about."

In light of fluctuating emotions, don't rush into making major decisions, getting remarried, or anything else! Instead, consider joining a grief-recovery group sponsored by your local church, hospital, or funeral home. You need time to find meaning in the past, to acknowledge your difficulties and resentments, to work through and share your grief, to adjust your old hopes to the new reality, to set new priorities. It is normal to experience grief at unexpected times, such as when you think you recognize a departed loved one on the street or hear your elder's voice, only to turn around and see that it was someone else. (See "The Caregiver's Grief" on pages 506-510 for specific help.)

If you were your spouse's caregiver, you might feel a mixture of relief, sadness, and guilt when the caregiving comes to an end.

It is usually best for a grieving spouse not to make important decisions about what to do with a home or estate for at least a year. If you receive a large payout from a life-insurance or pension-fund disbursement, put the money into a money-market account or CD until you can learn about making good investments. Find a trustworthy financial adviser or take an investment class at a community college.

You will need to attend to immediate financial matters, however, such as paying household bills. Survivors should plan *beforehand* to have money available for bills, food, etc. Don't wait until after your spouse is dead to find out how to access money. Take time to organize bank accounts, a safe-deposit box, mutual-fund and IRA holdings, pensions, vehicle titles, home mortgage, insurance, and social-security benefits. Gather and make an inventory of all assets and liabilities. Make sure your loved one's will is up-to-date.

Once you have a good idea of your financial situation, notify all concerned parties of your spouse's death, and transfer credit cards, licenses, titles, and bank accounts into your name. If your spouse died suddenly, see if she had accidental- or sudden-death benefits attached to her life-insurance policy, credit cards, bank accounts, or membership in unions or organizations. Take time to update your own will.

When Your Parent Loses a Spouse

If you are caring for a surviving parent, offer support but don't encourage your parent to grow overly dependent on you. It is not helpful to be too protective. Healing comes as a person begins to do things for himself that are consistent with his abilities. Try to help your parent to become as independent as possible without appearing to be insensitive or cold.

Start by evaluating your remaining parent's needs from every angle. What did he depend on his wife to do? Can he cook? Can he pay the bills? What did she depend on her husband to do? Is she aware of existing insurance policies? Can she prepare a tax return? By anticipating problems, you might be able to take steps to circumvent them. If, for example, your surviving parent has never mowed the lawn or changed the oil in the car, try to delegate those responsibilities to others. If she is too frail to drive a car, contact your Area Agency on Aging about transportation and food services for seniors.

As time goes on, encourage your surviving parent to remain—or become—active in outside interests, such as church-related activities, hobbies, and volunteer opportunities. One woman's parents volunteered part-time at a local rescue mission for years; her father offered financial advice and her mom helped with clerical duties. After her dad died, her mom became a full-time volunteer, helping with mailings and answering phones. "This involvement gives Mom a reason to get up and get dressed every day," says her daughter. "It gives her mental stimulation and provides a way for her to be productive, to contribute to the spiritual and physical needs of others."

In a support group, a survivor can find people who have gone through similar experiences.

Get Support

Bereavement groups are often very helpful for those who grieve. In a support group, a survivor can find people who have gone through similar experiences and can make new friends who will help him work through his loneliness. Call your local church or senior center to see if they offer bereavement support groups or group counseling.

Sometimes funeral homes offer bereavement classes for the family members they have served during the year. Some places offer a special class just before Christmas to help family members through the nostalgic holiday season.

The Caregiver's Grief

Everyone expects sadness to follow the death of a loved one, but bereavement brings a wide range of emotional and physical responses, including: crying, sleep disturbances (insomnia or desiring more sleep), inability to concentrate, withdrawal from social activities, lack of interest in normal routines (e.g., cooking, shopping, taking a walk), weight loss or weight gain, shortness of breath, tightness in the chest and throat, gastrointestinal problems, anxiety, or feelings of emptiness. Difficulty with intimacy on a number of levels may occur.

When the person you are grieving is someone you took care of, it means your role as a caregiver has come to an end, bringing on additional emotions. You may feel numbness, relief, exhaustion, anger, loneliness, guilt, sorrow, resentment, bitterness, irritability, fears, mood swings, or any combination of varying emotions. The emotions

---

BALANCING ACT

When my grandfather died, my grandmother was completely uninformed about their financial affairs. My grandfather had done everything. He'd taken care of all the finances, all the checkbooks—she didn't even know how to write a check. It was pretty tough on her for a while. Even figuring out how much money they had was a struggle. Her children spent many months trying to get it all figured out. As they worked on it they would educate her, and gradually she learned to balance a checkbook and do other things on her own, to the extent that she was able.

Patience is so important. I'm glad they didn't wrestle the checkbook away from Grandma.

Kate P.

you feel will depend on the relationship you had with your loved one. If the relationship between parent and child or husband and wife was not a good one, grief is often greater, as the hope of a healed relationship dies along with that other person. In that case, there is often significant ambivalence (grief mixed with relief). Keep in mind that any emotion you feel is okay. Emotions in themselves are not bad. What you feel is what you feel. It is how you deal with your emotions that matters. Consider the following common responses to grief:

Relief

"It sounds terrible to say, but life was easier after my father-in-law died," said one caregiver. "With the Parkinson's disease he was a handful. Plus he had been a very harsh person all his life. So it was almost a relief when he died, which is sad to say."

This caregiver's expression of relief is also tinged with guilt for feeling that way. Comments like this may be sad, but they are not terrible. It is not terrible to feel relief when a burden is lifted or when stress in family relationships is dramatically reduced. This kind of emotion is common, though maybe not commonly expressed.

A caregiver might also feel relieved when a loved one dies after suffering a painful or extended illness. One surviving spouse said, "When I get down, God reminds me of the relief it is for my husband to be freed of the bondage of his body and for me to be freed of the responsibility of having to take care of him."

LEARNING BY DOING

My husband was a very dominant person who made all the decisions. But later in life he developed a chronic, progressive disease that eventually affected his mind. This brilliant man who'd run several successful businesses got to the point where he couldn't run our own finances. But as he got worse, I got stronger at handling the affairs of the family and the finances. If he had died right when he first got the disease, I would have panicked and been completely helpless. But in the 14 years of his illness, I was able to learn to take over his responsibilities. I realize now that God was blessing me with that extra time.
                                                                              Nena T.

Guilt

Guilt is one of the most common emotions a caregiver has following the death of a loved one. Usually the guilt occurs when a caregiver thinks back and wishes he had said or done things differently.

It is also common for caregivers to have nagging doubts about whether they provided too much or too little care for an aging loved one. Regrets and "if-onlys" are common.

"I have many regrets, but that's life," says a caregiver named Ruth, whose husband was a pastor and battled leukemia for seven years. "As mortals, we're always going to say things we wish we hadn't. And the devil's a master at dredging up reasons to make us feel defeated. But the Holy Spirit doesn't do that. He's an encourager. Sure, He convicts when a person needs convicting, but not over something you can't do anything about."

When Ruth's husband was in a coma and on a respirator, she longed for another chance to hear his voice and talk together, but he never recovered. "His infection came on so fast, there wasn't time to communicate," Ruth says. "He knew I loved him, but I realize you can never say 'I love you' too many times."

You may be more vulnerable to guilty feelings when you are tired, not eating right, or not keeping active and involved.

If you have guilt or nagging doubts, it may be helpful to talk with a compassionate friend, pastor, or "Stephen's minister" from a local church. (Stephen's ministers are laypeople trained to minister to an individual's spiritual and emotional needs. For more information, see "What Churches Can Do for Your Loved One [and You]" on pages 313-321. Or see appendix to contact Stephen's Ministries.) Talking with another person may help you work through the issues one by one and identify the truth. You might decide to take any legitimate guilt to the cross for forgiveness and healing. Or you might conclude that you did the best you could given the information you had at the time. In either case, try not to get buried by guilt. Read a good book on dealing with guilt, such as *From Forgiven to Forgiving* by Jay Adams (Calvary Press, 1994) or *A Grief Observed* by C. S. Lewis (Zondervan, 1961). Also, keep in mind that you may be more vulnerable to guilty feelings when you are tired, not eating right, or not keeping active and involved with others. So turn your attention toward the living—yourself and those around you.

Anger and Tension

Often after a loved one dies, you must begin a process of sorting out his personal affairs. After his father's death, one man found his mother was nearly penniless. "I am so angry with my father for not taking better care of their finances. He always had a job, always had enough. He could have managed better. So now it's up to me to try to find some resources for Mom, to try to explain things to all her creditors."

A woman in Texas said, "After my grandmother died, there was a big fight between my father and his brothers over my grandmother's estate. 'She should not have left this to him,' or 'I deserved more.' It was pretty ugly."

Some families avoid this kind of tension by keeping a charitable attitude and staying in close communication. "My sisters and I just agreed we wouldn't fight over things," one woman said. "Some people have been really surprised at that. But we just agreed to talk things through. One person doesn't push on everybody else, and we don't push things on my mom."

Journaling can be a helpful way to process your feelings. One woman said, "After my mother died I had a lot of anger toward my sister for not attending our mother's funeral. As I wrote about it in my journal I found myself writing down other times she had let me down and I realized I wasn't just angry about Mother's funeral, but I was angry about a lifetime of disappointments. After taking the time to write it out like that, I realized I needed to talk with my sister."

While family members may have valid reasons for being angry or squabbling with each other, keep in mind that anger often leads to sin. The Bible gives this advice: "Let all bitterness, wrath, anger, clamor, and evil speaking be put away from you, with all malice. And be kind to one another, tenderhearted, forgiving one another, just as God in Christ forgave you" (Ephesians 4:31-32 NKJV). If arguments are over an elder's estate, consider getting a mediator to intervene. Better still, communicate with heirs beforehand if division of property might be a tender issue. Let your overriding principle be to "do nothing out of selfish ambition or vain conceit, but in humility consider others better than yourselves" (Philippians 2:3 NIV). In principle, it would be better to be wronged or cheated than to file a lawsuit against a relative (1 Corinthians 6:6-7).

However, if you believe a relative is thwarting your deceased loved one's wishes, consider getting outside help. Bring in a pastor, grief counselor, or other neutral party to help you work through the situation.

Introspection

For one man, the death of a great-aunt marked a personal crisis. He said, "I was trying to deal with the death of an entire generation of my family. It was not just people who were gone. An era had passed, and a chapter in my family history had closed forever. I found myself feeling strangely alone. When I first began to experience this emotion I began questioning myself, not God. I began to reflect upon my life—my accomplishments and failures. I examined my legacy. What would I leave to my family? The thought of what would be said about me at my funeral made me shudder. I began listening and praying. Psalm 139:16 says that I was put on the earth for a specific period of time. I no longer looked upon the passing of a generation as a time of grieving and feeling alone. Instead, I looked upon this as a call to service for God."

> *If you believe a relative is thwarting your deceased loved one's wishes, consider getting outside help.*

CHOOSING TO RECOVER

Take Time to Adjust

Caregiving can be a consuming task—emotionally and physically. When your loved one dies, give yourself some time off. There may be a lot of things you have been wanting to do, but it is highly recommended that you not rush into any new commitments. In the Old Testament, newlywed men were given a year off. Deuteronomy 24:5 says, "When a man takes a new wife, he shall not go out with the army, nor be charged with any duty; he shall be free at home one year" (NASB). If possible, give yourself the same privilege after your elder dies. Decide on an amount of "time off" and say no to all commitments for that length of time. It will be easier to say no if you determine to do so beforehand.

During this time, try to do things to recharge your batteries, such as getting more rest.

Another good thing to do is to prepare a list of things for friends to do. That way, when they say, "Let me know if I can do anything," you can ask them if they are serious and then show them the list of things you need done. Be sure the tasks are well-defined and limited (e.g., "bring a meal next Tuesday" or "mow the lawn this week"). Include a few very small tasks on the list, so people who were just "using an expression" when they offered to help can save face.

Doing things to renew your mind and spirit can be very helpful. For example, read books, go for walks, take a scenic drive, meditate on some of the promises of God (e.g., Proverbs 3:5-6, Jeremiah 33:3, Isaiah 57:18, and Matthew 6:33). Choose what is most helpful for *you*. One suggestion is to plan time for a spiritual retreat. It need not be anything elaborate—you could simply spend a day in the park with your Bible. Some people find that writing out their prayers is a helpful way to express their thoughts. And having a "prayer journal" enables you to look back at what you were thinking and feeling, and to note God's answers to your prayers.

"When I spend time in the Word of God and in prayer, it's like food," says Ruth (mentioned earlier in this chapter). "The Lord can provide a table in the wilderness. He can meet the need of the moment, just as He provided food for the Israelites when they had none."

The one thing that has remained a constant in Ruth's life since her husband died is church. "If I felt sorry for myself and got in my little cocoon and stayed away from church, I would miss out on many blessings. Since my husband was a pastor, I'm also very aware of my testimony and know that people are watching to see if the Lord is really real to me. But I've found that when I seek to minister to others, they, in turn, minister to me."

There may be a lot of things you have been wanting to do, but it is highly recommended that you not rush into any new commitments.

Process Your Thoughts and Emotions

Take time to sort through your feelings. You will benefit more by dealing with your emotions than by letting them slip by unattended. Consider confiding in a close friend or calling a pastor. When you are restless in the middle of the night, it is often helpful to talk to God and to thank Him for His help (Psalm 63:6). There may be great lessons in this time of bereavement that will help you in the future.

Getting together with close friends or others who have lost a loved one to share memories and feelings can be mutually beneficial. Sharing memories—of good things that happened and bad things you survived—

is often a good way to work through your loss. Being willing to forgive the past, such as the bad things your elder or others did to you, and confessing to God any bad things you did to them are important steps in recovery. Do you believe deep down that God accepts you unconditionally? Consider this heartfelt prayer of David: "Be gracious to me, O Lord, for to Thee I cry all day long. Make glad the soul of Thy servant, for to Thee, O Lord, I lift up my soul. For Thou, Lord, art good, and ready to forgive, and abundant in lovingkindness to all who call upon Thee" (Psalm 86:3-5 NASB). God forgives sins and heals the brokenhearted. He "saves those who are crushed in spirit" (Psalm 34:18 NASB), so it is possible to face the future with peace and freedom.

RECOMMENDED BOOKS ON GRIEF

- *When Your Soul Aches,* by Lois Rabey (Waterbrook Press, 2000).
- *Grieving the Loss of a Loved One,* by Kathe Wunnenberg (Zondervan, 2000).
- *Trusting God Through Tears,* by Jehu Burton (Baker, 2000).
- *In Light of Eternity: Perspectives on Heaven,* by Randy Alcorn (Waterbrook, 1999).
- *Though I Walk Through the Valley,* by Vance Havner (Baker Book House/ Spire, 1974).
- *Incredible Moments with the Savior,* by Ken Gire (Zondervan, 1990).
- *Recovering from the Losses of Life,* by H. Norman Wright (Baker Book House/ Spire, 1993).
- *Quiet Moments for Caregivers,* by Betty Free (Tyndale, 2002).
- *When Life Is Changed Forever,* by Rick Taylor (Harvest House, 1992).
- *My Companion Through Grief,* by Gary Kinnaman (Servant Publications, 1996).
- *Grieving the Loss of Someone You Love,* by Raymond R. Mitsch and Lynn Brookside (Servant Publications, 1993).
- *Roses in December,* by Marilyn Heavilin (Harvest House, 1987).
- *A Grief Unveiled,* by Gregory Floyd (Paraclete, 1999).
- *A Grief Observed,* by C. S. Lewis (Zondervan, 1961).
- *Through Troubled Waters,* by William Howard Armstrong (out of print, Harper & Brothers, 1957).

There may not be an easy answer to why God took your beloved friend home, but like Job in the Old Testament, you may learn to trust God more deeply, even when it is *beyond* human ability to understand.

One caregiver, who is now a widow, benefits by making a conscious decision to count her blessings. "I had a husband for 45 years, a family, a house, a car, food, as well as spiritual blessings," she says. "I'm learning to have an attitude of happy thankfulness and to keep in mind that the Lord got me through in days past and He will get me through in days to come."

Sharing memories—of good things that happened and bad things you survived—is often a good way to work through your loss.

WHAT NOW?

What Do You Want to Do?

After you have given yourself time to recharge your emotional batteries, you have the opportunity to ask, *What do I really want to do now?* The answer might be as simple as "live a normal life." Caregiving can disrupt families and households. Perhaps the thing most anticipated is getting back to business as usual. For others, life after caregiving might include the opportunity to renew friendships. Getting back into previous social activities or participating more fully in church programs might be just what you need. Asking, *What is God leading me to do?* may help you to focus your thoughts and prayers.

Maybe this phase of life gives you a freedom you have never had before. Is it time to go back to work? Time to pursue a new career? Time to volunteer in some capacity? Maybe you would enjoy the mental stimulation of going back to school. And the goal of higher education need not be a degree. Many people take classes that interest them just for the joy of learning. One helpful exercise is to try to imagine yourself five years from now. What would you like to be doing? Another important step is to pray about how you can use your time and talents for the Lord. What goals might you set to accomplish your dreams? Goal-setting is a way of promising yourself that you can go ahead and live a full life. The death of a loved one can be a catalyst for important changes.

What Have You Learned That Will Help You?

Having engaged in the task of caregiving, you have no doubt enlarged your understanding of the aging process. You now have the opportu-

HEAVENLY REMINDERS

Though the tragedy of death can be overwhelming, God provides solace, comfort, and many precious promises through His Word. These verses may help. Some find it especially meaningful to read them aloud.

1. Why are you cast down, O my soul? And why are you disquieted within me? Hope in God; for I shall yet praise Him, the help of my countenance and my God. (Psalm 42:11 NKJV)

2. God is our refuge and strength, a very present help in trouble. Therefore we will not fear, even though the earth be removed, and though the mountains be carried into the midst of the sea. (Psalm 46:1-2 NKJV)

3. From whence comes my help? My help comes from the Lord, who made heaven and earth. (Psalm 121:1-2 NKJV)

4. Precious in the sight of the Lord is the death of his saints. (Psalm 116:15 KJV)

5. But concerning the resurrection of the dead, have you not read what was spoken to you by God, saying, "I am the God of Abraham, the God of Isaac, and the God of Jacob"? God is not the God of the dead, but of the living. (Matthew 22:31-32 NKJV)

6. Jesus said . . . , "I am the resurrection and the life. He who believes in Me, though he may die, he shall live." (John 11:25 NKJV)

7. Let us therefore come boldly unto the throne of grace, that we may obtain mercy, and find grace to help in time of need. (Hebrews 4:16 KJV)

8. We are of good courage, I say, and prefer rather to be absent from the body and to be at home with the Lord. (2 Corinthians 5:8 NASB)

9. For our citizenship is in heaven, from which we also eagerly wait for the Savior, the Lord Jesus Christ, who will transform our lowly body that it may be conformed to His glorious body. (Philippians 3:20-21 NKJV)

10. For the Lord Himself will descend from heaven with a shout, with the voice of an archangel, and with the trumpet of God. And the dead in Christ will rise first. Then we who are alive and remain shall be caught up together with them in the clouds to meet the Lord in the air. And thus we shall always be with the Lord. (1 Thessalonians 4:16-17 NKJV)

11. Praise be to the God and Father of our Lord Jesus Christ! In his great mercy he has given us new birth into a living hope through the resurrection of Jesus Christ

from the dead, and into an inheritance that can never perish, spoil or fade— kept in heaven for you. (1 Peter 1:3-4 NIV)

12. Therefore, since we receive a kingdom which cannot be shaken, let us show gratitude, by which we may offer to God an acceptable service with reverence and awe. (Hebrews 12:28 NASB)

13. Teach us to number our days aright, that we may gain a heart of wisdom. (Psalm 90:12 NIV)

14. For I am convinced that neither death nor life, . . . nor anything else in all creation, will be able to separate us from the love of God that is in Christ Jesus our Lord. (Romans 8:38-39 NIV)

15. In the future there is laid up for me the crown of righteousness, which the Lord, the righteous Judge, will award to me on that day; and not only to me, but also to all who have loved His appearing. (2 Timothy 4:8 NASB)

16. This I recall to my mind, therefore have I hope. It is of the Lord's mercies that we are not consumed, because his compassions fail not. They are new every morning: great is thy faithfulness. The Lord is my portion, saith my soul; therefore will I hope in him. (Lamentations 3:21-24 KJV)

17. And I saw a new heaven and a new earth; for the first heaven and the first earth passed away, and there is no longer any sea. And I saw the holy city, new Jerusalem, coming down out of heaven from God, made ready as a bride adorned for her husband. And I heard a loud voice from the throne, saying, "Behold, the tabernacle of God is among men, and He shall dwell among them, and they shall be His people, and God Himself shall be among them, and He shall wipe away every tear from their eyes; and there shall no longer be any death; there shall no longer be any mourning, or crying, or pain; the first things have passed away." And He who sits on the throne said, "Behold, I am making all things new." (Revelation 21:1-5 NASB)

nity to look ahead to your own later years. You can plan your own retirement. It is a good time to review your options, taking into consideration your personal preferences and lifestyle, and make some tentative or general choices for the future. By doing your own planning early, you will have time to refine, change, and act on your plans.

The physical or mental limitations of old age can be a reminder that we should enjoy the blessings of life each day and appreciate all the things we are still able to do. Maybe it is time to take that trip you promised your spouse. Or it may be time to pursue a new hobby or sign up for an evangelism course or Bible study at your church. Many people use this time to remind family members, especially their own children, how much they mean to them and how important they are in their lives.

Try to imagine yourself five years from now. What would you like to be doing?

Also ask yourself, *Am I financially prepared for old age? Are my affairs in order? Do I have a will? Have I planned my funeral? Do I have a cemetery plot?* Planning ahead makes a huge difference, not only for you but also for your family.

What Have You Learned That Can Help Others?

There is a saying that "no experience is ever wasted"; this holds true in caring for the elderly. Caregiving may make you more sensitive to people in similar circumstances. One woman said, "Probably the greatest effect of caring for my mother has been that I am more aware of the sick and elderly. Calling on people in the hospital or those with terminal illnesses had never been something I did willingly. Now I know how much it means to them, and I know better how to act and what to say."

Another possibility is acting as a resource for other caregivers. You have probably accumulated a wealth of knowledge that can be put to good use. Let your minister know if you are willing to advise others; there will no doubt be occasion to call on you. Help someone cut through the Medicare red tape. Offer advice on the best doctors. Where did you take your mother to get her hair done? Simply listening to the frustrations of other caregivers could be an invaluable service.

In addition, you could be the one offering respite to an overworked caregiver. You know the value of a couple hours to run errands, to take in a grandchild's concert, or to go shopping. Your experience has probably given you the training you need to stay with someone else's elderly loved one for a time.

Do you have greater anticipation of heaven? Do you look forward to seeing your loved one and never being parted again? Consider compiling a list of Scriptural truths and promises that have been meaningful to you in your time of grief and sharing them with other seniors or caregivers you meet. (See "Heavenly Reminders" on pages 514-515.)

Perhaps your caregiving experience uncovered a gift or desire to work with the elderly in a more formal capacity. Perhaps you should pursue professional training. Is there a volunteer position you could fill at a nursing home or with a hospice?

On the other hand, it could be that after years of caring for your elderly loved one you need something completely different. As you consider the opportunities of service in your church, what are you really drawn to? What have you missed being able to do in recent years? Or maybe there is a community service in which you have become interested. Would you like to work part-time at the library? Do you want to become a guide at a museum? There are many exciting possibilities to explore now that you do not have as many limitations on your time.

Your circumstances are unique. But God knows your situation and will equip you to move forward with new purpose.

Your circumstances are unique. But God knows your situation and will equip you to move forward with new purpose. "'For I know the plans I have for you,' declares the Lord, 'plans to prosper you and not to harm you, plans to give you hope and a future'" (Jeremiah 29:11 NIV). He can use your experience for the good of others and for His glory. So cast your burdens on the Lord, seek wise counsel about your future, allow time to work through your grief, and reach out to others. No matter what, remember that you can go boldly to the throne of grace to receive mercy and to find grace to help in time of need (Hebrews 4:16 NKJV).

———— ✦ ————

When peace like a river attendeth my way,
When sorrows like sea-billows roll;
Whatever my lot, Thou hast taught me to say,
"It is well, it is well with my soul."

FROM "IT IS WELL WITH MY SOUL," BY HORATIO G. SPAFFORD

Current Commissions on Aging

The most current commissions on aging are listed below. The addresses and phone numbers should remain fairly constant through the years. You can start by contacting your state organization, or you can just go directly to a local senior center or your region's Area Agency on Aging for expert advice and referrals.

ALABAMA

Alabama Department
of Senior Services
RSA Plaza, Suite 470
770 Washington Avenue
Montgomery, AL 36130-1851
(334) 242-5743
fax: (334) 242-5594

ALASKA

Alaska Commission on Aging
Division of Senior Services
P.O. Box 110209
Juneau, AK 99811-0209
(907) 465-3250
fax: (907) 465-4716

ARIZONA

Aging and Adult Administration
Department of Economic Security
1789 West Jefferson Street, #950A
Phoenix, AZ 85007
(602) 542-4446
fax: (602) 542-6575

ARKANSAS

Arkansas Department
of Human Services
P.O. Box 1437, Slot S530
700 W. Main Street
Little Rock, AR 72203-1437
(501) 682-2441
fax: (501) 682-8155

CALIFORNIA

California Department of Aging
1600 K Street
Sacramento, CA 95814
(916) 322-5290
fax: (916) 324-1903

COLORADO

Department of Human Services
1575 Sherman St., Ground Floor
Denver, CO 80203
(303) 866-2800
fax: (303) 866-2696

CONNECTICUT

Department of Social Services
Elderly Services Division
25 Sigourney Street, 10th Floor
Hartford, CT 06106-5033
(860) 424-5277
fax: (860) 424-4966

DELAWARE

Department of Health
and Social Services
1901 North DuPont Highway
New Castle, DE 19720
(302) 577-4791
fax: (302) 577-4793

DISTRICT OF COLUMBIA

D.C. Office on Aging
One Judiciary Square
441 Fourth Street, N.W., Suite 900 South
Washington, DC 20001
(202) 724-5622
fax: (202) 724-4979

FLORIDA

Department of Elder Affairs
Building 4040, Suite 152
4040 Esplanade Way
Tallahassee, FL 32399-7000
(850) 414-2000
fax: (850) 414-2002

GEORGIA

Aging Services
Department of Human Resources
2 Peachtree Street N.W.
Atlanta, GA 30303-3176
(404) 657-5258
fax: (404) 657-5285

GUAM

Division of Senior Citizens
Department of Public Health
& Social Services
P.O. Box 2816
Agana, Guam 96910
011-671-475-0263
fax: 011-671-477-2930

HAWAII

Executive Office on Aging
250 South Hotel St., Suite 109
Honolulu, HI 96813-2831
(808) 586-0100
fax: (808) 586-0185

IDAHO

Idaho Commission on Aging
P.O. Box 83720-0007
338 Americana Terrace,
Suite 120
Boise, ID 83706
(208) 334-3833
fax: (208) 334-3033

ILLINOIS

Illinois Department on Aging
421 East Capitol Avenue,
Suite 100
Springfield, IL 62701-1789
(217) 785-3356
fax: (217) 785-4477

INDIANA

Division of Aging and
Rehabilitation Services
Family and Social Services
Administration
P.O. Box 7083
402 W. Washington Street, #W454
Indianapolis, IN 46207-7083
(317) 232-7020
fax: (317) 232-7867

IOWA

Iowa Department of Elder Affairs
Clemens Building, 3rd floor
200 Tenth Street
Des Moines, IA 50309-3609
(515) 242-3333
fax: (515) 242-3300

KANSAS

Kansas Department on Aging
New England Building
503 S. Kansas Ave.
Topeka, KS 66603-3404
(785) 296-4986
fax: (785) 296-0256

KENTUCKY

Office of Aging Services
Cabinet for Families and Children
Commonwealth of Kentucky
275 East Main Street, 5C-D
Frankfort, KY 40621
(502) 564-6930
fax: (502) 564-4595

LOUISIANA

Governor's Office of Elderly Affairs
P.O. Box 80374
Baton Rouge, LA 70898-0374
(225) 342-7100
fax: (225) 342-7133

MAINE

Department of Human Services
35 Anthony Avenue
State House - Station #11
Augusta, ME 04333
(207) 624-5335
fax: (207) 624-5361

MARYLAND

Maryland Department on Aging
State Office Building, Room 1007
301 West Preston Street
Baltimore, MD 21201
(410) 767-1100
fax: (410) 333-7943

MASSACHUSETTS

Massachusetts Executive Office of
Elder Affairs
One Ashburton Place, 5th floor
Boston, MA 02108-1518
(617) 727-7750
fax: (617) 727-6944

MICHIGAN

Michigan Office of Services
to the Aging
611 W. Ottawa, Ottawa Building,
3rd floor
P.O. Box 30676
Lansing, MI 48909-8176
(517) 373-8230
fax: (517) 373-4092

MINNESOTA

Minnesota Board on Aging
444 Lafayette Road, 4th floor
St. Paul, MN 55155-3843
(651) 296-2770 or (800) 882-6262
fax: (651) 297-7855

MISSISSIPPI

Mississippi Department
of Human Services
Division of Aging and Adult Services
750 North State Street
Jackson, MS 39202
(800) 948-3090 or (601) 359-4929
fax: (601) 359-9664

MISSOURI

Missouri Department of Health
and Senior Services
P.O. Box 1337
615 Howerton Court
Jefferson City, MO 65102-1337
(573) 751-3082
fax: (573) 751-8687

MONTANA

Department of Public Health
& Human Services
Senior and Long Term Care Division
P.O. Box 4210
111 N. Sanders
Helena, MT 59604
(406) 444-4077
fax: (406) 444-7743

NEBRASKA

Department of Health
and Human Services
P.O. Box 95044
301 Centennial Mall - South
Lincoln, NE 68509-5044
(402) 471-2307
fax: (402) 471-4619

NEVADA

Division for Aging Services
3100 W. Sahara Ave., Suite 103
Las Vegas, NV 89102
(702) 486-3545
fax: (702) 486-3572

NEW HAMPSHIRE

Department of Health
& Human Services
Division of Elderly and Adult Services
129 Pleasant Street, Brown Bldg.
Second Floor
Concord, NH 03301
(603) 271-4680
fax: (603) 271-4643

NEW JERSEY

Department of Health
and Senior Services
Division of Senior Affairs
P.O. Box 807
Trenton, NJ 08625-0807
(609) 943-3433 or (609) 943-3436
In state: (800) 792-8820 or
(877) 222-3737
fax: (609) 943-3343

NEW MEXICO

State Agency on Aging
La Villa Rivera Building
228 East Palace Avenue
Santa Fe, NM 87501
(505) 827-7640
In state: (800) 432-2080
fax: (505) 827-7649

NEW YORK

State Office for the Aging
2 Empire State Plaza
Agency Bldg. #2
Albany, NY 12223-1251
(518) 474-5731
In-state: (800) 342-9871
fax: (518) 474-0608

NORTH CAROLINA

Department of Health
& Human Services
2101 Mail Service Center
Raleigh, NC 27699-2101
(919) 733-3983
fax: (919) 733-0443

NORTH DAKOTA

North Dakota Department
of Human Services
Aging Services Division
600 South 2nd Street,
Suite 1C
Bismarck, ND 58504-5729
(701) 328-8910
fax: (701) 328-8989

NORTH MARIANA ISLANDS

CNMI Office on Aging
P.O. Box 2178
Commonwealth of the Northern
Mariana Islands
Saipan, MP 96950
(670) 233-1320
fax: (670) 233-1327

OHIO

Ohio Department of Aging
50 West Broad Street, 9th floor
Columbus, OH 43215-3363
(614) 466-5500
fax: (614) 466-5741

OKLAHOMA

Department of Human Services
Aging Services Division
312 N.E. 28th Street
Oklahoma City, OK 73125
(405) 521-2281 or (405) 521-2327
fax: (405) 521-2086

OREGON

Seniors and People with Disabilities
500 Summer Street, N.E., EO2
Salem, OR 97310-1073
(503) 945-5811
In state: (800) 282-8096
fax: (503) 373-7823

PALAU

State Agency on Aging
Attn: Mrs. Lilian Nakamura
Republic of Palau
Koror, PW 96940
011-680-488-2736
011-680-488-2165
fax: 011-680-488-1465
e-mail: myu@palaunet.com

PENNSYLVANIA

Department of Aging
Commonwealth of Pennsylvania
555 Walnut Street, 5th floor
Forum Place
Harrisburg, PA 17101-1919
(717) 783-1550
fax: (717) 783-6842

PUERTO RICO

Commonwealth of Puerto Rico
Governor's Office of Elderly Affairs
P.O. Box 50063 Old San Juan Station
San Juan, Puerto Rico 00902
(787) 721-5710 or (787) 721-4560 or
(787) 721-6121
fax: (787) 721-6510

RHODE ISLAND

Department of Elderly Affairs
160 Pine Street
Providence, RI 02903-3708
(401) 222-2858
fax: (401) 222-2130

AMERICAN SAMOA

Territorial Administration on Aging
Government of American Samoa
Pago Pago, American Samoa 96799
011-684-633-1251 or
011-684-633-1252
fax: 011-684-633-2533

SOUTH CAROLINA

Department of Health
& Human Services
Senior and Long-Term Care Services
P.O. Box 8206
Columbia, SC 29202-8206
(803) 898-2501
fax: (803) 898-4515

SOUTH DAKOTA

Department of Social Services
Office of Adult Services & Aging
700 Governors Drive
Pierre, SD 57501-2291
(605) 773-3656
fax: (605) 773-6834

TENNESSEE

Commission on Aging
Andrew Jackson Building, 9th floor
500 Deaderick Street
Nashville, TN 37243-0860
(615) 741-2056
fax: (615) 741-3309

TEXAS

Texas Department on Aging
4900 North Lamar Blvd., 4th floor
Austin, TX 78751-2316
(512) 424-6840
fax: (512) 424-6890

UTAH

Division of Aging & Adult Services
P.O. Box 45500
120 North 200 West, Suite 325
Salt Lake City, UT 84145-0500
(801) 538-3910
fax: (801) 538-4395

VERMONT

Department of Aging & Disabilities
Waterbury Complex
103 South Main Street
Waterbury, VT 05671-2301
(802) 241-2400
fax: (802) 241-2325

VIRGINIA

Department for the Aging
1600 Forest Avenue, Suite 102
Richmond, VA 23229
(804) 662-9333 or (800) 552-3402
fax: (804) 662-9354

VIRGIN ISLANDS

Senior Citizen Affairs
Virgin Islands Department
of Human Services
Knud Hansen Complex, Building A
1303 Hospital Ground
Charlotte Amalie, Virgin Islands 00802
(340) 774-0930
fax: (340) 774-3466

WASHINGTON

Department of Social & Health Services
Aging & Adult Services Administration
P.O. Box 45600
Olympia, WA 98504
(360) 725-2300 or (800) 422-3263
fax: (360) 407-0369

WEST VIRGINIA

West Virginia Bureau of Senior Services
1900 Kanawha Boulevard East
Holly Grove - Building 10
Charleston, WV 25305-0160
(304) 558-3317
fax: (304) 558-0004

WISCONSIN

Bureau of Aging & Long-Term
Care Resources
Department of Health and Family
Services
P.O. Box 7851
Madison, WI 53707
(608) 266-2536
fax: (608) 267-3203

WYOMING

Aging Division
6101 Yellowstone Rd., Room 259B
Cheyenne, WY 82002
(307) 777-7986
fax: (307) 777-5340

State Ombudsman Programs

In addition to state agencies on aging, most states also have what is called an "ombudsman" program to investigate complaints by the elderly on conditions in nursing homes or similar adult-care homes. If your aging loved one is in a nursing home and is concerned about the way it operates or about the care he is receiving, you can help him locate a local ombudsman. For your convenience, we have listed ombudsman programs below.

ALABAMA

State Long-Term Care Ombudsman
Commission on Aging
RSA Plaza, Suite 470
770 Washington Avenue
Montgomery, AL 36130-1851
(334) 242-5743
fax: (334) 242-5594

ALASKA

Office of the Long-Term Care
Ombudsman
550 W. 7th Ave., Suite 1830
Anchorage, AK 99501
(907) 334-4480;
In state: (800) 730-6393
fax: (907) 334-4486

ARIZONA

State Long-Term Care Ombudsman
Aging and Adult Administration
Department of Economic Security
1789 West Jefferson Street, 950A
Phoenix, AZ 85007
(602) 542-6452
fax: (602) 542-6575

ARKANSAS

State Long-Term Care Ombudsman
Arkansas Division of Aging & Adult
Services
P.O. Box 1437, Slot S530
700 W. Main Street
Little Rock, AR 72203-1437
(501) 682-2441
fax: (501) 682-8155

CALIFORNIA

State Long-Term Care Ombudsman
California Department of Aging
1600 K Street
Sacramento, CA 95814
(916) 322-5290
fax: (916) 323-7299

COLORADO

State Long-Term Ombudsman
The Legal Center
455 Sherman St., Suite 130
Denver, CO 80203
(303) 722-0300
fax: (303) 722-0720

CONNECTICUT

State Long-Term Care Ombudsman
Elderly Services Division
25 Sigourney Street, 10th floor
Hartford, CT 06106-5033
(860) 424-5200
fax: (860) 424-4966

DELAWARE

Division of Services for Aging and
Adults with Physical Disabilities
1901 North DuPont Highway
New Castle, DE 19720
(302) 577-4791
fax: (302) 577-4793

DISTRICT OF COLUMBIA

National Ombudsman
Resource Center
c/o NCCNHR
1424 16th St. N.W., Suite 202
Washington, D.C. 20036-2211
(202) 332-2275
fax: (202) 332-2949

FLORIDA

State Long-Term Care Ombudsman
Holland Building, Rm. 270
600 South Calhoun Street
Tallahassee, FL 32301
(850) 488-6190
fax: (850) 488-5657

GEORGIA

State Long-Term Care Ombudsman
Division of Aging Services
2 Peachtree St. NW, 9th Floor
Atlanta, GA 30303-3176
(404) 657-5319
fax: (404) 657-5285

HAWAII

State Long-Term Care Ombudsman
Executive Office on Aging
250 South Hotel St., Suite 107
Honolulu, HI 96813-2831
(808) 586-0100
fax: (808) 586-0185

IDAHO

State Long-Term Care Ombudsman
Office on Aging
P.O. Box 83720-0007
338 Americana Terrace, Suite 120
Boise, ID 83706
(208) 334-3833
fax: (208) 334-3033

ILLINOIS

State Long-Term Care Ombudsman
Illinois Department on Aging
421 East Capitol Avenue
Springfield, IL 62701-1789
(217) 785-3143
fax: (217) 524-9644

INDIANA

State Long-Term Care Ombudsman
Indiana Division of Aging &
Rehabilitative Services
P.O. Box 7083
402 W. Washington Street, #W454
Indianapolis, IN 46207-7083
In-state: (800) 622-4484
Out-of-state: (800) 545-7763, ext. 7134
fax: (317) 232-7867

IOWA

State LTC Ombudsman
Iowa Department of Elder Affairs
Clemens Building, 3rd Floor
200 Tenth Street
Des Moines, IA 50309-3609
(515) 242-3333
fax: (515) 242-3300

KANSAS

State LTC Ombudsman
Office of the State Long-Term Care
Ombudsman
610 SW 10th Avenue, 2nd Floor
Topeka, KS 66612-1616
(785) 296-3017
fax: (785) 296-3916

KENTUCKY

State LTC Ombudsman
Division of Aging Services
State LTC Ombudsman Office
275 East Main Street, 5C-D
Frankfort, KY 40621
(502) 564-6930
fax: (502) 564-4595

LOUISIANA

State LTC Ombudsman
Governor's Office of Elderly Affairs
P.O. Box 80374
412 N. 4th Street, 3rd floor
Baton Rouge, LA 70898-0374
(225) 342-7100
fax: (225) 342-7133

MAINE

State Long-Term Care Ombudsman
P.O. Box 128
Augusta, ME 04332
(207) 621-1079
fax: (207) 621-0509

MARYLAND

Long-Term Care Ombudsman
Office on Aging
State Office Building, Room 1007
301 West Preston Street
Baltimore, MD 21201
(410) 767-1091 or (410) 767-0705
fax: (410) 333-7943

MASSACHUSETTS

State Long-Term Care Ombudsman

Massachusetts Executive Office of Elder
Affairs
One Ashburton Place, 5th floor
Boston, MA 02108-1518
(617) 727-7750
fax: (617) 727-6944

MICHIGAN

State Long-Term Care Ombudsman
221 N. Pine St.
Lansing, MI 48933
(517) 485-9393; toll free: (866) 485-9393
fax: (517) 372-6401

MINNESOTA

State Long-Term Care Ombudsman
Office of Ombudsman for Older
Minnesotans
444 Lafayette Road, 4th floor
St. Paul, MN 55155-3843
(651) 296-0382
fax: (651) 297-7855

MISSISSIPPI

State Long-Term Care Ombudsman
Division of Aging and Adult Services
750 North State Street
Jackson, MS 39202
(601) 359-4929
fax: (601) 359-4370

MISSOURI

State Long-Term Care Ombudsman
Division on Aging
Department of Social Services
P.O. Box 1337
615 Howerton Court
Jefferson City, MO 65102-1337
(800) 309-3282 or (573) 526-0727
fax: (573) 751-8687

MONTANA

State Long-Term Care Ombudsman
Office on Aging
Department of Family Services
P.O. Box 4210
Helena, MT 59604
(406) 444-4077
fax: (406) 444-7743

NEBRASKA

State Long-Term Care Ombudsman
Department on Aging
P.O. Box 95044
301 Centennial Mall - South

Lincoln, NE 68509-5044
(402) 471-2307
fax: (402) 471-4619

NEVADA

State Long-Term Care Ombudsman
Division for Aging Services
3100 W. Sahara Ave., Suite 103
Las Vegas, NV 89102
(702) 486-3545
fax: (702) 486-3572

NEW HAMPSHIRE

State Long-Term Care Ombudsman
Department of Health & Human
Services
Office of the Ombudsman
129 Pleasant Street
Concord, NH 03301-6505
(603) 271-4375
fax: (603) 271-4771

NEW JERSEY

State Long-Term Care Ombudsman
P.O. Box 807
Trenton, NJ 08625-0807
(609) 943-4005
fax: (609) 943-3464

NEW MEXICO

State Long-Term Care Ombudsman
State Agency on Aging
La Villa Rivera Building
228 East Palace Avenue
Santa Fe, NM 87501
(505) 827-7640
fax: (505) 827-7649

NEW YORK

State Long-Term Care Ombudsman
State Office for the Aging
2 Empire State Plaza
Agency Bldg. #2
Albany, NY 12223-1251
(518) 474-0108
fax: (518) 474-7761

NORTH CAROLINA

State Long-Term Care Ombudsman
Division of Aging
2101 Mail Service Center
Raleigh, NC 27699-2101
(919) 733-3983
fax: (919) 733-0443

NORTH DAKOTA

State Long-Term Care Ombudsman
Aging Services Division, DHS
600 South 2nd Street, Suite 1C
Bismarck, ND 58504-5729
(701) 328-8915
fax: (701) 328-8989

OHIO

State Long-Term Care Ombudsman
Ohio Department of Aging
50 West Broad Street, 9th floor
Columbus, OH 43215-3363
(614) 466-1221
fax: (614) 466-5741

OKLAHOMA

State Long-Term Care Ombudsman
Aging Services Division, DHS
P.O. Box 25352
312 N.E. 28th Street, Suite 109
Oklahoma City, OK 73125
(405) 521-6734
fax: (405) 521-2086

OREGON

State Long-Term Care Ombudsman
Office of the Long-Term Care
Ombudsman
3855 Wolverine NE, Suite 6
Salem, OR 97305-1251
(503) 378-6533
fax: (503) 373-0852

PENNSYLVANIA

State Long-Term Care Ombudsman
Department of Aging
555 Walnut Street, 5th floor
Forum Place
Harrisburg, PA 17101-1919
(717) 783-7247
fax: (717) 772-3382

PUERTO RICO

State Long-Term Care Ombudsman
Governor's Office for Elderly Affairs
Call Box 50063, Old San Juan Station
San Juan, Puerto Rico 00902
(787) 725-1515
fax: (787) 721-6510

RHODE ISLAND

State Long-Term Care Ombudsman
Alliance for Better Long-Term Care
422 Post Road, Suite 204

Warwick, RI 02888
(401) 785-3340
fax: (401) 785-3391

SOUTH CAROLINA

State Long-Term Care Ombudsman
Division on Aging
P.O. Box 8206
Columbia, SC 29202-8206
(803) 898-2850
fax: (803) 898-4513

SOUTH DAKOTA

State Long-Term Care Ombudsman
Office of Adult Services & Aging
700 Governors Drive
Pierre, SD 57501-2291
(605) 773-3656
fax: (605) 773-6834

TENNESSEE

State Long-Term Care Ombudsman
Commission on Aging
Andrew Jackson Building, 9th Floor
500 Deaderick Street
Nashville, TN 37243-0860
(615) 741-2056
fax: (615) 741-3309

TEXAS

State Long-Term Care Ombudsman
Texas Department on Aging
P.O. Box 12786 Capitol Station
4900 North Lamar Blvd., 4th floor
Austin, TX 78711 (street address zip:
78751-2316)
(512) 424-6875
fax: (512) 424-6890

UTAH

State Long-Term Care Ombudsman
Division of Aging & Adult Services
Department of Social Services
P.O. Box 45500
120 North 200 West, Suite 325
Salt Lake City, UT 84145-0500
(801) 538-3910
fax: (801) 538-4395

VERMONT

State Long-Term Care Ombudsman
Vermont Legal Aid, Inc.
264 North Winooski
P.O. Box 1367

Burlington, VT 05402 (street address
zip: 05401)
(802) 863-5620
fax: (802) 863-7152

VIRGINIA

State Long-Term Care Ombudsman
Virginia Association of Area Agencies
on Aging
530 East Main Street, Suite 800
Richmond, VA 23219
(804) 644-2923 or (804) 644-2804
fax: (804) 644-5640

WASHINGTON

State Long-Term Care Ombudsman
Washington State Ombudsman
Program
1200 South 336th Street
Federal Way, WA 98003-7452
(800) 562-6028 or (253) 838-6810
fax: (253) 874-7831

WEST VIRGINIA

State Long-Term Care Ombudsman
Commission on Aging
1900 Kanawha Boulevard East
Holly Grove - Building 10
Charleston, WV 25305-0160
(304) 558-3317
fax: (304) 558-0004

WISCONSIN

State Long-Term Care Ombudsman
Bureau of Aging & Long-Term Care
Resources
214 North Hamilton Street
Madison, WI 53703-2118
(608) 266-8945
fax: (608) 261-6570

WYOMING

Deborah Alden
State Long-Term Care Ombudsman
Wyoming Senior Citizens, Inc.
P.O. Box 94
856 Gilchrist
Wheatland, WY 82201
(307) 322-5553
fax: (307) 322-3283

APPENDIX

Resource Directory

The organizations are listed alphabetically and by category. While these organizations may be of help to caregivers, inclusion in this list does not necessarily imply endorsement by Focus on the Family of an organization's material content or viewpoint. It would be wise to investigate any organization prior to using it as a resource.

ADULT DAY CARE

National Council on the Aging (see entry under Aging)

AGING

Administration on Aging (AoA)
330 Independence Avenue, SW
Washington, D.C. 20201
(202) 619-7501 (National Aging Information Center)
(800) 677-1116 (Eldercare Locator)
Web site: http://www.aoa.gov

The AoA, an agency of the U.S. Department of Health and Human Services, educates older people and their caregivers about the benefits and services available to help them. Call the Eldercare Locator for referrals to local services. Hours: Monday–Friday, 9 A.M. to 8 P.M. EST.

National Association of Area Agencies on Aging
927 15th Street NW
6th floor
Washington, D.C. 20005
(202) 296-8130
Web site: http://www.n4a.org

National Association of State Units on Aging
1201 15th Street, Suite 350
Washington, D.C. 20005
(202) 898-2578
Web site: http://www.nasua.org

National Council on the Aging (NCOA)
409 Third Street SW, Suite 200
Washington, D.C. 20024
(202) 479-1200
Web site: http://www.ncoa.org

Benefits Check*Up* Web site: http://www.benefitscheckup.org

This national, nonprofit organization works with area agencies on aging and other community organizations to promote the self-determination and well-being of older people through a variety of programs and services. BenefitsCheck*Up* is a free, on-line service to help older adults to access public-benefits programs.

National Institute on Aging
NIA Information Center
P.O. Box 8057
Gaithersburg, MD 20898-8057
(800) 222-2225
Web site: http://www.nia.nih.gov

Contact the NIA Information Center for a resource directory for older people and a list of free publications on aging-related topics.

ALCOHOL ABUSE

Al-Anon
1600 Corporate Landing Parkway
Virginia Beach, VA 23454-5617
(800) 356-9996
Web site: http://www.al-anon.org

Al-Anon helps families and friends of alcoholics recover from the effects of living with the problem drinking of a relative or friend.

Alcoholics Victorious
1045 Swift Avenue
Kansas City, MO 64116-4127
(816) 471-6433
Web site: http://www.av.iugm.org

Recovering alcoholics who recognize Jesus Christ as their "Higher Power"

gather together in support groups to share their experience, strength, and hope.

Freedom in Christ Recovery Ministry
Mike and Julia Quarles
4590 Mountain Creek Dr.
Roswell, GA 30075
(770) 998-6487
Web site: http://www.freedomfromaddiction.org

This nonprofit, Christ-centered ministry offers referrals and resources for addictive problems.

Overcomers Outreach
520 North Brookhurst Avenue, Suite 121
Anaheim, CA 92801
(800) 310-3001
Web site: http://www.overcomersoutreach.org

Overcomers Outreach support groups use the Bible and the 12 Steps of Alcoholics Anonymous to help individuals who are affected by alcoholism, sexual addiction, eating disorders, and other compulsive behaviors or dependencies.

ALZHEIMER S DISEASE

Alzheimer Society of Canada
20 Eglinton Ave. West, Suite 1200
Toronto, Ontario M4R 1K8
CANADA
(800) 616-8816 or (416) 488-8772
Web site: http://www.alzheimer.ca

Alzheimer's Association
919 North Michigan Ave., Suite 1100
Chicago, IL 60611-1676
(800) 272-3900 or (312) 335-8700

Web site: http://www.alz.org

Call the toll-free, 24-hour-a-day contact center for help with questions. A variety of brochures is available, including "Residential Care: A Guide to Choosing a New Home." The Web site has a helpful series of articles on how to compassionately handle someone with Alzheimer's disease.

Alzheimer's Disease Education and Referral (ADEAR) Center
P.O. Box 8250
Silver Spring, MD 20907-8250
(800) 438-4380 or (301) 495-3311
Web site: http://www.alzheimers.org

The ADEAR Center, a service of the National Institute on Aging (NIA), provides up-to-date information about Alzheimer's disease and related disorders. For an annually updated review of research on Alzheimer's Disease, you can download the NIA report "Progress Report on Alzheimer's Disease" from their Web site or order a copy by calling (800) 438-4380.

Geriatric Resources, Inc.
P.O. Box 239
Radium Springs, NM 88054
(800) 359-0390 or (505) 524-0250
Web site:
http://www.geriatric-resources.com

This company specializes in Alzheimer's caregiving resources and services.

American Music Therapy Association (AMTA)
8455 Colesville Road, Suite 1000
Silver Spring, MD 20910
(301) 589-3300
Web site: http://www.musictherapy.org

This nonprofit organization provides resources and information on the uses and benefits of music therapy. Contact AMTA for referrals, publications, and audiovisual materials.

ANEMIA

American Liver Foundation
(see entry under Digestive Diseases)

ANIMAL-ASSISTED THERAPY

Delta Society
289 Perimeter Road East
Renton, WA 98055-1329
(425) 226-7357
Web site: http://www.deltasociety.org

The Delta Society is a national, nonprofit organization whose mission is to improve human health through service and therapy animals. Its program, Pet Partners, brings volunteers and their pets to nursing homes and hospitals.

ARTHRITIS

Arthritis Foundation
P.O. Box 1616
Alpharetta, GA 30009
(800) 207-8633
Web site: http://www.arthritis.org

Contact this nonprofit, volunteer organization for information on arthritis and related diseases (such as lupus erythmatosus and rheumatism) and for referrals to local chapters, specialists, or support groups. Publications and videos are available on topics such as exercise therapy.

Arthritis Society (National Office)
393 University Avenue, Suite 1700
Toronto, Ontario M5G 1E6
CANADA
(416) 979-7228
Web site: http://www.arthritis.ca

The Arthritis Society provides information and emotional and practical support to people with arthritis and their loved ones.

National Institute of Arthritis and Musculoskeletal and Skin Diseases
1 AMS Circle
Bethesda, MD 20892
(877) 226-4267 (toll free)
Web site: http://www.niams.nih.gov

This clearinghouse offers printed information on arthritis and musculoskeletal and skin diseases.

ASSISTIVE DEVICES

Dynamic Living
1265 John Fitch Blvd., #9
South Windsor, CT 06074
(888) 940-0605 (toll free)

Web site:
http://www.dynamic-living.com

This company carries assistive devices for the home, such as emergency-response systems, dressing sticks, and toilet lift seats.

LifeLine Systems
111 Lawrence St.
Framingham, MA 01702
(800) 451-0525
Web site: http://www.lifelinesys.com

This for-profit company provides personal emergency-response-system products and services.

ASSISTED LIVING (SEE ALSO HOUSING)

Assisted Living Federation of America (ALFA)
11200 Waples Mill Road, Suite 150
Fairfax, VA 22030
(703) 691-8100
Web site: http://www.alfa.org

ALFA provides publications and an on-line directory for locating an assisted-living residence in your area.

Consumer Consortium on Assisted Living (CCAL)
P.O. Box 3375
Arlington, VA 22203
(703) 533-8121
Web site: http://www.ccal.org

This national, consumer-focused advocacy organization is dedicated to the needs and rights of assisted-living residents.

BLINDNESS & LOW VISION

American Foundation for the Blind
11 Penn Plaza, Suite 300
New York, NY 10001
(800) 232-5463 or (212) 502-7600
Web site: http://www.afb.org

Canadian National Institute for the Blind
Library for the Blind
1929 Bayview Avenue
Toronto, Ontario M4G 3E8
CANADA
(416) 480-7520
(800) 268-8818 (for reader services)

Web site: http://www.cnib.ca

This nonprofit, national organization offers free library services (braille books, talking books, and electronic and digital materials) to Canadians who are blind, visually impaired, or print-disabled.

EyeCare America (see entry under Eyes)

Lighthouse International
111 East 59th Street
New York, NY 10022-1202
(800) 829-0500 (information and resource service)
(212) 821-9200
Web site:
http://www.lighthouse.org/default.htm

Lighthouse International is a nonprofit organization based in New York that provides resources and information on the vision problems of the elderly.

Prevent Blindness America
500 East Remington Road
Schaumburg, IL 60173
(800) 331-2020 (information line)
E-mail: info@preventblindness.org
Web site: http://
www.preventblindness.org/

This leading volunteer eye-health-and-safety organization provides the latest information on diseases such as age-related macular degeneration, glaucoma, cataracts, and diabetic retinopathy.

BONE & JOINT DISEASES

American Academy of Orthopaedic Surgeons (AAOS)
6300 North River Road
Rosemont, IL 60018-4262
(847) 823-7186 or (800) 346-AAOS (2267)
Web site: http://www.aaos.org

AAOS is a nonprofit organization of doctors specializing in bones, joints, ligaments, muscles, and tendons. Contact AAOS for information on arthritis, osteoporosis, artificial joints, and prevention of hip fractures. Publications on orthopaedic medicine, many specifically for older people, are available.

American College of Obstetricians and

Gynecologists (see entry under Women's Health)

National Institutes of Health Osteoporosis and Related Bone Diseases National Resource Center
1232 22nd Street, NW
Washington, D.C. 20037-1292
(800) 624-BONE (2663)
Web site: http://www.osteo.org

The resource center provides free printed materials on osteoporosis, osteogenesis imperfecta, Paget's disease, and other metabolic bone diseases. It is not a health hot line.

National Osteoporosis Foundation
1232 22nd Street NW
Washington, D.C. 20037-1292
(800) 223-9994
Web site: http://www.nof.org.

Contact this foundation for information on bone health and osteoporosis prevention and treatment.

BRAIN DISEASES

National Brain Tumor Foundation
414 Thirteenth Street, Suite 700
Oakland, CA 94612
(800) 934-CURE (2873)
E-mail: nbtf@braintumor.org
Web site: http://www.braintumor.org

This foundation provides information and resources, support groups, conferences, access to a medical-advice nurse, and special caregiver training for family members and friends who are caring for a brain-tumor patient.

CANCER

American Cancer Society (ACS)
1599 Clifton Road, NE
Atlanta, GA 30329
(800) ACS-2345 (227-2345)
Web site: http://www.cancer.org

This national, volunteer health organization provides free publications on cancer and its prevention. ACS sponsors programs such as the Great American Smokeout (a day to quit smoking) and Man to Man (education and support for men with prostate cancer). Local ACS offices sponsor self-help groups, transportation programs,

and limited financial aid for cancer patients.

Cancer Treatment Centers of America
3150 Salt Creek Lane
Arlington Heights, IL 60005
(800) FOR-HELP (367-4357)
Web site: http://www.cancercenter.com

This nationwide network of hospitals and physicians provides innovative, comprehensive cancer care through a combination of medical, nutritional, physical, psychological, and spiritual therapies.

National Cancer Institute
NCI Public Inquiries Office
Building 31, Room 10A19
31 Center Drive
Bethesda, MD 20892-2580
(800) 4-CANCER (422-6237) (Cancer Information Service)
Web site: http://www.cancer.gov

NCI's toll-free service provides answers to specific questions about cancer as well as free publications and referrals to cancer specialists and local survivor groups.

CAREGIVING

Caregiver Media Group
6365 Taft Street, Suite 3006
Hollywood, FL 33024
(954) 893-0550
Web site: http://www.caregiver.com

This organization provides information, support, and guidance for caregivers; hosts annual "Sharing Wisdom" conferences for caregivers; and publishes *Today's Caregiver* magazine.

Caregiving.com/Caregiving Newsletter
P.O. Box 224
Park Ridge, IL 60068
(847) 823-0639
Web site: http://www.caregiving.com

This on-line resource and monthly print publication help persons who are caring for an aging relative.

CareGuide, Inc.
(888) 389-8839
Web site: http://www.careguide.com

CareGuide, a subsidiary of Coordinated

Care Solutions, provides access to care-management services and products designed to help elders remain independent in their own homes for as long as possible.

Center for Family Caregivers
P.O. Box 224
Park Ridge, IL 60068
(847) 823-0639
Web site:
http://www.familycaregivers.org

This nonprofit organization develops and distributes educational materials to help people throughout their caregiving role.

Children of Aging Parents (CAPS)
1609 Woodbourne Road, Suite 302A
Levittown, PA 19057
(800) 227-7294
Web site:
http://www.caps4caregivers.org

CAPS is a national, nonprofit referral-and-resource information organization dedicated to caregivers of the elderly, covering all aspects of caregiving.

Christian Caregivers
P.O. Box 2573
Elk Grove, CA 95759-2573
Web site:
http://www.Christiancaregivers.com

Christian Caregivers provides information and resources for caregivers and their families, including information about starting a caregiving ministry at church.

ElderWeb (see entry under Long-Term Care)

Eymann Publications, Inc.
P.O. Box 3577
Reno, NV 89505
(800) 354-3371 (toll free)
Web site: http://www.care4elders.com

This publisher specializes in newsletters related to aging issues and caring for elders.

Family Caregiver Alliance/National Center on Caregiving
690 Market Street, Suite 600
San Francisco, CA 94104
(800) 445-8106
Web site: http://www.caregiver.org

This alliance offers free information, publications, and support for caregivers.

National Alliance for Caregiving
4720 Montgomery Lane, Suite 642
Bethesda, MD 20814
Web site: http://www.caregiving.org

National Family Caregivers Association
10400 Connecticut Avenue, #500
Kensington, MD 20895-3944
(800) 896-3650
Web site: http://www.nfcacares.org

The NFCA provides emotional support for the family caregiver through educational materials and care-advisory support services.

Well Spouse Foundation
30 East 40th Street
New York, NY 10016
(800) 838-0879
Web site: http://www.wellspouse.org

This national, not-for-profit organization gives support to husbands, wives, and partners of the chronically ill and/or disabled.

CHARITIES

Canadian Council of Christian Charities
1 - 21 Howard Avenue
Elmira, Ontario N3B 2C9
CANADA
(519) 669-5137
Web site: http://www.cccc.org

This registered charitable organization is also an association, primarily of charities, within the evangelical Christian community in Canada. Its purpose is to integrate spiritual concerns of ministry with practical aspects of management, stewardship, and accountability.

Evangelical Council for Financial Accountability (ECFA)
440 West Jubal Early Drive, Suite 130
Winchester, VA 22601
(540) 535-0103
(800) 3BE-WISE (323-9473)
Web site: http://www.ecfa.org

This membership organization lists Christian nonprofit organizations that

meet its standards of responsible stewardship. A free *Giver's Guide* is available to help donors know what to look for—and what questions to ask—before giving to any charity.

CHRISTIAN MINISTRIES

American Bible Society
1865 Broadway
New York, NY 10023
(800) 32-BIBLE (322-4253)
Web site:
http://www.americanbible.org

The Bible League
P.O. Box 28000
Chicago, IL 60628
(866) TBL-INFO (825-4636) (toll free)
Web site: http://www.bibleleague.org

This nonprofit ministry, which provides Scriptures for discipleship around the world, has a Recycle Your Bible program (collecting complete used Bibles) and distributes a monthly prayer letter.

CASA (Christian Association of Senior Adult Ministries)
27601 Forbes Road, #49
Laguna Niguel, CA 92677
(888) 200-8552 (toll free)
Web site: http://www.gocasa.org

In addition to providing ministry resources and leadership training for pastors and leaders of seniors ministries, CASA encourages outreach and evangelism, service and assimilation, fellowship and spiritual/personal growth for all older adults.

Christian Seniors Fellowship
P.O. Box 46464
Cincinnati, OH 45246
(800) 35-ALIVE (352-5483)
Web site:
http://www.missionsalive.org/csf

With *Alive!* magazine, conferences, and materials, this organization strives to evangelize, revitalize, and equip seniors for ministry and service for Christ.

Focus on the Family
8605 Explorer Drive
Colorado Springs, CO 80920
(719) 531-3400

(800) A-FAMILY (for orders)
Web site: http://www.family.org

Focus on the Family publishes *LifeWise* magazine as part of its "Focus Over Fifty" ministry.

International Bible Society
P.O. Box 35700
Colorado Springs, CO 80935-3570
(800) 524-1588 (U.S. only)
(719) 867-2700
Web site: http://www.ibsdirect.com

This society offers large-print (14-point) Bibles; a spiral-bound *New Testament and Psalms for the Physically Disabled,* which can be turned with a mouth stick; *Access to God,* a 15-page booklet for rehabilitation or nursing-home ministry; and other resources.

National Bible Association
1865 Broadway
New York, NY 10023
(212) 408-1390
Web site: http://www.nationalbible.org

Contact the National Bible Association to read the Bible on-line or to order a daily Bible reading guide or daily Bible e-mail.

Stephen's Ministries (see entry under Counseling)

COMMUNITY-BASED CARE

National Association of Area Agencies on Aging (see entry under Aging)

CONSUMER INFORMATION

American Association of Retired Persons (AARP) (see entry under Senior Services)

BenefitsCheck*Up* (see entry under Senior Services)

Direct Marketing Association (DMA)
Mail Preference Service
P.O. Box 9008
Farmingdale, NY 11735-9008
Web site: http://www.the-dma.org/consumers/offmailinglist.html

This service allows consumers to have their names removed from mailing lists

and to decrease the amount of advertising mail they receive at home.

Direct Marketing Association (DMA)
Telephone Preference Service
P.O. Box 9014
Farmingdale, NY 11735-9014
Web site: http://www.the-dma.org/consumers/offtelephonelist.html

This service assists consumers in decreasing the number of national telephone marketing calls received at home.

TransUnion LLC's Name Removal Option
P.O. Box 97328
Jackson, MS 39288-7328
(888) 5OPTOUT (567-8688)
Web site: http://www.transunion.com/Contact.asp

To opt out of direct-mail offers by having your name removed from mailing lists offered by the main consumer credit-reporting agencies, call or write TransUnion.

COUNSELING

Biblical Counseling Foundation
42-600 Cook Street, Suite 100
Palm Desert, CA 92211-5143
(760) 773-2667
(877) 933-9333 (toll free, for orders)
Web site: http://www.bcfministries.org

This foundation publishes *Self-Confrontation,* a manual for in-depth biblical discipleship, which explains how to experience contentment in life's trials and to help others to face their problems biblically.

Focus on the Family's Counseling Department
(719) 531-3400

Focus on the Family provides professional counseling (a free, one-time service by phone) and referrals to Christian counselors nationwide. The phone line is open weekdays, 9 A.M. to 4:40 P.M. mountain time; ask for the counseling department at extension 2700.

Peacemaker Ministries
1537 Ave. D, Suite 352
Billings, MT 59102

(406) 256-1583
Web site: http://www.peacemakerministries.org/

This organization helps to equip and assist Christians and their churches to respond to conflict biblically.

Stephen's Ministries
2045 Innerbelt Business Center Drive
St. Louis, MO 63114
(314) 428-2600
Web site: http://www.stephenministries.com/

Stephen's Ministries helps congregations equip laypeople for spiritual growth and practical ministry. They offer Christ-centered training and resources that focus on one-to-one lay caregiving, spiritual gifts, small groups, evangelism, and spiritual growth.

CRIME

American Association of Retired Persons (AARP) (see entry under Senior Services)

American Red Cross (see entry under Emergency Assistance)

National Organization for Victim Assistance (NOVA)
1730 Park Road, NW
Washington, D.C. 20010
(800) TRY-NOVA (24-hour crisis line)
(202) 232-6682
Web site: http://www.try-nova.org

This nonprofit organization has publications on older crime victims and victim assistance, as well as a crisis hot line for victims of violent crime.

U.S. Department of Justice
Office for Victims of Crime
Web site: http://www.ojp.usdoj.gov/ovc/help/evresources.htm

This site has referrals to support services for crime victims.

DATABASES

American Self-Help Clearinghouse
Web site: http://www.selfhelpgroups.org

This Web site provides a searchable database of more than 1,000 national and international self-help support groups for addictions, bereavement, disabilities, abuse, caregiver concerns, and other stressful life situations.

DENTAL CARE

The Academy of General Dentistry
211 E. Chicago Ave., Suite 900
Chicago, IL 60611
(888) 243-3368
Web site: http://www.agd.org

The American Dental Association
211 E. Chicago Ave.
Chicago, IL 60611
(312) 440-2500
Web site: http://www.ada.org

DIABETES

American Diabetes Association
1701 North Beauregard Street
Alexandria, VA 22311
(800) DIABETES (342-2383)
(703) 549-1500
Web site: http://www.diabetes.org

National Diabetes Information Clearinghouse
1 Information Way
Bethesda, MD 20892-3560
(800) 860-8747 or (301) 654-3327
Web site: http://www.niddk.nih.gov (click on *diabetes* under Health Information)

This is an information-dissemination service of the National Institute of Diabetes and Digestive and Kidney Diseases, which is part of the National Institutes of Health.

DIGESTIVE DISEASES

American Liver Foundation
75 Maiden Lane, Suite 603
New York, NY 10038
(800) GO-LIVER (465-4837)
Web site: http:// www.liverfoundation.org

Contact this organization for information about hepatitis and other liver diseases, for physician referrals, and for chapter and support groups.

National Digestive Diseases Information Clearinghouse
2 Information Way

Bethesda, MD 20892-3570
(800) 891-5389 or (301) 654-3810
Web site: http://www.niddk.nih.gov (click on *digestive* under Health Information)

This clearinghouse is an information-dissemination service of the National Institute of Diabetes and Digestive and Kidney Diseases; it can provide you with information on constipation and treatment options.

DISABILITIES

Christian Council on Persons with Disabilities
7120 W. Dove Ct.
Milwaukee, WI 53223
Web site: http://www.ccpd.org

This evangelical Christian organization works with churches and disabled individuals, offering resources and referrals.

Joni and Friends
P.O. Box 3333
Agoura Hills, CA 91376
(818) 707-5664
TTY: (818) 707-9707
Web site: http//www.joniandfriends.org

This organization, founded by Joni Eareckson Tada, provides a broad range of materials, outreach, and training programs, equipping Christians to meet the needs of people with disabilities.

International Bible Society (see entry under Christian Ministries)

National Rehabilitation Information Center (see entry under Rehabilitation)

DIZZINESS

American Academy of Otolaryngology - Head and Neck Surgery, Inc. (AAO)
1 Prince Street
Alexandria, VA 22314
(703) 836-4444
Web site: http://www.entnet.org

This membership organization represents ear, nose, and throat specialists who diagnose and treat disorders of the ears, nose, throat, and related structures of the head and neck. They deal with issues such as dizziness,

hearing loss, swallowing disorders, sleep apnea, and head and neck cancer. Visit the Web site or contact AAO for patient-information leaflets or a list of doctors in your area.

Vestibular Disorders Association
P.O. Box 4467
Portland, OR 97208-4467
(800) 837-8428
Web site: http://www.vestibular.org

This nonprofit organization provides information, referrals, and support for people with inner-ear disorders such as Meniere's disease, BPPV, and labyrinthitis.

DRUG ABUSE

National Institute on Drug Abuse
National Institutes of Health
6001 Executive Boulevard, Room 5213
Bethesda, MD 20892
(301) 443-1124
Web site: http://www.drugabuse.gov

EDUCATION

American Association of Retired Persons (AARP) (see entry under Senior Services)

Elderhostel, Inc.
11 Avenue de Lafayette
Boston, MA 02111
(877) 426-8056 (toll free)
Web site: http://www.elderhostel.org

This not-for-profit, educational organization serves adults 55 years and older, offering classes and adventures nationwide and in 110 countries. Check their Web site or call to request a free catalog on upcoming educational programs.

SeniorNet
121 Second St., 7th floor
San Francisco, CA 94105
(415) 495-4990
Web site: http://www.seniornet.org

This nonprofit organization provides older adults with access to—and education about—computer technology and the Internet to enhance their lives.

ELDER ABUSE

National Center on Elder Abuse
1201 15th Street N.W., Suite 350
Washington, D.C. 20005-2800
(202) 898-2586
Web site:
http://www.elderabusecenter.org

Established by the Administration on Aging, the NCEA performs research studies, provides referrals and technical assistance on elder abuse, and operates the Clearinghouse on Abuse and Neglect of the Elderly (CANE), which collects information on elder abuse.

The National Elder Abuse Incidence Study
Web site:
http://www.aoa.dhhs.gov/abuse/report

EMERGENCY ASSISTANCE

American Red Cross
Web site: http://www.redcross.org

This volunteer organization provides relief to victims of disasters. Local chapters may provide programs for seniors, including disaster-preparedness education and health-and-safety classes such as first aid/CPR. Check the white pages (under *A* for American Red Cross) or the Web site above to find your local chapter.

MedicAlert Foundation (see entry under Medical Care)

EMPLOYMENT

Equal Employment Opportunity Commission
1801 L Street N.W.
Washington, D.C. 20507
(800) 669-3362 or (202) 663-4900
Web site: http://www.eeoc.gov

Green Thumb
2000 N. 14th Street, Suite 800
Arlington, VA 22201
(800) 901-7965 or (703) 522-7272

This national, not-for-profit organization is a leader in older-worker training, employment, and community service.

END-OF-LIFE CARE

Center for Bioethics and Human Dignity (see entry under Ethical Issues)

Heart Too Heart
220 34th Street W.
Billings, MT 59102

This organization does not buy or sell used pacemakers but rather salvages them for physicians to use in third-world countries at no charge to those who receive them.

International Task Force on Euthanasia and Assisted Suicide
P.O. Box 760
Steubenville, OH 43952
(740) 282-3810
Web site: http://www.internationaltaskforce.org

The Protective Medical Decisions Document (PMDD) is a durable power of attorney for health-care decisions.

MedicAlert Foundation (see entry under Medical Care)

EPILEPSY

Epilepsy Foundation
4351 Garden City Drive
Landover, MD 20785
(800) 332-1000
Web site:
http://www.epilepsyfoundation.org

Contact this foundation, which serves people with seizure disorders, for a list of local chapters, referrals to local specialists, support groups, camps, travel assistance, respite care, and employment assistance.

ESTATE PLANNING

Certified Financial Planner Board of Standards (see entry under Financial Planning & Assistance)

Colorado Bar Association
Web site: http://www.cobar.org/estateplanning.htm

A pamphlet on estate planning can be found at this Web address.

Kenneth Frenke & Co. (see entry under Financial Planning & Assistance)

Ronald Blue & Co. (see entry under Financial Planning & Assistance)

ETHICAL ISSUES

Center for Bioethics and Human Dignity
2065 Half Day Road
Bannockburn, IL 60015
(847) 317-8180
Web site: http://www.cbhd.org

The Center for Bioethics and Human Dignity affirms human dignity through bioethics by providing educational opportunities, renewing health-care professionalism, encouraging ethical scientific research, informing public policy, and equipping the world to uphold the God-given dignity of human beings.

The Christian Medical & Dental Associations
P.O. Box 7500
Bristol, TN 37621
(423) 844-1000
Web site: http://www.cmdahome.org

EUTHANASIA & ASSISTED SUICIDE

International Task Force on Euthanasia and Assisted Suicide (see entry under End-of-Life Care)

EXERCISE

American College of Sports Medicine (ACSM)
P.O. Box 1440
Indianapolis, IN 46206
(317) 637-9200
Web site: http://www.acsm.org

ACSM's *Active Aging Partnership* promotes education, research, and improving practice for those who work with older adults. For a free brochure on exercise for older people ("Fit Over Forty"), send a self-addressed, stamped envelope.

American Heart Association (see entry under Heart Disease)

Arthritis Foundation (see entry under Arthritis)

EYES

American Academy of Ophthalmology

P.O. Box 429098
San Francisco, CA 94142-9098
(877) 887-6327 (for brochures and
resources)
(800) 222-EYES (EyeCare America)
(800) 391-3937 (Glaucoma Project)
Web site: http://www.eyenet.org

EyeCare America, also known as the
National Eye Care Project, is a privately
funded program that offers referrals for
free ophthalmology care for qualified
seniors who are 65 and older, who have
not seen an ophthalmologist in the past
three years, and who do not have an
HMO, managed health care, or any
Veterans Administration benefits. The
Glaucoma Project is for seniors at high
risk for diabetes or glaucoma.

EyeCare America (see above)

Glaucoma Research Foundation
200 Pine St., Suite 200
San Francisco, CA 94104
(415) 986-3162
Web site: http://www.glaucoma.org

This private, nonprofit foundation is
dedicated to educating the public and
supporting research for glaucoma in
the scientific community.

Lighthouse International (see entry
under Blindness & Low Vision)

National Eye Care Project (see
American Academy of Ophthalmology
above)

FINANCIAL PLANNING & ASSISTANCE

**Certified Financial Planner
Board of Standards**
1700 Broadway, Suite 2100
Denver, CO 80290-2101
(888) CFP-MARK (237-6275)
(800) 487-1497
(303) 830-7500
Web site: http://www.cfp.net

This organization helps consumers
identify financial planners who have
met its professional and ethical
standards.

Crown Financial Ministries
P.O. Box 100
Gainesville, GA 30503

(866) 424-4000 (toll free)
(770) 534-1000
Web site: http://www.crown.org

This nondenominational organization,
which merged with Larry Burkett's
Christian Financial Concepts, provides
materials for churches and individuals,
seminars, four national radio programs,
an Internet Web site, and budget
counseling based on biblical principles
of finance.

Financial Planning Association (FPA)
3801 East Florida Avenue, #708
Denver, CO 80210
(800) 282-PLAN (7526)
Web site: http://www.fpanet.org

Consumers can contact the FPA to
obtain a list of certified financial
planners in their area or free brochures
on how to choose the right financial
planner and planning for long-term
health care.

Kenneth Frenke & Co.
15 Loop Road, Suite 105
Arden, NC 28704
(828) 654-9343 or (877) 940-9494

This fee-only wealth-management firm
applies biblical wisdom to time and
resources through its financial-
planning and investment services.

Moody's Investors Service, Inc.
99 Church Street
New York, NY 10007
Client services: (212) 553-1653
Web site: http://www.moodys.com

Moody's Investors Service, a global
credit rating, research, and risk-analysis
firm, publishes credit opinions,
research, and ratings on fixed-income
securities, bank loans, issuers of
securities, and other credit obligations.

**National Association
of Personal Financial Advisors**
355 West Dundee Road, Suite 200
Buffalo Grove, IL 60089
1-888-FEE-ONLY
Web site: http://www.napfa.org

**National Association
of Securities Dealers**
(800) 289-9999
Web site: http://www.nasdr.com

The NASD Regulation Public Disclosure
Program is intended to help investors
determine whether they wish to do business
with an individual broker or securities firm.
To check on the disciplinary history of an
NASD broker, go to the Web site's section
entitled "About Your Broker" and perform
an on-line search.

Ronald Blue & Co.
1100 Johnson Ferry Road, Suite 600
Atlanta, GA 30342
(800) 987-2987
Web site: http://www.ronblue.com
E-mail: clientservices@ronblue.com

This nationally recognized firm is
committed to providing *fee-only*
financial, estate, and investment
counsel from a biblical perspective.

**U.S. Securities and
Exchange Commission**
Office of Investor Education
and Assistance
450 Fifth Street, N.W.
Washington, D.C. 20549
Information Line: (202) 942-8088 or
(800) 732-0330
Web site: http://www.sec.gov

This organization's mission is to
protect investors and maintain the
integrity of the securities markets.
Contact the SEC to obtain free
publications and investor alerts or to
learn how to file a complaint.

FOOT CARE

**American Podiatric Medical
Association**
9312 Old Georgetown Road
Bethesda, MD 20814
(800) 366-8227 or (301) 581-9200
Web site: http://www.apma.org

This Web site has a "find a podiatrist"
locator service.

FRAUD & SCAMS

Better Business Bureau
4200 Wilson Boulevard, Suite 800
Arlington, VA 22203-1838
(703) 276-0100
Web site: http://www.bbb.org

Direct Marketing Association (see
entry under Consumer Information)

Equifax Credit Reporting Agency
P.O. Box 740241
Atlanta, GA 30374-0241
(800) 685-1111 (to order your
credit report)
(800) 525-6285 (to report fraud)
Web site: http://www.equifax.com

Experian Credit Reporting Agency
(formerly TRW)
Consumer Fraud Assistance
P.O. Box 2002
Allen, TX 75013
(888) 397-3742 (to report fraud or
order credit report)
Web site: http://www.experian.com

Federal Trade Commission (FTC)
600 Pennsylvania Avenue, N.W.
Washington, D.C. 20580
Toll-free Identity Theft Hot Line: (877)
ID-THEFT (438-4338)
Toll-free Consumer Response Center:
(877) FTC-HELP (382-4357)
Web site: http://www.ftc.gov

Call the FTC or check on-line to file a
complaint or to get free information on
consumer topics.

HHS Tips Fraud Hot Line
P.O. Box 23489
Washington, D.C. 20026
(800) 447-8477

Contact the Health and Human
Services Fraud Hot Line if you have
concerns about phony service
providers, door-to-door solicitations
for Medicare, or if Medicare paid for a
service that you believe was not
provided.

**Attorney General's Health Care
Fraud Division**
Patient Abuse for Criminal Complaints:
(800) 242-2873

Call this number if you have
information regarding criminal,
physical, or financial abuse in a licensed
nursing facility.

Social Security Administration (SSA)
Office of the Inspector General
Fraud Hot Line
P.O. Box 17768
Baltimore, MD 21235
(800) 269-0271 (fraud hot line)

(800) 772 1213 (main number)
Web site: http://www.ssa.gov/oig/

Contact the fraud hot line to report
fraud or to register a complaint about a
representive payee.

TransUnion
(800) 680-7289 (to report fraud)
(800) 916-8800 (consumer relations)
(800) 888-4212 (to order your credit
report)
Web site: http://www.transunion.com

GAMBLING

Freedom in Christ Recovery Ministry
(see entry under Alcohol Abuse)

**Gamblers Anonymous International
Service Office, Inc.**
P.O. Box 17173
Los Angeles, CA 90017
(213) 386-8789
Web site:
http://www.gamblersanonymous.org

This organization offers a 12-step self-
help program for compulsive gamblers.

Landrum Evangelistic Association
Chaplain to Mississippi Beach
44 Fleetwood Drive
Gulfport, MS 39503
(228) 831-1230

This ministry uses a Bible-based approach
to minister freedom from—not how to
cope with—a gambling addiction.

**National Coalition against Legalized
Gambling**
100 Maryland Avenue N.E., Room 311
Washington, D.C. 20002
(800) 664-2680
Web site: http://www.ncalg.org

GERIATRICS

**American Geriatrics Society
Foundation for Health in Aging**
350 Fifth Avenue, Suite 801
New York, NY 10018
(212) 308-1414
Web site: http://www.healthinaging.org

AGS's foundation provides an aging-
information clearinghouse and an on-
line manual called *Eldercare at Home.*

Geriatric Resources, Inc. (see entry
under Alzheimer's Disease)

**National Association of Professional
Geriatric Care Managers**
1604 North Country Club Road
Tucson, AZ 85716-3102
(520) 881-8008
Web site: http://www.caremanager.org

You can search this Web site for names
and credentials of geriatric care
managers in your elder's area.

GERONTOLOGY

Center for Social Gerontology
2307 Shelby Avenue
Ann Arbor, MI 48103
(734) 665-1126
Web site: http://www.tcsg.org

This organization encourages and
conducts research on various issues
important to the development of sound
social policy and programs. The
organization also disseminates
information and research findings on
issues in aging, such as standards for
guardianship services and elderly
tobacco use.

GRIEF

GOAL (Going Onward After Loss)
5109 Lucas-Perrysville Rd.
Perrysville, OH 44864
(419) 938-3475
E-mail: info@amazinggracellamas.com

GOAL offers help and information for
those grieving the death of an elderly
loved one or wishing to start a
Christian bereavement support group.

Stephen's Ministries (see entry under
Counseling)

GUARDIANSHIP

American Health Care Association (see
entry under Health Care)

Center for Social Gerontology (see
entry under Gerontology)

HEALTH & SPIRITUALITY

**International Center for the
Integration of Health & Spirituality**

(formerly the National Institute for Healthcare Research)
6110 Executive Blvd., Suite 908
Rockville, MD 20852
(301) 984-7162, ext. 301
Web site: http://www.icihs.org

The ICIHS is a leader in defining and advancing research-based integration of health and spirituality.

HEALTH CARE

Agency for Healthcare Research & Quality (AHRQ)
Publications Clearinghouse
P.O. Box 8547
Silver Spring, MD 20907-8547
(800) 358-9295
Web site: http://www.ahrq.gov

This federal organization's clearinghouse distributes free consumer publications on topics such as health-insurance choices, choosing and using a health plan, and preventing pressure ulcers.

American Health Care Association
Publications
P.O. Box 3161
Frederick, MD 21705-3161
(800) 628-8140 or (301) 846-7820
Web site: http://www.ahca.org

The AHCA offers a free consumer's guide to nursing facilities. This can be obtained by phone or on AHCA's Web site. Publications are also available about nursing homes, guardianship, assisted living, finances, and long-term-care services.

Joint Commission on Accreditation of Healthcare Organizations (JCAHO)
(630) 792-5800
Web site: http://www.jcaho.org
(click on *Quality Check* for performance reports on accredited health-care organizations)

This commission monitors health-care organizations to make sure they provide quality health care for the public. Accredited organizations have met with most of JCAHO's standards.

WebMD
400 The Lenox Building
3399 Peachtree Road NE
Atlanta, GA 30326

(404) 495-7600
Web site: http://www.webmd.com

WebMD provides on-line information for caregivers on stress, legal issues, assisted-living facilities, and other topics.

HEARING LOSS

American Academy of Otolaryngology - Head and Neck Surgery, Inc. (see entry under Dizziness)

American Speech-Language-Hearing Association (see entry under Speech Therapy)

Better Hearing Institute
515 King Street, Suite 420
Alexandria, VA 22314
(888) 432-7435
Web site: http://www.betterhearing.org

Contact this organization for brochures, information, and sources of financial aid, but *not* for comparisons of hearing-aid studies.

International Hearing Society (IHS)
16880 Middlebelt Road, Suite 4
Livonia, MI 48154
(800) 521-5247 (Hearing Aid Helpline)
Web site: http://www.ihsinfo.org

IHS is a professional organization providing assistance to consumers in locating a hearing-aid specialist as well as support and repair services.

National Association of the Deaf
814 Thayer Avenue, Suite 250
Silver Spring, MD 20910-4500
(301) 587-1788
TTY: (301) 587-1789
Web site: http://www.nad.org

This is an informational, referral, and advocacy organization for deaf and hard-of-hearing Americans.

HEART DISEASE

American Heart Association (AHA)
7272 Greenville Avenue
Dallas, TX 75231
(800) AHA-USA1 (242-8721)
Web site:
http://www.americanheart.org

The American Heart Association is a nonprofit organization dedicated to the diagnosis, treatment, and prevention of heart diseases and stroke. Contact AHA for free individual brochures on cholesterol, diet, nutrition, fitness, and heart-attack treatment.

HOME HEALTH CARE

Meals On Wheels Association of America (see entry under Senior Services)

National Association for Home Care (NAHC)
228 7th Street, S.E.
Washington, D.C. 20003
(202) 547-7424
Web site: http://www.nahc.org

Visit NAHC's Web site for a free consumer guide on how to choose a home-care provider.

National Association of Area Agencies on Aging (see entry under Aging)

National Association of Professional Geriatric Care Managers (see entry under Geriatrics)

Visiting Nurse Associations of America (see entry under Nurses)

HOSPICE

American Academy of Hospice and Palliative Medicine
4700 W. Lake Avenue
Glenview, IL 60025-1485
(847) 375-4712
Web site: http://www.aahpm.org

This professional society is for physicians involved in providing hospice and palliative care for the terminally ill, in conducting research, and in educating people.

Hospice Association of America
228 7th Street, S.E.
Washington, D.C. 20003
(202) 546-4759
Web site:
http://www.hospice-america.org

This organization represents the nation's home-care agencies and hospices.

Hospice Foundation of America
2001 S Street, N.W., Suite 300
Washington, D.C. 20009

(800) 854-3402
Web site:
http://www.hospicefoundation.org

This foundation offers information on choosing a hospice and assists those who are coping with terminal illness, death, and the process of grief.

National Hospice & Palliative Care Organization
Hospice Helpline: (800) 658-8898
Web site: http://www.nhpco.org
Web site: http://www.hospiceinfo.org

This organization provides free consumer information on hospice care as well as a searchable on-line database to "find a hospice."

HOUSING

National Resource and Policy Center on Housing and Long Term Care
University of Southern California
Andrus Gerontology Center
Los Angeles, CA 90089-0191
Web site:
http://www.aoa.dhhs.gov/housing

This Web site includes housing information for seniors, such as government-assisted housing programs for low-income older people and ideas for home modification and repairs.

Senior Alternatives for Living
Web site: http://
www.senioralternatives.com
Web site:
http://www.springstreet.com/seniors

Senior Alternatives, part of the Homestore.com Web site, offers information on different types of housing and care, on health and wellness, and on comparing Medicare health plans.

Tom Hom Group
4408 30th Street
San Diego, CA 92116
Phone: (619) 283-5515
Web site:
http://www.tomhomgroup.com

This company develops single-room-occupancy (SRO) housing in urban areas.

U.S. Department of Housing and Urban Development
451 7th Street S.W.
Washington, D.C. 20410
(202) 708-1112
TTY: (202) 708-1455
Web site: http://www.hud.gov/groups/seniors.cfm

Check here for financial-assistance resources and guides for making the right housing choice for an elderly loved one or to talk to a HUD-approved housing counselor.

HUNTINGTON S DISEASE

Huntington's Disease Society of America
158 West 29th Street, 7th floor
New York, NY 10001-5300
(800) 345-HDSA (4372)
Web site: http://www.hdsa.org

HDSA offers educational materials on Huntington's Disease, including practical hints for caregivers.

INCONTINENCE

National Association for Continence
P.O. Box 8310
Spartanburg, SC 29305-8310
(864) 579-7900 or (800) BLADDER (252-3337)
Web site: http://www.nafc.org

This not-for-profit organization offers a newsletter and products designed to improve the quality of life of people with incontinence.

INDEPENDENT LIVING

CareGuide, Inc. (see entry under Caregiving)

Independent Living USA
Web site: http://www.ilusa.com

A directory of resources for independent living, including information on employment, housing, assistive technology, advocacy, new technology, and travel.

INFECTIOUS DISEASES

Centers for Disease Control and Prevention (CDC)
1600 Clifton Road N.E.

Atlanta, GA 30333
(800) 311-3435
Web site: http://www.cdc.gov

Contact this government agency for fact sheets, statistics, and information on a wide variety of health topics, including senior health and disease-prevention guidelines.

National Institute of Allergy and Infectious Diseases (NIAID)
National Institutes of Health (NIH)
Building 31, Room 7A50
31 Center Drive, MSC 2520
Bethesda, MD 20892-2520
Web site: http://www.niaid.nih.gov

Contact NIAID for fact sheets and brochures on allergies, influenza and colds, and related illnesses.

INSURANCE

A.M. Best Company, Inc.
Ambest Road
Oldwick, NJ 08858
(908) 439-2200, ext. 5742
Web site: http://www.ambest.com

This Web site provides free ratings on insurance companies and their financial condition; the company will give a free rating over the phone for seniors who lack Internet access.

Health Insurance Association of America
1201 F Street, N.W., Suite 500
Washington, D.C. 20004-1204
(202) 824-1600
Web site: http://www.hiaa.org

HIAA publishes a series of guides on various types of insurance, such as health insurance, managed-care insurance, long-term-care insurance, and disability insurance.

National Association of Insurance Commissioners
Executive Headquarters
2301 McGee, Suite 800
Kansas City, MO 64108-2604
(816) 842-3600
Web site: http://www.naic.org

The NAIC helps regulate the insurance industry.

INTERGENERATIONAL PROGRAMS

Elder Craftsmen (EC)
610 Lexington Avenue
New York, NY 10022
(212) 319-8128
Web site:
http://www.eldercraftsmen.org

EC promotes the skills and creativity of seniors through craft-training programs, intergenerational programs, home-based community-service programs, and exhibits of finished artwork.

Family Friends
The National Council on the Aging
409 Third St. S.W., Suite 200
Washington, D.C. 20024
(202) 479-6675
Web site: http://www.ncoa.org/friends/family_friends.htm

Family Friends is an intergenerational volunteer program that matches older, mature men and women with children and families at risk.

KIDNEY DISEASES

National Kidney and Urologic Diseases Information Clearinghouse
3 Information Way
Bethesda, MD 20892-3580
(800) 891-5390 or (301) 654-4415
Web site: http://www.niddk.nih.gov
(click on *Kidney* or *Urologic* under Health Information)

This information-dissemination service of the National Institute of Diabetes and Digestive and Kidney Diseases responds to inquiries and offers booklets and brochures on kidney and urologic diseases.

National Kidney Foundation
30 East 33rd St., Suite 1100
New York, NY 10016
(800) 622-9010 or (212) 889-2210
Web site: http://www.kidney.org

LEGAL HELP

Advice & Counsel Incorporated
150 Shoreline Highway, Building E
P.O. Box 1739
Mill Valley, CA 94942-1739
(415) 331-1212

Web site: http://www.freeadvice.com

This legal site for consumers provides an attorney directory and general legal information to help people understand their legal rights on a variety of topics, such as estate planning.

American College of Trust & Estate Counsel (ACTEC)
3415 S. Sepulveda Blvd., Suite 330
Los Angeles, CA 90034-6060
(310) 398-1888
Web site: http://www.actec.org

ACTEC provides an on-line directory of attorneys who specialize in trusts and estate planning.

Christian Legal Society
4208 Evergreen Lane, Suite 222
Annandale, VA 22003
(703) 642-1070
For attorney referrals: (703) 642-1070, ext. 3700
Web site: http://www.clsnet.org

Call for referrals to Christian attorneys in your area.

FindLaw.com
Web site: http://www.findlaw.com

This Web site includes legal guides on aging topics and a nationwide lawyers directory.

FreeAdvice.com (see Advice & Counsel Incorporated above)

Legal Counsel for the Elderly (LCE)
American Association of Retired Persons (AARP)
601 E Street, N.W.
Washington, D.C. 20049
(202) 434-2120 (between 9:30 A.M. and 3 P.M.)
Web site: http://www.aarp.org

LCE works to expand the availability of legal services to older people.

National Academy of Elder Law Attorneys (NAELA)
1604 N. Country Club Road
Tucson, AZ 85716-3102
(520) 881-4005
Web site: http://www.naela.org

Check the Web site for a free listing of

elder-law attorneys, or you may purchase a copy of NAELA's directory for $15.

National Senior Citizens Law Center
1101 14th Street, N.W., Suite 400
Washington, D.C. 20005
(202) 289-6976
Web site: http://www.nsclc.org

NSCLC advocates nationwide to promote the independence and well-being of low-income elderly.

Nolo
950 Parker Street
Berkeley, CA 94710
(800) 728-3555
Web site: http://www.Nolo.com

This site provides articles and self-help law books written in plain English.

Weiss Research, Inc.
(800) 289-9222

This independent company offers ratings of insurance companies, banks, HMOs, mutual funds, and other companies in order to help consumers make sound, informed financial decisions.

LEISURE ACTIVITIES

American Association of Retired Persons (AARP) (see entry under Senior Services)

Christian Association of PrimeTimers (see entry under Senior Services)

LIVER DISEASE

American Liver Foundation
1425 Pompton Avenue
Cedar Grove, NJ 07009
(800) 223-0179
Web site:
http://www.liverfoundation.org

LONG-TERM CARE

Center for Long Term Care Financing
11418 Northeast 19th Street
Bellevue, WA 98004
(425) 467-6840
Web site: http://www.centerltc.org

This charitable, nonprofit organization promotes public policy that targets scarce public resources to the neediest people.

ElderWeb
1305 Chadwick Drive
Normal, IL 61761
(309) 451-3319
Web site: http://www.elderweb.com

This Web site—developed and authored by Karen Stevenson Brown, a CPA and elder-care expert—includes over 6,000 reviewed links to long-term-care information, as well as a library of articles, reports, news, and events.

Heartwarmers
6N534 Glendale Road
Medinah, IL 60157
(630) 893-5383
Web site: http://www.heartwarmers.org

This nonprofit company produces "sing-along" videos for seniors in long-term care.

LONG-TERM-CARE INSURANCE

Alexander, Hawes, and Audet, LLP
152 North Third St., Suite 600
San Jose, CA 95112
(408) 289-1776
Web site:
http://www.consumerlawpage.com

This Web site provides articles on long-term-care insurance and other legal issues.

General Electric Capital Assurance Company
Long-Term Care Division
Attention: Jill McGuire
4343 Commerce Court, Suite 100
Lisle, IL 60532
(800) 352-0140
Web site: http://www.gefn.com/longtermcare/index.jsp

GE's Long-Term Care Division offers a line of long-term-care insurance products.

LUNG DISEASES

American Cancer Society (see entry under Cancer)

American Lung Association
1740 Broadway
New York, NY 10019-4374
(212) 315-8700

Web site: http://www.lungusa.org

Centers for Disease Control and Prevention
National Center for Chronic Disease Prevention and Health Promotion
Office on Smoking and Health
Mail Stop K-50
4770 Buford Highway, N.E.
Atlanta, GA 30341-3717
(800) CDC-1311(232-1311)
Web site: http://www.cdc.gov/tobacco

Contact the CDC for free publications and information related to tobacco, smoking, and health.

Nicotine Anonymous World Service Office (see entry under Smoking Cessation)

MEDICARE & MEDICAID

Centers for Medicare and Medicaid Services (CMS) (formerly Health Care Financing Administration)
7500 Security Boulevard
Baltimore, MD 21244-1850
(800) MEDICARE (633-4227)
(410) 786-3000
Medicare Fraud Hot Line:
(800) 447-8477
Web site: http://www.medicare.gov

Contact CMS with questions about Medicare coverage, to obtain referrals for prescription drugs or for physicians who accept Medicare assignments, or to find out about Medigap policies.

MEDICAL CARE

American Board of Medical Specialties
1007 Church Street, Suite 404
Evanston, IL 60201-5913
(847) 491-9091
(866) ASK-ABMS (275-2267) (to verify doctor certification)
Web site: http://www.abms.org

You can find out whether a specific physician is certified in a particular medical specialty through the ABMS Web site (click "Who's Certified") or by calling their toll-free number.

American Medical Association
515 North State Street
Chicago, IL 60610
(312) 464-5000

Web site: http://www.ama-assn.org

American Academy of Family Physicians (AAFP)
11400 Tomahawk Creek Parkway
Leawood, KS 66201
(800) 274-2237 or (913) 906-6000
Web site: http://www.aafp.org

MedicAlert Foundation
2323 Colorado Avenue
Turlock, CA 95382
(800) 432-5378
Web site: http://www.medicalert.org

This nonprofit membership organization provides an emergency-medical-information service and advance-directive storage.

MEDLINEplus (see entry under Medicines)

MEDICINES

MEDLINEplus
U.S. National Library of Medicine
8600 Rockville Pike
Bethesda, MD 20894
Web site: http://www.medlineplus.gov

MEDLINEplus, a Web-based service, offers extensive health information from the world's largest medical library, the National Library of Medicine, as well as drug information and lists of hospitals and physicians.

MENTAL HEALTH

American Association for Geriatric Psychiatry
7910 Woodmont Ave., Suite 1050
Bethesda, MD 20814-3004
(301) 654-7850
Web site: http://www.aagponline.org

This organization is dedicated to promoting the mental health and well-being of older people and improving the care of those with late-life mental disorders.

American Association of Christian Counselors
P.O. Box 739
Forest, VA 24551
(800) 526-8673 (member services)
Web site: http://www.AACC.net

This organization's on-line store offers books and resources on lay counseling, marriage and family, and other topics.

National Alliance for the Mentally Ill (NAMI)
Colonial Place Three
2107 Wilson Blvd., Suite 300
Arlington, VA 22201
(800) 950-6264
Web site: http://www.nami.org

This alliance offers free fact sheets on mental illness and depression, including how these conditions affect older people.

National Institute of Mental Health
6001 Executive Blvd.
Room 8184, MSC 9663
Bethesda, MD 20892-9663
(800) 421-4211 or (301) 443-4513
Web site: http://www.nimh.nih.gov

Check the Web site or call the hot line for a variety of pamphlets on mental disorders.

MINORITY HEALTH

Agency for Healthcare Research & Quality (see entry under Health Care)

National Medical Association
1012 Tenth St., N.W.
Washington, D.C. 20001
(888) 662-7497 (physician referral)
(202) 347-1895
Web site: http://www.NMAnet.org

NMA primarily serves physicians who work with the underserved populations in urban areas, such as African-Americans and other minorities.

MOUTH CARE (SEE DENTAL CARE)

MULTIPLE SCLEROSIS

Multiple Sclerosis Association of America
706 Haddonfield Rd.
Cherry Hill, NJ 08002
(800) 532-7667 (help line)
Web site: http://www.msaa.com

NURSES

Deaconess Parish Nurse Ministries
475 E. Lockwood Avenue

St. Louis, MO 63119
(314) 918-2559
Web site: http://www.parishnurses.org

This ministry organization provides information on the network of parish nurses around the country who provide services through congregations that serve aging loved ones. They also provide information on starting a parish-nurse program.

Nurses Christian Fellowship and
Journal of Christian Nursing
Box 7895
Madison, WI 53707-7895
(608) 274-4834, ext. 402
E-mail: ncf@ivcf.org
Web site: http://www.ncf-jcn.org

This ministry provides local chapters, conferences, and resources that prepare nurses and students to view nursing through the eyes of Christian faith and to care for people in Christ's name.

Visiting Nurse Associations of America
11 Beacon Street, Suite 910
Boston, MA 02108
(800) 426-2547 (referral line for visiting nurses)
(617) 523-4042
Web site: http://www.vnaa.org

Visiting Nurse agencies provide home-health-care services to patients in the U.S. Their Web site can help you locate one of their agencies in your area.

NURSING HOMES

American Association of Homes and Services for the Aging
2519 Connecticut Avenue, N.W.
Washington, D.C. 20008-1520
(202) 783-2242
Web site: http://www.aahsa.org

American Health Care Association
Publications
P.O. Box 3161
Frederick, MD 21705-3161
(800) 628-8140 or (301) 846-7820
Web site: http://www.ahca.org

The AHCA offers a free consumer's guide to nursing facilities by phone or on its Web site.

Eden Alternative

742 Turnpike Road
Sherburne, NY 13460
(607) 674-5232
Web site:
http://www.edenalternative.com

Eden Alternative works to eliminate loneliness, helplessness, and boredom in nursing homes through an alternative philosophy of care for elders.

Heartwarmers (see entry under Long-Term Care)

National Citizens' Coalition for Nursing Home Reform
1424 16th Street N.W., Suite 202
Washington, D.C. 20036-2211
(202) 332-2275
Web site: http://www.nccnhr.org

This consumer/citizen action coalition provides information, advocacy, and guidance in selecting a nursing home and provides local referrals. A list of publications is available on request.

NUTRITION

American Dietetic Association
216 W. Jackson Blvd.
Chicago, IL 60606-6995
(800) 366-1655 or (312) 899-0040
Web site: http://www.eatright.org

The ADA's national referral service can link you with a registered dietician in your area.

Food and Drug Administration
5600 Fishers Lane
Rockville, MD 20857
(888) INFO-FDA (for information and referrals to other FDA centers)
Center for Drugs Evaluation and Research: (301) 827-4573 (pharmacists answer drug-related questions)
Center for Biologics Evaluation and Research: (800) 835-4709 (deals with vaccines or biological therapeutics for rheumatoid arthritis and other diseases)
Center for Food Safety and Applied Nutrition: (888) SAFE-FOOD
Center for Devices and Radiological Health: (800) 638-2041 (takes questions about cell phones, mammography machines, and other devices)
Center for Veterinary Medicine: (301) 594-1755 (takes pet-related calls)

Office of Special Health Issues: (301) 827-4460 (assists individuals with specific health-related needs, such as finding access to cancer therapies and clinical trials)
Web site: http://www.fda.gov

The FDA Web site has links to its five Centers, publications for seniors, and an alphabetical index to look up topics such as protecting yourself against health fraud.

Food and Nutrition Information Center
Agricultural Research Service, USDA National Agricultural Library, Room 105
10301 Baltimore Avenue
Beltsville, MD 20705-2351
Web site: http://www.nal.usda.gov/fnic

Meals On Wheels Association of America (see entry under Senior Services)

U.S. Department of Agriculture Center for Nutrition Policy and Promotion (CNPP)
1120 20th St., N.W.
Suite 200, North Lobby
Washington, D.C. 20036
(202) 418-2312
Web site: http://www.nal.usda.gov/fnic/Fpyr/pyramid.html

The CNPP develops and publishes information to help Americans put dietary guidelines into practice, such as the Food Guide Pyramid, available at this Web address.

U.S. Department of Agriculture Food Safety and Inspection Service
Washington, D.C. 20250-3700
(800) 535-4555 (USDA Meat and Poultry Hot Line)
(888) SAFE-FOOD (Food and Drug Administration Hot Line)
Web site: http://www.fsis.usda.gov/oa/consedu.htm
For "To Your Health: Food Safety for Seniors," check this Web site: http://www.foodsafety.gov/fsg/sr2.html

OCCUPATIONAL THERAPY

American Occupational Therapy Association, Inc. (AOTA)

4720 Montgomery Lane
P.O. Box 31220
Bethesda, MD 20824-1220
(301) 652-2682
Web site: http://www.aota.org

AOTA offers information on the role of occupational therapy in promoting functional independence, preventing disability, and maintaining health. Contact AOTA for referrals to local practitioners and therapy programs.

Visiting Nurse Associations of America (see entry under Nurses)

OSTEOPATHY

American Academy of Osteopathy
3500 DePauw Boulevard, Suite 1080
Indianapolis, IN 46268
(317) 879-1881
Web site: http://www.academyofosteopathy.org

This academy's goal is to teach, explore, advocate, and advance the science and art of total health-care management, emphasizing osteopathic principles, palpatory diagnosis, and osteopathic manipulative treatment.

OSTEOPOROSIS (SEE BONE & JOINT DISEASES)

PAIN

American Academy of Pain Management
13947 Mono Way, #A
Sonora, CA 95370
(209) 533-9744
Web site: http://www.aapainmanage.org
E-mail: aapm@aapainmanage.org

This is a membership and education society for health-care professionals. Their Web site includes a patient's bill of rights and a directory of pain-management programs and professionals.

American Chronic Pain Association
P.O. Box 850
Rocklin, CA 95677
(916) 632-0922
Web site: http://www.theacpa.org

American Pain Society
4700 W. Lake Ave.
Glenview, IL 60025
(847) 375-4715
Web site: http://www.ampainsoc.org

Chronic Pain Support Group
Web site: http://www.chronicpainsupport.org

This volunteer organization provides support through the Internet to those living in chronic pain.

Rest Ministries, Inc.
P.O. Box 502928
San Diego, CA 92150
(888) 751-REST (7378)
Web site: http://www.restministries.org

This nonprofit Christian organization serves people who live with chronic illness or pain by providing resources, articles, and programs on-line and through church "HopeKeeper" support groups.

PARKINSON S DISEASE

American Parkinson Disease Association
1250 Hylan Blvd., Suite 4B
Staten Island, NY 10305
(800) 223-2732
Web site: http://www.apdaparkinson.org

Parkinson's Disease Foundation
William Black Medical Building
Columbia Presbyterian Medical Center
710 West 168th Street
New York, NY 10032-9982
(800) 457-6676 or (212) 923-4700
Web site: http://www.pdf.org

PHYSICAL THERAPY

American Physical Therapy Association (APTA)
1111 North Fairfax Street
Alexandria, VA 22314
(800) 999-2782, ext. 3395 (toll free)
Web site: http://www.apta.org or http://www.geriatricspt.org

APTA is a national professional organization representing physical therapists and physical therapist assistants. APTA offers publications on topics such as osteoporosis; incontinence;

neck pain; carpal tunnel syndrome; hip, knee, or shoulder care; and what physical therapists can offer older adults.

PROSTATE DISEASES

American Foundation for Urologic Diseases (see entry under Urologic Diseases)

National Kidney and Urologic Diseases Information Clearinghouse (see entry under Kidney Diseases)

REHABILITATION

National Rehabilitation Information Center
1010 Wayne Avenue, Suite 800
Silver Spring, MD 20910
(800) 346-2742 or (301) 562-2400
Web site: http://www.naric.com

This center is funded by the National Institute on Disability and Rehabilitation Research (NIDRR) to serve the layperson or professional who is interested in disability issues and rehabilitation.

RESPITE CARE

Eldercare Locator (see entry under Senior Services)

Well Spouse Foundation (see entry under Caregiving)

RESTLESS LEGS

Restless Legs Syndrome Foundation
819 Second Street, S.W.
Rochester, MN 55902
(877) 463-6757
Web site: http://www.rls.org

This foundation is a nonprofit agency that provides information about restless legs syndrome. It develops support groups and seeks to find better treatments and a definitive cure.

RETIREMENT PLANNING (SEE ESTATE PLANNING)

SAFETY

U.S. Consumer Product Safety Commission
Office of Information and Public Affairs

4330 E. West Highway
Room 519
Bethesda, MD 20814
(800) 638-2772 or (301) 504-0580
Web site: http://www.cpsc.gov/cpscpub/pubs/701.html

A document entitled "Safety for Older Consumers Home Safety Checklist" is provided at this Web address.

SENIOR SERVICES

American Association of Retired Persons (AARP)
601 E. Street N.W.
Washington, D.C. 20049
(800) 424-3410 (membership)
(888) AARP-NOW (tax-aide site locator and "55 Alive" mature driving program)
Web site: http://www.aarp.org

AARP is a nonprofit, nonpartisan membership organization for people 50 and over. AARP offers a "55 Alive" mature driving safety program, an on-line tax-aide site locator, and other services. Publications are available on housing, health, exercise, retirement planning, money management, leisure, and travel.

BenefitsCheck*Up*
Web site:
http://www.benefitscheckup.org

This free, on-line service identifies federal and state assistance programs for older Americans in all 50 states. Sponsored by the National Council on the Aging (NCOA), BenefitsCheck*Up* was created to serve the millions of older adults who are eligible for benefits but do not know how to apply for them. Users complete a 10-minute survey and are then provided with an individual analysis of benefit programs.

Christian Association of PrimeTimers
P.O. Box 777
St. Charles, IL 60174-0777
(800) 443-0227
Web site:
http://www.christianprimetimers.org

This organization is a Christian alternative to AARP.

Eldercare Locator

927 15th St., N.W., 6th floor
Washington, D.C. 20005
(800) 677-1116 (9 A.M.–8 P.M., EST, Monday–Friday)
Web site:
http://www.n4a.org/locator.cfm

This is a free, nationwide service administered by the National Association of Area Agencies on Aging. The locator will direct you to state and local offices on aging that can help you find government-assistance programs and other senior services.

Meals On Wheels Association of America
1414 Prince Street, Suite 302
Alexandria, VA 20314
(703) 548-5558
Web site: http://www.mowaa.org

To locate a local program, to receive services, or to look for a place to volunteer, check out this Web site, which contains the nation's most comprehensive meal-program list.

National Council on the Aging (see entry under Aging)

Senior Resource
Web site:
http://www.seniorresource.com

This Web site provides information for seniors on housing options, retirement, finances, insurance, and other aging-related topics.

The White House
Greetings Office
Room 39
Washington, D.C. 20502-0039
(202) 456-5447

Upon request, the U.S. President sends anniversary and birthday cards to couples celebrating a 50th or subsequent anniversary and to individuals 80 and older.

United Seniors Health Council
409 Third Street, S.W.
Washington, D.C. 20024
(202) 479-6678
Web site:
http://www.unitedseniorshealth.org

The United Seniors Health Council

helps older consumers, caregivers, and professionals through a wide range of programs and services, including publications on financial planning, home care, long-term-care insurance, and other topics.

SKIN DISEASES

American Academy of Dermatology
930 N. Meachum Road
P.O. Box 4014
Schaumburg, IL 60168-4014
(847) 330-0230
Web site: http://www.aad.org

SLEEP DISORDERS

American Academy of Sleep Medicine (formerly American Sleep Disorders Association)
6301 Bandel Road, N.W., Suite 101
Rochester, MN 55901
(507) 287-6006
Web site: http://www.aasmnet.org

American Academy of Otolaryngology - Head and Neck Surgery, Inc. (see entry under Dizziness)

SMOKING CESSATION

Nicotine Anonymous World Service Office
419 Main Street, PMB #370
Huntington Beach, CA 92648
(415) 750-0328
Web site: http://www.nicotine-anonymous.org

This organization offers a 12-step program for quitting nicotine use.

SOCIAL SECURITY

Social Security Administration (SSA)
Office of Public Inquiries
6401 Security Boulevard
Baltimore, MD 21235
(800) 772-1213; outside U.S.: (410) 965-1910
Web site: http://www.ssa.gov

Contact SSA if you have questions regarding your social-security account, obtaining an application for benefits, or requesting free social-security benefit-information brochures.

SPEECH THERAPY

American Speech-Language-Hearing Association
10801 Rockville Pike
Rockville, MD 20852
(800) 638-8255 or (301) 897-5700, ext. 4524
Web site: http://www.asha.org

Provides free information on speech, language, and hearing disorders for aging populations.

STATISTICS

National Center for Health Statistics (NCHS)
Centers for Disease Control and Prevention
6525 Belcrest Road
Hyattsville, MD 20782-2003
(301) 458-4636
Web site: http://www.cdc.gov/nchs

This federal agency monitors the nation's health, producing reports on trends in health and aging, vital and health statistics, and other data.

STROKE

American Stroke Association
7272 Greenville Avenue
Dallas, TX 75231
(888) 4-STROKE (478-7653)
Web site: http://www.americanstroke.org

The American Stroke Association, a division of the American Heart Association, supports stroke survivors and their loved ones by providing resources, services, and information to improve quality of life.

National Stroke Association
9707 East Easter Lane
Englewood, CO 80112
(800) STROKES (787-6537) or (303) 649-9299
Web site: http://www.stroke.org

Call for information on strokes and for local stroke support-group listings.

SURGERY

American College of Surgeons (ACS)
633 North Saint Clair Street
Chicago, IL 60611-3211

(312) 202-5000
Web site: http://www.facs.org

ACS is a national organization offering educational materials and information about qualified surgeons and surgical treatments for many illnesses and injuries. Contact ACS on-line or by phone to locate a board-certified surgeon.

THYROID

American Academy of Otolaryngology - Head and Neck Surgery, Inc. (see entry under Dizziness)

Thyroid Foundation of America
350 Ruth Sleeper Hall, RSL 350
40 Parkman Street
Boston, MA 02114
(800) 832-8321
Web site: http://www.tsh.org

TRANSPORTATION

National Association of Area Agencies on Aging (see entry under Aging)

American Association of Retired Persons (AARP) (see entry under Senior Services)

TRAVEL

Elderhostel, Inc. (see entry under Education)

TREMOR

International Tremor Foundation (ITF)
7046 West 105th Street
Overland Park, KS 66212-1803
(888) 387-3667 (toll free)
Web site: http://www.essentialtremor.org

Contact ITF for referrals to medical specialists, a list of support groups by state, and information on more than 20 tremor disorders.

UROLOGIC DISEASES

American Foundation for Urologic Diseases
1128 North Charles Street
Baltimore, MD 21201
(410) 468-1800 or (800) 828-7866
Web site: http://www.afud.org

E-mail: admin@afud.org

American Urological Foundation, Inc.
1120 North Charles St.
Baltimore, MD 20201
(410) 727-1100
Web site: http://www.auanet.org

This organization's Web site provides an on-line referral service for finding a urologist.

National Kidney and Urologic Diseases Information Clearinghouse (see entry under Kidney Diseases)

VETERANS HEALTH

Department of Veterans Affairs (VA)
(800) 827-1000 (toll free)
Web site: http://www.va.gov

The VA provides benefits for eligible veterans and their families in outpatient clinics, medical centers, and nursing homes across the U.S. Contact the VA for information and publications on service locations and benefits, including comprehensive medical and dental care and pensions.

VOLUNTEERS

Association of Gospel Rescue Missions
1045 Swift Street
Kansas City, MO 64116-4127
(816) 471-8020
Web site: http://www.agrm.org

This association of 260 organizations

helps the homeless and other needy inner-city people by providing emergency food and shelter, youth and family services, rehabilitation programs for the addicted, education and job-training programs, and assistance to the elderly, the poor, and at-risk youth. Volunteer opportunities abound.

Corporation for National and Community Service
National Senior Service Corps
1201 New York Avenue, N.W.
Washington, D.C. 20525
(800) 424-8867 or (202) 606-5000
Web site:
http://www.nationalservice.org or
http://www.seniorcorps.org

This corporation oversees volunteer programs such as the National Senior Services Corps (helping older people get involved in community service), the Foster Grandparent Program (encouraging older people to work with children with special needs), and the Senior Companion Program (assisting older people with special needs in hospitals and other settings). Contact CNS for brochures, fact sheets, and program handbooks.

Delta Society (see entry under Animal-Assisted Therapy)

Meals On Wheels Association of

America (see entry under Senior Services)

National Council on the Aging (see entry under Aging)

The Salvation Army
Older Adult Ministries
615 Slaters Lane
Alexandria, VA 22313
(703) 684-5500
Web site: http://www.salvationarmy.org

Contact your local Salvation Army for information on adult day-care centers, feeding sites, senior residential housing, summer senior camps, senior clubs, or volunteer opportunities, such as the League of Mercy program for visiting nursing homes and hospitals.

WOMEN S HEALTH

American College of Obstetricians and Gynecologists (ACOG)
409 12th Street, S.W.
P.O. Box 96920
Washington, D.C. 20090-6920
(202) 863-2518 (resource center)
Web site: http://www.acog.org

ACOG is a professional society of doctors specializing in women's health care. Contact ACOG for referrals. For free pamphlets on osteoporosis, menopause, and hormone-replacement therapy, send a self-addressed, stamped envelope.

Endnotes

CHAPTER ONE: Facing a New Role

[1]Older Women's League, *Faces of Caregiving*, May 2001.

[2]William A. Davis, "The Burdens of . . . the Club Sandwich Generation. Welcome to the Golden Years: Caring for Parents, Children—Even Grandchildren," *Boston Globe,* 24 May 1994, sec. Living, p. 53.

[3]Karen S. Peterson, "Adult Kids in Crisis: What to Do with Mom, Dad? Hard Times for 'Sandwich Generation,'" *USA Today,* 18 April 1989, sec. A, p. 1.

[4]D. L. Wagner, "Long-Distance Caregiving for Older Adults," *Healthcare and Aging* (National Council on the Aging: Spring 1997).

CHAPTER TWO: Honoring Your Aging Loved Ones

[1]*Merriam-Websters Collegiate Dictionary,* Tenth Edition (Springfield, Mass.: Merriam-Webster, Inc., 1999).

[2]Age Wave IMPACT Inc., 2000 Powell St. #1180, Emeryville, CA 94608; Phone: (510) 601-7500; St. Jude Hospital, Fullerton, Calif.

[3]E. M. Brody, *Women in the Middle: Their Parent Care Years* (New York: Springer, 1990), 88–90.

[4]Senior Companion Program receives major funding through the Corporation for National and Community Service, a federal volunteer agency.

CHAPTER THREE: Your Circle of Support

[1]The Family Caregiver Alliance.

[2]The National Alliance for Caregiving and the American Association of Retired Persons, *Family Caregiving in the U.S.: Findings from a National Survey,* June 1997.

CHAPTER FOUR: Caring for Yourself

[1]"What a Friend We Have in Jesus," words by Joseph Medlicott Scriven, 1855.

[2]Gary & Dr. Greg Smalley, *Bound by Honor* (Wheaton, Ill.: Focus on the Family/Tyndale House Publishers, 1998), 114–15.

[3]Adapted with the permission of The Free Press, a Division of Simon & Schuster, Inc., from *Taking Care of Your Aging Family Members: A Practical Guide, Revised & Expanded* by Wendy Lustbader and Nancy R. Hooyman. Copyright © 1994 by Wendy Lustbader and Nancy R. Hooyman. Copyright © 1986 by The Free Press.

CHAPTER FIVE: Physical Changes in Aging—Part 1

[1]U.S. Department of Health and Human Services, National Center for Health Statistics, *Annual Report on Nation's Health Spotlights Elderly Americans* (13 October 1999).

[2]Centers for Disease Control and Prevention, *Unrealized Prevention Opportunities: Reducing the Health and Economic Burden of Chronic Disease* (1997: National Center for Chronic Disease Prevention and Health Promotion).

[3]National Institutes of Health, Osteoporosis and Related Bone Diseases National Resource Center.

[4]National Institute on Aging, *Age Page: Osteoporosis: The Bone Thief.*

[5]American College of Rheumatology, "Rheumatoid Arthritis," ACR Fact Sheet, 2000.

[6]David Armstrong and Lawrence A. Lavery, "Diabetic Foot Ulcers: Prevention, Diagnosis and Classification," *American Family Physician* (15 March 1998).

[7]Centers for Disease Control and Prevention, "Total Tooth Loss Among Persons Aged ≥ 65 Years—Selected States, 1995–1997," *Morbidity and Mortality Weekly Report,* 48 no. 10 (19 March 1999).

[8]Centers for Disease Control and Prevention, National Center for Health Statistics, "Leading Causes of Death," *National Vital Statistics Reports,* 49 no. 11 (12 October 2001).

CHAPTER SIX: Physical Changes in Aging—Part 2

[1]Terri L. Strassburger et al., "Interactive Effects of Age and Hypertension on Volumes of Brain Structures," *Stroke,* 28 (July 1997), 1410–1417.

[2]Federal Interagency Forum on Aging-Related Statistics' report, *Older Americans 2000: Key Indicators of Well-Being.*

[3]U.S. Environmental Protection Agency, Indoor Environments Division, "Indoor Air Quality," 2001.

[4]National Center for Health Statistics, "Trends in Asthma Morbidity and Mortality, January 2001," *Final Vital Statistics Report, 1979-1998.*

[5]L. J. Launer et al., "Rates and Risk Factors for Dementia and Alzheimer's Disease: Results from EURODEM Pooled Analyses, *Neurology,* 52 no. 78 (1999).

[6]American Lung Association, "What Are the Benefits of Quitting Smoking?" (2001). See <http://www.lungusa.org/tobacco/quit_ben.html>.

[7]National Heart, Lung, and Blood Institute, U.S. Department of Health and Human Services, Public Health Services, National Institutes of Health, "Check Your Smoking IQ," Publication No. 91-3031 (October 1991).

[8]Centers for Disease Control and Prevention, National Center for Health Statistics, *Health, United States, 1999, with Health and Aging Chartbook* (Hyattsville, Md.: 1999).

[9]Walter N. Kernan et al., "Phenylpropanolamine and the Risk of Hemorrhagic Stroke," *The New England Journal of Medicine,* 343 no. 25 (21 December 2000).

[10]National Institute on Aging, National Institutes of Health, *Progress Report on Alzheimer's Disease,* NIH Publication No. 00-4859 (2000).

[11]J. M. Hausdorff, "Power of Ageism on Physical Function of Older Persons," *Journal of American Geriatrics Society,* 47 no. 11 (November 1999), 1346.

[12]Albertson Owens et al., "Religion, Optimism, and Health in Older Adults," paper presented at the annual meeing of the Society for the Scientific Study of Religion (Raleigh, NC: October 1993).

[13]H. G. Koenig et al., "The Relationship between Religious Activites and Blood Pressure in Older Adults," *International Journal of Psychiatry in Medicine* 28, no. 2 (1998): 189–213.

[14]W. J. Strawbridge et al., "Frequent Attendance at Religious Services and Mortality over 28 Years," *American Journal of Public Health* 87, no. 6 (1997): 957–961.

CHAPTER SEVEN: Mental Change, Memory Loss, and Dementia

[1]Mary N. Haan et al., "The Role of APOE 4 in Modulating Effects of Other Risk Factors for Cognitive Decline in Elderly Persons," *JAMA,* 282 (1999), 40–46.

[2]K. W. Schaie, "The Course of Adult Intellectual Development," *American Psychologist,* 49 (1994), 304–313.

[3]D. J. Selkoe, "Aging Brain, Aging Mind," *Scientific American* (September 1992), 135–142.

[4]Ronald C. Petersen, PhD, MD et al., "Mild Cognitive Impairment," *Archives of Neurology,* 56 (1999), 303–308.

[5]"Alzheimers Is the Death of the Mind before the Death of the Body"; <www.efmoody.com/longterm/alzheimers.html>.

[6]The Alzheimer's Association; Centers for Disease Control and Prevention, National Center for Health Statistics, *National Vital Statistics Reports,* 48 no. 1 (12 October 2001).

[7]D. P. Rice et al., "The Economic Burden of Alzheimer's Disease Care," *Health Affairs,* 12 no. 2 (Summer 1993), 168.

[8]Alzheimer's Disease Education & Referral Center, U.S. Department of Health and Human Services, National Institute on Aging, *Alzheimer's Disease Genetics Fact Sheet,* Publication no. 97-4012 (August 1997).

[9]R. Mulnard et al., "Estrogen Replacement Therapy for Treatment of Mild to Moderate Alzheimer's Disease: A Randomized Controlled Trial," Alzheimer's Disease Cooperative Study, *JAMA* 283, no. 8 (23 February 2000): 1007–15.

CHAPTER EIGHT: Emotional Changes in Aging

[1]Mary C. Commerford and Marvin Reznikoff, "Relationship of Religion and Perceived Social Support to Self-Esteem and Depression in Nursing Home Residents," *Journal of Psychology,* 130 (1996), 35–50.

[2]Harold G. Koenig and David B. Larson, "Use of Hospital Services, Religious Attendance, and Religious Affiliation," *Southern Medical Journal,* 91 no. 10 (1998), 925–932.

[3]J. G. Spangler et al., "Church-Related Correlates of Tobacco Use Among Lumbee Indians in North Carolina," *Ethnicity & Disease,* 8 (1998), 73–80.

[4]Robert A. Hummer et al., "Religious Involvement and U.S. Adult Mortality," *Demography,* 36 no. 2 (1999) 1–13; R. W. Duff and L. K. Hong, "Age Density, Religiosity, and Death Anxiety in Retirement Communities, *Review of Religious Research,* 37 no. 1 (1995): 19–32.

[5]J. E. Birren, "Spiritual Maturity in Psychological Development," *Journal of Religious Gerontology* 7 (1990): 41–53.

CHAPTER TEN: Financial Care

[1]*A Profile of Older Americans: 1999,* prepared by the Program Resources Department, AARP and the Administration on Aging, U.S. Department of Health and Human Services.

[2]"Social Security Bulletin," *Annual Statistical Supplement* (2000).

[3]*Fast Facts and Figures about Social Security,* Social Security Administration, Office of Policy, Office of Research, Evaluation, and Statistics, SSA Publication No. 13-11785 (June 2001).

[4]Medicare Rights Center, *Medicare Appeals and Grievances: Strategies for System Simplification and Informed Consumer Decisionmaking,* (October 1996); see <www.medicarerights.org>.

CHAPTER ELEVEN: Legal Care and Estate Planning

[1]U.S. Trust Corporation, *U.S. Trust Survey of Affluent Americans: Retirement Planning* (May 1996); <www.ustrust.com/ustrust/html/knowledge/WealthManagementInsights/SurveyofAffluentAmericans>.

[2]Lorin Castleman, *Have You Done Proper Estate Planning?* (1999); <www.CA-Probate.com>. Prepared by Lorin Castleman, Attorney-at-Law, Castleman Law Firm, Pleasanton, Ca.

[3]Colorado Bar Association; <www.cobar.org/estateplanning.htm>. Used with permission.

CHAPTER TWELVE: Church, Religious Activity, and Spiritual Life

[1]J. S. Levin and R. J. Taylor, "Age Differences in Patterns and Correlates of the Frequency of Prayer," *The Gerontologist* 37 (February 1997), 75–88.

[2]The Gallup Organization, "Six in Ten Americans Read Bible at Least Occasionally," *Gallup News Service* (October 20, 2000).

[3]Barbara Payne, "Spiritual Maturity and Meaning-Filled Relationships: A Sociological Perspective," in James J. Seeber's (ed.) *Spiritual Maturity in the Later Years* (New York: Haworth Press, 1990).

[4]David G. Myers and Ed Diener, "Who is Happy?" *Psychological Science* 6, no. 1 (1995), 10–19.

[5]Kenneth I. Pargament et al., "Religious Struggle As a Predictor of Mortality among

Medically Ill Elderly Patients," *Archives of Internal Medicine* 161 (August 7, 2001), 1881–1885.

[6]S. A. Albertson Owens et al., "Religion, Optimism, and Health in Older Adults," 1993. Paper presented at the annual meeting of the Society for the Scientific Study of Religion, Raleigh, NC.

[7]U.S. Bureau of Census, Federal Interagency Forum on Aging-Related Statistics, *Older Americans 2000: Key Indicators of Well-Being.*

[8]D. E. Bradley, "Religious Involvement and Social Resources: Evidence from the Data Set 'Americans' Changing Lives.'" *Journal for the Scientific Study of Religion* 34, no. 2 (1995), 259–267.

[9]S. A. Albertson Owens et al., "The Relationship Between Cognitive Status and Religiosity in Older Adults," 1993. Paper presented at the annual meeting of the Society for the Scientific Study of Religion, Raleigh, NC.

[10]C. Collins and D. Frantz, "Let Us Prey," *Modern Maturity* (June 1994), 22–32.

[11]D. Briggs, "Study Says Older Americans Feel Neglected by Church," *Grand Rapids Press,* 17 September 1992, sec. B, p. 6.

[12]Juanita Westaby, "Tending Body and Soul," *Grand Rapids Press,* 20 February 1999, sec. B, p. 1.

CHAPTER THIRTEEN: Elder Abuse

[1]National Center on Elder Abuse, *The National Elder Abuse Incidence Study: Final Report* (Washington, D.C.: American Public Health Services Association, 1998).

[2]Council on Scientific Affairs, "Elder Abuse and Neglect," *JAMA* 257 (1987), 966–971.

[3]Charles E. Marshall, "Elder Abuse: Using Clinical Tools to Identify Clues of Mistreatment," *Geriatrics,* February 2000.

[4]K. Pillemer and D. Finkelhor, "The Prevalence of Elder Abuse: A Random Sample Survey," *Gerontologist* 28, no. 1 (1988), 51–57.

[5]T. Tatara, *Summaries of the Statistical Data on Elder Abuse in Domestic Settings for FY90 and FY91: A Final Report* (Washington, D.C.: National Aging Resource Center on Elder Abuse, 1993).

[6]T. Tatara, *Elder Abuse: Questions and Answers.* (Washington, D.C.: National Aging Resource Center on Elder Abuse, 1994).

[7]Lustbader and Hooyman, *Taking Care of Your Aging Family Members,* 40.

[8]K. Pillemer and D. W. Moore, "Abuse of Patients in Nursing Homes: Findings from a Survey of Staff," *Gerontologist* 29, 314–320.

CHAPTER FOURTEEN: Fraud, Scams, and Greed

[1]Jamie Stockwell, "ATM Scam Targeting Women in Suburbs," *Washington Post,* 9 February 2001, 1(B).

[2]U.S. Senate Special Committee on Aging, *Consumer Fraud and the Elderly: Easy Prey?* (Washington, D.C.: U.S. Government Printing Office, 1993).

[3]Federal Bureau of Investigation, "Protecting Yourself Against Identity Fraud" (2001). See <http://www.fbi.gov>.

[4]National Gambling Impact Study Commission, *Staff Generated Reports: Lotteries* (Washington, D.C., 1999), 7.

CHAPTER FIFTEEN: Helping Your Elder Remain at Home

[1]U.S. Bureau of the Census.

[2]Ada-Helen Bayer and Leon Harper, "Fixing to Stay: A National Survey on Housing and Home Modification Issues," (AARP Research Group and AARP Programs/ Applied Gerontology Group, May 2000).

[3]Flora Williams, "Value of Home Equity Used in Reverse Mortgages As a Potential Source of Income for Elderly Americans," *Journal of the Association for Financial Counseling and Planning Education* (April 1998).

CHAPTER SIXTEEN: When It's Time to Move

[1]U.S. Administration on Aging, *Profile of Older Americans: 2000.*

CHAPTER SEVENTEEN: Nursing-Home Care

[1]U.S. Department on Health and Human Services: Administration on Aging, *A Profile of Older Americans: 2000.*

[2]L. Osterkamp, "Family Caregiver: America's Primary Long-Term Care Resource," in *Annual Editions: Aging,* 7th ed. (Sluice Dock, Guilford, CT: Dushkin Publishing Group, 1991), 180–183.

[3]Nancy A. Krauss and Barbara M. Altman, "Characteristics of Nursing Home Residents—1996," *Medical Expenditure Panel Survey (MEPS)* from the Agency for Health Care Policy and Research.

[4]Ibid.

[5]National Alliance for Caregiving and the American Association of Retired Persons, *Family Caregiving in the U.S.: Findings from a National Survey* (1997), 17.

[6]Metropolitan Life Insurance Company, *The Met Life Study of Employer Costs for Working Caregivers* (Westport, CT: MetLife Mature Market Group, June 1997).

[7]National Alliance for Caregiving and the American Association of Retired Persons, *Family Caregiving in the U.S: Findings from a National Survey* (1997), 21.

[8]Family Caregiver Alliance and the Benjamin Rose Institute, *Making Hard Choices: Respecting Both Voices* (San Francisco [FCA] and Cleveland [BRI], 2000).

[9]Federal Interagency Forum on Aging-Related Statistics, *Older Americans 2000: Key Indicators of Well-Being* (Washington, D.C.: U.S. Government Printing Office, August 2000).

[10]Ibid.

[11]Victor Fuchs, "Health Care for the Elderly: How Much? Who Will Pay for It?" *Health*

Affairs (Center for Health Policy/Center for Primary Care and Outcomes Research, January/February 1999).

[12]Janemarie Mulvey and Barbara Stucki, *Who Will Pay for the Baby Boomers' Long-Term Care Needs?: Expanding the Role of Long-Term Care Insurance* (Washington, D.C.: American Council of Life Insurance, April 1998), 15.

[13]Robert J. Riekse and Henry Holstege, *Growing Older in America* (McGraw-Hill Companies, Inc., 1996), 389–390.

CHAPTER EIGHTEEN: End-of-Life Issues

[1]See the CitizenLink Web site at <www.family.org/cforum>.

[2]Christian Medical & Dental Associations, "Withholding or Withdrawing of Nutrition and Hydration," *CMDA Ethics Statements*, 3 May 1990; <www.cmdahome.org/index>.

[3]Advocates for Better Care, Food and Water: To Care or to Kill, 1996. P.O. Box 9145, Grand Rapids, MI 49509-0145.

[4]R. M. McCann et al., "Comfort Care for Terminally Ill Patients: The Appropriate Use of Nutrition and Hydration," *JAMA* 272, no. 16 (1994), 1263–1266; L. A. Printz, "Terminal Dehydration: A Compassionate Treatment," *Archives of Internal Medicine* 152, no. 4 (1992), 697–700.

[5]"Medical Decisions About the End of Life, I," "Report of the Committee to Study the Medical Practice Concerning Euthanasia, II," *The Study for the Committee on Medical Practice Concerning Euthanasia* (2 vols.), (The Hague: 19 September 1991).

[6]Oregon Health Division, *Oregon Death with Dignity Act: Three Years of Legalized Physician-Assisted Suicide,* 21 February 2001.

[7]Focus on the Family Physicians Resource Council, *Working Paper on Assisted Suicide and End-of-Life Care.*

[8]*Time* (15 April 1996), 82.

CHAPTER NINETEEN: When It's Time to Let Go

[1] A. McCarthy, "The Country of the Old," *Commonwealth* (1991), 505–506.

[2]C. Russell, "The Facts of Death," *American Demographics* (April 1989), 13–14.

[3]Elisabeth Kubler-Ross, *On Death and Dying* (New York: Macmillan, 1969).

[4]William L. Hendricks, *A Theology for Aging* (Broadman Press, 1986), 33.

CHAPTER TWENTY: Moving Forward

[1]J. William Worden, *Grief Counseling and Grief Therapy: A Handbook for the Mental Health Practitioner* (1991).

INDEX

FOCUS ON THE FAMILY®

Welcome to the Family!

Whether you received this book as a gift, borrowed it from a friend, or purchased it yourself, we're glad you read it! It's just one of the many helpful, insightful, and encouraging resources produced by Focus on the Family.

In fact, that's what Focus on the Family is all about—providing inspiration, information, and biblically based advice to people in all stages of life.

It began in 1977 with the vision of one man, Dr. James Dobson, a licensed psychologist and author of 16 best-selling books on marriage, parenting, and family. Alarmed by the societal, political, and economic pressures that were threatening the existence of the American family, Dr. Dobson founded Focus on the Family with one employee— an assistant—and a once-a-week radio broadcast, aired on only 36 stations.

Now an international organization, Focus on the Family is dedicated to preserving Judeo-Christian values and strengthening the family through more than 70 different ministries, including 8 separate daily radio broadcasts, television public service announcements, 10 publications, and a steady series of books and award-winning films and videos for people of all ages and interests.

Recognizing the needs of, as well as the sacrifices and important contributions made by, such diverse groups as educators, physicians, attorneys, crisis pregnancy center staff, and single parents, Focus on the Family offers specific outreaches to uphold and minister to these individuals too. And it's all done for one purpose, and one purpose only: to encourage and strengthen individuals and families through the life-changing message of Jesus Christ.

For more information about the ministry, or if we can be of help to your family, simply write to Focus on the Family, Colorado Springs, CO 80995, or call 1-800-A-FAMILY (1-800-232-6459). Friends in Canada may write Focus on the Family, P.O. Box 9800, Stn. Terminal, Vancouver, B.C. V6B 4G3 or call 1-800-661-9800. Visit our Web site (www.family.org) to learn more about Focus on the Family or to find out if there is an associate office in your country.

We'd love to hear from you!

Other Faith and Family Strengtheners
From *Focus on the Family*®

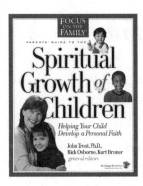

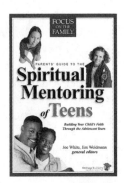

Quiet Moments For Caregivers

Betty Free Swanberg, who cared for both her parents, brings her insight and sensitivity to *Quiet Moments for Caregivers,* a loving tribute to those who devote themselves to a loved one's care. Filled with devotionals, prayers, and the questions that run through every caregiver's mind, it provides reassurance that God knows your situation and cares deeply.

Add Life to Your Years

While most Christians in the U.S. plan to retire, it's not a biblical concept. In fact, it's a life and passion killer. In *Add Life to Your Years,* you'll meet more than 40 unforgettable "senior citizens." Their exciting stories reveal the tremendous potential seniors have for serving the Lord.